펀펀리딩 – Did You Know?

지은이　전은지
펴낸이　허 민
펴낸곳　스텝업

기　획　구경모
디자인　김봉주
편　집　김현주
영문교열　Mathew Robert Dutra

초판 1쇄 발행 2013년 09월 02일
초판 2쇄 인쇄 2014년 09월 29일

출판신고 제 324-2012-000051호

TEL 02-747-7078
FAX 02-747-7079

www.stepupbook.net

ISBN 978-89-94553-07-8

가격은 뒤표지에 있습니다.
· 이 책의 무단전재 및 복사, 복제행위는 또는 독창적인 편집의 모방은 저작권법에 위반됩니다.
· 파본은 구입한 곳에서 교환이 가능합니다.

※ 스텝업은 (주)네오인의 어학전문 브랜드입니다.

전은지 지음

스텝업

Reading All In One
어휘+문법+독해+리스닝

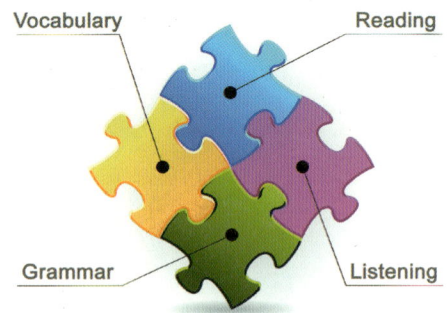

 흔히 한국인의 영어는 읽기 능력에 비해 말하기, 듣기 능력이 상대적으로 떨어진다고 합니다. 실제로 오랫동안 영어를 공부한 사람들 중에 문자로 된 글은 잘 읽고 이해하는데 외국인과 대면했을 때 자신의 의사를 제대로 전달하지 못하는 경우가 많습니다. 말하지 못하는 영어는 죽은 영어라는 인식과 함께, 요즘은 말하기 능력을 짧은 시간에, 가장 쉽고 효과적으로 향상시킬 수 있는 교재가 영어 교재 시장에서 큰 인기를 얻고 있습니다.

 그러나 영어를 포함한 외국어 학습을 논할 때, 읽기, 말하기, 듣기는 사실상 분리된 학습이라 볼 수 없습니다. 단어를 모르는 사람은 문장의 뜻을 이해할 수 없고, 개개의 단어 뜻은 알지만 문법을 알지 못하는 사람 역시 문장의 의미를 정확히 파악할 수 없습니다. 문자로 된 영문을 읽고 이해하지 못하는 사람은 영어로 잘 말할 수 없고, 발음을 제대로 알아듣지 못하는 사람은 제대로 된 발음으로 말할 수 없습니다. 이렇듯 외국어 학습에서 독해, 문법, 어휘, 듣기, 말하기는 서로 밀접하게 관련되어 있어서 이 중 일부분에만 치우친 학습은 올바른 외국어 학습이라 볼 수 없습니다.

 이 교재는 이러한 사실을 고려하여 독해를 기본으로 문법, 어휘, 듣기 학습이 동시에 효과적으로 이루어질 수 있도록 구성하였습니다. 여러 분야의 학습을 동시에 도모하는데 독해를 기본으로 한 데에는 이유가 있습니다. 어떤 글을 읽고 그 의미를 파악하고 이해하는 능력을 독해력이라고 하는데, 외국어 학습에서 독해력은 대단히 중요한 능력입니다. 외국어 학습의 목적과 목표는 개인마다 차이가 있겠지만, 독해 능력 향상은 누구에게나 외국어 학습의 중요한 목표 중 하나로 꼽힙니다. 대다수 외국어 관련 시험에서 독해 문항이 주를 이루는 것도 이 때문입니다.

독해 능력을 향상시키려면, 일단 어휘력이 기본이 되어야 합니다. 그러나 어휘 하나만으로 독해 능력을 높일 수 없고, 기본적인 문법, 구문에 대한 학습이 병행되어야 합니다. 그래서 독해력 향상을 위한 학습은 어휘, 문법, 구문 학습이 반드시 함께 이루어져야 합니다. 이렇게 읽기 능력을 키울 때 듣기와 말하기까지 병행된다면 가장 이상적인 외국어 학습이라 할 수 있습니다. 이 교재가 원어민이 읽어주는 지문 소리 파일을 제공하는 이유도 여기에 있습니다. 단순히 눈으로 읽고 의미를 파악하는 데서 끝나지 않고 귀로 듣고, 이를 따라서 소리 내어 반복적으로 읽는다면 독해서 한 권으로 읽기, 듣기, 말하기까지 학습할 수 있을 것입니다.

Interesting Scripts
재밌는 상식+다양한 분야별 지문

이 교재는 재미가 없으면 공부할 의욕이 생기질 않는 점을 고려하여 교재에서 다루는 100편의 지문을 흥미롭고 유익한 주제를 위주로 선별하였습니다. 또한, 아무리 재미있는 콘텐츠를 담고 있는 교재라도 그 교재를 학습하는 독자들에게 학습에 별 도움이 되지 못한다면 쓸모없는 교재가 되기 때문에, 선생님이 칠판에 판서하면서 수업하듯이 설명해주는 러닝보드(Learning Board)라는 코너를 마련하여 지문을 분석하고, 문장구조와 문법, 그리고 어휘의 첨삭설명을 통해 혼자서 공부하는데에도 큰 어려움이 없도록 배려하였습니다. 한 권의 독해교재를 통해 재미와 공부라는 두 마리 토끼를 모두 잡을 수 있도록 노력하였습니다.

영어가 어렵게만 와 닿고 흥미가 없어 영어 학습에 어려움을 겪고 있는 모든 분들에게 이 교재가 사막의 '오아시스'이자 영어의 바른 길잡이가 되길 바라며, 재미있게 읽으면서 문법, 어휘뿐 아니라 독해력, 청취력, 말하기 능력까지 향상되는 기회가 될 수 있기를 바랍니다.

Preview

본 교재는 지문을 읽고 문제를 풀고 복습할 수 있는 본서와 문제에 대한 정답과 해설을 실은 해설집으로 구성되어 있습니다.

1. 본서 구성 : 지문과 문제, 학습보드 & 어휘, 리스닝 & 딕테이션, 부록

① 독해 지문

독해지문은 총 100편으로, 크게 10개의 주제로 나눈 챕터에 각 10편의 지문이 들어 있습니다. 지문 내용은 일상생활에서 흔히 만날 수 있는 주제와 일반적인 상식, 그리고 재미와 흥미를 느낄 수 있는 토픽 위주로 구성되어 있습니다. 재미있게 읽으며 독해 학습도 하고 다양한 배경 지식도 쌓을 수 있는 기회가 될 것입니다.

02 Did You Know Painkillers Can Cause You A Wide Variety Of Pains?

Painkillers are supposed to kill pain. But unfortunately sometimes and in some cases, painkillers can cause you pain because they carry side effects like any type of drug. They can be dangerous even under normal use, so be careful not to misuse or abuse them.

Many people know that painkillers commonly cause constipation. So painkiller users should drink lots of water when taking them. Also painkillers can have an effect on both your heart and lungs. Some painkillers not only cause a feeling of sedation but also slow down the functioning of the heart and lungs. So if you have a problem with your cardiovascular or respiratory systems, you have to be extra careful. And some people complain of a feeling of sleepiness after taking them. That's because certain kinds of painkillers numb the receptors in the body that sense pain.

Aside from these, there are other side effects of painkillers such as addiction, difficulty sleeping and hallucinations. The best way to prevent possible side effects is to consult your doctor before use.

1 What is the main idea of this story?
  a. Painkillers may have unexpected side effects and cause pains.
  b. You should drink lots of water when taking painkillers.
  c. Painkillers are supposed to cause addiction and difficulty sleeping.
  d. Painkillers are evil so shouldn't be taken by anyone.

2 According to the article, almost every drug _____.
  a. slows down the function of many organs.
  b. can kill all kinds of pains.
  c. causes hallucinations.
  d. carries side effects.

3 Choose the correct words for each sentence.
  a. Government officials who misuse /mistreat /mistake power for their own benefits must be punished.
  b. Are there any the other / another / other students who want to try these pants on?
  c. Please tell me if you have a problem as / with / into the cardiovascular system.

② 연습문제

각 지문을 읽고 세 가지 형식의 문제를 풉니다. 문제는 1. 지문의 내용을 제대로 이해했는지 묻는 요지 또는 제목을 찾는 문제, 2. 세부적인 내용을 이해하였는지를 묻는 문제, 3. 지문에 나온 단어와 문법, 구문을 응용하여 맞는 표현을 고르는 문제(3~4문제)로 구성되어 있습니다. 문제를 푼 직후, 또는 모르는 문제가 나왔다고 해서 곧바로 정답을 확인하기보다는, 오른쪽의 Learning Board까지 모두 학습한 후 다시 한 번 문제를 풀어보고, 그 이후에 정답을 확인하는 것이 좋습니다. ※정답 및 해설은 해설집에 수록되어 있습니다.

마치 선생님이 강의하듯 시원하게 풀어 설명해주는 학습보드
& 관련어휘까지 깔끔히 정리된 어휘해설

③ 학습보드(Learning Board)

화이트보드의 형식으로 본문과 동일한 지문을 다시 한 번 보여주고, 본문 지문의 기본적인 문장 구조와 문법, 어휘 설명이 추가되어 있습니다. Learning Board에는 마치 선생님이 화이트보드에 판서하며 강의하듯 지문에 나온 구문, 어구에 대한 설명이 들어 있어서 학습자가 혼자서도 어렵지 않게 공부할 수 있습니다.

※ 초급단계에서 반드시 알고 있어야 할 필수 어휘는 형광색으로 표시해두었습니다. 아래 Words & Expressions에서 뜻을 꼭 확인하세요.

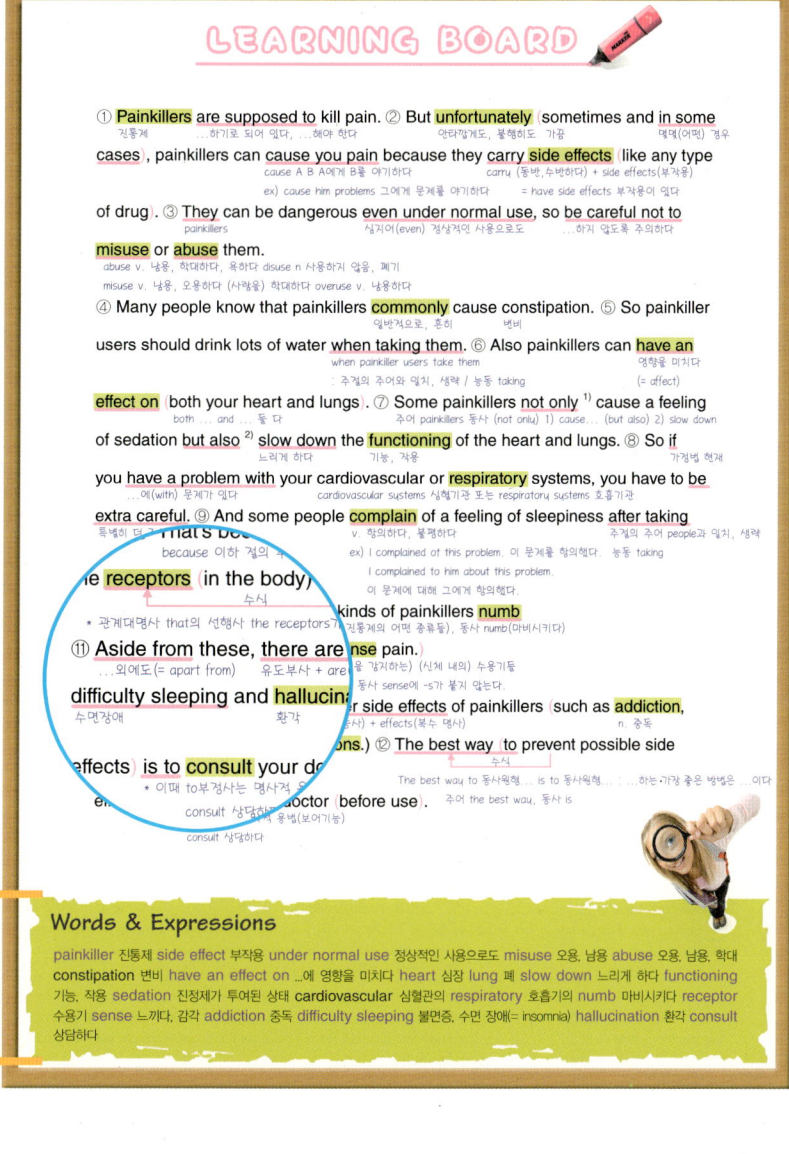

④ 어휘 (Words & Expressions)

학습한 어휘를 쉽게 복습할 수 있도록 본문에 나온 단어와 숙어, 관용어구뿐 아니라 학습보드에서 추가로 다룬 어휘까지 한꺼번에 정리되어 있는 코너입니다. 교재 뒷부분에 수록된 '부록 1. 이 책에서 배운 단어 정리'를 통해 다시 알파벳 순서로 복습하실 수 있습니다.

※ 굳이 외우지 않아도 되는 수준 높은 어휘는 회색처리 되어 있습니다.

지문 5개마다 제공되는 복습용 리스닝 프로그램 (하루 5개씩, 20일 1회독 완성)
& 듣고 싶을 때 바로 들을 수 있는 QR코드를 통해 리스닝과 복습효과 UP!

⑤ 듣기와 받아쓰기 (Listening with Dictation)

이 교재는 원어민이 지문을 읽어주는 MP3 파일이 함께 제공됩니다. Dictation은 본문 지문과 동일한 지문에 빈칸 처리가 되어 있습니다. 학습자는 소리 파일을 들으며 빈칸에 들어갈 단어, 표현을 받아 적습니다. Dictation은 듣기 훈련과 복습을 위해 마련된 것으로, 발음, 청취 측면에서 훈련이 필요한 단어나 표현, 그리고 본문에서 학습한 내용 위주로 빈칸 처리되어 있습니다. Dictation으로 듣기 훈련을 마친 후, 원어민 발음을 참고하여 소리 내어 지문을 다시 읽을 것을 추천합니다. 소리 파일을 듣고 소리 내어 읽는 과정을 반복하면 듣기와 말하기, 발음 훈련뿐 아니라 본문 내용을 복습하는 효과까지 얻을 수 있습니다.

※ 스마트폰에 QR코드를 인식하는 무료앱을 설치 후 QR코드를 스캔해주세요.

딕테이션의 정답 또한 바로 확인할 수 있도록 우측 페이지 하단에 배치되어 있습니다. 머리에서 잊기 전에 자연스럽게 복습할 수 있도록 5개의 지문을 학습할 때마다 이어서 5개의 딕테이션이 제공됩니다. 이에 맞춰, 독해를 집중적으로 공부할 경우 하루 5개 지문씩 20일 완성으로 교재를 1회독할 수 있습니다.

⑥ 부록 (Appendix)

1) 이 책에서 배운 단어 정리 : Words & Expressions에서 다룬 모든 단어를 알파벳순으로 나열하여 단어의 위치를 표시하였습니다. 단어만 복습하고자 할 때 복습용으로 활용할 수 있습니다.
2) 구두점의 쓰임 : 지문에 자주 등장하는 구두점의 정의와 용례를 정리하여 부록으로 담았습니다.

2. 해설집 구성 : 지문해석 & 정답 및 문제해설

① 지문 해석

지문 해석은 지나친 의역보다는 독해 학습에 맞도록 적절한 직역 위주로 번역되어 있습니다. Learning Board의 각 문장과 한글 해석에 번호를 매겨 놓았기 때문에 문장마다 앞에 표시된 번호로 영문과 해당 영문의 해석을 빠르고 쉽게 찾을 수 있습니다.

---

04 의사도 귀지가 생기는 정확한 이유를 잘 모른다는 거 아세요?

① 흥미롭게도 의사들은 귀지가 생기는 정확한 이유는 잘 모른다고 합니다. ② 하지만, 그 이유에 대한 몇 가지 이론은 있습니다. ③ 의사들은 귀지가 귀의 자가 청소 과정과 관련이 있으리라 생각합니다. ④ 또 귀지에 항바이러스 성질이 있다고 생각합니다. ⑤ 일반적으로 귀지가 먼지나 작은 벌레가 귀 안쪽으로 들어오지 못하게 막아 귀를 보호한다고 합니다. ⑥ 그리고 개인에 따라 귀지의 양이 차이 나는 확실한 이유 역시 아무도 모릅니다. ⑦ 어떤 사람은 귀지가 많이 생기는 데 반해, 어떤 사람은 전혀 생기지 않기도 합니다. ⑧ 물론 이유는 모릅니다. ⑨ 다행히 의사들은 너무 많이 생긴 귀지를 제거하는 가장 안전한 방법을 알고 있습니다. ⑩ 많은 사람들이 귀지를 제거하려고 면봉을 사용하지만, 의사들은 면봉이나 다른 작은 물건을 이도에 넣지 말 것을 권고합니다. ⑪ 그러다 귀지를 더 안쪽으로 밀어 넣을 수도 있고 또는 본의 아니게 이도나 고막 안쪽에 손상을 입힐 수도 있기 때문입니다. ⑫ 가장 좋은 방법은 젖은 수건을 사용하는 것입니다. ⑬ 손가락에 수건을 감고 귀 볼을 닦으세요. ⑭ 과도한 귀지를 제거하고 싶다면 따뜻한 물을 귀 안으로 흘려보낸 후 머리를 한쪽으로 기울여 귀지를 내 버리세요. ⑮ 그리고 부드럽고 마른 수건으로 귀 안쪽을 닦습니다.

문제 정답 및 해설

1. (c) 이 글의 요지를 고르세요.
   a. 의사들은 귀지에 대해 아는 게 하나도 없으니 그들의 말에 귀를 기울이지 말아야 한다. (not know beans about ...에 대해 아는 것이 하나도 없다)
   b. 귀지는 면봉처럼 작은 물건으로 제거되어야 한다.
   c. 우리에게 귀지가 생기는 정확한 이유는 아직 모르지만, 최선의 귀지 제거 방법은 알고 있다.
   d. 수건으로 여분의 귀지를 제거하는 것은 대단히 중요하다.

2. (a) 지문 내용과 맞지 않는 것을 고르세요.
   a. 의사들은 우리에게 귀지가 생기는 이유를 간신히 밝혀냈다. (manage to 간신히, 겨우, 힘겹게 ...를 해내다)
      ▶ 정확하고 확실한 이유는 밝혀내지 못했고, 이에 관한 몇 가지 이론만 있다.
   b. 면봉을 사용하는 것이 여분의 귀지를 제거하는 가장 안전한 방법이 아닐 수 있다.
   c. 모든 사람에게 같은 양의 귀지가 생기는 건 아니다.
   d. 우리에게 귀지가 생기는 이유에 관해 한 가지 이상의 이론이 있다.

a. (while) 네가 만든 사과 파이는 너무 달았지만, 반면 네 여동생이 만든 딸기 파이는 아주 맛있었다.
l mover over 게다가, in addition 덧붙여, 게다가, while 반면에

【해설】 앞 문장과 반대, 대조되는 내용이 이어지고 있기 때문에 while이 오는 것이 자연스럽다.

b. (does) 맥스에게 물어보세요. 그가 정말로 정답을 알고 있는데 그는 바로 저기에 있습니다.
【해설】 강조의 do : 본동사를 강조할 때 본동사 앞에 쓰이는데, 조동사처럼 시제와 인칭 변화가 do 동사에서 표현되고 본동사는 원형이 온다. 주어가 he(3인칭 단수 현재)이기 때문에 do가 아닌 does가 와야 한다. 'He knows the right answer...'에서 'knows'를 강조하기 위해 does know로 쓴 것이다. have나 get 등의 동사는 본동사를 강조하기 위한 동사로는 쓰이지 않고 have, get 바로 다음에 동사 원형이 오지 않는다. 단 사역동사로 쓰일 경우 목적어와 함께 원형 동사가 올 수 있다.

c. (as to why) 나는 그가 어제 그렇게 빨리 떠난 이유에 대한 그의 설명을 원한다.
【해설】 as to why ...에 대한 이유, ...의 이유에 대해
ex) There's no mystery as to why he broke up with her.
그가 그녀와 헤어진 이유에 대해 이해 못 할 건 없다.(이상할 것도 없다.)

---

② 문제 정답 및 해설

정답 및 해설 역시 영문 문항을 가급적 직역 위주로 해석하였으며, 문제 해설의 경우 정답뿐 아니라 오답도 정답이 될 수 없는 이유를 설명하여 풍부한 사고적 학습이 가능하도록 하였습니다. 또한 제시된 어휘나 문법을 공부할 때 함께 알아두면 유용한 관련 어휘와 문법을 자연스럽게 익힐 수 있도록 정리하였으며, 중요 표현 또는 문법의 쓰임을 정확히 이해할 수 있도록 예문도 함께 실었습니다.

Contents

Chapter 1. Health

01. **Did you know** Household Dust Is A Bunch Of Dead Skin Cells?
    집 먼지가 죽은 피부 세포 뭉치라는 거 아세요? `18`
02. **Did you know** Painkillers Can Cause You A Wide Variety Of Pains?
    진통제가 다양한 통증을 유발할 수 있다는 거 아세요? `20`
03. **Did you know** Cracking Your Knuckles Has Nothing To Do With Arthritis?
    손가락 관절 꺾기와 관절염은 아무 상관이 없다는 거 아세요? `22`
04. **Did you know** Doctors Don't Know Exactly Why We Have Earwax?
    의사도 귀지가 생기는 정확한 이유를 잘 모른다는 거 아세요? `24`
05. **Did you know** There Are 5,000,000 Red Blood Cells In One Drop Of Blood?
    피 한 방울에 5백만 개의 적혈구가 있다는 거 아세요? `26`

▷ Listening with Dictation `28`

06. **Did you know** Your Hands Can Tell You About Your Health?
    손이 당신의 건강에 관해 말해준다는 거 아세요? `30`
07. **Did you know** How Much Food You Can Eat After Gastric Bypass Surgery?
    위장우회수술 후 얼마나 먹을 수 있는지 아세요? `32`
08. **Did you know** Why Animal Activists Are Upset About Leech Therapy?
    동물 보호론자들이 왜 거머리 치료를 못마땅하게 여기는지 아세요? `34`
09. **Did you know** Not All Fish Are Good For Our Health?
    모든 생선이 다 건강에 좋은 건 아니라는 거 아세요? `36`
10. **Did you know** Why Carrot Juice Is Called Miracle Juice?
    왜 당근 주스가 기적의 주스라고 불리는지 아세요? `38`

▷ Listening with Dictation `40`

Chapter 2. Food

11. **Did you know** 'Sweetbread' Is Neither Sweet Nor Bread?
    스위트브레드가 달콤하지도 않고 빵도 아니라는 거 아세요? `44`
12. **Did you know** Vegetarians Do Not Eat Marshmallow?
    채식주의자들이 마시멜로를 먹지 않는다는 거 아세요? `46`
13. **Did you know** Shark Fin Soup Is As Dangerous As Sharks?
    상어 지느러미 수프가 상어만큼 위험하다는 거 아세요? `48`
14. **Did you know** Cambodians Like To Eat Fried Spiders?
    캄보디아 사람들은 튀긴 거미 먹기를 좋아한다는 거 아세요? `50`
15. **Did you know** Which Fruit Can Burn About 9 Pounds In A Month?
    한 달 안에 9파운드를 빼주는 과일이 무엇인지 아세요? `52`

▷ Listening with Dictation `54`

16. **Did you know** Fat-Free Foods Are Not Always Good For Your Health?
    무지방 음식이 항상 건강에 좋지는 않다는 거 아세요? `56`
17. **Did you know** Koreans Are Not The Only People Who Enjoy Soondae?
    우리만 순대를 좋아하는 게 아니라는 거 아세요? `58`
18. **Did you know** Chinese People Eat Pigeon Soup?
    중국인들이 비둘기 수프를 먹는다는 거 아세요? `60`
19. **Did you know** There Is A Nearly $200 Sandwich?
    약 200달러짜리 샌드위치가 있다는 거 아세요? `62`
20. **Did you know** The Most Expensive Coffee Is Made Of Cat Poo?
    가장 비싼 커피가 고양이 똥으로 만든다는 거 아세요? `64`

▷ Listening with Dictation `66`

Chapter 3.
Beauty

21. Did you know **Botox Is A Kind Of Poison?**
    보톡스가 일종의 독이라는 거 아세요? `70`
22. Did you know **The Basic Tips For Cleansing?**
    세안을 위한 기본 팁을 아세요? `72`
23. Did you know **How To Choose The Right Fat Burner?**
    어떻게 올바른 지방 연소제를 선택해야 하는지 아세요? `74`
24. Did you know **Three "Don'ts" For Healthy And Smooth Skin?**
    건강하고 매끄러운 피부를 위해 하지 말아야 할 세 가지가 무엇인지 아세요? `76`
25. Did you know **How To Prevent Split Ends?**
    갈라지는 머리끝을 방지하는 방법을 아세요? `78`

▷ Listening with Dictation `80`

26. Did you know **The Sweetest Way To Control Acne?**
    여드름을 관리하는 가장 달콤한 방법이 무엇인지 아세요? `82`
27. Did you know **Three Tips For Whiter Teeth?**
    더 하얀 치아를 갖기 위한 세 가지 팁을 아세요? `84`
28. Did you know **Why Removing Love Handles Is Difficult?**
    러브 핸들을 제거하는 게 왜 어려운지 아세요? `86`
29. Did you know **Which Hair Colors Can Make You Look Younger?**
    젊어 보이게 만드는 머리카락 색깔이 무엇인지 아세요? `88`
30. Did you know **There Are Exercises For Under-Eye Bags?**
    처진 눈 밑 살을 위한 운동이 있다는 거 아세요? `90`

▷ Listening with Dictation `92`

---

31. Did you know **That Calment's Secret Of Longevity Was Chocolate?**
    칼멘의 장수 비결이 초콜릿이라는 거 아세요? `96`
32. Did you know **What Happened To Karen Butler After Oral Surgery?**
    구강 수술 후 카렌 버틀러에게 어떤 일이 생겼는지 아세요? `98`
33. Did you know **How These Russian Girls Got The Wrong Parents?**
    어떻게 이 러시아 소녀들이 엉뚱한 부모와 살게 되었는지 아세요? `100`
34. Did you know **Why Jocelyn Wildenstein Is Famous?**
    조슬린 와일든스타인이 왜 유명한지 아세요? `102`
35. Did you know **How Rich Hollywood Stars Give Birth?**
    할리우드 스타들은 어떻게 출산하는지 아세요? `104`

▷ Listening with Dictation `106`

Chapter 4.
People

36. Did you know **What Nelson Mandela, Edgar Allan Poe, and Leo Tolstoy Have In Common?**
    넬슨 만델라, 에드거 앨런 포, 레오 톨스토이의 공통점이 무엇인지 아세요? `108`
37. Did you know **How Much This Eating Champion Weighs?**
    먹기 대회 우승자의 몸무게가 얼마인지 아세요? `110`
38. Did you know **How Cheval The Mailman Built 'Le Palais Ideal'?**
    우체부 슈발이 어떻게 '팔레 이데알'을 건축했는지 아세요? `112`
39. Did you know **Why Lali Was Worshiped As A Reincarnated God?**
    랄리가 왜 환생한 신으로 숭배 받았는지 아세요? `114`
40. Did you know **How Billie Bob Harrell, The Lottery Winner, Died?**
    복권 당첨자인 빌리 밥 하렐이 어떻게 죽었는지 아세요? `116`

▷ Listening with Dictation `118`

Chapter 5.
Animals & Nature

41. **Did you know** Not All Spiders Make Webs?
   모든 거미가 거미줄을 만드는 건 아니라는 사실 아세요? `122`
42. **Did you know** Where Oxygen Comes From?
   산소가 어디에서 나오는지 아세요? `124`
43. **Did you know** Cockroaches Are Kept As Pets?
   애완동물로 길러지는 바퀴벌레를 아세요? `126`
44. **Did you know** You Have To Pay A Fee Before Climbing The Himalayas?
   히말라야에 등반하기 전에 돈을 내야 한다는 거 아세요? `128`
45. **Did you know** Bats' Droppings Are Valuable To Humans?
   박쥐 똥이 인간에게 가치가 있다는 거 아세요? `130`

▷ Listening with Dictation `132`

46. **Did you know** How Hot The Hottest Hot Spring In The World Is?
   세계에서 가장 뜨거운 온천이 얼마나 뜨거운지 아세요? `134`
47. **Did you know** Why The Quagga, A Half Zebra And Half Horse, Went Extinct?
   반은 얼룩말, 반은 말인 콰가가 왜 멸종했는지 아세요? `136`
48. **Did you know** Whales Are Useful To The Bone?
   고래가 뼈까지 유용하다는 거 아세요? `138`
49. **Did you know** Animals Do Feel Sad?
   동물도 슬픔을 느낀다는 거 아세요? `140`
50. **Did you know** Sharks Can Play Opossum?
   상어가 주머니쥐 흉내를 낼 수 있다는 거 아세요? `142`

▷ Listening with Dictation `144`

Chapter 6.
Myth Or Fact

51. **Did you know** A Myth About The Common Cold?
   일반 감기에 관한 낭설을 아세요? `148`
52. **Did you know** 'Never Eat Before Exercise' Is A Myth?
   '운동 전에 먹으면 안 된다'는 게 낭설이라는 거 아세요? `150`
53. **Did you know** Reading In Dim Light Is Not A Cause Of Eye Damage?
   어두운 조명에서 글을 읽는다고 시력이 손상되는 건 아니라는 거 아세요? `152`
54. **Did you know** Whitening Toothpastes Do Not Whiten Your Teeth?
   미백 치약이 치아를 희게 만들지 않는다는 거 아세요? `154`
55. **Did you know** Coffee Won't Help You Sober Up?
   커피가 술 깨는데 도움이 안 된다는 거 아세요? `156`

▷ Listening with Dictation `158`

56. **Did you know** Cell Phones Have Nothing To Do With Gas Station Fires?
   휴대폰과 주유소 화재는 관계가 없다는 거 아세요? `160`
57. **Did you know** You Should Not Tilt Your Head Back When Your Nose Is Bleeding?
   코피가 날 때 머리를 뒤로 젖히면 안 된다는 거 아세요? `162`
58. **Did you know** What The Most Common Food Allergy Among Children Is?
   어린이들에게 가장 흔한 음식 알레르기가 무엇인지 아세요? `164`
59. **Did you know** The Majority Of The Sugar We Consume Is Not From Sweets?
   우리가 섭취하는 설탕 대부분이 단 과자에서 나오는 게 아니라는 거 아세요? `166`
60. **Did you know** There's No Need To Worry When You Die In Your Dreams?
   꿈에서 죽어도 걱정할 필요 없다는 거 아세요? `168`

▷ Listening with Dictation `170`

61. **Did You Know** There Is Palm Reading In Western Culture?
 서구 문화에서도 손금을 읽는다는 거 아세요? `174`
62. **Did You Know** How Copperfield Made The Statue Of Liberty Disappear?
 카퍼필드가 자유의 여신상을 어떻게 사라지게 했는지 아세요? `176`
63. **Did You Know** How American Psychic Readers List Their Ads?
 미국인 점술사들은 어떻게 광고하는지 아세요? `178`
64. **Did You Know** The Tarot Was Originally Used To Play Card Games?
 타로가 원래 카드 게임으로 사용되었다는 거 아세요? `180`
65. **Did You Know** There Was A Film In Which The Ghost Of A Dog Appeared?
 개 유령이 나타난 영화가 있다는 거 아세요? `182`

▷ Listening with Dictation `184`

Chapter 7. The Supernatural

66. **Did You Know** Your Face Reveals Your Personality?
 당신의 얼굴이 당신의 성격을 드러낸다는 거 아세요? `186`
67. **Did You Know** It's Bad Luck To Let Milk Boil Over?
 우유를 끓어 넘치게 하면 불운이라는 거 아세요? `188`
68. **Did You Know** How Friday The 13th Became The Worst Day?
 13일의 금요일이 어떻게 최악의 날이 되었는지 아세요? `190`
69. **Did You Know** How Many People Died Because Of The Salem Witch Trials?
 살렘 마녀 재판 때문에 몇 명이 사망했는지 아세요? `192`
70. **Did You Know** About The Mystery 'Ghost' House?
 미스터리 '유령'의 집을 아세요? `194`

▷ Listening with Dictation `196`

Chapter 8. Interesting Stories

71. **Did you know** What Animal Has 3 Hearts, 9 Brains, And Blue Blood?
 무슨 동물이 3개의 심장, 9개의 뇌, 그리고 파란 피를 갖고 있는지 아세요? `200`
72. **Did you know** St. Stephen's Clock Tower Is Leaning To One Side Just Like The Leaning Tower Of Pisa?
 성 스테판의 시계탑이 피사의 사탑처럼 한쪽으로 기울어지고 있다는 거 아세요? `202`
73. **Did you know** Why The Emperor Who Built The Taj Mahal Cut His Workers' Hands Off?
 타지마할을 건축한 황제가 일꾼들의 손을 자른 이유를 아세요? `204`
74. **Did you know** Why Fatemah Allowed Her Husband's Second Marriage?
 페이트마가 남편의 두 번째 결혼을 허락한 이유를 아세요? `206`
75. **Did you know** Who Can Be Mosquitoes' Favorites?
 누가 모기의 총애를 받는 사람이 되는지 아세요? `208`

▷ Listening with Dictation `210`

76. **Did you know** How Two Russians Made An Amazing Alien?
 두 명의 러시아인들이 놀라운 외계인을 어떻게 만들었는지 아세요? `212`
77. **Did you know** Why American-born Giant Pandas Were Sent Back To China?
 미국에서 태어난 자이언트 판다들이 왜 중국으로 돌려보내 졌는지 아세요? `214`
78. **Did you know** What The Kennedy Curse Is?
 케네디 저주가 무엇인지 아세요? `216`
79. **Did you know** Mount Rushmore Was Carved With The Help Of Dynamite?
 러슈모어산이 다이너마이트의 도움으로 조각되었다는 거 아세요? `218`
80. **Did you know** There Are Giraffe-looking Women?
 기린처럼 보이는 여성들이 있다는 거 아세요? `220`

▷ Listening with Dictation `222`

Chapter 9.
The Amazing Records

81. Did you know Who The Tallest Person In The World Is?
    세상에서 가장 큰 사람이 누구인지 아세요? 226
82. Did you know What Wolf Girl Wants To Be In The Future?
    늑대 소녀가 나중에 무엇이 되고 싶은지 아세요? 228
83. Did you know What The Most Dangerous Tree In The World Is?
    세상에서 가장 위험한 나무가 무엇인지 아세요? 230
84. Did you know How Long The Longest Tongue In The World Is?
    세상에서 가장 긴 혀가 얼마나 긴지 아세요? 232
85. Did you know How To Hold The World Record In The Field Of Marriage?
    결혼 분야에서 세계 기록을 보유하려면 어떻게 해야 하는지 아세요? 234

▷ Listening with Dictation 236

86. Did you know This Guinness Trivia?
    이런 기네스 기록도 있다는 거 아세요? 238
87. Did you know What Kind Of Record Dr. Marcel Petiot Held?
    마르셀 프티오 의사가 어떤 기록을 보유했는지 아세요? 240
88. Did you know The Shortest War Lasted Only 38 Minutes?
    가장 짧은 전쟁이 단 38분간 지속되었다는 거 아세요? 242
89. Did you know There Was A Mother Of 69 Children?
    69명의 자녀를 둔 어머니가 있다는 거 아세요? 244
90. Did you know How Fast Bruce Lee's Kicks Were?
    이소룡의 발차기가 얼마나 빨랐는지 아세요? 246

▷ Listening with Dictation 248

91. Did you know A Leopard Cannot Change Its Spots?
    표범이 자신의 점들을 바꿀 수 없다는 거 아세요? 252
92. Did you know You Can 'Paint The Town Red' Without A Paintbrush?
    붓 없이도 '시내를 빨갛게 칠할' 수 있다는 거 아세요? 254
93. Did you know What Can Kill The Cat With Nine Lives?
    목숨이 9개인 고양이를 죽일 수 있는 게 무엇인지 아세요? 256
94. Did you know You Can "Get The Axe" Without Receiving Any Actual Axe?
    실제 도끼를 받지 않고도 'get the axe' 할 수 있다는 거 아세요? 258
95. Did you know What Happens To Fish When They Go Belly-up?
    물고기가 배를 드러내면 어떻게 되는지 아세요? 260

▷ Listening with Dictation 262

Chapter 10.
Proverbs & Idioms

96. Did you know 'Gung Ho' Comes From Chinese Characters?
    'gung ho'가 한자라는 거 아세요? 264
97. Did you know The Meaning Of 'Easier Said Than Done'?
    'easier said than done'의 의미를 아세요? 266
98. Did you know The Meaning Of 'Blow It'?
    'blow it'의 의미를 아세요? 268
99. Did you know The Meaning Of 'Spill The Beans'?
    'spill the beans'의 의미를 아세요? 270
100. Did you know The Meaning Of 'Mind One's Ps And Qs'?
     'mind one's P's and Q's'의 의미를 아세요? 272

▷ Listening with Dictation 274

APPENDIX
1. 이 책에서 배운 단어 정리 278~293
2. 구두점의 쓰임 294~296

[해설집] ※ 책속의 책으로 제공

 **MP3 및 학습자료 다운로드 안내**

본 교재의 MP3 및 학습자료는 보카바이블닷컴에서 무료로 제공해드립니다.
아래 QR코드를 스캔하시거나 보카바이블닷컴에서 다운로드 받아 이용하실 수 있습니다.
(www.vocabible.com)

※ QR코드 상세 안내

 **원배속 원어민 녹음 MP3 다운받기**
(폰에서 다운로드 시 zip파일을 풀 수 있는 앱을 먼저 설치해주세요.)

 **타입별 MP3 다운받기/ 스트리밍 지원**
(챕터별/통합/개별 + 1.2배속 파일제공)

 **보카바이블닷컴 바로가기**
(www.vocabible.com)

▷ 원어민 MP3파일은 원배속과 1.2배속을 지원합니다.
　교재의 리스닝 코너에서도 QR코드를 통해 바로 들으실 수 있습니다.

Chapter 1. Health

01. Did You Know Household Dust Is A Bunch Of Dead Skin Cells?

집 먼지가 죽은 피부 세포 뭉치라는 거 아세요?

02. Did You Know Painkillers Can Cause You A Wide Variety Of Pains?

진통제가 다양한 통증을 유발할 수 있다는 거 아세요?

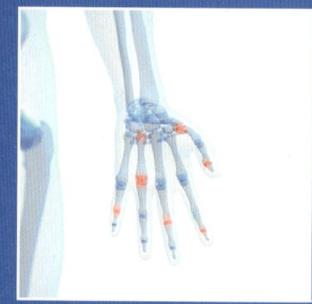

03. Did You Know Cracking Your Knuckles Has Nothing To Do With Arthritis?

손가락 관절 꺾기와 관절염은 아무 상관이 없다는 거 아세요?

04. Did You Know Doctors Don't Know Exactly Why We Have Earwax?

의사도 귀지가 생기는 정확한 이유를 잘 모른다는 거 아세요?

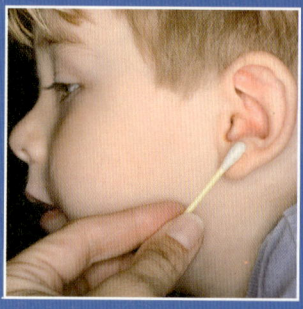

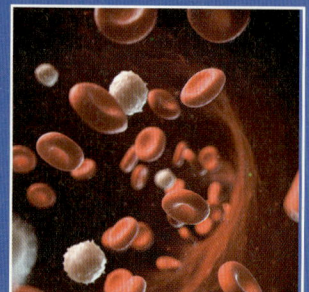

05. Did You Know There Are 5,000,000 Red Blood Cells In One Drop Of Blood?

피 한 방울에 5백만 개의 적혈구가 있다는 거 아세요?

※ 이 챕터의 원어민녹음 MP3를 들으시려면
스마트폰으로 우측 QR코드를 스캔해주세요

06. Did You Know Your Hands Can Tell You About Your Health?

손이 당신의 건강에 관해 말해준다는 거 아세요?

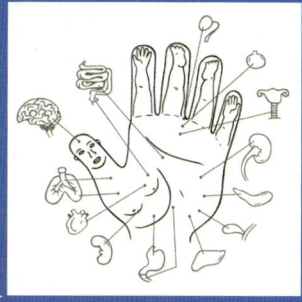

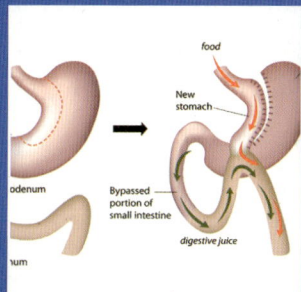

07. Did You Know How Much Food You Can Eat After Gastric Bypass Surgery?

위장우회수술 후 얼마나 먹을 수 있는지 아세요?

08. Did You Know Why Animal Activists Are Upset About Leech Therapy?

동물 보호론자들이 왜 거머리 치료를 못마땅하게 여기는지 아세요?

09. Did You Know Not All Fish Are Good For Our Health?

모든 생선이 다 건강에 좋은 건 아니라는 거 아세요?

10. Did You Know Why Carrot Juice Is Called Miracle Juice?

왜 당근 주스가 기적의 주스라고 불리는지 아세요?

01 Did You Know Household Dust Is A Bunch Of Dead Skin Cells?

Dust in your house is mostly made of dead skin cells. It is estimated that 30,000-40,000 dead skin cells are flaked off from your body per minute. Given the fact that the human body sheds dead skin cells constantly, we can say that common house dust is practically a bunch of dead skin cells.

Of course there are other things in household dust, such as the dried-up dead bodies of dust mites. Dust mites eat humans' dead skin cells and live in bedding, carpets and soft furnishings. When they are alive, they are the cause of allergies. After they die, they become part of household dust. It's not surprising that they are hated by everyone.

Another component is tiny fibers fallen from clothing, furniture fabrics and bedding. Furthermore, if you have pets in your house, your cute little pets will highly contribute to dust production since they drop all kinds of things. Pets drop dead skin cells and dried-up dead bodies of pet mites as well as hair. And if they wear dog clothing, they will also drop tiny bits of fiber.

1 What is the main idea of the story?

  a. Human body sheds over 30,000 dead skin cells per minute.
  b. Dust mites are bad because they eat humans' dead skin cells.
  c. Household dust mainly consists of dead skin cells.
  d. Raising pets inside the house is bad for your health.

2 Dust in your house is made of _____.

  a. dust mites and pets' hair
  b. dead skin cells, dried dead bodies of dust mites and tiny fibers
  c. clothing, furniture fabrics and bedding
  d. pet mites and dog clothing

3 Choose the correct words for each sentence.

  a. Due to the civil war, an estimated / estimate / estimation 3 million people were forced to live in unhealthy and dangerous places.
  b. I like cake as far as / as well as / as long as doughnuts, but sandwich is my most favorite.
  c. When I went into the shed, I shed tears of fear because there was a snake shedded / shedding / shed its skin.

LEARNING BOARD

① Dust in your house is mostly made of dead skin cells. ② It is estimated that 30,000-40,000 dead skin cells are flaked off from your body per minute. ③ Given the fact that the human body sheds dead skin cells constantly, we can say that common house dust is practically a bunch of dead skin cells. ④ Of course there are other things in household dust, (such as the dried-up dead bodies of dust mites. ⑤ Dust mites 1) eat humans' dead skin cells and 2) live in bedding, carpets and soft furnishings. ⑥ When they are alive, they are the cause of allergies. ⑦ After they die, they become part of household dust. ⑧ It's not surprising that they are hated by everyone. ⑨ Another component is tiny fibers (fallen from clothing, furniture fabrics and bedding). ⑩ Furthermore, if you have pets in your house, your cute little pets will highly contribute to dust production since they drop all kinds of things. ⑪ Pets drop 1) dead skin cells and 2) dried-up dead bodies of pet mites as well as 3) hair. ⑫ And if they wear dog clothing, they will also drop tiny bits of fiber.

Words & Expressions

dust 먼지 be made of …로 만들어지다 cell 1. 세포 2. 감방 3. 전지 skin cell 피부세포 It is estimated that …라고 추정되다 flake n. (떨어져 나온) 얇은 조각 v. 벗겨지다, 떨어져 나오다(off) per minute 1분당 shed n. 헛간 v. (피, 눈물, 땀) 흘리다, (허물을) 벗다 constantly 끊임없이 practically 실질적으로, 사실상 a bunch of 다수의(+ 복수 명사) dust mite 먼지 진드기 bedding 침구 soft furnishing 가정용 직물 the cause of allergy 알레르기의 원인 component 구성 요소 tiny 작은 fiber 섬유 fabric 직물, 천 furniture fabric 가구용 직물 pet 애완동물 contribute 공헌하다, 기여하다 highly contribute to …에 대단히 기여하다 dog clothing 애완견용 옷 tiny bits of fibers 작은 섬유 조각들

02 Did You Know Painkillers Can Cause You A Wide Variety Of Pains?

Painkillers are supposed to kill pain. But unfortunately sometimes and in some cases, painkillers can cause you pain because they carry side effects like any type of drug. They can be dangerous even under normal use, so be careful not to misuse or abuse them.

Many people know that painkillers commonly cause constipation. So painkiller users should drink lots of water when taking them. Also painkillers can have an effect on both your heart and lungs. Some painkillers not only cause a feeling of sedation but also slow down the functioning of the heart and lungs. So if you have a problem with your cardiovascular or respiratory systems, you have to be extra careful. And some people complain of a feeling of sleepiness after taking them. That's because certain kinds of painkillers numb the receptors in the body that sense pain.

Aside from these, there are other side effects of painkillers such as addiction, difficulty sleeping and hallucinations. The best way to prevent possible side effects is to consult your doctor before use.

1 What is the main idea of this story?
   a. Painkillers may have unexpected side effects and cause pains.
   b. You should drink lots of water when taking painkillers.
   c. Painkillers are supposed to cause addiction and difficulty sleeping.
   d. Painkillers are evil so shouldn't be taken by anyone.

2 According to the article, almost every drug _____.
   a. slows down the function of many organs.
   b. can kill all kinds of pains
   c. causes hallucinations.
   d. carries side effects.

3 Choose the correct words for each sentence.
   a. Government officials who misuse / mistreat / mistake power for their own benefits must be punished.
   b. Are there any the other / another / other students who want to try these pants on?
   c. Please tell me if you have a problem as / with / into the cardiovascular system.

LEARNING BOARD

① **Painkillers** are supposed to kill pain. ② But **unfortunately** (sometimes and in some cases), painkillers can cause you pain because they carry **side effects** (like any type of drug). ③ They can be dangerous even under normal use, so be careful not to **misuse** or **abuse** them.

④ Many people know that painkillers **commonly** cause constipation. ⑤ So painkiller users should drink lots of water when taking them. ⑥ Also painkillers can **have an effect on** (both your heart and lungs). ⑦ Some painkillers not only 1) cause a feeling of sedation but also 2) slow down the **functioning** of the heart and lungs. ⑧ So if you have a problem with your cardiovascular or **respiratory** systems, you have to be extra careful. ⑨ And some people **complain** of a feeling of sleepiness after taking them. ⑩ That's because certain kinds of painkillers **numb** the **receptors** (in the body) (that **sense** pain.)

⑪ Aside from these, there are other side effects of painkillers (such as **addiction**, difficulty sleeping and **hallucinations**.) ⑫ The best way (to prevent possible side effects) is to **consult** your doctor (before use).

Words & Expressions

painkiller 진통제 side effect 부작용 under normal use 정상적인 사용으로도 misuse 오용, 남용 abuse 오용, 남용, 학대 constipation 변비 have an effect on …에 영향을 미치다 heart 심장 lung 폐 slow down 느리게 하다 functioning 기능, 작용 sedation 진정제가 투여된 상태 cardiovascular 심혈관의 respiratory 호흡기의 numb 마비시키다 receptor 수용기 sense 느끼다, 감각 addiction 중독 difficulty sleeping 불면증, 수면 장애(= insomnia) hallucination 환각 consult 상담하다

21

03 Did You Know Cracking Your Knuckles Has Nothing To Do With Arthritis?

Knuckle cracking is an annoying bad habit. Its sound is unpleasant to hear, and the person who cracks his or her knuckles looks a little bit scary and bad. Moreover, there is a myth that knuckle cracking leads to arthritis. But that is not true for knuckle cracking does not cause arthritis. Maybe the cracking sound misleads us because people believe that if something cracks, it must be being damaged. But the truth is that nothing is cracked or damaged.

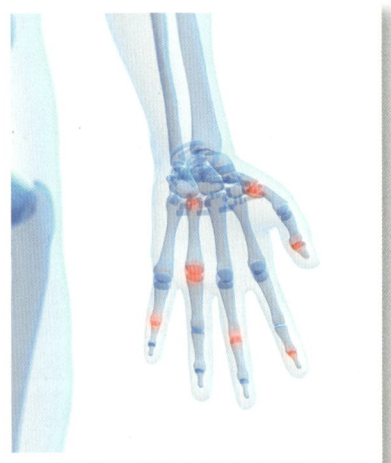

There were a few studies about this and the results indicated that knuckle cracking was not associated with arthritis. However, those studies also discovered that it would be better for knuckle crackers to stop it because it is associated with several hand problems. According to those studies, knuckle crackers are more likely to have weaker grip strength, hand swelling, or damage to the ligaments surrounding the joints than people who don't crack their knuckles.

1 What can be the best title of this story?

a. The Reason Why We Should Crack Our Knuckles
b. Start Cracking Your Knuckles For Your Hands
c. Hand swelling VS. Joint Damage
d. Knuckle Cracking : Not Related To Arthritis

2 According to the experts, knuckle crackers _____

a. tend to have weaker grip strength than who don't crack their knuckles.
b. are likely to be hospitalized because of arthritis.
c. have no choice but to have at least three hand problems.
d. must stop cracking their knuckles since knuckle cracking is annoying.

3 Choose the correct words for each sentence.

a. I think we have to wait several / a little / much more minutes for them.
b. The little boy looked scared because his teacher looked scared / scary / scare.
c. I just don't want to be associated / association / associate with those barbaric people.

LEARNING BOARD

① Knuckle cracking is an annoying bad habit. ② Its sound is unpleasant to hear, and the person (who cracks his or her knuckles) looks (a little bit) scary and bad. ③ Moreover, there is a myth that knuckle cracking leads to arthritis. ④ But that is not true for knuckle cracking does not cause arthritis. ⑤ Maybe the cracking sound misleads us because people believe that if something cracks, it must be being damaged. ⑥ But the truth is that nothing is cracked or damaged. ⑦ There were a few studies about this and the results indicated that knuckle cracking was not associated with arthritis. ⑧ However, those studies also discovered that it would be better (for knuckle crackers) to stop it because it is associated with several hand problems. ⑨ According to those studies, knuckle crackers are more likely to have weaker grip strength, hand swelling, or damage to the ligaments (surrounding the joints) than people who don't crack their knuckles.

Words & Expressions

have nothing to do with …와 관련이 없다 (↔ have something to do with …와 관련이 있다) crack 갈라지다, 깨지다 knuckle 관절 knuckle cracking 손가락 관절 꺾기 annoying 짜증 나는 habit 습관 unpleasant 불쾌한, 불편한 scary 무서운 myth 신화, 낭설 lead to …로 인도하다 mislead 잘못 인도하다, 오해하게 만들다 damage v. 손상을 주다 n. 손상, 피해, 손해배상금 arthritis 관절염 be associated with …와 관련이 있다 indicate 나타내다 grip 꽉 붙잡음, 이해, 움켜쥐다 strength 힘, 장점 swell 붓다, 불룩해지다 (swelling 부은 곳, 붓기 hand swelling 손이 붓는 것) ligament 인대 joint 관절

04 Did You Know Doctors Don't Know Exactly Why We Have Earwax?

Interestingly, it is said that doctors don't know exactly why we have earwax. However, there are several theories as to why. Doctors think that earwax might have something to do with the ear's self-cleaning process. They also think it could have antibacterial properties. Wax is generally believed to protect the ears by preventing dirts or small bugs from entering our inner ears. Additionally, no one knows for sure why the amount of earwax differs depending on the individual. Some people make lots of wax, while on the other hand, some don't make any wax. Of course, we don't know why that is.

Fortunately, doctors do know the safest way to remove extra earwax. Although many of us use cotton swabs to remove earwax, doctors recommend that we should not put any cotton swab or small object inside our ear canal. That's because you could push earwax in further or damage the inside of your ear canal or eardrum inadvertently. The best way is to use a moist washcloth. Just wrap it around your finger and clean your earlobes. If you want to remove excess earwax, let some warm water go into your ear, then tip your head to the side to dump it out. Then clean your inner ear with a soft, dry washcloth.

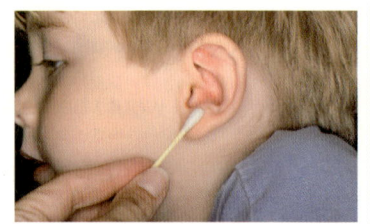

1 What is the main idea of the story?

a. Doctors don't know beans about earwax so we should not listen to them.
b. Earwax must be removed by small objects such as cotton swabs.
c. The exact reason why we have earwax is not known yet, but the best way to remove it is known.
d. It is absolutely critical to remove excess earwax with a washcloth.

2 According to the passage, which sentence is <u>wrong</u>?

a. Doctors managed to discover why we have earwax.
b. Using a cotton swab might not be the safest way to remove extra earwax.
c. Not everyone has the same amount of earwax.
d. There is more than one theory as to why we have earwax.

3 Choose the correct words for each sentence.

a. The apple pie you made was too sweet, <u>moreover / in addition / while</u> the strawberry pie your sister made was very tasty.
b. Ask Max. He <u>has / gets / does</u> know the right answer and he is right over there.
c. I want his explanation <u>as to why / as why / as of why</u> he left so soon yesterday.

LEARNING BOARD

① Interestingly, it is said that doctors don't know (exactly) why we have earwax. ② However, there are several theories as to why. ③ Doctors think that earwax might have something to do with the ear's self-cleaning process. ④ They also think it could have antibacterial properties. ⑤ Wax is generally believed to protect the ears by preventing dirts or small bugs from entering our inner ears. ⑥ Additionally, no one knows (for sure) why the amount of earwax differs (depending on the individual). ⑦ Some people make lots of wax, while on the other hand, some don't make any wax. ⑧ Of course, we don't know why that is. ⑨ Fortunately, doctors do know the safest way (to remove extra earwax). ⑩ Although many of us use cotton swabs to remove earwax, doctors recommend that we should not put any cotton swab or small object (inside our ear canal). ⑪ That's because you could 1) push earwax in further or 2) damage the inside of your ear canal or eardrum inadvertently. ⑫ The best way is to use a moist washcloth. ⑬ Just 1) wrap it around your finger and 2) clean your earlobes. ⑭ If you want to remove excess earwax, 1) let some warm water go into your ear, then 2) tip your head to the side to dump it out. ⑮ Then clean your inner ear (with a soft, dry washcloth).

Words & Expressions

interestingly 흥미롭게도 **earwax** 귀지 (또는 wax) **theory** 이론 **as to why** 이유, 원인에 관해 **self-cleaning** 자가 청소 **process** 과정 **antibacterial** 항균성의 **property** 성질, 특성 **dirt** 먼지 **differ** 다르다 **depending on the individual** 개인에 따라 **remove** 제거하다(= get rid of) **cotton swab** 면봉 **recommend** 권하다, 추천하다 **canal** 운하, 수로, 관 (ear canal 이도) **eardrum** 고막 **inadvertently** 본의 아니게 **moist** 습기, 수분 **washcloth** 수건 **wrap** 싸다, 포장하다 **earlobe** 귓불 **tip** 기울이다 **dump out** 갖다 버리다

25

Did You Know There Are 5,000,000 Red Blood Cells In One Drop Of Blood?

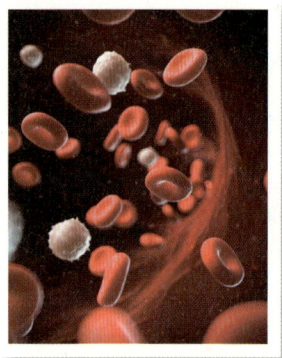

Amazingly there are about 5,000,000 red blood cells in just one drop of blood other than the 7,000 white blood cells and 450,000 platelet cells. And of course there are water, salt, fat, vitamins, sugar, and so on. No wonder blood is thicker than water. In fact, blood feels like warm soup. Blood is a little bit soupy and gooey because it is a mixture of liquid and lots and lots of cells. Many people think that the three main ingredients of blood are red blood cells, white blood cells and platelets. But actually, plasma, a yellow liquid material in the blood, makes up more than half of the blood.

Red blood cells carry oxygen around our body, white blood cells find and kill

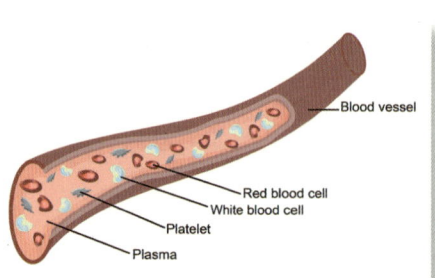

harmful germs, and platelets make blood clot to stop bleeding when we get injured. Here are some interesting facts about blood. Red blood cells live for about four months. White blood cells eat up not only bacteria and germs but also dead cells. And the factory that makes new red and white blood cells is bone marrow.

1 What is the main idea of the story?

a. The color of blood is red because of the platelets.
b. Blood is a mixture of lots of ingredients.
c. The platelet is the most important among blood ingredients.
d. The most essential ingredient in blood is bone marrow.

2 According to the article, you can guess _____.

a. red blood cells make up most of the blood
b. bone marrow plays an important role in making oxygen
c. without blood platelets, you could bleed to death
d. blood is useful due to its red color

3 Choose the correct words for each sentence.

a. White blood cells not only find <u>because / but also / however</u> kill harmful germs.
b. There <u>is / are / were</u> tons of cells in blood.
c. Plasma makes <u>up / off / over</u> more than half of the blood.

LEARNING BOARD

① **Amazingly** there are about 5,000,000 red blood **cells** in just one drop of blood other than the 7,000 white blood cells and 450,000 platelet cells. ② And (of course) there are water, salt, **fat,** vitamins, sugar, and so on. ③ No wonder blood is **thicker** than water. ④ In fact, blood feels like warm soup. ⑤ Blood is a little bit soupy and gooey because it is a **mixture** of **liquid** and lots and lots of cells. ⑥ Many people think that the three main ingredients of blood are 1) red blood cells, 2) white blood cells and 3) platelets. ⑦ But actually, plasma, (a yellow liquid material in the blood,) **makes up** more than half of the blood. ⑧ Red blood cells carry **oxygen** around our body, white blood cells find and kill **harmful germs**, and platelets make blood **clot** to stop **bleeding** when we get **injured**. ⑨ Here are some interesting facts about blood. ⑩ Red blood cells live for (about) four months. ⑪ White blood cells eat up not only bacteria and germs but also dead cells. ⑫ And the factory (that makes new red and white blood cells) is bone marrow.

Words & Expressions

amazingly 놀랍게도 **red blood cell** 적혈구 **other than** …외에, …말고 **white blood cell** 백혈구 **platelet** 혈소판 **fat** n. 지방 a. 뚱뚱한 **no wonder** 놀랄 일도 아니다, 당연하다 **thick** 진한, 두꺼운(↔ thin 연한, 얇은) **soupy** 수프 같은, 걸쭉한 **gooey** 끈끈한(= sticky) **mixture** 혼합물 (v. mix 혼합하다) **plasma** 혈장, 플라즈마 **liquid** 액체, 액체의 **material** 물질 **make up** 이루다, 형성하다, 구성하다 **more than half of** …의 반 이상 **oxygen** 산소 **harmful** 해로운 **germ** 세균 **bleed** 피가 나다 **clot** 엉기게 하다 (blood clot 혈전) **injure** 부상, 부상을 입다 **eat up** 먹어치우다 **factory** 공장 **bone marrow** 골수

27

Listening with Dictation

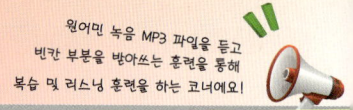

01 Did You Know Household Dust Is A Bunch Of Dead Skin Cells?

Dust in your house is mostly made of dead skin cells. _____ [1] 30,000-40,000 dead skin cells are _____ [2] your body per minute. _____ [3] the fact that the human body _____ [4] constantly, we can say that common house dust is _____ [5] a bunch of dead skin cells. Of course there are other things in household dust, such as the dried-up dead bodies of dust mites. Dust mites eat humans' dead skin cells and live in bedding, carpets and soft furnishings. When they are alive, they are _____ [6]. After they die, they become part of household dust. It's not surprising that they are hated by everyone. Another component is tiny fibers fallen from clothing, furniture fabrics and bedding. Furthermore, if you have pets in your house, your cute little pets will _____ [7] dust production since they drop _____ [8] things. Pets drop dead skin cells and dried-up dead bodies of pet mites _____ [9] hair. And if they wear dog clothing, they will also drop _____ [10] fiber.

02 Did You Know Painkillers Can Cause You A Wide Variety Of Pains?

Painkillers are supposed to kill pain. But unfortunately sometimes and in some cases, painkillers can cause you pain because they _____ [1] like any type of drug. They can be dangerous even _____ [2], so be careful not to misuse or abuse them. Many people know that painkillers _____ [3]. So painkiller users should drink lots of water _____ [4]. Also painkillers can have an effect on both your heart and lungs. Some painkillers not only cause _____ [5] but also slow down the functioning of the heart and lungs. So if you have a problem with your _____ [6] or _____ [7] systems, you have to be extra careful. And some people _____ [8] a feeling of sleepiness after taking them. That's because certain kinds of painkillers _____ [9] the receptors in the body that sense pain. Aside from these, there are other side effects of painkillers such as addiction, difficulty sleeping and _____ [10]. The best way to prevent possible side effects is to consult your doctor before use.

03 Did You Know Cracking Your Knuckles Has Nothing To Do With Arthritis?

Knuckle cracking is an _____ [1] bad habit. Its sound is _____ [2], and the person who cracks his or her knuckles looks a little bit scary and bad. Moreover, there is a myth that knuckle cracking _____ [3]. But that is not true for knuckle cracking does not cause arthritis. Maybe the cracking sound _____ [4] us because people believe that if something cracks, it _____ [5] damaged. But the truth is that nothing is cracked or damaged. There were a few studies about this and _____ [6] knuckle cracking _____ [7] arthritis. However, those studies also discovered that it _____ [8] knuckle crackers to stop it because it is associated with several hand problems. According to those studies, knuckle crackers _____ [9] have weaker grip strength, hand swelling, or _____ [10] the ligaments surrounding the joints than people who don't crack their knuckles.

28 Chapter 1 | Health

04 Did You Know Doctors Don't Know Exactly Why We Have Earwax?

Interestingly, it is said that doctors don't know exactly why we have earwax. However, there are several theories _____¹. Doctors think that earwax _____² the ear's self-cleaning process. They also think it could have antibacterial properties. Wax _____³ protect the ears by preventing dirts or small bugs from entering our inner ears. Additionally, no one knows for sure why the amount of earwax differs _____⁴. Some people make lots of wax, while on the other hand, some don't make any wax. Of course, we don't know why that is. Fortunately, doctors do know _____⁵ to remove extra earwax. Although many of us use _____⁶ to remove earwax, doctors recommend that we should not put any cotton swab or small object inside our ear canal. That's because you could push earwax _____⁷ or damage the inside of your ear canal or eardrum _____⁸. The best way is to use _____⁹. Just wrap it around your finger and clean your earlobes. If you want to remove excess earwax, let some warm water go into your ear, then tip your head to the side to _____¹⁰. Then clean your inner ear with a soft, dry washcloth.

05 Did You Know There Are 5,000,000 Red Blood Cells In One Drop Of Blood?

Amazingly there are about 5,000,000 red blood cells in just one drop of blood _____¹ the 7,000 white blood cells and 450,000 _____². And of course there are water, salt, fat, vitamins, sugar, and so on. No wonder _____³. In fact, blood _____⁴ warm soup. Blood is a little bit soupy and gooey because it is a mixture of liquid and lots and lots of cells. Many people think that the three main ingredients of blood are red blood cells, white blood cells and _____⁵. But actually, plasma, a yellow _____⁶ in the blood, makes up _____⁷ the blood. Red blood cells carry oxygen around our body, white blood cells find and kill harmful germs, and platelets _____⁸ to stop bleeding when we get injured. Here are some interesting facts about blood. Red blood cells live for about four months. White blood cells _____⁹ not only bacteria and germs but also dead cells. And the factory that makes new red and white blood cells is _____¹⁰.

---

01 정답
1. It is estimated that 2. flaked off from 3. Given 4. sheds dead skin cells 5. practically
6. the cause of allergies 7. highly contribute to 8. all kinds of 9. as well as 10. tiny bits of

02 정답
1. carry side effects 2. under normal use 3. commonly cause constipation 4. when taking them
5. a feeling of sedation 6. cardiovascular 7. respiratory 8. complain of 9. numb 10. hallucinations

03 정답
1. annoying 2. unpleasant to hear 3. leads to arthritis 4. misleads 5. must be being 6. the results indicated that 7. was not associated with 8. would be better for 9. are more likely to 10. damage to

04 정답
1. as to why 2. might have something to do with 3. is generally believed to 4. depending on the individual
5. the safest way 6. cotton swabs 7. in further 8. inadvertently 9. a moist washcloth 10. dump it out

05 정답
1. other than 2. platelet cells 3. blood is thicker than water 4. feels like 5. platelets
6. liquid material 7. more than half of 8. make blood clot 9. eat up 10. bone marrow

06 Did You Know Your Hands Can Tell You About Your Health?

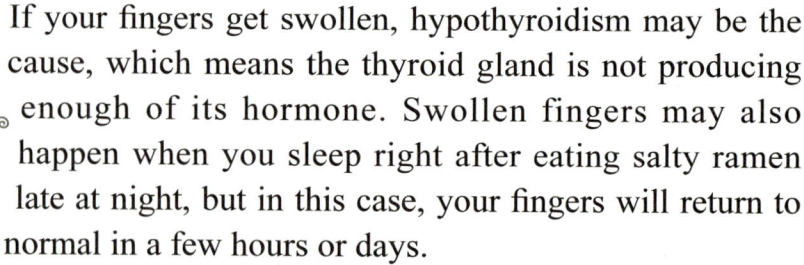

If your fingers get swollen, hypothyroidism may be the cause, which means the thyroid gland is not producing enough of its hormone. Swollen fingers may also happen when you sleep right after eating salty ramen late at night, but in this case, your fingers will return to normal in a few hours or days.

If your palms are redder than normal, you may have one of the following three problems. If you feel an itchy or burning pain, it's possible that you have eczema. Or, you may be allergic to something being worn or applied on your hands. Lastly, red palms could indicate that you have a problem with your liver. Not all people with red palms have a liver disease, but it's not a bad idea to get a checkup.

Generally, nails turn white when you press on them, then return to a pinkish color when you stop pressing. But if your nails stay white for a few minutes, you may have anemia or low iron. How about blue fingertips? Of course, this is not a good sign either. Although this symptom is common in women when it's cold, if it lasts more than an hour, you must go to the hospital right away.

1 What is the main idea of the story?
 a. Eating salty ramen late at night is not a good thing to do for your health.
 b. Hands as well as feet reveal various information about your health.
 c. If you see your hands, you will get lots of information about your health.
 d. People whose fingertips are blue must go to the hospital ASAP.

2 According to the passage, which sentence is wrong?
 a. The lack of thyroid hormone is the main cause of hypothyroidism.
 b. If you sleep right after eating salty ramen late at night, your fingers may be swollen.
 c. It is possible for people who have red palms to have a liver problem.
 d. During the winter, women's fingertips originally turn blue.

3 Choose the correct words for each sentence.
 a. If you feel faint again, please check your health diagnosis / syndromes / symptoms and signs with your doctor.
 b. After applying this ointment on / in / to my skin, I feel all itchy.
 c. Stop talking / to talk / talked, please. You have to be quiet because you are in a library.

LEARNING BOARD

① If your fingers get **swollen**, hypothyroidism may be the cause, which means the thyroid gland is not **producing** enough of its hormone. ② **Swollen fingers** may also happen when you sleep (right after eating **salty** ramen) late at night, but in this case, your fingers will return to normal (in a few hours or days.) ③ If your **palms** are redder than normal, you may have one of the following three problems.

④ If you feel an **itchy** or burning pain, it's possible that you have **eczema**.

⑤ Or, you may **be allergic to** something (being **worn** or **applied on** your hands).

⑥ Lastly, red palms could indicate that you have a problem with your **liver**.

⑦ Not all people (with red palms) have a liver **disease**, but it's not a bad idea to get a **checkup**. ⑧ Generally, nails turn white when you press on them, then return to a pinkish color when you stop pressing.

⑨ But if your nails stay white (for a few minutes), you may have **anemia** or low iron.

⑩ How about blue fingertips? ⑪ Of course, this is not a good sign either. ⑫ Although this **symptom** is common in women when it's cold, if it lasts more than an hour, you must go to the hospital **right away**.

Words & Expressions

get swollen 붓다 hypothyroidism 갑상선 기능 저하증 hormone 호르몬 thyroid 갑상선의 gland 분비선(샘) thyroid gland 갑상선 right after 직후 late at night 밤늦게 palm 손바닥 itchy 가려운 eczema 습진 be allergic to ...에 알레르기가 있다 liver 간 disease 질병 get a checkup (병원에서) 검사를 받다 pinkish 분홍빛의 anemia 빈혈 low iron 철분 부족 fingertip 손가락 끝 be not a good sign 좋은 징조가 아니다 symptom 증상, 징후 be in common in ...에게 흔하다 last 지속하다 right away 즉시

07 Did You Know How Much Food You Can Eat After Gastric Bypass Surgery?

Researches conducted by the U.S. doctors said that more than half of diabetes patients who underwent gastric bypass surgery were cured thanks to its effect on improving blood sugar control. Researchers at Imperial College London also recognized this effect, saying, "It's clear that gastric bypass surgery has a significant beneficial effect on glucose control." It seems that gastric bypass surgery will become more and more popular since obese patients with type 2 diabetes can lose weight and be cured at the same time. It's like 'killing two birds with one stone.'

Many obese patients with diabetes quit taking medication after this surgery. Naturally people are under the impression that this surgery is an easy way out of obesity and the risk of type 2 diabetes by just one operation. It sounds so easy and tempting. Yet the reality is not so easy and tempting. If you undergo this surgery, you will have a smaller stomach which is connected to the small intestine, which means your cute little stomach can only hold a very limited amount of food. If you eat more than a quarter of a cup of solid food, or eat some solid food with a cup of water, you may be sick because your small stomach can't handle that much food.

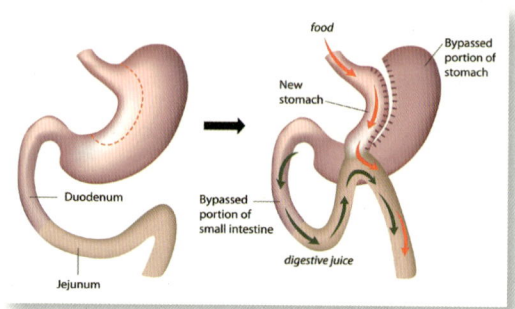

1 What can be the best title of this story?

a. Gastric Bypass Surgery : A Breakthrough For Obese Patients With Diabetes
b. Eating A Small Amount Of Food Can Be Dangerous
c. The Increase In Obese People With Type 2 Diabetes In The US
d. Type 2 Diabetes Patients Take The Easy Way Out

2 According to the passage, which sentence is right?

a. Obese people with type 2 diabetes must undergo gastric bypass surgery.
b. Gastric bypass surgery improve blood sugar control.
c. Doctors only in the US admit the awesome effect of gastric bypass surgery.
d. Gastric bypass surgery doesn't have any positive effect on glucose control.

3 Choose the correct words for each sentence.

a. You are supposed to <u>make / conduct / exam</u> scientific researches on this matter.
b. I hate my nose. I want to <u>undergo / be undergone / underwent</u> plastic surgery.
c. Mr. Witt has had an effect <u>to / on / for</u> me since I was 12 years old.
d. You are under the impression <u>during / while / that</u> I am rich, but I'm not.

LEARNING BOARD

① Researches conducted by the U.S. doctors said that more than half of diabetes patients who underwent gastric bypass surgery were cured thanks to its effect on improving blood sugar control. ② Researchers at Imperial College London also recognized this effect, saying, "It's clear that gastric bypass surgery has a significant beneficial effect on glucose control." ③ It seems that gastric bypass surgery will become more and more popular since obese patients with type 2 diabetes can 1) lose weight and 2) be cured at the same time. ④ It's like 'killing two birds with one stone.' ⑤ Many obese patients with diabetes quit taking medication after this surgery. ⑥ Naturally people are under the impression that this surgery is an easy way out of 1) obesity and 2) the risk of type 2 diabetes by just one operation. ⑦ It sounds so easy and tempting. ⑧ Yet the reality is not so easy and tempting. ⑨ If you undergo this surgery, you will have a smaller stomach which is connected to the small intestine, which means your cute little stomach can only hold a very limited amount of food. ⑩ If you 1) eat more than a quarter of a cup of solid food, or 2) eat some solid food with a cup of water, you may be sick because your small stomach can't handle that much food.

Words & Expressions

gastric 위(胃)의(gastric juice = stomach juice 위액) bypass 우회, 우회수술 gastric bypass surgery 위장우회수술 conduct (조사 등을) 하다 diabetes 당뇨병 undergo (...을) 겪다, 받다 blood sugar control 혈당 조절 significant 중요한, 특별한 beneficial 유익한 glucose 글루코스, 포도당 obese (사람이) 살찐, 비만한(cf. obesity 비만) quit 그만두다 medication 약물(치료) operation 수술 quarter 1/4(cf. quarter dollar 25센트) tempting 귀가 솔깃한, 유혹적인 an easy way out 쉬운 해결책 small intestine 소장 (large intestine 대장) stomach 위, 복부, 배 solid 단단한, 고체의 be sick 병이 나다 handle 다루다, 처리하다

33

08 Did You Know Why Animal Activists Are Upset About Leech Therapy?

Even today, not a few doctors are said to use leeches when practicing medicine, especially in Southeast Asia. Mostly, they use leeches to stimulate patients' blood circulation by draining excess blood to reduce the chance of blood congestion. It's called 'leech therapy.' In some cases, this unorthodox therapy has saved limbs by helping patients return the blood to normal circulation. In fact, if normal blood flow isn't restored within 48 hours after surgery, there will be a risk of amputation.

Leeches are also used to let blood out. Leeches have been used in medicine for centuries around the world since they are good at sucking blood. In the past,  people just put this thankful bloodsucker on the bite when assaulted by a venomous snake. Once the leeches had sucked enough blood to feel full, they voluntarily fell off. Then, they died from ingesting the venom and the patients survived.

These days, leech therapy continues to be practiced in the same way. That's why animal rights activists are upset about leech therapy because once the leeches have filled up on dirty blood and fallen off, the practitioners just throw them away to be destroyed.

1 What is the main idea of the story?

a. The normal blood circulation is absolutely important.
b. Leeches have been used to treat patients for many years.
c. Thankfully, all kinds of bloodsuckers are useful to humans.
d. Leeches and mosquitoes are creepy bloodsuckers.

2 According to the passage, which sentence is right?

a. These days, it's hard to find doctors who use leeches to treat patients.
b. The leech therapy is unorthodox, but it can save limbs of all patients bitten by venomous snakes.
c. Leeches had been used in medicine for many years only in Southeast Asia.
d. No need to worry about how to tear off leeches because they will fall off by themselves once they feel full.

3 Choose the correct words for each sentence.

a. Please do not waste wastes. We can save the Earth from / by / of recycling.
b. Demi Moore is said to use leeches to cleanse her body because she believes leeches help her stay / stayed / staying healthy.
c. Not a few / a little / much medical practitioners around the world have been using leeches.

LEARNING BOARD

① Even today, not a few doctors are said to use leeches when practicing medicine, especially in Southeast Asia. ② Mostly, they use leeches (to stimulate patients' blood circulation) (by draining excess blood) (to reduce the chance of blood congestion). ③ It's called 'leech therapy.' ④ In some cases, this unorthodox therapy has saved limbs by helping patients return the blood to normal circulation. ⑤ In fact, if normal blood flow isn't restored within 48 hours after surgery, there will be a risk of amputation. ⑥ Leeches are also used to let blood out. ⑦ Leeches have been used in medicine for centuries around the world since they are good at sucking blood. ⑧ In the past, people just put (this thankful bloodsucker) on the bite when assaulted by a venomous snake. ⑨ Once the leeches had sucked enough blood to feel full, they voluntarily fell off. ⑩ Then, they died from ingesting the venom and the patients survived. ⑪ These days, leech therapy continues to be practiced in the same way. ⑫ That's why animal rights activists are upset about leech therapy because once the leeches have 1) filled up on dirty blood and 2) fallen off, the practitioners just throw them away to be destroyed.

Words & Expressions

upset v. 속상하게(화나게) 만들다 a. 속상한 n. 배탈, 언짢음　leech 거머리　therapy 치료법　practice (의사가) 개업하다, 영업하다　medicine 의료, 약　stimulate 자극하다　circulation 순환, 유통, 배포　blood circulation 혈액 순환　drain (물, 액체) 빼내다, 비우다　congestion 혼잡, 막힘　unorthodox 비정통적인　limb 사지 (팔, 다리)　restore (이전 상태로) 회복시키다　normal blood flow 정상적인 혈액 흐름　amputate (수술로 팔이나 다리를) 절단하다 (n. amputation 사지 절단)　let out (소리 등을) 내다, 내보내다, 풀어주다　be good at …를 잘하다　suck 빨다　bloodsucker 흡혈귀, 피를 빠는 것　assault 공격하다　venom (뱀 등의) 독　venomous snake 독사 (=viper)　voluntarily 스스로, 자발적으로　feel full 배부름을 느끼다　fall off 떨어지다　ingest 삼키다, 먹다　survive 살아남다　animal (rights) activist 동물 (권익) 보호론자　fill up (가득) 채우다　practitioner 의술을 행하는 사람, 의사　throw away 버리다

35

09 Did You Know Not All Fish Are Good For Our Health?

We have heard a lot about the benefits of eating fish instead of meat. Fish oil completely differs from meat fat. It helps our cardiovascular system, joints, brain and so on. Although there is a multitude of benefits, you should think again before eating fish because nearly 40% of the fish available to us nowadays comes from fish farms.

Commonly, farmed fish are carnivorous such as salmon, tuna and shrimp. These farmed fish live in overcrowded and unclean conditions where there is a high risk of infection, contagion and contamination. According to a study, farmed salmon carry higher levels of contaminants like dioxins than wild salmon do. That means farmed salmon can be dangerous to humans since their polluted flesh can pollute our bodies when we eat it. There are also several other problems such as antibiotics and residues from chemicals used to clean fish farming nets.

But farmed fish are more widely available and cheaper than wild fish because farmed fish can be harvested all year round. So when shopping at the supermarket, choose wisely and carefully for the sake of your health.

1 What is the main idea of the story?

a. Carnivorous fish such as salmon is dangerous for its sharp teeth.
b. It would be better not to eat salmon or tuna due to its oil.
c. Farmed fish may not be a good choice for your health.
d. Farmed fish has to be cheaper than wild fish.

2 According to the passage, which sentence is right?

a. Fish oil is totally different from meat fat.
b. Fish is helpful for health, while on the other hand, fish oil is not helpful at all.
c. Wild fish is more vulnerable to infection than farmed fish.
d. Farmed fish is cheaper than wild fish because it is carnivorous.

3 Choose the correct words for each sentence.

a. Several medicines are <u>available / bearable / inexcusable</u> in any drugstore so you can easily buy them.
b. This technique will open up a multitude of new <u>possible / possibility / possibilities</u>.
c. You think you are ambitious but I think you are greedy. Ambition differs <u>with / from / as</u> greed, you know.

LEARNING BOARD

① We have heard a lot (about the benefits of eating fish) (instead of meat.) ② Fish oil completely differs from meat fat. ③ It helps our cardiovascular system, joints, brain and so on. ④ Although there is a multitude of benefits, you should think again before eating fish because nearly 40% of the fish (available to us nowadays) comes from fish farms. ⑤ Commonly, farmed fish are carnivorous (such as salmon, tuna and shrimp.) ⑥ These farmed fish live in (overcrowded and unclean) conditions (where there is a high risk of infection, contagion and contamination). ⑦ According to a study, farmed salmon carry higher levels of contaminants (like dioxins) than wild salmon do. ⑧ That means farmed salmon can be dangerous to humans since their polluted flesh can pollute our bodies when we eat it. ⑨ There are also several other problems (such as 1) antibiotics and 2) residues from chemicals) (used to clean fish farming nets). ⑩ But farmed fish are 1) more widely available and 2) cheaper than wild fish because farmed fish can be harvested (all year round). ⑪ So when shopping at the supermarket, choose (wisely and carefully) for the sake of your health.

Words & Expressions

benefit 이득, 이로움, 혜택 instead of … 대신 completely 완전히(= absolutely) differ from …와 다르다 cardiovascular 심혈관의 joint 관절 and so on 기타 등등 a multitude of 수많은 (+ 복수 명사) nearly 거의 available 입수 가능한 fish farm 어류 양식장 commonly 보통, 일반적으로 carnivorous 육식의 salmon 연어 tuna 참치 shrimp 새우 farmed fish 양식 어류 over-crowded 너무 붐비는 there is a high risk of …의 위험이 높다 infection 감염 contagion 전염, 전염병 contamination 오염 contaminant 오염물질 dioxin 다이옥신 pollute 오염시키다 antibiotics 항생제 residue 잔여물 chemical 화학물질 harvest 추수하다, 수확하다 all year round 일 년 내내

10 Did You Know Why Carrot Juice Is Called Miracle Juice?

Carrot juice is called miracle juice because its health-friendly effects are miraculous. As everybody already knows, drinking carrot juice, as well as eating carrots, is good for eyes and prevents night blindness. Carrot juice is also thought to reduce the risk of certain types of cancers including skin and breast cancer due to the high amount of beta carotene. Beta carotene changes to vitamin A in the body and there is a connection between vitamin A and cancer prevention.

Vitamin A is said to strengthen the bones, teeth and nails, and enhance your hair's condition. Drinking carrot juice is allegedly excellent for the liver since vitamin A reduces bile and fat in the liver. That's not all. Carrot juice aids in resistance to infections. Thanks to these properties of vitamin A, carrot juice is recommended as the best drink for pregnant women. When choosing carrots, you should choose the darker ones because the darker the color, the more carotene it contains. And one more thing. Although carrot juice is a miracle juice, just remember, 'Too much is as bad as too little.'

1 What can be the best title of this story?
  a. Amazing Benefits of Carrots
  b. Carrots VS. Carrot Juice : The Winner Is...
  c. The Richest Source of Vitamin A
  d. Too Much Is As Bad As Too Little

2 The reason why carrot juice is called miracle juice is because _____.
  a. only magicians can make carrot juice
  b. its nutritional effects are that good
  c. it can prevent all kinds of cancer
  d. it can make blind men see

3 Choose the correct words for each sentence.
  a. My aunt said she had no choice but to divorce him <u>because / since / due to</u> his erratic behavior.
  b. The boss had a hard time when he had to deal with <u>persistence / resistance / assistance</u> to change in his office.
  c. Some people think the more money you have, <u>the worst / the more / the most</u> you can express your opinion.

LEARNING BOARD

① **Carrot** juice is called **miracle** juice because its **health-friendly** effects are
당근　　　　　　　　　　n.기적　　　　　　　　　　= health-favoring 건강에 유익한
　　　　　　　　　　　　　　　　　　　　　　cf. environment-friendly 환경친화적인(eco-friendly) user-friendly 사용하기 편리한

miraculous. ② As everybody already knows, drinking carrot juice, (as well as eating
a. 기적적인　　　　3인칭 단수현재 + knows　　동명사 주어(당근 주스를 마시는 것)

carrots,) ¹⁾ is good for eyes and ²⁾ **prevents** night blindness. ③ Carrot juice is also
　　　　②번 문장의 동사 1) is, and 2) prevents v.예방하다 야맹증

thought to reduce the risk of certain types of **cancers** (including skin and breast
= be said to ...라고 한다　　　　　　　　수식　　　　　skin cancer 피부암
　　　　　　　　　　　　　　　　　　　　　　　　　　　breast cancer 유방암

cancer) (due to the high amount of beta carotene). ④ Beta carotene **changes to**
　　　= because of + 명사, 명사구　　　　　　　　　　　　　　　...로(to) 변하다

vitamin A (in the body) and there is a **connection between** vitamin A and cancer
　　　　　　　　　　　　　　　　...와 ...사이 (둘 사이)의 관계

prevention.
예방, 방지 n. prevention

⑤ Vitamin A is said to ¹⁾ **strengthen** (the bones, teeth and nails), and ²⁾ **enhance**
　　　　　　　　　　v. 강하게 하다 (a. strong 강한 n. strength 힘, 강도)　　v. 향상시키다
　　　　　　　　　　cf. lengthen v. 길게 하다 (a. long 긴 n. length 길이) /
　　　　　　　　　　widen v. 넓히다 (a. wide 넓은 n. width 폭) / deepen v. 깊어지다 (a. deep 깊은 n. depth 깊이)

your hair's condition. ⑥ Drinking carrot juice is allegedly **excellent for** the liver since
　　　　　　　　　　동명사 주어(마시는 것), 동사 is　be excellent(good) for ...에 좋다, 유익하다

vitamin A reduces bile and fat in the liver. ⑦ That's not all. ⑧ Carrot juice **aids** in
　　　　　　　　　　1. 담즙 2. 분노, 증오심　　　　이게 다가 아니다　　　　　　　　...에 도움을 주다

resistance to infections. ⑨ (Thanks to these **properties** of vitamin A), carrot juice is
...에 대한(to) 저항력　　　　(...덕분에, 때문에)　1. 소유물, 재산 2. 부동산 3. 특성 (여기서는 '특성')

recommended as the best drink for **pregnant** women. ⑩ When choosing carrots, you
...로 추천되다　　　　　　　= expectant mothers 임산부　주절의 주어 you와 일치, 생략
　　　　　　　　　　　　　pregnant 임신한　　　　　　능동 choosing

should choose the darker ones because the darker the color, the more carotene it
　　　　　　　　carrots　　the 비교급, the 비교급 ...할수록 ...하다　　　　= carrot
　　　　　　　　　　ex) The more you know, the more you hate him. 알면 알수록 그를 싫어하게 된다.
　　　　　　　　　　　　The smaller, the shrewder. 작을수록 더 기민하다, 작은 고추가 맵다 <속담>

contains. ⑪ And one more thing. ⑫ Although carrot juice is a miracle juice, just
　　　　　　　(There is) one more thing. 한 가지 더 있다.

remember, 'Too much is as bad as too little.'
명령형　　지나친 것(being too much)은 너무 모자라는 것(being too little)만큼이나 좋지 않다 (as bad as)
　　　　: 과유불급(過猶不及)

Words & Expressions

miracle 기적　**miraculous** 기적적인　**health-friendly** 건강에 유익한　**effect** 효과　**prevent** 예방하다(cf. prevention 예방, 방지)　**night blindness** 야맹증　**be thought to** ...라고 한다(= be said to)　**reduce** 줄이다　**breast cancer** 유방암　**the high amount of** 상당한 양의　**beta carotene** 베타카로틴　**connection** 관계, 연관　**strengthen** 강하게 하다　**nail** 손톱, 발톱 (fingernail 손톱, toenail 발톱)　**enhance** 향상시키다　**allegedly** 알려진 바에 의하면　**bile** 담즙　**liver** 간　**aid** 돕다　**resistance** 저항(성)　**property** 특성, 성질　**pregnant woman** 임산부　**Too much is as bad as too little.** 과유불급

Listening with Dictation

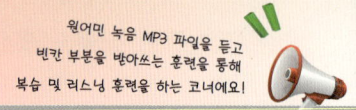

06 Did You Know Your Hands Can Tell You About Your Health?

If your fingers _____¹, hypothyroidism may be the cause, which means _____² is not producing enough of its hormone. Swollen fingers may also happen when you sleep right after eating salty ramen late at night, but in this case, your fingers will return to normal in a few hours or days. If your palms are redder than normal, you may have one of the following three problems. If you _____³ or burning pain, it's possible that you have _____⁴. Or, you may be allergic to something being worn or _____⁵ your hands. Lastly, red palms could _____⁶ that you have a problem with your liver. Not all people with red palms have a liver disease, but _____⁷ get a checkup. Generally, nails turn white when you press on them, then return to a pinkish color when you stop pressing. But if your nails stay white for a few minutes, you may have _____⁸. How about blue fingertips? Of course, this is not a good sign _____⁹. Although this symptom _____¹⁰ women when it's cold, if it lasts more than an hour, you must go to the hospital right away.

07 Did You Know How Much Food You Can Eat After Gastric Bypass Surgery?

Researches _____¹ the U.S. doctors said that more than half of diabetes patients who underwent gastric bypass surgery were cured thanks to its effect on improving _____². Researchers at Imperial College London also recognized this effect, saying, "It's clear that gastric bypass surgery _____³ glucose control." It seems that gastric bypass surgery will become more and more popular since _____⁴ type 2 diabetes can lose weight and be cured at the same time. _____⁵ 'killing two birds with one stone.' Many obese patients with diabetes _____⁶ after this surgery. Naturally people _____⁷ this surgery is an easy way out of obesity and the risk of type 2 diabetes by just one operation. It sounds so easy and tempting. Yet the reality is not so easy and tempting. If you _____⁸, you will have a smaller stomach which is connected to the small intestine, which means your cute little stomach can only hold _____⁹ food. If you eat more than _____¹⁰ a cup of solid food, or eat some solid food with a cup of water, you may be sick because your small stomach can't handle that much food.

08 Did You Know Why Animal Activists Are Upset About Leech Therapy?

Even today, _____¹ are said to use leeches when practicing medicine, especially in Southeast Asia. Mostly, they use leeches to stimulate patients' _____² by draining excess blood to reduce the chance of blood congestion. It's called 'leech therapy.' In some cases, this _____³ has saved limbs by helping patients return the blood to normal circulation. In fact, if normal blood flow isn't restored _____⁴ after surgery, there will be _____⁵. Leeches are also used to let blood out. Leeches have been used in medicine for centuries around the world since they are good at sucking blood. In the past, people just put this thankful bloodsucker _____⁶ when assaulted by a venomous snake. Once the leeches had sucked enough blood to feel full, they _____⁷ fell off. Then, they died from ingesting the venom and the _____⁸. These days, leech therapy continues to be practiced in the same way. That's why animal rights activists _____⁹ leech therapy because once the leeches have filled up on dirty blood and fallen off, the _____¹⁰ just throw them away to be destroyed.

09 Did You Know Not All Fish Are Good For Our Health?

We have heard a lot about the benefits of eating fish _____¹ meat. Fish oil completely differs from meat fat. It helps our cardiovascular system, joints, brain and so on. Although there is _____², you should think again before eating fish because nearly 40% of the fish _____³ nowadays comes from fish farms. Commonly, farmed fish are _____⁴ such as salmon, tuna and shrimp. These farmed fish live in _____⁵ conditions where there is _____⁶ infection, contagion and contamination. According to a study, farmed salmon carry higher levels of contaminants like dioxins than wild salmon do. That means farmed salmon can be dangerous to humans since their _____⁷ can pollute our bodies when we eat it. There are also several other problems such as _____⁸ and residues from chemicals used to clean fish farming nets. But farmed fish are more widely available and cheaper than wild fish because farmed fish can _____⁹. So when shopping at the supermarket, choose wisely and carefully _____¹⁰ your health.

10 Did You Know Why Carrot Juice Is Called Miracle Juice?

Carrot juice is called miracle juice because its _____¹ are miraculous. As everybody already knows, drinking carrot juice, as well as eating carrots, is good for eyes and prevents _____². Carrot juice is also thought to reduce the risk of certain types of cancers including skin and breast cancer due to the high amount of beta carotene. Beta carotene _____³ vitamin A in the body and there is _____⁴ vitamin A and cancer prevention. Vitamin A is said to _____⁵ the bones, teeth and nails, and _____⁶ your hair's condition. Drinking carrot juice _____⁷ the liver since vitamin A reduces bile and fat in the liver. That's not all. Carrot juice aids in _____⁸. Thanks to these properties of vitamin A, carrot juice is recommended as the best drink for pregnant women. When choosing carrots, you should choose the darker ones because the darker the color, the more carotene _____⁹. And one more thing. Although carrot juice is a miracle juice, just remember, '_____¹⁰'.

---

06 정답
1. get swollen 2. the thyroid gland 3. feel an itchy 4. eczema 5. applied on
6. indicate 7. it's not a bad idea to 8. anemia or low iron 9. either 10. is common in

07 정답
1. conducted by 2. blood sugar control 3. has a significant beneficial effect on 4. obese patients with 5. It's like 6. quit taking medication 7. are under the impression that 8. undergo this surgery 9. a very limited amount of 10. a quarter of

08 정답
1. not a few doctors 2. blood circulation 3. unorthodox therapy 4. within 48 hours 5. a risk of amputation
6. on the bite 7. voluntarily 8. patients survived 9. are upset about 10. practitioners

09 정답
1. instead of 2. a multitude of benefits 3. available to us 4. carnivorous 5. overcrowded and unclean
6. a high risk of 7. polluted flesh 8. antibiotics 9. be harvested all year round 10. for the sake of

10 정답
1. health-friendly effects 2. night blindness 3. changes to 4. a connection between 5. strengthen 6. enhance
7. is allegedly excellent for 8. resistance to infections 9. it contains 10. Too much is as bad as too little

Chapter 2. Food

11. Did you know 'Sweetbread' Is Neither Sweet Nor Bread?

스위트브레드가 달콤하지도 않고 빵도 아니라는 거 아세요?

12. Did you know Vegetarians Do Not Eat Marshmallow?

채식주의자들이 마시멜로를 먹지 않는다는 거 아세요?

13. Did you know Shark Fin Soup Is As Dangerous As Sharks?

상어 지느러미 수프가 상어만큼 위험하다는 거 아세요?

14. Did you know Cambodians Like To Eat Fried Spiders?

캄보디아 사람들은 튀긴 거미 먹기를 좋아한다는 거 아세요?

15. Did you know Which Fruit Can Burn About 9 Pounds In A Month?

한 달 안에 9파운드를 빼주는 과일이 무엇인지 아세요?

16. Did you know Fat-Free Foods Are Not Always Good For Your Health?

무지방 음식이 항상 건강에 좋지는 않다는 거 아세요?

17. Did you know Koreans Are Not The Only People Who Enjoy Soondae?

우리만 순대를 좋아하는 게 아니라는 거 아세요?

18. Did you know Chinese People Eat Pigeon Soup?

중국인들이 비둘기 수프를 먹는다는 거 아세요?

19. Did you know There Is A Nearly $200 Sandwich?

약 200달러짜리 샌드위치가 있다는 거 아세요?

20. Did you know The Most Expensive Coffee Is Made Of Cat Poo?

가장 비싼 커피가 고양이 똥으로 만든다는 거 아세요?

11 Did You Know 'Sweetbread' Is Neither Sweet Nor Bread?

Surprisingly, 'sweetbreads' are not a kind of bread; they are a kind of meat. More specifically speaking, sweetbread is a gland from young animals, frequently from piglets, calves, or lambs. People have used these glands as edible organ meats for a long time. You can make various sweetbreads depending on what ingredients are used. Sweetbread made from the thymus, an organ in the neck, is often called 'neck sweetbread', and sweetbread made from the pancreas, a belly organ near the stomach, is called 'belly sweetbread'. These are the two basic types of sweetbreads, but other glands are also eaten and also called 'sweetbreads'. For example, 'ear sweetbread' is made from one of the salivary glands in the mouth.

Mostly, sweetbreads are boiled first to remove a thin skin. While boiling, add salt, vinegar, or lemon juice. In some cases, people soak them in milk or water for several hours to remove all the blood.

1 What is the main idea of the story?
 a. It is barbaric and unacceptable to eat internal organs of young animals.
 b. It sounds like sweet-tasting bread but sweetbread is a kind of meat.
 c. Sweetbread is supposed to taste like sweet bread, but it tastes bitter.
 d. Sweetbread is a kind of meat but you can buy it at a local bakery.

2 Two basic types of sweetbread are _____.
 a. neck sweetbread and belly sweetbread
 b. ear sweetbread and neck sweetbread
 c. salivary sweetbread and throat sweetbread
 d. thymus sweetbread and piglet sweetbread

3 Choose the correct words for each sentence.
 a. The salary of the job I am applying for is between $5k and $6k <u>to say nothing of my experience / depending on experience / as far as my experience is concerned</u>.
 b. There are several fruits in the basket, <u>in addition / for example / moreover</u> mango, watermelon, and kiwi.
 c. Several calves <u>is / are / was</u> eating grass on the ground peacefully.

LEARNING BOARD

① **Surprisingly**, 'sweetbreads' are not a **kind** of bread; they are a kind of **meat**. ② More **specifically** speaking, sweetbread is a gland (from young animals), **frequently** (from piglets, calves, or lambs). ③ People have used these glands as **edible organ** meats **for a long time**. ④ You can make **various** sweetbreads **depending on** (what ingredients are used). ⑤ Sweetbread (made from the **thymus**, an organ in the neck, is often called 'neck sweetbread', and sweetbread (made from the **pancreas**), a belly organ near the stomach, is called 'belly sweetbread'. ⑥ These are the two basic types of sweetbreads, but other glands are also ¹⁾ eaten and also ²⁾ called 'sweetbreads'. ⑦ For example, 'ear sweetbread' is made from one of the salivary glands in the mouth.

⑧ **Mostly**, sweetbreads are boiled first to remove a **thin** skin. ⑨ While boiling, **add** salt, vinegar, or lemon juice. ⑩ In some cases, people **soak** them in milk or water for several hours (to remove all the blood).

Words & Expressions

surprisingly 놀랍게도 sweetbread 스위트브레드(어린 돼지, 양, 소의 췌장, 흉선) meat (식용) 고기 gland 분비선(샘) specifically 구체적으로 frequently 자주, 종종 piglet 아기 돼지 (pig 돼지) calf 송아지 (복수 calves) lamb 새끼 양 (sheep 양) edible 먹을 수 있는, 식용의(=eatable) organ 내장, 장기 for a long time 오랫동안, 장기간 various 다양한, 여러 가지의 depending on …에 따라 ingredient 재료 thymus 흉선 pancreas 췌장 belly 배 stomach 위장 salivary 침을 분비하는 (saliva n. 침) boil 끓이다 add 첨가하다, 추가하다, (말을) 덧붙이다 vinegar 식초 soak 담그다

12 Did You Know Vegetarians Do Not Eat Marshmallow?

Have you heard that vegetarians don't eat marshmallow? Not all vegetarians turn it down, but some vegetarians do refuse to eat it because it contains ingredients from animals.

There are several types of vegetarians, depending on what kinds of foods they eat.

Ovo-lacto vegetarians, for example, are vegetarians who choose not to eat meat of any kind, but do eat eggs and dairy products. They think it's OK to eat eggs, milk products, and honey because they can get those foods without killing animals.

On the other hand, vegans do not eat any kind of animal meat, eggs, or animal fat, nor dairy products like ice cream or yogurt. Their diet mainly includes fruits, vegetables and grains. So, they won't eat bread with butter, a chocolate cake covered with whipped cream, food cooked with lard (pigs' fat), or honey. There is one more thing vegans refuse to eat : gelatin. Gelatin is a kind of protein derived from the tissues, bones, and skins of animals, usually cows and pigs. That's why vegans refuse to eat desserts made with gelatin, such as jelly or marshmallow.

1 What can be the best title of this story?
  a. Shocking News : Marshmallow Is Meat?
  b. Three Types Of Vegetarians
  c. Desserts made of Animals
  d. Why Do Some Vegetarians Refuse To Eat Marshmallow?

2 According to the passage, which sentence is right?
  a. Some vegetarians refuse to eat marshmallow due to its disgusting taste.
  b. All vegetarians don't eat gelatin and marshmallow.
  c. Vegans will refuse to taste a small piece of milk chocolate.
  d. Ovo-lacto vegetarians think eggs and milk products are OK to eat since these foods taste too good to refuse.

3 Choose the correct words for each sentence.
  a. There is more than one way to skin a cat. Actually, there are <u>much / several / only one</u> ways of doing it.
  b. <u>Dairy / Diary / Daily</u> farms are farms where farmers raise cows to make milk or milk products.
  c. How much is a roasted potato <u>sprinkling / sprinkled / to sprinkle</u> lightly with cheese powder?
  d. I won't prepare food for you, <u>no / nor / not</u> for your family.

LEARNING BOARD

① Have you heard that vegetarians don't eat marshmallow? ② Not all vegetarians
...를 들어본 적이 있는가?   채식주의자 cf. vegetable 채소   마시멜로   부분 부정
(have pp: 현재완료-경험)   lacto-ovo vegetarian : 유제품과 알은 먹는 채식주의자
               vegan : 유제품과 알을 포함하여 일체의 동물성 음식을 먹지 않는 채식주의자

turn it down, but some vegetarians do refuse to eat it because it contains
거절하다(= refuse)   동사(refuse)를 강조하는 do   v. ...이 들어있다
ingredients (from animals).   n. container 그릇, 용기
  ↑ 수식   (동물에서 나온) 재료

③ There are several types of vegetarians, depending on (what kinds of foods they eat).
                                           (그들(vegetarians)이 어떤 종류의 음식을 먹느냐)에 따라

④ Ovo-lacto vegetarians, (for example), are vegetarians (who choose not to eat meat of
ovo → egg, lacto → milk   (예를 들어)   ↑ 수식   ...를 먹지 않기로 선택하다
유란 채식주의자 (계란과 유제품을 먹는 채식주의자)

any kind, but do eat eggs and dairy products). ⑤ They think it's OK to eat eggs, milk
        동사 eat을 강조하는 do   dairy 유제품의, 유제품 회사   (to)...하는 건 괜찮다
        but (choose to eat) eggs... cf. dairyman 낙농업자   it 가주어, to 진주어

products, and honey because they can get those foods (without killing animals).
        n. 꿀, (호칭) 여보   eggs, milk products, and honey   (동물을 죽이는 것 없이 → 동물을 죽이지 않고)

⑥ On the other hand, vegans do not eat any kind of animal meat, eggs, or animal
  반면에, 다른 한편으로   엄격한 채식주의자

fat, nor dairy products (like ice cream or yogurt). ⑦ Their diet mainly includes fruits,
    nor ...도 아니다   vegans의 식사
    → they do not eat dairy products either   diet 1. 식사, 식습관 2. 다이어트 (체중감량)

vegetables and grains. ⑧ So, they won't eat ¹⁾ bread with butter, ²⁾ a chocolate
채소, 식물인간   곡물, 낱알   chocolate a. 초콜릿으로 만든 + cake n. 명사
                                                         cake는 불가산 명사지만 형용사로 한정된 경우 a가 올 수 있다.

cake (covered with whipped cream), ³⁾ food (cooked with lard (pigs' fat)), or ⁴⁾
  ↑ 수식   cake (which is) covered with   ↑ 수식   food (which is) cooked with

honey. ⑨ There is one more thing (vegans refuse to eat) : gelatin. ⑩ Gelatin is a
        유도부사는 이어지는 실제 주어에 따라 동사가 결정된다.
        There are several types of vegetarians. 채식주의자는 몇 가지 종류가 있다. (복수)
        There is one thing (that) vegans refuse to eat. 비건들이 먹기를 거부하는 게 한 가지 있다. (단수)

kind of protein (derived from the tissues, bones, and skins of animals), usually cows
        ↑ 수식   protein (which is) derived from ...에서 나온 단백질   animals의 예
                derive from ...에서 나오다, 파생하다   : cows and pigs

and pigs. ⑪ That's why vegans refuse to eat desserts (made with gelatin), such as
                                                ↑ 수식   dessert which are made with

jelly or marshmallow.
desserts made with gelatin의 예 (gelatin의 예가 아니라 desserts의 예)

Words & Expressions

vegetarian 채식주의자 turn down 거절하다 contain ...이 들어 있다 refuse 거부, 거절하다 ingredient 재료, 성분
depending on ...에 따라 lacto-ovo vegetarian 유란 채식주의자 dairy 유제품의 (dairy product 유제품 = milk product) diet
1. 식사, 식습관 2. 다이어트 vegetable 채소, 식물인간 grain 곡물 whipped 매를 맞은, 거품이 인 lard 라드, 돼지기름 gelatin
젤라틴 protein 단백질 derive (from) ...에서 나오다, 파생하다 tissue (세포로 이루어진) 조직

13 Did You Know Shark Fin Soup Is As Dangerous As Sharks?

Shark fin soup is dangerous not because of a shark's sharp teeth, but because of its mercury content.

In China and Hong Kong, the popularity of shark fin soup has been rising among people. Many Chinese people think that shark fin soup is good for their health because it is highly nutritious. They believe that shark fin soup is rich in various vitamins and minerals, especially Vitamin A. But, lots of scientists and nutritionists disagree with their opinion. According to their research, it contains no Vitamin A at all, and the amount of minerals found in shark fin soup is not very high.

It is also widely believed that shark fin soup can prevent cancer. But scientifically, it is not proven that shark fin soup has cancer fighting abilities.

On the contrary, shark fin soup is said to be bad for our health due to its high mercury content. So, doctors recommend that pregnant women and young children avoid eating shark fins. Actually, dolphin meat and tuna are also considered to be dangerous because they also contain high levels of mercury.

1 What is the main idea of the story?
   a. Sharks are dangerous so never eat or touch them if you don't want to die.
   b. Doctors say shark fin soup is not healthful but dangerous for your health.
   c. Shark fin soup is expensive because of its mercury content.
   d. No wonder the popularity of shark fin soup has been rising.

2 Many scientists and nutritionists think _____.
   a. shark fin soup has cancer fighting abilities
   b. Chinese people must eat nutritious shark fin soup as often as possible
   c. shark fin soup is not rich in vitamins and minerals
   d. people who enjoy shark fin soup will die due to Vitamin A

3 Choose the correct words for each sentence.
   a. I am going to reveal top 10 reasons for fast food's popular / popularly / popularity.
   b. I don't want my two wobbly teeth / tooth / tooths to fall out. I just want them to stay as they are.
   c. The soil of this region is higher / high / highly rich in nitrogen and phosphorus.

LEARNING BOARD

① Shark fin soup is dangerous not because of a shark's sharp teeth, but because of its mercury content. ② In China and Hong Kong, the popularity (of shark fin soup) has been rising (among people). ③ Many Chinese people think that shark fin soup is good for their health because it is highly nutritious. ④ They believe that shark fin soup is rich in various vitamins and minerals, (especially Vitamin A). ⑤ But, lots of scientists and nutritionists disagree with their opinion. ⑥ According to their research, it contains no Vitamin A at all, and the amount of minerals (found in shark fin soup) is not very high. ⑦ It is also widely believed that shark fin soup can prevent cancer. ⑧ But scientifically, it is not proven that shark fin soup has cancer fighting abilities. ⑨ On the contrary, shark fin soup is said to be bad for our health (due to its high mercury content). ⑩ So, doctors recommend that pregnant women and young children avoid eating shark fins. ⑪ Actually, dolphin meat and tuna are also considered to be dangerous because they also contain high levels of mercury.

Words & Expressions

shark 상어 fin 지느러미 shark fin soup 상어 지느러미 수프, 샥스핀 teeth 이빨들 (단수 – tooth) mercury 수은 content 내용물, 함유량, 목차 popularity 인기 highly nutritious 영양가가 높은 nutritious 영양가가 높은(cf. nutrition 영양, 영양물) be rich in …이 풍부한 nutritionist 영양학자 disagree with …에 동의하지 않다 contain 함유하다 prevent 예방하다 scientifically 과학적으로 cancer fighting abilities 항암효과(능력) on the contrary 오히려, 반대로 recommend 권고하다, 추천하다 pregnant 임신한 (n. pregnancy 임신) avoid 피하다 dolphin 돌고래 tuna 다랑어, 참치

49

14 Did You Know Cambodians Like To Eat Fried Spiders?

Eating spiders? It sounds dangerous, but some people do it. Surprisingly, quite a few Cambodians think that spiders are tasty. In Cambodia, many people eat spiders almost everyday. They find them similar to fried chicken. They are said to eat fried spiders as an everyday snack. This may seem unbelievable, but it's true. It is easy to find edible spiders in Cambodia. There are spiders everywhere, especially in Skuon, a small town in Cambodia.

This town is famous for fried spiders. The villagers breed spiders in holes in the ground and hunt them in the forest as well. Usually, they cook the spiders with oil. Not all people are willing to eat deep-fried spiders. Some people like them, but some people don't. In fact, they don't look very appetizing. These spiders are as big as fists and look crisp on the outside.

Nobody knows for sure how they started eating spiders, but some scholars suggest that they might have been forced to eat them because they didn't have enough food to eat in the 1970s.

1. **What is the main idea of the story?**
   a. The taste of fried spiders is similar to fried chicken.
   b. Cambodians are strong because they have enough food to eat such as spiders.
   c. It is a poor decision to eat fried spiders because steamed spiders are much more delicious.
   d. It is not difficult to find people who eat fried spiders in Cambodia.

2. **According to the passage, which sentence is right?**
   a. Maybe Cambodians started eating spiders reluctantly for they didn't have much food.
   b. Fried chicken is the second most popular snack in Cambodia.
   c. Skuon, the capital city of Cambodia, has been raising spiders as a food resource.
   d. Deep-fried spiders are popular but not good for health.

3. **Choose the correct words for each sentence.**
   a. People think dogs bite strangers but the truth is not all dogs <u>bite / bites / biting</u> strangers.
   b. I cannot stand the idea of eating snail, but my friend Judy <u>found / made / have</u> it delicious.
   c. I told you to check his credit card first thing in the morning but you <u>don't / didn't / doesn't</u>.

LEARNING BOARD

① Eating spiders? ② It sounds dangerous, but some people do it. ③ Surprisingly, quite a few Cambodians think that spiders are tasty. ④ In Cambodia, many people eat spiders almost everyday. ⑤ They find them similar to fried chicken. ⑥ They are said to eat fried spiders as an everyday snack. ⑦ This may seem unbelievable, but it's true. ⑧ It is easy to find edible spiders in Cambodia. ⑨ There are spiders everywhere, especially in Skuon, (a small town in Cambodia.) ⑩ This town is famous for fried spiders. ⑪ The villagers 1) breed spiders in holes in the ground and 2) hunt them in the forest as well. ⑫ Usually, they cook the spiders with oil. ⑬ Not all people are willing to eat deep-fried spiders. ⑭ Some people like them, but some people don't. ⑮ In fact, they don't look very appetizing. ⑯ These spiders 1) are as big as fists and 2) look crisp on the outside. ⑰ Nobody knows (for sure) how they started eating spiders, but some scholars suggest that they might have been forced to eat them because they didn't have enough food (to eat) in the 1970s.

Words & Expressions

quite a few 상당히 많은 **Cambodian** 캄보디아인 **fried** 튀긴(fry 튀기다) **tasty** 맛있는(= delicious ↔ tasteless 맛이 없는) **edible** 식용의, 먹을 수 있는 **similar to** …와 비슷한 **snack** 간식 **unbelievable** 믿기 힘든 **villager** 마을 사람, 주민 **be famous for** …로 유명하다 **breed** 키우다, 사육하다 **deep-fried** 뜨거운 기름에 튀긴 **appetizing** 입맛을 돋우는 **fist** 주먹 **crisp** 바삭바삭한(= crispy) **scholar** 학자

51

15 Did You Know Which Fruit Can Burn About 9 Pounds In A Month?

You can shed 9 pounds in a month by eating African Mango. Thankfully, this special mango reduces bad cholesterol and burns an average of 2 inches of belly fat within a month. More thankfully, it is cheap compared to other diet foods, supplements, or diet pills. Of course, it's also a whole lot cheaper than gym membership fees. It costs less than a dollar per serving, so it's cheaper than a can of soda.

Dr. Oz was the person who made it famous in America. He called it a "breakthrough supplement" and a "miracle in your medicine cabinet" on his The Dr. Oz Show on September 13, 2010. Ever since then, many people have experienced its awesome effect. For instance, Dr. Tanya Edwards, M.D., called African Mango extract a "miracle pill" because she lost 7 pounds in a month with the help of it. She said she didn't make any changes to her eating habits or exercise routine.

With the recent popularity of African Mango, there are dozens of African Mango products being sold online. Be careful when you select one of these products, however, because not all of them are effective or trustworthy.

1 What is the main idea of the story?
a. Dr. Oz must be the salesperson who wants to sell African Mango.
b. Diet pills are better than African Mango.
c. African Mango can be a good solution to the obesity problem.
d. As far as African Mango is concerned, the cheaper, the better,

2 Dr. Oz was the person who _____.
a. spent millions of dollars annually trying to lose weight
b. called African Mango extract a "miracle pill"
c. experienced African Mango's miraculous effects
d. was the host of The Dr. Oz Show

3 Choose the correct words for each sentence.
a. As terrorists appeared at / in / on TV screen, passers-by stopped walking and watched the news.
b. Why are some methods so much more effective that / than / then others?
c. A myriad of bones and skeletons found near the crime scene have sheded / shed / shedding light on this murder case.
d. Can you believe this is her third served / serving / serves of macaroni and cheese?

LEARNING BOARD

① You can **shed** 9 pounds in a month by eating African Mango. ② Thankfully, this special mango ¹⁾ **reduces** bad cholesterol and ²⁾ **burns** an average of 2 inches of **belly** fat within a month. ③ More thankfully, it is **cheap compared to** other diet **foods, supplements,** or diet **pills**. ④ Of course, it's also **(a whole lot) cheaper than gym membership fees**. ⑤ It costs less than a dollar per serving, so it's cheaper than **a can of soda**.

⑥ Dr. Oz was the person (**who made it famous**) in America. ⑦ He called it a "**breakthrough** supplement" and a "miracle in your **medicine cabinet**" on his The Dr. Oz Show on September 13, 2010. ⑧ Ever since then, many people have experienced its **awesome** effect. ⑨ For instance, Dr. Tanya Edwards, M.D., called African Mango **extract** a "miracle pill" because she lost 7 pounds in a month with the help of it. ⑩ She said she didn't **make any changes to** her eating habits or exercise **routine**.

⑪ **With the recent popularity of** African Mango, there are **dozens of** African Mango products (**being sold online**). ⑫ Be careful when you select one of these products, however, because **not** all of them are effective or **trustworthy**.

Words & Expressions

shed (피·눈물을) 흘리다, 없애다, (옷·허물을) 벗다, (나뭇잎을) 떨어뜨리다, (빛을) 비추다 **thankfully** 고맙게도 **reduce** 줄이다, 감소시키다 **burn fat** 지방을 태우다, 연소시키다 **average** 평균 **belly** 배, 복부 **cheap** 싼 **compare to** ...와 비교하다 **supplement** 보조품, 보충제 **a whole lot** 대단히 **gym** 체육관 **fee** 요금 **per one serving** 1회 먹는 분량에, 일 인분에 **approximately** 대략 **annually** 매년 **lose weight** 체중을 감량하다 **breakthrough** 돌파구, 획기적 성공 **medicine cabinet** 약품 보관 찬장 **awesome** 굉장한, 대단한 **extract** n. 추출(물), 발췌 v. 뽑아내다, 추출하다 **eating habit** 식습관 **routine** 규칙적으로 하는 일, 일상 **exercise routine** 평소에 하는 운동 **trustworthy** 신뢰할 만한

Listening with Dictation

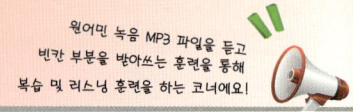

11 Did You Know 'Sweetbread' Is Neither Sweet Nor Bread?

Surprisingly, 'sweetbreads' are not a kind of bread; they are a kind of meat. _____¹, sweetbread is a gland from young animals, _____² from piglets, calves, or lambs. People have used these glands _____³ for a long time. You can make various sweetbreads _____⁴ what ingredients are used. Sweetbread _____⁵, an organ in the neck, is often called 'neck sweetbread', and sweetbread made from _____⁶, a belly organ near the stomach, is called 'belly sweetbread'. These are the two basic types of sweetbreads, but other glands _____⁷ and also called 'sweetbreads'. For example, 'ear sweetbread' is made from one of _____⁸ in the mouth. Mostly, sweetbreads are boiled first _____⁹. While boiling, add salt, vinegar, or lemon juice. In some cases, people _____¹⁰ them in milk or water for several hours to remove all the blood.

12 Did You Know Vegetarians Do Not Eat Marshmallow?

_____¹ vegetarians don't eat marshmallow? Not all vegetarians _____², but some vegetarians do refuse to eat it because it contains ingredients from animals. There are several types of vegetarians, depending on _____³. Ovo-lacto vegetarians, for example, are vegetarians who choose not to eat meat of any kind, but do eat eggs and _____⁴. They think _____⁵ eggs, milk products, and honey because they can get those foods _____⁶ animals. On the other hand, vegans do not eat any kind of animal meat, eggs, or animal fat, _____⁷ dairy products like ice cream or yogurt. Their diet mainly includes fruits, vegetables and grains. So, they won't eat bread with butter, a chocolate cake covered with whipped cream, _____⁸ (pigs' fat), or honey. There is one more thing vegans refuse to eat : gelatin. Gelatin is a kind of protein _____⁹ the tissues, bones, and _____¹⁰, usually cows and pigs. That's why vegans refuse to eat desserts made with gelatin, such as jelly or marshmallow.

13 Did You Know Shark Fin Soup Is As Dangerous As Sharks?

Shark fin soup is dangerous not because of a shark's sharp teeth, but because of its mercury content. In China and Hong Kong, the popularity of shark fin soup _____¹ among people. Many Chinese people think that shark fin soup _____² because it is _____³. They believe that shark fin soup _____⁴ various vitamins and minerals, especially Vitamin A. But, lots of scientists and nutritionists _____⁵ their opinion. According to their research, _____⁶ at all, and the amount of minerals found in shark fin soup is not very high. _____⁷ that shark fin soup can prevent cancer. But scientifically, it is not proven that shark fin soup has _____⁸. On the contrary, shark fin soup is said to be bad for our health _____⁹. So, doctors recommend that pregnant women and young children avoid eating shark fins. Actually, dolphin meat and tuna _____¹⁰ dangerous because they also contain high levels of mercury.

14 Did You Know Cambodians Like To Eat Fried Spiders?

Eating spiders? It sounds dangerous, but some people do it. Surprisingly, quite a few Cambodians think that spiders are tasty. In Cambodia, many people eat spiders almost everyday. They find them _____ ¹ fried chicken. They are said to eat fried spiders as an everyday snack. This may _____ ², but it's true. It is easy to find _____ ³ in Cambodia. There are spiders everywhere, especially in Skuon, a small town in Cambodia. This town is famous for fried spiders. The villagers _____ ⁴ spiders in holes in the ground and hunt them in the forest _____ ⁵. Usually, they cook the spiders with oil. Not all people _____ ⁶ deep-fried spiders. Some people like them, but some people don't. In fact, they don't _____ ⁷. These spiders are _____ ⁸ and look crisp on the outside. Nobody knows for sure how they started eating spiders, but some scholars suggest that they _____ ⁹ eat them because they _____ ¹⁰ in the 1970s.

15 Did You Know Which Fruit Can Burn About 9 Pounds In A Month?

You can _____ ¹ 9 pounds in a month by eating African Mango. Thankfully, this special mango _____ ² and burns an average of 2 inches of belly fat _____ ³. More thankfully, it is cheap compared to other diet foods, supplements, or diet pills. Of course, it's also _____ ⁴ gym membership fees. It costs less than a dollar per serving, so it's cheaper than a can of soda. Dr. Oz _____ ⁵ in America. He called it a "breakthrough supplement" and a "miracle in your medicine cabinet" _____ ⁶ his The Dr. Oz Show on September 13, 2010. Ever since then, many people have experienced its awesome effect. For instance, Dr. Tanya Edwards, M.D., called African Mango extract a "miracle pill" because she lost 7 pounds in a month with the help of it. She said she _____ ⁷ her eating habits or exercise routine. With _____ ⁸ of African Mango, there are _____ ⁹ African Mango products _____ ¹⁰. Be careful when you select one of these products, however, because not all of them are effective or trustworthy.

---

11 정답 1. More specifically speaking 2. frequently 3. as edible organ meats 4. depending on 5. made from the thymus 6. the pancreas 7. are also eaten 8. the salivary glands 9. to remove a thin skin 10. soak

12 정답 1. Have you heard that 2. turn it down 3. what kinds of foods they eat 4. dairy products 5. it's OK to eat 6. without killing 7. nor 8. food cooked with lard 9. derived from 10. skins of animals

13 정답 1. has been rising 2. is good for their health 3. highly nutritious 4. is rich in 5. disagree with 6. it contains no Vitamin A 7. It is also widely believed 8. cancer fighting abilities 9. due to its high mercury content 10. are also considered to be

14 정답 1. similar to 2. seem unbelievable 3. edible spiders 4. breed 5. as well 6. are willing to eat 7. look very appetizing 8. as big as fists 9. might have been forced to 10. didn't have enough food to eat

15 정답 1. shed 2. reduces bad cholesterol 3. within a month 4. a whole lot cheaper than 5. was the person who made it famous 6. on 7. didn't make any changes to 8. the recent popularity 9. dozens of 10. being sold online

16 Did You Know Fat-Free Foods Are Not Always Good For Your Health?

If you put yourself on a diet, or you have a health problem requiring weight loss, such as diabetes, watch out for fat-free or fat-reduced foods, diet sodas, and yogurt drinks. They sound healthy, but you had better not put these foods on your everyday menu because they may not be helpful for your diet or your health after all.

Fat-free or reduced-fat foods tend to be less flavorful than full-fat foods, which means they do not taste as good or as satisfying. So, if you set the table with these foods, you may have to eat more to feel full. In other words, these low-fat or zero-fat foods are likely to make you eat more than you need. Furthermore, foods labeled with the words like "light," "fat-free," "low-fat," "zero-calorie" or the like are prone to contain various sweeteners like extra sugar or corn syrup to make up for their unsatisfying flavor.

Recently, a Harvard research center published an article claiming that full-fat dairy products may actually lower the risk of diabetes. When it comes to books, we may 'not judge a book by its cover', but as for food, we would do well to 'judge food by its label'.

1 What can be the best title of this story?
   a. Must Choose Fat-Free Foods For Your Own Sake
   b. Be Aware : The Word 'Fat-Free' May Not Mean 'Healthy'
   c. Fat-Free : Totally Different From Low-Fat
   d. Don't Judge Drinks By Their Labels

2 According to the passage, which sentence is <u>wrong</u>?
   a. Fat-free or fat-reduced foods may not be beneficial to your health.
   b. If you have diabetes, you may want to eat full-fat dairy products.
   c. Ordinarily, people who try to cut down on fat have a tendency to choose low-fat or fat-free foods.
   d. Zero-fat drinks are good but they contain more salt and fat than you think.

3 Choose the correct words for each sentence.
   a. We have to <u>make out of / make our own / make up for</u> the deficit with bonuses.
   b. If you want to <u>low / lower / lowing</u> the danger of premature birth, Omega-3 fatty acids may help.
   c. Kay was diagnosed with type 2 diabetes which <u>are / were / is</u> different from type 1 diabetes.

LEARNING BOARD

① If ¹⁾ you put yourself on a diet, or ²⁾ you have a health problem requiring **weight loss**, (such as **diabetes**), watch out for ¹⁾ **fat-free** or **fat-reduced** foods, ²⁾ diet sodas, and ³⁾ yogurt drinks. ② **They** sound healthy, but you had better not put these foods on your everyday menu because they may not be helpful for your diet or your health **after all**. ③ (Fat-free or reduced-fat) foods **tend to** be less **flavorful** than full-fat foods, which means they do not **taste** as good or as **satisfying**. ④ So, if you set the table with these foods, you may have to eat more to feel full. ⑤ In other words, these low-fat or zero-fat foods **are likely to** make you eat more than you need. ⑥ Furthermore, foods (labeled with the words like "light," "fat-free," "low-fat," "zero-calorie" or the like) **are prone to** contain various **sweeteners** (like extra sugar or corn syrup) to **make up for** their unsatisfying **flavor**. ⑦ Recently, a Harvard research center published an **article** (claiming that full-fat dairy products may actually lower the risk of diabetes). ⑧ **When it comes to** books, we may 'not judge a book by its cover', but as for food, we would do well to 'judge food by its label'.

Words & Expressions

put … on a diet …에게 다이어트를 시키다 require 요구하다 weight loss 체중감량 diabetes 당뇨병 watch out for …을 주의하다, 조심하다 fat-free 무지방 fat-redued 지방을 줄인 (low-fat 저지방의) tend to …하는 경향이 있다 flavorful 풍미 있는, 맛이 좋은(=tasty) satisfying 만족스러운 taste 맛(=flavor) set the table 상을 차리다 feel full 배부름을 느끼다 in other words 즉, 다시 말해서 be likely to …하기 쉽다 furthermore 게다가, 더욱이 label 상표를 붙이다, (상표 등에) 필요한 정보를 적어 넣다 be prone to …하는 경향이 있다 sweetener 감미료 corn syrup 옥수수 시럽 make up for 벌충하다, 메우다 flavor 맛(=taste) article 기사, 논설 dairy product 유제품 when it comes to …에 관해서라면(=as for) don't judge a book by its cover 〈속담〉 책 표지만 보고 책을 판단하지 말라(외모만으로 판단하지 말라) do well to …하는 것이 현명하다

Did You Know Koreans Are Not The Only People Who Enjoy Soondae?

In Korea, Soondae has been a popular food for a long time. Amazingly, we can find foods very similar to Soondae in other countries.

Soondae is steamed pig's (or cow's) intestines stuffed with various ingredients. The common Korean Soondae generally contains cellophane noodles and pig's blood. Interestingly, people in Europe, North America, Latin America, and other Asian countries also enjoy this kind of food. It is called black pudding, blood pudding, or blood sausage, depending on the country. Their ingredients and recipes are similar to Korean Soondae.

Cows and pigs are preferred by countries such as Korea, China and Germany. But Tibetan people have used yaks, and several European countries have made black pudding out of sheep's intestines and blood. Typical European-style black pudding is filled with meat, blood, fat, bread, onions, and barley.

However, nowadays, unlike in Korea, sausages made of blood are not easy to find at local supermarkets or delis in western countries. It seems that westerners are no longer keen on food containing blood.

1 What is the main idea of the story?
  a. Unexpectedly, many people around the world enjoy foods similar to Korean Soondae.
  b. Soondae out of cows' intestines is more delicious than black pudding.
  c. European-styled black pudding is filled with cellophane noodles and pig's blood.
  d. Generally, Europeans don't like food containing blood

2 You can make Soondae by _____.
  a. cooking animals' intestines with lots of oil and spices
  b. steaming animals' intestines stuffed with cellophane noodles and pig's blood
  c. boiling sheep's intestines and blood in a large pan
  d. frying yaks' intestines filled with grains

3 Choose the correct words for each sentence.
  a. Some Europeans who love K-pop stars and Korean dramas are <u>keen on / likes to / desperate to</u> learning Korean.
  b. <u>Before long / Nowadays / For the time being</u> more and more children are addicted to computer games.
  c. These products are widely <u>preferred / prefer / to prefer</u> by customers around the world.

LEARNING BOARD

① In Korea, Soondae has been a popular food for a long time. ② Amazingly, we can find foods very similar to Soondae in other countries. ③ Soondae is steamed pig's (or cow's) intestines stuffed with various ingredients. ④ The common Korean Soondae generally contains cellophane noodles and pig's blood. ⑤ Interestingly, people in Europe, North America, Latin America, and other Asian countries also enjoy this kind of food. ⑥ It is called black pudding, blood pudding, or blood sausage, depending on the country. ⑦ Their ingredients and recipes are similar to Korean Soondae.

⑧ Cows and pigs are preferred by countries such as Korea, China and Germany. ⑨ But Tibetan people have used yaks, and several European countries have made black pudding out of sheep's intestines and blood. ⑩ Typical European-style black pudding is filled with meat, blood, fat, bread, onions, and barley. ⑪ However, nowadays, unlike in Korea, sausages made of blood are not easy to find at local supermarkets or delis in western countries. ⑫ It seems that westerners are no longer keen on food containing blood.

Words & Expressions

amazingly 놀랍게도 **similar to** …와 유사한 **steam** 증기, 증기로 익히다, 찌다 **intestine** 장, 창자 **stuffed with** …로 속을 채운 **various** 다양한, 여러 가지의 **ingredient** 재료, 성분 **cellophane noodles** 당면 **generally** 대개 **contain** …을 함유하다 **depending on** …에 따라 **recipe** 요리법, 레시피 **prefer** 선호하다 **onion** 양파 **barley** 보리 **nowadays** 요즘 **local** 동네의, 지역의 **deli** (=delicatessen) 식료품 가게, 식당 **be keen on** …를 좋아하다

18 Did You Know Chinese People Eat Pigeon Soup?

Chinese people eat pigeon soup. Many gourmets find it delicious, and it is relatively easy to make: prepare pigeon meat, chives, salt, and pepper, and then boil them together.

Pigeon soup is not that surprising compared to other exotic Chinese foods. Chinese cuisine is famous for being diverse and having amazing ingredients. Chefs are said to use almost everything edible in their cooking, including chicken hearts, monkey brains, bird's nests, bear paws, antlers, cockroaches, scorpions, cicadas, etc. People around the world enjoy and appreciate Chinese exotic and creative foods. But, some of them are not easy for foreigners to enjoy, because

they are too strange or unusual. For example, Stinky Tofu, made of fermented tofu, is popular in China but some cannot stand its strong odor. Also, it is not odd or strange to use animal's blood in Chinese dishes, while quite a few westerners think that's disgusting. Yet, many Chinese people allegedly believe that the blood of live snakes or turtles, and blood-dripping antlers are healthy foods.

1 What is the main idea of the story?

   a. The most horrible Chinese food is pigeon soup.
   b. Chinese food is diverse, creative and exotic.
   c. People who try to eat Stinky Tofu are likely to die of its terrible smell.
   d. Foreigners pretend to enjoy Chinese food but in fact, they don't.

2 According to the passage, which sentence is right?

   a. Many gourmets claim that pigeon soup is the most delicious food in China.
   b. The recipe of pigeon soup is quite simple but the ingredients cost very much.
   c. Chinese cuisines are nothing but normal so everyone can enjoy them without reserve.
   d. It seems that Chinese cooks are not afraid of using poisonous animals in their cooking.

3 Choose the correct words for each sentence.

   a. I'm so surprised that there are so many surprise / surprising / surprised six figure jobs out there.
   b. Many of my friends can sip / take a dip / appreciate fine wine and they are willing to pay hundreds of dollars to get a taste of it.
   c. Lady Gaga is famous for not only eccentric / being eccentric / eccentricity but also falling flat on her back during a show at Texas.

LEARNING BOARD

① Chinese people eat pigeon soup. ② Many gourmets find it delicious, and it is relatively easy to make: 1) prepare (pigeon meat, chives, salt, and pepper,) and then 2) boil them together. ③ Pigeon soup is not that surprising (compared to other exotic Chinese foods.) ④ Chinese cuisine is famous for 1) being diverse and 2) having amazing ingredients. ⑤ Chefs are said to use almost everything edible in their cooking, (including chicken hearts, monkey brains, bird's nests, bear paws, antlers, cockroaches, scorpions, cicadas, etc. ⑥ People (around the world) 1) enjoy and 2) appreciate Chinese (exotic and creative) foods. ⑦ But, some of them are not easy (for foreigners) to enjoy, because they are too strange or unusual. ⑧ For example, Stinky Tofu, (made of fermented tofu,) is popular in China but some cannot stand its strong odor. ⑨ Also, it is not odd or strange to use animal's blood in Chinese dishes, while quite a few westerners think that's disgusting. ⑩ Yet, many Chinese people allegedly believe that the blood (of live snakes or turtles) and blood-dripping antlers are healthy foods.

Words & Expressions

pigeon 비둘기 gourmet 미식가 relatively 비교적 pepper 후추 chive 차이브, 골파 boil 끓이다 surprising 놀라운 (surprised 놀란) exotic 이국적인 cuisine 요리법 diverse 다양한 chef 요리사, 주방장 edible 먹을 수 있는 chicken heart 닭의 심장, 겁쟁이 paw (동물) 발 antler 사슴뿔 cockroach 바퀴벌레 scorpion 전갈 cicada 매미 appreciate 1. 감상하다, 맛있게 먹다 2. 진가를 인정하다 3. 감사하다 creative 독창적인, 창의적인 unusual 특이한, 색다른 ferment 발효하다, 발효 stinky 악취가 나는 tofu 두부 can't stand 견딜 수 없다 odor 냄새 odd 이상한 dish 접시, 설거지거리, 요리 disgusting 구역질 나는 (disgust v. 역겹게 하다 n. 역겨움) allegedly ...라는 주장에 의하면, 이른바 blood-dripping 피가 뚝뚝 떨어지는

19 Did You Know There Is A Nearly $200 Sandwich?

You can find a sandwich worth $200 in the UK. Naturally, you have to pay 100 pounds (almost 200 USD) for ordering this special sandwich. This triple-layered sandwich is made of bread, chicken, quail eggs, ham, white truffles and so on. Of course, only the finest ingredients are used. Despite being fat and greasy, food fanatics all over the world speak very highly of its awesome taste.

Do you think a $200 sandwich is expensive? There are many more expensive foods out there. Saffron, a kind of spice, costs at least one thousand dollars per kilogram because it's very hard to get.

Spending over a thousand dollars on a spice sounds ridiculous, but there is something more ridiculous: whisky. This is not just any whisky, it is the most expensive whisky in the world. If you want to appreciate the rare taste of this 30-year-old whisky from the Macallan Fine Rare Vintage Collection, you may have to empty your bank account because the price per bottle is $38,000.

1 What is the main idea of the story?
   a. Spending thousands of dollars on one sandwich is a crazy thing to do.
   b. If you buy one bottle of the most expensive wine, you will go broke.
   c. There are unexpectedly expensive foods in the world.
   d. Greasy food is expensive but it's tasty.

2 If you want to order a $200 sandwich, you will have to _____.
   a. go to the UK
   b. keep your stomach empty
   c. withdraw $38,000 from your bank account
   d. go bankrupt

3 Choose the correct words for each sentence.
   a. I got the speeding ticket because I didn't know the speed limit was 35 miles per / every / in a hour.
   b. No wonder those bare / rare / scare handicrafts were sold at a high price. There were only three of them in the entire planet.
   c. I wanted to speak great / highly / good of his work, but I spoke ill of it in spite of myself.

LEARNING BOARD

① You can find a sandwich (worth $200) in the UK. ② Naturally, you have to pay
　　　　　　　　　　　　　↑수식　a sandwich which is worth $200　당연히　　　　　　　　pay (돈) for
　　　　　　　　　　200달러 가치의 샌드위치　* worth a. (얼마의) 가치가 있는　　　　　　　　…에 대해 돈을 내다

100 pounds (almost 200 USD) for ordering this special sandwich. ③ This
　　　　　　　　　　　　　　　　　　　　　　　　　　a $200 sandwich

triple-layered sandwich is made of bread, chicken, quail eggs, ham, white truffles
　(a)　　↑수식　↑(n)　* 완성품에서 재료를 알 수 있는 경우 made of (물리적 변화)　　송로버섯
triple 3 + layered 층(겹)의　　ex) This chair is made of wood. 이 의자는 나무로 만든 것이다.
(bi → 2, tri → 3, quad → 4)　* 완성품에서 재료를 알 수 없는 경우 made from (화학적 변화)
　　　　　　　　　　　　　　　　ex) Paper is made from wood. 종이는 나무로 만든다.

and so on. ④ Of course, only the finest ingredients are used. ⑤ Despite being fat
기타 등등(= etc.)　　　　최상의(the finest) 재료(ingredients) 만(only)　　despite + 명사/동명사
　　　　　　　　　　　　　　　　　　　　　　　　　　　　　　　　　　　= Despite the fact that this is fat and greasy

and greasy, food fanatics (all over the world) speak very highly of its awesome
기름기 많은　　fanatic 광신자　(전세계에서)　찬사를 보내다, 칭찬하다 (↔ speak ill of 흉을 보다)
　　　　　　　　　　　　　　　　　　　　　　　　　　　　　　　　　　　awesome 경탄할 만한, 굉장히 좋은
taste.
v. …맛이 나다, 맛보다 n. 맛, 취향 (a. tasty 맛있는 tasteless 아무 맛이 없는, 천박한) → 이 문장에서는 명사 '맛'

⑥ Do you think a $200 sandwich is expensive? ⑦ There are many more expensive
　　　　　　　　　　　　　　　　　비싼(↔ inexpensive)　유도부사(There) + 복수동사(are) + 복수명사(foods)

foods out there. ⑧ Saffron, (a kind of spice,) costs (at least) one thousand dollars
종류별 음식들　　　　　　= 동격　　　주어 Saffron (3인칭 단수 현재), 동사 costs
* 이때 food는 집합명사가 아니므로 복수가능.　　　　　　　　at least 최소한, 적어도

per kilogram because it's very hard to get.
1kg당　　　　　　　　　엉기(구하기) 어려운 = hard to come by, hard to obtain

⑨ Spending over a thousand dollars on a spice sounds ridiculous, but there is
동명사 주어 Spending (3인칭 단수 현재), 동사 sounds　어처구니없게 들리다 ridiculous a. 웃기는, 말도 안 되는
　spend 돈 on …에 돈을 쓰다　　　　　　　　　　　　　　ridicule n. 조롱, 조소

something more ridiculous: whisky. ⑩ This is not just any whisky, it is the most
　　　　　　　　= 동격　　　　　　　　　　　　　　　　음절이 긴 형용사의 최상급
　　　　　　　　　　　　　　　　　　　　　　　　the most expensive (↔ the cheapest)

expensive whisky (in the world). ⑪ If you want to appreciate the rare taste of this
　　　　　　　　　　　　　　　　　　　　　　　맛을 보다, 감상하다 …의 흔치 않은(rare) 맛

30-year-old whisky (from the Macallan Fine Rare Vintage Collection), you may have to
　(a)　↑수식　↑(n)　⑪번 문장구조 : 가정법 현재 if 주어(you) + 현재동사(want), 주어 + may + 동사원형(have to)
30-year-old : 30년 된 (형용사이므로 years로 쓰지 않도록 주의)

empty your bank account because the price (per bottle) is $38,000.
통장을 비우다, 통장의 돈을 모두 털다　　　　　(한 병당) 가격

Words & Expressions

worth of …가치의 naturally 당연히 pound 파운드 (계량 단위 1파운드 : 0.454kg, 영국의 화폐 단위) triple-layed 3중 겹의, 3층의 quail 메추라기 truffle 송로버섯, 트뤼플 and so on 기타 등등 greasy 기름기 많은 fanatic 광신자, …에 광적인 사람 speak highly of …를 칭찬하다 awesome 경탄할 만한, 굉장히 좋은 spice 향신료 hard to get 얻기(구하기) 어려운 sound ridiculous 어이없게 들리다 the rare taste of …의 흔치 않은 맛 empty one's bank account 통장을 털다 the price per bottle 한 병당 가격

Did You Know The Most Expensive Coffee Is Made Of Cat Poo?

Coffee made of cat poo is the most expensive coffee? You might say, 'No way!' but many people would say, 'Yes way.' Poo, or we can say 'feces', is supposed to be smelly and gross, but this cat poo coffee is nothing like that. Cat Poo Coffee (called "civet coffee" or "Kopi Luwak") is more expensive and tastier than Starbucks'. But, who would pay around $20 for a single cup of coffee brewed from an animal's poo? Unexpectedly, quite a few coffee lovers are willing to wait in line to get a taste of it.

It is not brewed from regular coffee beans. Its special beans are collected from the feces of the civet, which is not exactly a cat, but a cat-like mammal. The civet eats the coffee cherries that fall off the trees, then defecates. Brewers search through the droppings and pick out the cherries that have passed through its digestive system. It is expensive because only about 230kg of the beans are produced each year in the whole of Indonesia.

Generally, customers praise its strong aftertaste. Considering its origin, it's no wonder it has a strong aftertaste. In spite of that, some people have no reservations about paying 20 bucks for a cup of poo coffee, since its flavor is just that good.

1 What can be the best title of this story?

a. Eat Poo, Drink Poo, And Smell Poo
b. Cat, The Mysterious Animal
c. The Most Expensive Poo Ever
d. Coffee From Poo : Not Smelly But Fragrant

2 According to the passage, which sentence is <u>wrong</u>?

a. 'Feces' and 'poo' have the same meaning.
b. Poo is supposed to be smelly and dirty, but cat poo is not dirty, just smelly.
c. Coffee fanatics don't mind waiting in line to get a taste of Cat Poo Coffee.
d. Special beans of Kopi Luwak can be found in the droppings of the civet.

3 Choose the correct words for each sentence.

a. I have heard his lies quite a few <u>time / times / timing</u>. I can't believe whatever he says.
b. The nearest supermarket is Kristine's Fresh Market <u>which / who / when</u> is owned by my sister.
c. Considering <u>that his advanced age / his advanced age / as his advanced age</u>, he looks surprisingly young.
d. Bobby Brown, ex-husband of Whitney Houston who was found dead in her hotel room, <u>mourn / mourns / mourning</u> Houston's death.

LEARNING BOARD

① Coffee (made of cat poo) is the most expensive coffee? ② You might say, 'No way!' but many people would say, 'Yes way.' ③ Poo, (or we can say 'feces'), is supposed to be smelly and gross, but this cat poo coffee is nothing like that. ④ Cat Poo Coffee (called "civet coffee" or "Kopi Luwak") is more expensive and tastier than Starbucks'. ⑤ But, who would pay around $20 for a single cup of coffee (brewed from an animal's poo)?

⑥ Unexpectedly, quite a few coffee lovers are willing to wait in line to get a taste of it. ⑦ It is not brewed from regular coffee beans. ⑧ Its special beans are collected from the feces of the civet, (which is not exactly a cat, but a cat-like mammal.) ⑨ The civet [1] eats the coffee cherries (that fall off the trees), then [2] defecates. ⑩ Brewers [1] search through the droppings and [2] pick out the cherries (that have passed through its digestive system.) ⑪ It is expensive because only about 230kg of the beans are produced (each year) (in the whole of Indonesia). ⑫ Generally, customers praise its strong aftertaste. ⑬ Considering its origin, it's no wonder it has a strong aftertaste. ⑭ In spite of that, some people have no reservations about paying 20 bucks for a cup of poo coffee, since its flavor is just that good.

Words & Expressions

poo 대변(=feces, dropping) **be supposed to** ...하기로 되어 있다, 해야 한다 **smelly** 나쁜 냄새가 나는 **gross** 역겨운 **unexpectedly** 예상외로, 뜻밖에 **tasty** 맛있는 **brew** (커피, 차를) 우려내다 **get a taste of** ...의 맛을 보다 **coffee bean** 커피콩 **mammal** 포유류 **coffee cherry** 커피 열매 **defecate** 배변하다 **digestive system** 소화기관 **praise** 찬양하다 **strong aftertaste** 강한 뒷맛 **have no reservations** 주저하지 않다 **flavor** 맛, 향미

Listening with Dictation

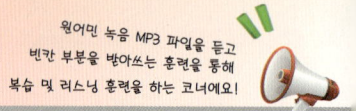

16 Did You Know Fat-Free Foods Are Not Always Good For Your Health?

If you _____¹, or you have a health problem _____² such as diabetes, watch out for fat-free or fat-reduced foods, diet sodas, and yogurt drinks. They sound healthy, but you _____³ put these foods on your everyday menu because they may not be helpful for your diet or your health after all. Fat-free or reduced-fat foods _____⁴ be less flavorful than full-fat foods, which means they do not taste as good or as satisfying. So, if you _____⁵ with these foods, you may have to eat more to feel full. In other words, these low-fat or zero-fat foods are likely to make you eat _____⁶. Furthermore, foods labeled with the words like "light," "fat-free," "low-fat," "zero-calorie" _____⁷ are prone to contain various sweeteners like extra sugar or corn syrup to _____⁸ their _____⁹. Recently, a Harvard research center published an article claiming that full-fat dairy products may actually _____¹⁰. When it comes to books, we may 'not judge a book by its cover', but as for food, we would do well to 'judge food by its label'.

17 Did You Know Koreans Are Not The Only People Who Enjoy Soondae?

In Korea, Soondae _____¹ for a long time. Amazingly, we can find foods very similar to Soondae in other countries. Soondae is steamed pig's (or cow's) intestines _____² various ingredients. The common Korean Soondae generally contains cellophane noodles and pig's blood. Interestingly, people in Europe, North America, Latin America, and other Asian countries also enjoy this kind of food. It is called black pudding, blood pudding, or blood sausage, _____³. Their ingredients and _____⁴ Korean Soondae. Cows and pigs _____⁵ countries such as Korea, China and Germany. But Tibetan people have used yaks, and several European countries have made black pudding _____⁶ sheep's intestines and blood. Typical European-style black pudding is filled with meat, blood, fat, bread, onions, and _____⁷. However, nowadays, _____⁸ in Korea, sausages made of blood are not easy to find at local supermarkets or _____⁹ in western countries. It seems that westerners _____¹⁰ food containing blood.

18 Did You Know Chinese People Eat Pigeon Soup?

Chinese people eat pigeon soup. Many gourmets _____¹, and it is relatively easy to make: prepare pigeon meat, chives, salt, and pepper, and then boil them together. Pigeon soup is not that surprising compared to other exotic Chinese foods. Chinese cuisine is famous for being diverse and having amazing ingredients. Chefs are said to _____² in their cooking, including chicken hearts, monkey brains, bird's nests, bear paws, antlers, cockroaches, scorpions, _____³, etc. People around the world enjoy and _____⁴ Chinese exotic and creative foods. But, some of them are not easy for foreigners to enjoy, because they are too strange or unusual. For example, Stinky Tofu, made of _____⁵ tofu, is popular in China but some _____⁶ its strong odor. Also, _____⁷ use animal's blood in Chinese _____⁸, while quite a few westerners think that's disgusting. Yet, many Chinese people _____⁹ that the blood of live snakes or turtles, and _____¹⁰ are healthy foods.

66 Chapter 2 | Food

19 Did You Know There Is A Nearly $200 Sandwich?

You can find a sandwich _____¹ in the UK. Naturally, you have to pay 100 pounds (almost 200 USD) _____² this special sandwich. This triple-layered sandwich is made of bread, chicken, _____³ eggs, ham, white truffles and so on. Of course, only _____⁴ are used. Despite being fat and greasy, food fanatics all over the world _____⁵ its awesome taste. Do you think a $200 sandwich is expensive? There are many more expensive foods out there. Saffron, a kind of spice, costs at least one thousand dollars per kilogram because _____⁶. Spending over a thousand dollars on a spice _____⁷, but there is something more ridiculous: whisky. This is not just any whisky, it is the most expensive whisky in the world. If you want to _____⁸ this 30-year-old whisky from the Macallan Fine Rare Vintage Collection, you may have to _____⁹ because _____¹⁰ is $38,000.

20 Did You Know The Most Expensive Coffee Is Made Of Cat Poo?

Coffee _____¹ cat poo is the most expensive coffee? You might say, 'No way!' but many people would say, 'Yes way.' Poo, or we can say '_____²' is supposed to be smelly and gross, but this cat poo coffee _____³. Cat Poo Coffee (called "civet coffee" or "Kopi Luwak") is more expensive and tastier than Starbucks'. But, who would pay around $20 _____⁴ coffee brewed from an animal's poo? Unexpectedly, quite a few coffee lovers are willing to wait in line _____⁵. It is not _____⁶ regular coffee beans. Its special beans are collected from the feces of the civet, which is not exactly a cat, but a cat-like mammal. The civet eats the coffee cherries that fall off the trees, then _____⁷. Brewers search through the droppings and pick out the cherries that have _____⁸. It is expensive because only about 230kg of the beans are produced each year in the whole of Indonesia. Generally, customers praise its strong aftertaste. Considering its origin, it's no wonder it _____⁹. In spite of that, some people _____¹⁰ paying 20 bucks for a cup of poo coffee, since its flavor is just that good.

---

16 정답 1. put yourself on a diet 2. requiring weight loss 3. had better not 4. tend to 5. set the table 6. more than you need 7. or the like 8. make up for 9. unsatisfying flavor 10. lower the risk of diabetes

17 정답 1. has been a popular food 2. stuffed with 3. depending on the country 4. recipes are similar to 5. are preferred by 6. out of 7. barley 8. unlike 9. delis 10. are no longer keen on

18 정답 1. find it delicious 2. use almost everything edible 3. cicadas 4. appreciate 5. fermented 6. cannot stand 7. it is not odd or strange to 8. dishes 9. allegedly believe 10. blood-dripping antlers

19 정답 1. worth $200 2. for ordering 3. quail 4. the finest ingredients 5. speak very highly of 6. it's very hard to get 7. sounds ridiculous 8. appreciate the rare taste of 9. empty your bank account 10. the price per bottle

20 정답 1. made of 2. feces 3. is nothing like that 4. for a single cup of 5. to get a taste of it 6. brewed from 7. defecates 8. passed through its digestive system 9. has a strong aftertaste 10. have no reservations about

Chapter 3. Beauty

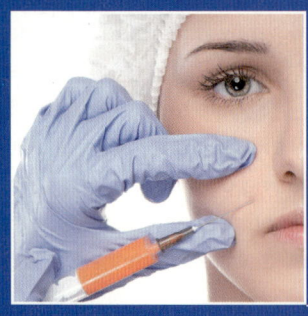

21. Did you know Botox Is A Kind Of Poison?

보톡스가 일종의 독이라는 거 아세요?

22. Did you know The Basic Tips For Cleansing?

세안을 위한 기본 팁을 아세요?

23. Did you know How To Choose The Right Fat Burner?

어떻게 올바른 지방 연소제를 선택해야 하는지 아세요?

24. Did you know Three "Don'ts" For Healthy And Smooth Skin?

건강하고 매끄러운 피부를 위해 하지 말아야 할 세 가지가 무엇인지 아세요?

25. Did you know How To Prevent Split Ends?

갈라지는 머리끝을 방지하는 방법을 아세요?

※ 이 챕터의 원어민녹음 MP3를 들으시려면
스마트폰으로 우측 QR코드를 스캔해주세요 ➡

26. Did you know The Sweetest Way To Control Acne?

여드름을 관리하는 가장 달콤한 방법이 무엇인지 아세요?

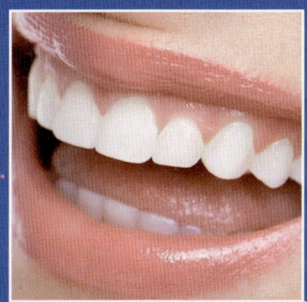

27. Did you know Three Tips For Whiter Teeth?

더 하얀 치아를 갖기 위한 세 가지 팁을 아세요?

28. Did you know Why Removing Love Handles Is Difficult?

러브 핸들을 제거하는 게 왜 어려운지 아세요?

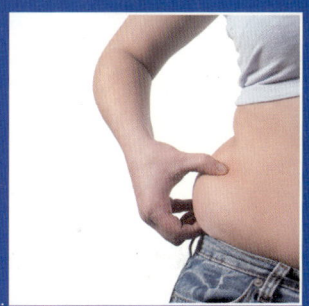

29. Did you know Which Hair Colors Can Make You Look Younger?

젊어 보이게 만드는 머리카락 색깔이 무엇인지 아세요?

30. Did you know There Are Exercises For Under-Eye Bags?

처진 눈 밑 살을 위한 운동이 있다는 거 아세요?

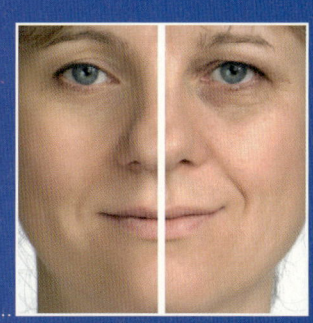

21 Did You Know Botox Is A Kind Of Poison?

Botox is the most popular non-surgical cosmetic procedure. Allegedly, millions of people have been getting Botox injections every year. As a matter of fact, more than 1.5 million North Americans received Botox injections in 2011.

Botox is the brand name of botulinum toxin A, and botulism is a serious form of food poisoning. The typical symptom of botulism is paralysis. In some cases, paralysis from botulism can be very dangerous, even fatal. Interestingly, Botox injections are a diluted form of botulism which is injected into facial muscles because they can paralyze or weaken the muscles that form wrinkles. For instance, when a person gets the injection in the muscles around the brows, those muscles

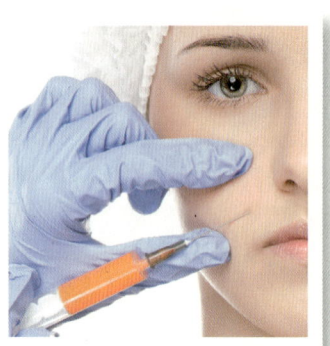

cannot contract for a period of time. They are paralyzed. After being given Botox injections, people can see the effects of the injections within a few hours to a couple of days.

Unfortunately, the amazing effects of Botox do not last long. If you want to maintain a wrinkle-free look throughout the year, you have to get the injections 3 to 4 times a year since the effects last about three to five months.

1 What is the main idea of the story?

  a. It is very dangerous and foolish to get Botox injections.
  b. Botox is the most expensive but popular non-surgical cosmetic procedure.
  c. Botox is fatal because it can paralyze the muscles.
  d. Botox is a diluted form of botulism which is a kind of dangerous toxin.

2 If you get a Botox injection into the muscles around your eye brows, _____.

  a. those muscles will be paralyzed
  b. you will go blind due to infection caused by the toxin
  c. your wrinkle-free skin will last for 5 years
  d. your facial muscles will contract very quickly.

3 Choose the correct words for each sentence.

  a. I think right side of my body is paralysis / paralyzed / paralyze. I can't move my right hand.
  b. Some patients with type 1 diabetes have to get insulin infections / injections / induction on a daily basis.
  c. Just be patient for a while. He will be here for / in / with a minute.

LEARNING BOARD

① Botox is the [1] most popular [2] non-surgical cosmetic procedure. ② Allegedly, millions of people have been getting Botox injections every year. ③ Botox is the brand name (of botulinum toxin A), and botulism is a serious form of food poisoning. ④ The typical symptom of botulism is paralysis. ⑤ In some cases, paralysis (from botulism) can be very dangerous, even fatal. ⑥ Interestingly, Botox injections are a diluted form (of botulism) (which is injected into facial muscles) because they can paralyze or weaken the muscles (that form wrinkles). ⑦ For instance, when a person gets the injection in the muscles around the brows, those muscles cannot contract (for a period of time). ⑧ They are paralyzed. ⑨ After being given Botox injections, people can see the effects of the injections (within a few hours to a couple of days). ⑩ Unfortunately, the amazing effects of Botox do not last long. ⑪ If you want to maintain a wrinkle-free look throughout the year, you have to get the injections (3 to 4 times) (a year) since the effects last about three to five months.

Words & Expressions

non-surgical 비수술적인, 수술을 하지 않는 surgical 수술의, 외과의 (cf. surgery 수술) cosmetic a. 성형의 n. 화장품 cosmetic procedure 미용 시술 injection 주입, 주사 botulism 보툴리눔 식중독 food poisoning 식중독 typical symptom 전형적인 증상 paralysis 마비 (v. paralyze 마비시키다) fatal 치명적인 dilute 희석하다, 묽게 하다 facial muscles 얼굴 근육 weaken 약하게 하다 (a. weak 약한) wrinkle (얼굴의) 주름 brow 이마 contract 수축하다, 계약서 (n. contraction 수축, 계약) for a period of time 한동안 effect 효과, 영향 last 지속하다 throughout the year 일 년 내내

22 Did You Know The Basic Tips For Cleansing?

First, you need to find the right cleanser for your skin. You can find a good cleanser for your skin type at drugstores or local cosmetic shops. The number one mistake people make when it comes to facial wash is thinking expensive ones are always better. But that is not always true. There is no need to spend over 50,000 won on a costly name-brand wash. However, you had better not choose bar soap because it generally dries out the skin.

And don't forget not to wash or cleanse too often. Nothing more than washing once or twice a day with a proper cleanser is needed. In the morning, just a splash of lukewarm water is enough.

One more thing: use a small amount of cleanser (just a dime-sized bit is sufficient to cleanse your face) and rinse with lukewarm water. Be careful not to wash your face with hot or cold water. Both can have a bad effect on your skin.

1 What can be the best title of this story?

a. The More You Wash, The Clearer Skin You Can Get
b. Cleanser : The Biggest Enemy For Your Skin
c. How To Wash Your Face & How To Choose Your Cleanser
d. All You Need To Know About Bar Soap

2 According to the passage, which sentence is <u>wrong</u>?

a. You had better not use bar soap and not wash your face more than twice a day.
b. No need to spend lots of money on expensive cleansers.
c. You can find an appropriate cleanser for your skin type only at drugstores.
d. You don't have to use any soap or cleanser when washing your face in the morning.

3 Choose the correct words for each sentence.

a. I do / make / have mistakes all the time but I try not to repeat the mistakes of the past.
b. When it comes about shopping / to shopping / to shop, my boyfriend is an expert.
c. Since my eyes are blurry, I have to be careful to not / not to / to not bump into something or someone.

LEARNING BOARD

① First, you need to find the right cleanser for your skin. ② You can find a good cleanser for your skin type (at drugstores or local cosmetic shops.) ③ The number one mistake (people make) (when it comes to facial wash) is thinking expensive ones are always better. ④ But that is not always true. ⑤ There is no need to spend (over) 50,000 won on a costly name-brand wash. ⑥ However, you had better not choose bar soap because it generally dries out the skin. ⑦ And don't forget not to wash or cleanse too often. ⑧ (Nothing more than) washing once or twice a day with a proper cleanser is needed. ⑨ In the morning, just a splash of lukewarm water is enough. ⑩ One more thing: 1) use a small amount of cleanser (just a dime-sized bit is sufficient to cleanse your face) and 2) rinse with lukewarm water. ⑪ Be careful not to wash your face with (hot or cold) water. ⑫ Both can have a bad effect on your skin.

Words & Expressions

cleansing 정화, 세척 cleanser 세안제, 비누(cf. detergent (세탁·주방용) 세제) drugstore 약국 local 동네의, 지역의 cosmetic shop 화장품 가게 when it comes to …에 관한 한 facial wash 세안용 비누 expensive 비싼(= costly) spend (money) on …에 돈을 쓰다 name-brand 브랜드가 있는, 유명 상표의 bar soap 고체 비누 splash (물을) 끼얹음, 첨벙, 철썩 뿌려진 물 lukewarm 미지근한 dime-sized 다임 동전 크기의 sufficient 충분한 rinse 헹구다 have a bad effect on …에 안 좋은 영향을 미치다

23 Did You Know How To Choose The Right Fat Burner?

Many diet and weight loss industries have been pocketing huge amounts of money because many people are willing to open their wallets for weight-loss products. People just want to lose weight easily and these products work.

Among the many dieting products, fat burners are gaining huge popularity, since these help users lose weight in a short time period without sweaty exercise or the horrible pain of dieting. The problem is that not everybody who spends money on fat burners tastes the joy of losing weight. So before choosing fat burners, consider the following points:

- Is it effective? - Fat burners are supposed to help you lose fat, not just water.
- Is it safe? - Check whether the ingredients are clinically safe and if there are any side effects. Choose only FDA-approved products.
- Are consumers satisfied with the product? - Review other users' opinions before buying. Hundreds of companies making and selling fat burners have been busted by the FDA for false advertising and using unhealthy ingredients.

1 What is the main idea of the story?

a. People who want to lose weight easily need to buy fat burners.
b. When choosing a fat burner, select the effective, safe and customer-approved one.
c. All diet products including fat burners must have been approved by the FDA.
d. Companies who advertise their products falsely must be busted by the FDA.

2 Fat burners are gaining popularity since _____.

a. they are cheaper than diet pills
b. they promise a miracle for a reasonable price
c. all of them are approved by the FDA and clinically safe
d. these can help users burn their fat in a not-so-difficult way

3 Choose the correct words for each sentence.

a. Surprisingly, his company pocket / pocketed / pockets nearly $3 million last year.
b. Why are you never satisfied with / satisfy about / satisfied by anything in your life?
c. If you cheat on a test, you will be bust / busted / to bust faster than you can say 'I'm busted!'

LEARNING BOARD

① Many (**diet** and **weight loss**) industries have been pocketing **huge** amounts of money
　　　　diet (industries) and weight loss industries　　　현재완료 진행　　　엄청난 금액의 돈 = a fortune
　　　　diet 식이요법, 다이어트를 하다　　　　　　　　　: ...를 (주머니에) 챙겨 넣고 있다 pocket n. 주머니 v. (주머니에) 넣다, 챙기다

because many people are willing to open their wallets for weight-loss products. ② People
　　　　　　　　　　　　　기꺼이 (be willing to) 지갑을 열다 (open one's wallets)

just want to **lose weight** easily and these products **work**. ③ Among the many dieting products,
　　　　　　　체중을 감량하다　　　　　　　　　효과가 있다　　between 둘 사이 among 둘 이상 사이
　　　　　　　(↔ gain weight 체중이 늘다)　ex) Does it work? 효과가 있니?　ex) between you and me 너랑 나 사이에
　　　　　　　　　　　　　　　　　　　　It did work. 정말 효과 있었어.　　among these people 이 사람들 사이에

fat burners are gaining huge **popularity**, since these help users lose weight (in a short time
　　　　　　현재진행 : 엄청난 인기를 얻고 있다　　　　　　　　help + 목적어(users) + 동사원형(lose) (짧은 시간에)
　　　　　　　　　　　　　　　　　　　　　　　　　　　　　: 사용자들(users)이 체중을 뺄(lose) 수 있도록 돕다(help)

period) (without ¹⁾ sweaty exercise or ²⁾ the horrible pain of dieting.) ④ The problem is that
　　　　　　　　　　땀 흘리는 운동　　　　　　　　　　　　　　　　　　　문제는 that 이하이다

not everybody (who spends money on fat burners) tastes the joy of losing weight.
　　부분 부정 ↑ 수식　　　　　　　　　　　　　　...의 즐거움(기쁨)을 맛보다
that 절의 주어 everybody, 동사 tastes

⑤ So before choosing fat burners, consider the following points:
　　　　before (you) chooseting　　　　명령형　다음의, 아래에 나오는

⑥ - Is it **effective**? - ⑦ Fat burners **are supposed to** help you lose fat, (not just water.)
　　　　a. 효과적인(↔ ineffective)　　　...하기로 되어 있다　help + 목적어(you) + 동사원형(lose)

⑧ - Is it safe? - ⑨ Check ¹⁾ whether the **ingredients** are **clinically** safe and ²⁾ if there are any
　　　　　　　　　1) whether... and 2) if there are...: (두 가지를) 확인하라
　　　　　　　　　whether the ingredients are clinically safe (or not) - 재료가 의학적으로 안전한지 아닌지

side effects. ⑩ Choose only FDA-approved products.
　부작용　　　　　　　　FDA 승인을 받은 approved 승인된, 공인된
　　　　　　　　　* FDA: 미식품의약국(Food and Drug Administration)

⑪ - Are **consumers satisfied with** the product? - ⑫ Review other users' opinions
　　사람주어 + be동사 + satisfied with (주어가) ...에 만족하다　　명령형
　　사물주어 + be동사 + satisfying (주어는) 만족스럽다 (satisfying은 형용사)

before buying. ⑬ Hundreds of companies (making and selling fat burners) have
= before you buy　　수백의　　　　　　　↑　수식　(fat burners를 만들고 판매하는) 회사들
　　　　　　　　　cf. dozens of 수십의 thousands of 수천의　　　주어 companies, 동사 have
　　　　　　　　　　　millions of 수백만의

been busted by the FDA for false advertising and using **unhealthy** ingredients.
현재완료 수동태 (have been pp by)　　false 거짓의 + advertising 광고 : 허위광고　a.건강에 해로운(↔healthy 건강에 좋은)
...에 의해 적발되고 있다 (for ... : 적발되는 이유)

Words & Expressions

fat burner 지방 연소 보조 제품 **diet** 식이요법, 다이어트를 하다 **weight loss industry** 체중 감량 산업 **pocket** 주머니에 넣다, 챙기다 **huge** 엄청난, 막대한 **be willing to** 기꺼이 ...하다 **open one's wallet** (돈을 내려고) 지갑을 열다 **weight-loss product** 체중 감량 제품 **lose weight** 체중을 감량하다 **work** 효과가 있다 **gain popularity** 인기를 얻다 **popularity** 인기 (cf. popular 인기 있는) **in a short time period** 짧은 시간 내에 **sweaty** 땀이 나는 (sweat 땀) **pain** 고통(=pang, agony) **taste the joy of** ...의 기쁨을 맛보다 **effective** 효과적인 **be supposed to** ...하기로 예정되어 있다 **ingredient** 성분, 재료, 요소 **clinically** 의학적으로 (clinic 병원, 진료) **side effect** 부작용 **approved** 승인을 받은 **customer** 고객 **bust** 단속하다 (be busted 단속에 걸리다) **false** 거짓의, 가짜의 **unhealthy** 건강에 해로운

24 Did You Know Three "Don'ts" For Healthy And Smooth Skin?

Don't smoke. If you are a smoker and don't have any intention to quit smoking in the near future, you had better prepare to get wrinkly and dry skin. Experts say sun exposure and smoking are the two main causes of skin damage. Kate Moss is the perfect example. Although she looks fabulous in pictures, and many skin experts have taken care of her skin with costly cosmetics, her bare skin is horrible because she is a longtime smoker.

Don't forget to moisturize. Skin needs moisture to stay healthy and smooth. Moisture-rich products and moisturizers help your skin lock in moisture. The best way to use moisturizers is to apply them while your skin is still damp.

Don't tan. Tanned skin looks great, but unfortunately tanned skin is damaged skin. Repeated or constant tanning or sunburn can not only accelerate the aging of the skin but also increase the risk of skin cancer.

1 What is the main idea of the story?

a. In order to get smooth skin, do not smoke or tan and do moisturize.
b. The most important thing to do for smooth skin is to moisturize.
c. Tanning and smoking are the main causes of skin cancer.
d. Kate Moss looks fabulous because she has used high-priced cosmetics.

2 According to the passage, which sentence is right?

a. A non-smoker is highly likely to have wrinkly and dry skin.
b. Kate Moss' bare skin is bad because she has smoked for a long time.
c. Skin experts recommend that you should apply moisturizers while taking a bath.
d. Repeated tanning is a good solution to skin cancer.

3 Choose the correct words for each sentence.

a. How can I steady cool / stay cool / keep cool in scorching hot temperatures?
b. Boy, I feel sorry for you because your workload looks brutally / brutality / brutal.
c. My wife has no intention of quitting smoke / smoking / smoked and that makes me crazy.

LEARNING BOARD

① Don't smoke. ② If you ¹⁾ are a smoker and ²⁾ don't have any intention to quit smoking (in the near future), you had better prepare to get (wrinkly and dry) skin.

③ Experts say sun exposure and smoking are the two main causes of skin damage. ④ Kate Moss is the perfect example. ⑤ Although ¹⁾ she looks fabulous in pictures, and ²⁾ many skin experts have taken care of her skin with costly cosmetics, her bare skin is horrible because she is a longtime smoker.

⑥ Don't forget to moisturize. ⑦ Skin needs moisture to stay healthy and smooth.

⑧ (Moisture-rich) products and moisturizers help your skin lock in moisture. ⑨ The best way to use moisturizers is to apply them while your skin is still damp.

⑩ Don't tan. ⑪ Tanned skin looks great, but unfortunately tanned skin is damaged skin. ⑫ (Repeated or constant) tanning or sunburn can not only ¹⁾ accelerate the aging of the skin but also ²⁾ increase the risk of skin cancer.

Words & Expressions

smoke v. 담배를 피우다 n. 연기 **smoker** 흡연자 **intention** 의도, 의사 **don't have any intention to** …할 의사가 없다 **quit** 그만두다, 중지하다 **in the near future** 가까운 미래에 **wrinkly** 주름진, 주름투성이의 (**wrinkle** 주름) **exposure** 노출 **damage** 손상 **fabulous** 멋진, 근사한 **costly** 비싼 **bare skin** 맨 피부 **longtime** 오랫동안의, 여러 해의 **moisturize** 수분을 주다 (**moisture** 수분 **moisturizer** 보습제) **smooth** 부드러운, 매끈한 **moisture-rich** 수분이 풍부한 **apply** 적용하다, (화장품) 바르다 **damp** 축축한 **tan** 피부를 태우다, 선탠하다 **repeated** 반복적인 **constant** 끊임없는, 계속되는 **sunburn** 햇볕에 의한 화상 **accelerate** 가속화하다 **cancer** 암

25 Did You Know How To Prevent Split Ends?

Women who have long and damaged hair are the most likely to have problems with split ends. Split ends happen when the tips of hairs lose their outer protective layer. The best and only way to remove current split ends is to cut them off. But, if you don't want to trim your hair frequently, refer to the following information.

First, do not use heated hair devices such as blow dryers, curling irons, hair straighteners, etc. These hot air tools dry out your hair and heat is the main cause of split ends. So, try not to use them or at least reduce the amount of time that you use them for. Second, lessen how often you dye your hair or get a perm. Both can damage hair, so avoid bleaching, dyeing, or getting a perm too often. Third, be careful when brushing. Brushing when it is wet, or brushing too often, or brushing with a fine-toothed comb can harm your hair. Inappropriate brushing can break pieces of your hair and eventually cause split ends. So do not brush wet hair, and use a wide-toothed comb.

1 What is the main idea of the story?

a. Long hair means damaged hair with split ends.
b. Heated hair devices have nothing to do with hair damage.
c. If you take precautions, split ends can be prevented.
d. A wide-toothed comb is always better than a fine-toothed comb.

2 People who hate to trim their hair frequently but have problems with split ends _____.

a. tend to brush their hair with a wide-toothed comb
b. must dye their hair as often as possible
c. have to use a fine-toothed comb
d. had better not use curling irons and hair straighteners

3 Choose the correct words for each sentence.

a. A proper exercise is a fine way <u>losing / to lose / for lost</u> weight and stay healthy.
b. <u>In order not to / In order to not / In not order to</u> break a large loaf of bread into pieces, she carried it with both hands.
c. How <u>often / much / long</u> do you work out? Let me guess. Twice a week?
d. The Smiths are <u>dying / dyeing / dyed</u> their hair black at the hair salon.

LEARNING BOARD

① Women (who have long and damaged hair) are the most likely to have problems with split ends. ② Split ends happen when the tips of hairs lose their outer protective layer. ③ The best and only way (to remove current split ends) is to cut them off. ④ But, if you don't want to trim your hair frequently, refer to the following information.

⑤ First, do not use heated hair devices (such as blow dryers, curling irons, hair straighteners, etc.) ⑥ These hot air tools dry out your hair and heat is the main cause of split ends. ⑦ So, ¹⁾ try not to use them or at least ²⁾ reduce the amount of time (that you use them for). ⑧ Second, lessen how often you dye your hair or get a perm. ⑨ Both can damage hair, so avoid bleaching, dyeing, or getting a perm (too often). ⑩ Third, be careful when brushing. ⑪ Brushing (when it is wet), or brushing (too often), or brushing (with a fine-toothed comb) can harm your hair. ⑫ Inappropriate brushing can ¹⁾ break pieces of your hair and eventually ²⁾ cause split ends. ⑬ So do not brush wet hair, and use a wide-toothed comb.

Words & Expressions

split ends 갈라진 머리끝 **split** 갈라지다. 쪼개지다. (남녀가) 헤어지다 **end** 끝 부분 **outer** 외부의. 외곽의 **layer** 층 **outer protective layer** 외부 보호층 **current** 현재의 **trim** 정리하다. 다듬다 **frequently** 자주 **refer to** …을 참조하다 **hair device** 모발 기구 **blow dryer** 헤어드라이어 **curl** (머리를) 곱슬곱슬하게 감다(말다) (curly 곱슬곱슬한) **iron** 철. 다리미 **straighten** 곧게 펴다 (straightener n. 곧게 펴는 것) **tool** 연장. 도구 **reduce** 줄이다(=lessen) **avoid** 피하다. 방지하다 **dye** 염색하다. 염료 (dyeing 염색) **bleach** 표백하다. 탈색하다 **brush** 솔질[빗질]하다 **a fine-toothed comb** 빗살이 촘촘한 빗 **inappropriate** 부적절한(↔ appropriate 적절한) **break pieces** 부수다 **eventually** 결국 **a wide-toothed comb** 빗살이 넓고 큰 빗

Listening with Dictation

21 Did You Know Botox Is A Kind Of Poison?

Botox is the most popular _____¹. Allegedly, millions of people have been getting Botox injections every year. As a matter of fact, more than 1.5 million North Americans received Botox injections in 2011. Botox is the brand name of botulinum toxin A, and botulism is _____² food poisoning. The _____³ of botulism is paralysis. In some cases, paralysis from botulism can be very dangerous, even fatal. Interestingly, Botox injections are _____⁴ botulism which is injected into facial muscles because they can _____⁵ the muscles that form wrinkles. For instance, when a person _____⁶ in the muscles around the brows, those muscles cannot contract _____⁷. They are paralyzed. After being given Botox injections, people can see the effects of the injections _____⁸. Unfortunately, the amazing effects of Botox do not last long. If you want to maintain a wrinkle-free look _____⁹, you have to get the injections 3 to 4 times a year since _____¹⁰ three to five months.

22 Did You Know The Basic Tips For Cleansing?

First, you need to find the right cleanser for your skin. You can find a good cleanser for your skin type _____¹ or local cosmetic shops. _____² when it comes to facial wash is thinking expensive ones are always better. But that is _____³. There is no need to spend over 50,000 won on a costly name-brand wash. However, you _____⁴ bar soap because it generally dries out the skin. And don't forget not to wash or cleanse too often. _____⁵ washing _____⁶ with a proper cleanser is needed. In the morning, just a splash of _____⁷ is enough. One more thing: use _____⁸ cleanser (just _____⁹ is sufficient to cleanse your face) and rinse with lukewarm water. Be careful not to wash your face with hot or cold water. Both can _____¹⁰ your skin.

23 Did You Know How To Choose The Right Fat Burner?

Many diet and weight loss industries have been pocketing huge amounts of money because many people _____¹ open their wallets for weight-loss products. People just want to _____² easily and these products _____³. Among the many dieting products, fat burners _____⁴, since these help users lose weight in a short time period without sweaty exercise or the horrible pain of dieting. The problem is that not everybody who _____⁵ fat burners _____⁶ losing weight. So before choosing fat burners, consider the following points: - Is it effective? - Fat burners are supposed to help you lose fat, not just water. - Is it safe? - Check whether the ingredients are _____⁷ and if there are any _____⁸. Choose only FDA-approved products. - Are consumers _____⁹ the product? - Review other users' opinions before buying. Hundreds of companies making and selling fat burners _____¹⁰ the FDA for false advertising and using unhealthy ingredients.

24. Did You Know Three "Don'ts" For Healthy And Smooth Skin?

Don't smoke. If you are a smoker and _____¹ quit smoking in the near future, you had better prepare to _____². Experts say sun exposure and smoking are the two main causes of skin damage. Kate Moss is the perfect example. Although she _____³ in pictures, and many skin experts _____⁴ her skin with costly cosmetics, her _____⁵ is horrible because she is a longtime smoker. Don't forget to moisturize. Skin needs moisture to _____⁶. Moisture-rich products and moisturizers help your skin lock in moisture. The best way to use moisturizers is to _____⁷ them while your skin is still damp. Don't tan. Tanned skin looks great, but unfortunately tanned skin is damaged skin. _____⁸ or constant tanning or sunburn can not only _____⁹ of the skin but also _____¹⁰.

25. Did You Know How To Prevent Split Ends?

Women who have long and damaged hair _____¹ have problems with split ends. Split ends _____² when the tips of hairs lose their outer protective layer. _____³ remove current split ends is to _____⁴. But, if you don't want to trim your hair frequently, refer to the following information. First, do not use heated hair devices such as blow dryers, curling irons, hair straighteners, etc. These _____⁵ dry out your hair and heat is the main cause of split ends. So, try not to use them or at least _____⁶ that you use them for. Second, _____⁷ how often you dye your hair or get a perm. Both can damage hair, so avoid bleaching, dyeing, or getting a perm too often. Third, be careful _____⁸. Brushing when it is wet, or brushing too often, or brushing with a fine-toothed comb can harm your hair. _____⁹ brushing can _____¹⁰ of your hair and eventually cause split ends. So do not brush wet hair, and use a wide-toothed comb.

---

21 정답 1. non-surgical cosmetic procedure 2. a serious form of 3. typical symptom 4. a diluted form of 5. payalyze or weaken 6. gets the injection 7. for a period of time 8. within a few hours to a couple of days 9. throughout the year 10. the effects last about

22 정답 1. at drugstores 2. The number one mistake people make 3. not always true 4. had better not choose 5. Nothing more than 6. once or twice a day 7. lukewarm water 8. a small amount of 9. a dime-sized bit 10. have a bad effect on

23 정답 1. are willing to 2. lose weight 3. work 4. are gaining huge popularity 5. spends money on 6. tastes the joy of 7. clinically safe 8. side effects 9. satisfied with 10. have been busted by

24 정답 1. don't have any intention to 2. get wrinkly and dry skin 3. look fabulous 4. have taken care of 5. bare skin 6. stay healthy and smooth 7. apply 8. Repeated 9. accelerate the aging 10. increase the risk of skin cancer

25 정답 1. are the most likely to 2. happen 3. The best and only way to 4. cut them off 5. hot air tools 6. reduce the amount of time 7. lessen 8. when brushing 9. inappropriate 10. break pieces

26 Did You Know The Sweetest Way To Control Acne?

Honey is an effective bacteria killer. So, honey has been used as a wound dressing because it can kill bacteria and help heal wounds. Bacteria in wounds are not the only kind honey can kill. Honey can also kill bacteria on your skin.

In fact, honey is one of the best ways to get clear and smooth skin. Thanks to honey's amazing healing properties — such as containing enzymes, antioxidants and anti-bacterial agents, — a honey facial mask is effective at removing acne scars, reducing redness, and moisturizing. In addition, it is very easy and simple. All you need is natural unfiltered honey.

First, wash your face. Make sure to remove all makeup and that your hands are clean. Apply the honey to your face. When applying honey, slowly rub the honey all over your face. Leave the honey on your face for about 15 minutes. Wash your face with warm water until all of the honey is removed, and lastly rinse with cool water to close your pores. Apply a honey mask 2-3 times a week or as desired.

1 What is the main idea of the story?
  a. Honey had been used to treat wounds but not any more.
  b. Honey can kill bacteria in wounds so we have to use honey as medicine.
  c. Filtered honey is not so effective compared to unfiltered honey.
  d. It is a good idea to use honey to treat acne or acne scars.

2 According to the passage, which sentence is right?
  a. In the past, people used honey only as a sweetener in replacement of sugar.
  b. Honey can kill all kinds of bacteria in the world thanks to antioxidants.
  c. If you have acne scars on your face, honey facial mask may be helpful.
  d. Honey facial mask needs lots of ingredients and costs much.

3 Choose the correct words for each sentence.
  a. You should read the directions carefully before making / getting / applying this ointment.
  b. 'Have a meeting three times a month / seven times a week / 24 hours a day?' You mean, we will have a meeting everyday?
  c. Meg is not the only one / the only person / not someone who can speak Spanish among us. Actually several people can speak Spanish as much as she does.

LEARNING BOARD

① Honey is an **effective** bacteria killer. ② So, honey has been used as a wound dressing because it can ¹⁾ kill bacteria and ²⁾ help **heal wounds**. ③ Bacteria (in wounds) are not the only kind (honey can kill). ④ Honey can also kill bacteria on your skin. ⑤ In fact, honey is one of the best ways to get (clear and smooth) skin. ⑥ Thanks to honey's amazing healing **properties** (—such as containing **enzymes**, antioxidants and anti-bacterial **agents**,—) a honey facial mask is effective at ¹⁾ removing **acne scars**, ²⁾ reducing redness, and ³⁾ moisturizing. ⑦ In addition, it is very easy and simple. ⑧ All you need is natural unfiltered honey. ⑨ First, wash your face. ⑩ Make sure ¹⁾ to remove all **makeup** and ²⁾ that your hands are clean. ⑪ **Apply** the honey to your face. ⑫ When applying honey, slowly rub the honey (all over your face). ⑬ Leave the honey on your face for about 15 minutes. ⑭ Wash your face with warm water until all of the honey is removed, and lastly rinse with cool water (to close your **pores**). ⑮ Apply a honey mask 2-3 times a week or as desired.

Words & Expressions

acne 여드름 **a wound dressing** 상처를 싸거나 덮는 도포제(드레싱) **heal** 치료하다 **wound** (흉기에 의한) 부상, 상처 **property** 특성, 성질, 부동산 **enzyme** 효소 **antioxidant** 산화방지제 **agent** 대리인, 중개상, 물질 **anti-bacterial agent** 항세균제 **scar** 흉, 상처 **unfiltered** 여과되지 않은 **makeup** 화장품(cf. make up 화장하다) **apply** (연고·로션 등을) 바르다, 적용하다, 신청하다 **rub** 문지르다, 비비다 **pore** 구멍, 모공(cf. porous 구멍이 많은) **as desired** 원하는 대로

27 Did You Know Three Tips For Whiter Teeth?

You can get your teeth whitened by your dentist. Professional whitening is the most effective and quickest way to get whiter teeth, but it costs you a lot. However, there are several inexpensive ways to get whiter teeth. Here are three tips for whiter teeth.

Brush And Rinse Often : Brushing your teeth is essential for keeping your teeth clean and white. So be sure to brush and rinse more than twice a day.

Avoid Drinking Colored Beverages : Colored beverages, such as coffee, tea, cola, wine, and juice, make you get yellow-stained teeth. So be sure to brush your teeth after drinking these beverages, not to mention trying to use a straw.

Stop Smoking. : No matter how often you get professional whitening treatments, and no matter how hard you try not to get yellow teeth, your teeth will get yellow again if you keep smoking. Cigarette smoke contains tar and many other chemicals which discolor your teeth. This is why some heavy and long-term smokers' teeth often appear not yellow but brown.

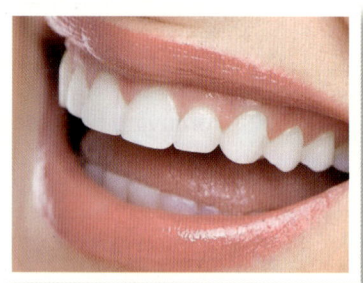

1 What can be the best title of this story?
   a. No Way To Get Whiter Teeth
   b. What You Can Do For Getting Whiter Teeth
   c. Smokers' Teeth : Teeth Of Hell
   d. A Smoker Found Unconscious After Brushing

2 Smokers cannot help getting yellow tinted teeth because _____.
   a. they hate all dentists and don't get a checkup
   b. cigarette smoke can discolor their teeth
   c. they never brush or rinse their teeth after eating
   d. they can't afford to get professional whitening

3 Choose the correct words for each sentence.
   a. My knees were swollen and bruised because I <u>got hurt / get to hurt / got hurted</u> by a soccer ball.
   c. If you keep <u>to shop / shop / shopping</u>, I'm sure you will be broke soon.
   d. I love his good character and his appearance, <u>as long as / not to mention / no matter how</u> his thick wallet.

LEARNING BOARD

① You can get your teeth whitened (by your dentist). ② Professional whitening is the most effective and quickest way to get whiter teeth, but it costs you a lot. ③ However, there are several inexpensive ways (to get whiter teeth). ④ Here are three tips for whiter teeth. ⑤ Brush And Rinse Often : ⑥ Brushing your teeth is essential for keeping your teeth clean and white. ⑦ So be sure to brush and rinse more than twice a day. ⑧ Avoid Drinking Colored Beverages : ⑨ Colored beverages, (such as coffee, tea, cola, wine, and juice,) make you get yellow-stained teeth. ⑩ So be sure to brush your teeth after drinking these beverages, not to mention trying to use a straw. ⑪ Stop Smoking : ⑫ No matter how often you get professional whitening treatments, and no matter how hard you try not to get yellow teeth, your teeth will get yellow again if you keep smoking. ⑬ Cigarette smoke contains tar and many other chemicals (which discolor your teeth). ⑭ This is why some heavy and long-term smokers' teeth often appear not yellow but brown.

Words & Expressions

dentist 치과의사 **professional** 전문적인 **whitening** 화이트닝, 미백 **effective** 효과적인 **cost** v. (값·비용을) 치르다 n. 비용 **inexpensive** 비싸지 않은 **tip** 1. 충고, 조언 2. (뾰족한) 끝 **brush** 솔질하다 **rinse** 헹구다 **essential** 필수적인 **beverage** 음료 **stain** 얼룩지게 하다, 얼룩, 더러움 **straw** 지푸라기, 빨대 **contain** …이 들어 있다 **chemical** 화학물질 **discolor** 변색시키다

85

28 Did You Know Why Removing Love Handles Is Difficult?

"Love handles" is a slang term for deposits of extra fat at the side of the waistline. We don't know how this sweet term was given to the saggy and flabby area on the sides. Whether this term is sweet or not, love handles bulging over your waistline don't look good.

Many people want to trim the love handle fat at their sides. But most of them say it's almost impossible to get rid of them. You can't have flat abs without getting your entire body into shape. Those chunks of fat are super stubborn. That's why you have to raise your metabolism by doing aerobic exercise to burn that extra fat. If you don't have the time or money to join a gym, there's no need to worry. Doing 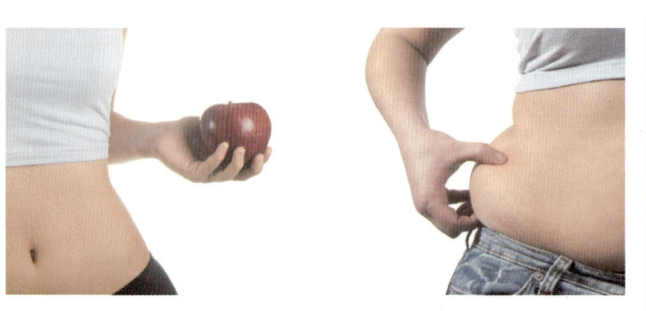 jumping jacks or running in place for about half an hour at home can be a good cardio workout for you. Of course, doing some other exercises that focus on the sides while doing basic exercise can help you remove love handles more effectively.

1 What can be the best title of this story?
   a. Solutions to Love Handles
   b. To Be Flabby Or To Be Saggy
   c. Effective Cardio Workouts For Everyone
   d. Remove Love Handles : A Mission Impossible

2 According to the passage, which sentence is right?
   a. Love handles are deposits of extra fat around the neck.
   b. The term 'love handles' is lovely because love handles look lovely.
   c. You have to get your body into shape before trying to get a flat ab.
   d. Doing exercises that focus only on the sides is effective to remove love handles.

3 Choose the right words for each sentence.
   a. After giving birth, I have this ugly flabby / chubby / stubby belly.
   b. Please tell me how and when to do / make / have exercises.
   c. You must decide while / whether / weather you go to the theater or stay home with your kids.

LEARNING BOARD

① "Love handles" is a slang term for deposits of extra fat (at the side of the waistline). ② We don't know how this sweet term was given to the (saggy and flabby) area on the sides. ③ Whether this term is sweet or not, love handles (bulging over your waistline) don't look good. ④ Many people want to trim the love handle fat at their sides. ⑤ But most of them say it's almost impossible to get rid of them. ⑥ You can't have flat abs without getting your entire body into shape. ⑦ Those chunks of fat are super stubborn. ⑧ That's why you have to raise your metabolism (by doing aerobic exercise to burn that extra fat). ⑨ If you don't have the time or money (to join a gym), there's no need to worry. ⑩ Doing jumping jacks or running in place (for about half an hour at home) can be a good cardio workout for you. ⑪ Of course, doing some other exercises (that focus on the sides) (while doing basic exercise) can help you remove love handles more effectively.

Words & Expressions

love handle 처진 뱃살, 늘어진 옆구리 살 **slang** 은어 **term** 1. 용어 2. 학기 3. 기간 4. 조건 **deposit** 축적물 **extra** 여분의, 가외의 **fat** 지방, 뚱뚱한 **side** 옆, 옆구리 **waistline** 허리선 **saggy** 축 처진 **flabby** 힘없이 늘어진 **bulge** 튀어나오다, 불거져 나오다 **trim** 다듬다, 잘라내다 **get rid of** 제거하다 **flat** 납작한 **abs** 복근 **get ... into shape** 건강한(맵시 있는) 몸매를 유지하다 **chunk** 덩어리 **stubborn** 완강한, 고집 센 **metabolism** 신진대사 **aerobic** 유산소의 (aerobic exercise = cardio exercise/workout 유산소 운동) **jumping jack** 팔 벌려 뛰기 **run in place** 제자리에서 뛰다 **cardio** (달리기 등 유산소 운동처럼) 심장을 강화시키는 운동 **workout** 운동(=exercise) **effectively** 효과적으로

Did You Know Which Hair Colors Can Make You Look Younger?

Did you know that dyeing your hair blonde can make you look older than you are? It can, since lighter hair color doesn't always go well with all shades of skin color. As we get older, our skin generally becomes yellowish and paler, and that is why it's not a very good idea to go blonde for people who are getting older but don't want to look old.

If you want to dye your hair in order to look younger than you are, consider   dyeing your hair dark brown, reddish brown, or black, since matching your hair to your skin tone is highly likely to make you look older than you are. As getting older usually leads to getting paler skin, it might be a good choice to dye your hair a color that's a little bit darker.

  Believe it or not, many Asians dye their hair black as they get older, and that surely makes them look younger than they are.

1 What can be the best title of this story?
  a. Dye Your Hair, And Your Hair Will Die
  b. Hair Colors Make You Look Younger Or Older
  c. Always Avoid Dyeing Your Hair Blonde
  d. Getting Old Means Getting Pale

2 For old people, it's not a nice idea to dye their hair blonde because _____.
  a. none of them wants to dye their hair dark brown
  b. people with pale skin have to go blonde for their own good
  c. matching their hair to their yellowish skin tone makes them look older
  d. old people always want to look old, not young

3 Choose the correct words for each sentence.
  a. Have you heard a guy who died while <u>dyeing / dying / dyed</u> his hair purple?
  b. I am afraid things aren't <u>making / going / becoming</u> well with the project.
  c. She arrived at the scene wearing her pinkish gown <u>around nineish / at nine sharp / at one to nine</u>. I don't remember the exact time.
  d. People who eat continuously tend to be <u>having / getting / doing</u> fatter and bigger.

LEARNING BOARD

① Did you know that dyeing your hair blonde can make you look older than you are? ② It can, since lighter hair color doesn't always go well with all shades of skin color. ③ As we get older, our skin generally becomes yellowish and paler, and that is why it's not a very good idea to go blonde (for people) (who [1] are getting older but [2] don't want to look old.)

④ If you want to dye your hair in order to look younger than you are, consider dyeing your hair [1] dark brown, [2] reddish brown, or [3] black, since matching your hair to your skin tone is highly likely to make you look older than you are. ⑤ As getting older usually leads to getting paler skin, it might be a good choice to dye your hair a color (that's a little bit darker).

⑥ Believe it or not, many Asians dye their hair black as they get older, and that surely makes them look younger than they are.

Words & Expressions

dye 염색하다 **blonde** 금발의 **look older** 더 늙어 보이다 **lighter** 더 밝은, 더 가벼운 **go well with** …와 잘 어울리다 **shade** 그늘, 빛 가리개, 색조 **get older** 나이가 들다 **yellowish** 노르스름한 **pale** 창백한 **go blonde** 금발로 하다 **look younger** 더 젊어 보이다 **consider** 고려하다 **dark** 어두운, 진한 **reddish** 불그스름한 **match** (어울리게) 맞추다 **tone** 색조 **be likely to** …하는 경향이 있다, …하기 쉽다 **highly** 매우, 대단히

89

30 Did You Know There Are Exercises For Under-Eye Bags?

As you get older, your skin becomes loose. Your eyelids are not an exception. If the area below the eyes becomes saggy, bags will appear under the eyes. That's why they are called 'eye bags,' because they are a kind of bag formed under the eyes. Of course, a plastic surgeon can lift saggy under-eye skin by surgery. But, there is a way to prevent saggy skin under the eyes without paying any money. Several facial exercises can help you improve your "bags under the eyes" problem.

1. Place your index fingers on the area under the eye. Try to lift the muscle of the eye with your fingers without wrinkling the skin around your brows. Maintain this pose for one second and repeat 15-20 times.

2. With the three middle fingers of each hand, tap lightly around your under-eye area. Tap from the outer corners of the eye to the inner corners, three to four times a day.

1 What is the main idea of the story?

a. Getting old means getting loose skin.
b. Some facial exercises can improve "bags under the eyes" problem.
c. When exercising, index fingers are the most important.
d. There is no way to remove eye bags other than plastic surgery.

2 According to the passage, which sentence is <u>wrong</u>?

a. Eye bags are formed under the eyes.
b. Plastic surgery can remove eye bags but it costs you.
c. Tapping gently the under-eye area may be helpful for "bags under the eyes" problem.
d. When doing facial exercises, you must use only index fingers.

3 Choose the right words for each sentence.

a. Can they take my personal information without <u>to let / let / letting</u> me know?
b. My boss wants to <u>give / place / submit</u> an ad in the newspapers and magazines.
c. Can I walk from here <u>until / with / to</u> the moon? or should I ride a bicycle?

LEARNING BOARD

① As you get older, your skin becomes loose. ② Your eyelids are not an exception.

③ If the area (below the eyes) becomes saggy, bags will appear under the eyes. ④ That's why they are called 'eye bags,' because they are a kind of bag formed under the eyes. ⑤ Of course, a plastic surgeon can lift (saggy under-eye) skin by surgery. ⑥ But, there is a way to prevent saggy skin (under the eyes) (without paying any money). ⑦ Several facial exercises can help you improve your "bags (under the eyes)" problem.

⑧ 1. Place your index fingers on the area (under the eye). ⑨ Try to lift the muscle of the eye (with your fingers) without wrinkling the skin (around your brows).

⑩ 1) Maintain this pose for one second and 2) repeat 15-20 times.

⑪ 2. With the three middle fingers of each hand, tap lightly around your under-eye area.

⑫ Tap (from the outer corners of the eye to the inner corners), (three to four times a day).

Words & Expressions

loose 헐거운 **eyelid** 눈꺼풀 **lid** 뚜껑, 덮개 **exception** 예외 **saggy** 축 처진, 늘어진 **bag** 주머니, 주머니처럼 늘어진 살 **appear** 나타나다 **form** 형성하다, 만들다 **plastic surgeon** 성형외과 의사 **plastic surgery** 성형수술 **lift** 들어 올리다 **by surgery** 수술로 **prevent** 막다, 예방하다 **facial exercise** 안면 운동 **improve** 개선하다, 좋아지게 하다 **place** 놓다, 두다 **index finger** 검지 **wrinkle** 주름지게 하다 **brows** 눈썹(= eye brows) **maintain** 유지하다 **pose** 자세 **repeat** 반복하다 **tap** 가볍게 두드리다 **under-eye area** 눈 밑 부위 **inner** 안쪽의

Listening with Dictation

26 Did You Know The Sweetest Way To Control Acne?

Honey is an effective bacteria killer. So, honey _____¹ a wound dressing because it can kill bacteria and help _____². Bacteria in wounds _____³ honey can kill. Honey can also kill bacteria on your skin. In fact, honey is one of the best ways to get clear and smooth skin. Thanks to honey's amazing healing properties – such as containing _____⁴, antioxidants and anti-bacterial agents, – a honey facial mask _____⁵ removing acne scars, reducing redness, and moisturizing. In addition, it is very easy and simple. _____⁶ natural unfiltered honey. First, wash your face. _____⁷ remove all makeup and that your hands are clean. Apply the honey to your face. _____⁸, slowly rub the honey all over your face. _____⁹ the honey on your face for about 15 minutes. Wash your face with warm water until all of the honey is removed, and lastly rinse with cool water to close your pores. Apply a honey mask 2-3 times a week or _____¹⁰.

27 Did You Know Three Tips For Whiter Teeth?

You can _____¹ by your dentist. Professional whitening is the most effective and quickest way to get whiter teeth, but _____². However, there are several inexpensive ways to get whiter teeth. Here are three tips for whiter teeth. Brush And Rinse Often : Brushing your teeth _____³ keeping your teeth clean and white. So be sure to brush and rinse _____⁴. Avoid Drinking Colored Beverages : _____⁵, such as coffee, tea, cola, wine, and juice, make you get yellow-stained teeth. So be sure to brush your teeth after drinking these beverages, _____⁶ trying to use a straw. Stop Smoking. : _____⁷ you get professional whitening treatments, and no matter how hard you try not to get yellow teeth, your teeth will get yellow again if you keep smoking. Cigarette smoke contains tar and _____⁸ which discolor your teeth. This is why some _____⁹ smokers' teeth _____¹⁰ not yellow but brown.

28 Did You Know Why Removing Love Handles Is Difficult?

"Love handles" is _____¹ deposits of extra fat _____² the waistline. We don't know how this sweet _____³ the saggy and flabby area on the sides. Whether this term is sweet or not, love handles _____⁴ your waistline don't look good. Many people want to _____⁵ at their sides. But most of them say it's almost impossible to get rid of them. You can't _____⁶ without getting your entire body into shape. Those chunks of fat are _____⁷. That's why you have to _____⁸ by doing aerobic exercise to burn that extra fat. If you don't have the time or money to join a gym, there's no need to worry. Doing jumping jacks or running in place _____⁹ at home can be a good cardio workout for you. Of course, doing some other exercises that focus on the sides while _____¹⁰ can help you remove love handles more effectively.

29 Did You Know Which Hair Colors Can Make You Look Younger?

Did you know that _____1 can make you _____2 you are? It can, since lighter hair color doesn't always _____3 all shades of skin color. _____4, our skin generally becomes yellowish and paler, and that is why it's not a very good idea to _____5 for people who are getting older but don't want to look old. If you want to dye your hair in order to look younger than you are, consider dyeing your hair dark brown, reddish brown, or black, since matching your hair to your skin tone _____6 make you look older than you are. As getting older usually _____7 getting paler skin, _____8 dye your hair a color that's a little bit darker. Believe it or not, many Asians dye their hair black as they get older, _____9 them look _____10.

30 Did You Know There Are Exercises For Under-Eye Bags?

As you get older, your skin _____1. Your eye lids are not an exception. If the area below the eyes becomes saggy, bags will _____2 under the eyes. That's why they are called 'eye bags,' because they are a kind of bag _____3 under the eyes. Of course, a plastic surgeon can lift saggy under-eye skin _____4. But, _____5 prevent saggy skin under the eyes _____6. Several facial exercises can help you improve your "bags under the eyes" problem. 1. _____7 your index fingers on the area under the eye. Try to lift the muscle of the eye with your fingers without wrinkling the skin around your brows. _____8 for one second and repeat 15-20 times. 2. With the three middle fingers of each hand, _____9 around your under-eye area. Tap from the outer corners of the eye to the inner corners, _____10.

---

26 정답
1. has been used as 2. heal wounds 3. are not the only kind 4. enzymes 5. is effective at
6. All you need is 7. Make sure to 8. When applying honey 9. Leave 10. as desired

27 정답
1. get your teeth whitened 2. it costs you a lot 3. is essential for 4. more than twice a day 5. Colored beverages
6. not to mention 7. No matter how often 8. many other chemicals 9. heavy and long-term 10. often appear

28 정답
1. a slang term for 2. at the side of 3. term was given to 4. bulging over 5. trim the love handle fat
6. have flat abs 7. super stubborn 8. raise your metabolism 9. for about half an hour 10. doing basic exercise

29 정답
1. dyeing your hair blonde 2. look older than 3. go well with 4. As we get older 5. go blonde 6. is highly likely to 7. leads to 8. it might be a good choice to 9. and that surely makes 10. younger than they are

30 정답
1. becomes loose 2. appear 3. formed 4. by surgery 5. there is a way to
6. without paying any money 7. Place 8. Maintain this pose 9. tap lightly 10. three to four times a day

Chapter 4. People

31. Did you know That Calment's Secret Of Longevity Was Chocolate?

칼멍의 장수 비결이 초콜릿이라는 거 아세요?

32. Did you know What Happened To Karen Butler After Oral Surgery?

구강 수술 후 카렌 버틀러에게 어떤 일이 생겼는지 아세요?

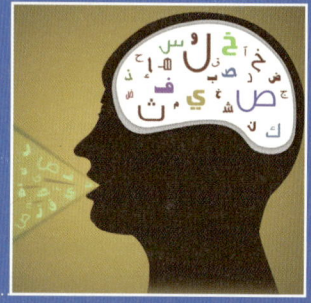

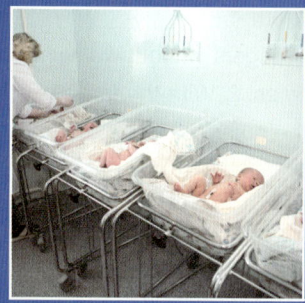

33. Did you know How These Russian Girls Got The Wrong Parents?

어떻게 이 러시아 소녀들이 엉뚱한 부모와 살게 되었는지 아세요?

34. Did you know Why Jocelyn Wildenstein Is Famous?

조슬린 와일든스타인이 왜 유명한지 아세요?

35. Did you know How Rich Hollywood Stars Give Birth?

할리우드 스타들은 어떻게 출산하는지 아세요?

36. Did you know What Nelson Mandela, Edgar Allan Poe, and Leo Tolstoy Have In Common?

넬슨 만델라, 에드거 앨런 포, 레오 톨스토이의 공통점이 무엇인지 아세요?

37. Did you know How Much This Eating Champion Weighs?

먹기 대회 우승자의 몸무게가 얼마인지 아세요?

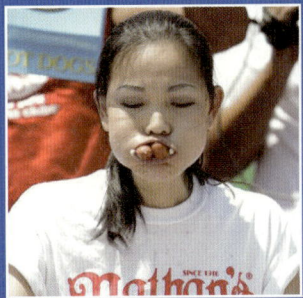

38. Did you know How Cheval The Mailman Built 'Le Palais Ideal'?

우체부 슈발이 어떻게 '발레 이데알'을 건축했는지 아세요?

39. Did you know Why Lali Was Worshiped As A Reincarnated God?

랄리가 왜 환생한 신으로 숭배 받았는지 아세요?

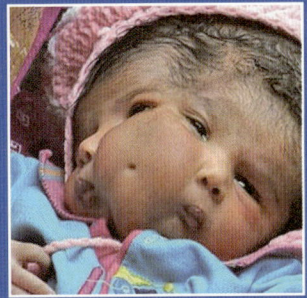

40. Did you know How Billie Bob Harrell, The Lottery Winner, Died?

복권 당첨자인 빌리 밥 하렐이 어떻게 죽었는지 아세요?

31 Did You Know That Calment's Secret Of Longevity Was Chocolate?

Jeanne Louise Calment was born in 1875 and died in 1997 in Arles, France. She died at the age of 122 years old. To be more exact, she lived 122 years and 164 days. Calment was listed in the Guinness Book of Records in 1988 and in 1995. Surprisingly, she lived longer than her only child and her only grandchild. She lived long enough to meet Vincent van Gogh when she was young. Later, she recalled him as "a dirty, badly dressed, and disagreeable man."

When people asked her about the secrets to her longevity, she said that the secrets might have been olive oil and chocolate. She was a longtime smoker, and allegedly not crazy about her health. But, she was healthy enough to ride a bicycle even at the age of 100, and she could take care of herself, by herself, until she was 110 years old. However, after causing a small fire while cooking in her flat, she was moved to a nursing home. She said she used lots of olive oil in her cooking and rubbed olive oil into her skin. She also ate about one kilogram of chocolate every week.

Jeanne Calment
- Lived 122 ½ years
- Ate 2 lbs of chocolate a week

1 What is the main idea of the story?
a. Calment's secret of longevity is chocolate and olive oil.
b. Calment could live longer than her grandchild thanks to riding a bicycle.
c. After meeting Gogh, Calment decided to live long.
d. Rubbing olive oil into the skin is the secret of longevity.

2 When Calment met Gogh, _____.
a. she envied Gogh because he was older than her
b. Gogh was not a clean or neat guy
c. she was 122 years old
d. she didn't want to share her chocolate with him

3 Choose the correct words for each sentence.
a. My little twin brothers have been crazy <u>about / at / of</u> baseball since they were 5.
b. It's safe to say that he is a <u>dirty / disagreeable / messy</u> man because he is always being rude, offensive and unamiable.
c. His colleagues recalled him <u>of / as / with</u> a nice and friendly guy and an excellent programmer.
d. What I want to <u>board / ride / make</u> is a big huge dinosaur, but all I have is an old bicycle.

LEARNING BOARD

① Jeanne Louise Calment was born in 1875 and died in 1997 in Arles, France. ② She died at the age of 122 years old. ③ To be more exact, she lived 122 years and 164 days. ④ Calment was listed in the Guinness Book of Records (in 1988 and in 1995). ⑤ Surprisingly, she lived longer than her only child and her only grandchild. ⑥ She lived long enough to meet Vincent van Gogh when she was young. ⑦ Later, she recalled him as "a (dirty, badly dressed, and disagreeable) man." ⑧ When people asked her about the secrets to her longevity, she said that the secrets might have been olive oil and chocolate. ⑨ She was 1) a longtime smoker, and allegedly 2) not crazy about her health. ⑩ But, she was healthy enough to ride a bicycle (even at the age of 100), and she could take care of herself, by herself, until she was 110 years old. ⑪ However, after causing a small fire while cooking in her flat, she was moved to a nursing home. ⑫ She said she 1) used lots of olive oil in her cooking and 2) rubbed olive oil into her skin. ⑬ She also ate about one kilogram of chocolate every week.

Words & Expressions

be born in (년도) …에 태어나다 die in (년도) …에 사망하다 recall 기억하다, 회고하다 disagreeable 불쾌한, 무뚝뚝한 longevity 장수, 오래 삶 a longtime smoker 오랜 흡연자 flat (영국) 아파트 a nursing home 양로원, 요양소 rub 문지르다, 비비다

32 Did You Know What Happened To Karen Butler After Oral Surgery?

Karen Butler, a 56-year-old American woman and lifelong resident of Oregon, developed an Irish accent after oral surgery. She had never been abroad, and never learned or tried to learn an Irish accent. But, when she awoke from sedation in 2009, she started speaking in an Irish accent. Actually, her accent was a mix of Irish, English, Scottish, and Australian. Anyway, the way she spoke was definitely not an American style.

Doctors suspect that she may be suffering from a rare case of foreign accent syndrome (FAS). This may sound like a 'hurriedly and newly coined term', but this kind of speech disorder really exists, though it is very rare. FAS is usually caused by some type of brain damage such as a stroke or brain hemorrhage.

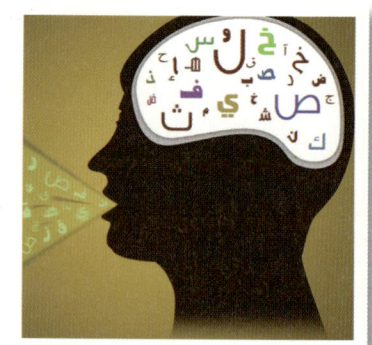

You can find other cases of FAS. A Norwegian woman also developed FAS after being hit by a bomb fragment during World War II. When she woke up, she was said to speak in a German accent. An American man also started speaking in a Scandinavian accent after a stroke. But, his accent faded after several months.

1 What is the main idea of the story?

a. FAS is a totally new term coined by a Norwegian woman.
b. There are thousands of people who suffer from FAS in the world.
c. Karen Butler developed a foreign accent after oral surgery.
d. If you were hit by something, you would speak in German accent.

2 According to the passage, which sentence is right?

a. Karen Butler has been living in Oregon since she was born in Oregon.
b. FAS is always caused by bomb fragments
c. Allegedly, a large number of North Americans suffer from FAS.
d. Ms. Butler got an Irish accent as a result of years of training.

3 Choose the correct words for each sentence.

a. I plan to be famous both at home and <u>outside / abroad / foreign</u>.
b. We must act with great haste because a <u>strike / stork / stroke</u> is a medical emergency.
c. The soldier has started bleeding after <u>shooted / being shot / shoot</u> by his enemy.

LEARNING BOARD

① Karen Butler, (a 56-year-old American woman and lifelong resident of Oregon,) developed an Irish accent after oral surgery. ② She had ¹⁾ never been abroad, and ²⁾ never learned or tried to learn an Irish accent. ③ But, when she awoke from sedation in 2009, she started speaking in an Irish accent. ④ Actually, her accent was a mix of Irish, English, Scottish, and Australian. ⑤ Anyway, the way (she spoke) was definitely not an American style.

⑥ Doctors suspect that she may be suffering from a rare case of foreign accent syndrome (FAS). ⑦ This may sound like a '(hurriedly and newly) coined term,' but this kind of speech disorder really exists, though it is very rare. ⑧ FAS is usually caused by some type of brain damage (such as a stroke or brain hemorrhage.)

⑨ You can find other cases of FAS. ⑩ A Norwegian woman also developed FAS after being hit by a bomb fragment during World War II. ⑪ When she woke up, she was said to speak in a German accent. ⑫ An American man also started speaking in a Scandinavian accent after a stroke. ⑬ But, his accent faded after several months.

Words & Expressions

oral 구강의, 구두의 lifelong 일생의, 평생 동안의 resident 주민 develop 발생하다, 생기다 accent 억양, 강세 surgery 수술, 외과 abroad 해외에(서), 해외로 awaken 깨어나다 sedation 진정제가 투여된 상태 suffer from (질병 등을) 앓다 rare 흔치 않은 coin 동전, (용어·표현을) 만들다 a newly coined term 신조어 speech disorder 언어장애 stroke 뇌졸중, 타박 hemorrhage 출혈 Norwegian 노르웨이의, 노르웨이인의 fragment 파편, 조각 fade 색이 바래다, 점점 사라지다

33 Did You Know How These Russian Girls Got The Wrong Parents?

In 2011, a pair of Russian teenage girls, Irina and Anya, and their family members were shocked because they found out that these two girls had been accidentally switched at birth, which means each girl's parents were not the real parents. Their mothers gave birth just 15 minutes apart in the same hospital in 1999. After being born, the two baby girls were given the wrong name tags by employees of the hospital.

The whole thing started when Irina's father thought that his daughter might not be his daughter because she looked nothing like him. A DNA test showed that neither of Irina's parents was her natural parent. With the help of the local police, Irina's mother started to search for her real daughter, who was living just a few miles away. Although the two girls were happy to meet their real parents, they

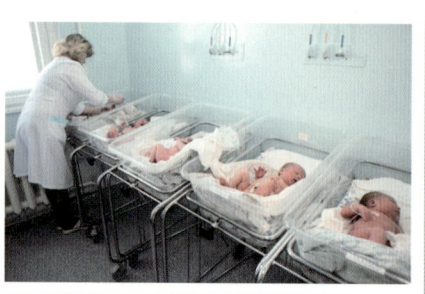

didn't want to leave the family they had grown up with. So, nothing changed for these two families. But, the hospital had to deal with a big change because both families decided to sue the hospital, demanding about $160,000 in damages. Nothing hurts like the truth, especially for that hospital.

1 What is the main idea of the story?
   a. Never give birth in Russia since all Russian hospitals are horrible.
   b. Finding natural parents is utmost important.
   c. The DNA test was supposed to be accurate but it wasn't.
   d. Two Russian girls who were switched at birth found their real parents.

2 The accident that happened to Irina and Anya _____.
   a. was a simple mistake of employees of the hospital
   b. became the main cause of the civil war
   c. was so tragic that Irina's parents had to divorce
   d. made both families go bankruptcy

3 Choose the correct words for each sentence.
   a. My boss who is famous for being short-tempered yells / demands / says an immediate and clear explanation.
   b. If there were damages / damage / much damages to pay, I should sell my car.
   c. Neither of them studies / study / studying hard to pass the exam even though they have much time to study.

LEARNING BOARD

① In 2011, a pair of Russian teenage girls, (Irina and Anya), and their family members were shocked because they found out that these two girls had been accidentally switched at birth, which means each girl's parents were not the real parents. ② Their mothers gave birth just 15 minutes apart in the same hospital in 1999. ③ After being born, the two baby girls were given the wrong name tags by employees of the hospital. ④ The whole thing started when Irina's father thought that his daughter might not be his daughter because she looked nothing like him. ⑤ A DNA test showed that neither of Irina's parents was her natural parent. ⑥ With the help of the local police, Irina's mother started to search for her real daughter, who was living just a few miles away. ⑦ Although the two girls were happy to meet their real parents, they didn't want to leave the family (they had grown up with). ⑧ So, nothing changed for these two families. ⑨ But, the hospital had to deal with a big change because both families decided to sue the hospital, demanding about $160,000 in damages. ⑩ Nothing hurts like the truth, especially for that hospital.

Words & Expressions

teenage 십대의 **accidentally** 우연히, 사고로 **switch** 바꾸다 **at birth** 태어날 때 **name tag** 이름표 **employee** 직원 **natural parents** 친부모 **search for** 찾다, 수색하다 **sue** 고소하다 **demand** 요구하다 **damages** 손해배상금 **nothing hurts like the truth** 〈속담〉 진실만큼 아픈 (고통스러운) 건 없다

34 Did You Know Why Jocelyn Wildenstein Is Famous?

She is kind of famous because she is a queen. She's not just any normal queen, such as Queen Elizabeth. She is the queen of plastic surgery. And again, she's not just any normal queen of plastic surgery — she is the queen of the worst plastic surgery nightmare!

Unusually, she was changed from a beauty into a beast by plastic surgery. You know, generally it is the other way around. More unusually, it was not an accident to get a monster-looking face. It was her choice.

Allegedly, she has spent a handsome amount of money on surgery over the years to look like a cat. Why? Because her rich husband liked his pet cats very much, and she didn't want to lose his love. So, she decided to change her face to look like a cat. And she did. However, her husband divorced her anyway. Even after the divorce, she couldn't stop getting plastic surgery. Now, she is over 60, and still keeps changing her face to look like a cat. Of course, it's getting worse and worse. Anyway, thank God her husband loved cats, not rabbits or elephants!

Jocelyn "cat woman" Wildenstein

1 What can be the best title of this story?
   a. Wildenstein : Changed Into The Beast To Look Like A Cat
   b. The Queen Of Plastic Surgery : Who Wouldn't Like Her?
   c. A Complete Flipflop : From The Monster To The Beauty Queen
   d. The Ultimate Cat Lover Turned Into A Cat

2 According to the passage, which sentence is <u>wrong</u>?
   a. Wildenstein has been famous for the worst plastic surgery nightmare.
   b. Wildenstein allegedly spent a fortune on plastic surgery.
   c. Wildenstein seems to be seriously addicted to plastic surgery.
   d. Wildenstein has been loved by her husband and his pet cats.

3 Choose the correct words for each sentence.
   a. The poverty problem in Africa is getting <u>better and better / worse to better / worse and worse,</u> and more and more people are starving.
   b. Butter is healthier than margarine? I thought it was <u>another / the other / others</u> way around.
   c. Maybe I should allow him to train my dog because I have nothing to <u>loose / lose / lost</u>.

LEARNING BOARD

① She is kind of famous because she is a queen. ② She's not just any normal queen, such as Queen Elizabeth. ③ She is the queen of plastic surgery. ④ And again, she's not just any normal queen of plastic surgery — she is the queen of the worst plastic surgery nightmare! ⑤ Unusually, she was changed from a beauty into a beast by plastic surgery. ⑥ You know, generally it is the other way around. ⑦ More unusually, it was not an accident to get a monster-looking face. ⑧ It was her choice. ⑨ Allegedly, she has spent a handsome amount of money on surgery (over the years) (to look like a cat). ⑩ Why? ⑪ Because 1) her rich husband liked his pet cats very much, and 2) she didn't want to lose his love. ⑫ So, she decided to change her face (to look like a cat). ⑬ And she did. ⑭ However, her husband divorced her anyway. ⑮ Even after the divorce, she couldn't stop getting plastic surgery. ⑯ Now, she 1) is over 60, and still 2) keeps changing her face (to look like a cat). ⑰ Of course, it's getting worse and worse. ⑱ Anyway, thank God her husband loved cats, not rabbits or elephants!

Words & Expressions

kind of 좀, 약간 queen 여왕 not just any 보통의 …은 아니다 normal 일반적인 plastic surgery 성형수술 nightmare 악몽 unusually 특이하게도 beast 야수 the other way around 반대로, 거꾸로 handsome 1. 잘생긴 2. 많은 a handsome amount of money 엄청난 금액의 돈 over the years 수년 동안, 수년에 걸쳐 divorce 이혼하다

35 Did You Know How Rich Hollywood Stars Give Birth?

Hollywood stars are too rich to give birth like everybody else does. Here are two rich star couples who gave birth in an unusual way.

The first too-rich Hollywood star couple is Beyonce Knowles and her hubby Jay-Z. They shelled out a whopping $1.3 million to rent an entire floor at the Lenox Hill Hospital in Manhattan. Hospital staff couldn't use their cell phones while working, since they might take disallowed pictures of the precious baby girl. Additionally, that floor's security cameras were covered to protect the couple's privacy, not to mention that a bunch of personal bodyguards were stood at every corner of the building.

Renting a whole floor of a hospital is nothing compared to this next couple. In 2006, the couple known as Brangelina flew to Namibia to give birth to their baby girl. This superstar couple and their unable-to-be-ugly baby were guarded by the 'government' of Namibia. The government gave their security personnel the right to punch or arrest anyone who tried to violate the couple's privacy. Furthermore, any journalists without proper permits were forbidden to enter the country. Of course, Jolie and Pitt spent a fortune during their stay in Namibia, including a hefty donation.

1 What is the main idea of the story?
   a. Brangelina couple is the richest and weirdest couple ever.
   b. Beyonce married Jay-Z since he owned a hospital in Manhattan.
   c. Some Hollywood stars don't spare their money when it comes to protecting their privacy.
   d. Jolie and Pitt asked the government of Namibia to forbid using cell phones.

2 To protect their privacy, Brangelina couple _____.
   a. flew to Namibia and gave birth to a girl there
   b. tried to arrest anyone who tried to punch their baby girl
   c. threatened the government of Namibia
   d. rent an entire floor of the hospital in Namibia

3 Choose the correct words for each sentence.
   a. Brian hasn't learn arithmetic, not to mention / not to mention that / not needy to mention of algebra.
   b. Korry was caught in another spacious / whopping / extensive lie. She is a born liar.
   c. The photographer made / took / had pictures of victims and put those pictures in the newspaper.

LEARNING BOARD

① Hollywood stars are too rich to give birth like everybody else does. ② Here are two rich star couples (who gave birth in an unusual way.) ③ The first too-rich Hollywood star couple is Beyonce Knowles and her hubby Jay-Z. ④ They shelled out (a whopping $1.3 million) to rent an entire floor (at the Lenox Hill Hospital) (in Manhattan). ⑤ Hospital staff couldn't use their cell phones while working, since they might take disallowed pictures of the precious baby girl. ⑥ Additionally, that floor's security cameras were covered (to protect the couple's privacy), not to mention that a bunch of personal bodyguards were stood at every corner of the building. ⑦ Renting a whole floor (of a hospital) is nothing compared to this next couple. ⑧ In 2006, the couple (known as Brangelina) flew to Namibia (to give birth to their baby girl). ⑨ This superstar couple and their unable-to-be-ugly baby were guarded by the 'government' of Namibia. ⑩ The government gave their security personnel the right to punch or arrest anyone who tried to violate the couple's privacy. ⑪ Furthermore, any journalists (without proper permits) were forbidden to enter the country. ⑫ Of course, Jolie and Pitt spent a fortune during their stay in Namibia, (including a hefty donation).

Words & Expressions

give birth 출산하다 **shell** 포격하다, 껍질을 까다 (shell out 큰돈을 들이다, 거금을 쓰다) **whopping** 무려, 자그마치 **rent** 빌리다 **floor** 층, 바닥 **disallowed** 허가(인정)받지 않은 **precious** 소중한, 귀중한 **privacy** 사생활 **not to mention** …는 말할 것도 없고 **a bunch of** 한 다발, 다수의 **personal bodyguard** 개인 경호원 **government** 정부 **punch** 주먹으로 치다; 펀치 **journalist** 언론인 **forbid** 금지하다 **spend a fortune** 많은 돈을 쓰다 **hefty** 많은, 두둑한 **donation** 기부, 기부금

105

Listening with Dictation

31 Did You Know That Calment's Secret Of Longevity Was Chocolate?

Jeanne Louise Calment _____¹ 1875 and died in 1997 in Arles, France. She died _____² 122 years old. To be more exact, she lived 122 years and 164 days. Calment was listed in the Guinness Book of Records in 1988 and in 1995. Surprisingly, she _____³ her only child and her only grandchild. She lived long enough to meet Vincent van Gogh when she was young. Later, she _____⁴ "a dirty, badly dressed, and _____⁵ man." When people asked her about _____⁶, she said that the secrets _____⁷ olive oil and chocolate. She was a longtime smoker, and allegedly not crazy about her health. But, she was healthy enough to _____⁸ even at the age of 100, and she could take care of herself, _____⁹, until she was 110 years old. However, after causing a small fire while cooking in her flat, she was moved to a nursing home. She said she used lots of olive oil in her cooking and _____¹⁰. She also ate about one kilogram of chocolate every week.

32 Did You Know What Happened To Karen Butler After Oral Surgery?

Karen Butler, a 56-year-old American woman and lifelong resident of Oregon, _____¹ an Irish accent after oral surgery. She _____², and never learned or tried to learn an Irish accent. But, when she _____³ sedation in 2009, she started speaking in an Irish accent. Actually, her accent was a mix of Irish, English, Scottish, and Australian. Anyway, _____⁴ was definitely not an American style. Doctors _____⁵ that she may be suffering from a rare case of foreign accent syndrome (FAS). This may sound like a 'hurriedly and _____⁶,' but this kind of speech disorder really exists, though it is very rare. FAS is usually caused by some type of brain damage such as a stroke or _____⁷. You can find other cases of FAS. A Norwegian woman also developed FAS _____⁸ a bomb fragment during World War II. When she woke up, she was said to speak in a German accent. An American man also _____⁹ a Scandinavian accent after a stroke. But, his accent _____¹⁰ after several months.

33 Did You Know How These Russian Girls Got The Wrong Parents?

In 2011, _____¹ Russian teenage girls, Irina and Anya, and their family members _____² because they found out that these two girls had been _____³ switched _____⁴, which means each girl's parents were not the real parents. Their mothers gave birth just 15 minutes apart in the same hospital in 1999. _____⁵, the two baby girls were given the wrong name tags by employees of the hospital. The whole thing started when Irina's father thought that his daughter _____⁶ because she looked nothing like him. A DNA test showed that neither of Irina's parents was her natural parent. With the help of the local police, Irina's mother started to search for her real daughter, who was living just a few miles away. Although the two girls were happy to meet their real parents, they didn't want to leave the _____⁷. So, nothing changed for these two families. But, the hospital had to _____⁸ because both families decided to sue the hospital, _____⁹ about $160,000 _____¹⁰. Nothing hurts like the truth, especially for that hospital.

106 Chapter 4 | People

34 Did You Know Why Jocelyn Wildenstein Is Famous?

She is _____¹ because she is a queen. She's not just any normal queen, such as Queen Elizabeth. She is the queen of _____². And again, she's not just any normal queen of plastic surgery– she is the queen of the worst plastic surgery nightmare! Unusually, she _____³ a beauty _____⁴ a beast by plastic surgery. You know, generally it is _____⁵. More unusually, it was not an accident to get a monster-looking face. It was her choice. Allegedly, she has spent _____⁶ money on surgery over the years to look like a cat. Why? Because her rich husband liked his pet cats very much, and she didn't want to lose his love. So, she decided to change her face to look like a cat. And she did. However, her husband _____⁷. Even after the divorce, she _____⁸ plastic surgery. Now, she is over 60, and still _____⁹ her face to look like a cat. Of course, it's getting worse and worse. Anyway, _____¹⁰ her husband loved cats, not rabbits or elephants!

35 Did You Know How Rich Hollywood Stars Give Birth?

Hollywood stars are _____¹ like everybody else does. Here are two rich star couples who gave birth _____². The first too-rich Hollywood star couple is Beyonce Knowles and her hubby Jay-Z. They _____³ a whopping $1.3 million to _____⁴ at the Lenox Hill Hospital in Manhattan. Hospital staff couldn't use their cell phones while working, since they might _____⁵ of the precious baby girl. Additionally, that floor's security cameras were covered to protect the couple's privacy, not to mention that _____⁶ personal bodyguards were stood _____⁷ the building. Renting a whole floor of a hospital is nothing compared to this next couple. In 2006, the couple known as Brangelina flew to Namibia to give birth to their baby girl. This superstar couple and their unable-to-be-ugly baby _____⁸ the 'government' of Namibia. The government gave their security personnel the right to punch or arrest anyone who tried to _____⁹. Furthermore, any journalists without proper permits were forbidden to enter the country. Of course, Jolie and Pitt _____¹⁰ during their stay in Namibia, including a hefty donation.

---

31 정답 1. was born in 2. at the age of 3. lived longer than 4. recalled him as 5. disagreeable 6. the secrets to her longevity 7. might have been 8. ride a bicycle 9. by herself 10. rubbed olive oil into her skin

32 정답 1. developed 2. had never been abroad 3. awoke from 4. the way she spoke 5. suspect 6. newly coined term 7. brain hemorrhage 8. after being hit by 9. started speaking in 10. faded

33 정답 1. a pair of 2. were shocked 3. accidentally 4. at birth 5. After being born 6. might not be his daughter 7. family they had grown up with 8. deal with a big change 9. demanding 10. in damages

34 정답 1. kind of famous 2. plastic surgery 3. was changed from 4. into 5. the other way around 6. a handsome amount of 7. divorced her anyway 8. couldn't stop getting 9. keeps changing 10. thank God

35 정답 1. too rich to give birth 2. in an unusual way 3. shelled out 4. rent an entire floor 5. take disallowed pictures 6. a bunch of 7. at every corner of 8. were guarded by 9. violate the couple's privacy 10. spent a fortune

36 Did You Know What Nelson Mandela, Edgar Allan Poe, and Leo Tolstoy Have In Common?

Other than these, Louis Armstrong (a jazz musician and trumpeter), Johann Sebastian Bach (a German composer), Marilyn Monroe (an actress), and Babe Ruth (a baseball player) also have this in common with them, too. These great people with great achievements were all orphans. They must have had a hard time when they were young, but as far as leaving their names in history was concerned, being orphans didn't matter to them.

Some people have a strong bias against orphans. They believe that orphans are highly likely to go wrong emotionally and financially, and tend to be bad or troubled people, like criminals. Orphans do have difficulties surviving in our society, since many of them don't receive parents' proper care, protection, or guidance. But, that doesn't mean every orphan has no choice but to be a bad or troubled person. Some of them become greater persons than people raised by both parents under very good conditions.

1 What is the main idea of the story?

a. It is impossible for orphans to leave their names in history as great figures.
b. All orphans are supposed to become great people and they do.
c. There are many orphans who turned out to be great figures in history.
d. The financial support for orphanages is utmost important.

2 According to the passage, which sentence is wrong?

a. There are many great people who were orphans but achieved great things.
b. Orphans are children who don't have rich parents or relatives.
c. Not all orphans become bad criminals.
d. It's possible for orphans to leave their names in history.

3 Choose the correct words for each sentence.

a. Some people claim that Greece is highly to like / like / likely to leave Euro due to the financial crisis.
b. Viki is a racist so she has a bias for / against / as African-Americans and Asians as well.
c. As far as me and my cousin is / are / was concerned, it doesn't matter whenever you go.

LEARNING BOARD

① Other than these, Louis Armstrong (a jazz musician and trumpeter), Johann Sebastian Bach (a German composer), Marilyn Monroe (an actress), and Babe Ruth (a baseball player) also have this in common with them, too. ② These great people (with great achievements) were all orphans. ③ They must have had a hard time when they were young, but as far as (leaving their names in history) was concerned, being orphans didn't matter to them. ④ Some people have a strong bias against orphans. ⑤ They believe that orphans 1) are highly likely to go wrong (emotionally and financially), and 2) tend to be (bad or troubled) people, (like criminals). ⑥ Orphans do have difficulties surviving in our society, since many of them don't receive parents' proper care, protection, or guidance. ⑦ But, that doesn't mean every orphan has no choice but to be a (bad or troubled) person. ⑧ Some of them become greater persons than people (raised by both parents under very good conditions.)

Words & Expressions

have in common 공통점이 있다 trumpeter 트럼펫 연주자 composer 작곡자 actress 여배우 orphan 고아 have a hard time 어려움을 겪다, 힘든 시기를 보내다 leave one's name in the history 역사에 이름을 남기다 bias 편견 (cf. biased 치우친, 편향된) have a strong bias against …에 대해 (부정적인) 편견을 가지다 go wrong 잘못되다 emotionally 정서적으로, 감정적으로 financially 경제적으로 criminal 범죄자 have a difficulty –ing …하는 데 어려움을 겪다 guidance 지도, 안내 under very good conditions 좋은 환경·조건에서

37 Did You Know How Much This Eating Champion Weighs?

Sonya Thomas (a Korean-born American, with the Korean name Lee Sun-kyung), a.k.a. The Black Widow, is a world champion eater.

She has won a whopping 37 times in eating competitions since 2003. In almost every eating competition she participated in, she set unbelievable world records. Her eye-popping and mouth-watering records are as follows:

11 pounds of cheesecake in 9 minutes in 2004, 183 chicken wings in 12 minutes in 2011, 65 hard boiled eggs in 6 minutes and 40 seconds in 2003, 44 lobsters totaling 11.4 pounds of lobster meat in 12 minutes in 2005, 38 Moonpies in 8 minutes in 2010, 552 oysters in 10 minutes in 2005, 6 and a half extra large slices of cheese pizza in 15 minutes in 2004, 41 Hot Dogs and Buns in 10 minutes in 2009, 183 Buffalo Wings in 12 minutes in 2011.

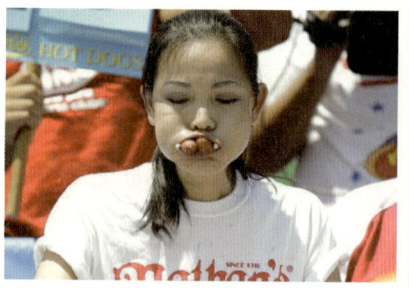

As everybody already must have noticed, she has never been a picky eater. She eats moonpies, tacos, clams, baked beans, anything; you name it, she can eat it.

What's surprising here is her size. She is 152cm tall and weighs 47kg.

1 What can be the best title of this story?
   a. Surprising Secrets To Become The Eating Champion
   b. The Eating Champion's Unbelievable Body Size
   c. Sonya Thomas, The Worst Eating Champion Ever
   d. Why She Was Called The Black Widow

2 In 2004, Sonya Thomas ate _____.
   a. hard boiled eggs and lobsters
   b. Buffalo wings and BBQ chicken wings
   c. cheese pizza and cheesecake
   d. Tacos, clams, baked beans

3 Choose the correct words for each sentence.
   a. I planned to participate with / participate in / participate of a race but I gave up because of injury.
   b. I have to buy the book titled 'How to stop being a heavy eater / picky eater / light eater' since my daughter says everything is yucky except chocolate.
   c. Almost every well in the village is drying out because it hasn't rained for three and half / three and a half / three a half years.

LEARNING BOARD

① Sonya Thomas (a Korean-born American), (with the Korean name Lee Sun-kyung), a.k.a. The Black Widow, is a world champion eater. ② She has won a whopping 37 times in eating competitions since 2003. ③ In almost every eating competition (she participated in), she set unbelievable world records. ④ Her (eye-popping and mouth-watering) records are as follows: ⑤ 11 pounds of cheesecake in 9 minutes in 2004, ⑥ 183 chicken wings in 12 minutes in 2011, ⑦ 65 hard boiled eggs in 6 minutes and 40 seconds in 2003, ⑧ 44 lobsters (totaling 11.4 pounds of lobster meat) in 12 minutes in 2005, ⑨ 38 Moonpies in 8 minutes in 2010, ⑩ 552 oysters in 10 minutes in 2005, ⑪ 6 and a half extra large slices of cheese pizza in 15 minutes in 2004, ⑫ 41 Hot Dogs and Buns in 10 minutes in 2009, ⑬ 183 Buffalo Wings in 12 minutes in 2011. ⑭ As everybody already must have noticed, she has never been a picky eater. ⑮ She eats moonpies, tacos, clams, baked beans, anything; you name it, she can eat it. ⑯ What's surprising here is her size. ⑰ She 1) is 152cm tall and 2) weighs 47kg.

Words & Expressions

Korean-born 한국 태생의 **a.k.a.**(=also known as) ...로도 알려진 **competition** 경쟁, 대회 **participate in** ...에 참가하다 **accomplish** 성취하다 **eye-popping** 눈알이 튀어나올 정도의, 놀라운 **mouth-watering** 군침 도는 **hard boiled egg** 삶은 달걀 **moonpie** 초코파이와 비슷한 파이 종류 **picky** 까다로운(=choosy) **picky eater** 입맛이 까다로운 사람 **clam** 조개 **name** 이름을 대다 **weigh** 무게가 ... 나가다

38 Did You Know How Cheval The Mailman Built 'Le Palais Ideal'?

Ferdinand Cheval (1836-1924) was a French mailman who built 'Le Palais Ideal' (The Ideal Palace) in Hauterives, which has been officially protected as a cultural landmark of France for its extraordinary architecture.

Cheval was a poor, uneducated mailman. He just delivered letters to people. But after he tripped on a stone in the street, his life began to change. He said the shape of the stone inspired him. The next day, he returned to the same spot where he had picked up the special stone to pick up some more. After that, Cheval collected stones and carried them home for the next 33 years. These stones became the building materials for his amazing Ideal Palace.

At first, he carried them in his pockets, but later he used a basket and then a wheelbarrow. It took him 33 years to complete his own dream palace. He just did

it by himself with his bare hands. Cheval died a year after finishing building it. He was buried in his palace, as he wished. Now, it's open to the public, and visitors from around the world become speechless due to the fact that this marvelous piece of architecture was built by one old man with stones.

1 What is the main idea of the story?

a. Amazingly, Cheval built the Ideal Palace by himself with bare hands.
b. Cheval was the most prominent architect in France.
c. Cheval tried to prove that stones can be excellent building materials.
d. Cheval made visitors speechless by carrying so many stones with bare hands.

2 According to the passage, which sentence is right?

a. Cheval delivered letters all day long so he couldn't do anything.
b. Cheval could build the Ideal Palace since he was a professional architect.
c. Cheval had collected tons of stones for his collection.
d. When Cheval was alive, he wanted to be buried in his own dream palace.

3 Choose the correct words for each sentence.

a. Your paintings left me talkative / speechless / unspeakable. It was just fantastic.
b. These books are for underprivileged children which / what / who can't afford to buy books.
c. It made me spend a while / It took me a while / I spent the time to learn how to play the guitar.

LEARNING BOARD

① Ferdinand Cheval (1836-1924) was a French mailman (who built 'Le Palais Ideal' (The Ideal Palace) in Hauterives), which has been officially protected as a cultural landmark of France for its extraordinary architecture. ② Cheval was a (poor, uneducated) mailman. ③ He just delivered letters to people. ④ But after he tripped on a stone in the street, his life began to change. ⑤ He said the shape (of the stone) inspired him. ⑥ The next day, he returned to the same spot (where he had picked up the special stone) to pick up some more. ⑦ After that, Cheval ¹⁾ collected stones and ²⁾ carried them home for the next 33 years. ⑧ These stones became the building materials for his amazing Ideal Palace. ⑨ (At first), he carried them in his pockets, but (later) he used ¹⁾ a basket and then ²⁾ a wheelbarrow. ⑩ It took him 33 years to complete his own dream palace. ⑪ He just did it by himself with his bare hands. ⑫ Cheval died a year after finishing building it. ⑬ He was buried in his palace, (as he wished). ⑭ Now, it's open to the public, and visitors (from around the world) become speechless due to the fact that this marvelous piece of architecture was built (by one old man) (with stones).

Words & Expressions

mailman 우체부 ideal 이상적인 palace 궁전 officially 공식적으로 protect 보호하다 landmark 주요 지형지물, 랜드마크 extraordinary 놀라운, 비범한 architecture 건축물 uneducated 교육을 받지 못한 deliver 배달하다 trip on …에 발이 걸려 넘어지다 inspire 영감을 주다 spot n. 장소, 점, 얼룩 v. 찾아내다, 발견하다 pick up …을 얻다 collected 수집한, 모은 complete 완성하다 by oneself 혼자서 bare hands 맨손 be buried 묻히다 (v. bury 묻다, 매장하다) speechless 말문이 막힌 it's open to the public 대중에 공개되다 marvelous 놀라운

39 Did You Know Why Lali Was Worshiped As A Reincarnated God?

Lali was born on March 11, 2008 in Northern India. When she was born, people believed she was a reincarnation of the god Ganesh, the Hindu god who is half person and half elephant. Not only local neighbors but also people around the world came to her little village to meet her. Many of them offered her parents money to ask for her blessing. This was very helpful for them because her young parents earned less than $2 a day, like many other neighbors in their village.

What was so special about this baby? Lali was born with two faces. She had one body and one head like other babies, but unlike other babies, she had two faces in one head. So, she had four eyes, two noses, and two mouths. Her young parents didn't agree to let the hospital perform a free CT scan or an MRI on her head. Lali's father said, "I accepted whatever God gives."

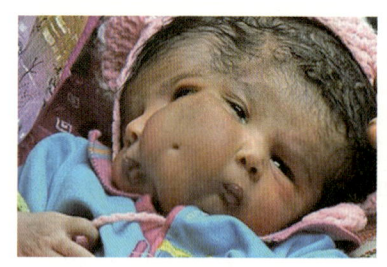

A baby with two faces is very rare but Lali was not the only baby with two faces. In 2011, another baby with two faces was born in Pakistan.

1 What is the main idea of the story?
   a. Lali's parents must be arrested for not paying Lali's hospital bill.
   b. God Ganesh, the God of Elephants, has two faces like Lali.
   c. A baby with two faces was worshipped since people believed she was a god.
   d. There was no other babies with two faces except Lali.

2 Lali was treated as the most special baby in her village because _____.
   a. she could earn money unlike other babies
   b. her appearance was very unique
   c. she could have a free CT scan
   d. she really was a reincarnation of the God Ganesh

3 Choose the correct words for each sentence.
   a. How can I clean my house in <u>further than / fewer than / less than</u> one hour?
   b. His visit surprised me since his visits were <u>mere / rare / scare</u> occasions.
   c. Megan broke up with Bill <u>because / although / despite</u> she thought Bill wasn't the only pebble on the beach.

LEARNING BOARD

① Lali was born on March 11, 2008 in Northern India. ② When she was born, people believed she was a **reincarnation** of the god Ganesh, (the Hindu god) (who is half person and half elephant.) ③ Not only local **neighbors** but also people around the world came to her little village (to meet her). ④ Many of them **offered** her parents money (to ask for her blessing). ⑤ This was very helpful for them because her young parents earned less than $2 (a day), (like many other neighbors in their village.)

⑥ What was so special about this baby? ⑦ Lali was born with two faces. ⑧ She had one body and one head (like other babies), but **unlike** other babies, she had two faces in one head. ⑨ So, she had four eyes, two noses, and two mouths.

⑩ Her young parents didn't agree to let the hospital **perform** a **free** CT scan or an MRI on her head. ⑪ Lali's father said, "I accepted whatever God gives."

⑫ A baby (with two faces) is very rare but Lali was not the only baby with two faces. ⑬ In 2011, another baby (with two faces) was born in Pakistan.

Words & Expressions

reincarnation 환생 local neighbor 동네 이웃 offer 제공하다 blessing 축복 earn 돈을 벌다 like other babies 다른 아기들처럼 free 무료의 perform 실행하다, 연기하다, 공연하다 perform a CT scan CT 촬영을 하다

Did You Know How Billie Bob Harrell, The Lottery Winner, Died?

Unfortunately, Billie Bob Harrell Jr., who held the only winning ticket to a Texas Lotto jackpot of $31 million in 1997, took his own life in 1999.

In 1997, Harrell and his family were having a hard time since Harrell was not good at earning money. So, he bought a lottery ticket, dreaming of hitting the jackpot. He did hit the jackpot, and it made him a millionaire. His hard times were officially over. He was so rich that he bought many things, such as big houses, a ranch, and fancy cars. Also, he contributed a large sum of his money. When somebody needed financial help, Harrell was there with cash. He just spent his time spending and lending money. However, his spending habits were

getting more and more out of control. Family, friends, and even strangers took advantage of him, while Harrell kind of enjoyed being used by them. Before long, his marriage began to crack and his bank account began to dry up.

Twenty months after hitting pay dirt, Harrell shot himself in his bedroom. After his death, his family members fought over the remaining money. But, there was not even enough money left to pay the taxes on his bank accounts.

1 What can be the best title of this story?
a. How To Win The Lottery & Change Your Life
b. Billie Bob Harrell, The Good Samaritan
c. The Tragic End Of The Lottery Winner
d. 20 Tips For Becoming A Lottery Winner

2 According to the passage, which sentence is <u>wrong</u>?
a. Billie Bob Harrell Jr. committed suicide two years after winning the lottery.
b. Even strangers tried to take advantage of Billie even though he was poor.
c. When Billie died, his money was almost gone.
d. Thanks to the lottery ticket, Billie went from rags to riches.

3 Choose the correct words for each sentence.
a. I am pretty good at solving others' problems but I am not so good <u>to solve / at solving / with solving</u> my own. Wonder why.
b. I had to spend two whole hours <u>doing / to do / do</u> my homework.
c. Two waiters were fired because they <u>fought over / struggled with / battled each other</u> some tips from customers.

LEARNING BOARD

① **Unfortunately**, Billie Bob Harrell Jr., (who held the only **winning** ticket to a Texas Lotto **jackpot** of $31 million in 1997,) **took his own life** in 1999. ② In 1997, Harrell and his family were **having a hard time** since Harrell was not good at earning money. ③ So, he bought a lottery ticket, (**dreaming of hitting the jackpot**). ④ He did hit the jackpot, and it made him a **millionaire**. ⑤ His hard times were officially over. ⑥ He was so rich that he bought many things, (such as big houses, a ranch, and **fancy** cars.) ⑦ Also, he **contributed** a large sum of his money. ⑧ When somebody needed financial help, Harrell was there with cash. ⑨ He just spent his time spending and lending money. ⑩ However, his spending habits were getting more and more **out of control**. ⑪ Family, friends, and even strangers **took advantage of** him, while Harrell (kind of) enjoyed being used by them. ⑫ Before long, his marriage began to **crack** and his **bank account** began to dry up. ⑬ Twenty months after **hitting pay dirt**, Harrell shot himself in his bedroom. ⑭ After his death, his family members fought over the remaining money. ⑮ But, there was not even enough **money left** **to pay the taxes** (on his bank accounts).

Words & Expressions

winning ticket 당첨 복권 **jackpot** (도박, 복권) 거액의 상금 **take one's own life** 스스로 목숨을 끊다 **have a hard time** 어려움을 겪다 **a lottery ticket** 복권 **hit the jackpot** 대박을 터트리다 **millionaire** 백만장자 **officially** 공식적으로 **ranch** (대규모) 농장 **fancy** 값비싼, 고급의 **contribute** 기부하다 **cash** 현금 **lend** 빌려주다 **spending habit** 소비습관 **out of control** 통제 불능의 **take advantage of** …를 이용/악용하다 **crack** 금이 가다 **bank account** 예금 계좌 **hit pay dirt** 노다지를 발견하다, 갑자기 큰 부자가 되다 **shoot** 총을 쏘다 **fight over** …를 두고 (가지려) 싸우다 **remaining** 남은, 남아 있는 **tax** 세금

117

Listening with Dictation

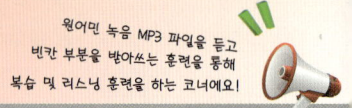

36 Did You Know What Nelson Mandela, Edgar Allan Poe, and Leo Tolstoy Have In Common?

_____¹ these, Louis Armstrong (a jazz musician and trumpeter), Johann Sebastian Bach (a German composer), Marilyn Monroe (an actress), and Babe Ruth (a baseball player) also _____² with them, too. These great people _____³ were all orphans. They _____⁴ when they were young, but as far as leaving their names in history was concerned, being orphans _____⁵. Some people have a strong bias _____⁶ orphans. They believe that orphans _____⁷ emotionally and financially, and tend to be bad or troubled people, like criminals. Orphans do _____⁸ in our society, since many of them don't receive parents' proper care, protection, or guidance. But, _____⁹ every orphan has no choice but to be a bad or troubled person. Some of them become greater persons than people raised by both parents _____¹⁰ very good conditions.

37 Did You Know How Much This Eating Champion Weighs?

Sonya Thomas (a Korean-born American, with the Korean name Lee Sun-kyung), a.k.a. The Black Widow, is a world champion eater. She has won _____¹ 37 times in eating competitions since 2003. In almost every eating competition she _____², she set unbelievable world records. Her eye-popping and _____³ records are as follows: 11 pounds of cheesecake in 9 minutes in 2004, 183 chicken wings in 12 minutes in 2011, 65 _____⁴ in 6 minutes and 40 seconds in 2003, 44 lobsters _____⁵ 11.4 pounds of lobster meat in 12 minutes in 2005, 38 Moonpies in 8 minutes in 2010, 552 _____⁶ in 10 minutes in 2005, 6 and a half _____⁷ cheese pizza in 15 minutes in 2004, 41 Hot Dogs and Buns in 10 minutes in 2009, 183 Buffalo Wings in 12 minutes in 2011. As everybody already must have noticed, she _____⁸. She eats moonpies, tacos, clams, baked beans, anything; you _____⁹ it, she can eat it. _____¹⁰ is her size. She is 152cm tall and weighs 47kg.

38 Did You Know How Cheval The Mailman Built 'Le Palais Ideal'?

Ferdinand Cheval (1836-1924) was a French mailman who built 'Le Palais Ideal' (The Ideal Palace) in Hauterives, which _____¹ as a cultural landmark of France for its _____² architecture. Cheval was a poor, uneducated mailman. He just _____³ to people. But after he _____⁴ in the street, his life began to change. He said the shape of the stone _____⁵ him. The next day, he returned to the same spot where he had picked up the special stone to pick up some more. After that, Cheval collected stones and carried them home _____⁶ 33 years. These stones became the building materials for his amazing Ideal Palace. At first, he carried them in his pockets, but later he used a basket and _____⁷ a wheelbarrow. _____⁸ 33 years to complete his own dream palace. He just did it by himself _____⁹. Cheval died a year after finishing building it. He was buried in his palace, as he wished. Now, it's open to the public, and visitors from around the world become speechless due to the fact that this marvelous _____¹⁰ was built by one old man with stones.

118 Chapter 4 | People

39 Did You Know Why Lali Was Worshiped As A Reincarnated God?

Lali was born _____¹ March 11, 2008 in Northern India. When she was born, people believed she was _____² the god Ganesh, the Hindu god who is half person and half elephant. Not only local neighbors but also people around the world came to her little village to meet her. Many of them offered her parents money to _____³. This was very _____⁴ them because her young parents _____⁵ less than $2 a day, like many other neighbors in their village. _____⁶ this baby? Lali was born with two faces. She had one body and one head like other babies, but _____⁷ other babies, she had two faces in one head. So, she had four eyes, two noses, and two mouths. Her young parents didn't agree to let the hospital perform a free CT scan or an MRI on her head. Lali's father said, "I accepted _____⁸ God gives." A baby with two faces is _____⁹ but Lali was _____¹⁰ with two faces. In 2011, another baby with two faces was born in Pakistan.

40 Did You Know How Billie Bob Harrell, The Lottery Winner, Died?

Unfortunately, Billie Bob Harrell Jr., who held the only winning ticket to a Texas Lotto jackpot of $31 million in 1997, _____¹ in 1999. In 1997, Harrell and his family were having a hard time since Harrell _____² money. So, he bought a lottery ticket, dreaming of hitting the jackpot. He did _____³, and it made him a millionaire. His hard times _____⁴. He was so rich that he bought many things, such as big houses, a ranch, and fancy cars. Also, he _____⁵ a large sum of his money. When somebody needed financial help, Harrell was there with cash. He just spent his time spending and lending money. However, his spending habits were getting more and more out of control. Family, friends, and even strangers _____⁶ him, while Harrell kind of _____⁷ them. Before long, his marriage began to crack and his bank account began to dry up. Twenty months _____⁸, Harrell shot himself in his bedroom. After his death, his family members _____⁹ the remaining money. But, there was _____¹⁰ to pay the taxes on his bank accounts.

---

36 정답 1. Other than 2. have this in common 3. with great achievements 4. must have had a hard time 5. didn't matter to them 6. against 7. are highly likely to go wrong 8. have difficulties surviving 9. that doesn't mean 10. under

37 정답 1. a whopping 2. participated in 3. mouth-watering 4. hard boiled eggs 5. totaling 6. oysters 7. extra large slices of 8. has never been a picky eater 9. name 10. What's surprising here

38 정답 1. has been officially protected 2. extraordinary 3. delivered letters 4. tripped on a stone 5. inspired 6. for the next 7. then 8. It took him 9. with his bare hands 10. piece of architecture

39 정답 1. on 2. a reincarnation of 3. ask for her blessing 4. helpful for 5. earned 6. What was so special about 7. unlike 8. whatever 9. very rare 10. not the only baby

40 정답 1. took his own life 2. was not good at earning 3. hit the jackpot 4. were officially over 5. contributed 6. took advantage of 7. enjoyed being used by 8. after hitting pay dirt 9. fought over 10. not even enough money left

Chapter 5. Animals & Nature

41. Did you know Not All Spiders Make Webs?

모든 거미가 거미줄을 만드는 건 아니라는 사실 아세요?

42. Did you know Where Oxygen Comes From?

산소가 어디에서 나오는지 아세요?

43. Did you know Cockroaches Are Kept As Pets?

애완동물로 길러지는 바퀴벌레를 아세요?

44. Did you know You Have To Pay A Fee Before Climbing The Himalayas?

히말라야에 등반하기 전에 돈을 내야 한다는 거 아세요?

45. Did you know Bats' Droppings Are Valuable To Humans?

박쥐 똥이 인간에게 가치가 있다는 거 아세요?

46. Did you know How Hot The Hottest Hot Spring In The World Is?

세계에서 가장 뜨거운 온천이 얼마나 뜨거운지 아세요?

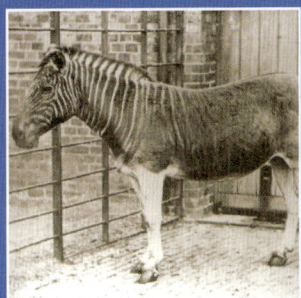

47. Did you know Why The Quagga, A Half Zebra And Half Horse, Went Extinct?

반은 얼룩말, 반은 말인 콰가가 왜 멸종했는지 아세요?

48. Did you know Whales Are Useful To The Bone?

고래가 뼈까지 유용하다는 거 아세요?

49. Did you know Animals Do Feel Sad?

동물도 슬픔을 느낀다는 거 아세요?

50. Did you know Sharks Can Play Opossum?

상어가 주머니쥐 흉내를 낼 수 있다는 거 아세요?

Did You Know Not All Spiders Make Webs?

Spiders are not insects. Unlike insects, spiders have two body parts, no antennae, no wings, and four pairs of legs. Insects have three body parts, two antennae, wings and three pairs of legs. Other arachnids, such as scorpions and ticks, have eight legs like spiders.

Not all spiders make webs. Only about half of all spiders use webs to catch prey. Certain spiders, like wolf spiders and crab spiders, just wait and pounce on prey from a close distance. Some spiders make webs, but their webs are not for hunting. Jumping spiders use webs to make resting places, and wolf spiders make egg sacs with their silk.

Maybe some of you watched the movie 'Charlotte's Web', and learned that spiders suck the juices, or we can say 'liquefied meat', from their prey rather than eating or crunching them. Some spider species do fill their stomachs by sucking, but some species actually eat their prey by chewing with their jaws.

1 What can be the best title of this story?

a. Facts About Spiders You May Misunderstand
b. Differences Between Spiders And Arachnids
c. Charlotte's Web : The Must Watch Movie
d. How To Make Liquefied Meat

2 Jumping spiders and wolf spiders _____.

a. use their webs to catch prey
b. don't use webs at all
c. don't use their webs when catching prey
d. have three pairs of wings and no antennae

3 Choose the correct words for each sentence.

a. At the crime scene, the police found human bones along with <u>two pair of glasses / two pairs of glasses / two glasses</u> and a watch.
b. You can <u>view / watch / look</u> free movies online.
c. This information about tax exemption is not <u>to / for / with</u> tax collectors but for tax payers.

LEARNING BOARD

① Spiders are not **insects**. ② Unlike insects, spiders have two body parts, no antennae, no wings, and four pairs of legs. ③ Insects have three body parts, two antennae, wings and three pairs of legs. ④ Other arachnids, (such as **scorpions** and ticks), have eight legs like spiders. ⑤ Not all spiders make **webs**. ⑥ Only about half of all spiders use webs to catch prey. ⑦ Certain spiders, (like wolf spiders and crab spiders,) just wait and **pounce** on prey (from a close distance). ⑧ Some spiders make webs, but their webs are not for hunting. ⑨ Jumping spiders use webs (to make **resting** places), and wolf spiders make egg sacs with their silk. ⑩ Maybe some of you ¹⁾ watched the movie 'Charlotte's Web', and ²⁾ learned that spiders **suck** the juices, (or we can say 'liquefied meat'), from their prey rather than eating or crunching them. ⑪ Some spider **species** do fill their **stomachs** by sucking, but some species actually eat their prey by chewing with their jaws.

Words & Expressions

spider 거미 **insect** 곤충 **antennae** 더듬이(antenna의 복수형) **arachnid** 거미류 **scorpion** 전갈 **tick** 진드기 **web** 거미줄 **prey** 먹이 **pounce** (공격하며) 덮치다(on) **at a close distance** 가까운 거리에서 **sac** (동식물 체내의) 주머니 **egg sac** 알주머니 **suck** 빨다 **liquefied** 액화된 **crunch** 오도독[와삭와삭] 씹다 **species** 종 **stomach** 배, 위 **fill one's stomach** 위장을 채우다 **chew** 씹다 **jaw** 턱

42 Did You Know Where Oxygen Comes From?

No one can survive without breathing, and we need oxygen to breathe. It is said that the human population hit 7 billion in October 2011. That means the amount of oxygen we need is beyond imagination.

Then, where does our oxygen come from? Oxygen is produced through photosynthesis in green plants, such as trees and flowers. South America's Amazon rain forest, a.k.a "the lungs of the world", is allegedly the single largest oxygen generator in the world. Some say it is providing more than 20% of the Earth's total oxygen. But some disbelieve this, saying that less than 10% of the world's oxygen is from the Amazon rain forest, and that the rest of it comes from the ocean. In fact, ocean plants, such as algae and plankton, generate an enormous amount of oxygen through photosynthesis. The exact amount is under debate, but some scientists claim that at least 50% of the world's atmospheric oxygen comes from the ocean.

For now, nobody knows whether the ocean produces more oxygen than the Amazon or not. But, one thing is for sure about oxygen. If we do not protect green plants on land and in the ocean, 7 billion human beings cannot survive.

1 What is the main idea of the story?

a. We have to protect the Amazon rain forest because it is the main source of the earth's oxygen.
b. Some claim the ocean is the largest oxygen generator but it's unclear that the ocean generates more oxygen than the Amazon.
c. All scientists agree that the single largest oxygen generator is the ocean.
d. We have to calculate the exact amount of oxygen produced by algae.

2 According to the passage, which sentence is right?

a. We cannot survive without Amazon rain forest since it's the lungs of the world.
b. Oxygen comes only from the ocean, that's why we have to protect the ocean.
c. Scientists found out the exact amount of oxygen produced by the ocean.
d. Green plants on land are not the only oxygen generator.

3 Choose the correct words for each sentence.

a. I hope this meeting can provide us / provide / provide with an opportunity to talk about our problem.
b. Breathe / Breathing / Breath deeply when you get nervous. That will help you relax.
c. Becoming rich over / beyond / with your wildest dream does not make you happy.

LEARNING BOARD

① No one can **survive** without **breathing**, and we need **oxygen** to **breathe**. ② It is said that the human **population** hit 7 billion in October 2011. ③ That means the amount of oxygen (we need) is beyond imagination. ④ Then, where does our oxygen **come from**?
⑤ Oxygen is produced through **photosynthesis** in green plants, (such as trees and flowers.)
⑥ South America's Amazon **rain forest**, (a.k.a "the lungs of the world",) is **allegedly** the single largest oxygen **generator** in the world.
⑦ Some say it is providing more than 20% of the Earth's total oxygen.
⑧ But some **disbelieve** this, saying ¹⁾ that less than 10% of the world's oxygen is from the Amazon rain forest, and ²⁾ that the rest of it comes from the ocean.
⑨ In fact, ocean plants, (such as algae and plankton), **generate** an **enormous** amount of oxygen through photosynthesis. ⑩ The exact amount is under debate, but some scientists claim that (at least) 50% of the world's **atmospheric** oxygen comes from the ocean. ⑪ For now, nobody knows whether the ocean produces more oxygen than the Amazon or not. ⑫ But, one thing is for sure about oxygen. ⑬ If we do not protect green plants (on land and in the ocean), 7 billion human beings cannot survive.

Words & Expressions

survive 살아남다 **breathe** 호흡하다, 숨 쉬다 **breathing** 호흡 (cf. breath 숨, 입김) **oxygen** 산소 (cf. hydrogen 수소 carbon dioxide 이산화탄소) **human population** 인구 **beyond one's imagination** …의 상상을 초월하는 **come from** …에서 나오다 **photosynthesis** 광합성 **allegedly** 전해진 바에 의하면 **be against** …에 반하다, 반대하다 **algae** 조류 **plankton** 플랑크톤 **generate** 생산하다 **enormous** 막대한 **be under debate** 논란의 여지가 있다 **atmospheric** 대기의 **for now** 현재로는, 우선은

43 Did You Know Cockroaches Are Kept As Pets?

Usually, cockroaches avoid people. They wander around the house at night to find something to eat. If they are caught by people, they will surely get sprayed with deadly poison. Quite a few people are willing to open their wallets to get rid of them from their houses.

But, a certain type of cockroach is kept and raised in the home as a pet. Unlike other kinds of cockroaches, this kind is able to make a hissing sound and doesn't have any wings. This big herbivore doesn't bite the hand that feeds it, since it is far from being aggressive, although its size is pretty big for an insect, reaching about 3 inches. That's why some people want to keep it as a pet.

It is the Madagascar hissing cockroach, also simply called 'Hisser'. Mostly, they eat fruits and vegetables, and can live up to 5 years if well cared for. If you want to keep them as pets, and you live in Florida, you will need to get a permit from the state. In the US, several states require permits to keep them as pets.

1 What is the main idea of the story?
a. We have to eliminate cockroaches at all costs.
b. Don't forget to get permits if you want to keep cockroaches as pets.
c. The Madagascar hissing cockroach is the best pet.
d. A certain kind of cockroach is being loved by people as a pet.

2 Hisser can be a good pet because _____.
a. people can catch it easily
b. it is mild and gentle
c. it carries all kinds of germs
d. it looks like a hissing snake

3 Choose the correct words for each sentence.
a. I'm glad every student <u>want to / is willing to / giving</u> chip in for charity.
b. My boy is too small <u>as / for / to</u> his age but he acts like an adult.
c. I am not able <u>for attending / to attend / of attendant</u> the meeting since something more important came up this morning.

LEARNING BOARD

① Usually, cockroaches avoid people. ② They wander around the house at night to find something to eat. ③ If they are caught by people, they will surely get sprayed with deadly poison. ④ Quite a few people are willing to open their wallets (to get rid of them from their houses).

⑤ But, a certain type of cockroach is ¹⁾ kept and ²⁾ raised in the home as a pet. ⑥ Unlike other kinds of cockroaches, this kind ¹⁾ is able to make a hissing sound and ²⁾ doesn't have any wings. ⑦ This big herbivore doesn't bite the hand that feeds it, since it is far from being aggressive, although its size is pretty big (for an insect), reaching about 3 inches. ⑧ That's why some people want to keep it as a pet.

⑨ It is the Madagascar hissing cockroach, (also simply called 'Hisser'). ⑩ Mostly, they ¹⁾ eat (fruits and vegetables), and ²⁾ can live up to 5 years if well cared for.

⑪ If ¹⁾ you want to keep them as pets, and ²⁾ you live in Florida, you will need to get a permit (from the state). ⑫ In the US, several states require permits to keep them as pets.

Words & Expressions

cockroach 바퀴벌레 **avoid** 피하다 **wander** 배회하다, 돌아다니다 **deadly** 치명적인 **open one's wallet** 지갑을 열다 **get rid of** 제거하다 **pet** 애완동물 **raise** 기르다, 키우다 (cf. rise 오르다, 증가) **make a hissing sound** 쉭쉭 소리를 내다 **herbivore** 초식동물 (cf. carnivore 육식동물 omnivore 잡식동물) **aggressive** 공격적인 **if well cared for** 잘 관리 받으면 **get permits** 허가를 받다 **require permits** 허가를 (받도록) 요구하다

Did You Know You Have To Pay A Fee Before Climbing The Himalayas?

Thorough preparation and training are not enough to climb the Himalayas. You also have to grab your wallet if you don't want to just return home without having done anything. It is called the 'peak royalty.' It differs depending on the peaks. If you plan to climb peaks of up to 6,500m, you must pay US $500. If you intend to go for peaks between 6,501m-7,000m, you will be charged US $2,000. Peaks above 7,001m cost you US $3,000. If you want to try to climb peaks in restricted areas, you have to go through the severest and harshest training, as well as withdraw US $4,000 from your bank account. Thankfully, these peak royalties are charged per group of 12 people. Don't say "phew!" too soon, because there are other expenses. US $400 will be charged as the environmental levy for each expedition, and US $500 will be charged for the Liaison Officers' equipment.

Even after going through the training and putting some money in your pocket, you have to do something else to climb the Himalayas, especially Mt. Everest. You must get a permit from the Nepalese government and submit an application, along with a recommendation from the concerned government or mountaineering association.

1 What is the main idea of the story?

a. All you need to climb the Himalayas is to get a permit from the government.
b. $4,000 is enough to pay all expenses to climb the Himalayas.
c. It costs a lot to climb the Himalayas.
d. Paying peak royalties is absurd and unfair.

2 According to the passage, which sentence is <u>wrong</u>?

a. Climbing the Himalayas is not as simple as it sounds.
b. Peak royalties differ depending only on the size of expedition teams.
c. Before trying to climb the Himalayas, you have to prepare some documents.
d. People who want to climb peaks above 7,001m have to pay roughly US $4,000.

3 Choose the correct words for each sentence.

a. I have never received a through / thorough / thoroughly evaluation on this matter.
b. You will charge / be charged / charging $500 or more per pair.
c. That's good / enough / all. We don't have enough time to do this. Please stop whining.

LEARNING BOARD

① Thorough preparation and training are not enough to climb the Himalayas. ② You also have to grab your wallet if you don't want to just return home (without having done anything). ③ It is called the 'peak royalty.' ④ It differs depending on the peaks. ⑤ If you plan to climb peaks of (up to) 6,500m, you must pay US $500. ⑥ If you intend to go for peaks between 6,501m-7,000m, you will be charged US $2,000. ⑦ Peaks (above 7,001m) cost you US $3,000. ⑧ If you want to try to climb peaks in restricted areas, you have to go through the severest and harshest training, as well as withdraw US $4,000 (from your bank account). ⑨ Thankfully, these peak royalties are charged per group of 12 people. ⑩ Don't say "phew!" too soon, because there are other expenses. ⑪ US $400 will be charged as the environmental levy for each expedition, and US $500 will be charged for the Liaison Officers' equipment. ⑫ Even after 1) going through the training and 2) putting some money in your pocket, you have to do something else to climb the Himalayas, especially Mt. Everest. ⑬ You must 1) get a permit from the Nepalese government and 2) submit an application, along with a recommendation from the concerned government or mountaineering association.

Words & Expressions

thorough 철저한 **preparation** 준비 **training** 훈련 **grab your wallet** 지갑을 챙기다 **peak** 정상, 꼭대기 **royalty** 로열티, 사용료 **depending on** ~에 따라 **go for** …을 시도하다, 애쓰다 **charge** 돈(값)을 청구하다 **restricted area** 제한 구역 **severe** 심한 **harsh** 혹독한, 힘든 **withdraw** (돈을) 인출하다 **account** 계좌, 설명, 회계 **thankfully** 다행히도, 고맙게도 **expense** 경비, 비용 **levy** (세금의) 추가 부담금 **environmental levy** 환경 부담금 **expedition** 탐험대, 원정대 **liaison officer** 연락담당관 **submit** 제출하다 **application** 신청서 **recommendation** 추천서 **concerned** 담당의, 관련된 **mountaineering** 등산 **association** 협회

45 Did You Know Bats' Droppings Are Valuable To Humans?

Bats' droppings are so valuable that we do not call them just 'excrement' or 'dung', but give them the name of 'guano.'

What's so special about their droppings? They are nutrient-rich droppings, which means humans use them as good fertilizers. Guano commonly refers to the excrement of bats. But, more exactly speaking, guano is the feces of bats, seals, and sea birds such as pelicans. Guano fertilizer has been popular due to its high levels of phosphorus and nitrogen. In addition, compared to other kinds of droppings, the odor of guano isn't so bad. So, many farmers prefer guano fertilizer to chemical fertilizers.

In spite of that, some critics say it's not a good thing to take bat guano from caves. When people collect bat guano, they disturb the bats' habitat and make them anxious and uneasy. It is said that some bats often drop their babies because of anxiety.

1 What can be the best title of this story?
a. Don't Waste Wastes From Bats
b. Which Is Worse : Bats' Droppings? Or Seals' Droppings?
c. Bats Drop Not Droppings But Babies
d. The Way To Find Good Fertilizers

2 The odor of guano is _____ compared to other kinds of droppings.
a. too good to go by
b. not so bad
c. obnoxious
d. like a fragrant flower

3 Choose the correct words for each sentence.
a. When he asked me to sit down, I said I preferred to be / preferred to / preferring stand.
b. Sorry but I don't know what exactly you are referring / referring to / referred.
c. Don't forget to collect fertilized eggs from the hen house and to buy some fertilize / fertilizers / fertilizing. I need to fertilize the garden.

LEARNING BOARD

① Bats' droppings are so **valuable** that we do not call **them** just 'excrement' or 'dung,' but give them the name (of 'guano.')

② What's so special about their droppings? ③ They are **nutrient**-rich droppings, which means humans use them as good **fertilizers**. ④ Guano commonly **refers to** the excrement of bats. ⑤ But, more exactly speaking, guano is the feces of bats, seals, and sea birds (such as pelicans). ⑥ Guano fertilizer has been **popular due to** its high levels of **phosphorus** and nitrogen. ⑦ In addition, **compared to** other kinds of droppings, the **odor** of guano isn't so bad. ⑧ So, many farmers **prefer** guano fertilizer to chemical fertilizers.

⑨ In spite of that, some **critics** say it's not a good thing to take bat guano from **caves**. ⑩ When people collect bat guano, they 1) **disturb** the bats' **habitat** and 2) make them **anxious** and uneasy. ⑪ It is said that some bats often drop their babies because of **anxiety**.

Words & Expressions

valuable 가치 있는 **excrement** 배설물 **dung** (큰 동물의) 똥 **guano** 구아노 (박쥐, 바닷새의 배설물) **dropping** 배설물 **nutrient** 영양분 **nutrient-rich** 양분이 풍부한 **fertilizer** 비료 **commonly** 일반적으로 **refer to** 가리키다 **feces** 배설물 **seal** 바다표범, 물개 **pelican** 펠리컨 **popular** 인기 있는 **due to** ~때문에 **phosphorus** 인 **nitrogen** 질소 **odor** 냄새 **chemical fertilizer** 화학비료 **critic** 비판하는 사람 **cave** 동굴 **disturb** 방해하다 **habitat** 거주지, 서식지 **anxious** 걱정하는, 불안해하는 **anxiety** 불안, 걱정

Listening with Dictation

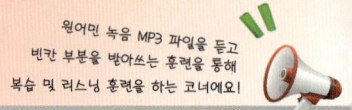

41 Did You Know Not All Spiders Make Webs?

Spiders are not insects. Unlike insects, spiders have two body parts, no _____¹ no wings, and _____² legs. Insects have three body parts, two antennae, wings and three pairs of legs. Other _____³, such as scorpions and ticks, have eight legs like spiders. Not all spiders make webs. Only _____⁴ all spiders use webs to catch prey. Certain spiders, like wolf spiders and crab spiders, just wait and pounce on prey from a close distance. Some spiders make webs, but their webs are not for hunting. Jumping spiders use webs to _____⁵, and wolf spiders _____⁶ with their silk. Maybe some of you watched the movie 'Charlotte's Web', and learned that spiders suck the juices, or we can say '_____⁷ meat', from their prey _____⁸ eating or crunching them. Some spider species do _____⁹ by sucking, but some species actually eat their prey by _____¹⁰.

42 Did You Know Where Oxygen Comes From?

No one can survive _____¹, and we need oxygen to breathe. It is said that the human population _____² in October 2011. That means the amount of oxygen we need is _____³. Then, where does our oxygen come from? Oxygen is produced through _____⁴ in green plants, such as trees and flowers. South America's Amazon rain forest, a.k.a "the lungs of the world", is allegedly _____⁵ oxygen generator in the world. Some say it is providing more than 20% of the Earth's total oxygen. But some disbelieve this, saying that less than 10% of the world's oxygen is from the Amazon rain forest, and that _____⁶ comes from the ocean. In fact, ocean plants, such as algae and plankton, generate an enormous amount of oxygen through photosynthesis. The exact amount _____⁷, but some scientists claim that at least 50% of the world's _____⁸ comes from the ocean. For now, nobody knows _____⁹ the ocean produces more oxygen than the Amazon or not. But, one thing _____¹⁰ oxygen. If we do not protect green plants on land and in the ocean, 7 billion human beings cannot survive.

43 Did You Know Cockroaches Are Kept As Pets?

Usually, cockroaches avoid people. They wander around the house _____¹ to find something to eat. If they are caught by people, they will surely _____² with deadly poison. _____³ are willing to open their wallets to get rid of them from their houses. But, a certain type of cockroach _____⁴ in the home as a pet. Unlike other kinds of cockroaches, this kind is able to make a hissing sound and doesn't have any wings. This big _____⁵ doesn't bite the hand that feeds it, since it is far from being aggressive, although its size is _____⁶, reaching about 3 inches. That's why some people want to keep it as a pet. It is the Madagascar hissing cockroach, _____⁷ 'Hisser'. Mostly, they eat fruits and vegetables, and can _____⁸ 5 years _____⁹. If you want to keep them as pets, and you live in Florida, you will need to _____¹⁰ from the state. In the US, several states require permits to keep them as pets.

132 Chapter 5 | Animals & Nature

44 Did You Know You Have To Pay A Fee Before Climbing The Himalayas?

_____¹ and training are not enough to climb the Himalayas. You also have to grab your wallet if you don't want to just return home _____². It is called the 'peak royalty.' _____³ depending on the peaks. If you plan to climb peaks of up to 6,500m, you must pay US $500. If you _____⁴ peaks between 6,501m-7,000m, you will be charged US $2,000. Peaks above 7,001m cost you US $3,000. If you want to try to climb peaks in restricted areas, you have to go through the severest and harshest training, _____⁵ withdraw US $4,000 from your bank account. Thankfully, these peak royalties are _____⁶ 12 people. Don't say "phew!" too soon, because _____⁷. US $400 will be charged as the _____⁸ for each expedition, and US $500 will be charged for the Liaison Officers' equipment. Even after going through the training and putting some money in your pocket, you have to do something else to climb the Himalayas, especially Mt. Everest. You must get a permit from the Nepalese government and _____⁹, along with a recommendation from the _____¹⁰ or mountaineering association.

45 Did You Know Bats' Droppings Are Valuable To Humans?

Bats' droppings are _____¹ we do not call them just 'excrement' or 'dung,' but give them the name of 'guano.' What's so special about their droppings? They are _____² droppings, which means humans use them as _____³. Guano _____⁴ the excrement of bats. But, more exactly speaking, guano is the feces of bats, seals, and sea birds such as pelicans. Guano fertilizer _____⁵ due to its high levels of _____⁶ and _____⁷. In addition, _____⁸ other kinds of droppings, the odor of guano isn't so bad. So, many farmers prefer guano fertilizer to chemical fertilizers. In spite of that, some critics say _____⁹ take bat guano from caves. When people collect bat guano, they disturb the bats' habitat and make them anxious and uneasy. It is said that some bats often drop their babies _____¹⁰.

---

41 정답
1. antennae 2. four pairs of 3. arachnids 4. about half of 5. make resting places
6. make egg sacs 7. liquefied 8. rather than 9. fill their stomachs 10. chewing with their jaws

42 정답
1. without breathing 2. hit 7 billion 3. beyond imagination 4. photosynthesis 5. the single largest
6. the rest of it 7. is under debate 8. atmospheric oxygen 9. whether 10. is for sure about

43 정답
1. at night 2. get sprayed 3. Quite a few people 4. is kept and raised 5. herbivore
6. pretty big for an insect 7. also simply called 8. live up to 9. if well cared for 10. get a permit

44 정답
1. Thorough preparation 2. without having done anything 3. It differs 4. intend to go for 5. as well as 6. charged per group 7. there are other expenses 8. environmental levy 9. submit an application 10. concerned government

45 정답
1. so valuable that 2. nutrient-rich 3. good fertilizers 4. commonly refers to 5. has been popular
6. phosphorus 7. nitrogen 8. compared to 9. it's not a good thing to 10. because of anxiety

46 Did You Know How Hot The Hottest Hot Spring In The World Is?

Brace yourself before putting your foot into this hot spring. It is literally a 'hot' spring — hot enough to boil some eggs. You can find the hottest hot spring in the world in Serbia. Its temperature is a whopping 111°C.

That is surely hot, but the largest hot spring can be found on another continent. Frying Pan Lake in New Zealand is the world's largest hot spring. The second largest is in Dominica, and the name is Boiling Lake. We don't know who named them, but their names express themselves very well since both of them are not only large but also very hot — hot enough to be described as 'frying' and 'boiling'.

Here's another amazing hot spring. It yields approximately 250 liters of hot water per second. This monstrous hot spring is actually a geyser in Yellowstone National Park in the US and its name is Excelsior Geyser Crater.

The Tamagawa Hot Spring holds the record for the highest flow rate in Japan. It has a flow rate of 150 liters per second. Its width is 3m and the temperature of its water is 98°C.

1 What is the main idea of the story?
   a. There are hot springs holding amazing records in the world.
   b. If you want to boil some eggs, go to the Boiling Lake.
   c. Japan's hot springs are not so hot, just big.
   d. The Excelsior Geyser Crater is called the monster hot spring.

2 According to the passage, which sentence is right?
   a. Hot springs in Japan are much hotter than hot springs in Yellowstone National Park.
   b. The second largest hot spring in the world is in New Zealand.
   c. The Boiling Lake was misnamed because its water is not hot but cold.
   d. The Excelsior Geyser Crater is famous for yielding so much hot water.

3 Choose the correct words for each sentence.
   a. It took me hours to measure the height / width / depth of a football field all by myself.
   b. I bought the book about Mother Teresa to know about the amazed / amazing / amaze life of hers.
   c. There is a yielding / yield / yielded sign next to the wheat field yielding 3 tones a hectare.

LEARNING BOARD

① Brace yourself before putting your foot into this hot spring. ② It is literally a 'hot' spring — hot enough to boil some eggs. ③ You can find the hottest hot spring (in the world) in Serbia. ④ Its temperature is a whopping 111°C.

⑤ That is surely hot, but the largest hot spring can be found on another continent.

⑥ Frying Pan Lake (in New Zealand) is the world's largest hot spring. ⑦ The second largest is in Dominica, and the name is Boiling Lake. ⑧ We don't know who named them, but their names express themselves very well since both of them are not only large but also very hot — hot enough to be described as 'frying' and 'boiling'.

⑨ Here's another amazing hot spring. ⑩ It yields approximately 250 liters of hot water (per second). ⑪ This monstrous hot spring is actually a geyser in Yellowstone National Park in the US and its name is Excelsior Geyser Crater.

⑫ The Tamagawa Hot Spring holds the record for the highest flow rate (in Japan). ⑬ It has a flow rate of 150 liters per second. ⑭ Its width is 3m and the temperature of its water is 98°C.

Words & Expressions

brace oneself 마음의 각오를 하다 **hot spring** 온천 **literally** 문자 그대로 **boil** 끓이다, 삶다 **temperature** 온도 **whopping** 엄청 큰 **continent** 대륙 **frying pan** 프라이팬 **the second largest** 두 번째로 큰 것 **amazing** 놀라운 **yield** 생산하다 **approximately** 대략 **per second** 초당 **monstrous** 거대한, 괴물 같은 **geyser** 간헐천 **flow rate** 유량 **width** 폭, 넓이

47 Did You Know Why The Quagga, A Half Zebra And Half Horse, Went Extinct?

The quagga, which was once found in great numbers on the plains of Africa, went extinct because people hunted them for their meat and hides. So, it was we humans who drove them to extinction.

The quagga was different from other zebras. It had distinct stripes only on the front part of its body. In the middle part of its body, the stripes faded into a plain brown. So, the quagga looked like a zebra and a horse at the same time.

Scholars were confused about how to categorize this species. Sadly, before they had made any decision about its species, the quagga became extinct. The last wild quagga was thought to have been shot and disappeared in the late 1870s, and the  very last quagga kept in captivity in Amsterdam died in 1883. But, scientists have continued to study it by its DNA. As a matter of fact, the quagga was the first extinct animal which left behind its DNA. Recently, genetic engineers revealed that the quagga was not a separate species. It had diverged from the plains zebra.

1 What is the main idea of the story?
 a. The quagga was totally different from the plains zebra.
 b. Ever since the quagga became extinct, scientists have studied about the cause of its extinction.
 c. The quagga looked the same as the zebra but its species was different.
 d. The quagga driven to extinction by human beings was the first extinct animal left behind its DNA.

2 In order to get _____, people had hunted the quagga at will.
 a. grass in the plains
 b. other zebras and horses
 c. meat and hides
 d. its DNA samples

3 Choose the correct words for each sentence.
 a. The hunters tried to catch seals for their hid / hides / hidden but seals hid under the ice.
 b. Those who did / came / made a decision to stay inside the house wouldn't leave the house.
 c. National treasures taken by Japan during the Japanese colonial era had come / came / coming back to Korea in 2001.
 d. Sue wore a plains / plain / plainly T-shirt, on the other hand, Demi wore a fancy colorful gown.

LEARNING BOARD

① The quagga, (which was once found in great numbers on the **plains** of Africa), went **extinct** because people hunted them for (their meat and **hides**). ② So, it was we humans who drove them to **extinction**. ③ The quagga was different from other zebras. ④ It had **distinct** stripes only on the front part of its body. ⑤ In the middle part of its body, the stripes **faded into** a **plain** brown. ⑥ So, the quagga looked like a zebra and a horse **at the same time**. ⑦ Scholars were **confused** about how to **categorize** this **species**. ⑧ Sadly, before they had made any decision about its species, the quagga became extinct. ⑨ The last wild quagga was thought to have been shot and disappeared in the late 1870s, and the very last quagga (kept in captivity in Amsterdam) died in 1883. ⑩ But, scientists have **continued** to study it by its DNA. ⑪ **As a matter of fact**, the quagga was the first extinct animal which left behind its DNA. ⑫ Recently, **genetic** engineers **revealed** that the quagga was not a **separate** species. ⑬ It had **diverged from** the plains zebra.

Words & Expressions

in great numbers 대량으로, 많은 수의 **extinct** 멸종한 **plain** n. 평원(cf. prairie 초원) a. 분명한, 꾸미지 않은, 못생긴, 무늬가 없는 **hide** n. 가죽 v. 숨다 **extinction** 멸종 **distinct** 뚜렷한, 선명한 **stripe** 줄무늬 **fade** 색이 바래다, 흐려지다 **plain brown** 평범한 갈색 **categorize** 분류하다 **species** 종 **become extinct** 멸종하다 **genetic** 유전의, 유전학의 **reveal** 밝히다, 드러내다 **separate** a. 별개의, 서로 다른, 독립된 v. 분리되다, 나누다, 헤어지다 **diverge** 갈라지다, 나뉘다

137

48 Did You Know Whales Are Useful To The Bone?

Whales have been useful to the bone for human beings, both figuratively as well as literally speaking.

Whales provide us with tons of meat. Considering their enormous size, it's no wonder they can give us an enormous amount of meat. They also provide us with their whalebones. Whalebone, also called baleen, is a kind of brush-looking filter inside the mouth of toothless whales. Whales eat tons of krill by filtering sea water through their whalebones. Whalebones have been variously used for a long time, in such products as umbrellas, brushes, women's corsets, fishing rods, and more.

The most important thing whales provide us is oil. In the past, whale oil was widely used as fuel in oil lamps and as candle wax. It was once a major food source for some people of the Pacific Northwest. Even today, it is still used in soap making and leather dressing. Most whale oil comes from blubber (sea animals' fat), but humans can extract oil from their baleen, meat, organs, bones, and even blood. From now on, maybe we should call them 'the giving whales.'

1 What is the main idea of the story?

a. Whale meat is delicious and highly nutritious.
b. Whales are endangered animals so we must protect them.
c. Whales have been useful for humans in various ways.
d. We must call whales 'the giving whales.'

2 According to the passage, which sentence is right?

a. Whales have been useful for human beings for a long time.
b. In many countries, in all ages, people have enjoyed eating whale meat.
c. Whalebones are still widely used as a major food source.
d. Whalebones are absolutely different from baleen.

3 Choose the correct words for each sentence.

a. The problem is that many government officials are deeply corrupt <u>through / to / into</u> the bone.
b. Since you insulted me in front of my family, <u>from time to time / from now on / till the end</u> you and I are no longer friends.
c. <u>Literally / figuratively / comparatively</u> speaking, you look like a hungry lion which has been starved for weeks.
d. The giving tree provided the boy <u>for / with / to</u> fruits and branches.

LEARNING BOARD

① Whales have been useful **to the bone** for human beings, both **figuratively** as well as **literally** speaking.

② Whales **provide** us **with** tons of meat. ③ **Considering** their **enormous** size, it's no wonder they can give us an enormous amount of meat. ④ They also provide us with their whalebones. ⑤ Whalebone, (also called baleen), is a kind of brush-looking filter (inside the mouth of **toothless** whales). ⑥ Whales eat tons of krill by filtering sea water (through their whalebones). ⑦ Whalebon have been **variously** used for a long time, in such products as umbrellas, brushes, women's corsets, fishing rods, and more. ⑧ The most important thing (whales provide us) is oil. ⑨ In the past, whale oil was widely used as 1) **fuel** in oil lamps and as 2) candle wax. ⑩ It was once a major food source for some people of the Pacific Northwest. ⑪ Even today, it is still used in soap making and **leather** dressing.

⑫ Most whale oil **comes from** blubber (sea animals' fat), but humans can **extract** oil from their baleen, meat, organs, bones, and even blood.

⑬ From now on, maybe we should call them 'the giving whales.'

Words & Expressions

useful 유용한 to the bone 뼈까지, 철저하게 figuratively 비유적으로 literally speaking 문자 그대로 말해서 provide 제공하다(with) enormous 거대한, 막대한 whalebone 고래수염(= baleen) toothless 이가 없는 filter 필터, 걸러내다 variously 다양하게 corset 코르셋 fishing rod 낚싯대 and more 그리고 더 있다 whale oil 고래기름 fuel 연료 a major food source 주요 식량원 soap making 비누 제작 leather dressing 가죽 무두질 extract 추출하다, 뽑아내다 come from …에서 나오다 blubber 바다 동물의 지방 from now on 지금부터

139

49 Did You Know Animals Do Feel Sad?

Not all animals feel sad, but some animals have shown signs of grief.

When one elephant dies, other elephants stand around the dead body and stare at it for a while. And, if a mother elephant loses her baby, she won't leave her dead baby, and touches it with her trunk from time to time.

In the case of chimpanzees and gorillas, they also feel sad when they lose their babies and vice versa. There was a baby chimpanzee who lost his mom. This baby chimp's sorrow was so deep that he refused to eat any food. Finally, he starved to death.

Parrots, which are faithful to their mates, also show sadness. When the mate dies, the other parrot seems disheartened and distressed by grief. Sometimes, they do not eat for a long time. Dogs are also said to grieve when sad things happen, like the deaths of their mate or owner.

1 What is the main idea of the story?
   a. Some animals show signs of grief because they have feelings of grief.
   b. Parrots feel sad when they lose their mates.
   c. All elephants grieve when their babies die.
   d. Chimpanzees and gorillas have so much in common.

2 _____ feel sad and show their grief.
   a. All animals
   b. Certain animals
   c. Only Elephants
   d. Most birds

3 Choose the correct words for each sentence.
   a. Tim and I promise to live together until dead / death / die separates us.
   b. I share my room with Jeff from time to time / now more than ever / at the same time and that makes me crazy.
   c. When I put down my pink trunk by a tree trunk to change clothes into swimming trunks, an elephant came close to me and touched my pink trunk with its trunks / trunk / a trunk.
   d. His dog is famous for being faithful with / to / for his owner. My dog? Definitely not.

LEARNING BOARD

① Not all animals feel sad, but some animals have shown signs of grief.
② When one elephant dies, other elephants ¹⁾ stand around the dead body and ²⁾ stare at it for a while. ③ And, if a mother elephant loses her baby, she ¹⁾ won't leave her dead baby, and ²⁾ touches it with her trunk from time to time.
④ In the case of chimpanzees and gorillas, they also feel sad when they lose their babies and vice versa. ⑤ There was a baby chimpanzee (who lost his mom).
⑥ This baby chimp's sorrow was so deep that he refused to eat any food. ⑦ Finally, he starved to death.
⑧ Parrots, (which are faithful to their mates,) also show sadness. ⑨ When the mate dies, the other parrot seems disheartened and distressed by grief. ⑩ Sometimes, they do not eat for a long time. ⑪ Dogs are also said to grieve when sad things happen, (like the deaths of their mate or owner.)

Words & Expressions

show signs of ...의 신호(조짐)를 보이다 grief n. 슬픔 (grieve v. 슬퍼하다) stare 빤히 쳐다보다(at) for a while 잠시 동안 lose 잃다 trunk (코끼리의) 코 from time to time 이따금 chimpanzee/chimp 침팬지 vice versa 반대의 경우도 그렇다 sorrow 슬픔 refuse 거절하다, 거부하다 starve to death 굶주리다, 굶어 죽다 parrot 앵무새 be faithful to ...에게 충실하다, 바람을 피우지 않다 mate 짝, 배우자, 친구 disheartened 낙심한 distressed 괴로운

141

50 Did You Know Sharks Can Play Opossum?

Sharks can make themselves look dead. It's understandable for opossums to "play possum." This comes as no surprise. But can sharks "play possum?"

Exactly speaking, sharks don't "play possum" of their own accord. But, they can enter a state of paralysis, and it is called 'tonic immobility' (a kind of apparent death).

Not all sharks display tonic immobility, but some sharks enter and remain in this state for about 10 to 15 minutes when inverted. During tonic immobility, sharks show no response when touched. Yet, after 15 minutes of this lifeless-looking state, they recover consciousness, turn themselves over quickly, and swim away.

So, you can make some sharks helpless for several minutes by turning them upside down; I mean, if you can. No one knows what causes this weird state.

Some scientists take advantage of this phenomenon to study sharks. Interestingly, scientists are not the only ones who use this tactic to take control of sharks. While hunting, killer whales often manage to invert sharks to eat them more easily.

1 What is the main idea of the story?

a. You can make shakes helpless by turning them into opossums.
b. In the state of tonic immobility, sharks can't swim fast.
c. Some sharks can play possum.
d. If you invert sharks, they will eat you up.

2 According to the passage, which sentence is wrong?

a. In the state of tonic immobility, sharks can't do anything.
b. Some sharks play possum, but some don't.
c. Killer whales often try to invert sharks while hunting them.
d. Tonic immobility lasts for 15 hours.

3 Choose the correct words for each sentence.

a. This shiny shirt will make me look / looking / to look good and young.
b. Paralysis / Paralyze / Paralyzed happens when something goes wrong with your body, especially your brain and muscles.
c. Tim was crying out loud while waited / waiting / to wait for his mom.

LEARNING BOARD

① Sharks can make themselves look dead. ② It's understandable for opossums to "play possum." ③ This comes as no surprise. ④ But can sharks "play possum?"

⑤ Exactly speaking, sharks don't "play possum" of their own accord. ⑥ But, they can enter a state of paralysis, and it is called 'tonic immobility' (a kind of apparent death).

⑦ Not all sharks display tonic immobility, but some sharks 1) enter and 2) remain in this state (for about 10 to 15 minutes) when inverted. ⑧ During tonic immobility, sharks show no response when touched. ⑨ Yet, after 15 minutes of this lifeless-looking state, they 1) recover consciousness, 2) turn themselves over quickly, and 3) swim away. ⑩ So, you can make some sharks helpless for several minutes by turning them upside down; I mean, if you can. ⑪ No one knows what causes this weird state. ⑫ Some scientists take advantage of this phenomenon (to study sharks). ⑬ Interestingly, scientists are not the only ones (who use this tactic to take control of sharks.) ⑭ While hunting, killer whales often manage to invert sharks to eat them more easily.

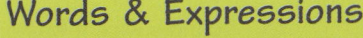

Words & Expressions

understandable 이해할 만한 **opossum** 주머니 쥐 **play possum** 죽은 척하다(= play dead) **come as no surprise** 놀랄 일도 아니다 **exactly speaking** 정확히 말하면 **of one's own accord** 자발적으로 **paralysis** 마비 **tonic immobility** 긴장성 부동 **apparent death** 가사상태 **display** 나타내다, 전시하다 **invert** 뒤집다 **show no response** 반응을 보이지 않다 **lifeless-looking** 죽은 것처럼 보이는 **recover** 회복하다 **consciousness** 의식 **helpless** 무력한 **weird** 기이한, 섬뜩한 **upside down** 위아래가 바뀐, 뒤집힌 **phenomenon** 현상 **tactic** 전략 **take control of** ...를 지배, 통제하다

Listening with Dictation

46 Did You Know How Hot The Hottest Hot Spring In The World Is?

_____ ¹ before putting your foot into this hot spring. It is _____ ² a 'hot' spring – _____ ³ some eggs. You can find the hottest hot spring in the world in Serbia. Its temperature is a whopping 111°C. That is surely hot, but the largest hot spring can be found _____ ⁴. Frying Pan Lake in New Zealand is the world's largest hot spring. The second largest is in Dominica, and the name is Boiling Lake. We don't know who named them, but their names _____ ⁵ very well since both of them are not only large but also very hot– hot enough to _____ ⁶ 'frying' and 'boiling'. Here's another amazing hot spring. It _____ ⁷ approximately 250 liters of hot water _____ ⁸. This monstrous hot spring is actually a _____ ⁹ in Yellowstone National Park in the US and its name is Excelsior Geyser Crater. The Tamagawa Hot Spring holds the record for the highest flow rate in Japan. It has a flow rate of 150 liters per second. Its width is 3m and the _____ ¹⁰ is 98°C.

47 Did You Know Why The Quagga, A Half Zebra And Half Horse, Went Extinct?

The quagga, which was once found _____ ¹ on the plains of Africa, went extinct because people hunted them for their meat and _____ ². So, it was we humans who _____ ³. The quagga was different from other zebras. It had distinct stripes only on the front part of its body. In the middle part of its body, the stripes _____ ⁴ a plain brown. So, the quagga looked like a zebra and a horse _____ ⁵. Scholars were confused about how to categorize this species. Sadly, before they had _____ ⁶ about its species, the quagga became extinct. The last wild quagga was thought to have been shot and disappeared in the late 1870s, and the very last quagga _____ ⁷ in Amsterdam died in 1883. But, scientists have continued to study it by its DNA. As a matter of fact, the quagga was the first extinct animal which _____ ⁸ its DNA. Recently, genetic engineers revealed that the quagga was not _____ ⁹. It had _____ ¹⁰ the plains zebra.

48 Did You Know Whales Are Useful To The Bone?

Whales have been useful to the bone for human beings, both _____ ¹ literally speaking. Whales _____ ² tons of meat. _____ ³ their enormous size, it's no wonder they can give us an enormous amount of meat. They also provide us with their whalebones. Whalebone, also called baleen, is a kind of brush-looking filter _____ ⁴ toothless whales. Whales eat tons of krill by filtering sea water through their whalebones. Whalebones _____ ⁵ for a long time, in such products as umbrellas, brushes, women's corsets, fishing rods, _____ ⁶. The most important thing whales provide us is oil. In the past, whale oil _____ ⁷ as fuel in oil lamps _____ ⁸ candle wax. It was once a major food source for some people of the Pacific Northwest. Even today, it is still used in soap making and leather dressing. Most whale oil comes from blubber (sea animals' fat), but humans can extract oil from their baleen, meat, _____ ⁹, bones, and even blood. _____ ¹⁰, maybe we should call them 'the giving whales.'

144 Chapter 5 | Animals & Nature

49. Did You Know Animals Do Feel Sad?

Not all animals feel sad, but some animals _____¹. When one elephant dies, other elephants stand around the dead body and _____² it for a while. And, if a mother elephant _____³, she won't leave her dead baby, and touches it with her trunk from time to time. In the case of chimpanzees and gorillas, they also feel sad when they lose their babies _____⁴. There was a baby chimpanzee who lost his mom. This baby chimp's _____⁵ he refused to eat any food. Finally, he _____⁶. Parrots, which _____⁷ their mates, also _____⁸. When the mate dies, the other parrot _____⁹ and distressed by grief. Sometimes, they do not eat for a long time. Dogs are also said to grieve when sad things happen, like _____¹⁰ or owner.

50. Did You Know Sharks Can Play Opossum?

Sharks can make themselves _____¹. It's understandable for opossums to "play possum." _____². But can sharks "_____³?" Exactly speaking, sharks don't "play possum" _____⁴. But, they can enter _____⁵, and it is called 'tonic immobility' (a kind of apparent death). Not all sharks display tonic immobility, but some sharks enter and remain in this state for about 10 to 15 minutes _____⁶. During tonic immobility, sharks _____⁷ when touched. Yet, after 15 minutes of this lifeless-looking state, they recover consciousness, turn themselves over quickly, and swim away. So, you can make some sharks helpless for several minutes by turning them upside down; I mean, if you can. No one knows what causes this weird state. Some scientists _____⁸ this phenomenon to study sharks. Interestingly, scientists _____⁹ use this tactic to _____¹⁰ sharks. While hunting, killer whales often manage to invert sharks to eat them more easily.

---

46 정답
1. Brace yourself 2. literally 3. hot enough to boil 4. on another continent 5. express themselves
6. be described as 7. yields 8. per second 9. geyser 10. temperature of its water

47 정답
1. in great numbers 2. hides 3. drove them to extinction 4. faded into 5. at the same time
6. made any decision 7. kept in captivity 8. left behind 9. a separated species 10. diverged from

48 정답
1. figuratively as well as 2. provide us with 3. Considering 4. inside the mouth of
5. have been variously used 6. and more 7. was widely used 8. and as 9. organs 10. From now on

49 정답
1. have shown signs of grief 2. stare at 3. loses her baby 4. and vice versa 5. sorrow was so deep that
6. starved to death 7. are faithful to 8. show sadness 9. seems disheartened 10. the deaths of their mate

50 정답
1. look dead 2. This comes as no surprise 3. play possum 4. of their own accord 5. a state of paralysis
6. when inverted 7. show no response 8. take advantage of 9. are not the only ones who 10. take control of

Chapter 6. Myth Or Fact

51. Did you know A Myth About The Common Cold?

일반 감기에 관한 낭설을 아세요?

52. Did you know 'Never Eat Before Exercise' Is A Myth?

'운동 전에 먹으면 안 된다'는 게 낭설이라는 거 아세요?

53. Did you know Reading In Dim Light Is Not A Cause Of Eye Damage?

어두운 조명에서 글을 읽는다고 시력이 손상되는 건 아니라는 거 아세요?

54. Did you know Whitening Toothpastes Do Not Whiten Your Teeth?

미백 치약이 치아를 희게 만들지 않는다는 거 아세요?

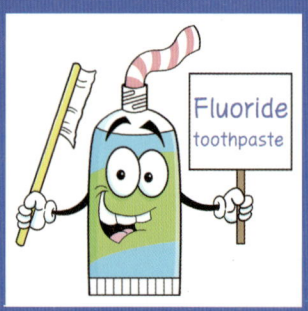

55. Did you know Coffee Won't Help You Sober Up?

커피가 술 깨는데 도움이 안 된다는 거 아세요?

56. Did you know Cell Phones Have Nothing To Do With Gas Station Fires?

휴대폰과 주유소 화재는 관계가 없다는 거 아세요?

57. Did you know You Should Not Tilt Your Head Back When Your Nose Is Bleeding?

코피가 날 때 머리를 뒤로 젖히면 안 된다는 거 아세요?

58. Did you know What The Most Common Food Allergy Among Children Is?

어린이들에게 가장 흔한 음식 알레르기가 무엇인지 아세요?

59. Did you know The Majority Of The Sugar We Consume Is Not From Sweets?

우리가 섭취하는 설탕 대부분이 단 과자에서 나오는 게 아니라는 거 아세요?

60. Did you know There's No Need To Worry When You Die In Your Dreams?

꿈에서 죽어도 걱정할 필요 없다는 거 아세요?

51 Did You Know A Myth About The Common Cold?

The most common myth about the cold is that vitamin C can prevent a cold. Many people are convinced that a large amount of vitamin C will prevent a cold or at least relieve cold symptoms. So, parents often make their kids eat fruits containing lots of vitamin C when they caught a cold.

Doctors and scientists have conducted many studies and experiments to test this common cold myth. The results said that it's just a myth. Currently, there is no conclusive data to prove that a large amount of vitamin C prevents a cold. But, the vitamin may still alleviate cold symptoms, even though there is no clear evidence of this. If you want to get over a cold sooner, a bowl of hot chicken soup can help. Chicken soup for colds is not a myth; it is a fact backed up with solid medical evidence, as it has an anti-inflammatory effect.

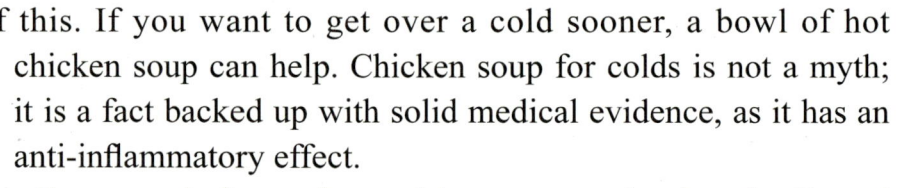

For your information, taking too much vitamin C, and for too long, may not be good for your health. Far from being good for health, it could actually be harmful, because excessive doses of vitamin C can cause diarrhea, which is very dangerous especially for elderly people and young children.

1 What is the main idea of the story?
   a. 'Taking a large amount of vitamin C prevents a cold' is a myth.
   b. Vitamin C is cheap but not effective, chicken soup is effective but pricey.
   c. As far as vitamin C is concerned, the more, the better.
   d. Taking vitamin C too much causes diarrhea.

2 A bowl of hot chicken soup can help you get over a cold sooner since _____.
   a. there is no an anti-inflammatory effect in it
   b. its anti-inflammatory properties are effective for a cold
   c. it can cause diarrhea and be harmful
   d. it has lots of good stuffs such as vitamin C

3 Choose the correct words for each sentence.
   a. It is said humans yawn in order to <u>alleviate / waste / removal</u> oxygen deficiency.
   b. I thought he would never <u>get over / make over / come over</u> the death of his sister.
   c. In one of the experiments <u>performed / conducted / taken</u> by HC Research Center, the shocking result was released.

LEARNING BOARD

① The most common **myth** (about the cold) is that vitamin C can **prevent** a **cold.** ② Many people are **convinced** that (a large amount of) vitamin C will ¹⁾ prevent a cold or (at least) ²⁾ **relieve** cold **symptoms.** ③ So, parents often **make** their kids **eat** fruits (containing lots of vitamin C) when they **caught a cold.** ④ Doctors and scientists have **conducted** many studies and **experiments** to **test** this common cold myth. ⑤ The results said that it's just a myth. ⑥ Currently, there is no **conclusive** data to prove that (a large amount of vitamin C) prevents a cold. ⑦ But, the vitamin may still **alleviate** cold symptoms, even though there is no clear **evidence** of this. ⑧ If you want to **get over** a cold sooner, a bowl (of hot chicken soup) can help. ⑨ Chicken soup for colds is not a myth; it is a fact **backed up** with **solid** medical evidence, as it has an anti-**inflammatory** effect. ⑩ For your information, ¹⁾ taking too much vitamin C, and ²⁾ for too long, may not be good for your health. ⑪ Far from being good for health, it could actually be **harmful**, because **excessive doses** of vitamin C can cause **diarrhea**, which is very dangerous especially for elderly people and young children.

Words & Expressions

myth 신화, (근거 없는) 믿음, 낭설 **common** 일반적인 **prevent** 예방하다 **convince** 확신시키다 **relieve** 경감하다, 완화시키다 **symptom** 증상, 징후 **conduct** 실시하다 **experiment** 실험 **test** 확인하다, 시험하다 **currently** 최근에 **conclusive** 결정적인 **alleviate** 완화하다 **clear evidence** 명백한 증거 **get over** 극복하다, (병이) 낫다 **back up** (이론을) 뒷받침하다 **be backed up with** …로 뒷받침되다 **solid** 확실한 **inflammatory** 염증의, 선동적인 **anti-inflammatory** 소염제의 **harmful** 해로운 **excessive** 지나친, 과도한 **dose** 약의 복용량 **diarrhea** 설사

52 Did You Know 'Never Eat Before Exercise' Is A Myth?

It is better to eat a small amount of food prior to starting a workout, because fuel is required to provide the needed energy for your body. You get that fuel from food and drinks. A proper portion of food will prepare your muscles for the activities that are to come. Fill up your tank with some fruits or drinks, such as bananas, nuts, or a cup of water.

There are other myths about exercise. People believe that you must stretch before a workout. But, several studies have shown that stretching sometimes leads to injury, since lengthened muscle fibers are more susceptible to strain.

Also, some women fear that if they work out, their fat will turn into muscle. They believe that lifting weights will surely make their bodies bulky and muscular. But, fat and muscle tissues are totally different, so that's an absolute myth and a lame excuse for not working out.

1 What is the main idea of the story?
   a. Eating something is very important to everyone, especially athletes.
   b. Before a workout, eat the proper amount of food and be careful about stretching.
   c. See what you eat before doing something hard.
   d. Eat less and exercise more.

2 According to the passage, which sentence is right?
   a. It would be better to eat some food before an exercise. Nuts can be a good choice.
   b. You have to stretch your legs and arms out several times right after a workout.
   c. The most recommended food before an exercise is a bunch of bananas.
   d. Fat tissues can turn into muscle tissues, that's why female athletes are muscly.

3 Choose the correct words for each sentence.
   a. Maria is nice and smart but her new boyfriend is so tall / handsome / lame.
   b. These sugary snacks make me fat, and this pair of jeans make / makes / made me look fat.
   c. I want to check out the latest movies that is / are / was to come.

LEARNING BOARD

① It is better to eat a small amount of food prior to starting a workout, because fuel is required to provide the needed energy for your body. ② You get that fuel from food and drinks. ③ A proper portion of food will prepare your muscles for the activities that are to come. ④ Fill up your tank with some fruits or drinks, (such as bananas, nuts, or a cup of water).

⑤ There are other myths about exercise. ⑥ People believe that you must stretch before a workout. ⑦ But, several studies have shown that stretching (sometimes) leads to injury, since lengthened muscle fibers are more susceptible to strain. ⑧ Also, some women fear that if they work out, their fat will turn into muscle. ⑨ They believe that lifting weights will surely make their bodies bulky and muscular. ⑩ But, fat and muscle tissues are totally different, so that's an absolute myth and a lame excuse for not working out.

Words & Expressions

prior to …전에 workout 운동(=exercise) fuel 연료 provide 제공하다 portion (음식의) 1인분, 몫 proper portion of …의 적당한 양 muscle 근육 activity 활동 that is(are) to come 이제 다가올, 가까운 미래의 exercise 운동(=workout) stretch 늘이다, 스트레칭하다 lead to …로 이어지다 lengthen 늘이다 muscle fiber 근섬유 susceptible to …에 취약한, 걸리기 쉬운 strain 부담, 압박, 염좌 lifting weights 역기 들기 bulky 우람한, 덩치 큰 muscular 근육의, 근육이 발달한 tissue 조직 absolute 완전한, 순전한 lame excuse 궁색한 변명

53 Did You Know Reading In Dim Light Is Not A Cause Of Eye Damage?

Reading in dim light, and reading very small print for a long time, are not causes of eye damage. Of course, your eyes will surely feel tired, exhausted, or uncomfortable, or become bloodshot by doing that. But, those bad reading habits will not cause permanent eye damage. Nevertheless, eye fatigue is not good for your eye health. Doctors do not exclude the possibility that eye fatigue from overuse or misuse can ruin your eyesight. Also, the way you use your eyes early in life can affect your vision. In order to reduce eye fatigue, read books or newspapers in a well-lit room, and take a break from time to time to let your eyes rest for a while.

Likewise, sitting too close to the TV or wearing someone else's glasses also will not hurt your eyes. Sitting close to the TV may lead to nearsightedness, but there is no evidence that these two behaviors cause permanent damage to your eyes.

There is another myth about eyes : carrots. Carrots are rich in beta carotene, which is changed into vitamin A in the body. Vitamin A is crucial for maintaining normal vision, so a vitamin A deficiency is a main cause of blindness. Despite this, eating supplementary carrots will not improve your eyesight.

1 What can be the best title of this story?
a. How To Protect Your Eyes From The TV
b. Keep An Eye On Your Eyes : Danger Everywhere
c. Unexpected Facts About Vitamin A
d. Facts & Myths About Eyes

2 If you want to reduce eye fatigue, you must _____.
a. wear others' glasses
b. overuse or misuse your eyes whenever possible
c. rest your eyes from time to time
d. read books in a dim-lit room

3 Choose the correct words for each sentence.
a. I wanted this affair to be settled without bloodshot / bloodshed / bloodstained.
b. Mr. Baker let me join his team despite / despite that / despite of the fact that my many faults.
c. We don't include / exclude / preclude the possibility of life on Mars even though there is no definite proof.

LEARNING BOARD

① ¹⁾ Reading (in dim light), and ²⁾ reading very small print (for a long time), are not causes of eye damage. ② Of course, your eyes will surely ¹⁾ feel tired, exhausted, or uncomfortable, or ²⁾ become bloodshot by doing that. ③ But, those bad reading habits will not cause permanent eye damage. ④ Nevertheless, eye fatigue is not good for your eye health. ⑤ Doctors do not exclude the possibility that eye fatigue (from overuse or misuse) can ruin your eyesight. ⑥ Also, the way (you use your eyes early in life) can affect your vision. ⑦ In order to reduce eye fatigue, ¹⁾ read books or newspapers in a well-lit room, and ²⁾ take a break (from time to time) to let your eyes rest for a while. ⑧ Likewise, ¹⁾ sitting (too close to the TV) or ²⁾ wearing someone else's glasses also will not hurt your eyes. ⑨ Sitting (close to the TV) may lead to nearsightedness, but there is no evidence that these two behaviors cause permanent damage to your eyes. ⑩ There is another myth about eyes : carrots. ⑪ Carrots are rich in beta carotene, which is changed into vitamin A in the body. ⑫ Vitamin A is crucial for maintaining normal vision, so a vitamin A deficiency is a main cause of blindness. ⑬ Despite this, eating supplementary carrots will not improve your eyesight.

Words & Expressions

dim 흐린, 어둑한 **cause** n. 원인 v. 초래하다, 일으키다 **damage** 손상 **tired** 지친, 피곤한 **uncomfortable** 불편한 **exhausted** 지친 **bloodshot** 핏발이 선 **permanent** 영구적인 **eye fatigue** 눈의 피로 **exclude** 배제하다, 제외하다 **overuse** 남용하다 **misuse** v. 오용하다 n. 남용, 오용 **ruin** 망치다, 손상시키다 **eyesight** 시력(=vision) **early in life** 인생 초기에, 어렸을 때 **affect** …에 영향을 미치다(=have an effect on) **vision** 시력(=eyesight), 통찰력 **reduce** 줄이다(=decrease) **well-lit** 조명이 잘 된 **take a break** 잠시 휴식을 취하다 **break** 휴식 **likewise** 마찬가지로 **nearsightedness** 근시 **crucial** 필수적인 **deficiency** 결핍, 부족 **supplementary** 추가의, 보충의 **improve** 개선하다, 좋아지게 하다

54 Did You Know Whitening Toothpastes Do Not Whiten Your Teeth?

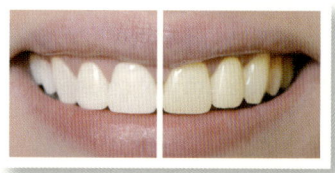

You know that not all commercials are true. Whitening tooth pastes wash the surfaces of your teeth, stained by coffee, tea, and food. Abrasive ingredients in the toothpaste remove the stains. This makes your teeth look whiter, not makes them white. So, what the commercials say is not only a myth, but also a kind of exaggerated advertisement.

There is another myth that toothpastes are all the same. That is a myth. Some toothpastes contain more abrasive materials, dyes, alcohol or artificial sweeteners and flavors than others. Some contain fluoride, some don't. According to the experts, toothpastes with no alcohol, no dyes, and less abrasives are better. Additionally, many people believe that fluoride toothpastes are better than non-fluoride toothpastes. This is not a myth, because it is true that the use of fluoride is closely related to fewer dental cavities. However, the common toothpaste myth of 'the more I use, the better' is not true. The more toothpaste you use, the more money you waste. The important things are the way you brush your teeth, and the quality of the toothpaste and the brush — not the amount of the toothpaste and foam.

1 What is the main idea of the story?
 a. You must buy fluoride tooth pastes for your teeth.
 b. An exaggerated advertisement is a serious crime.
 c. Tooth pastes are all different but their price is all the same.
 d. Whitening tooth pastes only make teeth look whiter, not make them white.

2 According to the passage, which sentence is <u>wrong</u>?
 a. Not all commercials are true and commercials of whitening tooth pastes are not an exception.
 b. Whitening tooth pastes do not make your teeth white to the core.
 c. All whitening tooth pastes contain the same amount of fluoride.
 d. The important thing is the way you brush your teeth, not the price of the paste.

3 Choose the correct words for each sentence.
 a. <u>What / When / Who</u> you just said is one of the most foolish remarks I have ever heard.
 b. The 4U center, a bona fide <u>no-profit / non-profit / not-profit</u> organization, is now recruiting volunteers.
 c. While some of her notes were spread all over the desk, some <u>didn't / wasn't / weren't</u>.

LEARNING BOARD

① You know that not all commercials are true. ② Whitening tooth pastes wash the surfaces of your teeth, (stained by coffee, tea, and food). ③ Abrasive ingredients (in the toothpaste) remove the stains. ④ This makes your teeth look whiter, not makes them white. ⑤ So, what the commercials say is not only a myth, but also a kind of exaggerated advertisement.

⑥ There is another myth that toothpastes are all the same. ⑦ That is a myth. ⑧ Some toothpastes contain more (abrasive materials, dyes, alcohol or artificial sweeteners and flavors) than others. ⑨ Some contain fluoride, some don't. ⑩ According to the experts, toothpastes (with no alcohol, no dyes, and less abrasives) are better. ⑪ Additionally, many people believe that fluoride toothpastes are better than non-fluoride toothpastes.

⑫ This is not a myth, because it is true that the use of fluoride is closely related to fewer dental cavities. ⑬ However, the common toothpaste myth (of 'the more I use, the better') is not true. ⑭ The more toothpaste you use, the more money you waste.

⑮ The important things are 1) the way you brush your teeth, and 2) the quality (of the toothpaste and the brush) — not the amount (of the toothpaste and foam).

Words & Expressions

whitening 화이트닝, 미백 **commercial** a. 상업의 n. 광고 (방송) **surface** 표면 **stain** 얼룩, 얼룩지게 하다 **abrasive** 연마재(의), 거친 **ingredient** 재료, 성분, 구성요소 **exaggerated** 과장된 **advertisement** 광고 **contain** 함유하다, (감정을) 억누르다 **dye** 염료, 염색하다 **artificial** 인공적인, 억지로 꾸민 **sweetener** 감미료 **flavor** 향, 향미료 **fluoride** 불소 **dental** 치아의 **cavity** 구멍, 충치 **quality** 질, 품질 **foam** 거품

55 Did You Know Coffee Won't Help You Sober Up?

Some people think coffee will help them sober up. They think if they drink a cup of coffee after drinking, the alcohol will wear off sooner than normal, or at least they can hide the effects of alcohol behind caffeine. But, that's a myth. No matter how much coffee you drink, the slow reaction time and poor judgment caused by alcohol cannot be worn off or hidden by caffeine.

Furthermore, the rumor about coffee's effect of increasing energy is also a myth. The reason why some feel that coffee makes them feel energized is that they think they feel less sleepy after drinking coffee. It is true that coffee does make you wake up and be more alert, because caffeine is a stimulant. So, you could work better or study late at night with the help of coffee.

The relation between anemia and coffee, however, is not a myth. As a matter of fact, coffee can cause a loss of vitamins and minerals such as vitamin C, calcium, zinc, and iron. So, if you suffer from anemia (iron deficiency), you should steer clear of coffee.

1 What is the main idea of the story?
  a. The caffeine in coffee is just a stimulant, not a cure-all.
  b. If you don't drink coffee while studying, you can't get a good grade.
  c. Coffee is absolutely dangerous because caffeine is a stimulant.
  d. You can hide the effects of alcohol behind caffeine.

2 Anemia and coffee _____.
  a. have nothing to do with each other
  b. have something in common
  c. have something to do with each other
  d. are not related to each other

3 Choose the correct words for each sentence.
  a. How long does it take for anesthesia to <u>wear off / go out / sober up</u>?
  b. How many children are <u>suffered by / suffering into / suffering from</u> hunger today?
  c. No matter what song you sing and no matter <u>how / what / when</u> well you do, I will not choose you as the winner.

LEARNING BOARD

① Some people think coffee will help them sober up. ② They think if they drink a cup of coffee after drinking, 1) the alcohol will wear off (sooner than normal), or (at least) 2) they can hide the effects of alcohol behind caffeine. ③ But, that's a myth. ④ No matter how much coffee you drink, 1) the slow reaction time and 2) poor judgment (caused by alcohol) cannot be 1) worn off or 2) hidden by caffeine. ⑤ Furthermore, the rumor (about coffee's effect of increasing energy) is also a myth. ⑥ The reason why some feel that coffee makes them feel energized is that they think they feel less sleepy after drinking coffee. ⑦ It is true that coffee does make you 1) wake up and 2) be more alert, because caffeine is a stimulant. ⑧ So, you could 1) work better or 2) study late at night with the help of coffee. ⑨ The relation between anemia and coffee, however, is not a myth. ⑩ As a matter of fact, coffee can cause a loss of vitamins and minerals (such as vitamin C, calcium, zinc, and iron). ⑪ So, if you suffer from anemia (iron deficiency), you should steer clear of coffee.

Words & Expressions

sober a. 술 취하지 않은 v. 정신이 들게 하다 **sober up** 술이 깨게 하다 **wear off** (서서히, 닳아) 없어지다, 사라지다 **slow reaction time** 느린 반응 속도 **increase** 증가시키다, 늘리다 **energize** 열기, 활력을 돋우다 **wake up** 잠을 깨우다, 정신이 들게 하다 **alert** 정신이 맑은, 경계하는 **stimulant** 자극제 **calcium** 칼슘 **zinc** 아연 **iron** 철, 철분 **anemia** 빈혈 **iron deficiency** 철분 결핍 **steer clear of** 피하다

Listening with Dictation

51 Did You Know A Myth About The Common Cold?

The most common myth about the cold is that vitamin C can prevent a cold. Many people _____ _____¹ a large amount of vitamin C will prevent a cold or at least _____². So, parents often make their kids eat fruits containing lots of vitamin C when they _____³. Doctors and scientists have conducted many studies and experiments to test this common cold myth. The results said that it's just a myth. _____ _____⁴, there is no conclusive data to prove that a large amount of vitamin C prevents a cold. But, the vitamin may still _____⁵ cold symptoms, even though _____⁶ this. If you want to get over a cold sooner, a bowl of hot chicken soup can help. Chicken soup for colds is not a myth; it is _____⁷ solid medical evidence, as it has an _____⁸. For your information, taking too much vitamin C, and for too long, may not be good for your health. _____⁹ good for health, it could actually be harmful, because excessive doses of vitamin C can cause _____¹⁰, which is very dangerous especially for elderly people and young children.

52 Did You Know 'Never Eat Before Exercise' Is A Myth?

It is better to eat a small amount of food _____¹ starting a workout, because fuel is required to _____² for your body. You _____³ food and drinks. _____⁴ food will prepare your muscles for the activities that are to come. Fill up your tank with some fruits or drinks, such as bananas, nuts, or a cup of water. There are other myths about exercise. People believe that you must stretch _____ _____⁵. But, several studies have shown that stretching sometimes _____⁶, since lengthened muscle fibers _____⁷ strain. Also, some women fear that if they work out, their fat will _____ _____⁸ muscle. They believe that lifting weights will surely make their bodies bulky and muscular. But, fat and muscle tissues _____⁹, so that's an absolute myth and _____¹⁰ not working out.

53 Did You Know Reading In Dim Light Is Not A Cause Of Eye Damage?

Reading _____¹, and reading very small print for a long time, are not causes of eye damage. Of course, your eyes will surely _____², exhausted, or uncomfortable, or become bloodshot by doing that. But, those bad reading habits will not cause permanent eye damage. Nevertheless, eye fatigue is not good for your eye health. Doctors _____³ that eye fatigue from overuse or misuse can _____ _____⁴. Also, the way you use your eyes early in life can affect your vision. In order to _____⁵, read books or newspapers in a _____⁶, and take a break from time to time to _____⁷. _____⁸, sitting too close to the TV or wearing someone else's glasses also will not hurt your eyes. Sitting close to the TV may lead to nearsightedness, but there is no evidence that these two behaviors cause permanent damage to your eyes. There is another myth about eyes : carrots. Carrots are rich in beta carotene, which is changed into vitamin A in the body. Vitamin A _____⁹ maintaining normal vision, so _____ _____¹⁰ is a main cause of blindness. Despite this, eating supplementary carrots will not improve your eyesight.

54 Did You Know Whitening Toothpastes Do Not Whiten Your Teeth?

You know that not all commercials are true. Whitening tooth pastes wash the surfaces of your teeth, _____¹ coffee, tea, and food. _____² in the toothpaste remove the stains. This makes your teeth look whiter, not makes them white. So, _____³ a not only a myth, but also a kind of _____⁴. There is another myth that toothpastes are all the same. That is a myth. Some toothpastes contain more abrasive materials, dyes, alcohol or _____⁵ and flavors than others. Some contain fluoride, some don't. According to the experts, toothpastes with no alcohol, no dyes, and less abrasives are better. _____⁶, many people believe that fluoride toothpastes are better than non-fluoride toothpastes. This is not a myth, because it is true that the use of fluoride is closely related to _____⁷. However, the common toothpaste myth of 'the more I use, the better' is not true. The more toothpaste you use, _____⁸. The important things are _____⁹ you brush your teeth, and the quality of the toothpaste and the brush – not the amount of the toothpaste and _____¹⁰.

55 Did You Know Coffee Won't Help You Sober Up?

Some people think coffee will help them _____¹. They think if they drink a cup of coffee after drinking, the alcohol will wear off sooner than normal, or at least they can hide the effects of alcohol behind caffeine. But, that's a myth. No matter how much coffee you drink, the slow reaction time and _____² caused by alcohol cannot _____³ or hidden by caffeine. Furthermore, the rumor about coffee's _____⁴ is also a myth. _____⁵ some feel that coffee makes them feel energized is that they think they _____⁶ after drinking coffee. It is true that coffee does make you wake up and be more alert, because caffeine is a stimulant. So, you could work better or study late at night with the help of coffee. _____⁷ anemia and coffee, however, is not a myth. As a matter of fact, coffee can _____⁸ vitamins and minerals such as vitamin C, calcium, zinc, and iron. So, if you _____⁹ (iron deficiency), you should _____¹⁰ coffee.

---

51 정답 1. are convinced that 2. relieve cold symptoms 3. caught a cold 4. Currently 5. alleviate 6. there is no clear evidence of 7. a fact backed up with 8. anti-inflammatory effect 9. Far from being 10. diarrhea

52 정답 1. prior to 2. provide the needed energy 3. get that fuel from 4. A proper portion of 5. before a workout 6. leads to injury 7. are more susceptible to 8. turn into 9. are totally different 10. a lame excuse for

53 정답 1. in dim light 2. feel tired 3. do not exclude the possibility 4. ruin your eyesight 5. reduce eye fatigue 6. well-lit room 7. let your eyes rest for a while 8. Likewise 9. is crucial for 10. a vitamin A deficiency

54 정답 1. stained by 2. Abrasive ingredients 3. what the commercials say 4. exaggerated advertisement 5. artificial sweeteners 6. Additionally 7. fewer dental cavities 8. the more money you waste 9. the way 10. foam

55 정답 1. sober up 2. poor judgment 3. be worn off 4. effect of increasing energy 5. The reason why 6. feel less sleepy 7. The relation between 8. cause a loss of 9. suffer from anemia 10. steer clear of

56 Did You Know Cell Phones Have Nothing To Do With Gas Station Fires?

Back in the 90s, a person who had lots of time sent phony e-mails to people claiming that Shell Oil issued a warning about the dangers of using cell phones at gas stations. Since then, quite a lot of people have blamed cell phones for sudden gasoline fires. However, Shell Oil didn't issue such a warning, and Shell said they have 'never heard of such incidents.'

The investigations proved that the cause of sudden fires at the pumps was actually static electricity. According to the experts, the static electricity emitted from cell phones is not strong enough to ignite the gasoline, which means the idea that 'cell phones cause fires at the pumps' is just a myth. But, using or turning on your cell phone can possibly release some static electricity. Although it's not enough to ignite anything, gas station owners and cell phone manufacturers tend to take the safer road. So, they ask their customers not to use cell phones while pumping gas, saying 'better safe than sorry.'

FYI, the warning that 'smoking can cause a fire at a gas station' is definitely not a myth. Never smoke at a gas station.

1 What can be the best title of this story?

a. Warning! Don't Even Think Of Using Cell Phones At The Pumps
b. Smokers, The Real Suspect
c. Another Myth Busted : You Can Smoke At The Pumps!
d. Sudden Gasoline Fires : Who Is To Blame?

2 According to the passage, which sentence is right?

a. Shell Oil issued a warning about the dangers of using cell phones at the pumps.
b. The cause of sudden fires at the pumps was static electricity released from cell phones.
c. You need strong static electricity to ignite the fire.
d. 'Smoking while pumping gas is dangerous' is a total myth.

3 Choose the correct words for each sentence.

a. No need to hurry up. You have a large number of / lots of / as many as time.
b. Dont' blame me on / for / to this. You just want to find someone to blame for your mistake.
c. How can you possible / possibly / possibility know what I said to my boss? I just talked to him a minute ago.

LEARNING BOARD

① Back in the 90s, a person (who had lots of time) sent phony e-mails to people claiming that Shell Oil issued a warning about the dangers of using cell phones at gas stations.

② Since then, quite a lot of people have blamed cell phones for sudden gasoline fires.

③ However, Shell Oil didn't issue such a warning, and Shell said they had 'never heard of such incidents.' ④ The investigations proved that the cause of sudden fires (at the pumps) was actually static electricity. ⑤ According to the experts, the static electricity (emitted from cell phones) is not strong (enough to ignite the gasoline), which means the idea (that 'cell phones cause fires at the pumps') is just a myth. ⑥ But, using or turning on your cell phone can possibly release some static electricity. ⑦ Although it's not enough to ignite anything, gas station owners and cell phone manufacturers tend to take the safer road. ⑧ So, they ask their customers not to use cell phones while pumping gas, saying 'better safe than sorry.' ⑨ FYI, the warning (that 'smoking can cause a fire at a gas station') is definitely not a myth.

⑩ Never smoke at a gas station.

Words & Expressions

phony 가짜의, 위조된(=fake) **issue** v. 발표하다. 공표하다. 발부하다. 발행하다 n. 주제, 안건, 문제, 발행 **gas station** 주유소 (= pump) **blame** 비난하다, …탓으로 돌리다 **investigation** 조사 **static** 고정된, 정적인 **static electricity** 정전기 **emit** (빛, 전기, 소리, 가스 등을) 내다. 내뿜다 **ignite** 점화하다. 불을 붙이다(cf. ignition 점화장치) **gasoline** 휘발유(=petrol), 가솔린(cf. diesel 디젤, 경유) **turn on** 켜다 **release** 방출하다 **manufacturer** 제조업자 **cell phone**(= cellular phone) 휴대폰 **take the safer road** 안전한 길을 선택하다 **customer** 손님, 고객(cf. consumer 소비자) **FYI** 참고로 (for your information) **definitely** 분명히, 틀림없이, 절대

57 Did You Know You Should Not Tilt Your Head Back When Your Nose Is Bleeding?

There are several medical myths you may want to know. When you have a nosebleed, it's not a very good idea to tilt your head back. Many people believe this will help stop the bleeding, but it's just a myth since it may actually cause blood to run into the throat and lead you to feel nauseous and vomit. The right way to stop a nosebleed is to tip your head forward and pinch your nostrils firmly with your fingers.

People think that when you are sick, you should lie down. Generally, this is true. But, sometimes it can be a myth, especially in the case of a heart attack. It sounds right that a person who is having a heart attack should lie down immediately, but lying down can make it more difficult to breathe. When having a heart attack, sitting with your knees bent is better than lying down before going to the hospital.

One more thing: quite a few parents still warn their kids not to swallow chewing gum. They believe the gum will stick to their intestines, but that's a myth. It is true that the gum base remains indigestible, but it passes out of the digestive system harmlessly.

1 What is the main idea of the story?
   a. Heart attack patients have to tilt their head back whenever possible.
   b. If you want your blood to run into the throat, buy a pack of chewing gum.
   c. Incorrect medical information can be dangerous or even fatal.
   d. When you suffer from a disease, you should lie down.

2 You will feel nauseous and vomit if you _____.
   a. pinch your nose strongly
   b. lie down in case of a heart attack
   c. tilt your head back when you have a nosebleed
   d. swallow chewing gums

3 Choose the correct words for each sentence.
   a. I almost vomited / throwing up / pukes after listening to Paul's cheesy pick-up lines such as 'your legs must be tired because you've been running through my mind all day.'
   b. Bleed / Bleeding / blood, a.k.a. hemorrhaging, means the loss of blood.
   c. First lay your book on the table and lie / lying / laid down on the couch.

LEARNING BOARD

① There are several medical myths you may want to know. ② When you have a nosebleed, it's not a very good idea to tilt your head back. ③ Many people believe this will help stop the bleeding, but it's just a myth since it may actually 1) cause blood to run into the throat and 2) lead you to feel nauseous and vomit. ④ The right way to stop a nosebleed is to 1) tip your head forward and 2) pinch your nostrils firmly with your fingers.

⑤ People think that when you are sick, you should lie down. ⑥ Generally, this is true. ⑦ But, sometimes it can be a myth, especially in case of a heart attack. ⑧ It sounds right that a person who is having a heart attack should lie down immediately, but lying down can make it more difficult to breathe. ⑨ When having a heart attack, sitting with your knees bent is better than lying down before going to the hospital.

⑩ One more thing: quite a few parents still warn their kids not to swallow chewing gum. ⑪ They believe the gum will stick to their intestines, but that's a myth. ⑫ It is true that the gum base remains indigestible, but it passes out of the digestive system harmlessly.

Words & Expressions

medical 의학의 **nosebleed** 코피 **tilt** 기울이다 **tilt one's head back** 고개를 뒤로 젖히다 **bleeding** 출혈 (cf. **bleed** 피를 흘리다) **blood** 피, 혈액) **nausea** 메스꺼움 **nauseous** 메스꺼운 **vomit** 토하다 **tip** v. 기울이다 n. 뾰족한 끝, 봉사료, 조언 **pinch** 꼬집다, 꽉 쥐다 **nostril** 콧구멍 **firmly** 꽉, 힘주어 **sick** 아픈, 병든 **lie down** (바닥에) 눕다 **heart attack** 심장마비 **immediately** 당장, 즉시, 즉각 **swallow** v. 삼키다 n. 제비 **chew** 씹다 **stick to** ...에 들러붙다 **indigestible** 소화되지 않은(=undigestible) **digestive system** 소화기관 **digest** 소화하다, 소화되다 **harmlessly** 해가 없이, 해롭지 않게

163

58 Did You Know What The Most Common Food Allergy Among Children Is?

Many people think a peanut allergy is the most common food allergy among children. That's not true. Although it is easy to find people who are allergic to peanuts, and allergic reactions to peanuts are highly threatening, the most common food allergy among children is a cow's milk allergy.

There's another myth about allergies. Some people say, 'I'm allergic to cat (or other furry animals) fur.' In many cases, they are allergic not to the fur but to a certain protein in the animal's saliva or in the flakes of its skin. Additionally, 'being too clean can be the cause of an allergy' might not be a myth since there is something called the hygiene hypothesis. The hygiene hypothesis suggests that super-clean modern lifestyles may be responsible for an increase in allergies among young children. Thanks to germ-free lifestyles, human bodies don't need to fight germs as much as they did in the past. As a result, the immune system, which hasn't been exposed to various bacteria or fungi, tends to overreact or respond sensitively to not-so-harmful substances such as pollen or mites. In fact, children who are frequently exposed to bacteria and viruses tend to have fewer allergies than children who aren't.

1 What is the main idea of the story?

a. People who are allergic to cat fur must avoid all kinds of furry animals.
b. There are several false myths about allergies.
c. An extremely-clean lifestyle is the main cause of a peanut allergy.
d. Human's immune system must be exposed to various bacteria.

2 According to the passage, which sentence is <u>wrong</u>?

a. The most common food allergy in children is a cow's milk allergy.
b. There is no such thing as the hygiene hypothesis, although some people think there is.
c. Allergic reactions to peanuts could be very dangerous and serious.
d. People who claim they are allergic to cat fur are likely to be allergic to a protein in its saliva.

3 Choose the correct words for each sentence.

a. Thanks to you helped us / your help / help us, we have tickets to the concert.
b. What part of the brain is responsible to / for / of memory?
c. I wonder, does Jack hate / dislikes / cursed me as much as he says he does?

LEARNING BOARD

① Many people think a peanut allergy is the most common food allergy among children. ② That's not true. ③ Although ¹⁾ it is easy to find people (who are allergic to peanuts), and ²⁾ allergic reactions to peanuts are highly threatening, the most common food allergy (among children) is a cow's milk allergy.

④ There's another myth about allergies. ⑤ Some people say, 'I'm allergic to cat (or other furry animals) fur.' ⑥ In many cases, they are allergic not to the fur but to a certain protein (in the animal's saliva or in the flakes of its skin). ⑦ Additionally, 'being too clean can be the cause of an allergy' might not be a myth since there is something (called the hygiene hypothesis). ⑧ The hygiene hypothesis suggests that super-clean modern lifestyles may be responsible for an increase in allergies (among young children). ⑨ Thanks to germ-free lifestyles, human bodies don't need to fight germs as much as they did in the past. ⑩ As a result, the immune system, (which hasn't been exposed to various bacteria or fungi,) tends to overreact or respond sensitively to not-so-harmful substances (such as pollen or mites). ⑪ In fact, children (who are frequently exposed to bacteria and viruses) tend to have fewer allergies than children (who aren't).

Words & Expressions

peanut 땅콩 **allergy** 알레르기 **be allergic to** …에 알레르기가 있다 **allergic reaction** 알레르기 반응 **threatening** 위협적인 (**threaten** 위협하다 **threat** 위협) **fur** (동물의) 털 **furry** 털로 덮인 **protein** 단백질 **saliva** 침 **flake** (떨어져 나온 얇은) 조각 **hygiene** 위생 (**hygienic** 위생적인) **hypothesis** 가설, 추측 **suggest** 말하다, (뜻을) 비치다 **be responsible for** …에 책임이 있다 **increase** 증가, 늘다 (↔ decrease, 감소, 줄다) **germ-free** 세균이 없는 **germ** 세균, 미생물 **immune system** 면역 체계 **be exposed to** …에 노출되다 **various** 다양한 **fungi** 곰팡이 (fungus의 복수형) **overreact** 과잉반응을 보이다 **respond** 반응하다, 대답하다 **sensitively** 민감하게 **pollen** 꽃가루 **mite** 진드기 **frequently** 자주, 흔히

165

59 Did You Know The Majority Of The Sugar We Consume Is Not From Sweets?

Parents tell their children 'cut down on sweets because they contain lots of sugar.' That's true. Many sweets contain too much sugar — that's why they are called 'sweets'. But at the same time, that's a myth. If you want to cut down on sugar, you have to stop drinking sodas and drinks like sports beverages. Those sweetened drinks are the major offenders. Most schools in the US haven't gotten rid of all soda vending machines in schools for nothing.

Furthermore, many adults believe that sugar makes their kids severely active. But, according to many studies, that's a myth. Kids are prone to go a bit crazy, bouncing on the sofa and yelling loudly during their birthday parties. That's not because they eat lots of sugary sweets such as cakes, cookies and candies, but

because kids just want to have fun. It has been officially proven that sugar doesn't make kids hyperactive.

However, several other rumors about sugar are true. For instance, sugar does cause heart diseases, raise your cancer risk, and even make you look old. So it's a good idea for your health not to eat too much sugar.

1 What is the main idea of the story?

  a. Sugar is evil because it makes kids crazy.
  b. The best way to cut down on sugar is to stop eating cookies and candies
  c. You had better watch out for sugar you consume and sodas you drink.
  d. If you want to look old, steer clear of sugar.

2 Many schools in the US get rid of soda vending machines in schools since _____.

  a. students are poor and sodas are expensive
  b. sodas turn students into fools and idiots
  c. sweet sodas make students hyperactive
  d. sodas contain an excessive amount of sugar

3 Choose the correct words for each sentence.

  a. You are building a house <u>for nothing / for something / for free</u> since nobody wants to live in.
  b. Before taking pictures, check how <u>many / much / few</u> light is there.
  c. Anyone who wants to raise chickens has to <u>rise / raise / rose</u> money to buy eggs and to build a hen house.

LEARNING BOARD

① Parents tell their children 'cut down on sweets because they contain lots of sugar.' ② That's true. ③ Many sweets contain too much sugar — that's why they are called 'sweets'. ④ But at the same time, that's a myth. ⑤ If you want to cut down on sugar, you have to stop drinking sodas and drinks (like sports beverages.) ⑥ Those sweetened drinks are the major offenders. ⑦ Most schools (in the US) haven't gotten rid of all soda vending machines in schools for nothing. ⑧ Furthermore, many adults believe that sugar makes their kids severely active. ⑨ But, according to many studies, that's a myth. ⑩ Kids are prone to go a bit crazy, (bouncing on the sofa and yelling loudly) during their birthday parties. ⑪ That's not because they eat lots of sugary sweets (such as cakes, cookies and candies), but because kids just want to have fun. ⑫ It has been officially proven that sugar doesn't make kids hyperactive. ⑬ However, several other rumors (about sugar) are true. ⑭ For instance, sugar does 1) cause heart diseases, 2) raise your cancer risk, and even 3) make you look old. ⑮ So it's a good idea for your health not to eat too much sugar.

Words & Expressions

cut down on ...를 줄이다 sweets 단 것, 단 음식들 contain 함유하다 at the same time 동시에 soda 탄산음료, 소다수 drink 음료, 마실 것 beverage 마실 것, 음료 sports beverage 스포츠음료 sweetened 단맛이 가미된 offender 범죄자 major offender (...의) 주범 get rid of 없애다 vending machine 자동판매기 severely 몹시, 심하게 (severe 엄한, 극심한) be prone to ...하는 경향이 있다 bounce 깡충깡충 뛰다, (수표가) 부도 처리되다 yell 고함치다 loudly 크게, 소란스럽게 officially 공식적으로 hyperactive 활동 과잉의 for instance 예를 들어 heart disease 심장병 cancer 암

167

Did You Know There's No Need To Worry When You Die In Your Dreams?

There is a myth that if you die in your dreams, you'll die in real life. Fortunately, that's just a myth. We often wake up suddenly while falling off a cliff, or everything abruptly stops at the moment of being hit by a bullet while dreaming. Those kinds of dreams are also included in dreams about dying. Given the fact that there are many dreams that we cannot remember, it's safe to say that almost every person has dreamed about dying. But, it's hard to find people who actually died after having a dream in which they died. So, if you have never dreamed those kinds of scary dreams yet, it's nothing to worry about.

By the way, there's an interesting myth about dreams. Some people say we can't control our dreams, but that's another false myth because some people can. It is called "lucid dreaming." Amazingly, approximately 10% of people can control their dreams or realize they are dreaming when they are dreaming. These people actually manage to control what they want to dream about, or change an existing dream into a different one.

1 What can be the best title of this story?

a. No Need To Worry About Dreams About Death
b. The Truth About Lucid Dreaming Finally Revealed
c. Control Your Dream? It's Like A Dream Comes True!
d. How To Control Your Dream

2 According to the passage, which sentence is right?

a. Almost every person has dreamed about dying.
b. If you train hard, you will control your dreams just as you wish.
c. It is impossible to change an existing dream into a different one.
d. The experts of lucid dreaming don't have a scary dream.

3 Choose the correct words for each sentence.

a. Sorry for being late. I just overslept and <u>waken / woke / wake</u> up late.
b. I am so depressed and exhausted that I can't do <u>which / what / when</u> I'm supposed to do.
c. About a couple of days ago, Nancy <u>dream / dreaming / dreamed</u> she was being attacked by her own brother.

LEARNING BOARD

① There is a myth that if you die in your dreams, you'll die in real life.

② Fortunately, that's just a myth. ③ We often wake up suddenly while falling off a cliff, or everything abruptly stops (at the moment of being hit) by (a bullet) while dreaming. ④ Those kinds of dreams are also included in dreams about dying.

⑤ Given the fact that there are many dreams (that we cannot remember), it's safe to say that almost every person has dreamed about dying. ⑥ But, it's hard to find people (who actually died after having a dream in which they died). ⑦ So, if you have never dreamed those kinds of scary dreams yet, it's nothing to worry about.

⑧ By the way, there's an interesting myth about dreams. ⑨ Some people say we can't control our dreams, but that's another false myth because some people can. ⑩ It is called "lucid dreaming." ⑪ Amazingly, approximately 10% of people can 1) control their dreams or 2) realize they are dreaming when they are dreaming.

⑫ These people actually manage to 1) control what they want to dream about, or 2) change an existing dream into a different one.

Words & Expressions

in real life 실제 현실(삶)에서 **fortunately** 다행스럽게도 **wake up** 잠에서 깨다, 깨우다 **cliff** 절벽 **abruptly** 갑자기, 불쑥 (=suddenly) **the moment of** …하는 순간 **bullet** 총알 **scary** 무서운 (cf. scared 겁먹은) **by the way** 그건 그렇고 **control** 통제 · 관리하다 **false** 잘못된, 틀린 **lucid** 명쾌한, 의식이 명확한 **amazingly** 놀랍게도 **approximately** 대략, 약

Listening with Dictation

56 Did You Know Cell Phones Have Nothing To Do With Gas Station Fires?

_____ ¹ in the 90s, a person who had lots of time _____ ² to people claiming that Shell Oil _____ ³ about the dangers of using cell phones at gas stations. Since then, quite a lot of people have blamed cell phones for sudden gasoline fires. However, Shell Oil didn't issue such a warning, and Shell said they had 'never heard of such incidents.' The investigations proved that the cause of sudden fires at the pumps was actually _____ ⁴. According to the experts, the static electricity _____ ⁵ cell phones is not strong enough to ignite the gasoline, which means the idea that 'cell phones cause fires at the pumps' is just a myth. But, using or _____ ⁶ can possibly release some static electricity. Although it's _____ ⁷ anything, gas station owners and cell phone manufacturers tend to _____ ⁸. So, they ask their customers not to use cell phones while pumping gas, saying '_____ ⁹.' FYI, the warning that 'smoking can _____ ¹⁰ at a gas station' is definitely not a myth. Never smoke at a gas station.

57 Did You Know You Should Not Tilt Your Head Back When Your Nose Is Bleeding?

There are several medical myths you may want to know. When you _____ ¹, it's not a very good idea to _____ ². Many people believe this will _____ ³, but it's just a myth since it may actually cause blood to run into the throat and lead you to _____ ⁴ and vomit. The right way to stop a nosebleed is to tip your head forward and pinch your nostrils firmly with your fingers. People think that when you are sick, you should lie down. Generally, this is true. But, sometimes it can be a myth, especially _____ ⁵ a heart attack. _____ ⁶ that a person who is having a heart attack should lie down immediately, but lying down can _____ ⁷ breathe. When having a heart attack, sitting with your knees bent is better than _____ ⁸ before going to the hospital. One more thing: quite a few parents still warn their kids not to swallow chewing gum. They believe the gum will stick to their intestines, but that's a myth. It is true that the gum base _____ ⁹, but it passes out of the _____ ¹⁰ harmlessly.

58 Did You Know What The Most Common Food Allergy Among Children Is?

Many people think a peanut allergy is _____ ¹ among children. That's not true. Although it is easy to find people who are allergic to peanuts, and _____ ² peanuts are _____ ³, the most common food allergy among children is a cow's milk allergy. There's another myth about allergies. Some people say, 'I'm allergic to cat (or other furry animals) fur.' In many cases, they are allergic not to the fur but to a certain protein in the animal's saliva or in the flakes of its skin. Additionally, 'being too clean can be the cause of an allergy' _____ ⁴ since there is something called the _____ ⁵. The hygiene hypothesis suggests that super-clean modern lifestyles may _____ ⁶ an increase in allergies among young children. Thanks to germ-free lifestyles, human bodies don't need to _____ ⁷ as much as they did in the past. As a result, _____ ⁸, which hasn't been exposed to various bacteria or fungi, tends to overreact or _____ ⁹ to not-so-harmful substances such as pollen or mites. In fact, children who _____ ¹⁰ bacteria and viruses tend to have fewer allergies than children who aren't.

59 Did You Know The Majority Of The Sugar We Consume Is Not From Sweets?

Parents tell their children '_____¹ sweets because they contain lots of sugar.' That's true. Many sweets contain too much sugar – that's why they are called 'sweets'. But at the same time, that's a myth. If you want to cut down on sugar, you have to _____² sodas and drinks like sports beverages. Those sweetened drinks are _____³. Most schools in the US _____⁴ all soda vending machines in schools for nothing. _____⁵, many adults believe that sugar makes their kids severely active. But, according to many studies, that's a myth. Kids _____⁶ go a bit crazy, bouncing on the sofa and yelling loudly during their birthday parties. That's not because they eat lots of sugary sweets such as cakes, cookies and candies, but because kids just want to have fun. _____⁷ that sugar doesn't _____⁸. However, several other rumors about sugar are true. For instance, sugar _____⁹ cause heart diseases, _____¹⁰, and even make you look old. So it's a good idea for your health not to eat too much sugar.

60 Did You Know There's No Need To Worry When You Die In Your Dreams?

There is a myth that if you die in your dreams, you'll die _____¹. Fortunately, that's just a myth. We often _____² while falling off a cliff, or everything abruptly stops _____³ being hit by a bullet while dreaming. Those kinds of dreams _____⁴ dreams about dying. _____⁵ there are many dreams that we cannot remember, it's safe to say that _____⁶ has dreamed about dying. But, it's hard to find people who actually died after having a dream in which they died. So, if you _____⁷ those kinds of scary dreams yet, it's nothing to worry about. By the way, there's an interesting myth about dreams. Some people say we can't control our dreams, but that's another false myth because some people can. It is called "_____⁸." Amazingly, _____⁹ 10% of people can control their dreams or realize they are dreaming when they are dreaming. These people actually _____¹⁰ what they want to dream about, or change an existing dream into a different one.

---

56 정답 1. Back 2. sent phony e-mails 3. issued a warning 4. static electricity 5. emitted from 6. turning on your cell phone 7. not enough to ignite 8. take the safer road 9. better safe than sorry 10. cause a fire

57 정답 1. have a nosebleed 2. tilt your head back 3. help stop the bleeding 4. feel nauseous 5. in case of 6. It sounds right 7. make it more difficult to 8. lying down 9. remains indigestible 10. digestive system

58 정답 1. the most common food allergy 2. allergic reactions to 3. highly threatening 4. might not be a myth 5. hygiene hypothesis 6. be responsible for 7. fight germs 8. the immune system 9. respond sensitively 10. are frequently exposed to

59 정답 1. cut down on 2. stop drinking 3. the major offenders 4. haven't gotten rid of 5. Furthermore 6. are prone to 7. It has been officially proven 8. make kids hyperactive 9. does 10. raise your cancer risk

60 정답 1. in real life 2. wake up suddenly 3. at the moment of 4. are also included in 5. Given the fact that 6. almost every person 7. have never dreamed 8. lucid dreaming 9. approximately 10. manage to control

Chapter 7. The Supernatural

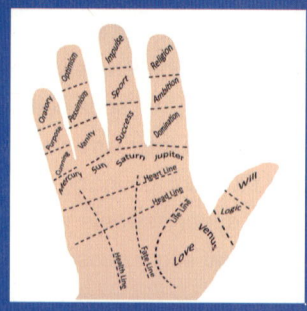

61. Did You Know There Is Palm Reading In Western Culture?

서구 문화에서도 손금을 읽는다는 거 아세요?

62. Did You Know How Copperfield Made The Statue Of Liberty Disappear?

카퍼필드가 자유의 여신상을 어떻게 사라지게 했는지 아세요?

63. Did You Know How American Psychic Readers List Their Ads?

미국인 점술사들은 어떻게 광고하는지 아세요?

64. Did You Know The Tarot Was Originally Used To Play Card Games?

타로가 원래 카드 게임으로 사용되었다는 거 아세요?

65. Did You Know There Was A Film In Which The Ghost Of A Dog Appeared?

개 유령이 나타난 영화가 있다는 거 아세요?

66. Did You Know Your Face Reveals Your Personality?

당신의 얼굴이 당신의 성격을 드러낸다는 거 아세요?

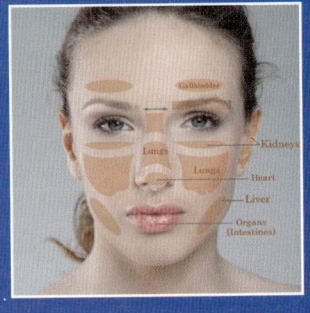

67. Did You Know It's Bad Luck To Let Milk Boil Over?

우유를 끓어 넘치게 하면 불운이라는 거 아세요?

68. Did You Know How Friday The 13th Became The Worst Day?

13일의 금요일이 어떻게 최악의 날이 되었는지 아세요?

69. Did You Know How Many People Died Because Of The Salem Witch Trials?

살렘 마녀 재판 때문에 몇 명이 사망했는지 아세요?

70. Did You Know About The Mystery 'Ghost' House?

미스터리 '유령'의 집을 아세요?

61 Did You Know There Is Palm Reading In Western Culture?

Do westerners believe in palm reading? Many people think that western culture is scientific and reasonable, far from being superstitious. But palm reading, also known as palmistry or chiromancy, has been practiced among western countries for a long time. Its roots can be found in Indian astrology and gypsy fortune-telling.

Some think they can see people's characters and futures by reading their palms. No one knows who started to study and read the lines on palms for the first time, but people around the world, including westerners, noticed there were lots of lines on palms and the lines were different from person to person. They thought these lines must have meant something and could reveal something.

Believe it or not, there are hundreds of books about palm reading in the US, Canada, UK, Germany, and others. It is easy to find some websites about palm reading on the Internet. Of course, you can also find palm readers in these western countries.

According to these sources, the four major lines are the heart line, the head line, the life line and the fate line. (Not everyone has the fate line.)

1 What can be the best title of this story?

a. To Read Or Not To Read : Everything About Palm Reading
b. Palm Readers : The messenger From Hell
c. Palm Readers In Custody
d. Palm Reading In Western Culture

2 Palm readers claim that they see people's character by _____.

a. reading some lines on their palms
b. searching hidden lines on their palms
c. making several lines on their palms
d. examining facial expressions

3 Choose the correct words for each sentence.

a. How much do I have to pay to place an ad <u>in / on / at</u> the internet?
b. Not everybody <u>have / has / having</u> a slim body like you.
c. Even though they believed <u>of / in / to</u> the broken mirror superstition, they pretended not to care about it.

174 **Chapter 7** | The Supernatural

LEARNING BOARD

① Do westerners believe in palm reading? ② Many people think that western culture is scientific and reasonable, far from being superstitious. ③ But palm reading, also known as palmistry or chiromancy, has been practiced among western countries for a long time. ④ Its roots can be found in Indian astrology and gypsy fortune-telling. ⑤ Some think they can see people's characters and futures by reading their palms. ⑥ No one knows who started to study and read the lines on palms for the first time, but people around the world, including westerners, noticed [1] there were lots of lines on palms and [2] the lines were different from person to person. ⑦ They thought these lines [1] must have meant something and [2] could reveal something. ⑧ Believe it or not, there are hundreds of books about palm reading in the US, Canada, UK, Germany, and others. ⑨ It is easy to find some websites about palm reading on the Internet. ⑩ Of course, you can also find palm readers in these western countries. ⑪ According to these sources, the four major lines are the heart line, the head line, the life line and the fate line. ⑫ Not everyone has the fate line.

Words & Expressions

palm 손바닥 palm reading 손금 읽기(= palmistry, chiromancy) westerner 서양사람 western 서구의 scientific 과학적인 reasonable 논리적인, 합리적인 superstitious 미신적인 astrology 점성술 fortune-telling 점 character 성격, 기질, 특징 from person to person 사람마다 reveal (비밀 등을) 드러내다 source 원천, 자료 fate 운명 fate line 운명선

Did You Know How Copperfield Made The Statue Of Liberty Disappear?

The Statue of Liberty did disappear in 1983. This magic show aired live on CBS and was performed by David Copperfield. When he made the statue disappear in front of the audience, viewers were amazed despite already being used to his awesome tricks such as the levitation of a car. How did he do it?

The audience sat in front of two pillars and the statue was seen in the distance between the two pillars. First, he lowered the curtain hung on the two pillars to make the audience unable to see the statue. When he raised the curtain, the people could no longer see the statue between the two pillars. It was absolutely shocking. Some claimed that the platform the audience was sitting on was a secretly moving platform like a turntable. They said it must have rotated very slowly while Copperfield had lowered the curtain. The audience and the TV viewers couldn't see the giant statue, but the fact would have been, they were looking at a duplicate of another stage. Or, Copperfield might have used a very bright light to make the audience temporarily become night blind for a few seconds.

Either way, the statue did not disappear after all. It was just not seen.

1 What is the main idea of the story?

a. Thanks to Copperfield, the Statue of Liberty should be rebuilt again.
b. Copperfield made the Statue of Liberty disappear by his trick.
c. The magician was under arrest for deceiving people around the world.
d. Copperfield was supposed to make the statute disappear, but he couldn't.

2 According to the passage, which sentence is right?

a. The Statue of Liberty disappeared in 1983 and never reappeared.
b. David Copperfield is famous but not popular due to his looks.
c. Some said Copperfield secretly used the moving platform to trick people.
d. Unlike the audience, the TV viewers weren't shocked when the statue disappeared.

3 Choose the correct words for each sentence.

a. The funeral for the president who died last weekend in London will be broadcasting at / aired on / airing through TV.
b. When I sat between / among / next to Jack and Jill, I totally felt like a third wheel.
c. Zack wanted to sue the chair manufacturer because the chair he sat on / sat / sitting in collapsed and he got injured.

LEARNING BOARD

① The Statue of Liberty did disappear in 1983. ② This magic show ¹⁾ aired live on CBS and ²⁾ was performed by David Copperfield. ③ When he made the statue disappear in front of the audience, viewers were amazed despite already being used to his awesome tricks (such as the levitation of a car). ④ How did he do it? ⑤ The audience sat (in front of two pillars), and the statue was seen in the distance between the two pillars. ⑥ First, he lowered the curtain (hung on the two pillars) to make the audience unable to see the statue. ⑦ When he raised the curtain, the people could no longer see the statue between the two pillars. ⑧ It was absolutely shocking. ⑨ Some claimed that the platform (the audience was sitting on) was a secretly moving platform (like a turntable). ⑩ They said it must have rotated very slowly while Copperfield had lowered the curtain. ⑪ The audience and the TV viewers couldn't see the giant statue, but the fact would have been, they were looking at a duplicate of another stage. ⑫ Or, Copperfield might have used a very bright light to make the audience (temporarily) become night blind (for a few seconds). ⑬ Either way, the statue did not disappear after all. ⑭ It was just not seen.

Words & Expressions

the Statue of Liberty 자유의 여신상 disappear 사라지다 air 방송하다 (on air 방송 중) audience 청중, 관객 viewer 시청자 awesome 경탄할 만한, 굉장한 (cf. awful 끔찍한, 지독한) trick 마술, 속임수 levitation 공중부양 pillar 기둥 raise 올리다, (자금을) 모금하다, 기르다 absolutely 굉장히, 참으로 claim 주장하다 rotate 회전하다 lower 낮추다, 내리다 duplicate 사본의, 똑같은, 사본 temporarily 일시적으로, 임시로 night blind 야맹(증)

63 Did You Know How American Psychic Readers List Their Ads?

There are psychic readers, or we can say, fortune-tellers in the USA, Canada, UK, and others. It's not hard to find their ads appearing on the Internet, in newspapers, or in magazines. Here is a sample of one such ad, to show how they promote their fortune-telling business.

Dora Charmcaster : Real Spiritual Psychic Reader, 35 years of experience.
Call today for a better tomorrow. Dora is here for you 24/7.
My services are 200% accurate, even other psychics consult me for advice.
- I offer various kinds of love spells, such as stay-faithful spells, make-someone-grow-feelings-for-me spells, prevent-my-lover-from-lying-to-me spells, and many more. You can also buy love potions for a reasonable price.
- I can help in all matters of life such as marriages, careers, law suits, health and even hair loss problems. I also do tarot card readings, aura cleansing, chakra balancing, and tea leaf readings. My specialty is past life readings.
* One free question for first time callers. Feel free to call me anytime. *

1 What can be the best title of this story?
a. How Western Psychic Readers Place Ads On The Internet
b. Dora Charmcaster : A Psychic Reader or A Psycho?
c. Call Dora Now For Your Better Future
d. Magical Love Potions For Sale

2 Other psychics seek Dora's advice because _____.
a. she is an accurate fortune teller
b. her love potions are cheap
c. the first time callers don't have to pay
d. Dora forces them to do that

3 Choose the correct words for each sentence.
a. After the storm clouds disappeared, the stars <u>appeared / appearing / were appeared</u> in the sky.
b. We need to do various <u>experiments / experiment / an experiment</u> to prove our theory.
c. Your <u>advise / advice / advised</u> for newlyweds is 'do not marry?'

LEARNING BOARD

① There are psychic readers, (or we can say, fortune-tellers) in the USA, Canada, UK, and others. ② It's not hard to find their ads appearing on the Internet, in newspapers, or in magazines. ③ Here is a sample of one such ad, to show how they promote their fortune-telling business. ④ Dora Charmcaster : Real Spiritual Psychic Reader, 35 years of experience. ⑤ Call today for a better tomorrow. ⑥ Dora is here for you 24/7. ⑦ My services are 200% accurate, even other psychics consult me for advice.

⑧ - I offer various kinds of love spells, (such as stay-faithful spells, make-someone-grow-feelings-for-me spells, prevent-my-lover-from-lying-to-me spells, and many more). ⑨ You can also buy love potions for a reasonable price.

⑩ - I can help in all matters of life (such as marriages, careers, law suits, health and even hair loss problems). ⑪ I also do 1) tarot card readings, 2) aura cleansing, 3) chakra balancing, and 4) tea leaf readings. ⑫ My specialty is past life readings.

⑬ * One free question for first time callers. ⑭ Feel free to call me anytime. *

Words & Expressions

psychic 초자연적인, 심령의 **psychic reader** 점 보는 사람, 심령술사(= fortune-teller) **ad** 광고(= advertisement) **magazine** 잡지 **promote** 홍보하다, 광고하다, 승진하다 **spiritual** 영적인 **experience** 경력, 경험 **accurate** 정확한 **consult** 상담하다 **advice** 조언, 충고 (cf advise 충고하다) **offer** 제공하다 **spell** 주문 **love spell** 사랑의 주문 **stay faithful** (상대가) 바람을 피우지 않다 **grow feelings for** ...에 대해 좋아하는 마음이 커지다 **and many more** 이외에 더 많다 **potion** 물약, 마법의 약 (cf. portion 몫, 1인분) **reasonable** 합리적인, 저렴한 **career** 직업, 직장생활 **law suit** 법적 소송 **hair loss** 탈모 **aura** (독특한) 분위기, 기운, 아우라 **cleansing** 정화, 깨끗하게 하기 **chakra** 차크라, 기 에너지 **tea leaf** 찻잎 **specialty** 전문, 전공 **past life** 전생

64 Did You Know The Tarot Was Originally Used To Play Card Games?

The tarot is a pack of cards now widely used in divination. But originally, the tarot was first used in games such as Triumphs and Italian tarocchini. Quite a few Europeans enjoyed these games during the 15th century. At that time, tarot cards were not used by occultists since they thought tarot cards did not have anything to do with magic or mysticism.

But from the late 18th century, people started to use tarot cards as a tool to gain insight into life issues or to read the future. It was said that a Swiss studied religious symbolism in the late 1700s. He thought the Tarot might be associated with Isis, a goddess in ancient Egypt, and Thoth, another of the ancient Egyptian deities. He claimed that the name "tarot" came from the Egyptian word meaning a "royal road". According to his claim, the tarot contained a royal road to secrets and hidden wisdom. Later, other scholars discovered that there was no foundation to prove his claim. Despite this, many people still firmly believe that the tarot is connected to the Egyptian Book of Thoth, and the tarot has been popularized by occult societies.

1 What can be the best title of this story?

a. The Tarot : From the Simple Game to the Tool for Divination
b. Tarot, A Royal Road To The Secret Hidden Wisdom
c. A Messenger From Thoth Meets The Tarot
d. The Secret Of The Tarot Revealed!

2 According to the passage, which sentence is right?

a. Generally, fortune-tellers and occultists use the tarot in divination.
b. The tarot has been used in both divination and games in all ages.
c. It was not until the early 18th century that people started to use the tarot to read the future.
d. Scholars finally figured out the relation between the tarot and the Egyptian Book of Thoth.

3 Choose the correct words for each sentence.

a. To my surprise, face transplants <u>now widely are accepted / are now widely accepted / are accepted now widely</u>.
b. <u>During the early 1900s / In the early 1900 / While early 1900s</u>, women's clothing was very much stylish and glamorous.
c. I thought his novel was <u>connected / connection / connect</u> to his personal experience but it had nothing to do with his experience.

LEARNING BOARD

① The tarot is a pack of cards (now widely used in divination). ② But originally, the tarot was first used in games (such as Triumphs and Italian tarocchini). ③ Quite a few Europeans enjoyed these games during the 15th century. ④ At that time, tarot cards were not used by occultists since they thought tarot cards did not have anything to do with magic or mysticism. ⑤ But from the late 18th century, people started to use tarot cards as a tool [1] to gain insight into life issues or [2] to read the future. ⑥ It was said that a Swiss studied religious symbolism (in the late 1700s). ⑦ He thought the Tarot might be associated with Isis, (a goddess in ancient Egypt), and Thoth, (another of the ancient Egyptian deities). ⑧ He claimed that the name "tarot" came from the Egyptian word (meaning a "royal road"). ⑨ According to his claim, the tarot contained a royal road to secrets and hidden wisdom. ⑩ Later, other scholars discovered that there was no foundation to prove his claim. ⑪ Despite this, many people still firmly believe that the tarot is connected to the Egyptian Book of Thoth, and the tarot has been popularized by occult societies.

Words & Expressions

tarot 타로 카드 originally 원래 a pack of cards 카드 한 팩(꾸러미) widely 널리 divination 점(= fortunetelling) occultist 비술(신비한 마술) 하는 사람 mysticism 신비주의 tool 도구 gain 얻다 insight 통찰력, 이해력 issues in life 삶의 문제 a Swiss 스위스 사람 religious 종교적인 symbolism 상징주의 goddess 여신 ancient 고대의 deity 신 ancient Egyptian deities 고대 이집트 신들 claim 주장하다; 주장 royal 왕족의 (cf. loyal 충성스러운) royal road 왕도 wisdom 지혜 scholar 학자 foundation 근거, 기초, 토대 firmly 굳게, 확고하게 be connected to …와 관련이 있다 popularize 대중화하다, 많은 사람들에게 알리다 occult 주술적인, 초자연적인 society 사회, 집단, 단체 occult society 주술인 모임[사회]

181

65 Did You Know There Was A Film In Which The Ghost Of A Dog Appeared?

In October 2011, some investigators claimed that they had found the spirit of a dog, Nigger, once owned by Guy Gibson, a heroic English pilot during the Second World War. The Dam Busters, filmed in 1954, was a war movie about the raid led by Wing Commander Guy Gibson. After this film was released, some people claimed that they could see a black dog running around behind the actors at the end of the film. People thought that the dog might be Nigger's ghost because there was no dog present during filming.

Before the film, there had been rumors that the black dog was seen near the burial place of Gibson, which is now part of the RAF Scampton Historical Museum. Furthermore, Gibson's old office, which hasn't been used for about 50 years, is said to be haunted by Gibson's ghost.

In 2011, the ghost hunters hit the road to find the spirit of Gibson's dog. Their search team, called Paranormal-lincs, investigated around the museum with equipment such as infra-red lights and video cameras in an attempt to catch a glimpse of the spirit of Gibson's dog. One of the investigators said that they felt 'the spectre of the dog's spirit' which tried to speak to them as they ran their electronic detection equipment.

1 What is the main idea of the story?

a. There is no such thing as the ghost of a dog or a haunted house.
b. There has been a rumor about the dog's ghost and some people claimed they felt it.
c. It is okay to go near the burying place of Gibson since nothing's there.
d. The Dam Busters was a war movie starred by Guy Gibson and Nigger.

2 When The Dam Busters was released, some people were surprised because _____.

a. the movie was filmed in the RAF Scampton Historical Museum, the haunted house
b. Nigger appeared on the movie with his owner Guy Gibson
c. the leading actor looked nothing like Guy Gibson
d. they saw the black dog in the movie although there was no dog during filming

3 Choose the correct words for each sentence.

a. I stayed up late last night to make / do / catch a glimpse of Helly's Commet.
b. It took me hours to set up lots of complicated equipments / complicated many equipment / lots of complicated equipment.
c. After the party pooper suddenly yelled 'the party is over!', people went home one by one and there was no one left at the end of the day / in the end that day / until the end of the day.
d. In Jacksville, there was a magic pear tree, owned to / by / from a greedy old farmer.

LEARNING BOARD

① In October 2011, some **investigators** claimed that they had **found** the **spirit** of a dog, Nigger, (once owned by Guy Gibson, a heroic English pilot) during the Second World War. ② The Dam Busters, (filmed in 1954), was a war movie about the **raid** (led by Wing **Commander** Guy Gibson). ③ After this **film** was **released**, some people claimed that they could see a black dog running around behind the actors at the end of the film. ④ People thought that the dog might be Nigger's ghost because there was no dog **present** during filming. ⑤ Before the film, there had been rumors that the black dog was seen near the **burial** place of Gibson, (which is now part of the RAF Scampton Historical Museum). ⑥ Furthermore, Gibson's old office, (which hasn't been used for about 50 years,) is said to **be haunted by** Gibson's **ghost**. ⑦ In 2011, the ghost hunters **hit the road** to find the spirit of Gibson's dog. ⑧ Their search team, (called Paranormal-lincs,) investigated around the museum with **equipment** (such as infra-red lights and video cameras) in an **attempt** to **catch a glimpse of** the spirit of Gibson's dog. ⑨ One of the investigators said that they felt 'the **spectre** of the dog's spirit' which tried to speak to them as they **ran** their **electronic** detection equipment.'

Words & Expressions

investigator 조사원, 수사관 **spirit** 유령, 영혼, 정신 **nigger** 흑인을 비하해 부르는 표현, 검둥이 (지문에서는 개의 이름으로 쓰였다) **own** 소유하다 **heroic** 영웅적인 **during the Second World War** 2차 세계 대전 중에 **dam** 댐 **buster** 폭파(파괴)시키는 것 **film** 영화, 영화를 찍다 **raid** 공습 **wing commander** (영국) 공군 중령 **release** (영화를) 개봉하다, 방출하다, 풀어주다 **burial place** 매장지 **haunt** 귀신이 출몰하다 **ghost hunter** 유령 사냥꾼 **hit the road** 출발하다, 길을 떠나다 **search team** 수색대 **investigate** 조사하다 (investigator 조사원) **equipment** 장비, 설비 **infra-red light** 적외선 **attempt** 시도 **catch a glimpse of** 잠깐(힐끗) 보다 **spectre/specter** 유령(=ghost) **electronic detection equipment** 전자 탐지 장비 **detection** 탐지

Listening with Dictation

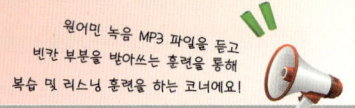

61 Did You Know There Is Palm Reading In Western Culture?

Do westerners _____¹ palm reading? Many people think that western culture is scientific and reasonable, _____². But palm reading, also known as palmistry or chiromancy, _____³ among western countries for a long time. Its roots can be found in Indian astrology and gypsy fortune-telling. Some think they can _____⁴ people's characters and futures _____⁵. No one knows who started to study and read the lines on palms for the first time, but people around the world, including westerners, noticed there were lots of lines on palms and the lines were different _____⁶. They thought these lines _____⁷ something and could reveal something. Believe it or not, there are hundreds of books about palm reading in the US, Canada, UK, Germany, and others. _____⁸ some websites about palm reading _____⁹. Of course, you can also find palm readers in these western countries. According to these sources, the four major lines are the heart line, the head line, the life line and the fate line. (_____¹⁰ the fate line.)

62 Did You Know How Copperfield Made The Statue Of Liberty Disappear?

The Statue of Liberty _____¹ in 1983. This magic show _____² CBS and was performed by David Copperfield. When he made the statue disappear in front of the audience, viewers were amazed _____³ his awesome tricks such as the levitation of a car. How did he do it? The audience sat in front of two pillars and the statue was seen in the distance between the two pillars. First, he _____⁴ the curtain hung on the two pillars to make the audience unable to see the statue. When he _____⁵ the curtain, the people _____⁶ the statue between the two pillars. It was absolutely shocking. Some claimed that the platform the audience was sitting _____⁷ was a secretly moving platform like a turntable. They said it must have rotated very slowly while Copperfield had lowered the curtain. The audience and the TV viewers couldn't see the giant statue, but the fact would have been, they were looking at _____⁸ another stage. Or, Copperfield might have used a very bright light to make the audience _____⁹ for a few seconds. _____¹⁰, the statue did not disappear after all. It was just not seen.

63 Did You Know How American Psychic Readers List Their Ads?

There are _____¹, or we can say, fortune-tellers in the USA, Canada, UK, and others. _____² their ads appearing on the Internet, in newspapers, or in magazines. Here is a sample of one such ad, to show how they promote their fortune-telling business. Dora Charmcaster : Real Spiritual Psychic Reader, 35 years of experience. Call today for a better tomorrow. Dora is here for you 24/7. My services are 200% accurate, even other psychics consult me _____³. - I _____⁴ various kinds of love spells, such as stay-faithful spells, make-someone-grow-feelings-for-me spells, prevent-my-lover-from-lying-to-me spells, and many more. You can also buy love potions _____⁵. - I can help in _____⁶ such as marriages, careers, _____⁷, health and even _____⁸ problems. I also do tarot card readings, aura cleansing, chakra balancing, and tea leaf readings. My _____⁹ is past life readings. * One free question for first time callers. _____¹⁰ call me anytime. *

64. Did You Know The Tarot Was Originally Used To Play Card Games?

The tarot is a pack of cards now widely used in divination. But _____¹, the tarot _____² games such as Triumphs and Italian tarocchini. Quite a few Europeans enjoyed these games during the 15th century. At that time, tarot cards were not used by occultists since they thought tarot cards _____³ magic or mysticism. But from the late 18th century, people started to use tarot cards as a tool to _____⁴ life issues or to read the future. It was said that a Swiss studied religious symbolism in the late 1700s. He thought the Tarot _____⁵ Isis, a goddess in ancient Egypt, and Thoth, another of the _____⁶. He claimed that the name "tarot" came from the Egyptian word meaning a "royal road". According to his claim, the tarot contained a royal road to secrets and hidden wisdom. Later, other scholars discovered that _____⁷ prove his claim. _____⁸ this, many people _____⁹ the tarot is connected to the Egyptian Book of Thoth, and the tarot _____¹⁰ occult societies.

65. Did You Know There Was A Film In Which The Ghost Of A Dog Appeared?

In October 2011, some investigators claimed that they had found the spirit of a dog, Nigger, _____¹ Guy Gibson, a heroic English pilot during the Second World War. The Dam Busters, _____² 1954, was a war movie about _____³ Wing Commander Guy Gibson. After this _____⁴, some people claimed that they could see a black dog running around behind the actors at the end of the film. People thought that the dog might be Nigger's ghost because _____⁵ during filming. Before the film, _____⁶ the black dog was seen near the burial place of Gibson, which is now part of the RAF Scampton Historical Museum. Furthermore, Gibson's old office, which _____⁷ for about 50 years, is said to be haunted by Gibson's ghost. In 2011, the ghost hunters _____⁸ to find the spirit of Gibson's dog. Their search team, called Paranormal-lincs, investigated around the museum with equipment such as infra-red lights and video cameras in an attempt to _____⁹ the spirit of Gibson's dog. One of the investigators said that they felt 'the spectre of the dog's spirit' which tried to speak to them as they _____¹⁰ their electronic detection equipment.

---

61 정답
1. believe in 2. far from being superstitious 3. has been practiced 4. see 5. by reading their palms
6. from person to person 7. must have meant 8. It is easy to find 9. on the Internet 10. Not everyone has

62 정답
1. did disappear 2. aired live on 3. despite already being used to 4. lowered 5. raised
6. could no longer see 7. on 8. a duplicate of 9. temporarily become night blind 10. Either way

63 정답
1. psychic readers 2. It's not hard to find 3. for advice 4. offer 5. for a reasonable price
6. all matters of life 7. law suits 8. hair loss 9. specialty 10. Feel free to

64 정답
1. originally 2. was first used in 3. did not have anything to do with 4. gain insight into 5. might be associated with
6. ancient Egyptian deities 7. there was no foundation to 8. Despite 9. still firmly believe that 10. has been popularized by

65 정답
1. once owned by 2. filmed in 3. the raid led by 4. film was released 5. there was no dog present
6. there had been rumors that 7. hasn't been used 8. hit the road 9. catch a glimpse of 10. ran

66 Did You Know Your Face Reveals Your Personality?

"Personology" or "physiognomy" believers think you can and should judge a book by its cover. These face readers believe they can know and judge you by your facial features since the features on your face reveal what kind of person you are.

For example, they can figure out a person's character by his or her eyebrows. People with dark black or bow-looking eyebrows are likely to have a good character. Flat and fat eyebrows mean 'cold-blooded' while soft and narrow eyebrows mean 'a daydreamer'. People with thin eyebrows are said to be arrogant, while people with thick and scattered eyebrows are thought to be aggressive. Additionally, face readers claim that they can uncover your health condition since they believe internal organs are related to facial parts. They think, for example, that the nose is related to the heart, and the lower lip is related to the intestines. So, if your lower lip bulges, face readers may say you have constipation or tend to have loose bowels.

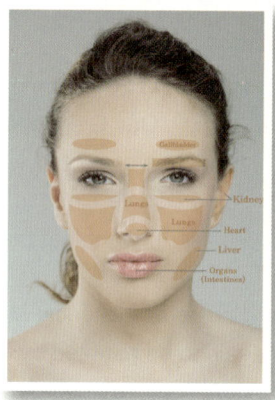

But face reading is not always right. There are generous and kind people with flat and fat eyebrows and people with bulging lower lips that can digest an enormous amount of food very well.

1 What can be the best title of this story?

a. The Relation Between Faces and Eye Brows
b. Watch Out the Deceitful Face Readers
c. Danger Of A Bulged Lower Lip
d. Your Face Reveals A Lot

2 According to the passage, which sentence is <u>wrong</u>?

a. Face readers guess your character and future simply by looking your face.
b. Face readers think people with black, bow-looking eyebrows are kind and nice.
c. Cold-blooded people always have flat and fat eyebrows. No exceptions.
d. Not everybody with thin eyebrows is arrogant and haughty.

3 Choose the correct words for each sentence.

a. I thought the poverty must be related <u>for / to / as</u> homelessness.
b. Reptiles are called '<u>cold-blood / cold-blooded / cold bloody</u> animals' because the temperature of all reptiles' blood is cold.
c. The way he teaches is telling what kind of teacher <u>is he / he is / was he</u>.

LEARNING BOARD

① "Personology" or "physiognomy" believers think you can and should judge a book by its cover. ② These face readers believe they can know and judge you by your facial features since the features on your face reveal what kind of person you are. ③ For example, they can figure out a person's character by his or her eyebrows. ④ People with dark black or bow-looking eyebrows are likely to have a good character. ⑤ Flat and fat eyebrows mean 'cold-blooded' while soft and narrow eyebrows mean 'a daydreamer'. ⑥ People with thin eyebrows are said to be arrogant, while people with thick and scattered eyebrows are thought to be aggressive. ⑦ Additionally, face readers claim that they can uncover your health condition since they believe internal organs are related to facial parts. ⑧ They think, for example, that the nose is related to the heart, and the lower lip is related to the intestines. ⑨ So, if your lower lip bulges, face readers may say you 1) have constipation or 2) tend to have loose bowels. ⑩ But face reading is not always right. ⑪ There are generous and kind people with flat and fat eyebrows and people with bulging lower lips that can digest an enormous amount of food very well.

Words & Expressions

personality 성격, 개성 **personology** 관상학(=physiognomy) **believer** 믿는 사람, 신자, 신봉자 **face reader** 관상 보는 사람 **facial feature** 얼굴의 특징 **reveal** 드러내다, 밝히다 **figure out** 이해하다, 알아내다 **eyebrows** 눈썹 (eyelash 속눈썹) **bow-looking** 화살처럼 생긴 **have a good character** 성격이 좋다 **flat** 납작한 **cold-blooded** 냉정한, 냉혈한의 **narrow** 좁은 **daydreamer** 공상가 **thin** 숱이 적은; 여윈, 가는 **thick** 숱이 많은; 두꺼운 **arrogant** 거만한 **scattered** 흩어진 **aggressive** 공격적인 **uncover** 벗기다, 알아내다 **internal organ** 장기, 내장기관 **bulge** 부풀다, 튀어나오다 **constipation** 변비 **loose bowels** 설사 **generous** 관대한, 너그러운 **digest** 소화하다 **enormous** 엄청난, 많은

67 Did You Know It's Bad Luck To Let Milk Boil Over?

Some believe it's bad luck to let milk boil over. It could be true, but no one knows for sure because it is just one of the many superstitions about luck. As a matter of fact, there are very many superstitions about luck in western culture. Superstitions bringing bad luck are as follows:

- Seeing an ambulance is highly unlucky. If you see an ambulance, you must pinch your nose or hold your breath until you see a black or a brown dog.
- It's bad luck to place a hat on a bed. It is also bad luck to walk under a ladder, or see an owl in the sunlight.
- If a robin or a white moth flies into a room through an open window, someone close to you will die soon.
- Don't say the word "pig" while fishing at sea because it brings misfortune.

- To break a mirror means 7 years of bad luck.
- A knife from a lover is not a nice gift since it suggests that the love will end sooner or later.
- Don't forget to cover your mouth when yawning. Your soul may leave your body when you open your mouth wide to yawn.

1 What is the main idea of the story?
   a. All superstitions about luck are absolutely true and accurate.
   b. There are many superstitions about luck in western culture.
   c. Believing superstitions about luck is a stupid thing to do.
   d. Never say words like 'pig' or 'broken mirror' since they bring misfortune.

2 If you see an ambulance, you may want to _____.
   a. pinch your cheeks as hard as you can
   b. cry because that means somebody is dying
   c. hold your breath until you see a black dog
   d. break mirrors and walk under a ladder

3 Choose the correct words for each sentence.
   a. I wonder, why do I have a stomachache while <u>to eat / eating / I ate</u>?
   b. Don't give up now. <u>For the time being / Sooner or later / From time to time</u> things will get better.
   c. We have no choice but to stay in her house <u>when / until / after</u> we find a place to live.
   d. Every morning, my husband never fails to say 'don't forget <u>locking / to lock / locked</u> the front door before you go out.'

LEARNING BOARD

① Some believe it's bad luck to let milk boil over. ② It could be true, but no one knows (for sure) because it is just one of the many superstitions about luck. ③ (As a matter of fact), there are very many superstitions about luck in western culture. ④ Superstitions (bringing bad luck) are as follows: ⑤ - Seeing an ambulance is highly unlucky. ⑥ If you see an ambulance, you must 1) pinch your nose or 2) hold your breath until you see a black or a brown dog. ⑦ - It's bad luck to place a hat on a bed. ⑧ It is also bad luck 1) to walk under a ladder, or 2) see an owl in the sunlight.

⑨ - If a robin or a white moth flies into a room through an open window, someone (close to you) will die soon.

⑩ - Don't say the word "pig" while fishing at sea because it brings misfortune.

⑪ - To break a mirror means 7 years of bad luck.

⑫ - A knife (from a lover) is not a nice gift since it suggests that the love will end sooner or later.

⑬ - Don't forget to cover your mouth when yawning. Your soul may leave your body when you open your mouth wide (to yawn.)

Words & Expressions

bad luck 불운 boil over 끓어 넘치다 for sure 확실히(=surely, certainly) superstition 미신 be as follows ...는 다음과 같다 pinch 꼬집다, 꽉 쥐다 hole one's breath 숨을 참다 ladder 사다리 sunlight 태양빛, 햇볕 robin 울새 (새 종류) moth 나방 at sea 바다에서 misfortune 불운, 불행 knife 칼 sooner or later 조만간 yawn 하품하다 open one's mouth wide 입을 크게 벌리다

189

68 Did You Know How Friday The 13th Became The Worst Day?

There are lots of superstitions about Fridays and many of them are negative such as 'If you sleep in a different bed on Friday, you will get nightmares.'

People can find many reasons why they have no choice but to hate Fridays in the Bible. Some believe a number of biblical incidents, like the collapse of the Tower of Babel, the death of Jesus Christ and Noah's Great Flood, all took place on Friday.

There are also lots of stories about the unlucky number 13. Judas, who betrayed Jesus, was the 13th guest at the Last Supper. In ancient Rome, 12 witches used to gather together and they considered the 13th as the devil.

In addition, in western culture, 12 is a perfect and complete number. That's why

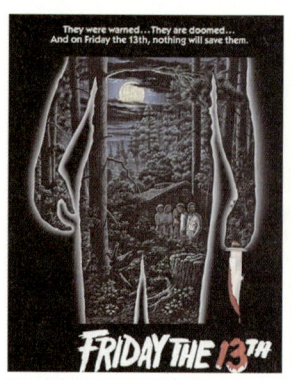

there are 12 months in a year, 12 signs of the zodiac, and 12 gods of Olympus. Meanwhile the number 13 has been connected with bad luck since it breaks the completeness of 12 with a surplus of 1. So, many cities don't have a 13th Street or a 13th Avenue and you won't find a room number 13 in hotels or hospitals.

It's only natural that Friday the 13th represents the worst because it is the combination of the worst day and the worst number.

1   What is the main idea of the story?

a. Both the Last Supper and Noah's Great Flood took place on Friday
b. 12 signs of zodiac have been connected with bad luck for a long time.
c. Friday the 13th is the combination of the worst day and the worst number.
d. 12 is the perfect and complete number and 13 is the evil and stupid number.

2   According to the passage, which sentence is right?

a. Many westerners have negative feelings towards Friday and the number 13.
b. People around the world believe that Noah's Great Flood happened on Friday the 13th.
c. Judas who betrayed Jesus 13 times did not attend the Last Supper.
d. It is not hard to find the room number 13 in hospitals in the US.

3   Choose the correct words for each sentence.

a. The rest of them had no choice but <u>return / to return / returning</u> home because the supervisor kicked them out.
b. The exact number of victims is not yet revealed, but the rumor says that a number of people <u>is / are / was</u> missing.
c. Considering the situation, I think you should have <u>considered / consideration / considerate</u> other options before spending a considerable amount of money on this.

LEARNING BOARD

① There are lots of superstitions about Fridays and many of them are negative such as 'If you sleep in a different bed on Friday, you will get nightmares.' ② People can find many reasons why they have no choice but to hate Fridays in the Bible. ③ Some believe a number of biblical incidents, like 1) the collapse of the Tower of Babel, 2) the death of Jesus Christ and 3) Noah's Great Flood, all took place on Friday.

④ There are also lots of stories about the unlucky number 13. ⑤ Judas, (who betrayed Jesus,) was the 13th guest at the Last Supper. ⑥ In ancient Rome, 12 witches used to gather together and they considered the 13th as the devil.

⑦ In addition, in western culture, 12 is a (perfect and complete) number. ⑧ That's why there are 12 months in a year, 12 signs of the zodiac, and 12 gods of Olympus.

⑨ Meanwhile the number 13 has been connected with bad luck since it breaks the completeness of 12 with a surplus of 1. ⑩ So, many cities don't have a 13th Street or a 13th Avenue and you won't find a room number 13 in (hotels or hospitals.)

⑪ It's only natural that Friday the 13th represents the worst because it is the combination of the worst day and the worst number.

Words & Expressions

Friday the 13th 13일의 금요일 **negative** 부정적인(↔ positive 긍정적인) **nightmare** 악몽 **a number of** 많은 (+ 복수명사) **biblical** 성경적인 **incident** 사건 **collapse** 붕괴, 무너지다, 폭락하다 **flood** 홍수 **take place** 발생하다, 개최되다 **betray** 배신하다 **last** 마지막의 **supper** 만찬 **witch** 마녀 **consider** …로 여기다 **complete** 완벽한, 완료하다, 끝마치다 (**completeness** 완전함) **zodiac** 황도 십이궁(=zodiac sign) **be connected with** …와 연관되다 **surplus** 잉여, 남는 것 **avenue** 거리, 길 **represent** 나타내다 **combination** 조합

69 Did You Know How Many People Died Because Of The Salem Witch Trials?

These horrific incidents were initiated not by ignorant poor people but by judges and doctors who were supposed to be intelligent, reasonable and fair. William Griggs, a village doctor, played an important role during the time of the Salem Witch Trials. He diagnosed some villagers as witches, and sent them to be tried. Once they were found guilty of witchcraft, they couldn't avoid being put to death. Under British law in the 17th century, those who were accused of being close to the devil or of being witches were considered as felons. They were regarded as criminals having committed a serious crime against the government.

One of the most famous Salem witch trials took place in 1692. About 180 people were arrested on a charge of witchcraft by the authorities. Among them, 29 people were convicted of the felony of witchcraft by the court. Most of them lost their lives by hanging. One man named Giles Corey, who refused to cooperate with the court, was pressed to death under heavy stones. At least seven other people reportedly died in prison.

1 What can be the best title of this story?

a. William Griggs, Assaulted by Ignorant Farmers
b. The Salem Witch Trials : Trials? Or Slaughter?
c. Witchcraft : The Most Serious Felon Against The Government
d. The Secret of Salem Witch Trials Finally Revealed

2 During the 17th century, people could be found guilty of _____.

a. doing something related to witchcraft
b. being close to the authorities
c. trying to cooperate with the court
d. being ignorant and poor

3 Choose the correct words for each sentence.

a. The guy who made / committed / did a crime must be thrown into jail.
b. When I hung up my coat on the hanger, saying 'hang on a minute,' she said her brother was sentenced to death by hanging / hung / hanged, which meant he was going to be hanged.
c. Those who are accused by / of / with racism, or we can say 'racists', are banned from entering our shop.

LEARNING BOARD

① These horrific incidents were initiated not by ignorant poor people but by judges and doctors (who were supposed to be intelligent, reasonable and fair). ② William Griggs, (a village doctor), played an important role during the time of the Salem Witch Trials. ③ He 1) diagnosed some villagers as witches, and 2) sent them to be tried. ④ Once they were found guilty of witchcraft, they couldn't avoid being put to death. ⑤ Under British law in the 17th century, those (who were accused 1) of being close to the devil or 2) of being witches) were considered as felons. ⑥ They were regarded as criminals (having committed a serious crime against the government.) ⑦ One of the most famous Salem witch trials took place in 1692. ⑧ About 180 people were arrested (on a charge of witchcraft) by the authorities. ⑨ Among them, 29 people were convicted of the felony of witchcraft by the court. ⑩ Most of them lost their lives by hanging. ⑪ One man (named Giles Corey), (who refused to cooperate with the court,) was pressed to death under heavy stones. ⑫ At least seven other people reportedly died in prison.

Words & Expressions

horrific 끔찍한 **incident** 사건, 일 **initiate** 시작하다 **ignorant** 무지한 **judge** 판사 **intelligent** 지적인 **reasonable** 이성적인, 합리적인 **fair** 공정한 **play an important role** 중요한 역할을 하다 **witch trial** 마녀 재판 **be found guilty of** (…라는 죄로) 유죄를 선고받다 **witchcraft** 마술 **avoid** 피하다 **put … to death** …를 사형에 처하다 **be accused of** …로 기소되다, 비난받다 **felon** 중죄인, 흉악범 (**felony** 중죄, 흉악 범죄) **criminal** 범죄자, 범인 **serious crime** 중죄, 무거운 죄 **commit a crime** 범죄를 저지르다 **arrest** 체포하다 **on a charge of** …의 혐의로 **authority** 권한, 당국, 권위자 **convict** 유죄를 선고하다 **be convicted of** …로 유죄 판결을 받다 **by hanging** 교수형으로 **cooperate** 협동하다, 협력하다 **press** 누르다 **reportedly** 소문에 따르면

193

Did You Know About The Mystery 'Ghost' House?

Sarah Winchester built a "Mystery House" because she was a super-rich widow and a huge believer in supernatural powers. After the death of her only baby daughter, she became mentally unstable. As worse came to worst, her dear husband and father-in-law passed away too. This made her the heiress to the Winchester Repeating Arms Company. Thanks to that, she could get $1,000 a day. (This amount of money is equivalent to about $25,000 a day in 2013.)

She was a moneybag; however, she was too sad to do anything. A psychic told her that the spirits who had died from Winchester rifles were starting to take revenge, and that she should build a house. Sarah believed that if she finished building her house, those spirits would kill her. From then on, she spent her fortune and time only on her house, which became known as the Winchester Mystery House. This house has many staircases and doors leading to nowhere. There are about 160 rooms and lots of maze-like corridors. She built her house like this to make the spirits confused. The construction of this house came to an end with her death. Sarah Winchester died in her sleep at the age of 83.

1 What is the main idea of the story?

  a. Although Winchester was not very rich, she was forced to build the huge house.
  b. Spirits loved the Mystery House since there were many rooms.
  c. Winchester had built the weird and absurd house to make ghosts confused.
  d. The Mystery House has been famous for being haunted.

2 According to the passage, which sentence is <u>wrong</u>?

  a. The founder of the Winchester Repeating Arms Company was Sarah Winchester.
  b. Sarah was rich but she couldn't do anything because she was sad.
  c. Sarah believed that the cause of her family's tragedy was the revenge of the ghosts.
  d. It was not that Sarah became strange until her daughter passed away.

3 Choose the correct words for each sentence.

  a. If you want to talk softly and politely, use the expression like '<u>pass away</u>' / '<u>pass by</u>' / '<u>pass out</u>' rather than 'kick the bucket.'
  b. David is too excited <u>to sitting / to sit / sat</u> down on his chair.
  c. The news about his death made me <u>surprised / to surprise / surprising</u>.

LEARNING BOARD

① Sarah Winchester built a "Mystery House" because she was a super-rich **widow** and a **huge** believer in **supernatural** powers. ② After the death of her **only baby** daughter, she became **mentally unstable**. ③ As worse came to worst, her dear husband and father-in-law **passed away** too. ④ This made her the **heiress** to the Winchester Repeating **Arms** Company. ⑤ **Thanks to that**, she could get $1,000 **a day**. ⑥ (This amount of money **is equivalent to** about $25,000 a day in 2013.) ⑦ She was a **moneybag**; however, she was **too** sad **to** do anything. ⑧ A **psychic** told her 1) that the **spirits** (who had died from Winchester rifles) were starting to take **revenge**, and 2) that she should build a house. ⑨ Sarah believed that if she finished building her house, those spirits would kill her. ⑩ **From then on**, she spent (her fortune and time) only on her house, (**which became known as** the Winchester Mystery House). ⑪ This house has many **staircases and doors** (leading to nowhere). ⑫ There are (about) 160 rooms and lots of **maze**-like corridors. ⑬ She built her house like this to make the spirits **confused**. ⑭ The construction of this house **came to an end with** her death. ⑮ Sarah Winchester **died in her sleep** at the age of 83.

Words & Expressions

mystery 수수께끼, 미스터리 **super-rich** 굉장히 부유한 **widow** 과부 **huge** 막대한 **supernatural** 초자연적인 **only daughter** 무남독녀 **mentally** 정신적으로 **unstable** 불안정한(↔ **stable** 안정된) **farther-in-law** 시아버지 **pass away** 세상을 떠나다, 죽다 **heiress** 상속녀(cf. **heir** 상속인) **repeating** 반복하는, (총) 연발의 **arms** 무기 **manufacture** 제조하다 **thanks to** …덕분에 **equivalent** (의미, 가치가) 동등한, …에 상응하는 **moneybag** 돈주머니, 부자 **psychic** 심령술사, 영매 **rifle** 소총 **spirit** 유령, 영혼 **revenge** 복수 **take revenge** 복수하다 **from then on** 그때부터 쭉 **staircase** 계단 **maze** 미로(=**labyrinth**) **maze-like** 미로 같은 **corridor** 복도 **confused** 혼란스러워하는 **construction** 건축 **come to an end** 끝나다

Listening with Dictation

66 Did You Know Your Face Reveals Your Personality?

"Personology" or "physiognomy" believers think you can and should _____¹. These face readers believe they can know and judge you by your facial features since the features on your face reveal _____². For example, they can _____³ a person's character by his or her eyebrows. People with dark black or bow-looking eyebrows are likely to have a good character. Flat and fat eyebrows mean 'cold-blooded' while soft and narrow eyebrows mean 'a daydreamer'. People with thin eyebrows are said to be _____⁴, while people with thick and scattered eyebrows are thought to be _____⁵. Additionally, face readers claim that they can _____⁶ since they believe internal organs _____⁷ facial parts. They think, for example, that the nose is related to the heart, and the lower lip is related to the intestines. So, if your lower lip bulges, face readers may say you _____⁸ or tend to have _____⁹. But face reading is not always right. There are generous and kind people with flat and fat eyebrows and people with bulging lower lips _____¹⁰ an enormous amount of food very well.

67 Did You Know It's Bad Luck To Let Milk Boil Over?

Some believe it's bad luck to _____¹. It could be true, but no one knows for sure because it is just one of the many superstitions about luck. As a matter of fact, there are very many superstitions about luck in western culture. Superstitions bringing bad luck are _____²: - Seeing an ambulance _____³. If you see an ambulance, you must pinch your nose or hold your breath until you see a black or a brown dog. - It's bad luck to _____⁴ on a bed. It is also bad luck to walk under a ladder, or see an owl in the sunlight. - If a robin or a white moth flies into a room through an open window, _____⁵ will die soon. - Don't say the word "pig" _____⁶ because it _____⁷. - To break a mirror means 7 years of bad luck. - A knife from a lover is not a nice gift since _____⁸ the love will end sooner or later. - Don't forget to cover your mouth when yawning. Your soul _____⁹ when you _____¹⁰ to yawn.

68 Did You Know How Friday The 13th Became The Worst Day?

There are _____¹ about Fridays and many of them are negative such as 'If you sleep in a different bed _____², you will get nightmares.' People can find many reasons why they have no choice but to hate Fridays in the Bible. Some believe _____³ biblical incidents, like the collapse of the Tower of Babel, the death of Jesus Christ and Noah's Great Flood, all took place on Friday. There are also lots of stories about the unlucky number 13. Judas, who betrayed Jesus, was the 13th guest _____⁴. In ancient Rome, 12 witches used to gather together and they considered the 13th as the devil. In addition, in western culture, 12 is a perfect and complete number. That's why there are 12 months in a year, 12 signs of the zodiac, and 12 gods of Olympus. Meanwhile the number 13 _____⁵ bad luck since it breaks the completeness of 12 _____⁶ 1. So, many cities don't have a 13th Street or a 13th Avenue and you won't find _____⁷ in hotels or hospitals. _____⁸ Friday the 13th _____⁹ because it is _____¹⁰ the worst day and the worst number.

Chapter 7 | The Supernatural

69 Did You Know How Many People Died Because Of The Salem Witch Trials?

These _____¹ incidents _____² not by ignorant poor people but by judges and doctors who were supposed to be intelligent, reasonable and fair. William Griggs, a village doctor, _____³ during the time of the Salem Witch Trials. He _____⁴ some villagers as witches, and _____⁵. Once they _____⁶ witchcraft, they couldn't _____⁷. Under British law in the 17th century, those who were accused of being close to the devil or of being witches were considered as felons. They were regarded as criminals having committed a serious crime _____⁸ the government. One of the most famous Salem witch trials took place in 1692. About 180 people were arrested on a charge of witchcraft by the authorities. Among them, 29 people _____⁹ witchcraft by the court. Most of them lost their lives by hanging. One man named Giles Corey, who refused to cooperate with the court, was pressed to death under heavy stones. At least _____¹⁰ reportedly died in prison.

70 Did You Know About The Mystery 'Ghost' House?

Sarah Winchester built a "Mystery House" because she was a super-rich _____¹ and a huge believer in supernatural powers. After the death of her only baby daughter, she became mentally unstable. _____², her dear husband and father-in-law _____³ too. This made her the heiress to the Winchester Repeating Arms Company. Thanks to that, she could get $1,000 a day. (This amount of money _____⁴ about $25,000 a day in 2013.) She was a moneybag; however, she was too sad to do anything. A psychic told her that the spirits who had died from Winchester rifles were starting to _____⁵, and that she should build a house. Sarah believed that if she _____⁶ her house, those spirits would kill her. From then on, she spent her fortune and time only on her house, _____⁷ the Winchester Mystery House. This house has many staircases and doors _____⁸. There are about 160 rooms and lots of _____⁹. She built her house like this to make the spirits confused. The construction of this house _____¹⁰ with her death. Sarah Winchester died in her sleep at the age of 83.

---

66 정답 1. judge a book by its cover 2. what kind of person you are 3. figure out 4. arrogant 5. aggressive 6. uncover your health condition 7. are related to 8. have constipation 9. loose bowels 10. that can digest

67 정답 1. let milk boil over 2. as follows 3. is highly unlucky 4. place a hat 5. someone close to you 6. while fishing at sea 7. brings misfortune 8. it suggests that 9. may leave your body 10. open your mouth wide

68 정답 1. lots of superstitions 2. on Friday 3. a number of 4. at the Last Supper 5. has been connected with 6. with a surplus of 7. a room number 13 8. It's only natural that 9. represents the worst 10. the combination of

69 정답 1. horrific 2. were initiated 3. played an important role 4. diagnosed 5. sent them to be tried 6. were found guilty of 7. avoid being put to death 8. against 9. were convicted of the felony of 10. seven other people

70 정답 1. widow 2. As worse came to worst 3. passed away 4. is equivalent to 5. take revenge 6. finished building 7. which became known as 8. leading to nowhere 9. maze-like corridors 10. came to an end

Chapter 8. Interesting Stories

71. Did you know What Animal Has 3 Hearts, 9 Brains, And Blue Blood?

무슨 동물이 3개의 심장, 9개의 뇌, 그리고 파란 피를 갖고 있는지 아세요?

72. Did you know St. Stephen's Clock Tower Is Leaning To One Side Just Like The Leaning Tower Of Pisa?

성 스테판의 시계탑이 피사의 사탑처럼 한쪽으로 기울어지고 있다는 거 아세요?

73. Did you know Why The Emperor Who Built The Taj Mahal Cut His Workers' Hands Off?

타지마할을 건축한 황제가 일꾼들의 손을 자른 이유를 아세요?

74. Did you know Why Fatemah Allowed Her Husband's Second Marriage?

페이트마가 남편의 두 번째 결혼을 허락한 이유를 아세요?

75. Did you know Who Can Be Mosquitoes' Favorites?

누가 모기의 총애를 받는 사람이 되는지 아세요?

76. Did you know How Two Russians Made An Amazing Alien?

두 명의 러시아인들이 놀라운 외계인을 어떻게 만들었는지 아세요?

77. Did you know Why American-born Giant Pandas Were Sent Back To China?

미국에서 태어난 자이언트 판다들이 왜 중국으로 돌려보내 졌는지 아세요?

78. Did you know What The Kennedy Curse Is?

케네디 저주가 무엇인지 아세요?

79. Did you know Mount Rushmore Was Carved With The Help Of Dynamite?

러슈모어산이 다이너마이트의 도움으로 조각되었다는 거 아세요?

80. Did you know There Are Giraffe-looking Women?

기린처럼 보이는 여성들이 있다는 거 아세요?

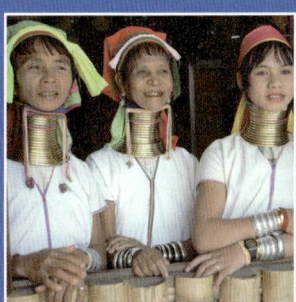

Did You Know What Animal Has 3 Hearts, 9 Brains, And Blue Blood?

This animal really does have 3 hearts, 9 brains, and blue blood. It is not a monster but a sea creature. We don't know if it is smart thanks to its 9 brains, but it is thought to be smarter than other sea creatures.

Its 9 brains are nothing compared to its muscles because 90% of its body is muscle. So, it has got the brains and the muscles! There is something amazing about its muscles. They can move even after being cut off. You can check it out for yourself. Chop up this muscular smart guy and put him in a pan with seasoning. You can see his arms continue to move for several minutes while being cooked.

So... it's got the brains, the muscles, and the moves. But unfortunately, it hasn't got the looks. It has no legs and no face, just many arms. However, it has a special

talent in its arms. When it gets attacked by a predator and loses one of its arms, it doesn't worry about it since its arms grow back. This guy is even scary and merciless enough to eat its own kind! Moreover, it has venom and can release ink.

Could you guess what it is? This amazing sea creature is the Giant Pacific octopus.

1 **What can be the best title of this story?**
a. The Reason Why The Giant Pacific Octopus Is Amazing
b. Warning! A Sea Monster Attack!
c. The Giant Pacific Octopus VS. Other Sea Creatures
d. Here Comes The Scary Creature : He Got The Muscles

2 **We can say the Giant Pacific octopus hasn't got the looks since _____.**
a. its face is all muscly and moving continuously
b. it has too many faces
c. its face is unbearably ugly
d. it doesn't have a face at all

3 **Choose the correct words for each sentence.**
a. I wonder how this paint got its / it's / it is color?
b. We can do anything together since you've got brains / the brains / a brain and I've got the muscles.
c. The robber appeared out of nowhere and he got robbed / robbed / had been robbed me of my money.

LEARNING BOARD

① This animal really does have 3 hearts, 9 brains, and blue blood. ② It is not a monster but a sea creature. ③ We don't know if it is smart thanks to its 9 brains, but it is thought to be smarter than other sea creatures. ④ Its 9 brains are nothing compared to its muscles because (90% of its body) is muscle. ⑤ So, it has got the brains and the muscles! ⑥ There is something amazing about its muscles. ⑦ They can move even after being cut off. ⑧ You can check it out for yourself. ⑨ ¹⁾ Chop up this muscular smart guy and ²⁾ put him in a pan with seasoning. ⑩ You can see his arms continue to move for several minutes while being cooked. ⑪ So... it's got the brains, the muscles, and the moves. ⑫ But unfortunately, it hasn't got the looks. ⑬ It has no legs and no face, just many arms. ⑭ However, it has a special talent in its arms. ⑮ When it ¹⁾ gets attacked by a predator and ²⁾ loses one of its arms, it doesn't worry about it since its arms grow back. ⑯ This guy is even scary and merciless enough to eat its own kind! ⑰ Moreover, it has venom and can release ink. ⑱ Could you guess what it is? ⑲ This amazing sea creature is the Giant Pacific octopus.

Words & Expressions

heart 심장 **brain** 뇌 **monster** 괴물 **sea creature** 바다생물 **smart** 똑똑한, 영리한 **compared to** ...에 비하면, ...와 비교하면 **muscle** 근육 **got the muscles** 근육이 있다. 즉 근육질이다 **amazing** 놀라운 **cut off** 잘라내다 **chop up** 잘게 썰다 **guy** 놈, 녀석 **seasoning** 양념 **got the moves** 멋진 동작(움직임. 춤. 무술 등)을 할 줄 안다 **have got the looks** 외모가 된다, 멋지다 **unfortunately** 불행하게도 **talent** 재능, 능력 **get attacked** 공격을 당하다 **predator** 포식자 **grow back** 다시 자라다 **scary** 무서운, 겁나는 **merciless** 무자비한 **venom** (뱀 등의) 독 cf. **venomous** 독이 있는(=poisonous) **release** 방출하다, 석방하다, 출시하다 **octopus** 문어

72 Did You Know St. Stephen's Clock Tower Is Leaning To One Side Just Like The Leaning Tower Of Pisa?

Experts acknowledged that St. Stephen's clock tower is leaning to one side just like the Leaning Tower of Pisa. They said St. Stephen's clock tower, the most famous landmark of London, leans 0.26 degrees to the north-west. That means the 315-feet-high tower is sinking into the banks of the river Thames. Although its tilt is visible to the naked eye, experts don't think they need to do anything right now. They say it would take around 4,000 years to reach the same angle as the Leaning Tower of Pisa. Mike McCann, the keeper of the tower, agreed with them.

The problem is that no one knows what causes it. Some claim that the London clay on which the tower was built might be the cause. It is thought that its clay foundation made the tower tilt while drying out. Or, it might be caused by work on the Underground near the tower, in spite of the fact that surveyors found no evidence of that.

Either way, people around the world hope that the future of the Elizabeth Tower is not at risk of sinking into the river Thames.

1 What is the main idea of the story?

a. St. Stephen's clock tower is sinking into the Han river.
b. The fate of St. Stephen's clock tower is safe for now.
c. The Elizabeth Tower is the largest clock in the world.
d. Mike McCann is the keeper of the Leaning Tower of Pisa.

2 According to the passage, which sentence is <u>wrong</u>?

a. The Elizabeth Tower is leaning to the side, but there is nothing we can do about it for now.
b. The height of St. Stephen's clock tower is 315 feet.
c. Although the tilt of the tower is so obvious, only experts can notice that.
d. St. Stephen's clock tower was built on the London clay.

3 Choose the correct words for each sentence.

a. There <u>is / are / were</u> no evidence for your theory. Please give me some information to prove it.
b. I saw Nedd, a tall and <u>leaning / lean / leaned</u> guy in my office, leaning against the wall.
c. We <u>surveied / surveyed / surveyied</u> 100 teachers last week and got the shocking result you might want to know.

LEARNING BOARD

① Experts acknowledged that St. Stephen's clock tower is leaning to one side just like the Leaning Tower of Pisa. ② They said St. Stephen's clock tower, (the most famous landmark of London), leans 0.26 degrees to the north-west. ③ That means the 315-feet-high tower is sinking into the banks of the river Thames. ④ Although its tilt is visible to the naked eye, experts don't think they need to do anything right now. ⑤ They say it would take around 4,000 years to reach the same angle as the Leaning Tower of Pisa. ⑥ Mike McCann, (the keeper of the tower,) agreed with them. ⑦ The problem is that no one knows what causes it. ⑧ Some claim that the London clay on which the tower was built might be the cause. ⑨ It is thought that its clay foundation made the tower tilt while drying out. ⑩ Or, it might be caused by work on the Underground near the tower, in spite of the fact that surveyors found no evidence of that. ⑪ Either way, people around the world hope that the future (of the Elizabeth Tower) is not at risk of sinking into the river Thames.

Words & Expressions

expert 전문가 acknowledge 인정하다. (수신을) 확인하다 St. Stephen's clock tower 성 스테판 시계탑 (영국 런던에 위치한 시계 탑. 거대한 시계 Big Ben이 있어서 Big Ben이라 불리기도 하는데, Big Ben은 2012년 엘리자베스 2세 여왕의 즉위 60주년을 기념하여 명칭이 Elizabeth Tower로 바뀌었다.) lean 기울다 landmark 주요 지형물 degree (각도 단위인) 도 sink 가라앉다, 함몰하다 bank 둑 tilt v. 기울다 n. 기울어짐 visible 눈으로 보이는 naked 벌거벗은 naked eye 육안, 맨눈 claim 주장하다 clay 진흙 foundation 근거, 기초, 토대 either way 어느 쪽이든 be at risk 위험에 처하다

Did You Know Why The Emperor Who Built The Taj Mahal Cut His Workers' Hands Off?

After his second wife Mumtaz Mahal passed away after giving birth to their 14th child in 1631, Shah Jahan, the fifth Mughal emperor, was devastated. Although she was one of his many wives and not a beauty queen at all, he loved her the most.

Six months later, he started to build the most magnificent tomb for her, the Taj Mahal. He didn't spare anything when it came to the Taj. He brought building materials from not only India but also several countries in central Asia. In order to transport the enormous amounts of material to the construction site, all available methods were used, including elephants. Over 20,000 people worked laboriously morning to night for 22 years on the tomb of their emperor's dead wife.

They did a wonderful job. The beauty of the Taj was perfect enough for it to become a UNESCO World Heritage Site in 1983. Additionally, the symmetry of this huge marble structure was so perfect that it was chosen as one of the New Seven Wonders of the World in 2007. Shah Jahan knew it was the best tomb ever and he didn't want anyone to build that kind of beautiful structure again.

So on his order, the hands of the master craftsmen were amputated.

1 What can be the best title of this story?
   a. Mumtaz Mahal's Bizzare Love for Tombs
   b. Shah Jahan : The Cruel Emperor Killed His Wife
   c. The Taj Mahal, The Most Beautiful and Perfect Tomb Ever
   d. The Miracle Of The River Yamuna

2 Shah Jahan cut the workers' hands off because _____.
   a. the master craftsmen were lazy and dishonest
   b. he didn't want anyone to build a beautiful tomb as the Taj
   c. UNESCO didn't choose the Taj as one of the New Seven Wonders of the world
   d. he was the most horrible and brutal emperor ever

3 Choose the correct words for each sentence.
   a. It's hard to understand how the storm ruined / spared / ruptured my house while nearby houses were totally destroyed.
   b. You must keep a fire extinguisher available / to no avail / being available at all times.
   c. The volcano eruption literally devastated my hometown. It was the most devastating / devastated / devastate disaster ever.

LEARNING BOARD

① After his second wife (Mumtaz Mahal) passed away after giving birth to their 14th child in 1631, Shah Jahan, (the fifth Mughal emperor), was devastated. ② Although she was one of his many wives and not a beauty queen at all, he loved her the most. ③ Six months later, he started to build the most magnificent tomb (for her), (the Taj Mahal). ④ He didn't spare anything when it came to the Taj. ⑤ He brought building materials from not only India but also several countries in central Asia. ⑥ In order to transport the enormous amounts of material to the construction site, all available methods were used, including elephants. ⑦ Over 20,000 people worked (laboriously morning to night for 22 years) on the tomb of their emperor's dead wife. ⑧ They did a wonderful job. ⑨ The beauty (of the Taj) was perfect enough (for it) to become a UNESCO World Heritage Site in 1983. ⑩ Additionally, the symmetry (of this huge marble structure) was so perfect that it was chosen as one of the New Seven Wonders of the World in 2007. ⑪ Shah Jahan knew it was the best tomb ever and he didn't want anyone to build that kind of beautiful structure again. ⑫ So on his order, the hands (of the master craftsmen) were amputated.

Words & Expressions

pass away 세상을 떠나다, 죽다 **emperor** 황제(남) (여황제 empress) **devastate** 완전히 파괴하다, 비탄에 빠지다 **beauty queen** 미인 대회 우승자, 예쁜 여자 **tomb** 무덤(= grave) **magnificent** 멋진, 웅장한 **spare** 아끼다 **when it comes to** …에 관해서라면 **building material** 건축자재 **transport** 수송하다, 실어 나르다 **enormous** 엄청난, 막대한 **site** 현장 **available** 입수 가능한 **laboriously** 힘들게, 어렵게 **do the job** 일을 하다, 해내다 **heritage** 유산 **additionally** 게다가 **symmetry** 대칭, 균형 **huge** 거대한 **marble structure** 대리석 건축물 **craftsman** 장인, 수공예가 **amputate** 손발을 자르다

205

74 Did You Know Why Fatemah Allowed Her Husband's Second Marriage?

Two Indonesians tied the knot in 2006 after getting approval from the High Court. Their marriage knocked everyone's socks off because of their age difference. Sudar, the groom, was 105 years old, and Ely, the bride, was 22. At the time, Sudar was still married to Fatemah, who was 69 and very much ill. Fatemah was said to welcome her husband's second wife, for she couldn't carry out her responsibilities as a wife, although she added that if she were not ill, she would never allow her husband's second marriage.

Ely allegedly felt sorry for Sudar since he had to take care of his ailing wife in spite of being very old and weak himself. She could help them as a friend or a maid, but she decided to marry him anyway.

It's hard to understand this whole situation, but you know what they say: nothing matters when it comes to true love. Ms. 22 must have loved Mr. 105 very much.

1 What can be the best title of this story?

a. The Oldest Man Finally Married
b. Ailing Wife Dumped By Vicious Husband
c. The Beauty And The Old Man : True and Touching Love Story
d. Mr. 105 Married Ms. 22 : Nothing Matters But Love

2 According to the passage, which sentence is right?

a. Sudar married Fatemah in 2006 although he has already been married to Ely.
b. Sudar's second marriage was illegal because the court didn't permit his marriage to Ely.
c. It seemed that Fatemah didn't welcome her husband's second wife wholeheartedly.
d. The age difference between the bridegroom and the bride was over 90.

3 Choose the correct words for each sentence.

a. I'm going to confess that I did something that <u>matters / matter / mattered</u> to you.
b. If it <u>was / were / is</u> not for him, she would fail the test.
c. When I asked John when he is going to tie the knot, he avoided answering my question, <u>tying the knot / tieing a knot / tying a knot</u> in a rope.

LEARNING BOARD

① Two Indonesians **tied the knot** in 2006 after getting **approval** from the High Court.
    tie the knot 결혼하다   주어가 주절의 주어(two Indonesians)와 일치, 생략
    cf. tie a knot 매듭을 묶다   능동이므로 getting/ get approval from ...로부터 허가를 받다

② Their marriage knocked everyone's socks off because of their age difference.
                  (모두를) 깜짝 놀라게 하다   나이 차이
    = Everyone was surprised[shocked] by their marriage.

③ Sudar, (**the groom**), was 105 years old, and Ely, (**the bride**), was 22. ④ At the time,
          = 동격   (bride) groom 신랑   = 동격   당시
Sudar was still married to Fatemah, who was 69 and very much ill. ⑤ Fatemah
    be [get] married to ...와 결혼한 상태이다   = and she(Fatemah)
    marry ...와 결혼하다 (with를 쓰지 않는다)

was said to welcome her husband's second wife, for she couldn't **carry out** her
    ...라고 한다   because, since   수행하다

responsibilities as a wife, although she added that if she were not ill, she would
carry out responsibilities as ...로서 책임을 다하다   (말을) 덧붙였다   가정법 과거 <현재의 반대 상황 가정>
responsibility 의무, 책임   if 과거동사/were, 주어 would/should + R

never allow her husband's second marriage.
    = She was ill, so she allowed her husband's second marriage.

⑥ Ely **allegedly** felt sorry for Sudar since he had to **take care of** his **ailing** wife
      알려진 바에 의하면   because, for   돌보다   a. 병든

in spite of being very old and weak himself. ⑦ She could help them as a friend
...에도 불구하고 (+ 동명사/명사)   = Ely   (자격) ...로서

or a **maid**, but she decided to marry him anyway.
    n. 하녀

⑧ It's hard to understand this whole situation, but you know what they say: nothing
   이해하기 어렵다(= it's difficult to understand)   이런 말도 있다

matters when it comes to true love. ⑨ Ms. 22 must have loved Mr. 105 very much.
              ...에 관해서라면   = Ely must have pp: = Sudar
                                                ...였음에 틀림없다 <과거 사실에 대한 강한 추측>

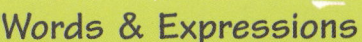

Words & Expressions

tie the knot 결혼하다(= marry) knot 매듭 approval 승인, 허락(cf. approve 승인하다) High Court 고등법원 marriage 결혼 knock someone's socks off 깜짝 놀라게 하다 age difference 나이 차이 (bride) groom 신랑 bride 신부 welcome 환영하다 responsibility 책임 ailing 병든 maid 하녀, 가정부 when it comes to ...에 관해서라면

207

75 Did You Know Who Can Be Mosquitoes' Favorites?

Mosquitoes are kind of picky eaters, so they do not suck just anybody's blood. They select their victims carefully before sticking in their long and thin mouths.

If you want to be the mosquitoes' favorite target and you are a brunette, consider dyeing your hair blonde or red since mosquitoes prefer blondes and redheads to brunettes. Furthermore, mosquitoes usually prefer to bite women over men. So, it's safe to say that blondies are mosquitoes' favorites.

If you don't want to dye your hair and you are not female, but still want to be their favorite, no need to worry. There is more than one way to be the chosen one.

Mosquitoes are attracted by smells, specifically, foul smells. So if you sweat a lot and keep your feet unwashed and stinky, you will have a much better chance at

donating blood to hungry mosquitoes than those who don't. There are two more things that attract mosquitoes : carbon dioxide and lactic acid. The more you produce these things, the more likely you can lure them to you. How? Simple: be obese or jittery, because overweight or fidgety people are said to produce more carbon dioxide and lactic acid than people who aren't.

1 What can be the best title of this story?
a. The Hidden Secret About Mosquitoes Revealed
b. The Best Way To Expel Mosquitoes
c. Tips For People Who Want To Be Mosquitoes' Favorites
d. Watch Out For Fidgety People

2 Mosquitoes tend to bite people who are _____.
a. blond or redhead and male
b. tall, thin and brunette
c. black-haired and female
d. blond and female

3 Choose the correct words for each sentence.
a. My wife prefers sports to reading, but I prefer to read books to / rather than / not to play sports outside.
b. When I saw two mosquitoes / mosquitos / mosquito on my arm, I slapped them.
c. Have you ever considered to move / moving / move to another country?

LEARNING BOARD

① Mosquitoes are kind of picky eaters, so they do not suck just anybody's blood.

② They select their victims carefully before sticking in their (long and thin) mouths.

③ If 1) you want to be the mosquitoes' favorite target and 2) you are a brunette, consider dyeing your hair blonde or red since mosquitoes prefer blondes and redheads to brunettes. ④ Furthermore, mosquitoes usually prefer to bite women over men. ⑤ So, it's safe to say that blondies are mosquitoes' favorites. ⑥ If 1) you don't want to dye your hair and 2) you are not female, but 3) still want to be their favorite, no need to worry. ⑦ There is more than one way to be the chosen one.

⑧ Mosquitoes are attracted by smells, (specifically), foul smells. ⑨ So if you 1) sweat a lot and 2) keep your feet unwashed and stinky, you will have a much better chance at donating blood to hungry mosquitoes than those who don't. ⑩ There are two more things that attract mosquitoes : carbon dioxide and lactic acid. ⑪ The more you produce these things, the more likely you can lure them to you. ⑫ How? ⑬ Simple: be obese or jittery, because (overweight or fidgety) people are said to produce more carbon dioxide and lactic acid than people who aren't.

Words & Expressions

mosquito 모기 **picky** 까다로운 (picky eater 식성이 까다로운 사람) **suck** 빨다 **victim** 희생자, 피해자 **stick** (뾰족한 것으로) 찌르다, 붙이다 **brunette** 흑갈색 머리를 가진 백인 여자 **prefer** 더 좋아하다, 선호하다 **redhead** 빨강 머리(를 가진 사람) **bite** 물다 **blondie** 금발 머리 여자 **favorite** 총애하는, 좋아하는 것(사람) **dye** 염색하다 (cf. die 죽다) **female** 여성, 암컷 (cf. male 수컷, 남성) **the chosen one** 선택받은 자 **attract** 마음을 끌다 **specifically** 구체적으로 **foul** 나쁜, 악취 나는 **sweat** 땀이 나다 **unwashed** 씻지 않은 **stinky** 악취가 나는 **donate** 기부하다 **carbon dioxide** 이산화탄소 **lactic acid** 젖산 **lure** 유혹하다 **obese** 비만한 **jittery** 안절부절못하는 **overweight** 과체중의 **fidgety** 가만히 있지 못하는 **produce** 만들어 내다

Listening with Dictation

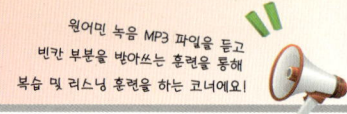

71 Did You Know What Animal Has 3 Hearts, 9 Brains, And Blue Blood?

This animal _____ ¹ 3 hearts, 9 brains, and blue blood. It is not a monster but a sea creature. We don't know if it is smart _____ ² its 9 brains, but _____ ³ be smarter than other sea creatures. Its 9 brains are nothing _____ ⁴ its muscles because 90% of its body is muscle. So, it _____ ⁵ the brains and the muscles! There is something amazing about its muscles. They can move even _____ ⁶. You can check it out for yourself. Chop up this muscular smart guy and put him in a pan with seasoning. You can see his arms _____ ⁷ for several minutes while being cooked. So... it's got the brains, the muscles, and the moves. But unfortunately, it _____ ⁸ the looks. It has no legs and no face, just many arms. However, it has a special talent in its arms. When _____ ⁹ by a predator and loses one of its arms, it doesn't worry about it since its arms grow back. This guy is even scary and merciless enough to eat its own kind! Moreover, it has venom and can release ink. Could you guess _____ ¹⁰? This amazing sea creature is the Giant Pacific octopus.

72 Did You Know Why St. Stephen's Clock Tower Is Leaning To One Side Just Like The Leaning Tower Of Pisa?

Experts acknowledged that St. Stephen's clock tower _____ ¹ one side just like the Leaning Tower of Pisa. They said St. Stephen's clock tower, the most famous landmark of London, leans 0.26 degrees to the north-west. That means the 315-feet-high tower is sinking into the _____ ² of the river Thames. Although its tilt is _____ ³, experts don't think they need to do anything right now. They say it would _____ ⁴ around 4,000 years to reach the same angle as the Leaning Tower of Pisa. Mike McCann, the keeper of the tower, _____ ⁵ them. The problem is that no one knows what causes it. Some claim that the London clay _____ ⁶ the tower was built might be the cause. It is thought that its clay foundation _____ ⁷ while drying out. Or, it might be caused by work on the Underground near the tower, _____ ⁸ the fact that surveyors _____ ⁹ of that. Either way, people around the world hope that the future of the Elizabeth Tower _____ ¹⁰ sinking into the river Thames.

73 Did You Know Why The Emperor Who Built The Taj Mahal Cut His Workers' Hands Off?

After his second wife Mumtaz Mahal passed away after _____ ¹ their 14th child in 1631, Shah Jahan, the fifth Mughal emperor, was devastated. Although she was _____ ² his many wives and not a beauty queen at all, he _____ ³. Six months later, he started to build the most magnificent tomb for her, the Taj Mahal. He _____ ⁴ when it came to the Taj. He brought building materials from not only India but also several countries in central Asia. In order to transport _____ ⁵ material to the construction site, _____ ⁶ were used, including elephants. Over 20,000 people _____ ⁷ morning to night for 22 years on the tomb of their emperor's dead wife. They did a wonderful job. The beauty of the Taj was perfect enough for it to become a UNESCO World Heritage Site in 1983. Additionally, the _____ ⁸ of this huge marble structure was so perfect that it was chosen as one of the New Seven Wonders of the World in 2007. Shah Jahan knew it was the best tomb ever and he didn't want anyone to build that kind of beautiful structure again. So _____ ⁹, the hands of the master craftsmen _____ ¹⁰.

74. Did You Know Why Fatemah Allowed Her Husband's Second Marriage?

Two Indonesians _____¹ in 2006 after _____² the High Court. Their marriage _____³ because of their age difference. Sudar, the groom, was 105 years old, and Ely, the bride, was 22. At the time, Sudar _____⁴ Fatemah, who was 69 and very much ill. Fatemah was said to welcome her husband's second wife, for she couldn't _____⁵ as a wife, although she added that if she _____⁶, she _____⁷ allow her husband's second marriage. Ely allegedly felt sorry for Sudar since he had to take care of his ailing wife in spite of _____⁸ and weak himself. She could help them as a friend or a maid, but she decided to marry him anyway. It's hard to understand this whole situation, but you know what they say: _____⁹ when it comes to true love. Ms. 22 _____¹⁰ Mr. 105 very much.

75. Did You Know Who Can Be Mosquitoes' Favorites?

Mosquitoes are _____¹ picky eaters, so they do not suck just anybody's blood. They _____² before sticking in their long and thin mouths. If you want to be the mosquitoes' favorite target and you are a brunette, _____³ your hair blonde or red since mosquitoes prefer blondes and redheads to brunettes. Furthermore, mosquitoes usually prefer to bite women over men. So , _____⁴ that blondies are mosquitoes' favorites. If you don't want to dye your hair and you are not female, but still want to be their favorite, no need to worry. _____⁵ be the chosen one. Mosquitoes are attracted by smells, _____⁶, foul smells. So if you _____⁷ and keep your feet unwashed and stinky, you will _____⁸ donating blood to hungry mosquitoes than those who don't. There are two more things that attract mosquitoes : carbon dioxide and lactic acid. The more you produce these things, _____⁹ you can lure them to you. How? Simple: be obese or jittery, because overweight or fidgety people _____¹⁰ more carbon dioxide and lactic acid than people who aren't.

---

71 정답
1. really does have 2. thanks to 3. it is thought to 4. compared to 5. has got
6. after being cut off 7. continue to move 8. hasn't got 9. it gets attacked 10. what it is

72 정답
1. is leaning to 2. banks 3. visible to the naked eye 4. take 5. agreed with
6. on which 7. made the tower tilt 8. in spite of 9. found no evidence 10. is not at risk of

73 정답
1. giving birth to 2. one of 3. loved her the most 4. didn't spare anything 5. the enormous amounts of
6. all available methods 7. worked laboriously 8. symmetry 9. on his order 10. were amputated

74 정답
1. tied the knot 2. getting approval from 3. knocked everyone's socks off 4. was still married to 5. carry out her responsibilities 6. were not ill 7. would never 8. being very old 9. nothing matters 10. must have loved

75 정답
1. kind of 2. select their victims carefully 3. consider dyeing 4. it's safe to say 5. There is more than one way to
6. specifically 7. sweat a lot 8. have a much better chance at 9. the more likely 10. are said to produce

76 Did You Know How Two Russians Made An Amazing Alien?

When two Russians posted their alien video on YouTube in April 2011, people around the world were taken aback.

Timur Hilall, 18, and Kirill Vlasov, 19, thought their alien video was funny so they expected to get some interesting comments on the Internet comment board. They did their job well enough to draw attention from around the world, including alien experts and the police. Although alien experts suspected the whole thing would be just another alien hoax, they thought it might be worth looking into because the alien in the video looked like the real deal. But the fact was that the "alien" was homemade bread. When the police visited their house, Timur and Kirill had to show them the alien made from flour, eggs and milk. The secret of its skin was also revealed: it was chicken skin. The teenagers had covered the oven-baked alien's body with chicken skin to look mysteriously biological. Brilliant.

UFO communities, which are already used to this kind of hoax, published a statement saying 'we don't know how to take this incredibly strange and perhaps enviably creative hoax.'

1 What is the main idea of the story?

a. The stupid UFO communities were tricked by Russian teenagers.
b. Alien experts complimented two Russians on their alien made from flour and milk.
c. Two Russians' so-called alien was turned out to be a fake.
d. Russian teenagers were enviably creative.

2 According to the passage, which sentence is right?

a. Two Russian teenagers were under arrest after making a fake alien.
b. Timur and Kirill just wanted to bake bread because they were hungry.
c. It seems that there are many other alien hoaxes in the world.
d. Alien experts tricked by these Russian teenagers hated chicken skin.

3 Choose the correct words for each sentence.

a. These are all wooden handicrafts. I guarantee that they are all ready-made / homemade / handmade.
b. I think there's no reason to make a fuss about Cathy's necklace. I know it's a real deal / really deal / real dealing but not a big deal.
c. I think this movie is worthwhile to watch, but that movie is not worth watching / to watch / watch.

LEARNING BOARD

① When two Russians posted their alien video on YouTube in April 2011, people (around the world) were taken aback. ② Timur Hilall, 18, and Kirill Vlasov, 19, thought their alien video was funny so they expected to get some interesting comments (on the Internet comment board). ③ They did their job well enough to draw attention from around the world, (including alien experts and the police). ④ Although alien experts suspected the whole thing would be just another alien hoax, they thought it might be worth looking into because the alien in the video looked like the real deal. ⑤ But the fact was that the "alien" was homemade bread. ⑥ When the police visited their house, Timur and Kirill had to show them the alien made from flour, eggs and milk. ⑦ The secret of its skin was also revealed: it was chicken skin. ⑧ The teenagers had covered the oven-baked alien's body with chicken skin to look mysteriously biological. ⑨ Brilliant. ⑩ UFO communities, (which are already used to this kind of hoax), published a statement saying 'we don't know how to take this incredibly strange and perhaps enviably creative hoax.'

Words & Expressions

alien 외계인 post (사진, 영상 등을 인터넷에) 올리다, 붙이다 comment 논평, 언급 internet comment board 인터넷 덧글 게시판 attention 주목, 관심 suspect 의심하다, 수상하게 여기다 hoax 거짓말, 장난질 be worth –ing …할 가치가 있다 real deal 실제, 진짜 homemade 집에서 만든 flour 밀가루 chicken skin 닭 껍질 oven-baked 오븐에 구운 mysteriously 신비하게 biological 생물학의, 생물체의 brilliant 근사한, 명석한 publish a statement 성명을 발표하다 incredibly 믿을 수 없을 정도로 enviably 부러울 정도로 creative 창의적인

77 Did You Know Why American-born Giant Pandas Were Sent Back To China?

In 2010, two American-born pandas, Mei Lan from Zoo Atlanta and Tai Shan from the Washington Zoo, were sent to China. Shortly after arriving in China, the super cuddly pandas were given a grand welcome. They even appeared on several TV programs just like they did in the United States.

Both of them had been loved so much by the American people ever since they were born in the US, and they served as goodwill ambassadors for China in the US. Then, why were they sent to China? It's because China has ownership of them. Ten years ago, China lent several giant pandas to the United States in exchange for ten million dollars. That's a very expensive price for borrowing something. Under the agreement between the US and China, China would retain ownership of the pandas and their future babies. So, Mei Lan and Tai Shan were

destined to return to China although they were born in the US through artificial insemination.

Then again, why did the US spend millions of dollars on borrowing (not buying) giant pandas? That's because so many people wanted to see these endangered animals, and the only way to come by them is through China.

1 What can be the best title of the story?

a. The Giant Panda : The Super Cutest Animal Ever
b. China's Unfair Trade Practices
c. The US Spent Exorbitant Money On Mei Lan
d. Two Giant Pandas Go Back To Their Homeland

2 Two America-born giant pandas were sent to China because _____.

a. they wanted to go back to their homeland
b. bamboo shoots in the US were not delicious
c. China had ownership of them
d. greedy China insisted all giant panda cubs belong to China

3 Choose the correct words for each sentence.

a. They are willing to borrow / lend / rent their support to noble and worthy causes.
b. If I have a library card and ask a librarian to lend me some books with my card, I can borrow / lend / rent them for free.
c. Ever since / During / While his wife was ill in bed, he has had a hard time.

LEARNING BOARD

① In 2010, two American-born pandas, Mei Lan from Zoo Atlanta and Tai Shan from the Washington Zoo, were sent to China. ② Shortly after arriving in China, the super cuddly pandas were given a grand welcome. ③ They even appeared on several TV programs just like they did in the United States. ④ Both of them had been loved so much by the American people ever since they were born in the US, and they served as goodwill ambassadors for China in the US. ⑤ Then, why were they sent to China? ⑥ It's because China has ownership of them. ⑦ Ten years ago, China lent several giant pandas to the United States in exchange for ten million dollars. ⑧ That's a very expensive price for borrowing something. ⑨ Under the agreement between the US and China, China would retain ownership of the pandas and their future babies. ⑩ So, Mei Lan and Tai Shan were destined to return to China although they were born in the US through artificial insemination. ⑪ Then again, why did the US spend millions of dollars on borrowing (not buying) giant pandas? ⑫ That's because so many people wanted to see these endangered animals, and the only way to come by them is through China.

Words & Expressions

shortly after …직후 cuddly 안아주고 싶은, 사랑스러운 give a grand welcome 크게 환영하다 appear 출연하다(on) good will 친선, 호의 ambassador 대사, 사절 goodwill ambassador 친선대사 ownership 소유권 lend 빌려주다(lend-lent-lent) cf. borrow 빌리다 in exchange for …와 교환하여 expensive 비싼(↔ inexpensive 비싸지 않은) retain 보유하다 be destined to …할 운명이다 artificial 인공의, 인위적인, 모조의 insemination 수정 artificial insemination 인공수정 endangered 멸종 위기에 처한 come by 얻다, 획득하다

78 Did You Know What The Kennedy Curse Is?

The Kennedy Curse is an expression used to describe tragic accidents which have happened to the Kennedy family. No one knows whether those unfortunate events have resulted from the curse or from sheer bad luck, but it is true that there have been many repeated and continual instances of misfortune in the Kennedy family.

Here are some of this family's tragic accidents. In 1963, then U.S. President John F. Kennedy was assassinated by Lee H. Oswald. And his older son John F. Kennedy, Jr died of a plane accident in 1999. His aircraft crashed into the Atlantic Ocean while he was in the cockpit. At that time he was only 39. Robert F. Kennedy, the younger brother of JFK, was also assassinated in 1968. He was shot by Sirhan Sirhan.

In 1984, David Anthony Kennedy died of a cocaine overdose and Michael Kennedy died in a skiing accident in 1997. Kara Kennedy Allen died of a heart attack while exercising in a health club in 2011. In 2012, Mary Richardson Kennedy, a wife of RFK Jr. (the son of the former U.S. senator Robert Kennedy) committed suicide.

1 What is the main idea of the story?
a. It is true there have been lots of tragic accidents in the Kennedy family.
b. The Kennedy curse is merely a superstition.
c. Many members of the Kennedy family were politicians.
d. John F. Kennedy, Jr and Kara Kennedy died because of the curse.

2 According to the passage, which sentence is right?
a. All family members in the Kennedy family are meant to die.
b. Nothing happened to the Kennedy family so the Kennedy curse is not true.
c. Both John F. Kennedy and his older son were killed by the same assassin.
d. It seemed that David Anthony Kennedy was a cocaine user.

3 Choose the correct words for each sentence.
a. An assassin / assassinate / assassinators is a person who murders someone prominent or important.
b. Julie was accused of fraud in 2013 by than / then / their her assistance and her close friend Maria.
c. A toddler fell to the floor while stomping / he stomped / to stomp her feet.
d. Michael, the former / late / early president of the World Trade from 2011 to 2013, was my father's friend.

LEARNING BOARD

① The Kennedy Curse is an expression used to describe tragic accidents (which have happened to the Kennedy family). ② No one knows whether those unfortunate events have resulted from the curse) or (from sheer bad luck), but it is true that there have been many (repeated and continual) instances (of misfortune) in the Kennedy family.

③ Here are some of this family's tragic accidents.

④ In 1963, then U.S. President John F. Kennedy was assassinated by Lee H. Oswald.

⑤ And his older son (John F. Kennedy, Jr) died of a plane accident in 1999. ⑥ His aircraft crashed into the Atlantic Ocean while he was in the cockpit. ⑦ At that time he was only 39. ⑧ Robert F. Kennedy, (the younger brother of JFK), was also assassinated in 1968. ⑨ He was shot by Sirhan Sirhan.

⑩ In 1984, David Anthony Kennedy died of a cocaine overdose and Michael Kennedy died in a skiing accident in 1997. ⑪ Kara Kennedy Allen died of a heart attack while exercising in a health club in 2011. ⑫ In 2012, Mary Richardson Kennedy, (a wife of RFK Jr.) (the son of the former U.S. Senator Robert Kennedy) committed suicide.

Words & Expressions

curse 저주 **expression** 표현 **describe** 묘사하다, 서술하다 **tragic** 비극적인 **unfortunate** 불운한 **event** 사건, 행사 **repeated** 반복된 **continual** 연속적인 **instance** 사례, 경우 **misfortune** 불운, 불행 **assassinate** 암살하다 **sheer** 순전한 **plane/airplane** 비행기 **aircraft** 항공기(날 수 있는 탑승물의 총칭) **crash** 추락하다 **cockpit** 조종석 **cocaine** 코카인 **overdose** 과다 복용 **die of a heart attack** 심장마비로 사망하다 **commit** (잘못된 일을) 저지르다 **commit suicide** 자살하다

217

Did You Know Mount Rushmore Was Carved With The Help Of Dynamite?

Mount Rushmore National Memorial, located in South Dakota, is a monumental super-giant granite sculpture of the heads of former U.S. presidents George Washington, Thomas Jefferson, Theodore Roosevelt and Abraham Lincoln. Its length from the top of the heads to the chins is a whopping 18m and you can see it from 90km away.

The man who designed the heads was Gutzon Borglum. He, and 400 people mustered for the most enormous carving project ever, painstakingly worked for years. The carving started in 1927 and ended in 1941. At that time, there was no road to the mountain, so the workers had to ride horses, walk, or even climb to get to the top of the mountain.

Interestingly, they didn't chip away the stone. To carve the huge heads into the face of Mount Rushmore, Borglum used dynamite. After blasting away large portions of rock with dynamite, Borglum and his workers carved the heads with drills, hammers, and chisels. The memorial is notable for not only its size, but also the fact that no one died during the carving, although it was a very dangerous job.

1 What is the main idea of the story?
   a. Mount Rushmore is famous for its height and beautiful scenery.
   b. While carving giant faces on Mount Rushmore, workers used dynamite.
   c. Explosives like dynamite must not be used under any circumstances.
   d. Borglum forced workers to use only hammers and chisels.

2 To carve four huge heads on Mount Rushmore, Borglum and workers _____.
   a. rode cars or wagons to get to the top of the mountain
   b. blasted large portions of rock away with the help of dynamites
   c. used only their hands and sticks for safety
   d. had chipped away the stone for over 10 years

3 Choose the correct words for each sentence.
   a. I need a proper carve / carving / carved knife to cut this big chunk of meat in half.
   b. The spleen is located in / locates in / located in the left upper part of the abdomen.
   c. All workers should start working at / in / on September 1 and finish their work during December.

LEARNING BOARD

① Mount Rushmore National Memorial, located in South Dakota, is a monumental super-giant granite sculpture of the heads of former U.S. presidents (George Washington, Thomas Jefferson, Theodore Roosevelt and Abraham Lincoln.) ② Its length (from the top of the heads to the chins) is a whopping 18m and you can see it from 90km away. ③ The man who designed the heads was Gutzon Borglum. ④ He, and 400 people mustered for the most enormous carving project ever, painstakingly worked for years. ⑤ The carving started in 1927 and ended in 1941. ⑥ At that time, there was no road to the mountain, so the workers had to 1) ride horses, 2) walk, or even 3) climb to get to the top of the mountain. ⑦ Interestingly, they didn't chip away the stone. ⑧ To carve the huge heads into the face of Mount Rushmore, Borglum used dynamite. ⑨ After blasting away large portions of rock with dynamite, Borglum and his workers carved the heads with drills, hammers, and chisels. ⑩ The memorial is notable for not only its size, but also the fact that no one died during the carving, although it was a very dangerous job.

Words & Expressions

memorial 기념비 monumental 기념비적인, (크기가) 엄청난 located in …에 위치한 super-giant 엄청나게 큰 granite 화강암 sculpture 조각 former 전의 length 길이 whopping 무려 muster 모으다, 소집하다 enormous 거대한(= huge) carving 조각 (cf. carve 조각하다) painstakingly 힘들게(= laboriously), 공들여 ride a horse 말을 타다 chip away 조금씩 (쪼아서) 깎아 내다 huge 거대한(= enormous) blast 폭파시키다 portion 부분, 몫 hammer 망치 chisel 끌 be notable for …로 유명하다(= be famous for)

80 Did You Know There Are Giraffe-looking Women?

Many Kayan people, a minority tribe of Burma, fled from Burma due to the brutal military regime. They had no choice but to live in the Thai border area as illegal immigrants. But, the authorities have let them live there because the giraffe-looking Kayan women attract tourists, and allow them to pocket some money.

Kayan women are famous as 'giraffe women' since their necks are much longer than normal. They actually make their necks longer on purpose. Traditionally, as far as women's necks are concerned, the longer, the better. So in order to have longer necks, most Kayan women wear brass (or silver) neck rings starting when they are young. They gradually add rings to their necks over the years. The heavy weight of the rings pushes down their shoulders, making their necks look longer.

The village where they live is an artificial village built by Thai businessmen. Most tourists visit there only to see the long-necked, exotic-looking Kayan women, and often refer to this village as a human zoo.

1 What can be the best title of this story?

   a. Thai Businessmen, The Archenemy of Kayan Women
   b. Illegal Immigrants Found Unconscious In The Thai Border
   c. Kayan Women : Why Are They Called "Giraffe Women?"
   d. Burma Military Regime Forced Kayan To Be Giraffes.

2 According to the passage, which sentence is wrong?

   a. The population of the Kayan tribe seems to be less than other tribes.
   b. Kayan people living in the Thai border area are illegal immigrants.
   c. Kayan women made their necks long to earn money.
   d. The reason Thai authorities allow Kayan people to live in their territory is money.

3 Choose the correct words for each sentence.

   a. My parents are migration / immigrants / emigrants. They left South Korea 10 years ago to start a new life here, North America.
   b. Many people think, as far as Hollywood starlets are concerned / concerning / concern thinner is better.
   c. Water is often referred to / with / for as the beginning of life.

LEARNING BOARD

① Many Kayan people, (a minority tribe of Burma,) fled from Burma (due to the brutal military regime). ② They had no choice but to live in the Thai border area as illegal immigrants. ③ But, the authorities have let them live there because the giraffe-looking Kayan women 1) attract tourists, and 2) allow them to pocket some money. ④ Kayan women are famous as 'giraffe women' since their necks are much longer than normal. ⑤ They actually make their necks longer on purpose. ⑥ Traditionally, as far as women's necks are concerned, the longer, the better. ⑦ So in order to have longer necks, most Kayan women wear brass (or silver) neck rings starting when they are young. ⑧ They gradually add rings to their necks over the years. ⑨ The heavy weight of the rings pushes down their shoulders, making their necks look longer. ⑩ The village (where they live) is an artificial village built by Thai businessmen. ⑪ Most tourists 1) visit there only to see the (long-necked, exotic-looking) Kayan women, and often 2) refer to this village as a human zoo.

Words & Expressions

minority 소수집단 tribe 부족, 종족 flee 도망가다 ('flea 벼룩'과 혼동하지 않도록 주의) brutal 잔혹한 military 군사의, 군대 regime 정권 border 국경(지역) illegal immigrant 불법 이주민 attract 끌어들이다(cf. attraction 관광명소) pocket some money 돈을 챙기다 on purpose 일부러 traditionally 전통적으로 brass 놋쇠, 금관 악기 gradually 서서히, 점차 artificial 인공적인 exotic 이국적인

221

Listening with Dictation

76 Did You Know How Two Russians Made An Amazing Alien?

When two Russians _____[1] their alien video on YouTube in April 2011, people around the world _____[2]. Timur Hilall, 18, and Kirill Vlasov, 19, thought their alien video was funny so they expected to get some interesting comments _____[3]. They did their job well enough to _____[4] from around the world, including alien experts and the police. Although alien experts _____[5] would be just another alien hoax, they thought it might _____[6] because the alien in the video looked like the real deal. _____[7] the "alien" was homemade bread. When the police visited their house, Timur and Kirill had to show them the alien _____[8] flour, eggs and milk. The secret of its skin was also revealed: it was chicken skin. The teenagers had covered the oven-baked alien's body with chicken skin to look _____[9]. Brilliant. UFO communities, which are already used to this kind of hoax, _____[10] saying 'we don't know how to take this incredibly strange and perhaps enviably creative hoax.'

77 Did You Know Why American-born Giant Pandas Were Sent Back To China?

In 2010, two American-born pandas, Mei Lan from Zoo Atlanta and Tai Shan from the Washington Zoo, _____[1] China. Shortly after arriving in China, the super cuddly pandas _____[2]. They even _____[3] several TV programs just like they did in the United States. Both of them had been loved so much by the American people _____[4] in the US, and they _____[5] goodwill ambassadors for China in the US. Then, why were they sent to China? It's because China has ownership of them. Ten years ago, China lent several giant pandas to the United States _____[6] ten million dollars. That's a very expensive price for borrowing something. _____[7] between the US and China, China would _____[8] the pandas and their future babies. So, Mei Lan and Tai Shan were destined to return to China although they were born in the US through _____[9]. Then again, why did the US spend millions of dollars on borrowing (not buying) giant pandas? That's because so many people wanted to see these endangered animals, and the only way to _____[10] is through China.

78 Did You Know What The Kennedy Curse Is?

The Kennedy Curse is an expression used to describe tragic accidents which have _____[1] the Kennedy family. No one knows whether those unfortunate events have _____[2] the curse or from _____[3], but it is true that there have been many repeated and continual instances of misfortune in the Kennedy family. Here are some of this family's tragic accidents. In 1963, _____[4] U.S. President John F. Kennedy _____[5] Lee H. Oswald. And his older son John F. Kennedy, Jr died of a plane accident in 1999. His aircraft crashed into the Atlantic Ocean while he _____[6]. At that time he was only 39. Robert F. Kennedy, the younger brother of JFK, was also assassinated in 1968. He _____[7] Sirhan Sirhan. In 1984, David Anthony Kennedy _____[8] cocaine overdose and Michael Kennedy died in a skiing accident in 1997. Kara Kennedy Allen died of _____[9] while exercising in a health club in 2011. In 2012, Mary Richardson Kennedy, a wife of RFK Jr. (the son of the former U.S. senator Robert Kennedy) _____[10].

79 Did You Know Mount Rushmore Was Carved With The Help Of Dynamite?

Mount Rushmore National Memorial, _____¹ South Dakota, is a _____² super-giant granite sculpture of the heads of former U.S. presidents George Washington, Thomas Jefferson, Theodore Roosevelt and Abraham Lincoln. Its length from the top of the heads to the chins is _____³ 18m and you can see it from 90km away. The _____⁴ designed the heads was Gutzon Borglum. He, and 400 people _____⁵ for the most enormous carving project ever, _____⁶ for years. The carving started in 1927 and ended in 1941. At that time, _____⁷ the mountain, so the workers had to ride horses, walk, or even climb to get to the top of the mountain. Interestingly, they didn't _____⁸ the stone. To carve the huge heads into the face of Mount Rushmore, Borglum used dynamite. After blasting away _____⁹ rock with dynamite, Borglum and his workers carved the heads with drills, hammers, and chisels. The memorial is notable for not only its size, but also _____¹⁰ no one died during the carving, although it was a very dangerous job.

80 Did You Know There Are Giraffe-looking Women?

Many Kayan people, _____¹ Burma, fled from Burma due to the brutal military regime. They _____² live in the Thai border area as _____³ . But, the authorities have let them live there because the giraffe-looking Kayan women attract tourists, and allow them to _____⁴. Kayan women are famous as 'giraffe women' since their necks are much longer than normal. They actually make their necks longer _____⁵. Traditionally, as far as women's necks are concerned, the longer, the better. So in order to have longer necks, most Kayan women _____⁶ brass (or silver) neck rings starting when they are young. They _____⁷ add rings to their necks over the years. The heavy weight of the rings pushes down their shoulders, making their necks look longer. The _____⁸ is an artificial village built by Thai businessmen. Most tourists visit there _____⁹ see the long-necked, exotic-looking Kayan women, and often _____¹⁰ a human zoo.

---

76 정답
1. posted 2. were taken aback 3. on the Internet comment board 4. draw attention 5. suspected the whole thing
6. be worth looking into 7. But the fact was that 8. made from 9. mysteriously biological 10. published a statement

77 정답
1. were sent to 2. were given a grand welcome 3. appeared on 4. ever since they were born 5. served as
6. in exchange for 7. Under the agreement 8. retain ownership of 9. artificial insemination 10. come by them

78 정답
1. happened to 2. resultd from 3. sheer bad luck 4. then 5. was assassinated by
6. was in the cockpit 7. was shot by 8. died of a 9. a heart attack 10. committed suicide

79 정답
1. located in 2. monumental 3. a whopping 4. man who 5. mustered
6. painstakingly worked 7. there was no road to 8. chip away 9. large portions of 10. the fact that

80 정답
1. a minority tribe of 2. had no choice but to 3. illegal immigrants 4. pocket some money 5. on purpose
6. wear 7. gradually 8. village where they live 9. only to 10. refer to this village as

223

Chapter 9. The Amazing Records

81. Did you know Who The Tallest Person In The World Is?

세상에서 가장 큰 사람이 누구인지 아세요?

82. Did you know What Wolf Girl Wants To Be In The Future?

늑대 소녀가 나중에 무엇이 되고 싶은지 아세요?

83. Did you know What The Most Dangerous Tree In The World Is?

세상에서 가장 위험한 나무가 무엇인지 아세요?

84. Did you know How Long The Longest Tongue In The World Is?

세상에서 가장 긴 혀가 얼마나 긴지 아세요?

85. Did you know How To Hold The World Record In The Field Of Marriage?

결혼 분야에서 세계 기록을 보유하려면 어떻게 해야 하는지 아세요?

86. Did you know This Guinness Trivia?

이런 기네스 기록도 있다는 거 아세요?

87. Did you know What Kind Of Record Dr. Marcel Petiot Held?

마르셀 프티오 의사가 어떤 기록을 보유했는지 아세요?

88. Did you know The Shortest War Lasted Only 38 Minutes?

가장 짧은 전쟁이 단 38분간 지속되었다는 거 아세요?

89. Did you know There Was A Mother Of 69 Children?

69명의 자녀를 둔 어머니가 있다는 거 아세요?

90. Did you know How Fast Bruce Lee's Kicks Were?

이소룡의 발차기가 얼마나 빨랐는지 아세요?

81 Did You Know Who The Tallest Person In The World Is?

Sultan Kosen, a Turk, is the tallest living person in the world, and he is still growing. When he was listed in Guinness World Records as the tallest person in 2009, he was 247cm tall. When Guinness measured his height again in his home town in 2011, his height measured 251cm.

His unusual growth is caused by a pituitary tumor affecting his growth hormone. Recently he underwent treatment for his tumor and is taking medication to control his excessive levels of growth hormone. Now, his hormone levels are said to be almost normal. But, he has already grown too much, so he must use crutches when walking.

He couldn't complete his schooling because of his uncontrollably ever-growing height. He couldn't go inside the school building due to the ceiling being too low for him. He also always has a hard time finding clothes and shoes that fit him, as well as fitting himself into a car. In spite of this, he says he enjoys a normal life, like playing computer games with his friends and helping his mom change light bulbs.

1 What is the main idea of the story?
   a. The tallest person has to use crutches all the time.
   b. Sultan Kosen became the tallest person because of his disease.
   c. A Turk named Sultan Kosen has the current biggest feet in the world.
   d. Kosen should have completed his schooling.

2 According to the article, a pituitary tumor _____.
   a. was measured 251cm
   b. was caused by his abnormal growth hormone
   c. was a kind of incurable cancer
   d. affected Kosen's height

3 Choose the correct words for each sentence.
   a. My job is to watch the rate of economic growth / grow / growing closely.
   b. The construction workers have already received / already have received / have received already their payment from their office.
   c. We measure his height once a week but his weight measure / is measured / measuring on a daily basis.

LEARNING BOARD

① Sultan Kosen, (a Turk), is the tallest living person in the world, and he is still growing. ② When he was listed in Guinness World Records as the tallest person in 2009, he was 247cm tall. ③ When Guinness measured his height again in his home town in 2011, his height measured 251cm. ④ His unusual growth is caused by a pituitary tumor (affecting his growth hormone). ⑤ Recently he 1) underwent treatment for his tumor and 2) is taking medication to control his excessive levels of growth hormone. ⑥ Now, his hormone levels are said to be almost normal. ⑦ But, he has already grown too much, so he must use crutches when walking. ⑧ He couldn't complete his schooling because of his uncontrollably ever-growing height. ⑨ He couldn't go inside the school building due to the ceiling being too low for him. ⑩ He also always has a hard time 1) finding clothes and shoes (that fit him), as well as 2) fitting himself into a car. ⑪ In spite of this, he says he enjoys a normal life, (like 1) playing computer games with his friends and 2) helping his mom change light bulbs).

Words & Expressions

measure 측정하다, (치수가) …이다 **height** 신장, 키 **unusual growth** 이상한 성장 **pituitary** 뇌하수체 **tumor** 종양 **affect** 영향을 미치다 **undergo** (…을) 겪다, 받다 **treatment** 치료, 처치 **take medication** 약을 복용하다 **medication** 약, 약물(치료) **excessive** 과도한 **growth hormone** 성장 호르몬 **hormone level** 호르몬 수치 **crutches** 목발 **complete one's schooling** 학업을 마치다 **uncontrollably** 통제할 수 없게 **ceiling** 천장 **light bulb** 전구

82 Did You Know What Wolf Girl Wants To Be In The Future?

This 11-year-old girl wants to become a doctor so she can help people. Maybe she wants to help patients with rare diseases like her. Supatra Sasuphan, known as Wolf Girl, was born with hypertrichosis, which causes an excessive amount of hair growth on her face and body. This syndrome is often called 'werewolf syndrome' and that's how she got the nickname Wolf Girl.

Her appearance is very extraordinary thanks to thick hair growing all over her face and body except on her two eyes and her mouth. The hair on her face and body is thick enough to make her hold the world record as the "Hairiest Girl in the World."

She said she was happy to be in the Guinness World Records. However, being the hairiest girl in the world is not easy or fun. She has undergone laser treatments to remove the hair, but after a short while it grows back. Also, she has been teased many times and called 'monkey face.' Fortunately, she has gradually been accepted by friends and neighbors since setting the world record. Although she enjoys being a record holder, her parents still want their little daughter to be cured. But, for now, there is no known cure for her condition.

1 What is the main idea of the story?

   a. The real name of Wolf Girl shouldn't be revealed to protect her privacy.
   b. The body of Supatra is pretty much covered with thick hair.
   c. Supatra's neighbors must avoid her because werewolf syndrome is contagious.
   d. Being the hairiest girl in the world is easy and fun.

2 According to the passage, which sentence is right?

   a. Supatra has more than one nick name and one of them is 'wolf face.'
   b. Supatra's appearance is abnormal but her friends have never made fun of her.
   c. Supatra can not afford to get treatments to remove her bushy hair.
   d. Supatra's entire body is covered with thick hair, but her eyes and mouth are an exception.

3 Choose the correct words for each sentence.

   a. You are safe forever / for instance / for now. But no one knows what will happen next.
   b. This robot was programmed to attack everyone only / toward / except the person who programmed it.
   c. We can say a 15 year old girl / a 15-year-old girl / a 15-years-old girl is on the brink of womanhood.
   d. These days, the number of patients of / with / for constipation is increasing day by day.

LEARNING BOARD

① This 11-year-old girl wants to become a doctor so she can help people. ② Maybe she wants to help patients with rare diseases (like her). ③ Supatra Sasuphan, (known as Wolf Girl,) was born with hypertrichosis, (which causes an excessive amount of hair growth) (on her face and body). ④ This syndrome is often called 'werewolf syndrome' and that's how she got the nickname Wolf Girl. ⑤ Her appearance is very extraordinary thanks to thick hair (growing all over her face and body except on her two eyes and her mouth). ⑥ The hair (on her face and body) is thick enough to make her hold the world record as the "Hairiest Girl in the World." ⑦ She said she was happy to be in the Guinness World Records. ⑧ However, being the hairiest girl (in the world) is not easy or fun. ⑨ She has undergone laser treatments (to remove the hair), but (after a short while) it grows back. ⑩ Also, she has been 1) teased many times and 2) called 'monkey face.' ⑪ Fortunately, she has gradually been accepted by friends and neighbors since setting the world record. ⑫ Although she enjoys being a record holder, her parents still want their little daughter to be cured. ⑬ But, for now, there is no known cure for her condition.

Words & Expressions

patient n. 환자 a. 인내심 있는 rare disease 희귀병 hypertrichosis 다모증 excessive 과도한 werewolf 늑대인간 syndrome 증후군 appearance 외모(=look) extraordinary 기이한, 색다른(↔ ordinary 평범한) thick 숱이 많은, 두꺼운, 걸쭉한(↔ thin 숱이 적은, 가는) undergo (수술 등을) 받다, 겪다 laser treatment 레이저 치료 after a short while 얼마 지나면 tease 놀리다(= make fun of) gradually 서서히, 점차 cure v. 낫게 하다, 치유하다 n. 치유, 치료법 condition 질환, 병, 상태, 조건

83 Did You Know What The Most Dangerous Tree In The World Is?

The most dangerous tree in the world is the Poison Guava, also called the manchineel. This tree is found in the Florida Everglades and sandy beaches of the Caribbean coast. So, if you visit there, be careful not to touch it or sit under this tree when it's raining. You should even hold your breath and cover your eyes when it is burned. Of course, don't even think of eating one of its sweet-smelling apple-like fruits. The best way to deal with it is to steer clear of it.

If the poisonous sap exuded from its trunk contacts your skin, it will cause serious blisters. If it touches your eyes, you may go blind, because of its highly acidic poison. Due to this same reason, it should never be your shelter from the rain. Raindrops containing its sap can be as dangerous as the sap itself. When this tree is burned, just run away from that area, because the smoke can irritate your eyes and even cause blindness. Although its fruits look good and smell good, they are fatal. Its leaves, bark, and sap (Anything! You name it!) are purely dangerous. That's why the Poison Guava ascended the throne as the most dangerous tree in the world.

1 What can be the best title of this story?

  a. The Manchineel, The Deadliest Tree
  b. The Poison Guava : Just Taste Its Ultimate Sweetness
  c. Stand Aside, Apples! Make Way For The Poison Guava!
  d. The Manchineel, Smells Good & Tastes Good

2 You must get away from the Poison Guava when it rains because _____.

  a. its poisonous sap makes you go bold
  b. its fruits are big and heavy
  c. you will get wet because its leaves are small and thin
  d. raindrops may contain its dangerous sap

3 Choose the correct words for each sentence.

  a. A couple of days ago, I had a <u>blister / cut / contusion</u> on my hand from tennis and I popped it.
  b. Two boys scratched their backs <u>itself / themselves / himself</u> although they could easily scratch each other's backs.
  c. The best and easiest way to learn about the cultural heritages <u>is / are / be</u> to read books about them.
  d. There are several factors that lead to bad <u>breathe / breath / breathing</u>.

LEARNING BOARD

① The most dangerous tree (in the world), is the Poison Guava, (also called the manchineel). ② This tree is found in ¹⁾ the Florida Everglades and ²⁾ sandy beaches of the Caribbean coast. ③ So, if you visit there, be careful not to ¹⁾ touch it or ²⁾ sit under this tree (when it's raining). ④ You should even ¹⁾ hold your breath and ²⁾ cover your eyes when it is burned. ⑤ Of course, don't even think of eating one of its (sweet-smelling apple-like) fruits. ⑥ The best way (to deal with it) is to steer clear of it. ⑦ If the poisonous sap (exuded from its trunk) contacts your skin, it will cause serious blisters. ⑧ If it touches your eyes, you may go blind, because of its highly acidic poison. ⑨ Due to this same reason, it should never be your shelter from the rain. ⑩ Raindrops (containing its sap) can be as dangerous as the sap itself. ⑪ When this tree is burned, just run away from that area, because the smoke can ¹⁾ irritate your eyes and even ²⁾ cause blindness. ⑫ Although its fruits look good and smell good, they are fatal. ⑬ Its leaves, bark, and sap (Anything! You name it!) are purely dangerous. ⑭ That's why the Poison Guava ascended the throne as the most dangerous tree in the world.

Words & Expressions

the manchineel 맨치닐 나무 **poison** 독, 독약 **sandy** 모래가 많은 **beach** 바닷가 **coast** 해안 **hold one's breath** 숨을 참다 **don't even think of** …할 생각도 마라 **steer clear of** 피하다 **poisonous** 독성의 **sap** 수액 **exude** 풍기다, (액체, 냄새) 흘리다 **trunk** 나무 몸통 (cf. branch/sprig/bough 가지) **contact** 접촉하다; 접촉, 연락 **blister** 수포 **highly acidic** 강한 산성의 **shelter** 피난처, 보호소, 주거지 **raindrop** 빗방울 **irritate** 따갑게 하다, 자극하다, 짜증나게 하다 **fatal** 치명적인 **bark** 나무껍질 **purely** 순전히, 전적으로, 오직 **ascend** 오르다 **throne** 왕좌

84 Did You Know How Long The Longest Tongue In The World Is?

The tongue of Chanel Tapper, a young female college student, is amazing enough to have achieved a Guinness World Record for the world's longest tongue. It's more like 'unbelievable' than 'amazing' because her tongue is as long as a 10cm ruler. To be more exact, her tongue is 9.75cm long. That is twice as long as average. When she sticks out her tongue, she kind of looks like a lizard.

She realized she had a long tongue when she was eight. She and her friends were taking pictures for Halloween, sticking their tongues out. When her pictures were printed, her tongue was noticeably outstanding because of its size and length.

When people around her saw the picture taken for the record, their reactions varied. But, there was something in common among their reactions : they were all surprised. She didn't do anything to lengthen her tongue; rather, she was born with it, and she doesn't think it's a family trait. She said she is always conscious of her extremely long tongue and it affects her friendships and relationships. But she thinks it's okay, because she got used to it and got paid for having the longest tongue in the world by Guinness.

1 What can be the best title of this story?
   a. The Shocking Secret About Chanel's Freaky Tongue
   b. A Normal Lady Who Has The Abnormal Tongue
   c. A Lizard Named Chanel Held The World's Record
   d. 10 Ways To Lengthen Your Tongue

2 According to the passage, which sentence is <u>right</u>?
   a. Unbelievably, Chanel's tongue looks like a long lizard.
   b. It was not until she was eight that she knew she had a extra large tongue.
   c. When people saw her picture of her long tongue, not all of them were surprised.
   d. Chanel's extremely long tongue is the result of years of training.

3 Choose the correct words for each sentence.
   a. Her tongue is so <u>amazing / amazed / amaze</u> that she was listed in the Guinness World Records.
   b. I want to show you our pictures <u>taking / taken / to take</u> recently in the park.
   c. Some say the euro zone is in crisis, but I say it's more <u>likely / like / liked</u> hell because it is far worse than just a crisis.

LEARNING BOARD

① The tongue of Chanel Tapper, (a young female college student), is amazing enough to have achieved a Guinness World Record for the world's longest tongue. ② It's more like 'unbelievable' than 'amazing' because her tongue is as long as a 10cm ruler. ③ To be more exact, her tongue is 9.75cm long. ④ That is twice as long as average. ⑤ When she sticks out her tongue, she (kind of) looks like a lizard. ⑥ She realized she had a long tongue when she was eight. ⑦ She and her friends were taking pictures (for Halloween), (sticking their tongues out). ⑧ When her pictures were printed, her tongue was noticeably outstanding because of its size and length. ⑨ When people (around her) saw the picture (taken for the record), their reactions varied. ⑩ But, there was something in common among their reactions : they were all surprised. ⑪ She didn't do anything to lengthen her tongue; (rather), she was born with it, and she doesn't think it's a family trait. ⑫ She said she is always conscious of her extremely long tongue and it affects her friendships and relationships. ⑬ But she thinks it's okay, because she ¹⁾ got used to it and ²⁾ got paid for having the longest tongue (in the world) (by Guinness).

Words & Expressions

tongue 혀 female 여성, 여성의(↔ male 남성, 남성의) amazing 놀라운 achieve 성취하다, 이루다 unbelievable 믿을 수 없을 정도로 놀라운 to be more exact 더 정확히 말하면 stick out 내밀다 lizard 도마뱀 noticeably 현저히 outstanding 두드러진, 뛰어난 reaction 반응 vary 다양하다, 가지각색이다 lengthen 길게 늘이다 trait 특징 be conscious of ...를 의식·자각하다 extremely 매우, 극히 affect 영향을 미치다 relation ship 관계 get paid for ...로 돈을 받다 get used to ...에 익숙하다

85 Did You Know How To Hold The World Record In The Field Of Marriage?

If you want to hold the world record in the field of marriage, you may have to register with your local gym right away.

Octavio Guillien and Adrian Martinez set the record for the longest engagement. When they were 15 years old, they got engaged. It was not until they hit 82 that they married. Their engagement happened in 1902 and their marriage took place in 1969. So, the period of their engagement was 67 years.

And, when our next couple married in June 2011, US President Obama sent a congratulatory card. Why? That's because the wedding ceremony took place on the 100th birthday of the bridegroom. The happy old groom, Forrest Lunsway, and his newly-wed, 90-year-old bride Rose Lunsway, officially became husband and wife after 30 years of living  together. But amazingly, Forrest Lunsway was not the oldest bridegroom. In 1984, Harry Steven set the record for the oldest bridegroom ever, and his record hasn't been broken yet. He married when he was 103 years old.

As you may have already noticed, if you want to set or break a record in the field of marriage, do not die early.

1 What can be the best title of this story?
 a. When To Engage & How To Marry
 b. Barak Obama Sent A Card To Whom?
 c. The Lunsways Broke The World Record
 d. A Useful Tip To Set The World's Record In The Field Of Marriage

2 If you want to set or break the record in the field of marriage, you _____.
 a. have to engage during elementary school
 b. must be healthy and live long
 c. will have to send a congratulatory card to Mr. President
 d. must die early along with your partner

3 Choose the correct words for each sentence.
 a. Until 2012 that / It was not until 2012 that / It was 2012 until my sister returned home and started to go to school.
 b. He said he sent me a letter two weeks ago, but I haven't received it still / yet / until.
 c. Which historical events took over / took part in / took place during the Baroque period?

LEARNING BOARD

① If you want to hold the world record in the field of marriage, you may have to register with your local gym right away. ② Octavio Guillien and Adrian Martinez set the record for the longest engagement. ③ When they were 15 years old, they got engaged. ④ It was not until they hit 82 that they married. ⑤ Their engagement happened in 1902 and their marriage took place in 1969. ⑥ So, the period of their engagement was 67 years. ⑦ And, when our next couple married in June 2011, US President Obama sent a congratulatory card. ⑧ Why? ⑨ That's because the wedding ceremony took place on the 100th birthday of the bridegroom. ⑩ The happy old groom, (Forrest Lunsway), and his newly-wed, 90-year-old bride (Rose Lunsway), officially became husband and wife after 30 years of living together. ⑪ But amazingly, Forrest Lunsway was not the oldest bridegroom. ⑫ In 1984, Harry Steven set the record for the oldest bridegroom ever, and his record hasn't been broken yet. ⑬ He married when he was 103 years old. ⑭ As you may have already noticed, if you want to set or break a record in the field of marriage, do not die early.

Words & Expressions

marriage 결혼 (marry 결혼하다) register 등록하다 gym 체육관(cf. gymnasium의 줄임말) engagement 약혼 get engaged 약혼하다 take place 개최되다, 발생하다 period 기간 congratulatory 축하의(cf. congratulation 축하) send a congratulation card 축하 카드를 보내다 wedding ceremony 결혼식 bridegroom/groom 신랑(↔ bride 신부) newly-wed 신혼의, 막 결혼한 officially 공식적으로 amazingly 놀랍게도

Listening with Dictation

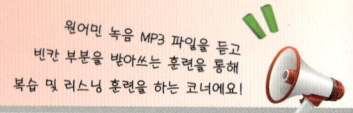

81 Did You Know Who The Tallest Person In The World Is?

Sultan Kosen, a _____¹, is the tallest living person in the world, and he is still growing. When he was listed in Guinness World Records as the tallest person in 2009, he was 247cm tall. When Guinness _____² his height again in his home town in 2011, his height measured 251cm. His unusual growth _____³ a pituitary tumor affecting his growth hormone. Recently he _____⁴ his tumor and is _____⁵ to control his excessive levels of growth hormone. Now, his hormone levels are said to be almost normal. But, he _____⁶ too much, so he must use crutches when walking. He couldn't complete his schooling because of his _____⁷. He couldn't go inside the school building _____⁸ being too low for him. He also always has a hard time finding clothes and shoes that fit him, as well as _____⁹. In spite of this, he says he enjoys a normal life, like playing computer games with his friends and helping his mom _____¹⁰.

82 Did You Know What Wolf Girl Wants To Be In The Future?

This 11-year-old girl wants to become a doctor so she can help people. Maybe she wants to help _____ _____¹ like her. Supatra Sasuphan, _____² Wolf Girl, was born with hypertrichosis, which causes _____³ hair growth on her face and body. This syndrome is often called 'werewolf syndrome' and that's how she _____⁴ Wolf Girl. Her appearance is very _____⁵ thanks to thick hair growing all over her face and body _____⁶ her two eyes and her mouth. The hair on her face and body is thick enough to make her hold the world record as the "Hairiest Girl in the World." She said she was happy to be _____⁷ the Guinness World Records. However, being the hairiest girl in the world is not easy or fun. She has undergone laser treatments to remove the hair, but after a short while it grows back. Also, she _____ _____⁸ many times and called 'monkey face.' Fortunately, she _____⁹ by friends and neighbors since setting the world record. Although she enjoys being a record holder, her parents still want their little daughter to be cured. But, for now, _____¹⁰ for her condition.

83 Did You Know What The Most Dangerous Tree In The World Is?

The most dangerous tree in the world is the Poison Guava, also called the manchineel. This tree _____ _____¹ the Florida Everglades and sandy beaches of the Caribbean coast. So, if you visit there, be careful not to touch it or sit under this tree when it's raining. You should even _____² and cover your eyes when it is burned. Of course, _____³ eating one of its sweet-smelling apple-like fruits. _____⁴ deal with it is to steer clear of it. If the poisonous sap _____⁵ its trunk contacts your skin, it will cause serious blisters. If it touches your eyes, you may go blind, because of its _____⁶. Due to this same reason, it should never be your shelter from the rain. Raindrops containing its sap can be _____⁷ the sap itself. When this tree is burned, just run away from that area, because the smoke can _____⁸ and even cause blindness. Although its fruits _____⁹, they are fatal. Its leaves, bark, and sap (Anything! You name it!) are purely dangerous. That's why the Poison Guava _____¹⁰ as the most dangerous tree in the world.

84. Did You Know How Long The Longest Tongue In The World Is?

The tongue of Chanel Tapper, a young female college student, _____¹ have achieved a Guinness World Record for the world's longest tongue. _____² 'unbelievable' than 'amazing' because her tongue is as long as a 10cm ruler. To be more exact, her tongue is 9.75cm long. That is _____³ average. When she _____⁴, she kind of looks like a lizard. She realized she had a long tongue when she was eight. She and her friends were taking pictures for Halloween, sticking their tongues out. When her _____⁵, her tongue was _____⁶ because of its size and length. When people around her saw _____⁷, their reactions varied. But, there was something in common among their reactions : they were all surprised. She didn't do anything to lengthen her tongue because; rather, she was born with it, and she doesn't think it's a family trait. She said she _____⁸ her extremely long tongue and it affects her friendships and relationships. But she thinks it's okay, because she _____⁹ and _____¹⁰ having the longest tongue in the world by Guinness.

85. Did You Know How To Hold The World Record In The Field Of Marriage?

If you want to hold the world record in the field of marriage, you may have to _____¹ right away. Octavio Guillien and Adrian Martinez set the record for the longest engagement. When they were 15 years old, they _____². It was not until they _____³ that they married. Their engagement happened in 1902 and their marriage took place in 1969. So, _____⁴ their engagement was 67 years. And, when our next couple married in June 2011, US President Obama _____⁵. Why? That's because the wedding ceremony _____⁶ 100th birthday of the bridegroom. The happy old groom, Forrest Lunsway, and his _____⁷, 90-year-old bride Rose Lunsway, _____⁸ husband and wife after 30 years of living together. But amazingly, Forrest Lunsway was not the oldest bridegroom. In 1984, Harry Steven set the record for the oldest bridegroom ever, and his _____⁹. He married when he was 103 years old. _____¹⁰, if you want to set or break a record in the field of marriage, do not die early.

---

81 정답
1. Turk 2. measured 3. is caused by 4. underwent treatment for 5. taking medication 6. has already grown 7. uncontrollably ever-growing height 8. due to the ceiling 9. fitting himself into a car 10. change light bulbs

82 정답
1. patients with rare diseases 2. known as 3. an excessive amount of 4. got the nickname 5. extraordinary 6. except on 7. in 8. has been teased 9. has gradually been accepted 10. there is no known cure

83 정답
1. is found in 2. hold your breath 3. don't even think of 4. The best way to 5. exuded from 6. highly acidic poison 7. as dangerous as 8. irritate your eyes 9. look good and smell good 10. ascended the throne

84 정답
1. is amazing enough to 2. It's more like 3. twice as long as 4. sticks out her tongue 5. pictures were printed 6. noticeably outstanding 7. the picture taken for the record 8. is always conscious of 9. got used to it 10. got paid for

85 정답
1. register with your local gym 2. got engaged 3. hit 82 4. the period of 5. sent a congratulatory card 6. took place on the 7. newly-wed 8. officially became 9. record hasn't been broken yet 10. As you may have already noticed

86 Did You Know This Guinness Trivia?

Darrell Best was listed in the Guinness Book of World Records as the reverend who has presided, at over 40 weddings, in the fastest and easiest way, with the help of his wedding chapel on wheels called "The Best Man." His ceremony doesn't take much time, and needs only two witnesses other than the bride and groom.

Rolf Iven, a young German, set the record for walking the longest distance over hot plates. Of course those hot plates were on while he walked on them! He set the world record by walking 22.90m on 'very hot' hot plates in Milan, Italy, on 18 April 2009.

Walking on hot plates must be very dangerous and scary, but not as dangerous and scary as this next challenge. Kanchana Ketkaew, a Thai woman, entered the Guinness Book of World Records as a person who lived in a glass room with 5,320 scorpions for 33 days and nights. From 22 December 2008 to 24 January 2009, she was stung thirteen times, although those particular scorpions were not deadly or harmful to humans.

1 What is the main idea of the story?

   a. The longest distance walking over hot plates was the hardest.
   b. To live in a glass room with scorpions, you have to fast at least 33 days.
   c. The most foolish thing to do is to live with scorpions in a glass room.
   d. Many people try to set the record in various ways.

2 According to the passage, which sentence is right?

   a. The Best Man of the rev. Best is a vehicle which can be used as a wedding chapel.
   b. When Rolf Iven was trying to set the record in 2009, hot plates were off.
   c. A Thai woman was listed as the most-stung-by-scorpions person in the world.
   d. Darrell Best is a German, so are Rolf Iven and Kanchana Ketkaew.

3 Choose the correct words for each sentence.

   a. This horror movie was supposed to be horrific but not as scared / scary / scare as I thought.
   b. Please turn off / on / into the lights. It's too dark to read my book.
   c. The principal of my school stepped forward to preside at / president for / presiding into the opening ceremony.

LEARNING BOARD

① Darrell Best was listed in the Guinness Book of World Records as the reverend (who has presided, at over 40 weddings, in the fastest and easiest way, with the help of his wedding chapel on wheels) called "The Best Man." ② His ceremony ¹⁾ doesn't take much time, and ²⁾ needs only two witnesses (other than the bride and groom).

③ Rolf Iven, (a young German), set the record for walking the longest distance over hot plates. ④ Of course those hot plates were on while he walked on them! ⑤ He set the world record by walking 22.90m on 'very hot' hot plates in Milan, Italy, on 18 April 2009.

⑥ Walking on hot plates must be very dangerous and scary, but not as (dangerous and scary) as this next challenge. ⑦ Kanchana Ketkaew, (a Thai woman), entered the Guinness Book of World Records as a person (who lived in a glass room with 5,320 scorpions for 33 days and nights). ⑧ From 22 December 2008 to 24 January 2009, she was stung thirteen times, although those particular scorpions were not deadly or harmful to humans.

Words & Expressions

reverend 목사 preside 사회를 보다, 주례를 서다 with the help of …의 도움으로 chapel (학교나 군대에 딸린) 예배당 ceremony 식, 의식 witness 증인 scary 무서운 scorpion 전갈 sting 쏘다 (be stung 쏘이다, 물리다) particular 특정한 deadly 치명적인 harmful 해로운

87 Did You Know What Kind Of Record Dr. Marcel Petiot Held?

Marcel Petiot was a doctor by day, a serial killer by night.

Nazi-occupied Paris was an absolutely horrible place to be during World War II. Many Jews wanted to escape from France because people were just "disappearing" so often. Dr. Petiot lured many Jews desperate to leave Paris. He got paid by them with the expectation of his helping them to leave for South America. But those poor Jews wouldn't set foot on South America, because they were instead savagely killed by Petiot. Most of the victims were dismembered and burned.

In 1944, neighbors of Petiot called the police and complained about the terrible smell coming from the chimney of his house. When the police entered his house and went down to the basement, they couldn't believe what they saw. Human remains, such as arms and legs, were scattered throughout the basement.

He was accused of murdering 27 people, but authorities suspected he might have killed as many as 150 people. He claimed that he was innocent, and he only had killed enemies of France like double-agents or German spies. But no judges or jurors believed him. On 25 May 1946, Petiot was beheaded on the guillotine.

1 **What is the main idea of the story?**

a. The enemies of France were beheaded on the guillotine.
b. During World War II, many Jews disappeared.
c. Marcel Petiot brutally killed many people.
d. Petiot's basement was his secret laboratory.

2 **Many Jews gave Petiot money because they thought _____.**

a. he would help them escape from Paris to South America
b. he was a good doctor who cured people for free
c. he was a double agent and German spy
d. he had a nice and spacious basement

3 **Choose the correct words for each sentence.**

a. Katie is a normal average mom <u>by / at / in the</u> day, a brave crimefighter by night.
b. She couldn't believe what she <u>heard / saw / smelled</u> even though she was watching it with her own eyes.
c. When are you going to leave your parents' house <u>for / with / at</u> the dormitory?
d. When Dean was accused of <u>burglary / he was a thief / he stole something</u>, he claimed that he was falsely accused.

LEARNING BOARD

① Marcel Petiot was a doctor by day, a serial killer by night. ② Nazi-occupied Paris was an absolutely horrible place to be during World War II. ③ Many Jews wanted to escape from France because people were just "disappearing" so often. ④ Dr. Petiot lured many Jews desperate to leave Paris. ⑤ He got paid by them with the expectation of his helping them to leave for South America. ⑥ But those poor Jews wouldn't set foot on South America, because they were instead savagely killed by Petiot. ⑦ Most of the victims were 1) dismembered and 2) burned. ⑧ In 1944, neighbors of Petiot 1) called the police and 2) complained about the terrible smell (coming from the chimney of his house). ⑨ When the police 1) entered his house and 2) went down to the basement, they couldn't believe what they saw. ⑩ Human remains, (such as arms and legs,) were scattered throughout the basement. ⑪ He was accused of murdering 27 people, but authorities suspected he might have killed as many as 150 people. ⑫ He claimed that 1) he was innocent, and 2) he only had killed enemies of France (like double-agents or German spies). ⑬ But no judges or jurors believed him. ⑭ On 25 May 1946, Petiot was beheaded on the guillotine.

Words & Expressions

by day 낮에는 serial killer 연쇄살인범 serial 연쇄적인, 연속 방송되는, 연속극 by night 밤에는 Nazi-occupied 나치가 지배하던 absolutely 극도로 horrible 무서운, 끔찍한 occupy 차지하다, 점령하다 Jews 유대인 escape 도망치다 lure 유혹하다, 꾀다 desperate 필사적인, 간절히 원하는 [to] leave for …로(향해) 떠나다 savagely 잔인하게 (savage 야만적인, 잔인한) victim 희생자 dismember 사지를 자르다 complain 불평하다, 항의하다 terrible 지독한, 끔찍한 chimney 굴뚝 basement 지하실 remains 유해, 남은 부분 scatter 흩뿌리다, 흩어지다 murder 살인하다 suspect 의심하다, 추정하다 innocent 죄가 없는, 결백한 double agent 이중 첩자 judge 판사 juror 배심원 behead 참수하다 guillotine 단두대

Did You Know The Shortest War Lasted Only 38 Minutes?

As far as a war is concerned, shorter is better. Then, how short did the shortest war last? The war between Zanzibar and England in 1896 was the shortest war in recorded history. It was called the 'Anglo-Zanzibar War'.

After the Sultan of Zanzibar died on 25 August 1896, his nephew Bargash rose to the throne, but the British Empire had another person in mind. The British thought this person would be much easier to manipulate. So, the British ordered Bargash to step down from the throne. Bargash refused.

The British sent the Royal Navy to the front of the palace where Bargash had just moved in. Despite the fact that Bargash made efforts to negotiate for a peaceful ending, the British Navy opened fire. The palace started to crumble and people, civilians and soldiers alike, started to die right in front of him. He knew he couldn't win this battle, so he made a hasty retreat to the German consulate.

After that, the British stopped firing and Zanzibar surrendered. This battle started at 9:00 am and lasted for just 38 to 45 minutes. Even though the British had won the battle pretty easily and got what they had wanted, they demanded Zanzibar to pay for the shells fired on Zanzibar.

1 What is the main idea of the story?
  a. The shortest war is the best war.
  b. Anglo-Zanzibar War, the shortest war, lasted for about 38 minutes.
  c. The British opened fire first so the British army was to blame for Anglo-Zanzibar War.
  d. The cause of Anglo-Zanzibar War was Bargash.

2 According to the passage, which sentence is right?
  a. Bargash was too scared to make efforts to negotiate for peace.
  b. Anglo-Zanzibar War was the best war in recorded history.
  c. The British Empire wanted Bargash to rise to the throne.
  d. Bargash, a member of the royal family, stepped up and became a sultan.

3 Choose the correct words for each sentence.
  a. Even though / During / When I have met him several times, I still can't remember his name.
  b. Pack up your belongings and go to the place where / when / who you belong.
  c. One man savagely killed the victim and the other just stood beside him. But both of them were guilty like / alike / likely.

LEARNING BOARD

① As far as a war is concerned, shorter is better. ② Then, how short did the shortest war last? ③ The war (between Zanzibar and England in 1896) was the shortest war in recorded history. ④ It was called the 'Anglo-Zanzibar War'. ⑤ After the Sultan of Zanzibar died on 25 August 1896, his nephew Bargash rose to the throne, but the British Empire had another person in mind. ⑥ The British thought this person would be much easier to manipulate. ⑦ So, the British ordered Bargash to step down from the throne. ⑧ Bargash refused. ⑨ The British sent the Royal Navy to the front of the palace (where Bargash had just moved in.) ⑩ Despite the fact that Bargash made efforts to negotiate for a peaceful ending, the British Navy opened fire. ⑪ The palace started to crumble and people, (civilians and soldiers alike,) started to die right in front of him. ⑫ He knew he couldn't win this battle, so he made a hasty retreat to the German consulate. ⑬ After that, the British stopped firing and Zanzibar surrendered. ⑭ This battle started at 9:00 am and lasted for just 38 to 45 minutes. ⑮ Even though the British 1) had won the battle pretty easily and 2) got what they had wanted, they demanded Zanzibar to pay for the shells (fired on Zanzibar.)

Words & Expressions

last 지속하다 in recorded history 기록된 역사 중 sultan 술탄 (이슬람교 지배자) nephew 남자 조카 throne 왕좌 rise to the throne 왕위에 오르다 have ... in mind ...를 마음에 두다 manipulate (사람, 사물) 조종하다, 다루다 step down 물러나다, 내려오다 palace 궁전 move in 이사해 오다 negotiate 협상하다 open fire 발포하다 crumble (건물이) 무너지다 civilian 시민 retreat 후회, 퇴각, 후퇴하다, 물러나다 make[beat] a retreat 물러가다, 도피하다 consulate 영사관 surrender 항복하다 demand 요구하다 shell 포탄, 조개껍데기

243

89 Did You Know There Was A Mother Of 69 Children?

Giving birth to 69 children? Sounds impossible. Actually it would have been almost impossible had she not given birth to twins or triplets... or quadruplets.

This super mom did give birth to a whopping 69 children with the help of multiple births. She had 16 pairs of twins, 7 sets of triplets, and 4 sets of quadruplets. It's no wonder that her name, Mrs. Feodor Vassilyev, was listed in the 2004 edition of the Guinness Book of World Records as the most prolific mom ever, although this unbelievable story happened in the 1700s. Her shocking record has not been broken yet. The Guinness Book acknowledged her improbable feat, but giving birth to 69 children... isn't that a little too much to believe? Some people doubt it. They think this story is a mere rumor or a made-up story. But what kind of people would have made this kind of story? And why on earth would they do such a thing?

Well, some people do make up this kind of story for various reasons. In 1983, a Chilean woman claimed that she had given birth to 58 children. But, after she died, police discovered that this prolific woman had lied in order to get government-provided food assistance. She had had only 16 children.

1 What can be the best title of this story?

 a. The Biggest Scam Ever : A Mom of 69 Children
 b. Who Are To Blame For Giving Birth To 69 Children?
 c. Believe It Or Not : The Unbelievably Prolific Mom
 d. The Government Takes Action To Feed 69 Children

2 Although Mrs. Vassilyev gave birth to 69 children in the 1700s, _____.

 a. a Chilean mom was acknowledged as the most living prolific mom ever
 b. the Guinness Book of World Records refused to acknowledge her record
 c. her story was introduced in the 2004 edition of the Guinness Book of World Records
 d. nobody has acknowledged her awesome feat for decades

3 Choose the correct words for each sentence.

 a. You have tried / Had you tried / Had tried you this diet, you could have lost some weight.
 b. All of my friends said nothing's going on between John and Kate, but I said, "I doubt / am doubt / take doubt it."
 c. What in the earth / on earth / at earth am I here for? And why in the world am I doing this thing?

LEARNING BOARD

① **Giving birth to** 69 children? ② **Sounds impossible**. ③ Actually it **would have been** almost impossible **had she not given** birth to **twins** or **triplets**... or **quadruplets**. ④ This super mom **did** give birth to a **whopping** 69 children with the help of **multiple** births. ⑤ She had 16 pairs of twins, 7 sets of triplets, and 4 sets of quadruplets. ⑥ It's no wonder that her name, (Mrs. Feodor Vassilyev,) was listed in the 2004 edition of the Guinness Book of World Records as the most **prolific** mom ever, although this **unbelievable** story happened **in the 1700s**. ⑦ Her shocking record **has not been broken** yet. ⑧ The Guinness Book **acknowledged** her **improbable** feat, but giving birth to 69 children... isn't that (a little) **too** much **to** believe? ⑨ Some people **doubt** it. ⑩ They think this story is ¹⁾ a **mere** rumor or ²⁾ a **made-up** story. ⑪ But (what kind of) people would have made this kind of story? ⑫ And why (on earth) would they do such a thing? ⑬ Well, some people do **make up** this kind of story for **various** reasons. ⑭ In 1983, a **Chilean** woman claimed that she had given birth to 58 children. ⑮ But, after she died, police discovered that this prolific woman had lied **in order to** get government-provided food **assistance**. ⑯ She **had had** only 16 children.

Words & Expressions

give birth (아기를) 낳다 impossible 불가능한 twin 쌍둥이 triplets 세 쌍둥이 quadruplets 네 쌍둥이 whopping 무려 multiple 많은, 다수의 multiple birth 다둥이 출산 pair 두 사람의 짝, 한 쌍 prolific 열매를 많이 맺는, 다작의, 다산의 acknowledge 인정하다 improbable 사실 같지 않은, 희한한 feat 공적 mere 그저, 단지 made-up story 지어낸 이야기 various 다양한 for various reasons 다양한 이유로 Chilean 칠레의, 칠레사람의 government-provided food assistance 정부가 제공하는 음식 지원 assistance 보조, 지원

90 Did You Know How Fast Bruce Lee's Kicks Were?

Bruce Lee, born in 1940 and died in 1973, was a martial artist, actor, martial arts instructor, director, and film producer, and was able to move with jaw-dropping speed. Literally, his speed was fast enough to make your jaw drop. How fast? His kicks were so fast that his films had to be slowed down, because people couldn't see his moves. The same goes for his punches.

Since his kicks and punches were extremely fast, some people tried to measure their speed. When Lee demonstrated a kick with his left leg in front of a video camera, his kick only took about a fifth of a second. The people who watched his demonstration on the spot were left speechless when they learned that it was Lee's right leg that was dominant.

Most action films, especially martial art films, are sped up to make their fight scenes look faster and more active. However, Lee's cases were the opposite. Film screeners had to run his films a little bit slower so audiences could see his kicks and punches.

1 What is the main idea of the story?

a. Many martial artists are right-handed.
b. Action films must be sped up to make them more active.
c. Bruce Lee could kick and punch extremely fast.
d. Bruce Lee was an excellent martial artist but not a good actor.

2 According to the passage, which sentence is <u>wrong</u>?

a. Lee was an actor, director and film producer as well.
b. Lee demonstrated his kick with his left leg in front of people.
c. Film makers ran Lee's films a little bit slower by mistake.
d. Generally, action films are sped up in order to make their scenes look more exciting.

3 Choose the correct words for each sentence.

a. It <u>took / made / had</u> him a week to solve this puzzle.
b. When I saw her room, I <u>left / was left / leave</u> speechless because it looked like a bomb hit it.
c. What I want to know is how to make my brother <u>do / to do / doing</u> what I want.

LEARNING BOARD

① Bruce Lee, (born in 1940 and died in 1973), was a martial artist, actor, martial arts instructor, director, and film producer, and was able to move with jaw-dropping speed. ② Literally, his speed was fast enough to make your jaw drop. ③ How fast? ④ His kicks were so fast that his films had to be slowed down, because people couldn't see his moves. ⑤ The same goes for his punches.

⑥ Since his kicks and punches were extremely fast, some people tried to measure their speed. ⑦ When Lee demonstrated a kick with his left leg in front of a video camera, his kick only took about a fifth of a second. ⑧ The people (who watched his demonstration on the spot) were left speechless when they learned that it was Lee's right leg (that was dominant.)

⑨ Most action films, (especially martial art films), are sped up to make their fight scenes look faster and more active. ⑩ However, Lee's cases were the opposite. ⑪ Film screeners had to run his films (a little bit) slower so audiences could see his kicks and punches.

Words & Expressions

martial artist 무술인 **instructor** 지도자 **director** 감독 **film producer** 영화 제작자 **jaw-dropping** 턱이 아래로 빠질 정도의, 놀라운 **slow down** 느리게 하다 **punch** 주먹으로 치다; 펀치 **extremely** 매우, 극히 **demonstrate** 보여주다, 입증하다, 시위에 참여하다 **demonstration** 실연, 증명, 데모 **a fifth of** 1/5의 **on the spot** 현장에서 **speechless** (너무 놀라) 말을 못 하는 **dominant** 우세한 **speed up** 속도를 빠르게 하다 **fighting scene** 격투 장면 **opposite** 반대편의, 반대의 것[사람] **screener** 스크리너 (화면을 검사하거나 가려내는 사람, 영화 화면을 조정하는 사람)

247

Listening with Dictation

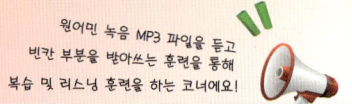

86 Did You Know This Guinness Trivia?

Darrell Best _____¹ the Guinness Book of World Records as the reverend who has presided, at over 40 weddings, in the fastest and easiest way, with the help of his _____² called "The Best Man." His ceremony doesn't _____³, and needs only two witnesses _____⁴ the bride and groom. Rolf Iven, a young German, set the record for walking the longest distance over hot plates. Of course those hot plates _____⁵ while he walked on them! He set the world record by walking 22.90m on 'very hot' hot plates in Milan, Italy, on 18 April 2009. Walking on hot plates _____⁶ and scary, but not as dangerous and scary as this next challenge. Kanchana Ketkaew, a Thai woman, _____⁷ the Guinness Book of World Records as a person who lived in a glass room with 5,320 scorpions _____⁸. From 22 December 2008 to 24 January 2009, she _____⁹, although those particular scorpions were not _____¹⁰ to humans.

87 Did You Know What Kind Of Record Dr. Marcel Petiot Held?

Marcel Petiot was a doctor by day, a serial killer by night. Nazi-occupied Paris was an absolutely horrible _____¹ during World War II. Many Jews wanted to escape from France because people were just "disappearing" so often. Dr. Petiot lured many Jews _____² Paris. He got paid by them _____³ his helping them to leave for South America. But those poor Jews wouldn't _____⁴ South America, because they were instead savagely killed by Petiot. Most of the victims were dismembered and burned. In 1944, neighbors of Petiot called the police and complained about the terrible smell coming from the chimney of his house. When the police entered his house and went down to the basement, they _____⁵. Human remains, such as arms and legs, were scattered _____⁶ the basement. He _____⁷ murdering 27 people, but authorities _____⁸ he might have killed _____⁹ 150 people. He claimed that he was innocent, and he only had killed enemies of France like double-agents or German spies. But no judges or jurors believed him. On 25 May 1946, Petiot was beheaded _____¹⁰.

88 Did You Know The Shortest War Lasted Only 38 Minutes?

As far as _____¹, shorter is better. Then, how short did the shortest war last? The war between Zanzibar and England in 1896 was the shortest war in recorded history. It was called the 'Anglo-Zanzibar War'. After the Sultan of Zanzibar died on 25 August 1896, his nephew Bargash _____², but the British Empire _____³. The British thought this person would be _____⁴. So, the British ordered Bargash to step down from the throne. Bargash refused. The British sent the Royal Navy to the front of the palace where Bargash had just moved in. _____⁵ Bargash _____⁶ negotiate for a peaceful ending, the British Navy opened fire. The palace started to crumble and people, _____⁷, started to die right in front of him. He knew he couldn't win this battle, so he _____⁸ to the German consulate. After that, the British stopped firing and Zanzibar surrendered. This battle _____⁹ 9:00 am and lasted for just 38 to 45 minutes. Even though the British had won the battle pretty easily and got _____¹⁰, they demanded Zanzibar to pay for the shells fired on Zanzibar.

89. Did You Know There Was A Mother Of 69 Children?

Giving birth to 69 children? _____1. Actually it would have been almost impossible _____2 birth to twins or triplets... or quadruplets. This super mom did give birth to a whopping 69 children _____3. She had 16 pairs of twins, 7 sets of triplets, and 4 sets of quadruplets. It's no wonder that her name, Mrs. Feodor Vassilyev, was listed in the 2004 edition of the Guinness Book of World Records as _____4, although this unbelievable story happened in the 1700s. Her shocking record has not been broken yet. The Guinness Book _____5, but giving birth to 69 children... isn't that _____6? Some people doubt it. They think this story is a mere rumor or _____7 But what kind of people would have made this kind of story? And why on earth would they _____8? Well, some people do make up this kind of story _____9. In 1983, a Chilean woman claimed that she had given birth to 58 children. But, after she died, police discovered that this prolific woman had lied in order to get government-provided _____10. She had had only 16 children.

90. Did You Know How Fast Bruce Lee's Kicks Were?

Bruce Lee, born in 1940 and died in 1973, was a _____1, actor, martial arts instructor, director, and film producer, and was able to _____2. Literally, his speed was _____3 make your jaw drop. How fast? His kicks were so fast that his films had to be slowed down, because people couldn't see his moves. _____4 his punches. Since his kicks and punches were extremely fast, some people tried to measure their speed. When Lee demonstrated a kick with his left leg in front of a video camera, his kick only took about _____5. The people who watched his demonstration _____6 were _____7 when they learned that it was Lee's right leg that was _____8. Most action films, especially martial art films, _____9 make their fight scenes look faster and more active. However, Lee's cases were _____10. Film screeners had to run his films a little bit slower so audiences could see his kicks and punches.

---

86 정답 1. was listed in 2. wedding chapel on wheels 3. take much time 4. other than 5. were on 6. must be very dangerous 7. entered 8. for 33 days and nights 9. was stung thirteen times 10. deadly or harmful

87 정답 1. place to be 2. desperate to leave 3. with the expectation of 4. set foot on 5. couldn't believe what they saw 6. throughout 7. was accused of 8. suspected 9. as many as 10. on the guillotine

88 정답 1. a war is concerned 2. rose to the throne 3. had another person in mind 4. much easier to manipulate 5. Despite the fact that 6. made efforts to 7. civilians and soldiers alike 8. made a hasty retreat 9. started at 10. what they had wanted

89 정답 1. Sounds impossible 2. had she not given 3. with the help of multiple births 4. the most prolific mom ever 5. acknowledged her improbable feat 6. a little too much to believe 7. a made-up story 8. do such a thing 9. for various reasons 10. food assistance

90 정답 1. martial artist 2. move with jaw-dropping speed 3. fast enough to 4. The same goes for 5. a fifth of a second 6. on the spot 7. left speechless 8. dominant 9. are sped up to 10. the opposite

Chapter 10. Proverbs & Idioms

91. Did you know A Leopard Cannot Change Its Spots?

표범이 자신의 점들을 바꿀 수 없다는 거 아세요?

92. Did you know You Can 'Paint The Town Red' Without A Paintbrush?

붓 없이도 '시내를 빨갛게 칠할' 수 있다는 거 아세요?

93. Did you know What Can Kill The Cat With Nine Lives?

목숨이 9개인 고양이를 죽일 수 있는 게 무엇인지 아세요?

94. Did you know You Can "Get The Axe" Without Receiving Any Actual Axe?

실제 도끼를 받지 않고도 'get the axe' 할 수 있다는 거 아세요?

95. Did you know What Happens To Fish When They Go Belly-up?

물고기가 배를 드러내면 어떻게 되는지 아세요?

96. Did you know 'Gung Ho' Comes From Chinese Characters?

'gung ho'가 한자라는 거 아세요?

97. Did you know The Meaning Of 'Easier Said Than Done'?

'easier said than done'의 의미를 아세요?

98. Did you know The Meaning Of 'Blow It'?

'blow it'의 의미를 아세요?

99. Did you know The Meaning Of 'Spill The Beans'?

'spill the beans'의 의미를 아세요?

100. Did you know The Meaning Of 'Mind One's Ps And Qs'?

'mind one's P's and Q's'의 의미를 아세요?

91 Did You Know A Leopard Cannot Change Its Spots?

A leopard cannot change its spots. Also, a tiger cannot change its stripes. A leopard has lots of spots on its fur. No matter how hard it tries to remove them, its spots will never vanish or become faint. Whether taking a bath, scrubbing with brushes, using all kinds of soap… it's "no can do," for it's not a matter you can solve by scrubbing the outside of its skin. Originally, this proverb came from the Bible.

"Can the Ethiopian change his skin, or the leopard his spots? Then may you also do good, that are accustomed to do evil." (Jeremiah 13:23)

It's impossible for a dark-skinned African to change his skin color to be like that of a fair-skinned European; neither can an evil person change his evil ways easily, because he is accustomed to do evil. Thus, you can use this proverb when you want to describe someone who cannot change his or her essential nature.

For example, there was a lazy guy and he was always late for work. When he arrived at his office, late as usual, he said that he was sorry and wouldn't be late again. But the next day, he was late as everybody had expected. Seeing him, his co-workers and boss said, "a leopard cannot change its spots."

1 What is the main idea of the story?
  a. It is not easy to change your essential nature.
  b. A dark-skinned African should not try to change his skin color.
  c. People who do good are likely to have spots on their skin.
  d. Lazy workers must scrub their skin with brushes.

2 According to Jeremiah 13:23, _____.
  a. The Ethiopian didn't use brushes when taking a bath
  b. The Ethiopian can't change his skin, neither can the leopard
  c. Tigers and leopards are evil animals
  d. The Ethiopian is accustomed to do evil

3 Choose the correct words for each sentence.
  a. Mark, who is <u>fair-skinned / fairy skin / skin of fair</u> and has fair hair, is a fair person.
  b. Normally, I am not accustomed <u>of / with / to</u> eating too much. So I think I have to stop eating now.
  c. He didn't care what was going on there and <u>neither she did / neither did she / she neither did</u>.

LEARNING BOARD

① A leopard cannot change its spots. ② Also, a tiger cannot change its stripes. ③ A leopard has lots of spots on its fur. ④ No matter how hard it tries to remove them, its spots will never vanish or become faint. ⑤ Whether ¹⁾ taking a bath, ²⁾ scrubbing with brushes, ³⁾ using all kinds of soap... it's "no can do," for it's not a matter (you can solve by scrubbing the outside of its skin). ⑥ Originally, this proverb came from the Bible. ⑦ "Can the Ethiopian change his skin, or the leopard his spots? ⑧ Then may you also do good, that are accustomed to do evil." (Jeremiah 13:23) ⑨ It's impossible for a dark-skinned African to change his skin color to be like that of a fair-skinned European; ⑩ neither can an evil person change his evil ways easily, because he is accustomed to do evil. ⑪ Thus, you can use this proverb when you want to describe someone (who cannot change (his or her) essential nature.) ⑫ For example, there was a lazy guy and he was always late for work. ⑬ When he arrived at his office, late as usual, he said that (he was sorry and wouldn't be late again). ⑭ But the next day, he was late as everybody had expected. ⑮ Seeing him, his co-workers and boss said, "a leopard cannot change its spots."

Words & Expressions

leopard 표범 **spot** 점 **stripe** 줄무늬 **proverb** 속담 **remove** 제거하다 **vanish** 사라지다 **become faint** 흐려지다 **rub** 문지르다 **brush** 솔 **no can do** 소용없다, 할 수 없다 **solve** (문제를) 해결하다 **originally** 원래 **Jeremiah** 예레미야(사람 이름, 구약 성경 예레미야서) **do good** 좋은 일을 하다, 이롭다 **fair-skinned** 피부가 밝은 **fair** 흰 피부의, 날씨가 맑은, 공정한, 상당한 **be accustomed to** 익숙하다 **essential nature** 본성 **as usual** 평소대로 **co-worker** 동료

92 Did You Know You Can 'Paint The Town Red' Without A Paintbrush?

You can 'paint the town red' not with a paintbrush but with lots of alcohol, because this expression has nothing to do with a paint job. It means, "to engage in a wild and riotous spree."

There is more than one suggestion as to the origin of this expression. The most well-known theory is that it was started by a nobleman named Henry. This guy was so mischievous that he ran riot in a Leicestershire town with a group of his friends, painting the town's buildings and bars red in the 1800s. Some claim that the 'red light district' might be the origin. In the past, the section of a town where bars and saloons were located was called the red light district. Thus they think the word 'red' might have come from 'red light district.' Or, it could have originated in red blood. In fact, some think this expression came from a kind of crazy behavior including shedding blood and painting walls and buildings with blood. Yet, no one knows which is the real origin.

Anyway, when the 2010 Winter Olympics was held in Vancouver, Canadians cheered on their athletes with the slogan 'paint the town red' since it also has the meaning of 'have lots of fun.'

1 What is the main idea of the story?
   a. Henry hated to live in the red light district
   b. 'Paint the town red' has nothing to do with the paint job.
   c. If you pain the town red, you will be under arrest by the local police.
   d. 'Paint the town red' means to shed blood.

2 According to the passage, which sentence is <u>wrong</u>?
   a. The expression 'paint the town red' has something to do with alcohol and parties.
   b. Henry was mischievous enough to paint buildings and bars red.
   c. There were many bars and pubs in the red light district.
   d. Everybody knows the origin of 'paint the town red.'

3 Choose the correct words for each sentence.
   a. <u>What / Which / That</u> one do you like more, coffee or tea?
   b. The new-comer told me that he came <u>after / from / again</u> the land of the ice and snow.
   c. I went to the church on Friday morning, where Dave's funeral <u>was held / hold / held</u>.

LEARNING BOARD

① You can 'paint the town red' not (with a paintbrush) but (with lots of alcohol,) because this expression has nothing to do with a paint job. ② It means, "to engage in (a wild and riotous spree."

③ There is more than one suggestion as to the origin of this expression. ④ The most well-known theory is that it was started by a nobleman (named Henry). ⑤ This guy was so mischievous that he ran riot in a Leicestershire town with a group of his friends, painting (the town's buildings and bars) red in the 1800s. ⑥ Some claim that the 'red light district' might be the origin. ⑦ In the past, the section of a town (where bars and saloons were located) was called the red light district. ⑧ Thus they think the word 'red' might have come from 'red light district.' ⑨ Or, it could have originated in red blood. ⑩ In fact, some think this expression came from (a kind of) crazy behavior (including 1) shedding blood and 2) painting walls and buildings with blood). ⑪ Yet, no one knows which is the real origin. ⑫ Anyway, when the 2010 Winter Olympics was held in Vancouver, Canadians cheered on their athletes with the slogan 'paint the town red' since it also has the meaning of 'have lots of fun.'

Words & Expressions

paint the town red 술 마시며 놀다 **paint** 물감, 색을 칠하다 **engage in** 참여하다, 관여하다 **riotous** 소란스러운 **spree** 흥청거리는 한바탕 놀음 **origin** 기원, 유래 **the most well-known** 가장 잘 알려진 **noble** 귀족 **mischievous** 장난꾸러기의 **run riot** 난동을 부리다 (**riot** 폭동, 소동) **red light district** 홍등가 **section** 구역, 지구, 부문 **bar** 술집 **saloon** 술집, 살롱 **locate** ...에 위치하다 **originate in** 비롯하다, 유래하다 **be held in** ...에서 개최되다 **cheer on** ...를 응원하다 **athlete** 운동선수 **have fun** 재미있게 즐기다

93 Did You Know What Can Kill The Cat With Nine Lives?

Cats are said to have nine lives. Then, what can kill cats? The answer can be found in the proverb 'curiosity killed the cat.' This means that curiosity or inquisitiveness can lead to dangerous situations. You can use this proverb when trying to stop someone from asking unwanted questions.

Cats are famous for being curious and for having nine lives. Generally, it is supposed to be almost impossible to kill something that has nine lives, but cats can be killed by their own curious natures. Cats are that curious! Maybe that's how this proverb came to be. But originally, what killed the cat was not 'curiosity' but 'care'. In this context, 'care' meant 'worry or sorrow.' In fact, 'care killed the cat' was used until the late 1800s.

It is very difficult to pinpoint exactly when this proverb started, or how the word 'care' replaced with 'curiosity.' All we know is that the original form of this proverb changed from 'care killed the cat' into 'curiosity killed the cat.'

Maybe we should stop being curious about the origin of this proverb. After all, curiosity killed the cat.

1 What is the main idea of the story?
   a. Don't even think of killing cats although cat meat is delicious.
   b. Cats are curious creatures, so there is a proverb like 'curiosity killed the cat.'
   c. Cats have nine lives so you will have to kill them ten times over if you want to eliminate them.
   d. The right expression is 'Care killed the cat', not 'Curiosity killed the cat."

2 During the 1800s, _____.
   a. people believed only curious cats had nine lives
   b. curious cats were killed by people
   c. many proverbs about cats were made
   d. people had used the proverb 'care killed the cat'

3 Choose the correct words for each sentence.
   a. It is easy <u>of saying / to say / into say</u> for you, Diane, but unfortunately it's not that easy for me.
   b. Hundreds of Indian girls shares the same name meaning "<u>wanted / savior / unwanted</u>" in Hindi since their parents wanted boys not girls.
   c. Much to my surprise, even I can change the world <u>from / into / as</u> a better place.

LEARNING BOARD

① Cats are said to have nine lives. ② Then, what can kill cats? ③ The answer can be found in the proverb 'curiosity killed the cat.' ④ This means that curiosity or inquisitiveness can lead to dangerous situations. ⑤ You can use this proverb when trying to stop someone from asking unwanted questions. ⑥ Cats are famous ¹⁾ for being curious and ²⁾ for having nine lives. ⑦ Generally, it is supposed to be almost impossible to kill something (that has nine lives,) but cats can be killed by their own curious natures. ⑧ Cats are that curious! ⑨ Maybe that's how this proverb came to be. ⑩ But originally, what killed the cat was not 'curiosity' but 'care'. ⑪ In this context, 'care' meant 'worry or sorrow.' ⑫ In fact, 'care killed the cat' was used until the late 1800s. ⑬ It is very difficult to pinpoint exactly ¹⁾ when this proverb started, or ²⁾ how the word 'care' replaced with 'curiosity.' ⑭ All we know is that the original form of this proverb changed from 'care killed the cat' into 'curiosity killed the cat.' ⑮ Maybe we should stop being curious about the origin of this proverb. ⑯ After all, curiosity killed the cat.

Words & Expressions

curiosity 호기심 inquisitiveness 꼬치꼬치 캐묻기 좋아함 unwanted 원치 않는 care 돌봄, 보살핌, 주의, 걱정 pinpoint 정확히 집어내다 replace 대체하다

257

Did You Know You Can "Get The Axe" Without Receiving Any Actual Axe?

You can 'get the axe' or 'give the axe' although there is no actual axe being given or taken away. It is possible because the word 'axe' has several different meanings.

An axe is a hand tool used for cutting wood or chopping down trees. It is also used as a verb, and its meaning is 'to chop, cut, or trim with an axe.' Its second meaning is a 'dismissal' especially from employment. So, words like 'discharge, removal, layoff...' are synonyms of 'axe'. That's how the expression 'to give the axe' got the meaning of 'to fire'. Similarly, 'to get the axe' means 'to get fired'.

Speaking of 'getting fired', there is another phrase you might want to know : the sack. 'Sack' is widely known as a kind of bag. But, it also has the meaning of dismissal, just like the word 'axe'. So to 'get the sack' is the same in meaning as to 'get the axe'.

One more thing: if you want to use the words 'sack' or 'axe' with the meaning of dismissal, do not omit the word 'the'. If you say, 'my boss gave me an axe (or a sack)', people will think that you received an actual axe (or sack) from your kind boss.

1 What is the main idea of the story?

a. If someone gives you the axe, you will have to pay for it.
b. 'Get the axe' means 'get fired.'
c. 'Get the axe' and 'give the sack' have the same meaning.
d. An axe is more expensive than a sack.

2 According to the passage, which sentence is right?

a. If you don't like one of your lazy employees, you can give him an axe.
b. The word 'axe' has at least five different meanings.
c. Synonyms of 'employment' are 'discharge' and 'layoff'.
d. 'Get the axe' is totally different from 'get an axe'.

3 Choose the correct words for each sentence.

a. You have to permit the <u>layoff / dismiss / sack</u> of some staff members due to budget cuts.
b. What religions <u>are commonly practiced / practiced are commonly / commonly are practiced</u> in Africa?
c. No way to play soccer under the scorching sun without <u>you get burned / getting burned / to get burning</u>.

LEARNING BOARD

① You can 'get the axe' or 'give the axe' although there is no actual axe (being given or taken away). ② It is possible because the word 'axe' has several different meanings.

③ An axe is a hand tool (used for 1) cutting wood or 2) chopping down trees).

④ It is also used as a verb, and its meaning is 'to chop, cut, or trim with an axe.'

⑤ Its second meaning is a 'dismissal' especially from employment. ⑥ So, words (like 'discharge, removal, layoff...') are synonyms of 'axe'. ⑦ That's how the expression 'to give the axe' got the meaning of 'to fire'. ⑧ Similarly, 'to get the axe' means 'to get fired'.

⑨ Speaking of 'getting fired', there is another phrase you might want to know : the sack. ⑩ 'Sack' is widely known as a kind of bag. ⑪ But, it also has the meaning of dismissal, just like the word 'axe'. ⑫ So to 'get the sack' is the same in meaning as to 'get the axe'.

⑬ One more thing: ⑭ if you want to use the words 'sack' or 'axe' with the meaning of dismissal, do not omit the word 'the'. ⑮ If you say, 'my boss gave me an axe (or a sack)', people will think that you received an actual axe (or sack) from your kind boss.

Words & Expressions

axe 도끼 get the axe 해고당하다 give the axe 해고하다 actual 실제 hand tool 수공구 split 쪼개다 chop 자르다 verb 동사 trim 다듬다 dismissal 해고 employment 고용 discharge 해고 removal 제거, 해고 layoff 일시 해고 synonym 유의어 fire 해고하다 get fired 해고당하다 similarly 유사하게, 마찬가지로 sack 가방 get the sack 해고당하다 be widely known as ...로 널리 알려지다 omit 빼다, 생략하다

259

95 Did You Know What Happens To Fish When They Go Belly-up?

If a fish goes belly-up, it's dead. Think about a dead fish. It doesn't swim or move its fins. It just floats upside-down on the water, showing its belly. The expression 'belly-up' means the same thing, since its origin is the floating position of a dead fish. So to 'go belly-up' means to 'be hopelessly ruined', 'fail' or 'go bankrupt'. Generally, this expression is used in financially difficult situations.

For example, you can say :

"Builders are on the verge of going belly-up because the price of cement is going higher and higher."

"He is certain that he won't go belly-up even though his debt problem is getting worse day by day."

"Many fish farmers are about to go belly-up since more and more fish in fish farms are literally going belly-up due to harmful pollutants being emitted from power plants."

But, there is no such thing as going 'belly-down.'

1 What is the main idea of the story?
a. You will go belly-up if you eat dead fish.
b. You can use the expression 'go belly-up' when someone suffers from stomach cancer.
c. The expression 'go belly-up' has something to do with fish and it means to 'fail'.
d. Fish farmers and builders are about to go belly-up.

2 The expression 'belly-up' comes from _____ .
a. the builder who has a debt problem
b. the position of fish swimming in the water
c. the floating position of a dead fish
d. the hopeless situation of being ruined

3 Choose the correct words for each sentence.
a. A group of fish is often called a school. So a school of fish <u>meaning / means / mean</u> the same as a group of fish.
b. My grocery bill is getting <u>better and better / higher and higher / larger and larger</u> due to inflation.
c. When the robber threatened to kill her, she called 911 and yelled, 'I'm about <u>to die / die / being dead</u>!'
d. My brother <u>was on the verge of / is about of / was planning to</u> nervous breakdown after failing to win the contest.

LEARNING BOARD

① If a fish goes belly-up, it's dead. ② Think about a dead fish. ③ It doesn't swim or move its fins. ④ It just floats upside-down on the water, showing its belly. ⑤ The expression 'belly-up' means the same thing, since its origin is the floating position of a dead fish. ⑥ So to 'go belly-up' means to 'be hopelessly ruined', 'fail' or 'go bankrupt'. ⑦ Generally, this expression is used in financially difficult situations.

⑧ For example, you can say:

⑨ "Builders are on the verge of going belly-up because the price of cement is going higher and higher."

⑩ "He is certain that he won't go belly-up even though his debt problem is getting worse day by day."

⑪ "Many fish farmers are about to go belly-up since more and more fish (in fish farms) are literally going belly-up due to harmful pollutants (being emitted from power plants)."

⑫ But, there is no such thing as going 'belly-down.'

Words & Expressions

belly 배 go belly-up 망하다, 파산하다, 배를 드러내다 fin 지느러미 float 물에 뜨다 upside-down 뒤집혀, 위아래가 바뀌어 ruin 망치다, 손상시키다 bankrupt 파산한(cf. bankruptcy 도산, 파산) financially 경제적으로 builder 건축업자 be on the verge of ...하기 직전이다 debt 빚 fish farmer 양식어민 literally 문자[말] 그대로 pollutant 오염물질 emit 방출하다 power plant 발전소

Listening with Dictation

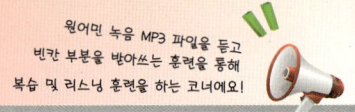

91 Did You Know A Leopard Cannot Change Its Spots?

A _____¹ cannot change its spots. Also, a tiger cannot change its stripes. A leopard has lots of spots on its fur. No matter how hard it tries to remove them, its spots will never _____². Whether taking a bath, scrubbing with brushes, using all kinds of soap... it's "_____³," for it's not a matter you can solve by scrubbing the outside of its skin. Originally, this proverb came from the Bible. "Can the Ethiopian change his skin, or the leopard his spots? Then may you also do good, that are accustomed to do evil." (Jeremiah 13:23) It's impossible for a dark-skinned African to change his skin color _____⁴ that of a _____⁵ European; _____⁶ can an evil person change his evil ways easily, because he _____⁷ do evil. Thus, you can use this proverb when you want to describe someone who cannot change his or her _____⁸. For example, there was a lazy guy and he was always late for work. When he arrived at his office, _____⁹, he said that he was sorry and wouldn't be late again. But the next day, he was late as everybody had expected. _____¹⁰, his co-workers and boss said, "a leopard cannot change its spots."

92 Did You Know You Can 'Paint The Town Red' Without A Paintbrush?

You can 'paint the town red' not with a paintbrush but with lots of alcohol, because this expression has nothing to do with a paint job. It means, "to engage in a wild and _____¹." There is more than one suggestion _____² the origin of this expression. The most well-known theory is that _____³ a nobleman named Henry. This guy was so _____⁴ that he _____⁵ in a Leicestershire town with a group of his friends, painting the town's buildings and bars red in the 1800s. Some claim that the 'red light district' might be the origin. In the past, the section of a town _____⁶ bars and saloons _____⁷ was called the red light district. Thus they think the word 'red' might have come from 'red light district.' Or, it could have _____⁸ in red blood. In fact, some think this expression came from a kind of crazy behavior including _____⁹ and painting walls and buildings with blood. Yet, no one knows which is the real origin. Anyway, when the 2010 Winter Olympics _____¹⁰ in Vancouver, Canadians cheered on their athletes with the slogan 'paint the town red' since it also has the meaning of 'have lots of fun.'

93 Did You Know What Can Kill The Cat With Nine Lives?

Cats _____¹ have nine lives. Then, what can kill cats? The answer can be found in the proverb 'curiosity killed the cat.' This means that curiosity or _____² can lead to dangerous situations. You can use this proverb when trying to stop someone from asking unwanted questions. Cats are famous for being curious and for having nine lives. Generally, it _____³ be almost impossible to kill something that has nine lives, but cats can be killed by their own _____⁴. Cats are that curious! Maybe that's how this proverb came to be. But originally, _____⁵ was not 'curiosity' but 'care'. In this context, 'care' meant 'worry or sorrow.' In fact, 'care killed the cat' was used _____⁶ 1800s. It is very difficult to _____⁷ this proverb started, or how the word 'care' _____⁸ 'curiosity.' _____⁹ the original form of this proverb changed from 'care killed the cat' into 'curiosity killed the cat.' Maybe we should _____¹⁰ about the origin of this proverb. After all, curiosity killed the cat.

262 Chapter 10 | Proverbs & Idioms

94. Did You Know You Can "Get The Axe" Without Receiving Any Actual Axe?

You can 'get the axe' or 'give the axe' although there is no actual axe _____¹ or _____². It is possible because the word 'axe' _____³. An axe is a hand tool used for cutting wood or chopping down trees. It is also used as a verb, and its meaning is 'to chop, cut, or trim with an axe.' Its second meaning is a '_____⁴' especially from employment. So, words like 'discharge, removal, layoff...' are synonyms of 'axe'. That's how the expression 'to give the axe' got the meaning of 'to fire.' _____⁵, 'to get the axe' means 'to get fired.' _____⁶ 'getting fired', there is another phrase you might want to know : the sack. 'Sack' _____⁷ a kind of bag. But, it also has the meaning of dismissal, just like the word 'axe'. So to 'get the sack' _____⁸ as to 'get the axe'. One more thing: if you want to use the words 'sack' or 'axe' with the meaning of dismissal, do not _____⁹ the word 'the'. If you say, 'my boss gave me an axe (or a sack)', people will think that you received an _____¹⁰ (or sack) from your kind boss.

95. Did You Know What Happens To Fish When They Go Belly-up?

If a fish _____¹, it's dead. Think about a dead fish. It doesn't swim or move its fins. It just floats _____² on the water, showing its belly. The expression 'belly-up' _____³, since its origin is the _____⁴ of a dead fish. So to 'go belly-up' means to 'be hopelessly ruined', 'fail' or '_____⁵ ' Generally, this expression is used in _____⁶. For example, you can say : "Builders _____⁷ going belly-up because the price of cement is going higher and higher." "He is certain that he won't go belly-up even though his debt problem is getting worse day by day." "Many fish farmers _____⁸ go belly-up since more and more fish in fish farms are literally going belly-up due to harmful pollutants being _____⁹ power plants." But, _____¹⁰ going 'belly-down.'

---

91 정답
1. leopard 2. vanish or become faint 3. no can do 4. to be like 5. fair-skinned
6. neither 7. is accustomed to 8. essential nature 9. late as usual 10. Seeing him

92 정답
1. riotous spree 2. as to 3. it was started by 4. mischievous 5. ran riot
6. where 7. were located 8. originated 9. shedding blood 10. was held

93 정답
1. are said to 2. inquisitiveness 3. is supposed to 4. curious natures 5. what killed the cat
6. until the late 7. pinpoint exactly when 8. replaced with 9. All we know is that 10. stop being curious

94 정답
1. being given 2. taken away 3. has several different meanings 4. dismissal 5. Similarly
6. Speaking of 7. is widely known as 8. is the same in meaning 9. omit 10. actual axe

95 정답
1. goes belly-up 2. upside-down 3. means the same thing 4. floating position 5. go bankrupt 6. financially difficult situations 7. are on the verge of 8. are about to 9. emitted from 10. there is no such thing as

96 Did You Know 'Gung Ho' Comes From Chinese Characters?

'Gung ho' comes from Chinese characters. Gung(工) means 'work' and Ho(合) means 'together, in harmony'. So, the literal meaning of 'gung ho' is 'work together.' However, if you look it up in the dictionary, you will read 'extremely enthusiastic, zealous.'

Actually, 'gung ho' has been used in English since 1942. Evans Carlson, the U.S. Marine Corps leader of World War II, admired the spirit of the Chinese Industrial Cooperative Society during his stay in China. So, when WW II began, he clipped this long Chinese-pronounced phrase to the two words 'gung ho' and took them as a slogan for his battalion. Since then, 'gung ho' has become an unofficial motto of the US Marine Corps as an expression of spirit and "can- do" attitude.

Have you never heard of this expression before? 'Gung ho' has been used more frequently than you think. The title of a 1986 comedy film, directed by Ron Howard, was 'Gung Ho'. You can find a book titled 'Gung Ho' by Ken Blanchard and Sheldon Bowles in a bookstore. And, there is a Japanese video game company named 'GungHo Online Entertainment.'

As you can see, quite a few people are gung ho about the expression 'gung ho.'

1 What is the main idea of the story?

a. Chinese characters have been frequently used by North Americans.
b. Carlson is the person who made the expression 'gungho' during his stay in Japan.
c. The expressions 'Gung ho' has been the slogan of Chinese Marine Corps since 1942.
d. The expression 'gung ho' made of Chinese characters means 'enthusiastic.'

2 According the passage, which sentence is right?

a. The figurative meaning of 'gung ho' is 'work together.'
b. You cannot find the expression 'gung ho' in the dictionary because it's not English.
c. 'Gung ho' has been the motto of the US Marine Corps since World War I.
d. 'Gung ho' is the title of the movie directed by Ron Howard.

3 Choose the correct words for each sentence.

a. When a robber shouted "freeze!", I had to run to the library to look <u>up / out / at</u> the word 'freeze' in the dictionary because I didn't know its meaning.
b. Just look at the window. You have no choice but to <u>admirable / admiral / admire</u> the beautiful scenery.
c. Rob and his brother <u>have enjoying / have enjoyed / has enjoyed</u> various sports since they were young.

LEARNING BOARD

① 'Gung ho' comes from Chinese characters. ② Gung(工) means 'work' and Ho(合) means 'together, in harmony'. ③ So, the literal meaning of 'gung ho' is 'work together.' ④ However, if you look it up in the dictionary, you will read 'extremely enthusiastic, zealous.' ⑤ Actually, 'gung ho' has been used in English since 1942. ⑥ Evans Carlson, (the U.S. Marine Corps leader of World War II,) admired the spirit of the Chinese Industrial Cooperative Society during his stay in China. ⑦ So, when WW II began, he 1) clipped (this long Chinese-pronounced phrase) to the two words 'gung ho' and 2) took them as a slogan for his battalion. ⑧ Since then, 'gung ho' has become an unofficial motto of the US Marine Corps as an expression of 1) spirit and 2) "can-do" attitude. ⑨ Have you never heard of this expression before? ⑩ 'Gung ho' has been used more frequently than you think. ⑪ The title (of a 1986 comedy film), directed by Ron Howard,) was 'Gung Ho'. ⑫ You can find a book (titled 'Gung Ho') (by Ken Blanchard and Sheldon Bowles) (in a bookstore). ⑬ And, there is a Japanese video game company (named 'GungHo Online Entertainment.') ⑭ As you can see, quite a few people are gung ho about the expression 'gung ho.'

Words & Expressions

Chinese character 한자 **in harmony** 조화로운, 협조하는 **literal meaning** 문자 그대로의 의미 **look up** (참고 도서, 사전 등) 찾아보다 **dictionary** 사전 **extremely** 매우, 극히 **enthusiastic** 열렬한, 열정적인 **zealous** 열성적인 **U.S. Marine Corps** 미 해병대 **admire** 존경하다 **spirit** 1. 기백, 정신 2. 마음 3. 유령, 영혼 **industrial** 산업의 **cooperative** 협동의 **clip** 자르다, 깎다 **slogan** 구호, 슬로건 **battalion** 대대, 부대 **unofficial** 비공식적인 **motto** 좌우명, 모토 **can-do attitude** 할 수 있다는 자세 **frequently** 자주, 종종 **be gung ho about** …에 열성적이다

97 Did You Know The Meaning Of 'Easier Said Than Done'?

Some mice had been living happily in a house for a long time until the owner of the house brought a big fat cat named Cutie. Cutie was misnamed because he was far from being cute. Cutie chased the mice all the time. The mice were so afraid of Cutie that they were having a hard time wandering around the house to find food.

One mouse, named Smartie, raised his hand. He was also misnamed because he was not smart but dumb. So, his friends called him Dumb Smartie.

Smartie said, "I've got a great idea. Just put a bell around Cutie's neck so he can't move around without making a ringing sound. If that nasty ugly guy comes near us, we'll be able to hear the sound and run away before he catches us."

Then Grandpa Mouse said, "That sounds easy. So when will you put the bell around his neck?"

Startled, Smartie said, "What? Me? No way. I will be surely eaten by Cutie if I try to put a bell around his neck."

"Easier said than done. Your friends don't call you Dumb Smartie for nothing," Grandpa Mouse answered.

1 What is the main idea of the story?

a. Mice don't stand a chance to defeat cats.
b. It is easy to say something, but not so easy to do that.
c. The best way to deal with a big cat is to put a bell around its neck.
d. Dumb people must not open their mouth to speak.

2 Both Cutie and Smartie were misnamed because _____.

a. Cutie was smart and Smartie was cute
b. they came from China, not the US
c. Cutie was dumb and Smartie was ugly
d. Cutie was not cute, Smartie was not smart

3 Choose the correct words for each sentence.

a. It should be 'Seoul', not 'Soul'. The name of the city is <u>misnamed / misspelled / misplaced</u> on the map.
b. My brother can do rope skipping without <u>touch / touching / he touches</u> the ground.
c. The <u>startling / startled / startle</u> students started to scream loudly, and that sound startled their teacher.

LEARNING BOARD

① Some mice had been living happily in a house for a long time until the owner of the house brought a big fat cat (named Cutie). ② Cutie was misnamed because he was far from being cute. ③ Cutie chased the mice all the time. ④ The mice were so afraid of Cutie that they were having a hard time wandering around the house (to find food). ⑤ One mouse, (named Smartie), raised his hand. ⑥ He was also misnamed because he was not smart but dumb. ⑦ So, his friends called him Dumb Smartie. ⑧ Smartie said, "I've got a great idea. ⑨ Just put a bell around Cutie's neck so he can't move around without making a ringing sound. ⑩ If that nasty ugly guy comes near us, we'll 1) be able to hear the sound and 2) run away before he catches us." ⑪ Then Grandpa Mouse said, "That sounds easy. ⑫ So when will you put the bell around his neck?" ⑬ Startled, Smartie said, "What? Me? No way. ⑭ I will be surely eaten by Cutie if I try to put a bell around his neck." ⑮ "Easier said than done. ⑯ Your friends don't call you Dumb Smartie for nothing," Grandpa Mouse answered.

Words & Expressions

mice 쥐들(mouse의 복수형) misname 이름을 잘못 붙이다 be far from ing …와 거리가 멀다 chase 뒤쫓다 wander 돌아다니다 smart 똑똑한 dumb 멍청한 ugly 못생긴 nasty 나쁜, 못된 run away 달아나다 startle 깜짝 놀라게 하다 easier said than done 행동보다 말이 쉽다

98 Did You Know The Meaning Of 'Blow It'?

It was Harry's seventh birthday. Harry was so excited and happy. Then things started to go wrong, but it wasn't his fault. He just did what he was told to do. He blew out the candles on a chocolate cake because his dad told him to do so. But, his blowing force was a bit strong, so his grandma, sitting on the opposite side, was covered with chocolate cream.

"Sorry, Grandma. I blew it," he apologized.

"Yes, you did," Grandma answered, wiping her face with a paper towel.

Then Harry blew up the balloons because his mom told him to do so. But, his blowing force was kind of strong, so the balloons popped and his little sister cried.

"Sorry, sis. I blew it," he apologized again.

"Yes, you did," his mom replied, comforting his crying sister.

His family should have been careful, then, when telling him to blow the little toy trumpet. Unfortunately, Harry blew it hard, although he hadn't meant to hurt his mom's ear.

"Sorry mom. I blew it," he apologized.

"Yes, you really did," his dad replied, taking his mom to the hospital.

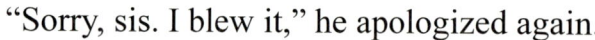

1 What can be the best title of this story?
   a. Mommy, The Promise Breaker
   b. Daddy, The Trumpet Maker
   c. Harry, The Super-Breath Boy
   d. Granny, The Party Pooper

2 According to the passage, which sentence is <u>wrong</u>?
   a. Harry's grandma attended his birthday party.
   b. The problem was that Harry looked for trouble and didn't do what he was told to do.
   c. It seemed that Harry's birthday party was over earlier than expected.
   d. Harry's grandma was covered with chocolate cream on her face.

3 Choose the correct words for each sentence.
   a. Some people say 'do as I say, not as I do. But I say, 'do as I <u>was told you to do / tell you not / tell you to do</u>, not as you want to do.'
   b. I'm sorry about lying to you. I <u>should let / should have let / shouldn't have let</u> you know the truth.
   c. As soon as I <u>apologize / apology / apologized</u> him about my mistake, he answered, 'your apology is accepted.'

LEARNING BOARD

① It was Harry's seventh birthday. ② Harry was so excited and happy. ③ Then things started to go wrong, but it wasn't his fault. ④ He just did what he was told to do. ⑤ He blew out the candles on a chocolate cake because his dad told him to do so. ⑥ But, his blowing force was a bit strong, so his grandma, (sitting on the opposite side,) was covered with chocolate cream. ⑦ "Sorry, Grandma. I blew it," he apologized. ⑧ "Yes, you did," Grandma answered, wiping her face with a paper towel. ⑨ Then Harry blew up the balloons because his mom told him to do so. ⑩ But, his blowing force was (kind of) strong, so the balloons popped and his little sister cried. ⑪ "Sorry, sis. I blew it," he apologized again. ⑫ "Yes, you did," his mom replied, comforting his crying sister.

⑬ His family should have been careful, then, when telling him to blow the little toy trumpet. ⑭ Unfortunately, Harry blew it hard, although he hadn't meant to hurt his mom's ear. ⑮ "Sorry mom. I blew it," he apologized.

⑯ "Yes, you really did," his dad replied, taking his mom to the hospital.

Words & Expressions

excited 신이 난, 흥분한(cf. **exciting** 흥미진진한, 신나게 하는) **go wrong** 잘못되다 **fault** 잘못, 실수 **blow out candles** 초를 입으로 불어 끄다 **blowing force** 후- 부는 힘 **a bit** 다소, 조금 **opposite** 반대편의 **apologize** 사과하다 **wipe** 닦다 **paper towel** 키친 타올 **pop** 뻥하고 터지다 **blow it** 실수하다, 망치다 **comfort** 달래다, 위로하다 **reply** 대답하다

99 Did You Know The Meaning Of 'Spill The Beans'?

Chris knew something was wrong, but didn't know what was wrong. He was late for work, so he had to run to the subway station. While running, he noticed that several people were looking at him. When he hopped on the subway, several people glanced sideways at him again. While taking the elevator in his office building, the people standing behind him giggled quietly. Chris was a little upset, but he didn't have time to find out what was going on, so he just rushed to his office.

When he entered the office, everybody simultaneously looked at him. He couldn't stand it anymore. "What is it? Why is everybody looking at me with a weird look?"

But no one would step forward to say what was going on.

"Please, come on, just spill the beans."

Then his co-workers began to open their mouths, one by one.

"Um... Your fly is down."

"And... your pants are ripped in the back."

"There is a large chunk of cheese in your hair."

"And... you are wearing mismatched socks."

1 What can be the best title of this story?
a. Never Wear Mismatched Socks
b. Chris, The Bean Spiller, Finally Arrested!
c. No Wonder Everybody Was Looking At Him
d. Chris Fed Up With His Rude Co-workers

2 Everybody looked at him with a weird look because _____.
a. he was wearing a Pororo tie
b. beans he spilled accidently were expensive
c. he arrived at his office very early
d. there's something seriously wrong with his appearance

3 Choose the correct words for each sentence.
a. When I wear this pair of jeans, I look like <u>a chunk of / a pack of / a bowl of</u> meat.
b. Put all your belongings <u>step by step / from time to time / one by one</u> on your desk. I have to check them carefully.
c. Yesterday, when my <u>fly / flew / flying</u> was open, a small fly flew into its hole.

LEARNING BOARD

① Chris knew something was wrong, but didn't know what was wrong. ② He was late for work, so he had to run to the subway station. ③ While running, he noticed that several people were looking at him. ④ When he hopped on the subway, several people glanced sideways at him again. ⑤ While taking the elevator in his office building, the people (standing behind him) giggled quietly. ⑥ Chris was a little upset, but he didn't have time to find out what was going on, so he just rushed to his office.

⑦ When he entered the office, everybody simultaneously looked at him. ⑧ He couldn't stand it anymore. ⑨ "What is it? Why is everybody looking at me with a weird look?"

⑩ But no one would step forward to say what was going on.

⑪ "Please, come on, just spill the beans."

⑫ Then his co-workers began to open their mouths, one by one.

⑬ "Um... Your fly is down."

⑭ "And... your pants are ripped in the back."

⑮ "There is a large chunk of cheese in your hair."

⑯ "And... you are wearing mismatched socks."

Words & Expressions

subway station 지하철역 hop 폴짝 뛰다 (hop on 깡충 뛰어 ...에 올라타다) glance sidewise at ...를 곁눈질로 보다 giggle 낄낄 웃다 upset 속상한 simultaneously 동시에 with a weird look 이상한 표정으로 (weird 이상한, 기이한) step forward to ...하려고 나서다 spill the beans (비밀을) 털어놓다 fly 바지 지퍼 rip 찢다 a large chunk of 커다란 덩어리 mismatched 잘못 짝지어진, 맞지 않는

Did You Know The Meaning Of 'Mind One's Ps And Qs'?

There was a little boy who wet his pants quite often and inadvertently. He knew that it was embarrassing, but he couldn't help it. One day, the boy's family attended a family reunion.

Before they left home, his dad said to him, "Hey, son. Mind your Ps and Qs. Whatever you do, don't forget to behave yourself, OK?"

"Dad, I don't want to go. What if I wet my pants again? Surely all the other cousins will laugh at me." He sounded like he was about to cry.

"Um... First and foremost, don't try to hold your urine in. If you even slightly feel like you need to go for a pee, do not hesitate and just rush to the toilet," replied his dad.

"But I can't go to an unfamiliar toilet alone..." he said.

"Just cue me. The moment you cue me, I will stop whatever I'm doing and go to the toilet with you."

"So all I have to do is to mind my pee and cue."

"As I told you, mind your Ps and Qs."

1 **What can be the best title of this story?**
 a. A Wet Blanket Wets His Pants
 b. Mind Pee And Cue Instead of Ps And Qs
 c. Oops! The Boy Did It Again
 d. Stop Whatever You Do

2 **The boy didn't want to go to the family reunion since _____.**
 a. he couldn't behave himself
 b. his cousins would surely laugh at him
 c. he was worried about wetting his pants in front of his family
 d. he couldn't go to the unfamiliar toilet

3 **Choose the correct words for each sentence.**
 a. I can see <u>familiar / unfamiliar / similar</u> faces among those people. I think I have never met them before.
 b. I told the police, "He is not dead yet, but he <u>is about to be / is going to dead / must have died</u>. He is dying!"
 c. You can do <u>whatever / however / whoever</u> you want and leave whenever you wish.

LEARNING BOARD

① There was a little boy who wet his pants (quite often and inadvertently).

② He knew that it was embarrassing, but he couldn't help it. ③ One day, the boy's family attended a family reunion.

④ Before they left home, his dad said to him, "Hey, son. Mind your Ps and Qs.

⑤ Whatever you do, don't forget to behave yourself, OK?"

⑥ "Dad, I don't want to go. ⑦ What if I wet my pants again? ⑧ Surely all the other cousins will laugh at me." ⑨ He sounded like he was about to cry.

⑩ "Um... First and foremost, don't try to hold your urine in. ⑪ If you even slightly feel like you need to go for a pee, 1) do not hesitate and just 2) rush to the toilet," replied his dad.

⑫ "But I can't go to an unfamiliar toilet alone..." he said.

⑬ "Just cue me.

⑭ The moment you cue me, I will 1) stop whatever I'm doing and 2) go to the toilet with you."

⑮ "So all I have to do is to mind my pee and cue."

⑯ "As I told you, mind your Ps and Qs."

Words & Expressions

wet one's pants 바지를 적시다, 오줌싸다 **quite** 꽤, 상당히 **inadvertently** 무심코 **embarrassing** 당혹스러운, 난처한 **reunion** (오랜만의) 만남, 모임 **mind one's P's and Q's** 예의 바르게 행동하다(=behave oneself) **cousin** 사촌 **laugh at** 비웃다 **first and foremost** 무엇보다 **hold one's urine** 소변을 참다 **slightly** 조금, 약간 **pee** 소변, 소변보다 (go for a pee 소변보다) **hesitate** 망설이다, 주저하다 **toilet** 화장실 **unfamiliar** 낯선, 익숙하지 않은 **cue** 신호를 보내다(=give a cue)

273

Listening with Dictation

96 Did You Know 'Gung Ho' Comes From Chinese Characters?

'Gung ho' comes from _____¹. Gung(工) means 'work' and Ho(合) means 'together, _____²' So, the literal meaning of 'gung ho' is 'work together.' However, if you _____³, you will read 'extremely _____⁴, zealous.' Actually, 'gung ho' has been used in English since 1942. Evans Carlson, the U.S. Marine Corps leader of World War II, admired the spirit of the Chinese Industrial Cooperative Society during his stay in China. So, when WW II began, he _____⁵ this long Chinese-pronounced phrase to the two words 'gung ho' and took them as a slogan for his battalion. Since then, 'gung ho' has become _____⁶ the US Marine Corps as an expression of spirit and "can- do" attitude. _____⁷ this expression before? 'Gung ho' _____⁸ than you think. The title of a 1986 comedy film, directed by Ron Howard, was 'Gung Ho'. You can find a book _____⁹ 'Gung Ho' by Ken Blanchard and Sheldon Bowles in a bookstore. And, there is a Japanese video game company named 'GungHo Online Entertainment.' As you can see, quite a few people _____¹⁰ the expression 'gung ho.'

97 Did You Know The Meaning Of 'Easier Said Than Done'?

Some mice had been living happily in a house for a long time _____¹ the owner of the house brought a big fat cat named Cutie. Cutie _____² because he was _____³. Cutie chased the mice all the time. The mice were so afraid of Cutie that they were having a hard time wandering around the house to find food. One mouse, named Smartie, _____⁴. He was also misnamed because he was not smart but dumb. So, his friends called him Dumb Smartie. Smartie said, "I've got a great idea. Just put a bell around Cutie's neck so he can't move around without making a ringing sound. If that nasty ugly guy _____⁵ us, we'll be able to hear the sound and run away _____⁶." Then Grandpa Mouse said, "That _____⁷. So when will you put the bell around his neck?" _____⁸, Smartie said, "What? Me? No way. I _____⁹ Cutie if I try to put a bell around his neck." "Easier said than done. Your friends don't call you Dumb Smartie _____¹⁰," Grandpa Mouse answered.

98 Did You Know The Meaning Of 'Blow It'?

It was Harry's seventh birthday. Harry was so excited and happy. Then things _____¹, but it wasn't his fault. He just did what he was told to do. He _____² on a chocolate cake because his dad _____³. But, his blowing force was a bit strong, so his grandma, sitting _____⁴, was covered with chocolate cream. "Sorry, Grandma. I blew it," he _____⁵. "Yes, you did," Grandma answered, wiping her face with a paper towel. Then Harry _____⁶ because his mom told him to do so. But, his blowing force was kind of strong, so the balloons popped and his little sister cried. "Sorry, sis. I blew it," he apologized again. "Yes, you did," his mom replied, comforting his crying sister. His family _____⁷, then, when telling him to _____⁸. Unfortunately, Harry blew it hard, although he _____⁹ hurt his mom's ear. "Sorry mom. I blew it," he apologized. "Yes, you really did," his dad _____¹⁰, taking his mom to the hospital.

Chapter 10 | Proverbs & Idioms

99 Did You Know The Meaning Of 'Spill The Beans'?

Chris knew _____¹, but didn't know _____². He was late for work, so he had to run to the subway station. While running, he noticed that several people were looking at him. When he _____³ the subway, several people _____⁴ him again. While _____⁵ in his office building, the people standing behind him _____⁶ quietly. Chris was a little upset, but he didn't have time to find out what was going on, so he just rushed to his office. When he entered the office, everybody _____⁷ looked at him. He couldn't stand it anymore. "What is it? Why is everybody looking at me with a weird look?" But no one would _____⁸ say what was going on. "Please, come on, just spill the beans." Then his co-workers began to open their mouths, one by one. "Um... Your _____⁹." "And... your pants are ripped in the back." "There is a large chunk of cheese in your hair." "And... you are wearing _____¹⁰."

100 Did You Know The Meaning Of 'Mind One's Ps And Qs'?

There was a little boy who _____¹ quite often and inadvertently. He knew that it was embarrassing, but he _____². One day, the boy's family attended a family reunion. Before they left home, his dad said to him, "Hey, son. Mind your Ps and Qs. Whatever you do, don't forget to _____³, OK?" "Dad, I don't want to go. _____⁴ I wet my pants again? Surely all the other cousins will laugh at me." He sounded like he was about to cry. "Um... _____⁵, don't try to _____⁶ your urine in. If you even _____⁷ feel like you need to _____⁸, do not hesitate and just rush to the toilet," replied his dad. "But I can't go to an unfamiliar toilet alone..." he said. "Just cue me. The moment you cue me, I will _____⁹ and go to the toilet with you." "So all I have to do is to mind my pee and cue." "As I told you, _____¹⁰."

---

96 정답 1. Chinese characters 2. in harmony 3. look it up in the dictionary 4. enthusiastic 5. clipped 6. an unofficial motto of 7. Have you never heard of 8. has been used more frequently 9. titled 10. are gung ho about

97 정답 1. until 2. was misnamed 3. far from being cute 4. raised his hand 5. comes near 6. before he catches us 7. sounds easy 8. Startled 9. will be surely eaten by 10. for nothing

98 정답 1. started to go wrong 2. blew out the candles 3. told him to do so 4. on the opposite side 5. apologized 6. blew up the balloons 7. should have been careful 8. blow the little toy trumpet 9. hadn't meant to 10. replied

99 정답 1. something was wrong 2. what was wrong 3. hopped on 4. glanced sideways at 5. taking the elevator 6. giggled 7. simultaneously 8. step forward to 9. fly is down 10. mismatched socks

100 정답 1. wet his pants 2. couldn't help it 3. behave yourself 4. What if 5. First and foremost 6. hold 7. slightly 8. go for a pee 9. stop whatever I'm doing 10. mind your Ps and Qs

Appendix 부록

1. 이 책에서 배운 단어 정리 278~291

2. 구두점의 쓰임 292~294

1. 이 책에서 배운 단어 정리

단어	페이지
a bit 다소, 조금	269
a bunch of 다수의 (+ 복수 명사)	19, 105
a fifth of 1/5의	247
a fine-toothed comb 빗살이 촘촘한 빗	79
a handsome amount of money 엄청난 금액의 돈	103
a large chunk of 커다란 덩어리	271
a longtime smoker 오랜 흡연자	97
a lottery ticket 복권	117
a major food source 주요 식량원	139
a multitude of 수많은 (+ 복수 명사)	37
a newly coined term 신조어	99
a number of 많은 (+ 복수명사)	191
a nursing home 양로원, 요양소	97
a pack of cards 카드 한 팩(꾸러미)	181
a Swiss 스위스 사람	181
a whole lot 대단히	53
a wide-toothed comb 빗살이 넓고 큰 빗	79
a wound dressing 상처를 싸거나 덮는 도포제(드레싱)	83
a.k.a.(=also known as) …로도 알려진	37
abrasive 연마재의, 거친	155
abroad 해외에(서), 해외로	99
abruptly 갑자기, 불쑥(=suddenly)	169
abs 복근	87
absolute 완전한, 순전한	151
absolutely 굉장히, 극도로, 참으로	177, 241
abuse 오용, 남용, 학대	21
accelerate 가속화하다	77
accent 억양, 강세	99
accidentally 우연히, 사고로	101
accomplish 성취하다	37
account 계좌, 설명, 회계	129
accurate 정확한	179
achieve 성취하다, 이루다	233
acknowledge 인정하다, (수신을) 확인하다	203, 245
acne 여드름	83
activity 활동	151
actress 여배우	109
actual 실제	259
ad 광고(= advertisement)	179
add 첨가하다, 추가하다, (말을) 덧붙이다	45
addiction 중독	21
additionally 게다가	205
admire 존경하다	265
advertisement 광고	155
advice 조언, 충고 (cf advise 충고하다)	179
aerobic 유산소의 (aerobic exercise = cardio exercise/workout 유산소 운동)	87
affect …에 영향을 미치다(=have an effect on)	153, 227, 233
after a short while 얼마 지나면	229
age difference 나이 차이	207
agent 대리인, 중개상, 물질	83
aggressive 공격적인	127, 187
aid 돕다	39
ailing 병든	207
air 방송하다 (on air 방송 중)	177
aircraft 항공기(날 수 있는 탑승물의 총칭)	217
alert 정신이 맑은, 경계하는	157
algae 조류	125
alien 외계인	213
all year round 일 년 내내	37
allegedly …라는 주장에 의하면, 알려진 바에 의하면, 이른바	39, 61, 125
allergic reaction 알레르기 반응	165
allergy 알레르기	165
alleviate 완화하다	149
amazing 놀라운	135, 201, 233
amazingly 놀랍게도	27, 59, 169, 235
ambassador 대사, 사절	215
amputate (수술로 팔이나 다리를) 절단하다 (n. amputation 사지 절단)	35, 205
an easy way out 쉬운 해결책	33
ancient Egyptian deities 고대 이집트 신들	181
ancient 고대의	181
and many more 이외에 더 많다	179
and more 그리고 더 있다	139
and so on 기타 등등	37, 63
anemia 빈혈	31, 157
animal (rights) activist 동물 (권익) 보호론자	35
annoying 짜증 나는	23
annually 매년	53
antennae 더듬이(antenna의 복수형)	123
anti-bacterial agent 항세균제	83
antibacterial 항균성의	25
antibiotics 항생제	37
anti-inflammatory 소염제의	149
antioxidant 산화방지제	83
antler 사슴뿔	61
anxiety 불안, 걱정	131
anxious 걱정하는, 불안해하는	131
apologize 사과하다	269
apparent death 가사상태	143
appear 나타나다, 출연하다(on)	91, 215
appearance 외모(=look)	229
appetizing 입맛을 돋우는	51
application 신청서	129
apply (연고·로션 등을) 바르다, 적용하다, 신청하다	77, 83
appreciate 1. 감상하다, 맛있게 먹다 2. 진가를 인정하다 3. 감사하다	61
approval 승인, 허락(cf. approve 승인하다)	207
approved 승인을 받은	75
approximately 대략, 약	53, 135, 169
arachnid 거미류	123
architecture 건축물	113
arms 무기	195
arrest 체포하다	193
arrogant 거만한	187
arthritis 관절염	23
article 기사, 논설	57
artificial insemination 인공수정	215

☐ artificial 인공의, 인위적인, 모조의 155, 215, 221	☐ be exposed to …에 노출되다 165
☐ as desired 원하는 대로 83	☐ be faithful to …에게 충실하다, 바람을 피우지 않다 141
☐ as to why 이유, 원인에 관해 25	☐ be famous for …로 유명하다 51
☐ as usual 평소대로 253	☐ be far from ing …와 거리가 멀다 267
☐ ascend 오르다 231	☐ be found guilty of (…라는 죄로) 유죄를 선고받다 193
☐ assassinate 암살하다 217	☐ be good at …를 잘하다 35
☐ assault 공격하다 35	☐ be gung ho about …에 열성적이다 265
☐ assistance 보조, 지원 245	☐ be held in …에서 개최되다 255
☐ association 협회 129	☐ be in common in …에게 흔하다 31
☐ astrology 점성술 175	☐ be keen on …를 좋아하다 59
☐ at a close distance 가까운 거리에서 123	☐ be likely to …하는 경향이 있다, …하기 쉽다 57, 89
☐ at birth 태어날 때 101	☐ be made of …로 만들어지다 19
☐ at sea 바다에서 189	☐ be not a good sign 좋은 징조가 아니다 31
☐ at the same time 동시에 167	☐ be notable for …로 유명하다(= be famous for) 219
☐ athlete 운동선수 255	☐ be on the verge of …하기 직전이다 261
☐ atmospheric 대기의 125	☐ be prone to …하는 경향이 있다 57, 167
☐ attempt 시도 183	☐ be responsible for …에 책임이 있다 165
☐ attention 주목, 관심 213	☐ be rich in …이 풍부한 49
☐ attract 끌어들이다(cf. attraction 관광명소) 209, 221	☐ be sick 병이 나다 33
☐ audience 청중, 관객 177	☐ be supposed to …하기로 되어 있다, 해야 한다 65, 75
☐ aura (독특한) 분위기, 기운, 아우라 179	☐ be thought to …라고 한다(= be said to) 39
☐ authority 권한, 당국, 권위자 193	☐ be under debate 논란의 여지가 있다 125
☐ available 입수 가능한 37, 205	☐ be widely known as …로 널리 알려지다 259
☐ avenue 거리, 길 191	☐ be willing to 기꺼이 …하다 75
☐ average 평균 53	☐ be worth –ing …할 가치가 있다 213
☐ avoid 피하다, 방지하다 49, 79, 127, 193	☐ beach 바닷가 231
☐ awaken 깨어나다 99	☐ beast 야수 103
☐ awesome 경탄할 만한, 굉장한 (cf. awful 끔찍한, 지독한) 53, 63, 177	☐ beauty queen 미인 대회 우승자, 예쁜 여자 205
☐ axe 도끼 259	☐ become extinct 멸종하다 137
☐ back up (이론을) 뒷받침하다 149	☐ become faint 흐려지다 253
☐ bad luck 불운 189	☐ bedding 침구 19
☐ bag 주머니, 주머니처럼 늘어진 살 91	☐ behead 참수하다 241
☐ bank account 예금 계좌 117	☐ believer 믿는 사람, 신자, 신봉자 187
☐ bank 둑, 은행 203	☐ belly 배, 복부 45, 53, 261
☐ bankrupt 파산한(cf. bankruptcy 도산, 파산) 261	☐ beneficial 유익한 33
☐ bar soap 고체 비누 73	☐ benefit 이득, 이로움, 혜택 37
☐ bar 술집 255	☐ beta carotene 베타카로틴 39
☐ bare hands 맨손 113	☐ betray 배신하다 191
☐ bare skin 맨 피부 77	☐ beverage 마실 것, 음료 27, 167
☐ bark 나무껍질 231	☐ beyond one's imagination …의 상상을 초월하는 125
☐ barley 보리 59	☐ bias 편견 (cf. biased 치우친, 편향된) 109
☐ basement 지하실 241	☐ biblical 성경적인 191
☐ battalion 대대, 부대 265	☐ bile 담즙 39
☐ be accused of …로 기소되다, 비난받다 193	☐ biological 생물학의, 생물체의 213
☐ be accustomed to 익숙하다 253	☐ bite 물다 209
☐ be against …에 반하다, 반대하다 125	☐ blame 비난하다, …탓으로 돌리다 161
☐ be allergic to …에 알레르기가 있다 31, 165	☐ blast 폭파시키다 219
☐ be as follows …는 다음과 같다 189	☐ bleach 표백하다, 탈색하다 79
☐ be associated with …와 관련이 있다 23	☐ bleed 피가 나다 27
☐ be at risk 위험에 처하다 203	☐ bleeding 출혈 (cf. bleed 피를 흘리다 blood 피, 혈액) 163
☐ be backed up with …로 뒷받침되다 149	☐ blessing 축복 115
☐ be born in (년도) …에 태어나다 97	☐ blister 수포 231
☐ be buried 묻히다 (v. bury 묻다, 매장하다) 113	☐ blonde 금발의 89
☐ be connected to …와 관련이 있다 181	☐ blondie 금발 머리 여자 209
☐ be connected with …와 연관되다 191	☐ blood circulation 혈액 순환 35
☐ be conscious of …를 의식·자각하다 233	☐ blood sugar control 혈당 조절 33
☐ be convicted of …로 유죄 판결을 받다 193	☐ blood-dripping 피가 뚝뚝 떨어지는 61
☐ be destined to …할 운명이다 215	☐ bloodshot 핏발이 선 153
	☐ bloodsucker 흡혈귀, 피를 빠는 것 35

☐ blow dryer 헤어드라이어	79
☐ blow it 실수하다, 망치다	269
☐ blow out candles 초를 입으로 불어 끄다	269
☐ blowing force 후- 부는 힘	269
☐ blubber 바다 동물의 지방	139
☐ boil over 끓어 넘치다	189
☐ boil 끓이다, 삶다	45, 61, 135
☐ bone marrow 골수	27
☐ border 국경(지역)	221
☐ botulism 보툴리눔 식중독	71
☐ bounce 깡충깡충 뛰다, (수표가) 부도 처리되다	167
☐ bow-looking 화살처럼 생긴	187
☐ brace oneself 마음의 각오를 하다	135
☐ brain 뇌	201
☐ brass 놋쇠, 금관 악기	221
☐ break pieces 부수다	79
☐ break 휴식	153
☐ breakthrough 돌파구, 획기적 성공	53
☐ breast cancer 유방암	39
☐ breathe 호흡하다, 숨 쉬다	125
☐ breathing 호흡 (cf. breath 숨, 입김)	125
☐ breed 키우다, 사육하다	51
☐ brew (커피, 차를) 우려내다	65
☐ bride 신부	207
☐ bridegroom/groom 신랑(↔ bride 신부)	207, 235
☐ brilliant 근사한, 명석한	213
☐ brow 이마	71
☐ brows 눈썹(= eye brows)	91
☐ brunette 흑갈색 머리를 가진 백인 여자	209
☐ brush 솔; 솔질[빗질]하다	79, 253
☐ brush 솔질하다	85
☐ brutal 잔혹한	221
☐ builder 건축업자	261
☐ building material 건축자재	205
☐ bulge 부풀다, 튀어나오다	87, 187
☐ bulky 우람한, 덩치 큰	151
☐ bullet 총알	169
☐ burial place 매장지	183
☐ burn fat 지방을 태우다, 연소시키다	53
☐ bust 단속하다 (be busted 단속에 걸리다)	75
☐ buster 폭파(파괴)시키는 것	183
☐ by day 낮에는	241
☐ by hanging 교수형으로	193
☐ by night 밤에는	241
☐ by oneself 혼자서	113
☐ by surgery 수술로	91
☐ by the way 그건 그렇고	169
☐ bypass 우회, 우회수술	33
☐ calcium 칼슘	157
☐ calf 송아지 (복수 calves)	45
☐ Cambodian 캄보디아인	51
☐ can't stand 견딜 수 없다	61
☐ canal 운하, 수로, 관 (ear canal 이도)	25
☐ cancer fighting abilities 항암효과(능력)	49
☐ cancer 암	77, 167
☐ can-do attitude 할 수 있다는 자세	265
☐ carbon dioxide 이산화탄소	209
☐ cardio (달리기 등 유산소 운동처럼) 심장을 강화시키는 운동	87
☐ cardiovascular 심혈관의	21, 37
☐ care 돌봄, 보살핌, 주의, 걱정	257
☐ career 직업, 직장생활	179
☐ carnivorous 육식의	37
☐ carving 조각 (cf. carve 조각하다)	219
☐ cash 현금	117
☐ catch a glimpse of 잠깐(힐끗) 보다	183
☐ categorize 분류하다	137
☐ cause n. 원인 v. 초래하다, 일으키다	153
☐ cave 동굴	131
☐ cavity 구멍, 충치	155
☐ ceiling 천장	227
☐ cell 1. 세포 2. 감방 3. 전지	19
☐ cell phone(= cellular phone) 휴대폰	161
☐ cellophane noodles 당면	59
☐ ceremony 식, 의식	239
☐ chakra 차크라, 기 에너지	179
☐ chapel (학교나 군대에 딸린) 예배당	239
☐ character 성격, 기질, 특징	175
☐ charge 돈(값)을 청구하다	129
☐ chase 뒤쫓다	267
☐ cheap 싼	53
☐ cheer on ...를 응원하다	255
☐ chef 요리사, 주방장	61
☐ chemical fertilizer 화학비료	131
☐ chemical 화학물질	37, 85
☐ chew 씹다	123, 163
☐ chicken heart 닭의 심장, 겁쟁이	61
☐ chicken skin 닭 껍질	213
☐ Chilean 칠레의, 칠레사람의	245
☐ chimney 굴뚝	241
☐ chimpanzee/chimp 침팬지	141
☐ Chinese character 한자	265
☐ chip away 조금씩 (쪼아서) 깎아 내다	219
☐ chisel 끌	219
☐ chive 차이브, 골파	61
☐ chop up 잘게 썰다	201
☐ chop 자르다	259
☐ chunk 덩어리	87
☐ cicada 매미	61
☐ circulation 순환, 유통, 배포	35
☐ civilian 시민	243
☐ claim 주장하다; 주장	177, 181, 203
☐ clam 조개	37
☐ clay 진흙	203
☐ cleanser 세안제, 비누(cf. detergent (세탁 · 주방용) 세제)	73
☐ cleansing 정화, 깨끗하게 하기	73, 179
☐ clear evidence 명백한 증거	149
☐ cliff 절벽	169
☐ clinically 의학적으로 (clinic 병원, 진료)	75
☐ clip 자르다, 깎다	265
☐ clot 엉기게 하다 (blood clot 혈전)	27
☐ coast 해안	231
☐ cocaine 코카인	217
☐ cockpit 조종석	217
☐ cockroach 바퀴벌레	61, 127
☐ coffee bean 커피콩	65
☐ coffee cherry 커피 열매	65
☐ coin 동전, (용어 · 표현을) 만들다	99

☐ cold-blooded 냉정한, 냉혈한의	187
☐ collapse 붕괴, 무너지다, 폭락하다	191
☐ collected 수집한, 모은	113
☐ combination 조합	191
☐ come as no surprise 놀랄 일도 아니다	143
☐ come by 얻다, 획득하다	215
☐ come from …에서 나오다	125, 139
☐ come to an end 끝나다	195
☐ comfort 달래다, 위로하다	269
☐ comment 논평, 언급	213
☐ commercial a. 상업의 n. 광고	155
☐ commit (잘못된 일을) 저지르다	217
☐ commit a crime 범죄를 저지르다	193
☐ commit suicide 자살하다	217
☐ common 일반적인	149
☐ commonly 보통, 일반적으로	37, 131
☐ compare to …와 비교하다	53
☐ compared to …에 비하면, …와 비교하면	201
☐ competition 경쟁, 대회	37
☐ complain 불평하다, 항의하다	241
☐ complete one's schooling 학업을 마치다	227
☐ complete 완벽한; 완료하다, 끝마치다 (completeness 완전함)	113, 191
☐ completely 완전히(= absolutely)	37
☐ component 구성 요소	19
☐ composer 작곡자	109
☐ concerned 담당의, 관련된	129
☐ conclusive 결정적인	149
☐ condition 질환, 병, 상태, 조건	229
☐ conduct (조사 등을) 하다	33, 149
☐ confused 혼란스러워하는	195
☐ congestion 혼잡, 막힘	35
☐ congratulatory 축하의(cf. congratulation 축하)	235
☐ connection 관계, 연관	39
☐ consciousness 의식	143
☐ consider …로 여기다, 고려하다	89, 191
☐ constant 끊임없는, 계속되는	77
☐ constantly 끊임없이	19
☐ constipation 변비	21, 187
☐ construction 건축	195
☐ consulate 영사관	243
☐ consult 상담하다	21, 179
☐ contact 접촉하다; 접촉, 연락	231
☐ contagion 전염, 전염병	37
☐ contain …이 들어 있다, …을 함유하다, (감정을) 억누르다	47, 49, 59, 85, 155, 167
☐ contaminant 오염물질	37
☐ contamination 오염	37
☐ content 내용물, 함유량, 목차	49
☐ continent 대륙	135
☐ continual 연속적인	217
☐ contract 수축하다, 계약서 (n. contraction 수축, 계약)	71
☐ contribute 공헌하다, 기여하다, 기부하다	19, 117
☐ control 통제ㆍ관리하다	169
☐ convict 유죄를 선고하다	193
☐ convince 확신시키다	149
☐ cooperate 협동하다, 협력하다	193
☐ cooperative 협동의	265
☐ corn syrup 옥수수 시럽	57
☐ corridor 복도	195
☐ corset 코르셋	139
☐ cosmetic a. 성형의 n. 화장품	71
☐ cosmetic procedure 미용 시술	71
☐ cosmetic shop 화장품 가게	73
☐ cost v. (값ㆍ비용을) 치르다 n. 비용	85
☐ costly 비싼	77
☐ cotton swab 면봉	25
☐ cousin 사촌	273
☐ co-worker 동료	253
☐ crack 금이 가다, 갈라지다, 깨지다	23, 117
☐ craftsman 장인, 수공예가	205
☐ crash 추락하다	217
☐ creative 독창적인, 창의적인	61, 213
☐ criminal 범죄자, 범인	109, 193
☐ crisp 바삭바삭한(= crispy)	51
☐ critic 비판하는 사람	131
☐ crucial 필수적인	153
☐ crumble (건물이) 무너지다	243
☐ crunch 오도독[와삭와삭] 씹다	123
☐ crutches 목발	227
☐ cuddly 안아주고 싶은, 사랑스러운	215
☐ cue 신호를 보내다(=give a cue)	273
☐ cuisine 요리법	61
☐ cure v. 낫게 하다, 치유하다 n. 치유, 치료법	229
☐ curiosity 호기심	257
☐ curl (머리를) 곱슬곱슬하게 감다(말다) (curly 곱슬곱슬한)	79
☐ current 현재의	79
☐ currently 최근에	149
☐ curse 저주	217
☐ customer 손님, 고객(cf. consumer 소비자)	75, 161
☐ cut down on …를 줄이다	167
☐ cut off 잘라내다	201
☐ dairy product 유제품	57
☐ dairy 유제품의 (dairy product 유제품 = milk product)	47
☐ dam 댐	183
☐ damage v. 손상을 주다 n. 손상, 피해	23, 77, 153
☐ damages 손해배상금	101
☐ damp 축축한	77
☐ dark 어두운, 진한	89
☐ daydreamer 공상가	187
☐ deadly 치명적인	127, 239
☐ debt 빚	261
☐ deep-fried 뜨거운 기름에 튀긴	51
☐ defecate 배변하다	65
☐ deficiency 결핍, 부족	153
☐ definitely 분명히, 틀림없이, 절대	161
☐ degree (각도 단위인) 도	203
☐ deity 신	181
☐ deli(=delicatessen) 식료품 가게, 식당	59
☐ deliver 배달하다	113
☐ demand 요구하다	101, 243
☐ demonstrate 보여주다, 입증하다, 시위에 참여하다	247
☐ demonstration 실연, 증명, 데모	247
☐ dental 치아의	155
☐ dentist 치과의사	85
☐ depending on ~에 따라	45, 47, 59, 129
☐ depending on the individual 개인에 따라	25
☐ deposit 축적물	87

281

□ derive (from) …에서 나오다, 파생하다 47	□ drugstore 약국 73
□ describe 묘사하다, 서술하다 217	□ due to ~때문에 131
□ desperate 필사적인, 간절히 원하는[to] 241	□ dumb 멍청한 267
□ detection 탐지 183	□ dump out 갖다 버리다 25
□ devastate 완전히 파괴하다, 비탄에 빠지다 205	□ dung (큰 동물의) 똥 131
□ develop 발생하다, 생기다 99	□ duplicate 사본의, 똑같은, 사본 177
□ diabetes 당뇨병 33, 57	□ during the Second World War 2차 세계 대전 중에 183
□ diarrhea 설사 149	□ dust 먼지 19
□ dictionary 사전 265	□ dust mite 먼지 진드기 19
□ die in (년도) …에 사망하다 97	□ dye 염색하다, 염료 79, 89, 155, 209
□ die of a heart attack 심장마비로 사망하다 217	□ dyeing 염색 79
□ diet 1. 식사, 식습관 2. 다이어트(를 하다) 47, 75	□ eardrum 고막 25
□ differ from …와 다르다 37	□ earlobe 귓불 25
□ differ 다르다 25	□ early in life 인생 초기에, 어렸을 때 153
□ difficulty sleeping 불면증, 수면 장애(= insomnia) 21	□ earn 돈을 벌다 115
□ digest 소화하다, 소화되다 163, 187	□ earwax 귀지 (또는 wax) 25
□ digestive system 소화기관 65, 163	□ easier said than done 행동보다 말이 쉽다 267
□ dilute 희석하다, 묽게 하다 71	□ eat up 먹어치우다 27
□ dim 흐린, 어둑한 153	□ eating habit 식습관 53
□ dime-sized 다임 동전 크기의 73	□ eczema 습진 31
□ dioxin 다이옥신 37	□ edible 먹을 수 있는, 식용의(=eatable) 45, 51, 61
□ director 감독 247	□ effect 효과, 영향 39, 71
□ dirt 먼지 25	□ effective 효과적인 75, 85
□ disagree with …에 동의하지 않다 49	□ effectively 효과적으로 87
□ disagreeable 불쾌한, 무뚝뚝한 97	□ egg sac 알주머니 123
□ disallowed 허가(인정)받지 않은 105	□ either way 어느 쪽이든 203
□ disappear 사라지다 177	□ electronic detection equipment 전자 탐지 장비 183
□ discharge 해고 259	□ embarrassing 당혹스러운, 난처한 273
□ discolor 변색시키다 85	□ emit (빛, 전기, 소리, 가스 등을) 내다, 내뿜다, 방출하다 161, 261
□ disease 질병 31	□ emotionally 정서적으로, 감정적으로 109
□ disgusting 구역질 나는 (disgust v. 역겹게 하다 n. 역겨움) 61	□ emperor 황제(남) (여황제 empress) 205
□ dish 접시, 설거지거리, 요리 61	□ employee 직원 101
□ disheartened 낙심한 141	□ employment 고용 259
□ dismember 사지를 자르다 241	□ empty one's bank account 통장을 털다 63
□ dismissal 해고 259	□ end 끝 부분 79
□ display 나타내다, 전시하다 143	□ endangered 멸종 위기에 처한 215
□ distinct 뚜렷한, 선명한 137	□ energize 열기, 활력을 돋우다 157
□ distressed 괴로운 141	□ engage in 참여하다, 관여하다 255
□ disturb 방해하다 131	□ engagement 약혼 235
□ diverge 갈라지다, 나뉘다 137	□ enhance 향상시키다 39
□ diverse 다양한 61	□ enormous 거대한(= huge), 막대한, 엄청난 125,139, 187, 205, 219
□ divination 점(= fortunetelling) 181	□ enthusiastic 열렬한, 열정적인 265
□ divorce 이혼하다 103	□ enviably 부러울 정도로 213
□ do good 좋은 일을 하다, 이롭다 253	□ environmental levy 환경 부담금 129
□ do the job 일을 하다, 해내다 205	□ enzyme 효소 83
□ do well to …하는 것이 현명하다 57	□ equipment 장비, 설비 183
□ dog clothing 애완견용 옷 19	□ equivalent (의미, 가치가) 동등한, …에 상응하는 195
□ dolphin 돌고래 49	□ escape 도망치다 241
□ dominant 우세한 247	□ essential nature 본성 253
□ don't even think of …할 생각도 마라 231	□ essential 필수적인 85
□ don't have any intention to …할 의사가 없다 77	□ event 사건, 행사 217
□ don't judge a book by its cover 〈속담〉 책 표지만 보고 책을 판단하지 말라(외모만으로 판단하지 말라) 57	□ eventually 결국 79
□ donate 기부하다 209	□ exactly speaking 정확히 말하면 143
□ donation 기부, 기부금 105	□ exaggerated 과장된 155
□ dose 약의 복용량 149	□ exception 예외 91
□ double agent 이중 첩자 241	□ excessive 지나친, 과도한 149, 227, 229
□ drain (물, 액체) 빼내다, 비우다 35	□ excited 신이 난, 흥분한(cf. exciting 흥미진진한, 신나게 하는) 269
□ drink 음료, 마실 것 167	□ exclude 배제하다, 제외하다 153
□ dropping 배설물 131	□ excrement 배설물 131
	□ exercise routine 평소에 하는 운동 53

exercise 운동(=workout)	151
exhausted 지친	153
exotic 이국적인	61, 221
expedition 탐험대, 원정대	129
expense 경비, 비용	129
expensive 비싼(= costly ↔ inexpensive 비싸지 않은)	73, 215
experience 경력, 경험	179
experiment 실험	149
expert 전문가	203
exposure 노출	77
expression 표현	217
extinct 멸종한	137
extinction 멸종	137
extra 여분의, 가외의	87
extract n. 추출(물), 발췌 v. 뽑아내다, 추출하다	53, 139
extraordinary 놀라운, 비범한; 기이한, 색다른 (↔ ordinary 평범한)	113, 229
extremely 매우, 극히	233, 247, 265
exude 풍기다, (액체, 냄새) 흘리다	231
eye fatigue 눈의 피로	153
eyebrows 눈썹 (eyelash 속눈썹)	187
eyelid 눈꺼풀	91
eye-popping 눈알이 튀어나올 정도의, 놀라운	37
eyesight 시력(=vision)	153
fabric 직물, 천	19
fabulous 멋진, 근사한	77
face reader 관상 보는 사람	187
facial exercise 안면 운동	91
facial feature 얼굴의 특징	187
facial muscles 얼굴 근육	71
facial wash 세안용 비누	73
factory 공장	27
fade 색이 바래다, 흐려지다, 점점 사라지다	99, 137
fair 흰 피부의, 날씨가 맑은, 공정한, 상당한	193, 253
fair-skinned 피부가 밝은	253
fall off 떨어지다	35
false 거짓의, 가짜의; 잘못된, 틀린	75, 169
fanatic 광신자, …에 광적인 사람	63
fancy 값비싼, 고급의	117
farmed fish 양식 어류	37
farther-in-law 시아버지	195
fat burner 지방 연소 보조 제품	75
fat n. 지방 a. 뚱뚱한	27, 87
fatal 치명적인	71, 231
fate line 운명선	175
fate 운명	175
fat-free 무지방	57
fat-redued 지방을 줄인 (low-fat 저지방의)	57
fault 잘못, 실수	269
favorite 총애하는, 좋아하는 것(사람)	209
feat 공적	245
feces 배설물	131
fee 요금	53
feel full 배부름을 느끼다	35, 57
felon 중죄인, 흉악범 (felony 중죄, 흉악 범죄)	193
female 여성, 여성의(↔ male 남성, 남성의)	209, 233
ferment 발효하다, 발효	61
fertilizer 비료	131
fiber 섬유	19
fidgety 가만히 있지 못하는	209
fight over …를 두고 (가지려고) 싸우다	117
fighting scene 격투 장면	247
figuratively 비유적으로	139
figure out 이해하다, 알아내다	187
fill one's stomach 위장을 채우다	123
fill up (가득) 채우다	35
film producer 영화 제작자	247
film 영화, 영화를 찍다	183
filter 필터, 걸러내다	139
fin 지느러미	49, 261
financially 경제적으로	109, 261
fingertip 손가락 끝	31
fire 해고하다	259
firmly 꽉, 힘주어; 굳게, 확고하게	163, 181
first and foremost 무엇보다	273
fish farm 어류 양식장	37
fish farmer 양식어민	261
fishing rod 낚싯대	139
fist 주먹	51
flabby 힘없이 늘어진	87
flake n. (떨어져 나온) 얇은 조각 v. 벗겨지다, 떨어져 나오다(off)	19, 165
flat (영국) 아파트	97
flat 납작한	87, 187
flavor 맛(=taste), 향미	57, 65, 155
flavorful 풍미 있는, 맛이 좋은(=tasty)	57
flee 도망하다 (cf. flea 벼룩)	221
float 물에 뜨다	261
flood 홍수	191
floor 층, 바닥	105
flour 밀가루	213
flow rate 유량	135
fluoride 불소	155
fly 바지 지퍼	271
foam 거품	155
food poisoning 식중독	71
for a long time 오랫동안, 장기간	45
for a period of time 한동안	71
for a while 잠시 동안	141
for instance 예를 들어	167
for now 현재로는, 우선은	125
for sure 확실히(=surely, certainly)	189
for various reasons 다양한 이유로	245
forbid 금지하다	105
form 형성하다, 만들다	91
former 전의	219
fortunately 다행스럽게도	169
fortune-telling 점	175
foul 나쁜, 악취 나는	209
foundation 근거, 기초, 토대	181, 203
fragment 파편, 조각	99
free 무료의	115
frequently 자주, 종종	45, 79, 165, 265
Friday the 13th 13일의 금요일	191
fried 튀긴(fry 튀기다)	51
from now on 지금부터	139
from person to person 사람마다	175
from then on 그때부터 쭉	195
from time to time 이따금	141
frying pan 프라이팬	135

283

☐ fuel 연료	139, 151
☐ functioning 기능, 작용	21
☐ fungi 곰팡이 (fungus의 복수형)	165
☐ fur (동물의) 털	165
☐ furniture fabric 가구용 직물	19
☐ furry 털로 덮인	165
☐ furthermore 게다가, 더욱이	57
☐ FYI 참고로 (for your information)	161
☐ gain popularity 인기를 얻다	75
☐ gain 얻다	181
☐ gas station 주유소 (= pump)	161
☐ gasoline 휘발유(=petrol), 가솔린(cf. diesel 디젤, 경유)	161
☐ gastric bypass surgery 위장우회수술	33
☐ gastric 위(胃)의(gastric juice = stomach juice 위액)	33
☐ gelatin 젤라틴	47
☐ generally 대개	59
☐ generate 생산하다	125
☐ generous 관대한, 너그러운	187
☐ genetic 유전의, 유전학의	137
☐ germ 세균, 미생물	27, 165
☐ germ-free 세균이 없는	165
☐ get ... into shape 건강한(맵시 있는) 몸매를 유지하다	87
☐ get a checkup (병원에서) 검사를 받다	31
☐ get a taste of ...의 맛을 보다	65
☐ get attacked 공격을 당하다	201
☐ get engaged 약혼하다	235
☐ get fired 해고당하다	259
☐ get older 나이가 들다	89
☐ get over 극복하다, (병이) 낫다	149
☐ get paid for ...로 돈을 받다	233
☐ get permits 허가를 받다	127
☐ get rid of ...을 없애다, 제거하다	87, 127, 167
☐ get swollen 붓다	31
☐ get the axe 해고당하다	259
☐ get the sack 해고당하다	259
☐ get used to ...에 익숙하다	233
☐ geyser 간헐천	135
☐ ghost hunter 유령 사냥꾼	183
☐ giggle 킬킬 웃다	271
☐ give a grand welcome 크게 환영하다	215
☐ give birth 출산하다	105, 245
☐ give the axe 해고하다	259
☐ glance sidewise at ...를 곁눈질로 보다	271
☐ gland 분비선(샘)	31, 45
☐ glucose 글루코스, 포도당	33
☐ go belly-up 망하다, 파산하다, 배를 드러내다	261
☐ go blonde 금발로 하다	89
☐ go for ...을 시도하다, 애쓰다	129
☐ go well with ...와 잘 어울리다	89
☐ go wrong 잘못되다	109, 269
☐ goddess 여신	181
☐ goodwill ambassador 친선대사	215
☐ goodwill 친선, 호의	215
☐ gooey 끈끈한(= sticky)	27
☐ got the moves 멋진 동작(움직임, 춤, 무술 등)을 할 줄 안다	201
☐ got the muscles 근육이 있다, 즉 근육질이다	201
☐ gourmet 미식가	61
☐ government 정부	105
☐ government-provided food assistance 정부가 제공하는 음식 지원	245
☐ grab your wallet 지갑을 챙기다	129
☐ gradually 서서히, 점차	221, 229
☐ grain 곡물	47
☐ granite 화강암	219
☐ greasy 기름기 많은	63
☐ grief n. 슬픔 (grieve v. 슬퍼하다)	141
☐ grip 꽉 붙잡음, 이해, 움켜쥐다	23
☐ gross 역겨운	65
☐ grow back 다시 자라다	201
☐ grow feelings for ...에 대해 좋아하는 마음이 커지다	179
☐ growth hormone 성장 호르몬	227
☐ guano 구아노 (박쥐, 바닷새의 배설물)	131
☐ guidance 지도, 안내	109
☐ guillotine 단두대	241
☐ guy 놈, 녀석	201
☐ gym 체육관(cf. gymnasium의 줄임말)	53, 235
☐ habit 습관	23
☐ habitat 거주지, 서식지	131
☐ hair device 모발 기구	79
☐ hair loss 탈모	179
☐ hallucination 환각	21
☐ hammer 망치	219
☐ hand tool 수공구	259
☐ handle 다루다, 처리하다	33
☐ handsome 1. 잘생긴 2. 많은	103
☐ hard boiled egg 삶은 달걀	37
☐ hard to get 얻기(구하기) 어려운	63
☐ harmful 해로운	27, 149, 239
☐ harmlessly 해가 없이, 해롭지 않게	163
☐ harsh 혹독한, 힘든	129
☐ harvest 추수하다, 수확하다	37
☐ haunt 귀신이 출몰하다	183
☐ have ... in mind ...를 마음에 두다	243
☐ have a bad effect on ...에 안 좋은 영향을 미치다	73
☐ have a difficulty -ing ...하는 데 어려움을 겪다	109
☐ have a good character 성격이 좋다	187
☐ have a hard time 어려움을 겪다, 힘든 시기를 보내다	109, 117
☐ have a strong bias against ...에 대해 (부정적인) 편견을 가지다	109
☐ have an effect on ...에 영향을 미치다	21
☐ have fun 재미있게 즐기다	255
☐ have got the looks 외모가 된다, 멋지다	201
☐ have in common 공통점이 있다	109
☐ have no reservations 주저하지 않다	65
☐ have nothing to do with ...와 관련이 없다 (↔ have something to do with ...와 관련이 있다)	23
☐ heal 치료하다	83
☐ health-friendly 건강에 유익한	39
☐ heart attack 심장마비	163
☐ heart disease 심장병	167
☐ heart 심장	21, 201
☐ hefty 많은, 두둑한	105
☐ height 신장, 키	227
☐ heiress 상속녀(cf. heir 상속인)	195
☐ helpless 무력한	143
☐ hemorrhage 출혈	99

☐ herbivore 초식동물		127
(cf. carnivore 육식동물 omnivore 잡식동물)		
☐ heritage 유산		205
☐ heroic 영웅적인		183
☐ hesitate 망설이다, 주저하다		273
☐ hide n. 가죽 v. 숨다		137
☐ High Court 고등법원		207
☐ highly acidic 강한 산성의		231
☐ highly contribute to …에 대단히 기여하다		19
☐ highly nutritious 영양가가 높은		49
☐ highly 매우, 대단히		89
☐ hit pay dirt 노다지를 발견하다, 갑자기 큰 부자가 되다		117
☐ hit the jackpot 대박을 터트리다		117
☐ hit the road 출발하다, 길을 떠나다		183
☐ hoax 거짓말, 장난질		213
☐ hold one's breath 숨을 참다		231
☐ hold one's urine 소변을 참다		273
☐ hole one's breath 숨을 참다		189
☐ homemade 집에서 만든		213
☐ hop 폴짝 뛰다 (hop on 깡충 뛰어 …에 올라타다)		271
☐ hormone level 호르몬 수치		227
☐ hormone 호르몬		31
☐ horrible 무서운, 끔찍한		241
☐ horrific 끔찍한		193
☐ hot spring 온천		135
☐ huge 거대한, 엄청난(= enormous)	75, 195 , 205, 219	
☐ human population 인구		125
☐ hygiene 위생 (hygienic 위생적인)		165
☐ hyperactive 활동 과잉의		167
☐ hypertrichosis 다모증		229
☐ hypothesis 가설, 추측		165
☐ hypothyroidism 갑상선 기능 저하증		31
☐ ideal 이상적인		113
☐ if well cared for 잘 관리 받으면		127
☐ ignite 점화하다, 불을 붙이다(cf. ignition 점화장치)		161
☐ ignorant 무지한		193
☐ illegal immigrant 불법 이주민		221
☐ immediately 당장, 즉시, 즉각		163
☐ immune system 면역 체계		165
☐ impossible 불가능한		245
☐ improbable 사실 같지 않은, 희한한		245
☐ improve 개선하다, 좋아지게 하다	91, 153	
☐ in a short time period 짧은 시간 내에		75
☐ in exchange for …와 교환하여		215
☐ in great numbers 대량으로, 많은 수의		137
☐ in harmony 조화로운, 협조하는		265
☐ in other words 즉, 다시 말해서		57
☐ in real life 실제 현실(삶)에서		169
☐ in recorded history 기록된 역사 중		243
☐ in the near future 가까운 미래에		77
☐ inadvertently 무심코, 본의 아니게	25, 853	
☐ inappropriate 부적절한(↔ appropriate 적절한)		79
☐ incident 사건, 일	191, 193	
☐ increase 증가(시키다), 늘다 (↔decrease 감소, 줄다)	157, 165	
☐ incredibly 믿을 수 없을 정도로		213
☐ index finger 검지		91
☐ indicate 나타내다		23
☐ indigestible 소화되지 않은(=undigestible)		163
☐ industrial 산업의		265
☐ inexpensive 비싸지 않은		85

☐ infection 감염	37
☐ inflammatory 염증의, 선동적인	149
☐ infra-red light 적외선	183
☐ ingest 삼키다, 먹다	35
☐ ingredient 성분, 재료, 요소	45, 47, 59, 75, 155
☐ initiate 시작하다	193
☐ injection 주입, 주사	71
☐ injure 부상, 부상을 입다	27
☐ inner 안쪽의	91
☐ innocent 죄가 없는, 결백한	241
☐ inquisitiveness 꼬치꼬치 캐묻기 좋아함	257
☐ insect 곤충	123
☐ insemination 수정	215
☐ insight 통찰력, 이해력	181
☐ inspire 영감을 주다	113
☐ instance 사례, 경우	217
☐ instead of … 대신	37
☐ instructor 지도자	247
☐ intelligent 지적인	193
☐ intention 의도, 의사	77
☐ interestingly 흥미롭게도	25
☐ internal organ 장기, 내장기관	187
☐ internet comment board 인터넷 덧글 게시판	213
☐ intestine 장, 창자	59
☐ invert 뒤집다	143
☐ investigate 조사하다 (investigator 조사원)	183
☐ investigation 조사	161
☐ investigator 조사원, 수사관	183
☐ iron deficiency 철분 결핍	157
☐ iron 철, 철분, 다리미	79, 157
☐ irritate 따갑게 하다, 자극하다, 짜증나게 하다	231
☐ issue v. 발표하다, 공표하다, 발부하다, 발행하다 n. 주제, 안건, 문제, 발행	161
☐ issues in life 삶의 문제	181
☐ It is estimated that …라고 추정되다	19
☐ it's open to the public 대중에 공개되다	113
☐ itchy 가려운	31
☐ jackpot (도박, 복권) 거액의 상금	117
☐ jaw 턱	123
☐ jaw-dropping 턱이 아래로 빠질 정도의, 놀라운	247
☐ Jeremiah 예레미야(사람 이름, 구약 성경 예레미야서)	253
☐ Jews 유대인	241
☐ jittery 안절부절못하는	209
☐ joint 관절	23, 37
☐ journalist 언론인	105
☐ judge 판사	193, 241
☐ jumping jack 팔 벌려 뛰기	87
☐ juror 배심원	241
☐ kind of 좀, 약간	103
☐ knife 칼	189
☐ knock someone's socks off 깜짝 놀라게 하다	207
☐ knot 매듭	207
☐ knuckle cracking 손가락 관절 꺾기	23
☐ knuckle 관절	23
☐ Korean-born 한국 태생의	37
☐ label 상표를 붙이다, (상표 등에) 필요한 정보를 적어 넣다	57
☐ laboriously 힘들게, 어렵게	205
☐ lactic acid 젖산	209
☐ ladder 사다리	189
☐ lamb 새끼 양 (sheep 양)	45

☐ lame excuse 궁색한 변명	151
☐ landmark 주요 지형지물, 랜드마크	113, 203
☐ lard 라드, 돼지기름	47
☐ laser treatment 레이저 치료	229
☐ last 마지막의; 지속하다	31, 71, 191, 243
☐ late at night 밤늦게	31
☐ laugh at 비웃다	273
☐ law suit 법적 소송	179
☐ layer 층	79
☐ layoff 일시 해고	259
☐ lead to …로 이어지다, 인도하다	23, 151
☐ lean 기울다	203
☐ leather dressing 가죽 무두질	139
☐ leave for …로(향해) 떠나다	241
☐ leave one's name in the history 역사에 이름을 남기다	109
☐ leech 거머리	35
☐ lend 빌려주다(lend-lent-lent) cf. borrow 빌리다	117, 215
☐ length 길이	219
☐ lengthen (길게) 늘이다	151, 233
☐ leopard 표범	253
☐ let out (소리 등을) 내다, 내보내다, 풀어주다	35
☐ levitation 공중부양	177
☐ levy (세금의) 추가 부담금	129
☐ liaison officer 연락담당관	129
☐ lid 뚜껑, 덮개	91
☐ lie down (바닥에) 눕다	163
☐ lifeless-looking 죽은 것처럼 보이는	143
☐ lifelong 일생의, 평생 동안의	99
☐ lift 들어 올리다	91
☐ lifting weights 역기 들기	151
☐ ligament 인대	23
☐ light bulb 전구	227
☐ lighter 더 밝은, 더 가벼운	89
☐ like other babies 다른 아기들처럼	115
☐ likewise 마찬가지로	153
☐ limb 사지 (팔, 다리)	35
☐ liquefied 액화된	123
☐ liquid 액체, 액체의	27
☐ literal meaning 문자 그대로의 의미	265
☐ literally speaking 문자 그대로 말해서	139
☐ literally 문자[말] 그대로	135, 261
☐ liver 간	31, 39
☐ lizard 도마뱀	233
☐ local neighbor 동네 이웃	115
☐ local 동네의, 지역의	59, 73
☐ locate …에 위치하다	255
☐ located in …에 위치한	219
☐ longevity 장수, 오래 삶	97
☐ longtime 오랫동안의, 여러 해의	77
☐ look older 더 늙어 보이다	89
☐ look up (참고 도서, 사전 등을) 찾아보다	265
☐ look younger 더 젊어 보이다	89
☐ loose bowels 설사	187
☐ loose 헐거운	91
☐ lose weight 체중을 감량하다	53, 75
☐ lose 잃다	141
☐ loudly 크게, 소란스럽게	167
☐ love handle 처진 뱃살, 늘어진 옆구리 살	87
☐ love spell 사랑의 주문	179
☐ low iron 철분 부족	31
☐ lower 낮추다, 내리다	177
☐ lucid 명쾌한, 의식이 명확한	169
☐ lukewarm 미지근한	73
☐ lung 폐	21
☐ lure 유혹하다, 꾀다	209, 241
☐ made-up story 지어낸 이야기	245
☐ magazine 잡지	179
☐ magnificent 멋진, 웅장한	205
☐ maid 하녀, 가정부	207
☐ mailman 우체부	113
☐ maintain 유지하다	91
☐ major offender (…의) 주범	167
☐ make a hissing sound 쉭쉭 소리를 내다	127
☐ make up for 벌충하다, 메우다	57
☐ make up 이루다, 형성하다, 구성하다	27
☐ make[beat] a retreat 물러가다, 도피하다	243
☐ makeup 화장품 (cf. make up 화장하다)	83
☐ mammal 포유류	65
☐ manipulate (사람, 사물) 조종하다, 다루다	243
☐ manufacture 제조하다	195
☐ manufacturer 제조업자	161
☐ marble structure 대리석 건축물	205
☐ marriage 결혼 (marry 결혼하다)	207, 235
☐ martial artist 무술인	247
☐ marvelous 놀라운	113
☐ match (어울리게) 맞추다	89
☐ mate 짝, 배우자, 친구	141
☐ material 물질	27
☐ maze 미로 (=labyrinth)	195
☐ maze-like 미로 같은	195
☐ measure 측정하다, (치수가) …이다	227
☐ meat (식용) 고기	45
☐ medical 의학의	163
☐ medication 약, 약물(치료)	33, 227
☐ medicine cabinet 약품 보관 찬장	53
☐ medicine 의료, 약	35
☐ memorial 기념비	219
☐ mentally 정신적으로	195
☐ merciless 무자비한	201
☐ mercury 수은	49
☐ mere 그저, 단지	245
☐ metabolism 신진대사	87
☐ mice 쥐들(mouse의 복수형)	267
☐ military 군사의, 군대	221
☐ millionaire 백만장자	117
☐ mind one's P's and Q's 예의 바르게 행동하다 (= behave oneself)	273
☐ minority 소수집단	221
☐ miracle 기적	39
☐ miraculous 기적적인	39
☐ mischievous 장난꾸러기의	255
☐ misfortune 불운, 불행	189, 217
☐ mislead 잘못 인도하다, 오해하게 만들다	23
☐ mismatched 잘못 짝지어진, 맞지 않는	271
☐ misname 이름을 잘못 붙이다	267
☐ misuse v. 오용하다 n. 남용, 오용	21, 153
☐ mite 진드기	165
☐ mixture 혼합물 (v. mix 혼합하다)	27
☐ moist 습기, 수분	25
☐ moisture-rich 수분이 풍부한	77

- moisturize 수분을 주다 (moisture 수분 moisturizer 보습제) 77
- moneybag 돈주머니, 부자 195
- monster 괴물 201
- monstrous 거대한, 괴물 같은 135
- monumental 기념비적인, (크기가) 엄청난 219
- moonpie 초코파이와 비슷한 파이 종류 37
- more than half of …의 반 이상 27
- mosquito 모기 209
- moth 나방 189
- motto 좌우명, 모토 265
- mountaineering 등산 129
- mouth-watering 군침 도는 37
- move in 이사해 오다 243
- multiple birth 다둥이 출산 245
- multiple 많은, 다수의 245
- murder 살인하다 241
- muscle fiber 근섬유 151
- muscle 근육 151, 201
- muscular 근육의, 근육이 발달한 151
- muster 모으다, 소집하다 219
- mysteriously 신비하게 213
- mystery 수수께끼, 미스터리 195
- mysticism 신비주의 181
- myth 신화, (근거 없는) 믿음, 낭설 23, 149
- nail 손톱, 발톱(fingernail 손톱, toenail 발톱) 39
- naked eye 육안, 맨눈 203
- naked 벌거벗은 203
- name tag 이름표 101
- name 이름을 대다 37
- name-brand 브랜드가 있는, 유명 상표의 73
- narrow 좁은 187
- nasty 나쁜, 못된 267
- natural parents 친부모 101
- naturally 당연히 63
- nausea 메스꺼움 163
- nauseous 메스꺼운 163
- Nazi-occupied 나치가 지배하던 241
- nearly 거의 37
- nearsightedness 근시 153
- negative 부정적인(↔ positive 긍정적인) 191
- negotiate 협상하다 243
- nephew 남자 조카 243
- newlywed 신혼의, 막 결혼한 235
- nigger 흑인을 비하해 부르는 표현, 검둥이
  (지문에서는 개의 이름으로 쓰였다) 183
- night blind 야맹(증) 177
- night blindness 야맹증 39
- nightmare 악몽 103, 191
- nitrogen 질소 131
- no can do 소용없다, 할 수 없다 253
- no wonder 놀랄 일도 아니다, 당연하다 27
- noble 귀족 255
- non-surgical 비수술적인, 수술을 하지 않는 71
- normal blood flow 정상적인 혈액 흐름 35
- normal 일반적인 103
- Norwegian 노르웨이의, 노르웨이인의 99
- nosebleed 코피 163
- nostril 콧구멍 163
- not just any 보통의 …은 아니다 103
- not to mention …는 말할 것도 없이 105
- nothing hurts like the truth
  〈속담〉 진실만큼 아픈 (고통스러운) 건 없다 101
- noticeably 현저히 233
- nowadays 요즘 59
- numb 마비시키다 21
- nutrient 영양분 131
- nutrient-rich 양분이 풍부한 131
- nutritionist 영양학자 49
- nutritious 영양가가 높은(cf. nutrition 영양, 영양물) 49
- obese (사람이) 살찐, 비만한(cf. obesity 비만) 33, 209
- occult society 주술인 모임[사회] 181
- occult 주술적인, 초자연적인 181
- occultist 비술(신비한 마술) 하는 사람 181
- occupy 차지하다, 점령하다 241
- octopus 문어 201
- odd 이상한 61
- odor 냄새 61, 131
- of one's own accord 자발적으로 143
- offender 범죄자 167
- offer 제공하다 115, 179
- officially 공식적으로 113, 117, 167, 235
- omit 빼다, 생략하다 259
- on a charge of …의 혐의로 193
- on purpose 일부러 221
- on the contrary 오히려, 반대로 49
- on the spot 현장에서 247
- onion 양파 59
- only daughter 무남독녀 195
- open fire 발포하다 243
- open one's mouth wide 입을 크게 벌리다 189
- open one's wallet (돈을 내려고) 지갑을 열다 75, 127
- operation 수술 33
- opossum 주머니 쥐 143
- opposite 반대편의, 반대의 것[사람] 247, 269
- oral 구강의, 구두의 99
- organ 내장, 장기 45
- origin 기원, 유래 255
- originally 원래 181, 253
- originate in 비롯하다, 유래하다 255
- orphan 고아 109
- other than …외에, …말고 27
- out of control 통제 불능의 117
- outer protective layer 외부 보호층 79
- outer 외부의, 외곽의 79
- outstanding 두드러진, 뛰어난 233
- oven-baked 오븐에 구운 213
- over the years 수년 동안, 수년에 걸쳐 103
- over-crowded 너무 붐비는 37
- overdose 과다 복용 217
- overreact 과잉반응을 보이다 165
- overuse 남용하다 153
- overweight 과체중의 209
- ovo-lacto vegetarian 유란 채식주의자 47
- own 소유하다 183
- ownership 소유권 215
- oxygen 산소
  (cf. hydrogen 수소 carbon dioxide 이산화탄소) 27, 125
- pain 고통(=pang, agony) 75

287

☐ painkiller 진통제	21
☐ painstakingly 힘들게(= laboriously), 공들여	219
☐ paint the town red 술 마시며 놀다	255
☐ paint 물감, 색을 칠하다	255
☐ pair 두 사람의 짝, 한 쌍	245
☐ palace 궁전	113, 243
☐ pale 창백한	89
☐ palm reading 손금 읽기(= palmistry, chiromancy)	175
☐ palm 손바닥	31, 175
☐ pancreas 췌장	45
☐ paper towel 키친 타올	269
☐ paralysis 마비 (v. paralyze 마비시키다)	71, 143
☐ parrot 앵무새	141
☐ participate in …에 참가하다	37
☐ particular 특정한	239
☐ pass away 세상을 떠나다, 죽다	195, 205
☐ past life 전생	179
☐ patient n. 환자 a. 인내심 있는	229
☐ paw (동물) 발	61
☐ peak 정상, 꼭대기	129
☐ peanut 땅콩	165
☐ pee 소변, 소변보다 (go for a pee 소변보다)	273
☐ pelican 펠리컨	131
☐ pepper 후추	61
☐ per minute 1분당	19
☐ per one serving 1회 먹는 분량에, 일 인분에	53
☐ per second 초당	135
☐ perform a CT scan CT 촬영을 하다	115
☐ perform 실행하다, 연기하다, 공연하다	115
☐ period 기간	235
☐ permanent 영구적인	153
☐ personal bodyguard 개인 경호원	105
☐ personality 성격, 개성	187
☐ personology 관상학(=physiognomy)	187
☐ pet 애완동물	19, 127
☐ phenomenon 현상	143
☐ phony 가짜의, 위조된 (=fake)	161
☐ phosphorus 인	131
☐ photosynthesis 광합성	125
☐ pick up …을 얻다	113
☐ picky eater 입맛이 까다로운 사람	111, 209
☐ picky 까다로운(=choosy)	111, 209
☐ pigeon 비둘기	61
☐ piglet 아기 돼지 (pig 돼지)	45
☐ pillar 기둥	177
☐ pinch 꼬집다, 꽉 쥐다	163, 189
☐ pinkish 분홍빛의	31
☐ pinpoint 정확히 집어내다	257
☐ pituitary 뇌하수체	227
☐ place 놓다, 두다	91
☐ plain brown 평범한 갈색	137
☐ plain n. 평원(cf. prairie 초원) a. 분명한, 꾸미지 않은, 못생긴, 무늬가 없는	137
☐ plane/airplane 비행기	217
☐ plankton 플랑크톤	125
☐ plasma 혈장, 플라즈마	27
☐ plastic surgeon 성형외과 의사	91
☐ plastic surgery 성형수술	91, 103
☐ platelet 혈소판	27
☐ play an important role 중요한 역할을 하다	193
☐ play possum 죽은 척하다(= play dead)	143
☐ pocket some money 돈을 챙기다	221
☐ pocket 주머니에 넣다, 챙기다	75
☐ poison 독, 독약	231
☐ poisonous 독성의	231
☐ pollen 꽃가루	165
☐ pollutant 오염물질	261
☐ pollute 오염시키다	37
☐ poo 대변(=feces, dropping)	65
☐ pop 뻥하고 터지다	269
☐ popular 인기 있는	131
☐ popularity 인기	49, 75
☐ popularize 대중화하다, 많은 사람들에게 알리다	181
☐ pore 구멍, 모공(cf. porous 구멍이 많은)	83
☐ portion (음식의) 1인분, 부분, 몫	151, 219
☐ pose 자세	91
☐ post (사진, 영상 등을 인터넷에) 올리다, 붙이다	213
☐ potion 물약, 마법의 약 (cf. portion 몫, 1인분)	179
☐ pounce (공격하며) 덮치다(on)	123
☐ pound 파운드 (계량 단위 1파운드 : 0.454kg, 영국의 화폐 단위)	63
☐ power plant 발전소	261
☐ practically 실질적으로, 사실상	19
☐ practice (의사가) 개업하다, 영업하다	35
☐ practitioner 의술을 행하는 사람, 의사	35
☐ praise 찬양하다	65
☐ precious 소중한, 귀중한	105
☐ predator 포식자	201
☐ prefer 더 좋아하다, 선호하다	59, 209
☐ pregnant woman 임산부	39
☐ pregnant 임신한 (n. pregnancy 임신)	49
☐ preparation 준비	129
☐ preside 사회를 보다, 주례를 서다	239
☐ press 누르다	193
☐ prevent 막다, 예방하다(cf. prevention 예방, 방지)	39, 49, 91, 149
☐ prey 먹이	123
☐ prior to …전에	151
☐ privacy 사생활	105
☐ process 과정	25
☐ produce 만들어 내다	209
☐ professional 전문적인	85
☐ prolific 열매를 많이 맺는, 다작의, 다산의	245
☐ promote 홍보하다, 광고하다, 승진하다	179
☐ proper portion of …의 적당한 양	151
☐ property 특성, 성질, 부동산	25, 39, 83
☐ protect 보호하다	113
☐ protein 단백질	47, 165
☐ proverb 속담	253
☐ provide 제공하다(with)	139, 151
☐ psychic reader 점 보는 사람, 심령술사 (= fortune-teller)	179
☐ psychic 초자연적인, 심령의; 심령술사, 영매	179, 195
☐ publish a statement 성명을 발표하다	213
☐ punch 주먹으로 치다; 펀치	105, 247
☐ purely 순전히, 전적으로, 오직	231
☐ put … on a diet …에게 다이어트를 시키다	57
☐ put … to death …를 사형에 처하다	193
☐ quadruplets 네 쌍둥이	245

quail 메추라기	63
quality 질, 품질	155
quarter 1/4(cf. quarter dollar 25센트)	33
queen 여왕	103
quit 그만두다, 중지하다	33, 77
quite a few 상당히 많은	51
quite 꽤, 상당히	273
raid 공습	183
raindrop 빗방울	231
raise 올리다, (자금을) 모금하다, 기르다, 키우다 (cf. rise 오르다, 증가)	127, 177
ranch (대규모) 농장	117
rare disease 희귀병	229
rare 흔치 않은	99
reaction 반응	233
real deal 실제, 진짜	213
reasonable 이성적인, 합리적인, 저렴한	175, 179, 193
recall 기억하다, 회고하다	97
receptor 수용기	21
recipe 요리법, 레시피	59
recommend 권하다, 추천하다	25, 49
recommendation 추천서	129
recover 회복하다	143
red blood cell 적혈구	27
red light district 홍등가	255
reddish 불그스름한	89
redhead 빨강 머리(를 가진 사람)	209
reduce 줄이다, 감소시키다(=lessen, decrease)	39, 53, 79, 153
refer to …을 참조하다, 가리키다	79, 131
refuse 거절하다, 거부하다	47, 141
regime 정권	221
register 등록하다	235
reincarnation 환생	115
relation ship 관계	233
relatively 비교적	61
release (영화를) 개봉하다, 방출하다, 석방하다, 출시하다	161, 183, 201
relieve 경감하다, 완화시키다	149
religious 종교적인	181
remaining 남은, 남아 있는	117
remains 유해, 남은 부분	241
removal 제거, 해고	259
remove 제거하다(= get rid of)	25, 253
rent 빌리다	105
repeat 반복하다	91
repeated 반복된, 반복적인	77, 217
repeating 반복하는, (총) 연발의	195
replace 대체하다	257
reply 대답하다	269
reportedly 소문에 따르면	193
represent 나타내다	191
require permits 허가를 (받도록) 요구하다	127
require 요구하다	57
resident 주민	99
residue 잔여물	37
resistance 저항(성)	39
respiratory 호흡기의	21
respond 반응하다, 대답하다	165
responsibility 책임	207
restore (이전 상태로) 회복시키다	35
restricted area 제한 구역	129
retain 보유하다	215
retreat 후회, 퇴각, 후퇴하다, 물러나다	243
reunion (오랜만의) 만남, 모임	273
reveal (비밀 등을) 드러내다, 밝히다	137, 175, 187
revenge 복수	195
reverend 목사	239
ride a horse 말을 타다	219
rifle 소총	195
right after 직후	31
right away 즉시	31
rinse 헹구다	73, 85
riotous 소란스러운	255
rip 찢다	271
rise to the throne 왕위에 오르다	243
robin 울새 (새 종류)	189
rotate 회전하다	177
routine 규칙적으로 하는 일, 일상	53
royal road 왕도	181
royal 왕족의 (cf. loyal 충성스러운)	181
royalty 로열티, 사용료	129
rub 문지르다, 비비다	83, 97, 253
ruin 망치다, 손상시키다	153, 261
run away 달아나다	267
run in place 제자리에서 뛰다	87
run riot 난동을 부리다 (riot 폭동, 소동)	255
sac (동식물 체내의) 주머니	123
sack 가방	259
saggy 축 처진, 늘어진	87, 91
saliva 침	165
salivary 침을 분비하는	45
salmon 연어	37
saloon 술집, 살롱	255
sandy 모래가 많은	231
sap 수액	231
satisfying 만족스러운	57
savagely 잔인하게 (savage 야만적인, 잔인한)	241
scar 흉, 상처	83
scary 무서운, 겁나는 (cf. scared 겁먹은)	23, 169, 201, 239
scatter 흩뿌리다, 흩어지다	241
scattered 흩어진	187
scholar 학자	51, 181
scientific 과학적인	175
scientifically 과학적으로	49
scorpion 전갈	61, 123, 239
screener 스크리너 (화면을 검사하거나 가려내는 사람, 영화 화면을 조정하는 사람)	247
sculpture 조각	219
sea creature 바다생물	201
seal 바다표범, 물개	131
search for 찾다, 수색하다	101
search team 수색대	183
seasoning 양념	201
section 구역, 지구, 부문	255
sedation 진정제가 투여된 상태	21, 99
self-cleaning 자가 청소	25
send a congratulation card 축하 카드를 보내다	235
sense 느끼다, 감각	21
sensitively 민감하게	165

separate a. 별개의, 서로 다른, 독립된	137
v. 분리되다, 나누다, 헤어지다	
serial killer 연쇄살인범	241
serial 연쇄적인, 연속 방송되는, 연속극	241
serious crime 중죄, 무거운 죄	193
set the table 상을 차리다	57
severe 심한	129
severely 몹시, 심하게 (severe 엄한, 극심한)	167
shade 그늘, 빛 가리개, 색조	89
shark fin soup 상어 지느러미 수프, 샥스핀	49
shark 상어	49
shed n. 헛간 v. (피·눈물을) 흘리다, 없애다, (옷·허물을) 벗다, (나뭇잎을) 떨어뜨리다, (빛을) 비추다	19, 53
sheer 순전한	217
shell n. 포탄, 조개껍데기 v. 포격하다, 껍질을 까다 (shell out 큰돈을 들이다, 거금을 쓰다)	105, 243
shelter 피난처, 보호소, 주거지	231
shoot 총을 쏘다	117
shortly after … 직후	215
show no response 반응을 보이지 않다	143
show signs of …의 신호(조짐)를 보이다	141
shrimp 새우	37
sick 아픈, 병든	163
side effect 부작용	21, 75
side 옆, 옆구리	87
significant 중요한, 특별한	33
similar to …와 비슷한, 유사한	51, 59
similarly 유사하게, 마찬가지로	259
simultaneously 동시에	271
sink 가라앉다, 함몰하다	203
site 현장	205
skin cell 피부세포	19
slang 은어	87
slightly 조금, 약간	273
slogan 구호, 슬로건	265
slow down 느리게 하다	21, 247
slow reaction time 느린 반응 속도	157
small intestine 소장 (large intestine 대장)	33
smart 똑똑한, 영리한	201, 267
smelly 나쁜 냄새가 나는	65
smoke v. 담배를 피우다 n. 연기	77
smoker 흡연자	77
smooth 부드러운, 매끈한	77
snack 간식	51
soak 담그다	45
soap making 비누 제작	139
sober a. 술 취하지 않은 v. 정신이 들게 하다	157
sober up 술이 깨게 하다	157
society 사회, 집단, 단체	181
soda 탄산음료, 소다수	167
soft furnishing 가정용 직물	19
solid 단단한, 고체의, 확실한	33, 149
solve (문제를) 해결하다	253
sooner or later 조만간	189
sorrow 슬픔	141
sound ridiculous 어이없게 들리다	63
soupy 수프 같은, 걸쭉한	27
source 원천, 자료	175
spare 아끼다	205

speak highly of …를 칭찬하다	63
specialty 전문, 전공	179
species 종	123, 137
specifically 구체적으로	45, 209
spectre/specter 유령 (=ghost)	183
speech disorder 언어장애	99
speechless (너무 놀라) 말을 못 하는, 말문이 막힌	113, 247
speed up 속도를 빠르게 하다	247
spell 주문	179
spend (money) on …에 돈을 쓰다	73
spend a fortune 많은 돈을 쓰다	105
spending habit 소비습관	117
spice 향신료	63
spider 거미	123
spill the beans (비밀을) 털어놓다	271
spirit 1. 기백, 정신 2. 마음 3. 유령, 영혼	183, 195, 265
spiritual 영적인	179
splash (물을) 끼얹다, 첨벙, 철썩 뿌려진 물	73
split ends 갈라진 머리끝	79
split 갈라지다, 쪼개(지)다, (남녀가) 헤어지다	79, 259
sports beverage 스포츠음료	167
spot n. 장소, 점, 얼룩 v. 찾아내다, 발견하다	113, 253
spree 흥청거리는 한바탕 놀음	255
St. Stephen's clock tower 성 스테판 시계탑	203
stain 얼룩지게 하다, 얼룩, 더러움	85, 155
staircase 계단	195
stare 빤히 쳐다보다(at)	141
startle 깜짝 놀라게 하다	267
starve to death 굶주리다, 굶어 죽다	141
static electricity 정전기	161
static 고정된, 정적인	161
stay faithful (상대가) 바람을 피우지 않다	179
steam 증기, 증기로 익히다, 찌다	59
steer clear of 피하다	157, 231
step down 물러나다, 내려오다	243
step forward to …하려고 나서다	271
stick (뾰족한 것으로) 찌르다, 붙이다	209
stick out 내밀다	233
stick to …에 들러붙다	163
stimulant 자극제	157
stimulate 자극하다	35
sting 쏘다 (be stung 쏘이다, 물리다)	239
stinky 악취가 나는	61, 209
stomach 위, 복부, 배	33, 45, 123
straighten 곧게 펴다 (straightener n. 곧게 펴는 것)	79
strain 부담, 압박, 염좌	151
straw 지푸라기, 빨대	85
strength 힘, 장점	23
strengthen 강하게 하다	39
stretch 늘이다, 스트레칭하다	151
stripe 줄무늬	137, 253
stroke 뇌졸중, 타법	99
strong aftertaste 강한 뒷맛	65
stubborn 완강한, 고집 센	87
stuffed with …로 속을 채운	59
submit 제출하다	129
subway station 지하철역	271
suck 빨다	35, 123, 209
sue 고소하다	101
suffer from (질병 등을) 앓다	99

☐ sufficient 충분한	73
☐ suggest 말하다, (뜻을) 비치다	165
☐ sultan 술탄 (이슬람교 지배자)	243
☐ sunburn 햇볕에 의한 화상	77
☐ sunlight 태양빛, 햇볕	189
☐ super-giant 엄청나게 큰	219
☐ supernatural 초자연적인	195
☐ super-rich 굉장히 부유한	195
☐ superstition 미신	189
☐ superstitious 미신적인	175
☐ supper 만찬	191
☐ supplement 보조제, 보충제	53
☐ supplementary 추가의, 보충의	153
☐ surface 표면	155
☐ surgery 수술, 외과	99
☐ surgical 수술의, 외과의(cf. surgery 수술)	71
☐ surplus 잉여, 남는 것	191
☐ surprising 놀라운 (surprised 놀란)	61
☐ surprisingly 놀랍게도	45
☐ surrender 항복하다	243
☐ survive 살아남다	35, 125
☐ susceptible to …에 취약한, 걸리기 쉬운	151
☐ suspect 의심하다, 수상하게 여기다, 추정하다	213, 241
☐ swallow v. 삼키다 n. 제비	163
☐ sweat 땀이 나다	209
☐ sweaty 땀이 나는 (sweat 땀)	75
☐ sweetbread 스위트브레드(어린 돼지, 양, 소의 췌장, 흉선)	45
☐ sweetened 단맛이 가미된	167
☐ sweetener 감미료	57, 155
☐ sweets 단 것, 단 음식들	167
☐ swell 붓다, 불룩해지다 (swelling 부은 곳, 붓기 hand swelling 손이 붓는 것)	23
☐ switch 바꾸다	101
☐ symbolism 상징주의	181
☐ symmetry 대칭, 균형	205
☐ symptom 증상, 징후	31, 149
☐ syndrome 증후군	229
☐ synonym 유의어	259
☐ tactic 전략	143
☐ take a break 잠시 휴식을 취하다	153
☐ take advantage of …를 이용/악용하다	117
☐ take control of …를 지배, 통제하다	143
☐ take medication 약을 복용하다	227
☐ take one's own life 스스로 목숨을 끊다	117
☐ take place 개최되다, 발생하다	191, 235
☐ take revenge 복수하다	195
☐ take the safer road 안전한 길을 선택하다	161
☐ talent 재능, 능력	201
☐ tan 피부를 태우다, 선탠하다	77
☐ tap 가볍게 두드리다	91
☐ tarot 타로 카드	181
☐ taste the joy of …의 기쁨을 맛보다	75
☐ taste 맛(=flavor)	57
☐ tasty 맛있는(= delicious ↔ tasteless 맛이 없는)	51, 65
☐ tax 세금	117
☐ tea leaf 찻잎	179
☐ tease 놀리다(= make fun of)	229
☐ teenage 십대의	101
☐ teeth 이빨들 (단수 – tooth)	49
☐ temperature 온도	135
☐ temporarily 일시적으로, 임시로	177
☐ tempting 귀가 솔깃한, 유혹적인	33
☐ tend to …하는 경향이 있다	57
☐ term 1. 용어 2. 학기 3. 기간 4. 조건	87
☐ terrible 지독한, 끔찍한	241
☐ test 확인하다, 시험하다	149
☐ thankfully 다행히도, 고맙게도	53, 129
☐ thanks to …덕분에	195
☐ that is(are) to come 이제 다가올, 가까운 미래의	151
☐ the cause of allergy 알레르기의 원인	19
☐ the chosen one 선택받은 자	209
☐ the high amount of 상당한 양의	39
☐ the manchineel 맨치닐 나무	231
☐ the moment of …하는 순간	169
☐ the most well-known 가장 잘 알려진	255
☐ the other way around 반대로, 거꾸로	103
☐ the price per bottle 한 병당 가격	63
☐ the rare taste of …의 흔치 않은 맛	63
☐ the second largest 두 번째로 큰 것	135
☐ the Statue of Liberty 자유의 여신상	177
☐ theory 이론	25
☐ therapy 치료법	35
☐ there is a high risk of …의 위험이 높다	37
☐ thick 진한, 두꺼운, 숱이 많은, 걸쭉한	27, 187, 229
☐ thin 숱이 적은; 여윈, 가는	187
☐ thorough 철저한	129
☐ threatening 위협적인 (threaten 위협하다 threat 위협)	165
☐ throne 왕좌	231, 243
☐ throughout the year 일 년 내내	71
☐ throw away 버리다	35
☐ thymus 흉선	45
☐ thyroid gland 갑상선	31
☐ thyroid 갑상선의	31
☐ tick 진드기	123
☐ tie the knot 결혼하다(= marry)	207
☐ tilt one's head back 고개를 뒤로 젖히다	163
☐ tilt v. 기울다 n. 기울어짐	163, 203
☐ tiny bits of fibers 작은 섬유 조각들	19
☐ tiny 작은	19
☐ tip v. 기울이다 n. 뾰족한 끝, 봉사료, 조언	25, 85, 163
☐ tired 지친, 피곤한	153
☐ tissue (세포로 이루어진) 조직	47, 151
☐ to be more exact 더 정확히 말하면	233
☐ to the bone 뼈까지, 철저하게	139
☐ tofu 두부	61
☐ toilet 화장실	273
☐ tomb 무덤(= grave)	205
☐ tone 색조	89
☐ tongue 혀	233
☐ tonic immobility 긴장성 부동	143
☐ Too much is as bad as too little. 과유불급	39
☐ tool 연장, 도구	79, 181
☐ toothless 이가 없는	139
☐ traditionally 전통적으로	221
☐ tragic 비극적인	217
☐ training 훈련	129
☐ trait 특징	233
☐ transport 수송하다, 실어 나르다	205
☐ treatment 치료, 처치	227
☐ tribe 부족, 종족	221

단어	페이지
trick 마술, 속임수	177
trim 정리하다, 다듬다, 잘라내다	79, 87, 259
trip on …에 발이 걸려 넘어지다	113
triple-layed 3중 겹의, 3층의	63
triplets 세 쌍둥이	245
truffle 송로버섯, 트뤼플	63
trumpeter 트럼펫 연주자	109
trunk (코끼리의) 코, 나무 몸통 (cf. branch/sprig/bough 가지)	141, 231
trustworthy 신뢰할 만한	53
tumor 종양	227
tuna 다랑어, 참치	37, 49
turn down 거절하다	47
turn on 켜다	161
twin 쌍둥이	245
typical symptom 전형적인 증상	71
U.S. Marine Corps 미 해병대	265
ugly 못생긴	267
unbelievable 믿을 수 없을 정도로 놀라운	51, 233
uncomfortable 불편한	153
uncontrollably 통제할 수 없게	227
uncover 벗기다, 알아내다	187
under normal use 정상적인 사용으로도	21
under very good conditions 좋은 환경·조건에서	109
under-eye area 눈 밑 부위	91
undergo (…을) 겪다, 받다	33, 227, 229
understandable 이해할 만한	143
uneducated 교육을 받지 못한	113
unexpectedly 예상외로, 뜻밖에	65
unfamiliar 낯선, 익숙하지 않은	273
unfiltered 여과되지 않은	83
unfortunate 불운한	217
unfortunately 불행하게도	201
unhealthy 건강에 해로운	75
unofficial 비공식적인	265
unorthodox 비정통적인	35
unpleasant 불쾌한, 불편한	23
unstable 불안정한(↔ stable 안정된)	195
unusual growth 이상한 성장	227
unusual 특이한, 색다른	61
unusually 특이하게도	103
unwanted 원치 않는	257
unwashed 씻지 않은	209
upset v. 속상하게(화나게) 만들다 a. 속상한 n. 배탈, 언짢음	35, 851
upside down 위아래가 바뀐, 뒤집힌	143
upside-down 뒤집혀, 위아래가 바뀌어	261
useful 유용한	139
valuable 가치 있는	131
vanish 사라지다	253
various 다양한, 여러 가지의	45, 59, 165, 245
variously 다양하게	139
vary 다양하다, 가지각색이다	233
vegetable 채소, 식물인간	47
vegetarian 채식주의자	47
vending machine 자동판매기	167
venom (뱀 등의) 독 cf. venomous 독이 있는(=poisonous)	35, 201
venomous snake 독사(=viper)	35
verb 동사	259
vice versa 반대의 경우도 그렇다	141
victim 희생자, 피해자	209, 241
viewer 시청자	177
villager 마을 사람, 주민	51
vinegar 식초	45
visible 눈으로 보이는	203
vision 시력(=eyesight), 통찰력	153
voluntarily 스스로, 자발적으로	35
vomit 토하다	163
waistline 허리선	87
wake up 잠에서 깨다, 깨우다, 정신이 들게 하다	157, 169
wander 배회하다, 돌아다니다	127, 267
washcloth 수건	25
watch out for …을 주의하다, 조심하다	57
weaken 약하게 하다 (a. weak 약한)	71
wear off (서서히, 닳아) 없어지다, 사라지다	157
web 거미줄	123
wedding ceremony 결혼식	235
weigh 무게가 … 나가다	37
weight loss industry 체중 감량 산업	75
weight loss 체중감량	57
weight-loss product 체중 감량 제품	75
weird 기이한, 섬뜩한	143
welcome 환영하다	207
well-lit 조명이 잘 된	153
werewolf 늑대인간	229
western 서구의	175
westerner 서양사람	175
wet one's pants 바지를 적시다, 오줌싸다	273
whale oil 고래기름	139
whalebone 고래수염 (=baleen)	139
when it comes to …에 관한 한, …에 관해서라면 (=as for)	57, 73, 205, 207
whipped 매를 맞은, 거품이 인	47
white blood cell 백혈구	27
whitening 화이트닝, 미백	85, 155
whopping 무려, 자그마치; 엄청 큰	105, 135, 219, 245
widely 널리	181
widow 과부	195
width 폭, 넓이	135
wing commander (영국) 공군 중령	183
winning ticket 당첨 복권	117
wipe 닦다	269
wisdom 지혜	181
witch trial 마녀 재판	193
witch 마녀	191
witchcraft 마술	193
with a weird look 이상한 표정으로 (weird 이상한, 기이한)	271
with the help of …의 도움으로	239
withdraw (돈을) 인출하다	129
witness 증인	239
work 효과가 있다	75
workout 운동(=exercise)	87, 151
worth of …가치의	63
wound (흉기에 의한) 부상, 상처	83
wrap 싸다, 포장하다	25

- □ wrinkle (얼굴의) 주름; 주름지게 하다　　71, 91
- □ wrinkly 주름진, 주름투성이의　　77
- □ yawn 하품하다　　189
- □ yell 고함치다　　167
- □ yellowish 노르스름한　　89
- □ yield 생산하다　　135
- □ zealous 열성적인　　265
- □ zinc 아연　　157
- □ zodiac 황도 십이궁(=zodiac sign)　　191

2. 구두점의 쓰임

1. 콤마(,)

1) 동격을 표현할 때
- Mike McCann, the keeper of the tower, agreed with them.
  탑의 관리인인 마이크 맥캔은 그들과 의견이 같았다.
  (Mike McCann = the keeper of the tower)
- Shah Jahan, the fifth Mughal emperor, was devastated.
  다섯 번째 무굴 황제인 샤 자한은 상심했다.
  (Shah Jahan = the fifth Mughal emperor)

2) 두 문장 또는 구와 이어지는 문장을 분리할 때
- If they are caught by people, they will surely get sprayed with deadly poison.
  그들은 사람들에게 잡히면, 분명 치명적인 독 세례를 받을 것이다.
- After that, the British stopped firing and Zanzibar surrendered.
  이후, 영국은 포격을 중단했고 잔지바르는 항복했다.

3) 두 독립절을 접속사로 연결할 때 접속사 앞에 콤마
- It could be true, but no one knows for sure.
  사실일 수도 있지만, 아무도 확실히 모른다.
- The vitamin may alleviate cold symptoms, even though there is no clear evidence of this.
  비타민이 감기 증상을 완화시킬 수도 있지만, 이에 관한 명백한 증거는 없다.

4) 콤마 + 관계대명사 – 계속적인 용법 (앞 문장과 뒤 문장을 계속 이어 해석한다.)
- They are nutrient-rich droppings, which means humans use them as good fertilizers.
  그것들은 영양이 풍부한 똥인데, 이 말은 인간이 이를 좋은 비료로 사용한다는 뜻이다.
- Sudar was still married to Fatemah, who was 69 and very much ill.
  수다는 여전히 페이트마와 결혼한 상태였는데, 페이트마는 69살로 대단히 아팠다.

5) 셋 이상 열거할 때
- Bruce Lee was a martial artist, actor, martial arts instructor, director, and film producer.
  이소룡은 무술인, 배우, 무술 지도자, 감독, 그리고 영화 제작자였다.
- Vegans do not eat any kind of animal meat, eggs, or animal fat.
  비건은 어떤 종류든 육류, 계란, 또는 동물성 지방을 먹지 않는다.

6) 단어, 구, 절 등을 문장 사이에 추가, 삽입할 때
- Mosquitoes are attracted by smells, specifically, foul smells.
  모기는 냄새, 특히 지독한 냄새에 끌린다.

- Other arachnids, such as scorpions and ticks, have eight legs like spiders.
  전갈, 틱과 같은 다른 거미류들은 거미처럼 다리가 8개이다.
- Mount Rushmore National Memorial, located in South Dakota, is a monumental super-giant granite sculpture.
  사우스 다코타에 위치한 러슈모어산 국립 기념비는 엄청나게 큰 기념비적인 화강암 조각이다.
- They think, for example, that the nose is related to the heart.
  예를 들어, 그들은 코가 심장과 관련이 있다고 생각한다.

7) 날짜를 표기할 때 (month date(아라비아 숫자) + , + year)
- on his The Dr. Oz Show on September 13, 2010
  2010년 9월 13일, 그의 닥터 오즈 쇼에서

8) 콤마 + 분사 (주절의 주어와 일치할 때 주어 생략, 능동일 때 동사에 -ing)
- Its size is pretty big for an insect, reaching about 3 inches.
  이것의 크기는 곤충치고 꽤 커서 약 3인치에 달한다.
- They ask their customers not to use cell phones while pumping gas, saying 'better safe than sorry.'
  그들은 주유 중 휴대전화를 사용하지 말 것을 당부하며 '불편해도 안전한 게 낫다'고 말한다.
- She and her friends were taking pictures for Halloween, sticking their tongues out.
  그녀와 친구들은 할로윈 때 혀를 내밀고 사진을 찍었다.

2. 하이픈(hyphen) : 짧은 가로선(-)으로 단어와 단어를 연결할 때 사용

thirty-three people 32명의 사람들 ex-wife 전 부인 wrinkle-free 주름 없는 moisture-rich 수분이 풍부한 environmental-friendly 환경친화적인 fat-free or fat-reduced foods 무지방 또는 저지방 음식 a six-year-old boy 6살짜리 소년 government-provided food assistance 정부 지원 음식 보조 with jaw-dropping speed 턱이 떨어질 정도의(놀라운) 속도로 FDA-approved products FDA의 승인을 받은 제품들 typical European-style black pudding 전형적인 유럽식 블랙 푸딩 blood-dripping antlers 피가 뚝뚝 떨어지는 사슴뿔 a cat-like mammal 고양이와 비슷한 포유류

3. 대시(dash) : 긴 가로선(—)으로 문장 안에서 부가, 추가설명 시 사용

- It is literally a 'hot' spring — hot enough to boil some eggs.
  말 그대로 '뜨거운' 샘인데, 얼마나 뜨거운지 계란을 삶을 수 있을 정도입니다.
- Many sweets contain too much sugar — that's why they are called 'sweets'.
  많은 단 것들은 너무 많은 설탕이 들어 있는데, 그래서 '단 것'이라 불립니다.

4. **세미콜론(;)** : 밀접하게 관련된 두 개의 완전한 문장(독립절)을 연결할 때 사용. 그래서 세미콜론 뒤에는 and, but so, or 등의 등위 접속사가 나오지 않지만, 부사나 연결사는 올 수 있다. 세미콜론 뒤에는 항상 소문자로 시작한다.

- She was a moneybag; however, she was too sad to do anything.
  그녀는 거부였다. 하지만, 너무 슬퍼서 아무것도 할 수 없었다.
- Chicken soup for colds is not a myth; it is a fact backed up with solid medical evidence.
  감기에 닭고기 수프는 낭설이 아니다. 이는 확고한 의학적 증거가 뒷받침된 사실이다.
- Sweetbreads are not a kind of bread; they are a kind of meat.
  스위트브레드는 빵 종류가 아니다. 이는 고기 종류이다.

5. **콜론(:)** : 목록을 늘어놓거나 인용문을 표시할 때, 앞의 문장에 대한 보충 설명을 할 때 사용. 세미콜론이 두 독립절을 연결하는 데 반해, 콜론 다음에는 단어, 구, 절 모두 올 수 있다.

- There is another myth about eyes: carrots.
  눈에 관한 또 다른 낭설이 있는데, 바로 당근이다.
- One more thing: quite a few parents still warn their kids not to swallow chewing gum.
  한 가지 더. 많은 어머니들이 아직도 아이들에게 껌을 삼키지 말라고 경고한다.
- But, there was something in common among their reactions: they were all surprised.
  그러나 그들의 반응에 공통된 것이 있었으니, 모두들 놀랐다는 것이다.

Fun! Fun! Reading!

DID YOU KNOW?

펀펀 리딩

전은지 지음

www.vocabible.com

재미와 공부를 한방에! 독해 초급에서 중급까지 20일 완성!
- **Fun & Amusing** | 흥미로운 내용으로 독해공부하는 재미가 쏠쏠
- **Learning Board** | 선생님이 칠판에 풀어서 설명해주는 학습보드로 이해가 쏙쏙
- **All in One Reading** | 어휘&숙어, 문법, 구문, 독해가 한방에 팍팍
- **Listening & Dictation** | 딕테이션을 통해 듣기 실력까지 쑥쑥
- **MP3 & Support** | QR 코드를 스캔하면 원어민 MP3가 쌩쌩
- **Basic to Intermediate** | 내신, 수능, 토플, 편입, 공무원 독해 입문서

해설집

스텝업

전은지 지음

Chapter 1. Health

 집 먼지가 죽은 피부 세포 뭉치라는 거 아세요?

① 집 안 먼지는 대부분 죽은 피부 세포로 이루어져 있습니다. ② 일분마다 우리 몸에서 떨어지는 죽은 피부 세포가 대략 3만–4만 개 정도로 추정됩니다. ③ 우리 몸이 끊임없이 죽은 피부 세포를 흘린다는 걸 감안할 때, 일반적인 집 먼지는 실질적으로 죽은 피부 세포 뭉치라고 할 수 있습니다. ④ 물론 집 먼지 중에는 다른 것들도 있는데, 이를테면 죽은 먼지 진드기의 마른 시체를 들 수 있습니다. ⑤ 먼지 진드기는 인간의 죽은 피부 세포를 먹으며 침구, 카펫, 직물 등에서 삽니다. ⑥ 살아 있을 때는 알레르기의 원인이 됩니다. ⑦ 그리고 죽은 후에는 집 먼지가 됩니다. ⑧ 먼지 진드기가 모두에게 미움을 받는 것도 당연합니다. ⑨ 또 다른 성분은 옷, 천 가구, 침구에서 떨어진 작은 섬유입니다. ⑩ 게다가 집 안에 애완동물이 있는 경우 작고 귀여운 애완동물이 집안 먼지 생산에 크게 기여한다고 보면 되는데, 애완동물은 온갖 종류의 것들을 다 떨어뜨리기 때문입니다. ⑪ 애완동물은 죽은 피부 세포, 말라버린 애완동물 진드기 시체뿐 아니라 털도 떨어뜨립니다. ⑫ 애완동물이 개 옷을 입고 있다면, 작은 섬유 조각도 떨어뜨릴 겁니다.

문제 정답 및 해설

1. (c) 이 글의 요지를 고르세요.
   a. 인간의 몸은 일 분에 3만개 이상의 죽은 피부 세포를 떨어뜨린다.
   b. 먼지 진드기가 나쁜 이유는 인간의 죽은 피부 세포를 먹기 때문이다.
   c. 집 먼지는 대부분 죽은 피부 세포로 이루어져 있다.
   d. 집 안에서 애완동물을 키우는 건 건강에 해롭다.

2. (b) 집안의 먼지는 _____ 로 이루어져 있다.
   a. 먼지 진드기와 애완동물의 털
   b. 죽은 피부 세포, 죽은 먼지 진드기의 마른 시체와 작은 섬유 조각
   c. 옷, 가구용 직물과 침구
   d. 애완동물 진드기와 애견용 옷

3. 각 문장에 알맞은 표현을 고르세요.

   a. (estimated) 내전으로 인해, 대략 3백만 명의 사람들이 어쩔 수 없이 건강에 해롭고 위험한 곳에서 살아야 했다.
   | civil war 내전 / an estimated 3 million people 대략 3백만 명 정도의 사람들 / live in unhealthy and dangerous places 건강에 해롭고 위험한 곳에 살다

   【해설】 estimated a. 견적의, 추측의 / estimate v. 추산하다 n. 견적서, 추산 / estimation n. (가치, 자격 등) 판단, 평가(치) ▶ 3 million people을 꾸며주는 형용사 estimated가 쓰여야 맞다.

   b. (as well as) 나는 도넛뿐만 아니라 케이크도 좋아하지만, 제일 좋아하는 건 샌드위치이다.
   【해설】 as far as …만큼 멀리 / as well as …뿐만 아니라 / as long as …하는 한, …이기만 한다면 ▶ 문맥상 as well as가 가장 적당하다.

   c. (shedding) 헛간에 들어갔을 때, 허물 벗는 뱀이 있어서 나는 두려움의 눈물을 흘렸다.
   【해설】 첫 번째 shed: n. 헛간, 두 번째 shed: v. (눈물, 피) 흘리다 (shed의 과거형은 shed, shedded 둘 다 쓰이는데, 이 문장에서는 과거형 shed로 쓰인 것이다), 세 번째 shed: v. (뱀 등이 허물을) 벗다 '뱀이 허물을 벗는 것'은 능동이므로 shedded가 아닌 shedding을 쓴다.

진통제가 다양한 통증을 유발할 수 있다는 거 아세요?

① 진통제는 통증을 없애야 합니다. ② 하지만 안타깝게도 가끔 그리고 어떤 경우 진통제가 통증을 유발하기도 하는데 다른 약이 그렇듯 진통제에도 부작용이 있기 때문입니다. ③ 정상적인 사용으로도 위험할 수 있기 때문에 남용, 오용하지 않도록 조심해야 합니다. ④ 진통제가 일반적으로 변비를 일으킨다는 건 많이 알고 있습니다. ⑤ 그러니 진통제 사용자들은 복용 시 물을 많이 마셔야 합니다. ⑥ 또한, 진통제는 심장과 폐 모두에 영향을 미칠 수 있습니다. ⑦ 어떤 진통제는 진정되는 느낌만 드는 게 아니라 심장과 폐 기능을 느리게 만들기도 합니다. ⑧ 그래서 심혈관계나 호흡기에 문제가 있다면 각별히 더 조심해야 합니다. ⑨ 그리고 진통제를 복용한 후 졸음을 호소하는 사람들이 있습니다. ⑩ 그건 진통제 중 어떤 종류는 통증을 감지하는 신체의 수용기를 마비시키기 때문입니다. ⑪ 이 외에도 진통제의 다른 부작용들이 있는데, 중독, 불면증, 환각을 들 수 있습니다. ⑫ 이런 가능한 부작용을 예방하는 최선의 방법은 사용하기 전에 의사와 상의하는 것입니다.

문제 정답 및 해설

1. (a) 이 글의 요지를 고르세요.
   a. 진통제에 예상치 못한 부작용이 있거나 통증을 유발할 수도 있다.
   b. 진통제 복용 시 물을 많이 마셔야 한다.
   c. 진통제는 중독과 불면증을 유발한다.
   d. 진통제는 사악하기 때문에 어느 누구도 복용하면 안 된다.

2. (d) 지문에 의하면 거의 모든 약이 _____.
   a. 많은 기관의 기능을 느리게 한다
   b. 모든 종류의 통증을 없앨 수 있다
   c. 환각을 일으킨다
   d. 부작용을 동반한다

3. 각 문장에 알맞은 표현을 고르세요.

   a. (misuse) 자신의 이익을 위해 권력을 남용하는 정부 관리들은 반드시 처벌받아야 한다.
   【해설】 misuse 남용하다 / mistreat 사람이나 동물을 학대하다 / mistake 실수, 오해하다, 잘못 판단하다 ▶ 'misuse power for one's own ends [benefits] 자신의 이득을 위해 권력을 남용하다'

   b. (other) 이 바지를 입어보고 싶은 다른 학생들이 있습니까?
   【해설】 특정한 대상, 특정한 것의 나머지를 가리키는 것이 아니기 때문에 the other가 아닌 other를 쓴다. students(복수명사)와 another는 함께 올 수 없다. (other + 복수, another + 단수)

   c. (with) 심혈관계 문제가 있으면 저에게 말씀해주십시오.
   ∥ cardiovascular system 심혈관계
   【해설】 have a problem with ...에 문제가 있다(= have an issue with)

 손가락 관절 꺾기와 관절염은 아무 상관이 없다는 거 아세요?

① 손가락 관절 꺾기는 짜증나는 나쁜 버릇입니다. ② 소리도 듣기에 좋지 않고, 손가락 관절을 꺾는 사람은 좀 무섭고 불량해 보입니다. ③ 게다가 손가락 관절 꺾기를 하면 관절염에 걸린다는 설도 있습니다. ④ 그러나 그건 낭설이며, 손가락 관절 꺾기가 관절염을 일으키지는 않습니다. ⑤ 아마 꺾는 소리 때문에 잘못 생각하게 된 것 같은데, 사람들은 무언가 꺾이는 소리가 나면 손상되는 것이라 믿기 때문입니다. ⑥ 하지만, 사실 꺾이거나 손상되는 건 없습니다. ⑦ 이에 관해 연구한 몇 가지 조사 결과를 보면, 손가락 관절 꺾기는 관절염과 아무 상관이 없습니다. ⑧ 하지만, 그 연구에서는 손가락 관절을 꺾는 사람들은 그 버릇을 그만두는 게 좋다는 사실도 발견했는데 몇 가지 손 문제와 관련이 있기 때문입니다. ⑨ 앞의 연구 결과에 의하면, 손가락 관절을 꺾는 사람들은 그렇지 않은 사람들보다 잡는 힘이 약해지고 손이 붓고, 관절을 둘러싼 인대가 손상될 가능성이 더 높다고 합니다.

문제 정답 및 해설

1. (d) 지문의 제목으로 적당한 것을 고르세요.
   a. 우리가 관절을 꺾어야만 하는 이유
   b. 당신의 손을 위해 관절 꺾기를 시작하라
   c. 부은 손 vs. 관절 손상
   d. 손 관절 꺾기 : 관절염과 관련 없다

2. (a) 전문가들에 의하면, 손가락 관절을 꺾는 사람들은 _____.
   a. 손가락 관절을 꺾지 않는 사람들에 비해 쥐는 힘이 더 약한 경향이 있다.
   b. 관절염 때문에 입원할 가능성이 있다. ▶ 관절꺾기와 관절염은 상관이 없다. be hospitalized 병원에 입원하다
   c. 최소한 세 가지의 손 문제를 가질 수밖에 없다. ▶ 'According to those studies, knuckle crackers are more likely to have weaker grip strength…'라는 표현에서도 나와 있듯이 손가락 관절 꺾기를 한다고 반드시 손 문제가 생기는 건 아니고, 단지 그럴 가능성이 더 높아진다.
   d. 관절 꺾기는 짜증 나기 때문에 관절 꺾는 걸 반드시 그만두어야 한다. ▶ 짜증나기 때문이 아니라 '손 문제를 야기할 수 있기 때문에 그만두는 게 좋다'고 나온다.

3. 각 문장에 알맞은 표현을 고르세요.

   a. (several) 나는 그들을 위해 몇 분 더 기다려야 한다고 생각한다.
   【해설】several, a few, few, many + 셀 수 있는 명사 (복수형)
   a little, little, much + 셀 수 없는 명사 (단수형)

   b. (scary) 작은 소년은 선생님이 무서워 보였기 때문에 겁에 질린 듯 보였다.
   【해설】scare v. 겁주다, 무서워하다 / scared 무서워하는, 겁먹은 / scary 무서운, 겁나는
   주어 + look scary : 주어가 무섭게 보이다
   주어 + look scared : 주어가 무서워하는 듯 보이다
   ex) 주어 + look frightening : 주어가 무서워 보이다
   주어 + look frightened : 주어가 무서워하는 듯 보이다

   c. (associated) 저 야만적인 사람들과 엮이고 싶지 않다.
   | barbaric 야만적인 (barbarian n. 야만인)
   【해설】be associated with …와 관련되다

 의사도 귀지가 생기는 정확한 이유를 잘 모른다는 거 아세요?

① 흥미롭게도 의사들은 귀지가 생기는 정확한 이유는 잘 모른다고 합니다. ② 하지만, 그 이유에 대한 몇 가지 이론은 있습니다. ③ 의사들은 귀지가 귀의 자가 청소 과정과 관련이 있으리라 생각합니다. ④ 또 귀지에 항바이러스 성질이 있다고 생각합니다. ⑤ 일반적으로 귀지가 먼지나 작은 벌레가 귀 안쪽으로 들어오지 못하게 막아 귀를 보호한다고 합니다. ⑥ 그리고 개인에 따라 귀지의 양이 차이 나는 확실한 이유 역시 아무도 모릅니다. ⑦ 어떤 사람은 귀지가 많이 생기는 데 반해, 어떤 사람은 전혀 생기지 않기도 합니다. ⑧ 물론 이유는 모릅니다. ⑨ 다행히 의사들은 너무 많이 생긴 귀지를 제거하는 가장 안전한 방법을 알고 있습니다. ⑩ 많은 사람들이 귀지를 제거하려고 면봉을 사용하지만, 의사들은 면봉이나 다른 작은 물건을 이도에 넣지 말 것을 권고합니다. ⑪ 그러다 귀지를 더 안쪽으로 밀어 넣을 수도 있고 또는 본의 아니게 이도나 고막 안쪽에 손상을 입힐 수도 있기 때문입니다. ⑫ 가장 좋은 방법은 젖은 수건을 사용하는 것입니다. ⑬ 손가락에 수건을 감고 귀 볼을 닦으세요. ⑭ 과도한 귀지를 제거하고 싶다면 따뜻한 물을 귀 안으로 흘려보낸 후 머리를 한쪽으로 기울여 귀지를 내 버리세요. ⑮ 그리고 부드럽고 마른 수건으로 귀 안쪽을 닦습니다.

문제 정답 및 해설

1. (c) 이 글의 요지를 고르세요.
   a. 의사들은 귀지에 대해 아는 게 하나도 없으니 그들의 말에 귀를 기울이지 말아야 한다. (not know beans about ...에 대해 아는 것이 하나도 없다)
   b. 귀지는 면봉처럼 작은 물건으로 제거되어야 한다.
   c. 우리에게 귀지가 생기는 정확한 이유는 아직 모르지만, 최선의 귀지 제거 방법은 알고 있다.
   d. 수건으로 여분의 귀지를 제거하는 것은 대단히 중요하다.

2. (a) 지문 내용과 맞지 않는 것을 고르세요.
   a. 의사들은 우리에게 귀지가 생기는 이유를 간신히 밝혀냈다. (manage to 간신히, 겨우, 힘겹게 ...를 해내다)
   ▶ 정확하고 확실한 이유는 밝혀내지 못했고, 이에 관한 몇 가지 이론만 있다.
   b. 면봉을 사용하는 것이 여분의 귀지를 제거하는 가장 안전한 방법이 아닐 수 있다.
   c. 모든 사람에게 같은 양의 귀지가 생기는 건 아니다.
   d. 우리에게 귀지가 생기는 이유에 관해 한 가지 이상의 이론이 있다.

3. 각 문장에 알맞은 표현을 고르세요.

   a. (while) 네가 만든 사과 파이는 너무 달았지만, 반면 네 여동생이 만든 딸기 파이는 아주 맛있었다.
   I mover over 게다가, in addition 덧붙여, 게다가, while 반면에
   【해설】앞 문장과 반대, 대조되는 내용이 이어지고 있기 때문에 while이 오는 것이 자연스럽다.

   b. (does) 맥스에게 물어보세요. 그가 정말로 정답을 알고 있는데 그는 바로 저기에 있습니다.
   【해설】강조의 do : 본동사를 강조할 때 본동사 앞에 쓰이는데, 조동사처럼 시제와 인칭 변화가 do 동사에서 표현되고 본동사는 원형이 온다. 주어가 he(3인칭 단수 현재)이기 때문에 do가 아닌 does가 와야 한다. 'He knows the right answer...'에서 'knows'를 강조하기 위해 does know로 쓴 것이다. have나 get 등의 동사는 본동사를 강조하기 위한 동사로는 쓰이지 않고 have, get 바로 다음에 동사 원형이 오지 않는다. 단 사역동사로 쓰일 경우 목적어와 함께 원형 동사가 올 수 있다.

   c. (as to why) 나는 그가 어제 그렇게 빨리 떠난 이유에 대한 그의 설명을 원한다.
   【해설】as to why ...에 대한 이유, ...의 이유에 대해
   ex) There's no mystery as to why he broke up with her.
   그가 그녀와 헤어진 이유에 대해 이해 못 할 건 없다.(이상할 것도 없다.)

피 한 방울에 5백만 개의 적혈구가 있다는 거 아세요?

① 놀랍게도 단 한 방울의 피안에 5백만 개의 적혈구 외에 7천 개의 백혈구, 45만 개의 혈소판이 들어 있습니다. ② 물론 물, 소금, 지방, 비타민, 설탕 등도 들어 있습니다. ③ 물이 피보다 진할 만도 하지요. ④ 사실 피는 따뜻한 수프 같은 느낌이 납니다. ⑤ 피는 약간 질척하고 끈적거리는데, 이는 피가 액체와 엄청나게 많은 세포의 혼합물이기 때문입니다. ⑥ 많은 사람들이 피의 세 가지 주요 성분이 적혈구, 백혈구, 혈소판으로 알고 있습니다. ⑦ 하지만, 실제 피의 노란색 액체 물질인 혈장(플라즈마)이 피의 반 이상을 차지합니다. ⑧ 적혈구는 온몸에 산소를 운반하고, 백혈구는 해로운 세균을 찾아 죽이며 혈소판은 상처가 났을 때 피가 멎도록 피를 엉기게 만듭니다. ⑨ 피에 관한 재미있는 사실이 있습니다. ⑩ 적혈구는 약 4달 정도 삽니다. ⑪ 백혈구는 박테리아와 세균뿐 아니라 죽은 세포도 먹어 치웁니다. ⑫ 그리고 새 적혈구와 백혈구를 만드는 공장은 골수입니다.

문제 정답 및 해설

1. (b) 이 글의 요지를 고르세요.
   a. 혈액의 색깔이 빨간 이유는 혈소판 때문이다.
   b. 혈액은 수많은 요소들의 혼합물이다.
   c. 혈소판은 혈액 요소들 중 가장 중요하다.
   d. 혈액에서 가장 핵심적인 요소는 골수이다.

2. (c) 지문을 읽고 추측할 수 있는 것은 _____
   a. 적혈구가 혈액의 대부분을 차지한다.
   b. 골수는 산소 생산에 중요한 역할을 한다.
   c. 혈소판이 없으면 출혈로 사망할 수 있다.
   d. 혈액은 빨간 색깔 때문에 유용하다.

3. 각 문장에 알맞은 표현을 고르세요.

   a. (but also) 백혈구 세포는 해로운 세균을 찾을 뿐 아니라 죽이기도 한다.
   【해설】not only A but also B 구문 : A뿐 아니라 B도

   b. (are) 혈액 안에 수 톤의 (매우 많은) 세포가 있다.
   【해설】tons of : 수 톤의, 아주 많은 / a ton of : '1톤의' 일반적으로 '매우 많은'의 뜻으로 쓰인다. ▶ 셀 수 있는 명사, 셀 수 없는 명사 모두 함께 쓰일 수 있다. a tone of의 경우는 단수 동사가 오며, 비슷한 의미지만 형태가 복수인 tons of는 복수 동사가 온다.
   ex) How much is a ton of money?
   　　엄청난 돈이라면 얼마나 많은 것인가?
   　　There are tons of work to do.
   　　할 일이 아주 많다.

   c. (up) 혈장은 혈액의 반 이상을 차지한다.
   【해설】make up 이루다, 형성하다 / make off 떠나다, 도망가다 / make over 양도하다, 바꾸다

손이 당신의 건강에 관해 말해준다는 거 아세요?

① 손가락이 부었다면, 갑상선이 호르몬을 충분히 생산하지 못해서 생기는 갑상선기능저하 때문일 수 있습니다. ② 밤 늦게 짠 라면을 먹은 직후 잠이 들어도 손가락이 부을 수 있지만 이런 경우는 몇 시간 혹은 며칠 내에 손가락이 정상으로 돌아옵니다. ③ 손바닥이 정상보다 더 붉다면 다음 세 가지 문제 중 하나일 수 있습니다. ④ 가려움이나 후끈한 통증이 느껴지면 습진일 가능성이 있습니다. ⑤ 또는 손에 끼고 있거나 손에 바른 무언가에 알레르기가 있을 수도 있습니다. ⑥ 마지막으로 붉은 손바닥은 간에 문제가 있을 수도 있다는 뜻입니다. ⑦ 손바닥이 붉은 사람은 모두 간에 질병이 있다는 건 아니지만, 그래도 한 번 검사를 받는 게 나쁘지 않을 겁니다. ⑧ 일반적으로 손톱을 누르면 희게 변했다가 누르지 않으면 손톱은 다시 분홍빛으로 돌아옵니다. ⑨ 하지만, 희게 변한 손톱이 몇 분간 계속된다면 빈혈이나 철분 부족일 수 있습니다. ⑩ 손톱 끝이 푸른색인 건 어떨까요? ⑪ 당연히 좋은 징조가 아닙니다. ⑫ 추울 때 여성들에게 흔한 징후이긴 하지만, 이것이 한 시간 이상 지속될 경우에는 즉시 병원에 가야 합니다.

문제 정답 및 해설

1. (c) 이 글의 요지를 고르세요.
   a. 늦은 밤 짠 라면을 먹는 건 건강에 좋지 않다.
   b. 발뿐 아니라 손은 건강에 관한 다양한 정보를 나타낸다.
   c. 손을 보면 건강에 관해 많은 정보를 얻을 수 있다.
   d. 손가락 끝이 푸른 사람들은 당장 병원에 가야만 한다.

2. (d) 지문 내용과 맞지 않는 것을 고르세요.
   a. 갑상선 호르몬의 부족이 갑상선 기능 저하증의 주요 원인이다.
   b. 밤늦게 짠 라면을 먹은 직후 자면, 손가락이 부을 수 있다.
   c. 손바닥이 붉은 사람들은 간 문제가 있을 수 있다.
   d. 겨울에 여성들 손가락 끝은 원래 파랗게 변한다. originally turn blue 원래 파랗게 변한다 ▶ 겨울에 여성의 손가락 끝이 파랗게 변하는 경우가 흔하긴 하지만 원래 모두가 다 그런 것은 아니다.

3. 각 문장에 알맞은 표현을 고르세요.

   a. (symptoms) 또 어지러우면 제발 의사와 당신 건강의 징후와 증상을 확인하시오. l feel faint 어지러움을 느끼다, 현기증이 나다

【해설】 diagnosis 진단 (v. diagnose) / syndrome 증후군 / symptom 징후, 증상 ▶ 문맥상 symptoms가 적당하다

b. (on) 이 연고를 피부에 바른 후 온몸이 가렵다.
l apply (로션, 연고 등을) 바르다, 적용하다 ointment 연고
【해설】 apply on ...에 바르다 ▶ 피부 같은 표면 위에 바를 때 전치사 on

c. (talking) 말을 그만 하십시오. 도서관에 계시기 때문에 조용하셔야 합니다. l be in a library 도서관에 있다
【해설】 stop + to부정사: ...하기 위해 (걸음이나 하던 일을) 멈추다
stop + -ing: ...하는 것을 멈추다
ex) stop to smoke 담배 피우기 위해 (하던 일을) 멈추다
   stop smoking 담배 피우는 것을 멈추다, 금연하다

 **위장우회수술 후 얼마나 먹을 수 있는지 아세요?**

① 미국의 의사들이 실시한 연구조사에서 위장우회수술을 받은 당뇨병 환자들 중 반 이상이 혈당 조절을 개선시키는 이 수술의 효과 덕분에 병이 치료되었다고 합니다. ② 임페리얼 칼리지 런던의 연구원들 역시 이 효과를 확인하면서 '위장우회수술이 포도당 조절에 대단하고 유익한 효과를 낸다'고 말했습니다. ③ 위장우회수술의 인기가 점점 더 높아질 것 같은데, 2형 당뇨병을 가진 비만한 환자들이 살도 빼고 동시에 치료도 받을 수 있기 때문입니다. ④ 일석이조라 할 수 있습니다. ⑤ 당뇨병을 가진 많은 비만한 환자들은 이 수술 후 약 복용도 끊었습니다. ⑥ 사람들이 이는 단 한 번의 수술로 비만과 2형 당뇨병의 위험에서 쉽게 벗어날 수 있는 방법이라 생각하는 것도 당연합니다. ⑦ 너무 쉽고 유혹적으로 들리니까요. ⑧ 하지만, 현실은 그다지 쉽지도, 유혹적이지도 않습니다. ⑨ 이 수술을 받으면, 작은창자에 연결된 더 작은 위장을 갖게 되는데, 이 말은 작고 귀여운 위장에 대단히 제한적인 양의 음식만 들어갈 수 있다는 뜻입니다. ⑩ 단단한 음식을 1/4컵 이상 먹거나 단단한 음식을 물 한 컵과 함께 먹으면 병이 날 수도 있는데, 왜냐하면 작은 위장이 그렇게 많은 음식을 처리할 수 없기 때문입니다.

문제 정답 및 해설

1. (a) 지문의 제목으로 적당한 것을 고르세요.
   a. 위장우회수술 : 비만한 당뇨병 환자들을 위한 돌파구
   b. 적은 양의 음식을 먹는 것이 위험할 수 있다.
   c. 미국에서 2형 당뇨병을 가진 비만인들 증가
   d. 2형 당뇨병 환자들 쉬운 길을 선택하다

2. (b) 지문 내용과 맞는 것을 고르세요.
   a. 2형 당뇨병을 앓는 비만인들은 위장우회수술을 반드시 받아야 한다. ▶ 체중 감소와 혈당 조절에 긍정적인 효과가 있으나 모든 환자들이 반드시 받아야 한다는 것은 아니다.
   b. 위장우회수술은 혈당 조절을 개선시킨다.
   c. 오직 미국의 의사들만 위장우회수술의 놀라운 효과를 인정한다. ▶ 미국뿐 아니라 영국(임페리얼 칼리지 런던)에서도 인정했다.
   d. 위장우회수술은 포도당 조절에 어떤 긍정적인 영향도 미치지 않는다. ▶ 위장우회수술이 포도당 조절에 긍정적인 영향을 미친다.

3. 각 문장에 알맞은 표현을 고르세요.

   a. (conduct) 너는 이 문제에 관해 과학적인 조사를 하기로 되어있다. l conduct researches on …에 관해 조사하다 (또는 conduct a research on)
   【해설】conduct scientific researches 과학적인 조사를 실시하다
   ▶ 동사 conduct가 쓰인다.

   b. (undergo) 내 코가 싫다. 성형 수술을 받고 싶다.
   l plastic surgery 성형수술 = cosmetic surgery
   【해설】undergo는 수동태로 쓰지 않는다.
   수술 받다 : undergo surgery (O) be undergone surgery (X)

   c. (on) 위트 씨는 내가 12살 때부터 나에게 영향을 미쳐왔다.
   【해설】have an effect on …에 영향을 미치다 ▶ 현재 완료 (has had an effect on) + since 주어 + 과거동사 (I was) : …이래로 (since) …해왔다

   d. (that) 너는 내가 부자라고 생각하지만 나는 부자가 아니다.
   【해설】be under the impression that 주어 + 동사 : that 이하…라고 생각하다.

08 동물 보호론자들이 왜 거머리 치료를 못마땅하게 여기는지 아세요?

① 심지어 오늘날에도, 특히 동남아시아의 적지 않은 의사들이 의료 시술 때 거머리를 사용한다고 합니다. ② 대부분의 경우 이들은 추가적인 혈액을 뽑아내 환자의 혈액 순환을 촉진하고 혈액 응고의 가능성을 줄이기 위해 거머리를 사용합니다. ③ 이를 '거머리 치료'라고 부릅니다. ④ 어떤 경우, 비정통적인 이 치료법이 환자의 혈액 순환이 정상으로 돌아오는데 도움을 주어 실제 사지절단에서 구해주기도 합니다. ⑤ 사실 수술 후 48시간 이내 혈액 순환이 정상으로 돌아오지 않으면 사지절단의 위험이 있습니다. ⑥ 또한, 거머리는 피를 빼내는데도 사용됩니다. ⑦ 거머리들은 수백 년간 전 세계에서 의학에 사용되었는데, 거머리들이 피를 아주 잘 빨기 때문입니다. ⑧ 과거에는 사람들이 독사의 공격을 받으면 고마운 이 흡혈 동물을 물린 부위에 올려놓았습니다. ⑨ 거머리들은 일단 배부를 정도로 피를 빤 후에는 스스로 떨어집니다. ⑩ 그러면 거머리들은 뱀독을 먹어서 죽고, 환자는 살아남았습니다. ⑪ 요즘 거머리 치료도 이와 같은 방식으로 계속되고 있습니다. ⑫ 그래서 동물 권익 보호론자들이 거머리 치료법에 광분하는 것인데, 더러운 피로 배를 채운 거머리가 떨어져 나가면 시술자들이 거머리가 죽게 내다 버리기 때문입니다.

문제 정답 및 해설

1. (b) 이 글의 요지를 고르세요.
   a. 정상적인 혈액 순환은 대단히 중요하다.
   b. 거머리들은 오랫동안 환자를 치료하는데 사용되고 있다.
   c. 다행히도 모든 종류의 흡혈 동물들은 인간에게 유용하다.
   d. 거머리와 모기는 소름 끼치는 흡혈귀들이다.

2. (d) 지문 내용과 맞는 것을 고르세요.
   a. 요즘 환자를 치료할 때 거머리를 이용하는 의사를 찾기가 쉽지 않다. ▶ 요즘도 특히 동남아시아에서 거머리를 치료에 이용하는 의사들이 꽤 있다.
   b. 거머리 치료는 비정통적이지만, 독사에 물린 모든 환자들의 팔다리를 구할 수 있다. ▶ 지문에 독사에 물린 모든 환자들(all patients)을 다 구했다고는 나오지 않았다.
   c. 거머리는 오직 동남아시아에서만 수년 동안 의술에 활용되었다. ▶ 거머리 치료는 특히 동남아시아에서 많이 활용되었고, 현재도 활용되고 있다. 문제의 문장은 과거완료로 되어 있어 '현재는 시술되지 않는다'는 의미이다.
   d. 거머리를 어떻게 떼어낼 것인지 고민할 필요가 없는데, 일단 배가 차면 스스로 떨어지기 때문이다. (by oneself 스스로)

3. 각 문장에 알맞은 표현을 고르세요.

   a. (by) 쓰레기를 버리지 맙시다. 재활용으로 지구를 구할 수 있습니다.
   【해설】save the Earth by …로(수단, 방법) 지구를 구하다 / recycling 재활용

   b. (stay) 데미 무어는 신체를 깨끗하게 하는데 거머리를 이용했다고 하는데, 그녀는 거머리가 건강을 유지하는 데 도움이 된다고 믿는다.
   【해설】help + 목적어 + (to 생략) 동사원형: …하는 걸(동사) 돕다 (도움이 되다)
   ex) help her stay healthy 그녀가 건강을 유지하는 데 도움이 되다
       help my dad stop smoking 아빠가 금연하는데 돕다

   c. (not a few) 전 세계의 적지 않은 의료인들이 거머리를 이용해 왔다.
   【해설】not a few 적지 않은, 꽤 많은 + 가산 명사의 복수형
   (a little, much는 불가산 명사와 함께 쓰인다.)

모든 생선이 다 건강에 좋은 건 아니라는 거 아세요?

① 육류 대신 생선을 섭취할 때의 이점에 관해 우리는 많이 들어왔습니다. ② 생선 기름은 육류 지방과는 완전히 다릅니다. ③ 생선 기름은 심장혈관계, 관절, 뇌 등에 도움이 됩니다. ④ 이렇게 유익한 점이 많은데도 불구하고 생선을 먹기 전에 한 번 더 생각해야 하는 이유는, 오늘날 우리가 구할 수 있는 생선의 약 40%가 양어장에서 오기 때문입니다. ⑤ 보통 양어장 생선은 연어, 참치, 새우처럼 육식성입니다. ⑥ 이들 양식어는 너무 붐벼서 비좁고 더러운 환경에서 생활하는데, 그래서 감염, 전염, 오염의 위험이 높습니다. ⑦ 한 연구에 의하면, 양식된 연어는 자연산 연어보다 다이옥신 같은 오염물질 함유율이 더 높다고 합니다. ⑧ 이 말은 양식 연어의 오염된 살을 우리가 먹으면 우리 몸도 오염되기 때문에 양식 연어가 인간에게 위험할 수 있다는 뜻입니다. ⑨ 또 항생제와 양식 어망 청소에 쓰인 화학품의 잔여물 같은 또 다른 문제도 있습니다. ⑩ 하지만, 양식어는 자연산 생선보다 구하기도 쉽고 값도 싼데, 이는 양식어가 일 년 내내 수확되기 때문입니다. ⑪ 그러니 슈퍼마켓에서 장을 볼 때 건강을 위해 지혜롭고 신중하게 선택하세요.

문제 정답 및 해설

1. (c) 이 글의 요지를 고르세요.
   a. 연어 같은 육식어류는 날카로운 이빨 때문에 위험하다.
   b. 기름 때문에 연어나 참치는 먹지 않는 게 좋다.
   c. 양식된 어류는 건강에 좋은 선택이 아닐 수 있다.
   d. 양식된 어류는 야생 어류보다 더 저렴해야만 한다.

2. (a) 지문 내용과 맞는 것을 고르세요.
   a. 어류 기름은 육류 기름과 완전히 다르다.
   b. 어류는 건강에 도움이 되는 반면, 어류 기름은 전혀 도움이 되지 않는다. ▶ 어류 기름은 심장혈관계, 관절, 뇌 등에 도움이 된다.
   c. 야생 어류는 양식 어류보다 감염에 더 취약하다. ▶ 비좁고 비위생적인 환경에서 양식되는 양식 어류가 야생 어류보다 감염에 더 취약하다
   d. 양식 어류는 육식성이기 때문이 야생 어류보다 더 저렴하다. ▶ 양식 어류 중 육식어류가 많은 건 맞지만, 값이 저렴한 이유는 일 년 내내 수확되기 때문이다.

3. 각 문장에 알맞은 표현을 고르세요.

   a. (available) 몇몇 약품은 아무 가게에서나 구할 수 있어서 쉽게 살 수 있다. ▎drugstore 가게, 슈퍼, 약국

   【해설】available 입수, 사용 가능한, 구할 수 있는 / bearable 견딜 수 있는 / inexcusable 용서할 수 없는 ▶ 문맥상 available이 적당하다.

   b. (possibilities) 이 기술은 새로운 무수한 가능성을 열어줄 것이다.
   【해설】a multitude of + 복수 명사 : 많은
   cf). a lot of, plenty of, a great deal of, a large number of, a myriad of = (아주) 많은

   c. (from) 너는 네가 야망이 있다고 생각하지만 나는 네가 탐욕스럽다고 생각한다. 알겠지만 야망은 탐욕과 다르다.
   ▎ambitious 야망이 있는 ambition 야망 greedy 탐욕스러운 greed 탐욕
   【해설】A differ from B = A is different from B A는 B와 다르다

왜 당근 주스가 기적의 주스라고 불리는지 아세요?

① 당근 주스는 기적의 주스라고 불리는데, 왜냐하면 당근 주스가 지닌 건강에 유익한 효능이 기적적이기 때문입니다. ② 다들 이미 알고 있듯이 당근 주스를 마시거나 당근을 섭취하면 눈에 좋고 야맹증을 예방할 수 있습니다. ③ 그리고 당근 주스가 피부암과 유방암 같은 암의 위험을 줄여준다고 알려진 건 베타카로틴 함량이 높기 때문입니다. ④ 베타카로틴은 몸 안에서 비타민 A로 바뀌는데, 비타민 A와 암 예방은 관련이 있습니다. ⑤ 비타민 A는 뼈, 치아, 손톱을 강화시켜 주고 머릿결도 좋아지게 한다고 합니다. ⑥ 당근 주스를 마시면 비타민 A가 간의 담즙과 지방을 줄여주기 때문에 간에도 좋다고 알려져 있습니다. ⑦ 이게 다가 아닙니다. ⑧ 당근 주스는 감염에 저항하는데도 도움을 줍니다. ⑨ 이러한 특성과 비타민 A 때문에 당근 주스는 임신한 여성에게 가장 좋은 음료로 추천받고 있습니다. ⑩ 당근을 고를 때 색이 더 진한 걸 고르는 게 좋은데, 색이 진할수록 카로틴 함량이 높기 때문입니다. ⑪ 그리고 한 가지 더. ⑫ 당근 주스가 기적의 주스인 건 맞지만, '과유불급'이란 말을 잊지 마세요.

문제 정답 및 해설

1. (a) 지문의 제목으로 적당한 것을 고르세요.
   a. 놀라운 당근의 유익
   b. 당근 대 당근 주스 - 승자는...
   c. 비타민 A의 최대 보고(寶庫)
   d. 과유불급

2. (b) 당근 주스가 기적의 주스라 불리는 이유는 _____ 때문이다.
   a. 오직 마법사만 당근 주스를 만들 수 있기
   b. 영양학적 효과가 그만큼 좋기
   c. 모든 종류의 암을 예방할 수 있기
   d. 앞을 못 보는 사람을 보게 만들 수 있기

3. 각 문장에 알맞은 표현을 고르세요.

   a. (due to) 고모는 그의 이상한 행동 때문에 이혼하지 않을 수 없었다고 말했다. l erratic 이상한 behavior 행동
   【해설】because, since (때문에) + 주어 + 동사 (절) / due to, because of (때문에) + 명사 (구) ▶ 문제에서 his erratic behavior가 명사구이기 때문에 because나 since는 올 수 없다.

   b. (resistance) 사장은 사무실 내 변화에 대한 저항을 해결하기 힘들었다. l have a hard time ...하는데 어려움을 겪다 deal with 다루다, 해결하다
   【해설】persistence n. 고집, 지속 / resistance n. ...에 대한(to) 저항 / assistance n. 도움, 원조 ▶ 문맥상 resistence가 가장 적당하다. (resistance to change 변화에 대한 거부/저항)

   c. (the more) 어떤 이들은 돈을 많이 가질수록 자기 의견을 더 많이 표현할 수 있다고 생각한다.
   l express one's opinion 의견을 표현하다
   【해설】the 비교급, the 비교급 구문: 더 ...할수록 더 ...하다
   ex) The thinner, the better. 날씬할수록 더 좋다
   The more you eat, the fatter you become. 많이 먹을수록 더 살이 찌게 된다.

Chapter 2. Food

11 '스위트브레드'가 달콤하지도 않고 빵도 아니라는 거 아세요?

① 놀랍게도 스위트브레드는 빵 종류가 아니라 고기 종류입니다. ② 더 구체적으로 말하면, 스위트브레드는 새끼 돼지, 송아지, 새끼 양 같은 어린 동물의 분비선입니다. ③ 사람들은 오랫동안 동물의 분비선을 식용 가능한 내장기관 고기로 사용해왔습니다. ④ 사용하는 재료에 따라 다양한 스위트브레드를 만들 수 있습니다. ⑤ 흉선(목구멍의 장기)으로 만든 스위트브레드는 종종 '목 스위트브레드'라 불리고, 췌장이나 위장과 가까운 복부 장기로 만든 스위트브레드는 '배 스위트브레드'라고 불립니다. ⑥ 이는 스위트브레드의 기본적인 두 종류인데 다른 분비선들 역시 식용되고 있으며, 역시 '스위트브레드'라고 불립니다. ⑦ 예를 들어 '귀 스위트브레드'는 입속 침샘 중 하나로 만든 것입니다. ⑧ 대부분의 경우 스위트브레드는 얇은 피막을 제거하기 위해 먼저 끓입니다. ⑨ 끓일 때 소금, 식초 또는 레몬즙을 첨가합니다. ⑩ 어떤 경우 피를 모두 제거하기 위해 몇 시간 동안 우유나 물에 담그는 사람들도 있습니다.

문제 정답 및 해설

1. (b) 이 글의 요지를 고르세요.
   a. 어린 동물의 내장 기관을 먹는다는 건 야만적이고 용납할 수 없다.
   b. 듣기에는 달콤한 맛이 나는 빵 같지만 스위트브레드는 고기 종류이다.
   c. 스위트브레드는 달콤한 빵 같은 맛이 나야 하지만 쓴맛이 난다.
   d. 스위트브레드는 고기 종류지만 동네 빵집에서 구매할 수 있다.

2. (a) 스위트브레드의 기본적인 두 가지 종류는 _____ 이다.
   a. 목 스위트브레드와 배 스위트브레드
   b. 귀 스위트브레드와 목 스위트브레드
   c. 침샘 스위트브레드와 목구멍 스위트브레드
   d. 흉선 스위트브레드와 새끼 돼지 스위트브레드

3. 각 문장에 알맞은 표현을 고르세요.

   a. (depending on experience) 내가 지원하는 직장의 급여는 경력에 따라 5,000달러에서 6,000달러 사이이다.
   | salary 급여, 봉급 apply for 지원하다 * 5k = 5000 (K는 1000을 뜻한다.)
   【해설】to say nothing of ...는 말할 필요도 없고 / depending on ...에 따라 / as far as ... be concerned ...에 관한 한 ▶ 문맥 상 depending on experience가 가장 적당하다

   b. (for example) 바구니 안에 몇 가지 과일이 있는데, 예를 들면 망고, 수박, 그리고 키위이다.
   【해설】in addition 게다가 / for example 예를 들어(= for instance) / moreover 게다가 ▶ 바구니에 든 과일이 구체적으로 무엇인지 예를 들고 있으므로 for example이 적당하다.
   * in addition to + 명사/동명사: ...이외에, ...에 더하여

   c. (are) 송아지 몇 마리가 평화롭게 땅에서 풀을 먹고 있다.
   | calves 송아지들 peacefully 평화롭게
   【해설】calf의 복수형 ▶ calves (당연히 복수 동사가 와야 한다.)
   calf처럼 -f /-fe로 끝나는 명사의 복수형: f/fe가 v로 변하고 -es가 붙는다.
   ex) scarf – scarves / knife – knives / wife – wives / shelf – shelves
   (-f/fe로 끝나는 모든 단어가 이와 같이 복수형이 되는 것은 아니며, chiefs, chefs처럼 그냥 -s가 오는 단어도 있다.)

채식주의자들이 마시멜로를 먹지 않는다는 거 아세요?

① 채식주의자들이 마시멜로를 먹지 않는다는 거 들어보셨나요? ② 모든 채식주의자들이 이를 거부하는 건 아니지만, 일부 채식주의자들은 이것에 동물에서 나온 재료가 들어 있다는 이유로 정말 먹기를 거부합니다. ③ 채식주의자는 그들이 어떤 음식을 먹느냐에 따라 몇 가지 종류가 있습니다. ④ 예를 들어 유란 채식주의자는 모든 종류의 고기는 먹지 않지만, 계란과 유제품은 먹는 채식주의자들입니다. ⑤ 이들은 계란, 유제품, 그리고 꿀은 동물을 죽이지 않고 얻을 수 있는 음식이기 때문에 먹어도 괜찮다고 생각합니다. ⑥ 반면 비건은 모든 종류의 동물 고기, 계란, 동물 지방은 물론이요, 아이스크림, 요구르트 같은 유제품도 먹지 않습니다. ⑦ 이들의 식단은 주로 과일, 야채, 곡물이 들어갑니다. ⑧ 그래서 버터 바른 빵, 휘핑크림이 덮인 초콜릿 케이크, 라드(돼지기름)로 요리한 음식과 꿀은 먹지 않습니다. ⑨ 비건이 먹기를 거부하는 게 한 가지 더 있는데, 바로 젤라틴입니다. ⑩ 젤라틴은 일종의 단백질로 동물, 보통 소와 돼지의 조직, 뼈, 가죽에서 나옵니다. ⑪ 그래서 비건들이 젤리, 마시멜로 같은 젤라틴으로 만든 디저트 먹기를 거부하는 겁니다.

문제 정답 및 해설

1. (d) 지문의 제목으로 적당한 것을 고르세요.
   a. 놀라운 소식 : 마시멜로가 고기?
   b. 세 종류의 채식주의자 (지문에는 유란 채식주의자와 비건, 두 종류가 소개되었다.)
   c. 동물로 만든 디저트
   d. 왜 채식주의자들은 마시멜로 먹기를 거부하는가?

2. (c) 지문 내용과 맞는 것을 고르세요.
   a. 어떤 채식주의자들은 마시멜로의 끔찍한 맛 때문에 먹기를 거부한다. ▶ 맛 때문이 아니라 마시멜로가 동물의 뼈와 가죽에서 나왔기 때문에 먹기를 거부하는 것이다.
   b. 모든 채식주의자들은 젤라틴과 마시멜로우를 먹지 않는다. ▶ 모든 채식주의자들이 아니라 그중에서 비건이 젤라틴과 마시멜로우를 먹지 않는다.
   c. 비건은 밀크초콜릿의 작은 조각도 맛보기를 거부할 것이다. ▶ vegan은 철저한 채식주의자로 밀크초콜릿에 우유가 들어가기 때문에 거부할 것이다.
   d. 유란 채식주의자들이 달걀과 유제품은 괜찮다고 생각하는 건 이 음식들이 너무 맛있어서 거부할 수 없기 때문이다. ▶ 맛 때문이 아니라 생물을 죽이지 않고 얻을 수 있는 음식이기 때문에 계란과 유제품을 먹는 것이다.

3. 각 문장에 알맞은 표현을 고르세요.
   a. (several) 고양이 가죽을 벗기는 데 한 가지 방법만 있는 건 아니다. 사실 그렇게 하는데 몇 가지 방법이 있다.

【해설】 'There is more than one way to skin a cat.' 〈속담〉 '무언가를 하는데 반드시 한 가지 방법만 있는 건 아니다.' 이 문장에서 동사가 is로 쓰인 건 is에 걸리는 주어가 one way (단수)이기 때문이다. 두 번째 문장에서는 ways가 복수이기 때문에 are가 쓰였다. ways 앞에 much나 only one은 올 수 없다. much는 셀 수 없는 명사를 수식하기 때문에 ways와 같이 복수형-s가 붙은 단어 앞에 올 수 없고, 마찬가지로 단수의 의미인 only one 역시 ways 앞에 올 수 없다.

b. (Dairy) 낙농장은 농부들이 우유를 짜거나 유제품을 만들기 위해 소를 키우는 농장이다.
【해설】 dairy 유제품의 / diary 일기 / daily 매일의 ▶ 발음과 철자가 헷갈리는 표현이므로 사용에 주의. '낙농장'은 dairy farm

c. (sprinkled) 치즈 가루가 가볍게 뿌려진 구운 감자는 얼마입니까?
I how much is …는 (가격이) 얼마입니까? roasted 구워진 sprinkle 뿌리다 lightly 가볍게, 약간 cheese powder 치즈 가루
【해설】 a roasted potato (which is) sprinkled lightly with cheese powder에서 which is가 생략된 것이다. 누군가에 의해 치즈 가루가 '뿌려진' 구운 감자, 즉 수동의 의미이기 때문에 pp 형태가 쓰여야 한다.

d. (nor) 나는 당신이나 당신의 친구들을 위해서 음식을 준비하지 않을 것이다.
【해설】 부정어 또는 neither + … nor: …도 또한 아니다
ex) This job can't be done by me nor you. 이 일은 나나 당신이 할 수 없다.

13 상어 지느러미 수프(샥스핀)가 상어만큼이나 위험하다는 거 아세요?

① 상어 지느러미 스프가 위험한 이유는 상어의 날카로운 이빨 때문이 아니라 수은 함량 때문입니다. ② 중국과 홍콩에서 상어 지느러미 수프의 인기가 사람들 사이에서 높아지고 있습니다. ③ 많은 중국인들은 상어 지느러미가 영양가가 높기 때문에 건강에 유익하다고 생각합니다. ④ 이들은 상어 지느러미 수프에 다양한 비타민과 미네랄, 특히 비타민 A가 풍부하다고 믿고 있습니다. ⑤ 하지만, 많은 과학자들과 영양학자들은 이들의 의견에 동의하지 않습니다. ⑥ 이들의 연구에 따르면 상어 지느러미에는 비타민 A가 전혀 없고, 상어 지느러미 수프에 든 미네랄의 양은 높지 않다고 합니다. ⑦ 또한, 상어 지느러미 수프가 암을 예방한다고 널리 믿고 있습니다. ⑧ 그러나 과학적으로 상어 지느러미 수프에 항암 효능이 있다고 밝혀진 바 없습니다. ⑨ 반대로 상어 지느러미 수프는 수은 함량 때문에 건강에 해롭습니다. ⑩ 그래서 의사들은 임산부와 어린이들은 상어 지느러미 제품 섭취를 피하라고 권합니다. ⑪ 실제 돌고래 고기와 참치 역시 높은 수은 함량 때문에 위험하다고 간주되고 있습니다.

문제 정답 및 해설

1. (b) 이 글의 요지를 고르세요.
   a. 상어는 위험하기 때문에 죽고 싶지 않다면 먹지도, 만지지도 마라.
   b. 의사들은 상어 지느러미 수프가 건강에 좋은 게 아니라 건강에 위험하다고 말한다.
   c. 상어 지느러미 수프는 수은 함량 때문에 비싸다.
   d. 상어 지느러미 수프의 인기가 높아지는 건 당연하다.

2. (c) 많은 과학자들과 영양학자들은 _____ 생각한다.
   a. 상어 지느러미 수프에 암을 예방하는 능력이 있다고
   b. 중국인들은 영양가 높은 상어 지느러미 수프를 가능한 한 자주 먹어야 한다고
   c. 상어 지느러미 수프는 비타민과 미네랄이 풍부하지 않다고
   d. 상어 지느러미 수프를 즐기는 사람들은 비타민 A 때문에 죽을 것이라고

3. 각 문장에 알맞은 표현을 고르세요.

   a. (popularity) 나는 패스트푸드의 인기에 대한 상위 10가지 이유를 밝힐 예정이다. ❙ reveal 밝히다 reason 이유

   【해설】popular a. 인기 있는 / popularly ad. 일반적으로 / popularity n. 인기 ▶ 명사인 popularity가 와야 맞다.

   b. (teeth) 나는 흔들리는 이 두 개가 빠지는 걸 원치 않는다. 그것들이 그대로 있으면 좋겠다.
   ❙ wobbly 흔들리는 fall out 빠지다 stay (그대로) 유지하다
   【해설】tooth 이빨 하나 (단수) teeth 이빨 두 개 이상 (복수) ▶ 흔들리는 이가 두 개라고 나오기 때문에 teeth로 써야 한다. 이와 같은 복수형을 취하는 다른 단어로는 'foot(발) – feet, goose(거위) – geese'등이 있다. cf. blood – bleed의 경우는 단수, 복수가 아니라 blood(명사 : 피) – bleed(동사 : 피를 흘리다)

   c. (highly) 이 지역의 토양에는 질소와 인이 매우 풍부하다.
   ❙ soil 흙, 토양 region 지역 be rich in …가 풍부하다 nitrogen 질소 phosphorus 인
   【해석】형용사 rich를 수식하는 부사 highly가 와야 한다. highly(매우) + rich(풍부한)

14 캄보디아인들이 튀긴 거미 먹기를 좋아한다는 거 아세요?

① 거미를 먹는다? ② 위험한 것 같지만 어떤 사람들은 먹습니다. ③ 놀랍게도 상당히 많은 캄보디아인들이 거미를 맛있다고 생각합니다. ④ 캄보디아에서는 많은 사람들이 거의 매일 거미를 먹습니다. ⑤ 이들은 거미 맛이 튀긴 닭고기와 비슷하다고 생각합니다. ⑥ 이들은 매일 먹는 간식으로 튀긴 거미를 먹는다고 합니다. ⑦ 믿기 힘들지만 사실입니다. ⑧ 캄보디아에서 식용 거미는 쉽게 찾을 수 있습니다. ⑨ 사방 어디에서나 거미를 찾을 수 있는데 특히 캄보디아의 한 작은 마을 스쿠온이 그렇습니다. ⑩ 이 마을은 튀긴 거미로 유명합니다. ⑪ 마을 사람들은 땅의 구멍에 거미를 키우기도 하고 숲에서 거미를 사냥하기도 합니다. ⑫ 일반적으로 이들은 기름으로 거미를 요리합니다. ⑬ 모든 사람들이 튀긴 거미를 기꺼이 먹는 건 아닙니다. ⑭ 어떤 이들은 좋아하지만 어떤 이들은 그렇지 않습니다. ⑮ 사실 거미는 그다지 맛있어 보이지 않습니다. ⑯ 이 거미는 주먹 크기만 하고 겉이 바삭해 보입니다. ⑰ 어떻게 해서 이들이 거미를 먹게 되었는지 확실하게 아는 사람은 없지만, 일부 학자들은 1970년대에 먹을 게 부족해서 어쩔 수 없이 먹게 된 게 아닌가 생각합니다.

문제 정답 및 해설

1. (d) 이 글의 요지를 고르세요.
   a. 튀긴 거미의 맛은 튀긴 닭고기와 비슷하다.
   b. 캄보디아인들이 힘이 센 건 거미처럼 먹을 게 풍부하기 때문이다.
   c. 튀긴 거미를 먹는 건 좋은 결정이 아닌데, 찐 거미가 훨씬 더 맛있기 때문이다.
   d. 캄보디아에서 튀긴 거미를 먹는 사람들을 찾는 건 어렵지 않다.

2. (a) 지문 내용과 맞는 것을 고르세요.
   a. 아마도 캄보디아인들은 먹을 게 많지 않기 때문에 어쩔 수 없이 거미를 먹기 시작했을 것이다. ▶ 마지막 문장을 통해 먹을 게 충분치 않아 먹기 시작한 것으로 추측할 수 있다.
   b. 튀긴 닭고기는 캄보디아에서 두 번째로 인기 있는 간식이다. ▶ 튀긴 거미가 인기 있는 간식이고 닭고기와 비슷한 맛이라는 내용은 나오지만, 인기 순위는 나오지 않았다.
   c. 캄보디아의 수도 스쿠온은 식량자원으로 거미를 사육해오고 있다. ▶ 스쿠온이 캄보디아 수도라는 말은 없으며, 그냥 작은 마을(small town)이라고만 나온다.
   d. 기름에 튀긴 거미는 인기가 좋지만, 건강에는 좋지 않다. ▶ 거미 튀김이 건강과 어떤 관련이 있는지는 나오지 않았다.

3. 각 문장에 알맞은 표현을 고르세요.

   a. (bite) 사람들은 개가 낯선 사람들을 문다고 생각하지만, 사실 모든 개가 낯선 사람들을 무는 건 아니다.
   【해설】 부분 부정일 때 함께 나온 주어에 동사를 맞춘다. not all dogs + 복수 동사 / not all people + 복수 동사 / not everyone + 단수 동사

   b. (found) 나는 달팽이를 먹는다는 생각을 견딜 수 없지만, 내 친구 주디는 그게 맛있다고 생각한다. I cannot stand the idea of –ing/명사 ...라는 생각을 견딜 수 없다
   【해설】 find it 형용사: 그것이 ...하다는 걸 알게 되다, ...라고 생각하다
   ex) I find it cute when boys yawn. 나는 남자아이들이 하품할 때 귀엽다고 생각한다.
   My dad found it boring to cook food for himself. 아빠는 자신을 위해 음식을 만드는 건 지루하다는 걸 알게 되었다.

   c. (didn't) 내가 너에게 아침에 제일 먼저 그의 신용카드를 확인하라고 말했는데 너는 그러지 않았.
   I check 확인하다 credit card 신용카드 first thing in the morning 아침에 제일 먼저, 무엇보다 먼저
   【해설】 일단 주어가 you(2인칭)이기 때문에 doesn't가 올 수 없고, 시제가 과거이기 때문에 don't도 올 수 없다.

15 한 달 안에 9파운드를 빼주는 과일이 무엇인지 아세요?

① 아프리카 망고를 먹으며 한 달에 9파운드를 뺄 수 있습니다. ② 고맙게도 이 특별한 망고는 나쁜 콜레스테롤을 줄여주고 한 달 안에 평균 2인치의 복부 지방을 연소시킵니다. ③ 더욱 고마운 것은 다른 다이어트 음식, 보조제, 다이어트 약품과 비교했을 때 가격이 싸다는 겁니다. ④ 물론 헬스클럽 회원 이용료보다 훨씬 더 쌉니다. ⑤ 1회분 가격이 1달러도 못 되니까 음료수 한 캔보다 쌉니다. ⑥ 이를 유명하게 만든 사람은 오즈 박사입니다. ⑦ 그는 2010년 9월 13일 자신의 〈닥터 오즈 쇼〉에서 이를 "획기적 보조제" 그리고 "의약품 보관 찬장 안의 기적"이라 불렀습니다. ⑧ 이후 많은 사람들이 아프리카 망고의 놀라운 효과를 경험하고 있습니다. ⑨ 예를 들어 의학박사 타냐 에드워즈는 아프리카 망고 추출물을 "기적의 알약"이라 불렀는데, 이것의 도움으로 한 달에 7파운드를 감량했기 때문입니다. ⑩ 그녀는 식습관과 평소 하던 운동에 어떤 변화도 주지 않았다고 합니다. ⑪ 최근 아프리카 망고의 인기에 영합해 수십 종의 아프리카 망고 제품이 온라인상에서 팔리고 있습니다. ⑫ 그러나 이런 제품 중 하나를 고를 때 주의해야 하는데, 모든 제품이 다 효과적이거나 믿을 만한 건 아니기 때문입니다.

문제 정답 및 해설

1. (c) 이 글의 요지를 고르세요.
   a. 오즈 박사는 아프리카 망고를 판매하려는 판매원이 분명하다.
   b. 다이어트 알약이 아프리카 망고보다 더 낫다.
   c. 아프리카 망고는 비만 문제의 좋은 해결책이 될 수 있다.
   d. 아프리카 망고에 관한 한, 저렴할수록 더 좋다.

2. (d) 오즈 박사는 _____ 이었다.
   a. 체중을 감량하기 위해 매년 수백만 달러를 쓴 사람 ▶ 오즈 박사가 체중 감량을 위해 돈을 썼다는 내용은 나오지 않는다.
   b. 아프리카 망고 추출물을 "기적의 알약"이라 불렀던 사람 ▶ 아프리카 망고 추출물을 "기적의 알약"이라 부른 사람은 의학박사 타냐 에드워즈
   c. 아프리카 망고의 기적적인 효과를 경험한 사람 ▶ 오즈 박사는 아프리카 망고의 효과를 직접 경험한 것이 아니라 이를 소개한 사람으로, 이를 경험한 사람이 많은데 그 중 한 예로 타냐 에드워즈가 소개되었다.
   d. '더 닥터 오즈 쇼'의 진행자 ▶ 'on his The Dr. Oz Show'라는 표현에서 Dr. Oz. Show의 진행자가 오즈 박사임을 알 수 있다.

3. 각 문장에 알맞은 표현을 고르세요.

   a. (on) 테러리스트들이 TV 화면에 나오자, 행인들은 걸음을 멈추고 뉴스를 시청했다. ▎terrorist 테러리스트 passer-by 지나가는 사람, 행인 (복수형 passers-by)
   【해설】 appear on TV screen 텔레비전 화면에 나오다 ▶ 화면에 무언가 나올 때 전치사 on을 쓴다. ex) on TV / on the screen

   b. (than) 왜 어떤 방법들은 다른 것(방법)들보다 훨씬 더 효과적인가?
   【해설】 비교급 more가 쓰였으므로 than이 오는 것이 적당하다.
   more effective than ... : ...보다 더 효과적인 (so much는 more effective를 꾸며주며 강조하는 부사 : 훨씬 더 효과적인)

   c. (shed) 사건 현장 부근에서 발견된 수많은 뼈와 해골들은 이번 살인 사건에 실마리를 제공했다. ▎a myriad of 수많은 skeleton 뼈대, 골격 crime scene 사건 현장 shed light on ...에 빛을 비추다, 밝히다, 해결의 실마리를 제공하다 murder case 살인 사건
   【해설】 shed는 현재, 과거, 과거분사 형태를 동일하게 쓰거나 shedded로 쓴다. 현재완료 (have+pp)이기 때문에 shedding은 쓸 수 없고, shed의 과거분사 shed 또는 shedded로 써야 한다.

   d. (serving) 이게 그녀가 세 번째 갖다 먹는 마카로니 앤 치즈라는 게 믿어지나요?
   【해설】 serving n. 한 번 먹는 양, 일 회분, 일인분(의 음식)
   ex) One serving of food at this restaurant is not sufficient for me.
   이 식당의 1인분 음식은 나에게 부족하다.

16 무지방 음식이 항상 건강에 좋은 건 아니라는 사실 아세요?

① 만약 다이어트 중이거나 당뇨처럼 체중 감량이 요구되는 건강 문제를 안고 있다면, 무지방 또는 저지방 음식, 다이어트 음료와 요구르트 음료를 조심하세요. ② 이런 음식들은 건강에 좋은 것 같지만 매일 먹는 식단에 올리지 않는 게 좋은데, 결과적으로 다이어트나 건강에 도움이 안 될 수도 있기 때문입니다. ③ 무지방 또는 저지방 음식은 지방이 다 들어간 음식들에 비해 맛이 떨어지는 경향이 있는데, 이 말은 맛과 만족감이 좋지 않다는 뜻입니다. ④ 그래서 이런 음식들로 상을 차릴 경우 배부른 느낌이 들려면 더 많이 먹어야 합니다. ⑤ 달리 말하면, 저지방, 무지방 음식들은 필요 이상의 음식을 먹게 만듭니다. ⑥ 게다가 "라이트" "무지방" "저지방" "제로 칼로리" 등과 같은 단어가 라벨에 적힌 음식들은 만족스럽지 못한 맛을 보충하기 위해 다양한 감미료와 과도한 설탕 또는 옥수수 시럽이 들어 있을 가능성이 높습니다. ⑦ 최근 하버드 연구 센터는 한 기사를 통해 지방이 그대로 다 들어 있는 유제품이 당뇨의 위험을 낮출 수도 있다고 주장합니다. ⑧ 책에 관해서는 '책 표지만 보고 책을 판단하지 말아야' 하지만, 음식에 관해서는 '라벨을 보고 음식을 판단하는' 게 현명한 것 같습니다.

문제 정답 및 해설

1. (b) 지문의 제목으로 적당한 것을 고르세요.
   a. 당신 자신을 위해 무지방 음식을 선택하라
   b. 주의 : '무지방'이란 단어가 '건강'을 뜻하지 않을 수도 있다
   c. 무지방 : 저지방과 완전 별개
   d. 상표만 보고 음료를 판단하지 말라.

2. (d) 지문 내용과 맞지 않는 것을 고르세요.
   a. 무지방 또는 지방을 줄인 음식이 건강에 유익하지 않을 수도 있다.
   b. 당뇨병이 있다면, 지방이 다 들어간 유제품을 먹고 싶을 수도 있다. ▶ 지문에 지방이 다 들어간 유제품이 오히려 당뇨병에 나을 수도 있다는 내용이 나온다.
   c. 일반적으로 지방 섭취를 줄이려는 사람들은 저지방이나 무지방 음식을 선택하는 경향이 있다.
   d. 무지방 음료는 좋은 것이지만 생각보다 많은 소금과 지방을 함유하고 있다. ▶ 소금과 지방이 아니라 설탕이 많이 들어 있다.

3. 각 문장에 알맞은 표현을 고르세요.

   a. (make up for) 우리는 보너스로 적자를 벌충해야 한다.
   ▌deficit 적자, 부족액

【해설】 make out of ...로 만들다 / make up for 벌충하다(compensate) ▶ 내용상 make up for가 적당하다.

b. (lower) 조산의 위험을 낮추고 싶다면 오메가 3 지방산이 도움이 될 것이다. ▌premature birth 조산 fatty acid 지방
【해설】 low a. 낮은 / lower v. 낮추다 / lowing a. 음매 하고 우는 n. 음매 울음소리
▶ 문제에서는 want to 다음에 동사 원형이 와야 하고, 문맥상 '낮추다'라는 lower 동사가 와야 적당하다.

c. (is) 케이는 2형 당뇨 진단을 받았는데, 이는 1형 당뇨와 다르다. ▌be diagnosed with ...로 진단받다 be different from ...와 다르다
【해설】 diabetes는 '병명'으로 –es로 끝나서 복수명사 같지만 단수명사이다. which는 앞에 나온 diabetes를 받기 때문에 단수 동사 is를 써야 한다.

우리만 순대를 좋아하는 게 아니라는 거 아세요?

① 한국에서 순대는 오랫동안 인기 있는 음식이었습니다. ② 놀랍게도 다른 나라에서도 순대와 매우 비슷한 음식들을 찾을 수 있습니다. ③ 순대는 다양한 재료를 채워 넣어 익힌 돼지 (또는 소의) 창자입니다. ④ 한국의 일반적인 순대는 대개 당면과 돼지 피로 만듭니다. ⑤ 재미있게도, 유럽, 북아메리카, 라틴 아메리카와 다른 아시아 국가들 역시 이런 종류의 음식을 즐겨왔습니다. ⑥ 나라에 따라 흑푸딩, 피푸딩, 또는 피 소시지라고 불립니다. ⑦ 재료와 조리법은 한국의 순대와 비슷합니다. ⑧ 한국, 중국, 독일과 같은 많은 나라들이 소와 돼지를 선호합니다. ⑨ 하지만, 티베트 사람들은 야크를 사용하고, 일부 유럽 국가들은 양의 창자와 피로 흑푸딩을 만들어왔습니다. ⑩ 전형적인 유럽 스타일의 흑푸딩은 고기, 피, 지방, 빵, 양파, 보리 등을 채워 넣어 만듭니다. ⑪ 하지만, 한국과는 달리, 오늘날 서구 국가들의 슈퍼마켓이나 음식점에서 피로 만든 소시지를 찾기가 쉽지 않습니다. ⑫ 서구인들은 피가 들어간 음식은 더 이상 좋아하지 않는 것 같습니다.

문제 정답 및 해설

1. (a) 이 글의 요지를 고르세요.
   a. 의외로 전 세계의 많은 사람들이 한국의 순대와 비슷한 음식을 즐긴다.
   b. 소 내장으로 만든 순대는 블랙 푸딩보다 맛있다.
   c. 유럽식 블랙 푸딩은 당면과 돼지 피가 들어간다.
   d. 일반적으로 유럽인들은 피가 들어간 음식은 좋아하지 않는다.

2. (b) 순대는 _____ 만든다.
   a. 동물 창자를 많은 기름과 향료로 요리해서
   b. 당면과 돼지 피를 채워 넣은 동물 창자를 쪄서
   c. 커다란 팬에 양 창자와 피를 끓여서
   d. 곡물을 채워 넣은 야크의 창자를 튀겨서

3. 각 문장에 알맞은 표현을 고르세요.

   a. (keen on) K-팝 스타들과 한국 드라마를 좋아하는 일부 유럽인들이 한국어를 배우고 싶어 한다.
   l be keen on + 명사/-ing 좋아하다, ...하기 원하다
   【해설】주어는 Europeans, 동사는 are이기 때문에 likes to가 올 수 없고, desperate to는 뒤에 동사원형이 와야 하므로 learning Korean과 이어질 수 없다. 'be desperate to 동사원형 또는 for 명사 (필사적으로, 간절하게 ... 원하다)'

   b. (Nowadays) 요즘 점점 더 많은 아이들이 컴퓨터 게임에 중독되고 있다. l more and more 점점 더 많은 be addicted to ...에 중독되다
   【해설】before long 오래지 않아 / nowadays 요즘 / for the time being 당분간 ▶ 문맥상 nowadays가 적당하다.

   c. (preferred) 이 제품들은 전 세계 고객들로부터 널리 사랑받는다.
   【해설】prefer (to) 더 좋아하다, 더 선호하다 ▶ 문제에서는 수동태로 쓰였다. be동사 + 부사(widely) + pp(preferred) + by
   * 'prefer to 동사원형'과 'prefer A to B'를 혼동하지 않도록 주의
   1) prefer to : I think I would prefer to walk home.
      나는 걸어서 집에 가는 게 좋겠다고 생각한다.
   2) prefer A to B : I prefer walking to running.
      나는 뛰기보다 걷기를 더 좋아한다. (to를 사용해서 walking과 running을 비교)

18. 중국인들이 비둘기 수프를 먹는다는 거 아세요?

① 중국인들은 비둘기 수프를 먹습니다. ② 많은 미식가들이 이를 맛있다고 생각하고, 비교적 만들기도 쉬운데, 비둘기 고기, 차이브(골파), 소금과 후추를 준비한 뒤 이를 끓이면 됩니다. ③ 비둘기 수프는 중국의 다른 이색적인 음식과 비교할 때 그리 놀라운 음식이 아닙니다. ④ 중국 요리는 다양성과 놀라운 재료로 유명합니다. ⑤ 요리사들은 먹을 수 있는 건 거의 모든 걸 요리에 사용한다는데, 닭 심장, 원숭이 뇌, 새 둥지, 곰 발바닥, 사슴뿔, 바퀴벌레, 전갈, 매미 등을 들 수 있습니다. ⑥ 전 세계 사람들은 중국의 이색적이고 창의적인 음식을 즐기고 맛있게 먹습니다. ⑦ 하지만, 그 중 어떤 음식들은 너무 이색적이고 특이해서 외국인들이 먹기 힘든 것도 있습니다. ⑧ 예를 들어 발효된 두부로 만든 취두부는 중국에서는 인기가 좋지만, 취두부의 강한 냄새를 견디지 못하는 사람도 있습니다. ⑨ 또 중국 요리에서 동물의 피를 사용하는 건 이상하거나 특이한 일이 아니지만, 상당한 서구인들은 이를 끔찍하다고 여깁니다. ⑩ 그러나 많은 중국인들은 살아 있는 뱀이나 거북의 피, 그리고 피가 뚝뚝 떨어지는 사슴뿔을 건강식이라고 믿습니다.

문제 정답 및 해설

1. (b) 이 글의 요지를 고르세요.
   a. 가장 끔찍한 중국 음식은 비둘기 수프다.
   b. 중국 음식은 다양하고 창의적이고 이국적이다.
   c. 취두부를 먹으려고 시도한 사람들은 끔찍한 냄새로 사망하기 쉽다.
   d. 외국인들은 중국 음식을 즐기는 척하지만, 사실은 그렇지 않다.

2. (d) 지문 내용과 맞는 것을 고르세요.
   a. 많은 미식가들은 비둘기 수프가 중국에서 가장 맛있는 음식이라고 주장한다. ▶ 미식가들이 비둘기 수프를 맛있다고 생각하지만, 중국에서 제일 맛있다고는 하지 않았다.
   b. 비둘기 수프 조리법은 꽤 간단하지만, 재료는 아주 비싸다. ▶ 재료 가격에 대한 내용은 나오지 않았다.
   c. 중국 요리는 평범해서 모두가 거리낌 없이 즐길 수 있다. ▶ 외국인들 중에는 평범하지 않은 중국 요리를 즐기지 못하는 경우도 있다. (nothing but 단지, 그저 normal 평범한 without reserve 거리낌 없이)
   d. 중국 요리사들은 독이 있는 동물을 요리에 이용하는 걸 두려워하지 않는 것 같다. ▶ 요리 재료 중에 전갈이 나온 것으로 보아 그렇다고 추측할 수 있다. (cook n. 요리사 v. 요리하다)

3. 각 문장에 알맞은 표현을 고르세요.

   a. (surprising) 세상에 급여가 몇십만 달러인 놀라운 직업이 많다는 데 놀랐다.
   | six figure 6자리 숫자 (six figure job 급여가 6자리(십만 단위)인 직업)
   【해설】 surprise ▶ 사람 주어 + be 동사 + surprised: 주어가 놀라다 (I am surprised...)
   사물 주어 + be 동사 + surprising: 주어가 놀랍다 (It is surprising..) 형용사 surprising : 놀라운 (명사 수식)
   문장 앞부분에서는 I am surprised that... '나는 ...에 놀랐다.' that 이하의 주어는 there, 동사는 are ▶ many 많은 (부사) + surprising (형용사) + jobs (명사) : 많은 놀라운 직업들

   b. (appreciate) 많은 내 친구들은 좋은 포도주를 맛볼 줄 알아서 그 맛을 보기 위해 수백 달러도 기꺼이 내놓는다.
   | fine wine 좋은 포도주 get a taste of ...의 맛을 보다
   【해설】 sip 홀짝홀짝(조금씩) 마시다 / take a dip 잠시 수영하다 (dip 살짝 담그다) / appreciate 진정한 가치를 알아보다, 고마워하다 -> 내용상 appreciate가 적당하다.

   c. (being eccentric) 레이디 가가는 특이한 것으로 유명할 뿐만 아니라 텍사스에서 쇼 중에 뒤로 벌렁 넘어진 것으로도 유명하다.
   | eccentric 독특한 fall flat on one's back 뒤로 벌렁 넘어지다
   【해설】 be famous for + 명사/-ing : be famous for 다음에 형용사가 직접 올 수 없기 때문에 be동사의 -ing형인 'being + 형용사' 형태로 와야 한다.
   ex) He is famous for handsome. (X) He is famous for being handsome. (O)
   그는 잘생긴 것으로 유명하다.

19 약 200달러짜리 샌드위치가 있다는 거 아세요?

① 영국에서 200달러 가치의 샌드위치를 찾을 수 있습니다. ② 당연히 이 특별한 샌드위치를 주문하려면 100파운드(미국 달러로 거의 200달러)를 지불해야 합니다. ③ 세 겹으로 된 이 샌드위치는 빵, 닭고기, 메추라기 알, 햄, 화이트 트뤼플 등으로 만듭니다. ④ 물론 최고의 재료만 사용됩니다. ⑤ 매우 기름지지만 전 세계 음식 마니아들은 최상의 맛이라며 극찬합니다. ⑥ 샌드위치에 200달러라는 게 비싸다고 생각하나요? ⑦ 세상에는 그보다 더 비싼 음식이 아주 많습니다. ⑧ 일종의 향신료인 사프란은 워낙 얻기 어려운 탓에 1kg에 최소 1천 달러 이상을 지불해야 합니다. ⑨ 향신료 하나에 수천 달러를 쓴다는 게 어이없는 짓 같지만, 더 어이없는 게 있으니 바로 위스키입니다. ⑩ 그냥 위스키가 아니라 전 세계에서 가장 비싼 위스키입니다. ⑪ 맥켈란 파인 레어 빈티지 컬렉션의 30년 된 이 위스키의 흔치 않은 맛을 보려면 통장을 털어야 할지도 모르는데, 한 병당 가격이 38,000달러이기 때문입니다.

문제 정답 및 해설

1. (c) 이 글의 요지를 고르세요.
   a. 샌드위치 하나에 수천 달러를 쓰는 건 미친 짓이다.
   b. 가장 비싼 포도주 한 병을 산다면 파산할 것이다.
   c. 세상에는 예상 밖으로 비싼 음식들이 있다.
   d. 기름진 음식은 비싸지만 맛은 좋다.

2. (a) 200달러짜리 샌드위치를 주문하고 싶다면 _____ 한다.
   a. 영국에 가야
   b. 빈 위장을 계속 유지해야(속을 비워둬야)
   c. 통장에서 38,000달러를 인출해야
   d. 파산해야

3. 각 문장에 알맞은 표현을 고르세요.

   a. (per) 속도 제한이 시간당 35마일이라는 걸 몰랐기 때문에 과속 딱지를 떼었다.
   | speeding ticket 속도위반 딱지 speed limit 속도 제한
   【해설】 한 시간당 per hour: 35 miles per hour ▶ 한 시간에 35마일 갈 수 있는 속도
   ex) This cloth is three dollars per yard. 이 옷감은 1야드에 3달러이다.

   Admission fee is 1000 won per person. 입장료는 1인당 천 원이다.
   Gasoline cost 80 cents per gallon last week. 가솔린 값이 지난주 1갤런당 80센트였다.

   b. (rare) 흔치 않은 그 수공예품들이 높은 가격에 팔린 것도 당연하다. 지구상에 단 세 개밖에 없으니 말이다.
   | no wonder 당연하다, 놀랄 일도 아니다 handicraft 수공예품, 손으로 만든 공예품 be sold at a high price 높은 가격에 팔리다 in the entire planet 전 세계에서, 이 행성에서
   【해설】 bare 벌거벗은, 맨 / rare 흔하지 않아서 귀한, 드문, (고기) 살짝 익힌 / scare 겁주다 ▶ '지구상에 세 개뿐'이라는 표현이 힌트

   c. (highly) 나는 그의 작품을 좋게 말하고 싶었지만, 나도 모르게 나쁘게 말해버렸다.
   | work 일하다, 작품 in spite of oneself 자신도 모르게
   【해설】 speak highly of …를 좋게 말하다, 칭찬하다 / speak ill of …를 나쁘게 말하다, 혹평하다

가장 비싼 커피가 고양이 똥으로 만든다는 거 아세요?

① 고양이 똥으로 만든 커피가 가장 비싼 커피? ② 여러분은 '말도 안 돼!'라고 말할지 모르지만, '말이 된다'고 할 사람이 많습니다. ③ '배설물'이라고도 하는 똥은 냄새나고 더러워야 하지만 고양이 똥 커피는 전혀 그렇지 않습니다. ④ 고양이 똥 커피(시벳 커피 또는 코피 루왁)는 스타벅스 커피보다 더 비싸고 더 맛있습니다. ⑤ 하지만, 20달러나 내고 동물 똥에서 추출한 커피 한 컵을 먹겠다는 사람이 누가 있을까요? ⑥ 의외로, 상당한 커피 애호가들이 그 맛을 보기 위해 기꺼이 줄을 서서 기다립니다. ⑦ 이 커피는 평범한 커피콩에서 추출하지 않습니다. ⑧ 특별한 콩은 시벳(사향고양이)의 똥에서 모을 수 있는데, 시벳은 정확히 고양이는 아니고 고양이와 비슷한 포유동물입니다. ⑨ 시벳은 나무에서 떨어진 커피 열매를 먹고 똥을 쌉니다. ⑩ 커피 만드는 사람들은 똥을 뒤져 시벳의 소화 기관을 통과한 열매를 골라냅니다. ⑪ 이 커피가 비싼 이유는 매년 인도네시아 전역에서 겨우 230kg 정도만 생산되기 때문입니다. ⑫ 보통 고객들은 이 커피의 강한 뒷맛에 찬사를 보냅니다. ⑬ 어디에서 나온 것인지 감안할 때 뒷맛이 강할 만도 하지요. ⑭ 그럼에도 불구하고 조금도 주저하지 않고 똥 커피 한 컵에 20달러를 내는 사람들이 있는데, 풍미가 그만큼 좋기 때문입니다.

문제 정답 및 해설

1. (d) 지문의 제목으로 적당한 것을 고르세요.
   a. 똥을 먹고, 똥을 마시고 그리고 똥 냄새를 맡다
   b. 고양이, 신비로운 동물
   c. 세계에서 가장 비싼 똥
   d. 똥에서 나온 커피 : 구리지 않고 향기롭다

2. (b) 지문 내용과 맞지 않는 것을 고르세요.
   a. '배설물' 과 '똥'은 같은 의미이다.
   b. 똥은 냄새나고 더러워야 하지만 고양이 똥은 냄새만 지독할 뿐 더럽지 않다. ▶ 고양이 똥 자체가 더럽거나 냄새나지 않는다고는 나오지 않았고 시벳 고양이 똥에서 나온 '커피'의 맛과 향이 좋다고 나온다.
   c. 커피 애호가들은 고양이 똥 커피를 맛보기 위해 줄을 서서 기다리는 것도 마다하지 않는다.
   d. 코피 루왁의 특별한 콩은 시벳 고양이의 똥에서 찾을 수 있다.

3. 각 문장에 알맞은 표현을 고르세요.
   a. (times) 그의 거짓말을 수차례 들어왔다. 그가 무슨 말을 하든 나는 믿을 수 없다.
   【해설】quite a few times = many times 수차례, 여러 번 (quite a few + 복수명사 + 복수동사)

   b. (which) 가장 가까운 슈퍼마켓은 크리스틴의 후레쉬 마켓인데 그곳은 내 누이가 주인이다.
   【해설】Kristine's Fresh Market이라는 사물을 선행사로 하는 관계대명사는 which 또는 that이 적당하다.

   c. (his advanced age) 연로한 그의 나이를 생각할 때 그는 놀랄 만큼 젊어 보인다. ▌considering ...를 감안할 때 advanced age 연로한 나이 look young 젊어 보이다
   【해설】considering + 명사/동명사 / considering that + 주어 + 동사 ▶ considering that 다음에는 his advanced age라는 명사구가 아닌 주어+동사 절이 온다. 그래서 considering his advanced age로 쓰거나, 아니면 considering that he is quite old (그가 꽤 나이가 들었다는 걸 감안할 때)로 써야 한다.

   d. (mourns) 자신의 호텔 방에서 사망한 채 발견된 휘트니 휴스턴의 전 남편 바비 브라운은 휴스턴의 죽음을 애도한다. ▌ex-husband 전 남편 be found dead 사망한 채 발견되다 mourn 애도하다
   【해설】주어가 Bobby Brown(3인칭 단수)이기 때문에 동사가 현재시제라면 mourns, 과거라면 mourned가 와야 하고, 원형 동사 mourn은 올 수 없다. 주어와 동사의 위치가 멀리 떨어져 있을 때 주의.

Chapter 3. Beauty

21 보톡스가 일종의 독이라는 거 아세요?

① 보톡스는 가장 인기 있는 비수술적인 미용 시술입니다. ② 알려진 바에 의하면 매년 수백만의 사람들이 보톡스 시술(주사)을 받는다고 합니다. ③ 보톡스는 보툴리눔 독소 A의 상표로, 보툴리눔 식중독은 심각한 식중독의 한 형태입니다. ④ 보툴리눔 식중독의 전형적인 증상은 마비입니다. ⑤ 어떤 경우 보툴리눔 식중독으로 인한 마비는 대단히 위험해서, 심지어 치명적일 수도 있습니다. ⑥ 흥미롭게도, 보툴리눔 식중독을 희석시킨 것을 얼굴에 주입하는 게 보톡스 시술인데, 이것이 주름을 형성하는 근육을 마비시키거나 약화시키기 때문입니다. ⑦ 예를 들어 눈썹 주위 근육에 이 시술을 받는다면, 주변 근육은 일정 기간 동안 수축할 수 없게 됩니다. ⑧ 근육이 마비된 것입니다. ⑨ 보톡스 주입을 받고 난 후, 사람들은 몇 시간에서 이틀 이내에 시술의 효과를 볼 수 있습니다. ⑩ 불행히도 보톡스의 놀라운 효과는 오래 지속되지 않습니다. ⑪ 일 년 내내 주름 없는 모습을 유지하고 싶다면 일 년에 3-4회 시술을 받아야 하는데, 효과가 3달에서 5달 정도만 유지되기 때문입니다.

문제 정답 및 해설

1. (d) 이 글의 요지를 고르세요.
   a. 보톡스 주사를 맞는 건 매우 위험하고 어리석은 짓이다.
   b. 보톡스는 가장 비싸지만 인기 있는 비수술적 미용 시술이다.
   c. 보톡스는 근육을 마비시킬 수 있기 때문에 치명적이다.
   d. 보톡스는 위험한 독소 종류인 보툴리즘을 희석한 형태이다.

2. (a) 눈썹 주변 근육에 보톡스 주사를 맞으면 _____.
   a. 그 근육이 마비될 것이다
   b. 독소에 의한 감염으로 장님이 될 것이다
   c. 주름 없는 피부가 5년간 지속될 것이다
   d. 얼굴 근육이 매우 빨리 수축될 것이다.

3. 각 문장에 알맞은 표현을 고르세요.

   a. (paralyzed) 내 몸의 오른쪽 부분이 마비된 것 같다. 오른손을 움직일 수 없다.
   【해설】paralyze v. 마비시키다 paralysis n. 마비 ▶ 문제의 문장은 수동태(내 몸이 마비되다)로 be동사 + pp 형태이므로 paralyzed가 와야 한다.

   b. (injections) 1형 당뇨병 환자들 중 일부는 매일 인슐린 주사를 맞아야 한다.
   | patient 환자 type 1 diabetes 1형 당뇨병 insulin 인슐린
   【해설】infection 감염 / injection 주사, 주입 / induction 유도, 인도, 귀납
   get insulin injections 인슐린 주사를 맞다

   c. (in) 잠깐만 참아라. 그는 조금 있으면 여기 올 것이다.
   | patient a. 인내하는, 참는 n. 환자 for a while 잠시 동안
   【해설】in a minute 일 분 안에 (within a minute), 조금 있으면 / for a minute 일 분 동안 ▶ '...이내에' 라는 뜻의 in이 와야 맞다.

세안을 위한 기본 팁을 아세요?

① 먼저 자기 피부에 맞는 클렌저(세안제품)를 찾을 필요가 있습니다. ② 약국이나 동네 화장품 가게에서 자기 피부 타입에 맞는 좋은 클렌저를 찾을 수 있습니다. ③ 피부 세안에 관해 사람들이 가장 많이 저지르는 실수는 비싼 제품이 항상 좋다고 생각하는 것입니다. ④ 하지만, 언제나 그런 건 아닙니다. ⑤ 고가의 유명 브랜드 세안 제품 하나에 5만 원 이상의 돈을 쓸 필요는 없습니다. ⑥ 하지만, 고체 비누는 고르지 않는 게 좋은데, 일반적으로 고체 비누가 피부를 건조시키기 때문입니다. ⑦ 그리고 너무 자주 씻거나 세안하지 말아야 한다는 걸 잊지 마세요. ⑧ 적당한 클렌저로 하루에 한두 번 세안하면 되지 그 이상은 필요 없습니다. ⑨ 아침에는 미지근한 물만 한 번 뿌리듯 세안하는 걸로 충분합니다. ⑩ 한 가지 더. 클렌저 양을 적게 사용하고 (얼굴을 닦는데 다임 동전 하나 크기면 충분) 미지근한 물로 헹궈 냅니다. ⑪ 뜨겁거나 찬물로 닦지 않도록 주의하세요. ⑫ 두 가지 모두 피부에 안 좋은 영향을 미칠 수 있습니다.

문제 정답 및 해설

1. (c) 지문의 제목으로 적당한 것을 고르세요.
   a. 닦으면 닦을수록 더 투명한 피부를 얻을 수 있다
   b. 클렌저 : 피부의 최대 적
   c. 어떻게 세안할 것인가 & 어떻게 클렌저를 선택할 것인가
   d. 고체 비누에 대해 당신이 알아야 할 모든 것

2. (c) 지문 내용과 맞지 않는 것을 고르세요.
   a. 고체 비누를 사용하지 않는 게 좋고 하루에 두 번 이상 세안하지 않는 게 좋다.
   b. 비싼 세안제에 많은 돈을 쓸 필요가 없다.
   c. 자기 피부에 맞는 적당한 세안제는 오직 약국에서만 찾을 수 있다. ▶ 약국과 동네 화장품 가게에서 구매할 수 있다.
   d. 아침에 세수할 때 고체 비누나 세안제를 쓸 필요가 없다.

3. 각 문장에 알맞은 표현을 고르세요.

   a. (make) 나는 항상 실수를 하지만 과거의 실수를 반복하지 않으려고 노력한다. l mistake 실수 repeat 반복하다
   【해설】 make a mistake / make mistakes 실수하다 ▶ do a mistake 혹은 have a mistake 등과 같이 쓰지 않고 항상 make a mistake로 쓴다. 마찬가지로 do one's homework (숙제하다)라는 표현도 항상 do 동사를 써야 하고, take a break (쉬다) 역시 take 동사와만 쓰인다. 이렇게 특정 동사와 쓰이는 표현은 따로 암기해야 한다.
   * make와 함께 쓰이는 표현: make a wish 소원을 빌다 make a reservation 예약하다 make a decision 결정하다 make a fuss 야단법석을 떨다 make a phone call 전화하다 make a living 생계를 꾸리다, 벌어 먹고살다

   b. (to shopping) 쇼핑에 관해서라면 내 남자친구는 전문가이다.
   【해설】 when it comes to 명사 ...에 관해서라면 ▶ 이 표현에서 to는 'to 동사원형 (to 부정사)'이 아니므로 주의한다.

   c. (not to) 내 눈이 흐리기 때문에 나는 무언가 또는 누군가와 부딪치지 않도록 조심해야 한다. l blurry 흐릿한, 모호한 bump 부딪치다
   【해설】 to 부정사의 부정: to 부정사 앞에 부정어 not이 온다.
   ex) try to run 달리려고 노력하다 ▶ try not to run 달리지 않으려고 노력하다
     be careful not to 동사원형: ...않도록 조심하다
     – be careful not to fail 실패하지 않도록 조심하다
     – be careful not to catch a cold 감기 걸리지 않도록 조심하다

 올바른 지방 연소제를 어떻게 선택해야 하는지 아세요?

① 다이어트와 체중 감량 산업이 엄청난 돈을 챙기는 건 많은 사람들이 체중 감량 제품에 기꺼이 지갑을 열기 때문입니다. ② 사람들은 그저 쉽게 체중을 감량하고 싶은데 이런 제품들은 효과가 있습니다. ③ 많은 다이어트 제품들 중에 지방 연소제가 엄청난 인기를 얻고 있는데, 이유는 이 제품들은 땀 흘리는 운동이나 끔찍한 다이어트의 고통 없이 짧은 시간에 체중을 감량할 수 있게 도와주기 때문입니다. ④ 문제는 지방 연소제에 돈을 쓰는 사람들 모두가 체중 감량의 기쁨을 맛보는 건 아니라는 점입니다. ⑤ 그래서 지방 연소제를 선택하기 전에 다음 사항을 고려해야 합니다. ⑥ – 효과적인가? – ⑦ 지방 연소제는 지방을 빼줘야지 물만 빼주면 안 됩니다. ⑧ – 안전한가? – ⑨ 성분이 의학적으로 안전한지, 부작용은 없는지 확인해야 합니다. ⑩ FDA 승인을 받은 제품을 선택합니다. ⑪ – 소비자들이 그 제품에 만족하는가? – ⑫ 구매 전에 다른 사용자들의 의견을 살펴보세요. ⑬ 지방 연소제를 만들어 판매하는 수백 군데의 업체들이 허위 광고와 건강에 해로운 재료를 사용해서 FDA에 적발되고 있습니다.

문제 정답 및 해설

1. (b) 이 글의 요지를 고르세요.
   a. 쉽게 살을 빼려는 사람들은 지방 연소제를 구매할 필요가 있다.
   b. 지방 연소제를 고를 때 효과적이고 안전하며 소비자가 승인한 제품을 선택하라.
   c. 지방 연소제를 포함한 모든 다이어트 제품은 FDA의 승인을 받은 게 틀림없다.
   d. 허위로 제품을 광고하는 회사들은 FDA에 적발당해야 한다.

2. (d) 지방 연소제들이 인기를 얻고 있는 이유는 _____ 때문이다.
   a. 다이어트 알약보다 저렴하기
   b. 저렴한 값으로 기적을 약속하기
   c. 모든 제품이 FDA의 승인을 받았고 의약적으로 안전하기
   d. 사용자들이 그리 어렵지 않은 방법으로 지방을 연소하도록 돕기

3. 각 문장에 알맞은 표현을 고르세요.

   a. (pocketed) 놀랍게도 그의 회사는 지난해 거의 3백만 달러를 벌었다. l pocket v. 주머니에 넣다, 챙기다

   【해설】주어 his company가 3인칭 단수이기 때문에 시제가 현재라면 pockets로, 과거라면 pocketed로 와야 한다. last year라는 표현이 있으므로 문장의 시제는 과거.

   b. (satisfied with) 왜 너는 네 삶에 무엇이든 만족하는 법이 없느냐?
   【해설】사람 주어 + be satisfied with …에 만족하다 (반드시 전치사 with가 온다.) 반대 표현인 dissatisfied 역시 전치사 with와 함께 쓰인다.
   ex) There are many customers who are dissatisfied with this product.
   이 제품에 만족하지 않는 고객들이 많다.

   c. (busted) 시험에서 커닝을 하면 '걸렸다' 라고 말하기도 전에 걸릴 것이다. l cheat on a test 시험 볼 때 커닝하다 bust 적발하다 faster than you can say …라고 말하기도 전에, …라고 말하는 것보다 더 빨리
   【해설】문맥상 수동태로 써야 맞다. ▶ be busted 걸리다, 적발당하다

24 건강하고 매끄러운 피부를 위해 하지 말아야 할 세 가지가 무엇인지 아세요?

① 담배를 피우지 마세요. ② 만약 당신이 흡연자이고 조만간 담배를 끊을 생각이 없다면, 주름지고 메마른 피부를 갖게 될 각오를 하는 게 좋습니다. ③ 전문가들은 태양 노출과 흡연이 피부 손상의 주요 두 가지 원인이라고 말합니다. ④ 케이트 모스가 완벽한 예입니다. ⑤ 사진에서는 근사해 보이고 많은 피부 전문가들이 비싼 화장품으로 피부 관리를 해주고 있음에도 불구하고 모스의 맨 피부가 끔찍한 건, 그녀가 오랜 흡연자이기 때문입니다. ⑥ 보습을 잊지 마세요. ⑦ 건강하고 매끈한 피부를 유지하려면 수분이 필요합니다. ⑧ 수분이 많이 함유된 제품과 보습제는 피부의 수분이 빠져나가지 않게 막는 데 도움이 됩니다. ⑨ 최선의 보습제 사용법은 피부가 촉촉할 때 바르는 것입니다. ⑩ 선탠을 하지 마세요. ⑪ 선탠한 피부가 보기에는 좋지만, 불행히도 선탠한 피부는 손상된 피부입니다. ⑫ 반복적으로 또는 지속적으로 선탠하거나 태양에 피부를 그을리면 피부 노화가 가속될 뿐만 아니라 피부암의 위험도 높아집니다.

문제 정답 및 해설

1. (a) 이 글의 요지를 고르세요.
   a. 매끄러운 피부를 가지려면, 흡연이나 선탠을 하지 말고 보습을 하라.
   b. 매끄러운 피부를 위해 해야 할 가장 중요한 것은 보습이다.
   c. 태닝과 흡연은 피부암의 주요 요인이다.
   d. 케이트 모스가 멋져 보이는 건 고가의 화장품을 사용하기 때문이다.

2. (b) 지문 내용과 맞는 것을 고르세요.
   a. 비흡연자는 주름지고 건조한 피부를 갖게 될 가능성이 매우 높다. ▶ 비흡연자가 아니라 흡연자의 피부가 주름지고 건조해질 가능성이 높다.
   b. 케이트 모스의 맨 피부가 나쁜 건 오랫동안 흡연했기 때문이다.
   c. 피부 전문가들은 목욕 중에 보습제를 바르라고 권한다. ▶ '목욕 중'이 아니라 '목욕 직후' 피부가 촉촉할 때 바르라고 권한다.
   d. 반복적인 태닝은 피부암의 좋은 해결책이다. ▶ 반복적인 태닝은 피부암의 위험을 높인다.

3. 각 문장에 알맞은 표현을 고르세요.

   a. (stay cool) 타는 듯 뜨거운 온도에서 어떻게 하면 시원함을 유지할 수 있을까? ∥ stay (...상태를) 유지하다 scorching 타는 듯 무더운 temperature 온도, 체온
   【해설】stay cool 시원한 상태를 유지하다 / keep cool 냉정함(침착성)을 잃지 않다 ▶ 문맥상 stay cool이 적당하다

   b. (brutal) 이런, 너 정말 안 됐다. 업무량이 장난 아니구나. ∥ workload 업무량, 일해야 할 것들 brutal 잔혹한, 인정사정없는
   【해설】look + 형용사: ...처럼/...로 보이다
   ex) look great 근사해 보이다 look brutal 끔찍해 보이다 look troubled 근심이 있어 보이다

   c. (smoking) 내 아내는 담배를 끊을 생각이 없는데, 그것 때문에 미치겠다. ∥ have no intention of –ing/명사 ...할 생각(의도)가 없다 drive someone crazy (nuts) ...를 미치게(화나게) 하다
   【해설】quit (그만두다)은 –ing를 취한다.
   ex) quit talking 말을 그만두다 quit drinking 술을 그만 마시다

25 갈라지는 머리끝을 방지하는 방법을 아세요?

① 길고 손상된 모발을 가진 여성은 머리끝이 갈라지는 문제를 겪을 가능성이 아주 높습니다. ② 머리끝 부분이 외부 보호층을 잃으면 머리끝이 갈라지게 됩니다. ③ 현재 갈라진 끝 부분을 제거하는 최상의, 그리고 유일한 방법은 잘라내는 것입니다. ④ 하지만, 자주 머리카락을 다듬고 싶지 않다면, 아래 정보를 참조하세요. ⑤ 먼저, 바람으로 말리는 드라이어, 컬링 아이론, 헤어 스트레이트너 등 열을 이용한 모발 기구를 사용하지 않습니다. ⑥ 이렇게 뜨거운 바람을 이용한 모발 용품들은 머리카락을 마르게 만들고, 열은 머리끝이 갈라지는 주요 원인입니다. ⑦ 그래서 이러한 용품을 사용하지 않도록, 최소한 이를 사용하는 시간을 줄이도록 노력합니다. ⑧ 두 번째로 염색 또는 파마 횟수를 줄입니다. ⑨ 두 가지 모두 모발을 손상시킬 수 있으니 탈색, 염색 또는 파마를 너무 자주 하지 않도록 합니다. ⑩ 세 번째, 빗질할 때 주의합니다. ⑪ 머리카락이 젖었을 때 빗질하거나 너무 자주 빗질하거나 촘촘한 빗으로 빗질하는 것 모두 모발을 손상시킬 수 있습니다. ⑫ 부적절한 빗질은 모발을 부수고 결과적으로 머리끝이 갈라지는 원인이 됩니다. ⑬ 그러니 젖은 머리를 빗지 말고 빗살이 넓은 빗을 사용합니다.

문제 정답 및 해설

1. (c) 이 글의 요지를 고르세요.
   a. 긴 머리는 머리끝이 갈라진 손상된 머리를 뜻한다.
   b. 열을 사용하는 헤어 제품과 머리카락 손상은 아무 상관없다.
   c. 예방 조치를 취하면 갈라진 머리끝은 예방할 수 있다.
   d. 빗살이 넓은 빗이 촘촘한 빗보다 항상 좋다.

2. (d) 머리를 자주 다듬기는 싫지만, 머리끝이 갈라지는 문제를 안고 있는 사람들은 _____.
   a. 빗살이 넓은 빗으로 머리를 빗는 경향이 있다.
   b. 가능한 한 자주 머리카락 염색을 해야 한다
   c. 빗살이 촘촘한 빗을 사용해야 한다.
   d. 컬링 아이론과 헤어 스트레이트너를 사용하지 않는 게 좋다

3. 각 문장에 알맞은 표현을 고르세요.

   a. (to lose) 적당한 운동은 체중을 줄이고 건강을 유지하는 좋은 방법이다. | proper 적당한 exercise 운동 a fine way 좋은 방법 lose weight 체중을 감량하다 stay heathy 건강을 유지하다
   【해설】 a fine[best, good] way to 동사 [또는 of –ing] …하는 좋은 방법 ▶ to lose가 오거나 of losing이 와야 한다.

   b. (In order not to) 커다란 빵 덩어리를 산산조각내지 않기 위해 그녀는 양손으로 빵을 옮겼다. | in order to = to …하기 위해 a large loaf of bread 큰 덩어리의 빵 break into pieces 산산조각이 나다
   【해설】 in order to의 부정은 to 부정사의 부정과 마찬가지로 to 앞에 부정어 not이 온다. ▶ in order not to …하지 않기 위해

   c. (often) 얼마나 자주 운동을 합니까? 내가 맞추어 보겠습니다. 일주일에 두 번? | work out 운동하다 twice a week 일주일에 두 번
   【해설】 how often 얼마나 자주 how much 얼마나 많이 how long 얼마나 오래(길게)
   ex) How long did it take? (시간이) 얼마나 오래 걸렸습니까?
   How much do you get paid? (급여를) 얼마나 많이 받습니까?

   d. (dyeing) 스미스 부부는 미용실에서 머리카락을 검게 염색하고 있다. | dye 염색하다 hair salon 미용실(= beauty salon)
   【해설】 dye 동사의 과거형은 dyed, –ing형은 dyeing이다. (dying은 die의 –ing형) 문제에서는 'be 동사 + ing 현재 진행형'이기 때문에 dyed가 아닌 dyeing이 정답이다.

여드름을 관리하는 가장 달콤한 방법이 무엇인지 아세요?

① 꿀은 효과적인 박테리아 킬러입니다. ② 그래서 꿀이 상처 도포제로 사용되고 있는데, 꿀이 박테리아를 죽이고 상처가 낫는 데 도움이 되기 때문입니다. ③ 꿀이 상처의 박테리아만 죽일 수 있는 게 아닙니다. ④ 꿀은 여러분 피부의 박테리아도 죽일 수 있습니다. ⑤ 사실 꿀은 깨끗하고 매끄러운 피부를 얻는 가장 좋은 방법 중 하나입니다. ⑥ 이를테면 효소와 산화방지제, 항세균제를 함유한 꿀의 놀라운 치유적 속성들 덕분에 꿀 페이셜 마스크는 여드름 흉터를 없애고 붉어지는 현상을 완화시키며 보습에도 효과적입니다. ⑦ 게다가 아주 쉽고 간단합니다. ⑧ 필요한 건 걸러지지 않은 천연 꿀 뿐입니다. ⑨ 먼저 얼굴을 씻습니다. ⑩ 반드시 화장을 완전히 지우고 손을 깨끗이 해야 합니다. ⑪ 얼굴에 꿀을 바릅니다. ⑫ 꿀을 바를 때 얼굴 전체에 꿀을 천천히 문지르며 바릅니다. ⑬ 그리고 약 15분 정도 그대로 꿀을 얼굴에 둡니다. ⑭ 꿀을 완전히 씻어낼 때까지 따뜻한 물로 얼굴을 씻고 마지막으로 모공을 닫기 위해 시원한 물로 씻습니다. ⑮ 꿀 마스크는 일주일에 2-3번, 혹은 원하는 대로 시행합니다.

문제 정답 및 해설

1. **(d)** 이 글의 요지를 고르세요.
   a. 꿀은 상처 치료에 쓰이곤 했지만 더 이상은 그렇지 않다.
   b. 꿀은 상처의 박테리아를 죽일 수 있으므로 꿀을 약품으로 사용해야 한다.
   c. 여과된 꿀은 여과되지 않은 꿀에 비해 그리 효과적이지 않다.
   d. 여드름이나 여드름 상처를 치료하는데 꿀을 사용하는 건 좋은 생각이다.

2. **(c)** 지문 내용과 맞는 것을 고르세요.
   a. 과거에 사람들은 설탕 대신 감미료로만 꿀을 사용했다.
      ▶ 감미료로 꿀을 사용한 내용은 나오지 않는다.
   b. 꿀은 항산화제 덕분에 세상 모든 종류의 박테리아를 다 죽일 수 있다. ▶ 모든 박테리아를 다 죽인다는 말은 나오지는 않았다.
   c. 얼굴에 여드름 흉터가 있다면 꿀 페이셜 마스크가 도움이 될 수 있다.
   d. 꿀 페이셜 마스크는 필요한 재료가 많고 돈도 많이 든다. ▶ 재료가 unfiltered honey 한 가지뿐이다.

3. 각 문장에 알맞은 표현을 고르세요.

   a. **(applying)** 이 연고를 바르기 전에 설명을 잘 읽어야 한다. l direction 설명서, 사용서, ointment 연고
   【해설】로션, 연고 등을 피부에 바를 때 ▶ 동사 apply를 쓴다.

   b. **(seven times a week)** '일주일에 일곱 번 회의를 한다고요?' 그럼 매일 회의를 할 거라는 뜻인가요?
   l have a meeting 회의를 하다
   【해설】'we will have a meeting everyday'라는 표현이 힌트. 매일 회의를 한다는 건 일주일에 일곱 번 회의를 한다는 뜻. three times a month 한 달에 세 번 / seven times a week 일주일에 일곱 번 / 24 hours a day 하루 24시간

   c. **(not the only one)** 메그는 우리 중에 스페인어를 할 줄 아는 유일한 사람이 아니다. 사실 몇 사람이 그녀만큼 스페인어를 할 줄 안다.
   【해설】'언어를 말하다'라고 할 땐 speak 동사만 쓸 수 있다. (speak Spanish, speak Japanese 등) tell Spanish (X), say Spanish (X) /
   주어 + be not the only one who : 주어만 ...한 건 아니다.
   ex) You are not the only one who couldn't pass the test.
   시험에 통과하지 못한 사람이 너뿐만이 아니다.

더 하얀 치아를 갖기 위한 세 가지 팁을 아세요?

① 치과 의사를 통해 치아를 희게 만들 수 있습니다. ② 전문 미백은 치아를 하얗게 만드는 가장 효과적이고 빠른 방법이지만 돈이 많이 듭니다. ③ 하지만, 저렴하게 흰 치아를 가질 수 있는 몇 가지 방법이 있습니다. ④ 여기 더 흰 치아를 위한 세 가지 팁을 소개합니다. ⑤ 자주 양치하고 입을 헹군다. : ⑥ 양치는 치아를 깨끗하고 희게 유지하는 데 필수적입니다. ⑦ 그래서 반드시 하루에 두 번 이상 양치하고 입을 헹구도록 합니다. ⑧ 색깔이 있는 음료 마시는 걸 피한다. : ⑨ 색깔이 있는 음료, 예를 들어 커피, 차, 콜라, 포도주, 그리고 주스 같은 음료는 노랗게 얼룩진 치아를 갖게 합니다. ⑩ 그러니 빨대를 이용하려고 노력하는 건 말할 필요도 없고, 이런 음료를 마신 후에는 반드시 양치를 하세요. ⑪ 금연한다. : ⑫ 전문 미백 치료를 아무리 자주 받는다 해도, 치아가 노랗게 되지 않게 아무리 열심히 노력한다 해도, 계속 담배를 피우면 다시 치아가 노랗게 될 것입니다. ⑬ 담배 연기에는 치아를 변색시키는 타르와 다른 많은 화학 물질이 들어 있습니다. ⑭ 오랫동안 담배를 많이 피운 애연가들의 치아가 노란 정도가 아니라 갈색으로 보이기도 하는 건 이 때문입니다.

문제 정답 및 해설

1. (b) 지문의 제목으로 적당한 것을 고르세요.
   a. 더 흰 치아를 갖는 건 불가능
   b. 더 흰 치아를 위해 당신이 할 수 있는 일
   c. 흡연자의 치아 : 지옥의 치아
   d. 흡연자, 양치 후 의식을 잃은 채 발견되다

2. (b) 흡연자들이 노랗게 변색된 치아를 가질 수밖에 없는 건 _____ 때문이다.
   a. 그들이 모든 치과의사를 싫어하고 검사를 받지 않기
   b. 담배 연기가 치아를 변색시키기
   c. 식사 후 양치를 하거나 입을 헹구지 않기
   d. 그들이 전문 미백을 받을 돈이 없기

3. 각 문장에 알맞은 표현을 고르세요.

   a. (got hurt) 내 무릎이 붓고 멍들었는데 축구공에 부상당했기 때문이다. l swollen 부은 bruised 멍든
   【해설】 get + pp + by : be동사 대신 get을 이용한 수동태 ▶ hurt는 과거, 과거 분사 형태가 동일한 불규칙 동사이다. (hurt – hurt – hurt)

   b. (shopping) 계속 쇼핑을 한다면 나는 네가 곧 파산하리라 확신한다. l shop 쇼핑하다 go[be] broke 파산하다
   【해설】 keep –ing 계속 …하다
   ex) keep studying 계속 공부하다
   　　 keep going 계속 하다(가다)

   c. (not to mention) 나는 그의 좋은 성격과 그의 외모를 좋아하고, 그의 두툼한 지갑은 말할 필요도 없다.
   l character 성격 appearance 외모
   【해설】 as long as …이기만 하면, …인 한 / not to mention …는 말할 것도 없고 / no matter how 얼마나 …한다 해도 ▶ 문맥상 not to mention이 적당하다.

28 러브 핸들을 제거하는 게 왜 어려운지 아세요?

① 러브 핸들은 허리선의 옆구리에 붙은 여분의 지방 축적물을 뜻하는 은어입니다. ② 어쩌다 옆구리의 힘없이 늘어진 부위가 이렇게 사랑스러운 이름을 갖게 되었는지는 모를 일입니다. ③ 이름이 사랑스럽든 아니든 허리 밖으로 불거져 나온 러브 핸들은 전혀 좋아 보이지 않습니다. ④ 많은 이들이 옆구리의 러브 핸들 지방만 빼길 원합니다. ⑤ 하지만, 대부분이 이를 제거하기가 거의 불가능하다고 말합니다. ⑥ 몸 전체의 체형을 관리하지 않고 평평한 복근을 가질 수는 없습니다. ⑦ 그 지방 덩어리들은 보통 질긴 게 아니니까요. ⑧ 이것이 과도한 지방을 연소시키려면 유산소 운동으로 신진대사를 올려야 하는 이유입니다. ⑨ 체육관에 갈 시간이나 돈이 없어도 걱정할 필요 없습니다. ⑩ 집에서 팔 벌려 뛰기나 제자리에서 30분 정도 뛰는 것도 좋은 유산소 운동이 됩니다. ⑪ 물론 기본 운동을 하면서 옆구리에 초점을 맞춘 다른 운동을 해주는 건 러브 핸들을 더 효과적으로 제거하는 데 도움이 됩니다.

문제 정답 및 해설

1. (a) 지문의 제목으로 적당한 것을 고르세요.
   a. 러브 핸들 해결책
   b. 처질 것인가, 늘어질 것인가
   c. 모두를 위한 효과적인 유산소 운동
   d. 러브 핸들 제거 : 불가능한 임무

2. (c) 내용과 맞는 것을 고르세요.
   a. 러브 핸들은 목 주변의 과도한 지방 축적물이다. ▶ 러브 핸들은 목이 아니라 옆구리에 쌓인 지방이다.
   b. 러브 핸들이라는 용어가 사랑스러운 이유는 러브 핸들이 사랑스럽게 보이기 때문이다. ▶ 러브 핸들이라는 말 자체는 사랑스럽지만 러브 핸들은 보기에 좋지 않다.
   c. 납작한 배를 갖고자 노력하기 전에 몸매를 균형 있게 가꾸어야 한다. ▶ 전체적으로 몸매가 균형 있게 유지되어야 특정 부위 관리가 가능하다.
   d. 오직 옆구리에만 초점을 맞춘 운동을 하는 건 러브 핸들을 제거하는 데 효과적이다. ▶ 기본적인 전신 유산소 운동을 하면서 옆구리에 초점을 맞춘 운동을 해야 효과적으로 러브 핸들을 제거할 수 있다.

3. 각 문장에 알맞은 표현을 고르세요.

   a. (flabby) 출산 후, 나는 보기 흉한 처진 배를 갖게 되었다.

   【해설】 flabby 처진, 늘어진 / chubby 귀엽게 통통한 / stubby 뭉툭한, 땅딸막한 ▶ ugly라는 표현이 함께 나오고 있기 때문에 chubby보다는 flabby가 더 적당하고, 뱃살을 표현하는 형용사로 stubby보다 flabby가 더 적당하다.

   b. (do) 어떻게 그리고 언제 운동을 해야 할지 누가 나에게 말씀해주십시오.

   【해설】 '운동을 하다'라는 표현은 do an exercise / do exercises로 쓰고 do 외에 have, make와 같은 동사를 혼용해 쓰지 않는다. 이런 식으로 do 동사만을 취하는 표현으로는 'do a favor 부탁하다, do one's homework 숙제하다, do one's hair 머리 손질하다, do one's best 최선을 다하다' 등이 있다.

   c. (whether) 너는 극장에 갈 것인지 집에서 아이들과 있을 것인지 결정해야 한다. ▎whether A or B : A할 것인지, B할 것인지

   【해설】 weather는 whether와 발음이 비슷하지만, 의미는 전혀 다른 '날씨'라는 뜻이다.

29. 젊어 보이게 만드는 머리카락 색깔이 무엇인지 아세요?

① 머리카락을 금발로 염색하면 실제보다 더 늙어 보일 수 있다는 사실을 아세요? ② 그럴 수 있는데, 이는 더 밝은 색 머리카락이 모든 피부 색조와 언제나 잘 어울리는 건 아니기 때문입니다. ③ 나이가 들면 보통 우리 피부는 노르스름해지고 더 창백해지는데, 이런 이유로 나이는 들지만 늙어 보이고 싶지 않은 사람이 금발을 하는 건 그다지 좋은 생각이 아닙니다. ④ 실제보다 더 젊어 보이기 위해 머리카락을 염색하고 싶다면, 머리카락 색깔과 피부 톤을 맞추면 실제보다 더 늙어 보일 가능성이 높아지므로 진한 갈색, 붉은 갈색, 또는 검정색 염색을 고려해보세요. ⑤ 나이가 들면 일반적으로 피부가 더 창백해지므로, 좀 진한 색깔로 머리카락을 염색하는 게 좋은 선택이라 할 수 있습니다. ⑥ 믿거나 말거나지만, 많은 아시아인들은 나이가 들수록 검정색으로 머리카락을 염색하는데 이들은 실제보다 확실히 더 젊어 보입니다.

문제 정답 및 해설

1. (b) 지문의 제목으로 적당한 것을 고르세요.
   a. 머리카락을 염색하라. 그럼 당신의 머리카락이 죽을 것이다.
   b. 더 젊어 보이거나 더 늙어 보이는 머리카락 색깔
   c. 금발로 염색하는 것을 항상 피하라
   d. 늙는다는 건 창백해진다는 뜻

2. (c) 연로한 분들에게 금발로 염색하는 건 좋은 생각이 아닌데, _____ 때문이다.
   a. 그들 중 아무도 짙은 갈색으로 염색하길 원하지 않기
   b. 창백한 피부를 가진 사람들은 그들 자신을 위해 금발을 해야만 하기
   c. 머리카락과 노르스름한 피부 톤을 맞추면 더 늙어 보이기
   d. 연로한 분들은 젊어 보이는 게 아니라 항상 늙어 보이길 원하기

3. 각 문장에 알맞은 표현을 고르세요.

   a. (dyeing) 머리카락을 보라색으로 염색하다 죽은 남자 얘기 들었니?
   【해설】'dye 염색하다'의 -ing형은 dyeing이다. dying은 'die 죽다'의 -ing형.

   b. (going) 프로젝트가 잘 안 되는 것 같다.
   【해설】things are(aren't) going well with ...가 잘 되다(잘 되지 않다)

   go well 잘 되다, 잘 어울리다 / go wrong 잘 못 되다

   c. (around nineish) 그녀는 아홉 시쯤 분홍색 톤의 드레스를 입고 현장에 나타났다. 정확한 시간은 기억하지 않는다.
   l at the scene 현장에 pinkish 분홍색 비슷한 색깔의 gown 드레스 exact time 정확한 시간
   【해설】색깔 + ish ...와 비슷한 색깔의 – pinkish, reddish, blueish, brownish...
   마찬가지로 시간을 나타내는 숫자 뒤에 -ish를 붙이면 '...시간 쯤의, ...경'의 뜻으로 around와 자주 쓰인다. threeish 3시경 tenish 10시쯤, noonish 정오쯤 ▶ 'I don't remember the exact time'이라는 표현으로 보아 at nine sharp, at one to nine은 정답이 아니다. around nineish 9시경 / at nine sharp 9시 정각에 / at one to nine 9시 1분 전에

   d. (getting) 끊임없이 먹는 사람들은 점점 살이 찌고 거대해지는 경향이 있다. l continuously 끊임없이 tend to ...하는 경향이 있다.
   【해설】be getting + 비교급: 점점 더 ...해지다
   ex) My back is getting better every day.
       내 등이 매일 좋아지고 있다.
       Ever since his wife died, he has been getting weaker by the day.
       아내가 세상을 떠난 이후, 그는 매일 약해지고 있다.
   * by the day 하루하루

30  처진 눈 밑 살을 위한 운동이 있다는 거 아세요?

① 나이가 들면 피부가 느슨해집니다. ② 눈꺼풀도 예외는 아닙니다. ③ 눈 아랫부분이 처지면 주머니 같은 게 눈 밑에 생깁니다. ④ 그래서 이를 처진 눈 밑 살 (눈 밑 주머니)이라고 부르는데, 눈 아래에 형성된 일종의 주머니이기 때문입니다. ⑤ 물론 성형외과 의사가 수술로 처진 눈꺼풀을 올려줄 수 있습니다. ⑥ 하지만, 돈을 내지 않고도 처지지 않은 눈꺼풀을 가질 수 있는 방법이 있습니다. ⑦ 몇 가지 안면 운동이 "눈 밑 살 문제"를 개선하는 데 도움이 될 수 있습니다. ⑧ 1. 검지를 눈 아래 부위에 올립니다. ⑨ 눈썹 주변 피부에 주름을 만들지 않고 손가락으로 아래 눈꺼풀 근육을 올려보세요. ⑩ 그 자세를 1초 유지하고 15-20회 반복합니다. ⑪ 2. 각 손의 가운데 세 손가락을 이용하여 눈 아래 부위를 가볍게 두드립니다. ⑫ 눈 모서리의 바깥쪽에서부터 안쪽으로 두드리는 게 좋고 하루에 3-4회 실시합니다.

문제 정답 및 해설

1. (b) 이 글의 요지를 고르세요.
   a. 늙는다는 것은 헐거운 피부를 갖는다는 뜻이다.
   b. 몇 가지 안면 운동으로 처진 눈 밑 살 문제를 개선할 수 있다.
   c. 운동할 때 검지가 가장 중요하다.
   d. 성형 수술 외에 처진 눈 밑 살을 제거할 방법이 없다.

2. (d) 지문 내용과 맞지 않는 것을 고르세요.
   a. 처진 눈 밑 살은 눈 아래에 형성된다.
   b. 성형 수술로 처진 눈 밑 살을 제거할 수 있지만 비용이 든다.
   c. 눈 밑 부위를 가볍게 두드리는 건 처진 눈 밑 살 문제를 개선시킬 수 있다. ▶ eye bags를 개선할 수 있는 안면 운동 중 두 번째로 소개된 운동이다.
   d. 안면 운동을 할 때 반드시 검지만 사용해야 한다. ▶ 검지만 사용해야 한다는 내용은 나오지 않았고 두 번째로 소개된 운동에서는 가운데 세 손가락(검지, 중지, 약지)을 사용하라고 나온다.

3. 각 문장에 알맞은 표현을 고르세요.

   a. (letting) 그들이 내게 알리지 않고 내 개인 정보를 가져갈 수 있습니까?
   | personal information 개인 정보 let someone know …에게 알리다, 알게 하다
   【해석】without은 전치사이기 때문에 다음에 동사의 -ing형이나 명사(구)가 와야 한다.

   b. (place) 사장님은 신문과 잡지에 광고를 싣기 원하신다.
   【해석】광고를 내다(싣다) : place an ad (advertisement)
   * place 대신 put, list를 쓸 수도 있다.

   c. (to) 여기에서 달까지 걸어갈 수 있습니까, 아니면 자전거를 타야 합니까?
   【해석】from A to B : A에서 B까지
   ex) from Seoul to Pusan 서울에서 부산까지
   from here to there 여기에서 저기까지

Chapter 4. People

31 칼멘의 장수 비결이 초콜릿이라는 거 아세요?

① 잔 루이스 칼멘은 프랑스 아를에서 1875년에 태어나 1997년에 사망했습니다. ② 122살의 나이로 세상을 떠난 겁니다. ③ 더 정확히 말하면 122년 164일을 살았습니다. ④ 칼멘은 1988년과 1995년에 기네스 세계 기록에 올랐습니다. ⑤ 놀랍게도 그녀는 하나밖에 없는 자식과 하나밖에 없는 손주보다 더 오래 살았습니다. ⑥ 그녀는 어린 시절 빈센트 반 고흐를 만났을 정도로 오래 살았습니다. ⑦ 나중에 그녀는 고흐를 '더럽고 옷을 잘 못 입었으며 무뚝뚝한 남자'로 기억했습니다. ⑧ 사람들이 그녀에게 장수 비결을 물었을 때 그녀는 비법이 올리브기름과 초콜릿일지도 모른다고 말했습니다. ⑨ 그녀는 오랜 흡연자였고 알려진 바에 의하면 건강에 지나치게 신경 쓰지도 않았다고 합니다. ⑩ 하지만, 100살 때 자전거를 탈 정도로 꽤 건강했고, 110살 때까지 혼자서 생활할 수 있었습니다. ⑪ 하지만, 아파트에서 요리하다 작은 화재를 낸 이후, 그녀는 양로원으로 이주했습니다. ⑫ 그녀는 음식에 올리브기름을 많이 사용했으며 피부에 올리브기름을 발랐다고 합니다. ⑬ 또 매주 1kg 정도의 초콜릿을 먹었다고 합니다.

문제 정답 및 해설

1. (a) 이 글의 요지를 고르세요.
   a. 칼멘의 장수 비결은 초콜릿과 올리브 오일이다.
   b. 칼멘은 자전거를 탄 덕분에 손주보다 더 오래 살 수 있었다.
   c. 고흐를 만난 후 칼멘은 오래 살기로 결심했다.
   d. 올리브 오일을 피부에 문지르는 게 장수 비결이다.

2. (b) 칼멘이 고흐를 만났을 때, _____.
   a. 고흐가 그녀보다 나이가 많아서 그를 부러워했다
   b. 고흐는 깔끔하거나 말쑥한 남자가 아니었다
   c. 그녀는 122살이었다
   d. 그녀는 자기 초콜릿을 그에게 나눠주고 싶지 않았다

3. 각 문장에 알맞은 표현을 고르세요.

   a. (about) 내 쌍둥이 남동생들은 5살 때부터 야구에 정신을 팔고 산다.
   【해설】crazy는 형용사로 '1. 미친, 2. 미친 듯 화가 난 3. …에 열광하는'의 뜻이 있다.
   전치사 about과 함께 쓰이면 'be crazy about …를 대단히 좋아하다(= be mad about), …에 열광하다'

   b. (disagreeable) 그는 항상 무례하고, 공격적이고 퉁명스럽기 때문에 그를 불쾌한 사람이라 불러도 된다.
   It's safe to say that …라고 말해도 된다
   【해설】'rude 무례한, offensive 공격적인, 모욕적인, unamiable 퉁명스러운' 등 표현이 이어진 것으로 보아 '지저분한'이라는 뜻의 dirty, messy보다는 disagreeable(불쾌한)이 더 적당하다.

   c. (as) 그의 동료들은 그를 착하고 친절한 사람, 훌륭한 프로그래머로 기억했다.
   【해설】recall은 명사로 '기억, 회수, 소환', 동사로는 '기억해내다, 생각나게 하다'의 뜻이 있다. recall A as B : A를 B로 기억, 회상하다 ▶ 전치사 as가 와야 한다.

   d. (ride) 내가 타고 싶은 건 아주 거대한 공룡이지만 내가 가진 건 낡은 자전거뿐이다.
   【해설】동물, 자동차, 자전거 등을 탈 때에는 ride : ride a horse 말 타다, ride a bicycle 자전거 타다 ride a subway 지하철 타다 ride a bus 버스 타다
   배, 비행기를 탈 때에는 board : board a plane 비행기를 타다 board a cruise ship 여객선을 타다

32. 구강 수술 후 카렌 버틀러에게 어떤 일이 생겼는지 아세요?

① 일평생 오리건 주민으로 살아온 56세의 미국인 여성 카렌 버틀러는 구강 수술 후 아일랜드 억양이 생겼습니다. ② 그녀는 외국에 나간 적도 없고, 아일랜드 억양을 배운 적도, 배우려고 시도한 적도 없습니다. ③ 하지만, 2009년 진정제에서 깨어났을 때 그녀는 아일랜드 억양으로 말하기 시작했습니다. ④ 사실 그녀의 억양은 아일랜드에 영국식, 스코틀랜드식, 그리고 호주식이 섞여 있습니다. ⑤ 어쨌든 그녀가 말하는 방식이 미국식이 아닌 건 확실합니다. ⑥ 의사들은 그녀가 희귀한 경우인 외국인 억양 증후군(FAS)을 앓을지도 모른다고 추측하고 있습니다. ⑦ '급하게 새로 만들어 낸 용어'처럼 들릴지도 모르겠는데, 매우 희귀하긴 하지만 이런 종류의 언어 장애가 정말 존재합니다. ⑧ FAS는 일반적으로 뇌졸중 또는 뇌출혈 등 일종의 뇌 손상으로 야기됩니다. ⑨ FAS의 다른 예들도 찾을 수 있습니다. ⑩ 한 노르웨이인 여성 역시 2차 세계대전 중 폭탄 파편에 맞은 후 외국인 억양 증후군이 생겼습니다. ⑪ 그녀가 정신을 차렸을 때 그녀는 독일식 억양으로 말했다고 합니다. ⑫ 미국인 남성 역시 뇌졸중을 앓은 후 스칸디나비아식 억양으로 말하기 시작했습니다. ⑬ 하지만, 그의 억양은 몇 달 후 없어졌습니다.

문제 정답 및 해설

1. **(c)** 이 글의 요지를 고르세요.
   a. FAS는 한 노르웨이 여성에 의해 만들어진 완전히 새로운 용어이다.
   b. 전 세계에 FAS를 앓는 사람들이 수천 명이다.
   c. 카렌 버틀러는 구강 수술 후 외국어 억양이 생겼다.
   d. 무언가에 맞으면 독일식 억양으로 말하게 될 것이다.

2. **(a)** 지문 내용과 맞는 것을 고르세요.
   a. 카렌 버틀러는 오리건에서 태어난 이래 계속 오리건에서 살고 있다. ▶ a lifelong resident of Oregon이라는 표현에서 오리건 태생으로 계속 오리건에 살고 있음을 알 수 있다.
   b. 항상 폭탄 파편에 의해서 발생된다. ▶ FAS는 뇌 손상에 의해 야기된다.
   c. 알려진 바에 의하면 수많은 북미인들이 FAS를 앓고 있다. ▶ 매우 희귀한 질병으로 FAS 환자는 많지 않다.
   d. 버틀러 여사는 수년간의 훈련으로 아일랜드 억양을 갖게 되었다. ▶ 아일랜드 억양을 시도하거나 배우려 한 적이 없다고 나온다.

3. 각 문장에 알맞은 표현을 고르세요.

   a. **(abroad)** 나는 국내와 해외 모두에서 유명해지기로 계획을 세웠다.
   【해설】'국내외에서'란 표현은 'at home and abroad'를 쓴다. 이때 home은 '가정, 집'이 아니라 '국내'라는 뜻, abroad는 부사로 '해외에(서), 해외로'라는 뜻이다.
   ex) go abroad 해외로 나가다 / study abroad 외국에서 공부하다

   b. **(stroke)** 뇌졸중은 의학적 응급상황이기 때문에 대단히 빨리 행동해야 한다.
   ┃ with great haste 대단히 서둘러, 빨리 medical 의학적인 emergency 응급상황
   【해설】strike v. 때리다, 치다 / stork n. 황새 / stroke n. 뇌졸중
   ▶ 문맥상 stroke가 적당하다. 동사 strike의 과거형은 struck

   c. **(being shot)** 군인은 적의 총에 맞은 후 피가 나기 시작했다.
   【해설】군인이 총에 맞은 것, 즉 수동의 의미이다. 원래는 after the soldier was shot by his enemy에서 after절의 주어가 주절의 주어 the soldier와 일치해서 생략되고, 수동의 의미이기 때문에 was shot이 being shot으로 바뀐 것이다. 또한 shoot의 과거형은 shooted가 아닌 shot이다. (shoot-shot-shot)

33 어떻게 이 러시아 소녀들이 엉뚱한 부모와 살게 되었는지 아세요?

① 2011년, 러시아인 십대 소녀 두 명인 아이리나와 아냐, 그리고 가족들은 두 소녀들이 우연히 태어날 때 바뀌었다는 걸 알고 깜짝 놀랐는데, 이 말은 각 소녀의 부모가 진짜 부모가 아니라는 뜻입니다. ② 이들의 어머니들은 1999년 같은 병원에서 15분 간격으로 출산했습니다. ③ 태어난 후 두 아기 딸들은 병원 직원에 의해 엉뚱한 이름표를 받았던 것입니다. ④ 이 모든 일은 아이리나의 아버지가 딸이 자기 딸이 아닐 수도 있다고 생각하면서 시작되었는데 딸이 아버지와 전혀 닮지 않았기 때문이었습니다. ⑤ DNA 테스트 결과 아이리나의 부모 중 누구도 아이리나의 친부모가 아니라고 나왔습니다. ⑥ 지방 경찰의 도움으로 아이리나의 어머니는 친딸을 찾기 시작했는데 그 딸은 불과 몇 마일 거리에 살고 있었습니다. ⑦ 두 소녀는 친부모를 만나 기뻤지만, 그들이 함께 성장했던 가족을 떠나길 원치 않았습니다. ⑧ 그래서 이 두 가족에게 변한 건 없었습니다. ⑨ 하지만, 병원은 엄청난 변화를 맞이해야 했는데 두 가족이 병원을 상대로 16만 달러의 손해배상을 청구하기로 결정했기 때문입니다. ⑩ 특히 그 병원에게 있어서 진실만큼 고통스러운 것은 없는 것 같습니다.

문제 정답 및 해설

1. (d) 이 글의 요지를 고르세요.
   a. 러시아 병원은 모두 끔찍하기 때문에 러시아에서 출산하지 마라.
   b. 친부모를 찾는 건 가장 중요하다.
   c. DNA 테스트는 정확해야 했지만 그렇지 않았다.
   d. 출생 시 바뀐 두 러시아 소녀가 친부모를 찾았다.

2. (a) 아이리나와 아냐에게 일어났던 사건은 _____.
   a. 병원 직원들의 단순한 실수였다
   b. 내전의 주요 원인이 되었다
   c. 너무 비극적이어서 아이리나의 부모는 이혼할 수밖에 없었다
   d. 두 가족을 파산하게 만들었다.

3. 각 문장에 알맞은 표현을 고르세요.

   a. (demands) 성질 급하기로 소문난 내 상사는 즉각적이고 명확한 설명을 요구했다.
   I short-tempered 성질이 급한, 성격이 불같은 immediate 즉각적인 explanation 설명

   【해설】yell v. 크게 소리치다 / demand v. 요구하다 / say v. 말하다 ▶ 문맥상 demand가 적당하다 * demand an explanation 설명·해명을 요구하다

   b. (damages) 지불해야 할 손해배상액이 있다면, 내 차를 팔아야 한다.
   【해설】If 주어 과거 동사 (또는 were), 주어 + could/would/should + 동사원형 ▶ 가정법 과거 : 현재 사실의 반대
   '손해배상액'이라는 뜻의 damages는 항상 복수형으로 쓴다.

   c. (studies) 공부할 시간이 많은데도 그들 중 아무도 시험을 통과하기 위해 열심히 공부하지 않는다.
   【해설】neither of 복수명사 + 단수동사: 양쪽 (둘) 모두 …아니다
   ex) Neither of us is hungry. 우리 중 배고픈 사람은 없다.

조슬린 와일든스타인이 왜 유명한지 아세요?

① 그녀는 여왕이라서 좀 유명합니다. ② 엘리자베스 여왕 같은 일반적인 여왕이 아닙니다. ③ 그녀는 성형수술의 여왕입니다. ④ 또 그냥 일반적인 성형수술의 여왕이 아니라, 그녀는 최악의 성형수술 악몽의 여왕입니다! ⑤ 이상하게도 그녀는 성형수술로 미녀에서 야수로 바뀌었습니다. ⑥ 그 반대가 일반적인데도 말입니다. ⑦ 더 이상한 건 그녀가 괴물 같은 얼굴이 된 게 사고가 아니라는 겁니다. ⑧ 그건 그녀의 선택이었습니다. ⑨ 알려진 바에 의하면 그녀는 수년간 고양이처럼 보이기 위한 수술에 엄청난 금액의 돈을 썼다고 합니다. ⑩ 왜냐고요? ⑪ 그녀의 돈 많은 남편이 애완 고양이들을 아주 좋아했고 그녀는 그의 사랑을 잃고 싶지 않았기 때문이었습니다. ⑫ 그래서 그녀는 고양이처럼 보이도록 얼굴을 바꾸기로 결심했습니다. ⑬ 그리고 그렇게 했습니다. ⑭ 그런데도 남편은 그녀와 이혼했습니다. ⑮ 심지어 이혼 이후에도 그녀는 성형수술 받는 걸 멈출 수 없었습니다. ⑯ 현재 60살이 넘었는데 여전히 고양이처럼 보이도록 얼굴을 바꾸고 있습니다. ⑰ 물론 갈수록 더 끔찍해지고 있습니다. ⑱ 어쨌든 그녀의 남편이 토끼나 코끼리가 아닌 고양이를 좋아했다는 게 다행입니다!

문제 정답 및 해설

1. (a) 지문의 제목으로 적당한 것을 고르세요.
   a. 와일든스타인 : 고양이처럼 보이기 위해 야수로 변하다
   b. 성형수술의 여왕 : 누가 그녀를 싫어하겠는가?
   c. 완전 변신 : 괴물에서 여신으로
   d. 고양이를 극도로 사랑하는 사람, 고양이가 되다

2. (d) 지문 내용과 맞지 않는 것을 고르세요.
   a. 와일든스타인은 최악의 성형수술 악몽으로 유명하다.
   b. 와일든스타인은 엄청난 돈을 성형수술에 썼다고 한다.
   c. 와일든스타인은 성형수술에 심각하게 중독된 것 같다.
   d. 와일든스타인은 남편과 애완 고양이들의 사랑을 받고 있다.

3. 각 문장에 알맞은 표현을 고르세요.

   a. (worse and worse) 아프리카의 빈곤 문제가 갈수록 심각해지고 있으며 점점 더 많은 사람들이 굶어 죽어 간다.
   | poverty 가난 starve 굶어 죽다

   【해설】better and better 점점 좋아지는 / worse and worse 점점 더 나빠지는 / worse to better 나빠지다가 좋아지는 ▶ 이후 이어지는 내용을 고려할 때 is getting worse and worse가 적당하다.

   b. (the other) 버터가 마가린보다 더 건강에 좋다고? 나는 그 반대인 줄 알았는데.
   【해설】the other way around 반대의, 거꾸로의

   c. (lose) 내가 손해 볼 것도 없으니 그가 내 개를 훈련시키도록 허락해야 할 것 같아.
   【해설】nothing to lose 잃어버릴 것 없는, 손해 볼 것 없는
   loose a. 헐거운, 풀린 / lose v. 잃다 / lost v. lose의 과거형, a. 잃어버린

35 할리우드 스타들은 어떻게 출산하는지 아세요?

① 할리우드 스타들은 너무 부자라서 일반인들처럼 출산할 수 없습니다. ② 평범하지 않은 방식으로 출산한 돈 많은 할리우드의 부부 두 쌍을 소개합니다. ③ 너무 돈이 많은 첫 번째 할리우드 스타 커플은 비욘세 놀즈와 남편 제이지입니다. ④ 이들은 무려 천삼백만 달러를 들여 맨해튼의 레녹스 힐 병원의 한 층 전체를 빌렸습니다. ⑤ 병원 직원들은 병원에서 일하는 동안 휴대 전화를 사용할 수 없었는데, 이는 허락 없이 그들의 소중한 딸 아기의 사진을 찍을 수 있기 때문입니다. ⑥ 물론 그 층의 보안 카메라 모두 이 커플의 사생활 보호를 위해 가려졌고, 건물 구석구석마다 수많은 개인 경호원들이 보초 선 건 말할 것도 없습니다. ⑦ 병원 한 층을 다 빌린 것도 이 커플에 비하면 아무것도 아닙니다. ⑧ 2006년 브란젤리나(브래드 피트와 안젤리나 졸리 커플을 가리키는 표현-주) 커플은 딸을 낳기 위해 나미비아로 날아갔습니다. ⑨ 이 슈퍼스타 커플과 예쁘지 않을 수 없는 이들의 아기는 나미비아 '정부'의 보호를 받았습니다. ⑩ 정부는 이들의 개인 경호원들에게 이들의 사생활을 침해하려는 사람에게 주먹을 날리거나 체포할 수 있는 권한을 주었습니다. ⑪ 그리고 적당한 허가증이 없는 언론인은 아예 입국을 금지했습니다. ⑫ 물론 졸리와 피트는 나미비아에 머무는 동안 거액의 기부를 포함해 상당한 돈을 썼습니다.

문제 정답 및 해설

1. (c) 이 글의 요지를 고르세요.
   a. 브란젤리나 커플은 가장 부유하고 이상한 커플이다.
   b. 비욘세가 제이지와 결혼한 건 그가 맨해튼에 병원을 소유했기 때문이었다.
   c. 어떤 할리우드 스타들은 사생활 보호에 관해서라면 돈을 아끼지 않는다.
   d. 졸리와 피트는 나미비아 정부에 휴대폰 사용을 금지하도록 요구했다.

2. (a) 사생활 보호를 위해 브란젤리나 커플은 _____.
   a. 나미비아로 날아가 거기서 딸을 출산했다
   b. 그들의 딸을 때리려는 사람은 누구든 체포하려 했다
   c. 나미비아 정부를 협박했다
   d. 나미비아의 병원 한 층을 전부 임대했다

3. 각 문장에 알맞은 표현을 고르세요.

   a. (not to mention) 브라이언은 대수학은 말할 것도 없고 연산도 배우지 않았다.
   ▎arithmetic 산수 연산 algebra 대수학

   【해설】 not to mention + 명사(구), not to mention (the fact) that 주어 + 동사 ▶ algebra라는 명사가 이어지기 때문에 not to mention that은 올 수 없다.

   b. (whopping) 코리는 또 다른 엄청난 거짓말을 했다는 게 걸렸다. 그녀는 못 말리는 거짓말쟁이이다.
   ▎be caught in a lie 거짓말하다 걸리다 a born liar 타고난 거짓말쟁이
   【해설】 spacious 넓은 / whopping 굉장한, 엄청난, 무려 / extensive 광범위한 ▶ 의미상 whopping이 가장 적당하다. 형용사 whopping 외에 big lies, humongous lies 등으로도 '엄청난 거짓말'이라는 의미를 표현할 수도 있다.

   c. (took) 사진사는 희생자들의 사진을 찍어 신문에 사진을 실었다.
   【해설】 '사진 찍다'는 take a picture 또는 take pictures / '...를 신문에 싣다'는 put something in the newspaper

36 넬슨 만델라, 에드거 앨런 포, 레오 톨스토이의 공통점이 무엇인지 아세요?

① 이들 외에도, 루이 암스트롱(재즈 음악가, 트럼펫 연주가), 요한 세바스찬 바흐(독일 작곡가), 마릴린 먼로(배우), 베이브 루스(야구 선수) 역시 이들과 공통점을 갖고 있습니다. ② 엄청난 업적을 이룬 엄청난 이 사람들 모두 고아였습니다. ③ 이들은 어렸을 때 어려운 시절을 보냈을 게 분명하지만, 역사에 이름을 남기는 데 있어서 고아라는 건 이들에게 아무 문제가 되지 않았습니다. ④ 어떤 사람들은 고아에 관해 강한 편견을 가지고 있습니다. ⑤ 이들은 고아들이 정서적, 경제적으로 잘못될 가능성이 매우 높기 때문에 범죄자처럼 나쁜 사람 또는 문제를 가진 사람이 되는 경향이 있다고 믿습니다. ⑥ 고아들 중 많은 경우 부모의 적절한 보살핌과 보호, 지도를 받지 못하기 때문에 사회에서 살아가기가 어려운 게 사실입니다. ⑦ 하지만, 그렇다고 모든 고아가 나쁜 사람이나 범죄자가 될 수밖에 없다는 뜻은 아닙니다. ⑧ 어떤 고아들은 아주 좋은 환경에서 양부모의 양육을 받고 자란 사람보다 더 훌륭하게 자라기도 합니다.

문제 정답 및 해설

1. (c) 지문의 제목으로 적당한 것을 고르세요.
   a. 고아들이 위대한 인물로 역사에 이름을 남기는 건 불가능하다.
   b. 모든 고아들은 위대한 인물이 되기로 되어 있고 다들 그렇게 된다. be supposed to 동사 : …하기로 되어 있다
   c. 역사에 남는 위대한 인물이 된 많은 고아들이 있다. turn out (to be) 명사/형용사 : …로 판명되다. (결과가) …이 되다
   d. 고아원들을 위한 경제적인 지원은 굉장히 중요하다.

2. (b) 지문 내용과 맞지 않는 것을 고르세요.
   a. 고아지만 위대한 업적을 이룬 위인들이 많다.
   b. 고아들이란 부유한 부모나 친척이 없는 어린이들이다.
      ▶ 지문에는 고아의 정의에 대해 나오지 않았다.
   c. 모든 고아들이 다 나쁜 범죄자들이 되는 건 아니다.
   d. 고아들이 역사에 이름을 남기는 건 가능하다.

3. 각 문장에 알맞은 표현을 고르세요.

   a. (likely) 어떤 사람들은 그리스가 경제 위기 때문에 유로를 떠날 가능성이 높다고 주장한다.
   ▎due to …때문에 financial crisis 경제 위기

【해설】be likely to …할 가능성이 높다 ▶ likely를 더욱 강조하는 부사 highly와 함께 쓰려면 be highly likely to …할 가능성이 매우 높다

b. (against) 비키는 인종차별주의자라서 아프리카계 미국인은 물론 아시아인에 대한 편견을 갖고 있다.
▎racist 인종차별주의자 bias 편견 African-American 아프리카계 미국인, 흑인
【해설】have a bias against …에 대해 비우호적인 (반하는) 편견을 가지다
have a bias towards …에 대해 (일반적인) 편견을 가지다

c. (are) 나랑 내 사촌은 네가 언제 떠나도 상관없다.
【해설】as far as ( ) be concerned …에 관한한 ▶ be 동사는 ( )에 맞춘다. 문제의 경우 'me and my cousin' 두 명이기 때문에 단수 동사 is나 was가 올 수 없고 시제가 현재이기 때문에 과거 was가 올 수 없다.

37 먹기 대회 우승자의 몸무게가 얼마인지 아세요?

① 블랙 위도우로 알려진 소냐 토마스(한국 태생의 미국인으로 한국 이름은 이선경)는 먹기 대회 세계 챔피언입니다. ② 그녀는 2003년부터 먹기 대회에서 무려 37번이나 우승했습니다. ③ 그녀는 참여한 거의 모든 먹기 대회에서 믿기 힘든 세계 기록을 달성했습니다. ④ 눈이 튀어나올 만하고 입에 군침이 도는 그녀의 기록은 다음과 같습니다. ⑤ 2004년 9분 동안 11파운드의 치즈 케이크, ⑥ 2011년 12분 동안 닭 날개 183개, ⑦ 2003년 6분 40초 동안 삶은 달걀 65개, ⑧ 2005년 12분 동안 랍스터 44개 고기 무게로 총 11.4파운드, ⑨ 2010년 8분 동안 문파이 38개, ⑩ 2005년 10분 동안 굴 552개, ⑪ 2004년 15분 동안 초대형 치즈 피자 6 1/2조각, ⑫ 2009년 10분 동안 핫도그와 번즈 41개, ⑬ 2011년 12분 동안 버팔로 윙 183조각. ⑭ 다들 눈치챘겠지만, 그녀는 한 번도 식성이 까다로운 적이 없습니다. ⑮ 문 파이, 타코, 조개, 베이크드 빈즈, 어떤 것을 말하든 그녀는 먹을 수 있습니다. ⑯ 여기서 놀라운 건 그녀의 사이즈입니다. ⑰ 그녀는 152cm 키에 체중은 47kg입니다.

문제 정답 및 해설

1. (b) 지문의 제목으로 적당한 것을 고르세요.
   a. 먹기 대회 우승자가 되기 위한 놀라운 비밀
   b. 먹기 대회 우승자의 믿을 수 없는 체형
   c. 소냐 토마스, 최악의 먹기 대회 우승자
   d. 왜 그녀는 검은 과부라 불리는가

2. (c) 2004년에 소냐 토마스는 _____ 먹었다.
   a. 삶은 달걀과 바다 가재를
   b. 버팔로 윙과 BBQ 치킨 윙을
   c. 치즈 피자와 치즈케이크를
   d. 타코, 조개, 베이크드 빈즈를

3. 각 문장에 알맞은 표현을 고르세요.

   a. (participate in) 나는 달리기 경주에 참가할 계획이었지만 부상 때문에 포기했다.
   【해설】 participate in …에 참가하다(= take part in) participate는 전치사 in과 함께 쓰인다. (take part 역시 in과 함께 쓰여 '참가하다'의 의미)

   b. (picky eater) 나는 '까다롭게 먹는 사람이 되지 않는 법'이라는 제목의 책을 사야만 하는데, 내 딸이 초콜릿을 제외하고 모든 게 다 맛이 없다고 말하기 때문이다.
   | yucky 지독히 맛없는, 역겨운
   【해설】 heavy eater 대식가 / picky eater 까다롭게 먹는 사람 / light eater 소식가 ▶ 문맥상 picky eater가 적당하다.

   c. (three and a half) 마을의 거의 모든 우물이 말라가고 있는데 3년 반 동안 비가 오지 않고 있기 때문이다.
   【해설】 a half : 반, 1/2 ▶ '…의 반'이라는 의미로 half 앞에 'a'가 반드시 들어가야 한다.

38. 우체부 슈발이 어떻게 '발레 이데알'을 건축했는지 아세요?

① 페르디낭 슈발 (1836-1924)은 오뜨리브에 '발레 이데알'(이상의 궁전)을 건축한 프랑스인 우체부인데, 이는 파리의 문화적 지형물이며 특별한 건축물로 공식적인 보호를 받고 있습니다. ② 슈발은 가난하고 교육을 받지 못한 우체부였습니다. ③ 그는 그저 편지를 배달할 뿐이었습니다. ④ 그러나 거리에서 돌에 발이 걸린 이후, 그의 인생은 바뀌기 시작했습니다. ⑤ 그는 그 돌의 모양이 그에게 영감을 주었다고 말했습니다. ⑥ 다음 날, 그는 특별한 돌을 주웠던 장소에 더 많이 줍기 위해 돌아가 보았습니다. ⑦ 이후 슈발은 33년 동안 돌을 모아 집으로 가져갔습니다. ⑧ 바로 그 돌들이 그의 놀라운 '이상의 궁전' 건축 재료가 되었습니다. ⑨ 처음에는 주머니에 돌을 넣어 나르다가 나중에는 바구니와 손수레를 이용했습니다. ⑩ 그가 자신만의 꿈의 궁전을 완공하는 데 33년이 걸렸습니다. ⑪ 그가 혼자서 맨손으로 이루어낸 것입니다. ⑫ 건축을 끝낸 후 일 년 뒤에 슈발이 사망했습니다. ⑬ 그는 원하던 대로 자신의 궁전에 묻혔습니다. ⑭ 현재 이곳은 대중에 공개되고 있는데, 전 세계의 방문객들은 이 놀라운 건축물이 한 노인에 의해 돌로 지어졌다는 사실에 말을 잇지 못합니다.

문제 정답 및 해설

1. (a) 이 글의 요지를 고르세요.
   a. 놀랍게도 슈발은 맨손으로 혼자서 이상의 궁전을 건축했다.
   b. 슈발은 프랑스에서 가장 저명한 건축가였다.
   c. 슈발은 돌멩이가 훌륭한 건축자재가 될 수 있음을 증명하고자 했다.
   d. 슈발은 맨손으로 아주 많은 돌멩이들을 옮겨서 방문객들의 말문이 막히게 했다.

2. (d) 지문 내용과 맞는 것을 고르세요.
   a. 슈발은 하루 종일 편지를 배달해야 해서 아무것도 할 수 없었다. ▶ 우체부로 일하면서 33년간 돌을 주워 이상의 궁전을 지었다.
   b. 슈발이 이상의 궁전을 지을 수 있었던 건 그가 전문 건축가였기 때문이다. ▶ 그는 건축가가 아닌 우체부였고 교육을 받지 못한 사람이라고 나온다.
   c. 슈발은 수집을 위해 수 톤의 돌멩이를 모았다. ▶ 단순히 수집을 위해 모은 게 아니라 이상의 궁전을 건축하기 위해 모은 것이다.
   d. 슈발이 살아 있을 때 그는 자신의 꿈의 궁전에 묻히기를 원했다.

3. 각 문장에 알맞은 표현을 고르세요.

a. (speechless) 네 그림에 내 말문이 막혔다. 정말 멋지다.
【해설】talkative 수다스러운 / speechless (놀람, 공포, 기쁨, 감동, 분노 등의 감정으로) 말문이 막힌 / unspeakable (무언가 너무 끔찍하거나 좋지 않아서) 말할 수도 없는 ▶ 이어지는 문장에서 fantastic이라고 했기 때문에 문맥상 speechless가 적당하다.
cf. leave someone speechless …의 말문이 막히게 만들다 become speechless 말문이 막히다 make someone speechless 누군가를 말문이 막히게 만들다

b. (who) 이 책들은 책을 살 여력이 없는 가난한 어린이들을 위한 것이다.
l underprivileged 사회, 경제적으로 혜택을 받지 못하는 can't afford to 동사원형: …할 경제적인 능력이 없다, …할 돈이 없다
【해설】underprivileged children 사람을 받는 관계대명사 ▶ who

c. (it took me a while) 기타 치는 법을 배우는데 시간이 꽤 걸렸다.
【해설】시간이 얼마 걸리다 ▶ it takes (took) 사람 + 걸린 시간 + to 동사
ex) It took him three hours to solve this problem.
    그가 이 문제를 푸는 데 3시간이 걸렸다.
* spent 동사를 쓰려면 I spent some time learning… 으로 써야 한다. (spend + ing)

39 랄리가 왜 환생한 신으로 숭배받았는지 아세요?

① 랄리는 2008년 3월 북부 인도에서 태어났습니다. ② 소녀가 태어났을 때 사람들이 랄리를 반은 인간, 반은 코끼리인 힌두신 가네쉬가 환생했다고 믿었습니다. ③ 동네 사람들뿐 아니라 전 세계의 사람들이 랄리를 만나러 작은 마을로 왔습니다. ④ 대부분의 사람들은 랄리의 축복을 받고자 부모에게 돈을 주었습니다. ⑤ 그건 랄리의 부모에게 큰 도움이 되었는데, 이유인즉 랄리의 젊은 부모는 그 마을의 다른 이웃들처럼 하루에 2달러도 못 벌기 때문입니다. ⑥ 이 아기의 무엇이 그렇게 특별했을까요? ⑦ 랄리는 얼굴이 두 개로 태어났습니다. ⑧ 랄리는 다른 아기들처럼 하나의 몸과 하나의 머리를 갖고 있지만, 다른 아기들과는 달리 하나의 머리에 얼굴이 두 개입니다. ⑨ 그래서 눈이 네 개, 코가 두 개, 입도 두 개입니다. ⑩ 랄리의 젊은 부모는 병원이 랄리의 머리를 무료로 CT 스캔 혹은 MRI를 찍어주겠다는 데 동의하지 않았습니다. ⑪ 랄리의 아빠는 "나는 신이 주신 건 무엇이든 그대로 받아들이겠습니다," 라고 말했습니다. ⑫ 두 얼굴을 가진 아기는 매우 희귀하지만 랄리만이 두 얼굴을 가진 아기는 아닙니다. ⑬ 2011년 파키스탄에서도 두 얼굴을 가진 아기가 태어났습니다.

문제 정답 및 해설

1. (c) 이 글의 요지를 고르세요.
   a. 랄리의 부모는 랄리의 병원비를 내지 않아 체포되어야 한다.
   b. 가네쉬라는 코끼리의 신은 랄리처럼 두 개의 얼굴을 가졌다.
   c. 얼굴이 둘인 아기가 숭배 받았는데, 사람들이 아기를 신으로 믿었기 때문이다.
   d. 랄리를 제외하고 얼굴이 두 개인 아기는 없다.

2. (b) 랄리가 동네에서 가장 특별한 아기로 취급받은 이유는 _____ 때문이다.
   a. 다른 아기들과는 달리 돈을 벌 수 있었기
   b. 외모가 매우 남달랐기
   c. 공짜 CT 촬영을 받을 수 있었기
   d. 정말로 가네쉬 신의 환생이었기

3. 각 문장에 알맞은 표현을 고르세요.

   a. (less than) 어떻게 하면 한 시간 이내에 집을 청소할 수 있는가?
   【해설】 further than (일반적으로) 거리를 비교할 때 (...보다 더 멀리) / fewer than 셀 수 있는 명사를 비교할 때 (...보다 더 적은) ▶ 시간은 셀 수 없는 명사로 few 또는 fewer와 함께 쓰이지 않는다.

   less than an hour = within an hour 한 시간 이내에, 한 시간이 걸리지 않게 (opp. more than an hour 한 시간 이상)
   ex) Unlike my expectation, his presentation took more than an hour. 내 예상과는 달리 그의 발표는 한 시간 이상 걸렸다.

   b. (rare) 그의 방문이 나를 놀라게 했던 건, 그의 방문은 드문 일이기 때문이다.
   ▌ mere 단지, 그저 rare 드문, 희귀해서 진귀한 scare 겁주다
   【해설】 문맥상 rare가 가장 적당하다. rare와 혼동하기 쉬운 단어로 scarce가 있다. rare와 scarce 모두 '드문'의 뜻이지만, rare에 비해 scarce는 '부족해서 드문'이라는 어감이 있다. ex) rare occasions 드문 일 rare disease 희귀병 scarce resources 많지 않은 자원

   c. (because) 메간이 빌과 헤어진 건 세상에는 빌 말고도 남자는 많다고 생각했기 때문이었다.
   ▌ break up with ...와 헤어지다 not the only pebble on the beach 해변 가의 유일한 돌이 아니다, 즉 세상에 많다
   【해설】 "메간이 빌과 헤어졌다." _____ "빌 말고도 세상에 남자는 많다고 생각하다."
   이 두 문장을 이어주는 적절한 접속사는 because(인과관계)이다. (although + 절 ...임에도 불구하고, despite + ing, 명사 ...임에도 불구하고)

복권 당첨자 빌리 밥 하렐이 어떻게 사망했는지 아세요?

① 불행히도 1997년 3천1백만 달러가 걸린 텍사스 로또의 유일한 당첨 복권을 소유했던 빌리 밥 하렐 주니어는 1999년 자살했습니다. ② 1997년, 하렐이 돈을 잘 벌지 못해 하렐과 그의 가족은 힘들게 생활했습니다. ③ 그래서 그는 대박의 꿈을 안고 복권을 구매했습니다. ④ 그는 정말 대박을 터트렸고 덕분에 백만장자가 되었습니다. ⑤ 그의 힘든 시절은 공식적으로 끝난 것입니다. ⑥ 그는 너무 부자라 큰 집들, 목장, 멋진 자동차 등 많은 것을 사들였습니다. ⑦ 그리고 상당한 돈을 기부했습니다. ⑧ 경제적인 도움이 필요한 사람에게는 현금을 든 하렐이 있었습니다. ⑨ 그는 돈을 쓰고 빌려주는데 시간을 보냈습니다. ⑩ 그러다 그의 소비 습관은 점점 통제 불능이 되어갔습니다. ⑪ 가족, 친구, 심지어 모르는 사람들도 그를 이용했고, 하릴은 이들에게 갈취당하는 걸 즐기기도 했습니다. ⑫ 얼마 지나지 않아 그의 결혼 생활에 금이 가기 시작했고 그의 통장도 마르기 시작했습니다. ⑬ 대박을 터트린 지 20개월 후, 하렐은 자기 침실에서 권총으로 자살했습니다. ⑭ 그가 사망한 후 그의 가족들은 남은 그의 돈을 두고 싸웠습니다. ⑮ 하지만, 그의 통장에 남은 돈은 세금 내기에도 부족했습니다.

문제 정답 및 해설

1. (c) 지문의 제목으로 적당한 것을 고르세요.
   a. 어떻게 복권에 당첨되어 인생을 바꿀 것인가
   b. 빌리 밥 하렐, 선한 사마리아인
   c. 복권 당첨자의 비극적 종말
   d. 복권 당첨자가 되기 위한 20가지 힌트

2. (b) 지문 내용과 맞지 않는 것을 고르세요.
   a. 빌리 밥 하렐 주니어는 복권에 당첨된 지 2년 후에 자살했다.
   b. 빌리가 가난한데도 불구하고 모르는 사람들이 빌리를 이용해 먹으려 했다. ▶ 복권 당첨으로 부자가 되었을 때 모르는 사람까지 빌리를 악용하려 들었다.
   c. 빌리가 사망했을 때 그의 돈은 거의 없어진 상태였다.
   d. 복권 덕분에 빌리는 가난뱅이에서 부자가 되었다. (go from rags to riches 거지에서 부자가 되다)

3. 각 문장에 알맞은 표현을 고르세요.

   a. (at solving) 나는 남의 문제를 해결하는 건 꽤 잘하는데 내 문제를 해결하는 건 썩 잘하지 못한다. 왜 그런지 모르겠다.
   【해설】 be good at –ing = be excellent at –ing …를 잘하다
   be not good at –ing = be bad at –ing = be terrible at –ing …를 잘 못하다

   b. (doing) 나는 숙제하는데 꼬박 두 시간을 보내야 했다.
   【해설】 spend + 목적어 (돈, 시간) + –ing …하는데 시간을 보내다.
   spend my time doing nothing 내 시간을 아무것도 하지 않고 보내다

   c. (fought over) 두 명의 웨이터가 해고당했는데, 손님이 준 팁을 놓고 싸웠기 때문이었다.
   struggle 투쟁하다, 애쓰다 battle 전투하다, 싸우다
   【해설】 fight over …를 두고 서로 갖겠다고 싸우다 / struggle with …와 다투다 (with 다음에 주어와 다투는 상대가 나온다.) / battle each other 서로 (둘이서) 싸우다
   ex) John and I have never fought for a girl.
   　존과 나는 여자를 두고 싸운 적이 없다.

Chapter 5. Animals & Nature

 모든 거미가 거미줄을 만드는 건 아니라는 사실 아세요?

① 거미는 곤충이 아닙니다. ② 다른 곤충들과는 달리 거미는 몸이 두 부분이고, 더듬이와 날개가 없고 다리는 네 쌍입니다. ③ 곤충은 몸이 세 부분이고 2개의 더듬이, 날개, 다리는 세 쌍입니다. ④ 전갈, 틱과 같은 다른 거미류 역시 거미처럼 8개의 다리를 갖고 있습니다.

⑤ 그리고 모든 거미가 거미줄을 만드는 건 아닙니다. ⑥ 모든 거미 중 반 정도는 거미줄로 먹이를 잡습니다. ⑦ 늑대거미나 게 거미 같은 거미들은 그냥 기다렸다가 가까운 거리에서 먹이에게 달려듭니다. ⑧ 어떤 거미는 거미줄을 만들긴 하지만 사냥을 위한 건 아닙니다. ⑨ 깡충거미는 쉴 곳을 만들기 위해 거미줄을 사용하고, 늑대거미는 거미줄로 알주머니를 만듭니다.

⑩ 여러분 중 어떤 분들은 '샬럿의 거미줄' 영화를 보고 거미가 먹이를 먹거나 씹는 게 아니라 주스, 또는 '물처럼 만든 고기'를 빨아 먹는다는 사실을 배웠을 겁니다. ⑪ 어떤 거미 종류는 빨아서 배를 채우지만, 어떤 종류는 실제 턱으로 씹어서 먹이를 먹기도 합니다.

문제 정답 및 해설

1. (a) 지문의 제목으로 적당한 것을 고르세요.
   a. 당신이 오해하고 있을 수도 있는 거미에 대한 사실들
   b. 거미와 곤충의 차이점
   c. 샬럿의 거미줄 : 필수 시청 영화
   d. 액화된 고기 만드는 법

2. (c) 깡충 거미와 늑대거미는 _____.
   a. 먹이를 잡을 때 거미줄을 사용한다
   b. 거미줄을 전혀 사용하지 않는다
   c. 먹이를 잡을 때 거미줄을 사용하지 않는다
   d. 세 쌍의 날개가 있고 더듬이는 없다

3. 각 문장에 알맞은 표현을 고르세요.

   a. (two pairs of glasses) 범죄 현장에서 경찰은 안경 두 벌, 손목시계 한 개와 함께 사람의 뼈를 발견했다.
   I crime scene 범죄 현장 along with ...와 함께
   【해설】a pair of (한 쌍, 한 벌) + glasses, pants, shoes (명사의 복수형 등)이 올 수 있고, 복수로 표현할 때에는 'two pairs of, three pairs of...' 로 쓴다.

   b. (watch) 온라인으로 무료 영화를 볼 수 있다.
   【해설】view, watch, look 모두 '보다'라는 뜻이지만, 특히 영화, 텔레비전을 볼 때는 watch 동사를 쓴다.

   c. (for) 면제에 관한 이 정보는 세금 징수원이 아니라 납세자들을 위한 것이다. I exemption 면제, 세금 공제 tax exemption 면세 tax collector 세금 징수원 tax payer 납세자
   【해설】be for ...를 위한 것이다 / not A but B: A가 아니라 B
   ex) It is not for playing, but for studying.
      이것은 놀기 위한 것이 아니라 공부하기 위한 것이다.

산소가 어디에서 나오는지 아세요?

① 숨을 쉬지 않고 살 수 있는 사람은 없기 때문에 우리는 숨을 쉴 산소가 필요합니다. ② 2011년 10월 인구가 70억 명에 도달했다고 합니다. ③ 이 말은 우리가 필요로 하는 산소의 양이 상상을 초월한다는 뜻입니다. ④ 그럼 산소는 어디에서 오는 것일까요? ⑤ 산소는 나무나 꽃 같은 녹색 식물의 광합성을 통해 생산됩니다. ⑥ "지구의 허파"라고도 알려진 남아메리카 아마존 열대 우림은 전 세계의 단일 최대 산소 발전소라고 합니다. ⑦ 어떤 이들은 이곳에서 지구의 전체 산소 중 20% 이상을 제공한다고 말합니다. ⑧ 하지만, 어떤 이들은 이를 믿지 않고, 세계 산소량의 10% 미만이 아마존 열대 우림에서 나오고 나머지는 바다에서 나온다고 말합니다. ⑨ 실제로 조류와 플랑크톤 같은 해양 식물이 광합성을 통해 엄청난 양의 산소를 생산합니다. ⑩ 정확한 양은 논란의 여지가 있지만, 일부 과학자들은 전 세계 대기권 산소의 최소 50%가 바다에서 나온다고 주장합니다. ⑪ 현재 바다에서 아마존보다 더 많은 산소를 생산하는지 여부는 아무도 모릅니다. ⑫ 하지만, 산소에 관해 확실한 것이 하나 있습니다. ⑬ 만약 우리가 육지와 바다의 녹색 식물을 보호하지 않으면 70억 인구는 생존할 수 없다는 것입니다.

문제 정답 및 해설

1. (b) 이 글의 요지를 고르세요.
   a. 아마존 열대 우림은 지구 산소의 주요 원천이기 때문에 반드시 보호해야 한다.
   b. 바다가 최대 산소 발생소라고 주장하는 사람들이 있지만 바다가 아마존 보다 더 많은 산소를 생산한다는 건 확실치 않다.
   c. 많은 과학자들은 단일 최대 산소 발생소가 바다라는데 동의한다.
   d. 우리는 조류에 의해 생산되는 산소의 정확한 양을 계산해야 한다.

2. (d) 지문 내용과 맞는 것을 고르세요.
   a. 아마존 열대 우림 없이 우리가 생존할 수 없는 이유는 이곳이 세계의 허파이기 때문이다. ▶ 아마존 열대 우림이 세계의 폐라 불리는 건 맞지만, 아마존 없이 생존할 수 없다는 내용은 나오지 않았다.
   b. 산소는 오직 바다에서만 나오기 때문에 우리는 바다를 보호해야만 한다. ▶ 산소는 육지와 바다의 녹색 식물에서 나온다.
   c. 과학자들은 바다에서 생산되는 산소의 정확한 양을 알아냈다. ▶ 바다에서 생산되는 산소의 정확한 양은 논란의 여지가 있다고 나온다.
   d. 오직 육지의 녹색 식물만 산소를 만들어내는 건 아니다. ▶ 육지 뿐 아니라 바다의 녹색 식물도 산소를 생산한다.

3. 각 문장에 알맞은 표현을 고르세요.

   a. (provide) 이번 회의가 우리 문제에 대해 이야기할 기회를 줄 수 있기를 바란다.
   【해설】'우리에게 기회를 제공하다'라고 쓰려면 1) provide us with an opportunity 2) provide an opportunity to us로 써야 한다.

   b. (Breathe) 긴장될 때 심호흡을 하라. 그럼 긴장을 푸는데 도움이 될 것이다.
   【해설】breathe v. 숨을 쉬다, 호흡하다 breath n. 숨, 호흡
   breathe = take a breath 호흡하다, 숨을 쉬다
   breathe deeply = take a deep breath 심호흡을 하다 (부사 deeply가 동사 breathe 를 수식)

   c. (beyond) 상상을 초월하는 부자가 되는 게 당신을 행복하게 만들어주지는 않는다.
   【해설】beyond ...이상의, ...를 초월하는 * beyond one's wildest dream 상상을 초월하는

애완동물로 길러지는 바퀴벌레를 아세요?

① 일반적으로 바퀴벌레는 사람을 피합니다. ② 먹을 것을 찾아 밤에 집 안을 돌아다니지요. ③ 만약 사람들에게 걸리면 치명적인 독 스프레이 세례를 받을 게 확실합니다. ④ 상당히 많은 사람들이 집 안의 바퀴벌레를 없애기 위해 기꺼이 지갑을 엽니다.
⑤ 하지만 어떤 종류의 바퀴벌레는 애완동물로 집 안에서 길러집니다. ⑥ 다른 종류의 바퀴벌레들과는 달리, 이 종류는 쉭쉭 소리를 낼 수 있고 날개가 없습니다. ⑦ 큰 초식동물인 이 바퀴는 약 3인치 정도로 벌레 치고 크기가 큰 편이지만 공격적이지 않아서 먹이 주는 사람의 손을 물지 않습니다. ⑧ 그래서 어떤 사람들은 이 바퀴벌레를 애완동물로 키우길 원합니다.
⑨ 이는 마다가스카르 히싱 바퀴벌레로, 간단히 '히서'라고도 불립니다. ⑩ 대부분 과일과 야채를 먹고, 잘 돌보아주면 5년까지 살 수 있습니다. ⑪ 당신이 이 바퀴벌레를 애완동물로 키우고 싶은데 플로리다에 살고 있다면, 주(state)의 허가를 받아야 할 것입니다. ⑫ 미국의 몇몇 주는 이들을 애완동물로 키우려면 허가를 받도록 요구하고 있습니다.

문제 정답 및 해설

1. (d) 이 글의 요지를 고르세요.
   a. 무슨 수를 써서라도 바퀴벌레는 제거해야 한다. (at all costs 무슨 수를 써서라도)
   b. 바퀴벌레를 애완동물로 키우고 싶다면 허가받는 걸 잊지 마라.
   c. 마다가스카르 히싱 바퀴벌레는 최고의 애완동물이다.
   d. 어떤 종류의 바퀴벌레는 애완동물로 사람들의 사랑을 받고 있다.

2. (b) 히서가 좋은 애완동물이 될 수 있는 건 _____ 때문이다.
   a. 사람들이 이를 쉽게 잡을 수 있기
   b. 순하고 얌전하기
   c. 온갖 종류의 세균을 옮기기
   d. 쉭쉭소리를 내는 뱀과 비슷하게 생겼기

3. 각 문장에 알맞은 표현을 고르세요.

   a. (is willing to) 모든 학생이 자선을 위해 기꺼이 돈을 모금해서 기쁩니다.

【해설】주어가 every student(3인칭 단수 현재)이기 때문에 동사가 want일 경우 wants가 와야 하고, give라면 gives로 와야 한다.

   b. (for) 내 아들은 나이에 비해 아주 작지만, 어른처럼 행동한다.
【해설】small for one's age 나이에 비해 작은 / big for one's age 나이에 비해 큰
ex) fat for a model 모델치고 뚱뚱한
    old for an athlete 운동선수치고 나이가 많은

   c. (to attend) 오늘 아침에 더 중요한 일이 생겨서 회의에 참석할 수 없습니다.
【해설】be able to 동사원형 : ...할 수 있다(=can, be capable of + -ing)

44. 히말라야에 등반하기 전에 돈을 내야 한다는 거 아세요?

① 히말라야에 등반하는데 철저한 준비와 훈련만으로는 부족합니다. ② 아무것도 하지 않고 그냥 집으로 돌아오고 싶지 않다면 지갑 챙겨야 합니다. ③ 이를 '정상 로열티'라고 부릅니다. ④ 이는 정상이 어디냐에 따라 다릅니다. ⑤ 만약 6,500미터 이하의 정상을 오를 계획이라면, 미국 달러로 500달러를 내야 합니다. ⑥ 6,501미터에서 7,000미터 사이의 정상에 도전할 생각이라면, 2,000달러를 내야 합니다. ⑦ 7,001미터 이상의 정상일 경우 3,000달러를 내야 합니다. ⑧ 만약 제한 구역 내의 정상에 오르고자 시도하고 싶다면, 가장 혹독하고 어려운 훈련을 거쳐야 하고 통장에서 4,000달러도 인출해야 합니다. ⑨ 다행히도 이 로열티는 12명으로 이루어진 한 그룹당 내는 돈입니다. ⑩ 다른 추가 비용도 있으니까 너무 빨리 '휴-'하지 마십시오(안도의 한숨을 쉬지 마십시오). ⑪ 매번 원정 때마다 환경 부담금 400달러, 연락 담당관 장비 비용 500달러도 내야 합니다. ⑫ 훈련도 하고 주머니에 돈도 챙겨 넣은 이후에도 히말라야, 특히 에베레스트 산을 오르려면 해야 할 일이 더 있습니다. ⑬ 네팔 정부로부터 허가를 받아야 하고, 지원서와 함께 당국 정부의 추천서 혹은 등반협회의 추천서를 제출해야 합니다.

문제 정답 및 해설

1. (c) 이 글의 요지를 고르세요.
   a. 히말라야를 등반하기 위해 해야 할 일은 정부로부터 허가를 받는 것뿐이다.
   b. 4천 달러면 히말라야 등반에 필요한 모든 경비를 대는데 충분하다.
   c. 히말라야를 등반하는데 돈이 많이 든다.
   d. 정상 로열티를 낸다는 건 말도 안 되고 부당하다.

2. (b) 지문 내용과 맞지 않는 것을 고르세요.
   a. 히말라야 등반은 말처럼 간단하지 않다. ▶ 등반 훈련만 해야 하는 게 아니라 비용도 내야하고 서류도 준비해야 한다.
   b. 정상 로열티는 오직 원정팀의 크기에 따라 다르다. ▶ 오직 원정팀 크기에 따라 달라지는 것이 아니라 정상의 고도에 따라 다르다.
   c. 히말라야 등반 시도 전에 몇 가지 서류를 준비해야 한다. ▶ 지원서, 추천서 등을 내야 한다.
   d. 7,001미터 이상의 정상을 오르고 싶은 사람은 약 4,000달러를 내야 한다. ▶ 정상 로열티 3,000달러, 환경 부담금 400달러, 연락 담당관 장비 비용 500달러 등 약 3,900달러 정도 내야 한다.

3. 각 문장에 알맞은 표현을 고르세요.

a. (thorough) 나는 이 문제에 대한 빈틈없는 평가를 받아본 적이 없다. l receive 받다 evaluation 평가
【해설】through ...를 통과하여 / thorough 철저한, 빈틈없는 (ad. thoroughly) 명사인 evaluation을 수식하기 때문에 부사 thoroughly는 쓸 수 없다.

b. (be charged) 당신은 한 켤레 당 500달러 또는 그 이상을 내야 할 것이다. l or more 또는 그 이상 per pair 쌍당, 켤레당
【해설】charge 값을 요구하다, 청구하다 ▶ 주어 you에게 청구되는 것, 즉 you가 청구당하는 수동이므로 'be charged' 수동태가 되어야 맞다.

c. (enough) 그만 하시오. 이럴 시간 여유가 없습니다. 징징대는 것 좀 그만 두시오. l whine 징징대다
【해설】That's enough. 그것으로 충분하다, 더 이상 하지 마라 / That's great. 그것 참 좋다 / That's all. 그것이 전부이다. ▶ 문맥상 That's enough.가 적당하다.

45 박쥐 똥이 인간에게 가치가 있다는 거 아세요?

① 박쥐 똥은 너무 가치가 있어서 그냥 '배설물' 또는 '똥'이라 부르지 않고 '구아노'라는 이름을 붙여주었습니다. ② 그들의 똥이 뭐가 그리 특별할까요? ③ 영양가가 풍부한 똥이라 인간이 사용할 수 있는 훌륭한 비료가 됩니다. ④ 구아노는 일반적으로 동굴 바닥에서 수집된 박쥐 배설물을 의미합니다. ⑤ 하지만, 더 정확히 말하면 구아노는 펠리컨 같은 바닷새, 박쥐, 물개의 배설물입니다. ⑥ 구아노 비료는 인과 질소 함량이 높아서 인기가 좋습니다. ⑦ 게다가 다른 종류의 똥과 비교할 때 구아노 냄새는 그리 지독하지 않습니다. ⑧ 그래서 많은 농부들이 화학비료보다 구아노 비료를 더 좋아합니다.

⑨ 그럼에도 불구하고 일부 비판가들은 동굴에서 박쥐 구아노를 가져오는 게 좋은 일이 아니라고 말합니다. ⑩ 사람들이 박쥐 구아노를 모을 때, 박쥐의 서식지를 혼란시키고 박쥐들을 불안하고 어수선하게 만듭니다. ⑪ 어떤 박쥐는 불안감 때문에 아기를 떨어뜨린다고 합니다.

문제 정답 및 해설

1. (a) 지문의 제목으로 적당한 것을 고르세요.
   a. 박쥐에게서 나온 쓰레기를 버리지 말라
   b. 어느 것이 더 지독할까 : 박쥐 똥? 아니면 물개 똥?
   c. 박쥐는 똥이 아니라 아기를 떨어뜨린다
   d. 좋은 비료를 찾는 방법

2. (b) 구아노의 냄새는 다른 종류의 배설물에 비해 _____.
   a. 그냥 지나치기에는 너무 좋다
   b. 그다지 나쁘지 않다
   c. 불쾌하다 (obnoxious 불쾌한)
   d. 꽃처럼 향기롭다 (fragrant 향기로운)

3. 각 문장에 알맞은 표현을 고르세요.

   a. (preferred to) 그가 나에게 앉으라고 했을 때 나는 서는 게 좋다고 말했다.
   【해설】prefer to 동사원형: …하기를 더 좋아하다 / prefer A to B: B보다 A를 더 좋아하다 ▶ prefer to stand 서 있는 게 더 좋다

   b. (referring to) 죄송하지만 정확히 무엇을 언급하시는지 모르겠습니다.
   【해설】'조회하라, 참조하다, 위탁하다, 언급하다'등의 뜻을 가진 동사 refer는 전치사 to와 함께 쓰인다. 문제에서는 '언급하다'의 뜻으로 쓰였다.

   c. (fertilizers) 닭장에서 수정란 모아 오는 것과 비료 약간 사오는 걸 잊지 말아라. 정원에 비료를 주어야겠다.
   【해설】fertilize 1. 수정시키다 2. 비료를 주다
   fertilized egg 수정란, fertilize a garden 정원에 비료를 주다, fertilizer 비료

 세계에서 가장 뜨거운 온천이 얼마나 뜨거운지 아세요?

① 이 온천에 발을 넣기 전에 마음의 준비를 단단히 해야 합니다. ② 말 그대로 '뜨거운' 샘인데, 얼마나 뜨거운지 계란을 삶을 수 있을 정도입니다. ③ 세상에서 가장 뜨거운 온천은 세르비아에 있습니다. ④ 온도가 무려 섭씨 111도라고 합니다. ⑤ 그 정도면 상당히 뜨겁지만 가장 큰 온천은 다른 대륙에서 찾을 수 있습니다. ⑥ 뉴질랜드의 '프라잉 팬 레이크'가 세상에서 가장 큰 온천입니다. ⑦ 두 번째로 큰 것은 도미니카에 있고 이름은 '보일링 레이크'입니다. ⑧ 누가 이름을 지었는지는 모르지만 프라잉 팬 레이크와 보일링 레이크라는 이름은 온천을 아주 잘 표현하는 이름인데, 이유인즉 둘 다 거대할 뿐만 아니라 'frying(튀기는)'과 'boiling(끓는)'이라 묘사될 정도로 꽤 뜨겁기 때문입니다. ⑨ 여기 또 다른 놀라운 온천이 있습니다. ⑩ 이 온천은 1초당 뜨거운 물이 약 250리터나 나온다고 합니다. ⑪ 거대한 이 온천은 사실 미국의 옐로스톤 국립공원에 있는 간헐천으로 이름은 엑셀시오 가이저 크레이터입니다. ⑫ 타마가와 온천은 일본에서 가장 많은 유량 기록을 보유하고 있습니다. ⑬ 이 온천은 1초에 150리터의 물이 흘러나옵니다. ⑭ 온천 폭은 3미터, 물의 온도는 섭씨 98도입니다.

문제 정답 및 해설

1. (a) 이 글의 요지를 고르세요.
   a. 세상에는 놀라운 기록을 보유한 온천들이 있다.
   b. 계란을 삶고 싶다면 보일링 레이크로 가라.
   c. 일본의 온천은 매우 뜨겁지는 않고 크긴 크다.
   d. 엑셀시오 가이저 크레이터는 괴물 온천이라 불린다.

2. (d) 지문 내용과 맞는 것을 고르세요.
   a. 일본의 온천은 옐로스톤 국립공원의 온천보다 더 뜨겁다. ▶ 옐로스톤의 엑셀시오 가이저 크레이터의 온천 온도는 지문에 나오지 않았다.
   b. 세계에서 두 번째로 큰 온천은 뉴질랜드에 있다. ▶ 두 번째로 큰 온천은 도미니카에 있다.
   c. 보일링 레이크는 물이 뜨겁지 않고 차갑기 때문에 이름이 잘못 붙여졌다. ▶ boiling이라는 이름에 걸맞게 물이 뜨겁다고 나온다.
   d. 엑셀시오 가이저 크레이터는 아주 많은 뜨거운 물이 나오기로 유명하다. ▶ 1초당 뜨거운 물이 약 250리터나 나온다고 한다.

3. 각 문장에 알맞은 표현을 고르세요.

   a. (width) 혼자서 풋볼 경기장의 폭을 재는 데 몇 시간이 걸렸다.

   【해설】height 높이 / width 넓이 / depth 깊이 ▶ 혼자서 풋볼 경기장의 깊이나 높이를 재기는 힘들기 때문에 문맥상 width가 적당하다.
   * measure the width / height / depth of …의 폭/높이/깊이를 재다, 측정하다

   b. (amazing) 나는 테레사 수녀에 관한 책을 샀는데, 그녀의 놀라운 삶에 관해 알기 위해서였다.
   【해설】놀라운 삶 amazing (a) + life (n)
   ex) I was amazed when I knew about her life. Her life was amazing. 나는 그녀의 삶에 관해 알았을 때 놀랐다. 그녀의 삶은 놀랍다.

   c. (yield) 1헥타르당 3톤을 생산하는 밀밭 옆에 양보 표지판이 있다.
   【해설】a yield sign 도로에 있는 '양보' 표지판 ▶ yield sign에서 yield는 '양보'라는 뜻의 명사, 'yielding 3 tones a hectare'에서 yield는 '생산하다'라는 뜻의 동사

47 반은 얼룩말, 반은 말인 콰가가 왜 멸종했는지 아세요?

① 한 때 아프리카 초원에서 많은 수가 발견되었던 콰가는 사람들이 고기와 가죽을 얻기 위해 사냥하는 바람에 멸종되었습니다. ② 그러니까 콰가를 멸종으로 내몬 건 바로 우리 인간입니다. ③ 콰가는 다른 얼룩말과는 다릅니다. ④ 몸 앞부분에만 선명한 줄무늬가 있었습니다. ⑤ 몸의 중간 부분에서 줄무늬가 흐려지면서 그냥 갈색이 됩니다. ⑥ 그래서 콰가는 얼룩말과 말을 동시에 닮았습니다. ⑦ 학자들은 이 종을 어떻게 분류할지 몰랐습니다. ⑧ 안됐지만, 학자들이 이 종에 대한 어떤 결정도 내리기 전에, 콰가가 멸종되었습니다. ⑨ 마지막 야생 콰가는 1870년대 후반에 총에 맞아 사라진 것으로 알려져 있고, 암스테르담의 동물원에 있던 진짜 마지막 콰가는 1883년에 사망했습니다. ⑩ 하지만, 과학자들은 콰가의 DNA로 콰가에 대한 연구를 계속하고 있습니다. ⑪ 사실 콰가는 DNA를 남긴 최초의 멸종 동물입니다. ⑫ 최근 유전공학자들은 콰가가 분리된 종이 아니라는 것을 밝혀냈습니다. ⑬ 콰가는 초원 얼룩말에서 나온 종이었습니다.

문제 정답 및 해설

1. (d) 이 글의 요지를 고르세요.
   a. 콰가는 초원 얼룩말과 완전히 다르다
   b. 콰가가 멸종한 이후, 과학자들은 멸종 원인에 대해 연구하고 있다.
   c. 콰가는 얼룩말과 똑같이 생겼지만, 종은 달랐다.
   d. 인간에 의해 멸종당한 콰가는 DNA를 남긴 최초의 멸종 동물이다.

2. (c) _____를/을 얻기 위해 사람들은 마음대로 콰가를 사냥했었다.
   a. 초원의 풀
   b. 다른 얼룩말과 말
   c. 고기와 가죽
   d. 이것의 DNA 샘플

3. 각 문장에 알맞은 표현을 고르세요.

   a. (hides) 사냥꾼들은 가죽을 얻기 위해 물개를 잡으려 했지만, 물개들은 얼음 아래로 숨었다.
   【해설】첫 번째 hides는 '가죽'이라는 뜻의 명사(복수형), 두 번째 hid는 '숨다'라는 뜻의 동사 hide의 과거형이다.

   b. (made) 집 안에 머무르기로 결정한 사람들은 집을 나서지 않으려 했다.
   ▌those who ...한/인 사람들 make a decision 결정하다
   【해설】make 동사만 취하는 표현들(have, get 등의 동사와 혼용되지 않는다):
   make a wish 소원을 빌다, make a reservation 예약하다, make an effort 노력하다

   c. (come) 일제 강점기 때 일본에 빼앗겼던 국보들이 2001년 한국으로 되돌아왔다.
   ▌national treasure 국보 the Japanese colonial era 일제 강점기
   【해설】과거 완료 문장 had + pp : come (come–came–come)의 과거분사는 come

   d. (plain) 수가 평범한 티셔츠를 입은 반면 데미는 화려하고 다양한 색의 드레스를 입었다.
   【해설】plain a. 1) 밋밋한, 무늬가 없는 2) 분명한, 명확한 3) 솔직한 4) 소박한, 매력이 없는 ▶ 문제에서는 '밋밋한'의 뜻 (plainly ad. 밋밋하게, 솔직하게 / plains a. 평원 지대의)

48 고래가 뼈까지 유용하다는 거 아세요?

① 고래가 인간에게 뼈까지 철저하게 유용하다는 건 비유적으로 한 말이든 축어적으로 한 말이든 다 맞는 말입니다. ② 고래는 우리에게 수 톤의 고기를 제공합니다. ③ 고래의 엄청난 크기를 감안할 때 고래가 엄청난 양의 고기를 제공한다는 건 놀랄 일도 아닙니다. ④ 그리고 고래는 고래수염(baleen)도 우리에게 제공해왔습니다. ⑤ 이는 치아가 없는 고래의 입안에 있는 솔처럼 생긴 일종의 필터입니다. ⑥ 고래는 고래수염을 통해 바닷물을 걸러 수 톤의 크릴새우를 먹습니다. ⑦ 고래수염은 우산, 솔, 여성의 코르셋, 낚싯대 등과 같은 제품에서 오랫동안 다양하게 이용되어 왔습니다. ⑧ 고래가 우리에게 제공하는 가장 중요한 건 기름입니다. ⑨ 과거에 고래 기름은 램프의 발광제와 양초 왁스로 널리 애용되었습니다. ⑩ 한 때 태평양 북서지역의 일부 사람들의 주요 식량자원이기도 했습니다. ⑪ 지금도 비누 제작과 가죽 무두질에 고래 기름이 쓰이고 있습니다. ⑫ 대부분의 고래 기름은 블러버 (해양 동물의 지방)에서 나오지만, 인간은 고래의 수염, 고기, 내장, 뼈, 심지어 혈액에서도 기름을 뽑아냅니다. ⑬ 지금부터 우리는 고래를 '아낌없이 주는 고래'라고 불러야 할 것 같습니다.

문제 정답 및 해설

1. (c) 이 글의 요지를 고르세요.
   a. 고래 고기는 맛있고 매우 영양가가 높다.
   b. 고래는 멸종 위기 동물이기 때문에 우리가 보호해야 한다.
   c. 고래는 여러 가지 면에서 인간에게 유용하다.
   d. 우리는 고래를 '아낌없이 주는 고래'라고 불러야 한다.

2. (a) 지문 내용과 맞는 것을 고르세요.
   a. 고래는 오랫동안 인간에게 유용하게 쓰여 왔다.
   b. 많은 나라에서, 예나 지금이나 사람들은 고래 고기를 즐기고 있다. ▶ 고래가 고기를 많이 제공한다는 말은 나왔지만, 예나 지금이나 많은 국가에서 고래 고기를 즐긴다는 내용은 나오지 않았다.
   c. 고래수염은 여전히 주요 식량 자원으로 널리 쓰이고 있다. ▶ 예전에 식량 자원으로 쓰인 적이 있지만, 현재까지 그렇다고는 나오지 않았다.
   d. whalebones와 baleen은 완전히 다르다. ▶ whalebone과 baleen은 '고래수염'의 뜻을 가진 동의어이다.

3. 각 문장에 알맞은 표현을 고르세요.

   a. (to) 문제는 많은 정부 관리들이 철저하게 매우 부패했다는 것이다. l government official 정부 관리
   【해설】 to the bone = to the core 중심까지, 철저하게 ▶ be deeply corrupt to the bone (to the core) 뼛속까지 철저하게 부패하다

   b. (from now on) 네가 내 가족 앞에서 나를 모욕했으니 이제부터 너와 나는 더 이상 친구가 아니다.
   【해설】 from time to time 때때로(= sometimes) / from now on 이제부터 / till the end 끝까지 ▶ 문맥상 from now on이 적당하다

   c. (figuratively) 비유적으로 말하면, 너는 몇 주간 굶은 배고픈 사자 같다.
   【해설】 literally speaking 문자 그대로 말하면 / figuratively speaking 비유적으로 말하면 / comparatively speaking 비교해서 말하면 ▶ 사람을 배고픈 사자에 비유했기 때문에 문맥상 figuratively speaking이 적당하다.

   d. (with) 아낌없이 주는 나무는 소년에게 열매와 가지를 제공했다.
   【해설】 provide 사람 with 물건: 사람에게 물건을 제공하다

49 동물도 슬픔을 느낀다는 거 아세요?

① 모든 동물이 슬픔을 느끼는 건 아니지만, 일부 동물은 슬픔을 표현합니다.
② 코끼리 중 한 마리가 죽으면 다른 코끼리들은 시체 주위에 둘러서서 한동안 동료를 바라봅니다. ③ 그리고 엄마 코끼리는 아기를 잃으면 죽은 아기 곁을 떠나지 않고 가끔씩 코로 아기를 만집니다.
④ 침팬지와 고릴라의 경우, 이들 역시 아기를 잃거나 그 반대의 경우 슬픔을 느낍니다. ⑤ 엄마를 잃은 아기 침팬지가 있었습니다. ⑥ 그 아기 침팬지의 슬픔이 얼마나 심했는지 먹기를 거부했습니다. ⑦ 마침내 아기는 굶어 죽었습니다.
⑧ 배우자에게 헌신적인 앵무새 역시 슬픔을 표현합니다. ⑨ 짝이 죽으면 남은 앵무새는 슬픔으로 상심하고 고통스러운 듯 보입니다. ⑩ 가끔은 오랫동안 먹지 않기도 합니다. ⑪ 개들 역시 짝이나 주인의 죽음처럼 슬픈 일이 생기면 슬퍼한다고 합니다.

문제 정답 및 해설

1. (a) 이 글의 요지를 고르세요.
   a. 일부 동물은 슬픔의 감정을 갖고 있기 때문에 슬픔을 표현한다.
   b. 앵무새는 짝을 잃으면 슬픔을 느낀다. (맞는 내용이지만 전체 지문의 요지로 보기 힘들다.)
   c. 모든 코끼리들은 새끼를 잃으면 슬퍼한다. (모든 코끼리라고는 나오지 않았으며, 요지로 볼 수도 없다.)
   d. 침팬지와 고릴라는 공통점이 아주 많다.

2. (b) _____ 은(는) 슬픔을 느끼고 슬픔을 나타낸다.
   a. 모든 동물들
   b. 어떤 동물들
   c. 오직 코끼리
   d. 대부분의 새들

3. 각 문장에 알맞은 표현을 고르세요.

   a. (death) 팀과 나는 죽음이 우리를 갈라놓을 때까지 함께 살기로 약속한다.
   【해설】death n. 죽음 / die v. 죽다 / dead a. 죽은 ▶ 명사 death(3인칭 단수 현재)가 until 이하 문장의 주어로 쓰였다. 그래서 동사는 separates로 쓰였다.

   b. (from time to time) 나는 이따금 제프와 방을 같이 쓰는데, 그건 정말 나를 미치게 한다.
   【해설】now more than ever 그 어느 때보다 지금이 더 / at the same time 동시에 / from time to time 가끔, 때때로 ▶ 문맥상 from time to time이 가장 적당하다

   c. (trunk) 수영복으로 갈아입기 위해 나무 몸통 옆에 내 분홍 트렁크 가방을 내려놓았을 때, 한 코끼리가 가까이 다가와 자기 코로 내 분홍 트렁크 가방을 만졌다.
   【해설】my pink trunk 분홍색 가방, 트렁크 가방 / a tree trunk 나무 몸통 / swimming trunks 남성용 사각 수영복 (shorts 반바지, pants 바지 등을 복수형으로 쓰는 것과 마찬가지로 사각 수영복 역시 복수형(-s)으로 쓴다.) / its trunk = elephant's trunk 코끼리의 코

   d. (to) 그의 개는 주인에게 충성스러운 것으로 유명하다. 내 개는? 전혀 그렇지 않다.
   【해설】be faithful to ...에게 충성스럽다, 충실하다. (배우자에게) 바람을 피우지 않다

상어가 주머니쥐 흉내를 낼 수 있다는 거 아세요?

① 상어는 자신을 죽은 것처럼 보이게 할 수 있습니다. ② 주머니쥐가 "죽은 척 한다"는 건 이해할만합니다. ③ 놀랄 일도 아니지요. ④ 하지만, 상어가 주머니쥐 흉내를? ⑤ 정확히 말하면 상어는 스스로 주머니쥐 흉내(죽은 척하기)를 내지 않습니다. ⑥ 하지만 마비 상태에 들어가긴 하는데, 이를 '긴장성 부동'이라고 합니다. (일종의 가사상태) ⑦ 모든 상어가 긴장성 부동을 보이는 건 아니지만, 일부 상어는 몸이 뒤집히면 이런 상태가 되어 10분에서 15분 정도 유지합니다. ⑧ 긴장성 부동 상태일 때 상어는 누가 건드려도 반응을 보이지 않습니다. ⑨ 물론 죽은 것처럼 보이는 이 15분이 지난 후 상어는 정신을 차리고 얼른 몸을 뒤집어 수영해 가버립니다. ⑩ 그래서, 할 수만 있다면, 상어를 뒤집어 놓으면 몇 분 동안 상어를 무력하게 만들 수 있습니다. ⑪ 무엇이 이런 이상한 상태를 유발하는지는 아무도 모릅니다. ⑫ 일부 과학자들은 상어를 연구하는데 이 현상을 이용합니다. ⑬ 재미있게도 과학자들만 상어를 통제하려고 이런 전략을 활용하는 게 아닙니다. ⑭ 범고래들은 사냥할 때 쉽게 상어를 잡아먹기 위해 종종 상어를 뒤집습니다.

문제 정답 및 해설

1. (c) 이 글의 요지를 고르세요.
   a. 상어를 주머니쥐로 만들어 무력하게 만들 수 있다.
   b. 부동성 긴장 상태일 때 상어는 빨리 수영할 수 없다.
   c. 어떤 상어는 죽은 척할 수 있다.
   d. 상어를 뒤집으면 상어가 당신을 잡아먹을 것이다.

2. (d) 지문 내용과 맞지 않는 것을 고르세요.
   a. 긴장성 부동 상태일 때 상어는 아무것도 하지 못한다.
      ▶ 움직이지 못하는 가사상태에 빠진다.
   b. 어떤 상어는 죽은 척하지만 어떤 상어는 그렇지 않다.
      ▶ Not all sharks display... 라고 나온다. 즉 모든 상어가 다 긴장성 부동 상태를 보이는 건 아니다.
   c. 범고래들은 사냥할 때 종종 상어를 뒤집으려고 시도한다. ▶ 지문 후반부에 범고래가 상어를 쉽게 잡아먹기 위해 뒤집는다고 나온다.
   d. 긴장성 부동은 15시간 동안 지속된다. ▶ 15 hours가 아니라 15 minutes이다.

3. 각 문장에 알맞은 표현을 고르세요.

   a. (look) 이 반짝이는 셔츠는 나를 멋지고 젊어 보이게 해줄 것이다.
   【해설】 사역동사 make + 목적어 + 동사원형: 목적어가 ...하게 만들다
   make me look + 형용사: 내가 ...처럼 보이게 만들다
   ex) make her look fat 그녀를 뚱뚱하게 보이게 하다
       make you look angry 네가 화가 난 것처럼 보이게 하다

   b. (Paralysis) 마비는 몸, 특히 뇌와 근육에 문제가 생겼을 때 발생한다.
   something goes wrong with ...에 문제가 생기다, 잘못 되다
   【해설】 paralysis n. 마비 / paralyze v. 마비시키다 ▶ happens는 동사, when 부사절이 이어지므로 이 문장에 주어가 필요하다. 따라서 명사인 paralysis가 정답이다.

   c. (waiting) 팀은 엄마를 기다리는 동안 큰 소리로 울었다.
   【해설】 문장의 주어는 Tim, wait 동사의 주체 역시 Tim으로 주절의 주어 Tim과 일치한다. 이런 경우 while절의 주어를 생략할 수 있다. 동사가 능동이면 –ing로, 수동이면 (being) pp 형으로 바꾸어 쓴다. 문제에서는 주어인 Tim이 기다리는 것, 즉 능동이므로 while waiting으로 쓸 수 있다. * wait은 자동사이므로 수동태 불가
   ex) A little girl had to stand up while being punished for lying.
       어린 소녀는 거짓말로 벌을 받는 동안 서 있어야 했다.
   * 'while she was punished...'에서 주절의 주어와 while 절 주어가 일치하므로 생략, 수동태 was punished는 being punished로 바뀌었다.

Chapter 6. Myth Or Fact

51 일반 감기에 관한 낭설을 아세요?

① 감기에 관한 가장 흔한 낭설은 비타민 C가 감기를 예방한다는 것입니다. ② 많은 사람들이 많은 양의 비타민 C가 감기를 예방하거나 최소한 감기 증상을 완화시킨다고 확신합니다. ③ 그래서 부모들은 아이가 감기에 걸리면 보통 비타민 C가 많이 함유된 과일을 먹입니다. ④ 의사들과 과학자들은 감기에 관해 널리 알려진 낭설을 확인하기 위해 많은 연구와 실험을 해왔습니다. ⑤ 그 결과 그건 낭설일 뿐입니다. ⑥ 현재까지 많은 양의 비타민 C가 감기를 예방한다고 증명된 결정적인 자료는 없습니다. ⑦ 명백한 증거는 없지만 그래도 비타민이 감기 증상을 경감시킬 수도 있습니다. ⑧ 감기가 빨리 낫고 싶다면 따뜻한 닭고기 수프 한 그릇이 도움이 될 수 있습니다. ⑨ 감기에 닭고기 수프를 먹는 건 낭설이 아니라 확실한 의학적 증거가 뒷받침된 사실인데, 닭고기 수프에는 소염 효과가 있기 때문입니다. ⑩ 참고로 비타민 C를 너무 많이, 너무 오랫동안 섭취하면 건강에 좋지 않을 수 있습니다. ⑪ 건강에 좋은 건 고사하고 오히려 해로울 수 있는데, 과도한 양의 비타민 C는 설사를 유발하기 때문으로, 설사는 특히 연로한 어르신들과 어린이들에게 매우 위험합니다.

문제 정답 및 해설

1. (a) 이 글의 요지를 고르세요.
   a. '많은 양의 비타민 C를 복용하는 게 감기를 예방한다'는 건 낭설이다.
   b. 비타민 C는 저렴하지만 효과적이지 않고, 닭고기 수프는 효과적이지만 비싸다.
   c. 비타민 C에 관해서라면 많을수록 좋다. (the more, the better. 많으면 많을수록 좋다.)
   d. 비타민 C를 너무 많이 복용하는 건 설사를 일으킨다.

2. (b) 뜨거운 닭고기 수프 한 그릇은 감기를 빨리 낫게 하는 데 도움이 될 수 있는데 이유는 _____ 때문이다.
   a. 소염 효과가 전혀 들어 있지 않기
   b. 소염 특성이 감기에 효과적이기
   c. 설사를 유발하고 위험할 수 있기
   d. 비타민 C 같은 좋은 물질이 많이 들어 있기

3. 각 문장에 알맞은 표현을 고르세요.

   a. (alleviate) 인간은 산소 부족을 경감하기 위해 하품을 한다고 한다. | yawn 하품하다 alleviate 경감하다 waste 낭비하다 removal 제거 (v. remove) oxygen 산소 deficiency 결핍

【해설】in order to + 동사원형: …하기 위해 ▶ in order to 다음에 동사 원형이 오기 때문에 removal은 올 수 없고, 의미상 waste보다 alleviate가 적당하다.

b. (get over) 나는 그가 누이의 죽음을 결코 극복하지 못하리라 생각했다.
【해설】get over 극복하다 / make over 양도하다, 고치다 / come over 갑자기 …기분이 들다, 엄습하다, …에 들르다 ▶ 문맥상 get over가 적당하다.

c. (conducted) HC 리서치 센터에서 실시한 실험 중 하나에서 놀라운 결과가 나왔다.
【해설】conduct the experiment 실험을 하다 ▶ 문제의 문장은 '…the experiments (which were) conducted by HC Research Center'에서 'which were'가 생략된 형태로 보면 된다.

 '운동 전에 먹으면 안 된다'는 게 낭설이라는 거 아세요?

① 운동을 시작하기 전에 적은 양의 음식을 먹는 게 좋은데, 이유는 몸에 필요한 에너지를 공급하려면 연료가 필요하기 때문입니다. ② 그 연료는 음식과 음료에서 얻을 수 있습니다. ③ 적당한 양의 음식은 근육이 이제 시작할 활동을 준비할 수 있게 합니다. ④ 바나나, 견과, 물 한 컵 등 약간의 과일과 음료로 연료 탱크를 채우세요. ⑤ 운동에 관한 낭설이 더 있습니다. ⑥ 사람들은 운동 전에 반드시 스트레칭을 해야 한다고 믿습니다. ⑦ 하지만, 몇몇 연구에 따르면 가끔은 스트레칭이 부상으로 이어지기도 하는데, 늘어난 근육 섬유가 염좌에 더 취약해지기 때문입니다. ⑧ 몇몇 여성들은 운동하면 지방이 근육이 될 수도 있다고 생각합니다. ⑨ 그들은 역기를 하면 근육질의 우람한 몸이 된다고 생각합니다. ⑩ 하지만, 지방과 근육 조직은 완전히 다르기 때문에 그건 말도 안 되는 낭설이고, 운동을 하지 않으려는 궁색한 변명입니다.

문제 정답 및 해설

1. (b) 이 글의 요지를 고르세요.
   a. 무언가 먹는 것은 모두에게, 특히 운동선수에게 매우 중요하다.
   b. 운동 전에, 적당한 양의 음식을 먹고 스트레칭에 주의하라.
   c. 무언가 힘든 일을 하기 전에 무엇을 먹는지 확인하라.
   d. 덜 먹고 더 운동하라.

2. (a) 지문 내용과 맞는 것을 고르세요.
   a. 운동 전에 음식을 약간 먹는 게 좋다. 견과류가 괜찮다.
   b. 운동 직후 팔과 다리를 수차례 스트레칭 해야 한다. ▶ 운동 후에 관해서는 지문에 언급되지 않았다.
   c. 운동 전 먹는 음식으로 바나나 한 다발이 가장 추천된다. ▶ 바나나 한 다발이 아니라 바나나 몇 개.
   d. 지방 조직이 근육 조직으로 바뀔 수 있기 때문에 여성 운동선수들이 근육질이다. ▶ 지방 조직과 근육 조직은 전혀 다른 것으로 서로 바뀌지 않는다.

3. 각 문장에 알맞은 표현을 고르세요.

   a. (lame) 마리아는 멋지고 똑똑하지만, 그녀의 새 남자친구는 정말 형편없다.

I lame a. 다리를 저는, 형편없는, 말이 안 되는
【해설】접속사 but이 있기 때문에 nice and smart와 반대되는 표현이 와야 자연스럽다.

b. (makes) 설탕이 들어간 이 간식은 나를 뚱뚱하게 만들고, 이 청바지 한 벌은 나를 뚱뚱해 보이게 만든다. I sugary 설탕이 들어간, 너무 달콤한 a pair of 한 벌의 jeans 청바지
【해설】and 뒤에 이어지는 문장에서 주어는 this pair(한 벌)이다. 즉 주어가 3인칭 단수 현재라서 동사는 makes가 와야 한다. a pair of jeans: 단수(청바지 한 벌) two pairs of jeans: 복수(청바지 두 벌)

c. (are) 곧 개봉할 최신 영화들을 확인해보고 싶다.
【해설】that이 앞서 나온 movies(복수)를 받기 때문에 복수 동사 are가 쓰여야 맞다.

어두운 불빛에서 글을 읽는다고 시력이 손상되는 건 아니라는 거 아세요?

① 어두운 불빛에서 글을 읽거나 아주 작은 글자를 오랫동안 읽는 게 눈이 손상되는 원인은 아닙니다. ② 물론 그렇게 하면 눈이 분명 피로하고 힘들고 불편해지며 충혈됩니다. ③ 하지만, 그런 나쁜 독서 습관이 눈에 영구적인 손상을 가하는 건 아닙니다. ④ 그럼에도 불구하고 눈의 피로는 눈 건강에 좋지 않습니다. ⑤ 의사들은 남용이나 오용으로 인한 눈의 피로로 시력이 안 좋아질 가능성을 배제하지 않습니다. ⑥ 그리고 어린 시절 눈을 어떻게 사용하느냐가 시력에 영향을 미칠 수 있습니다. ⑦ 눈의 피로를 줄이려면, 조명이 잘 된 방에서 책이나 신문을 읽고 눈이 잠깐 쉴 수 있도록 가끔씩 쉬는 시간을 가집니다. ⑧ 마찬가지로 텔레비전에 너무 가까이 앉거나 남의 안경을 쓰는 것 역시 눈을 손상시키는 건 아닙니다. ⑨ 텔레비전에 가까이 앉으면 근시가 생기겠지만, 이런 두 가지 행동이 눈에 영구 손상을 입힌다는 증거는 없습니다. ⑩ 눈에 관한 낭설이 하나 더 있는데, 바로 당근입니다. ⑪ 당근은 베타카로틴이 풍부한데, 이는 몸 안에서 비타민 A로 바뀝니다. ⑫ 비타민 A는 정상 시력을 유지하는데 필수적이라서 비타민 A 부족은 실명의 주요 원인입니다. ⑬ 그렇지만 추가적인 당근을 먹는다고 시력이 좋아지는 건 아닙니다.

문제 정답 및 해설

1. (d) 지문의 제목으로 적당한 것을 고르세요.
   a. TV로부터 어떻게 눈을 보호할 것인가
   b. 눈에 주의하라 : 사방에 도사리는 위험 (keep an eye on 지켜보다, 주의하며 주시하다)
   c. 예상치 못한 비타민 A에 관한 사실들
   d. 눈에 관한 사실과 낭설

2. (c) 눈의 피로를 줄이고 싶다면 _____ 한다.
   a. 다른 사람들의 안경을 써야
   b. 가능할 때마다 눈을 남용하고 오용해야
   c. 가끔씩 눈을 쉬게 해야
   d. 조명이 어두운 방에서 책을 읽어야

3. 각 문장에 알맞은 표현을 고르세요.

   a. (bloodshed) 나는 이 문제가 유혈 사태 없이 해결되기를 바랐다.
   【해설】bloodshot a. 핏발이 선 / bloodshed n. 유혈사태 / bloodstained a. 핏자국이 있는, 피투성이의 ▶ without 다음에 형용사나 절이 올 수 없고 명사/명사구가 온다.
   * be settled without bloodshed 유혈 사태 없이 해결되다

   b. (despite) 베이커 씨는 나의 많은 결점에도 불구하고 팀에 나를 넣어 주었다.
   【해설】despite + 명사(구) (= in spite of + 명사(구)) …에도 불구하고 despite that 또는 despite the fact that + 주어 + 동사
   ex) despite my many faults 나의 많은 결점에도 불구하고
   = despite (the fact) that I have many faults
   * 'in spite of'와 혼동하여 despite 다음에 of를 넣기 쉽지만, despite 다음에는 of가 오지 않는다. (despite = in spite of)

   c. (exclude) 명확한 증거물은 없지만, 화성에 생명체가 있을 가능성을 배제하지 않는다.
   【해설】include 포함하다 / exclude 배제하다 / preclude …못하게 하다 ▶ even though 이하 내용으로 보아 문맥상 exclude가 와야 자연스럽다.

54 미백 치약이 치아를 희게 만들지 않는다는 거 아세요?

① 모든 광고가 다 사실은 아니라는 거 아실 겁니다. ② 미백 치약은 커피, 차, 음식으로 얼룩진 치아의 표면을 닦아줍니다. ③ 치약 속의 연마제 성분이 얼룩을 제거하는 것뿐입니다. ④ 그건 치아를 더 희게 보이도록 만들 뿐, 치아를 희게 만드는 건 아닙니다. ⑤ 그러니까 광고에서 하는 말은 낭설일 뿐 아니라 일종의 과대광고입니다. ⑥ 치약은 다 그게 그거라는 낭설이 있습니다. ⑦ 낭설입니다. ⑧ 어떤 치약은 다른 치약에 비해 연마성분, 염색제, 알코올, 인공 감미료나 향이 더 많이 들어 있습니다. ⑨ 또 어떤 것은 불소가 들었고, 어떤 것은 들어 있지 않습니다. ⑩ 전문가들에 의하면 알코올과 염색제가 없고 연마제가 적게 들어 있는 게 좋은 치약입니다. ⑪ 덧붙이자면 많은 사람들이 불소가 없는 것보다 있는 게 더 좋은 치약이라고 믿습니다. ⑫ 이건 낭설이 아닌데, 불소 사용이 충치가 적게 생기는 것과 밀접한 관련이 있기 때문입니다. ⑬ 그러나 '더 많이 사용할수록 더 좋다'라는 일반적인 치약 낭설은 사실이 아닙니다.
⑭ 치약은 더 많이 사용할수록 돈만 더 낭비할 뿐입니다. ⑮ 중요한 건 양치 방법, 치약과 칫솔의 품질이지, 치약과 거품의 양이 아닙니다.

문제 정답 및 해설

1. (d) 이 글의 요지를 고르세요.
   a. 치아를 위해 불소 함유 치약을 구매해야 한다.
   b. 과대광고는 중범죄이다.
   c. 치약은 다 다르지만 가격은 다 똑같다.
   d. 화이트닝 치약은 이를 희게 보이게 할 뿐 이를 희게 만들지는 않는다.

2. (c) 지문 내용과 맞지 않는 것을 고르세요.
   a. 모든 상업 광고가 다 사실은 아니며 화이트닝 치약 광고도 예외는 아니다.
   b. 화이트닝 치약이 근본적으로 이를 희게 만들어주는 건 아니다.
   c. 모든 화이트닝 치약은 동일한 양의 불소를 함유하고 있다. ▶ 불소가 든 것도 있고 들지 않는 것도 있다.
   d. 중요한 점은 칫솔질하는 방법이지 치약 가격이 아니다.

3. 각 문장에 알맞은 표현을 고르세요.

   a. (what) 네가 방금 한 말은 내가 들어본 가장 어리석은 말 중 하나이다.
   【해설】 이 문장의 주어는 'What you just said(네가 지금 한 말)', 동사는 is. What은 선행사를 포함한 관계대명사로 'The thing that you just said'의 의미이다.

   b. (non-profit) 진짜 비영리 단체인 4U 센터가 현재 자원봉사자들을 모집 중이다.
   ▎bona fide 진짜의 non-profit 비영리의 organization 단체 recruit (사원, 신병, 회원을) 모집하다 volunteer 자원봉사자
   【해설】 non- '…이 아닌'의 의미를 만드는 접두어로 non 대신 no, not이 쓰이지 않는다.
   ex) nonsense 터무니없는 말 / non-fiction 실화 / non-verbal 비언어적인 / non-oil 석유 이외의 / non-taxable 비과세 대상의 (하이픈 없이 사용하기도 한다.)

   c. (weren't) 그녀의 쪽지 중 일부는 책상 위에 다 흩어져 있었지만, 일부는 그렇지 않았다.
   【해설】 be spread 흩어지다(수동태) spread는 과거, 과거분사 형태가 동일하다. ▶ 앞 문장의 동사, 시제와 일치시켜야 한다. some were spread… some weren't (spread).

커피가 술 깨는데 도움이 안 된다는 거 아세요?

① 어떤 사람들은 커피가 술 깨는 데 도움이 된다고 생각합니다. ② 그들은 술 마신 후 커피 한 잔을 마시면 술기운이 평소보다 빨리 없어지거나 최소한 카페인 뒤로 술기운을 숨길 수 있다고 생각합니다. ③ 하지만, 그건 낭설입니다. ④ 아무리 많은 커피를 마셔도, 알코올로 인한 느린 반응 시간과 안 좋은 판단력은 카페인으로 없어지지도 않고 감출 수도 없습니다. ⑤ 게다가 커피가 힘을 북돋는다는 소문 역시 낭설입니다. ⑥ 커피가 힘이 나게 한다고 느끼는 이유는 커피를 마시면 잠이 덜 온다고 느끼기 때문입니다. ⑦ 커피가 잠을 깨고 정신을 차리게 하는 건 맞지만, 그건 카페인이 자극제이기 때문입니다. ⑧ 그래서 커피의 힘으로 일을 더 잘할 수 있고 또는 밤늦게까지 공부할 수 있는 것입니다. ⑨ 하지만, 빈혈과 커피의 관계는 낭설이 아닙니다. ⑩ 실제 커피는 비타민 C, 칼슘, 아연, 철분 같은 비타민과 미네랄 손실을 야기합니다. ⑪ 그래서 빈혈(철분 결핍)이 있다면 커피를 피해야 합니다.

문제 정답 및 해설

1. (a) 이 글의 요지를 고르세요.
   a. 커피의 카페인은 단순히 자극제일 뿐, 만병통치약은 아니다.
   b. 공부할 때 커피를 마시지 않으면 좋은 성적을 받을 수 없다.
   c. 카페인이 자극제이기 때문에 커피는 대단히 위험하다.
   d. 알코올의 효과를 커피 뒤로 숨길 수 있다.

2. (c) 빈혈과 커피는 _____.
   a. 서로 아무 관련이 없다
   b. 공통점이 있다
   c. 서로 관련이 있다
   d. 서로 아무 관련이 없다

3. 각 문장에 알맞은 표현을 고르세요.
   a. (wear off) 마취가 풀리는데 (마취제 효과가 없어지는데) 얼마나 오래 걸립니까? | how long does it take …하는데 시간이 얼마나 걸리는가? anesthesia 마취제
   【해설】 wear off (서서히 조금씩, 닳아서) 없어지다 / go out 나가다 / sober up 술이 깨다 ▶ 문맥상 wear off가 적당하다.

b. (suffering from) 얼마나 많은 어린이들이 기아로 고통당하고 있습니까?
【해설】 suffer는 번역하면 수동의 의미 같지만 수동태 (be suffered by)로 쓰지 않는다.
ex) I suffer from insomnia. (O) 나는 불면증을 앓고 있다.
    I am suffered from insomnia. (X)

c. (how) 네가 어떤 노래를 부르든 간에 그리고 얼마나 잘하든 간에 나는 너를 우승자로 뽑지 않을 것이다.
【해설】 no matter 의문사 + 주어 + 동사 ▶ 양보의 의미를 가진 부사절로 의문사는 이어지는 문맥에 따라 적절히 사용한다.
* how의 경우 형용사나 부사 위치는 how뒤에 온다는 점에 주의 (no matter how (형용사/부사) + 주어 + 동사)
ex) no matter how good she looks
    그녀가 얼마나 멋지게 보이든 상관없이
    no matter where you go 네가 어디를 가든 상관없이
    no matter who comes 누가 오든 상관없이

휴대폰과 주유소 화재는 관계가 없다는 거 아세요?

① 과거 90년대에, 시간 많은 어떤 사람이 사람들에게 가짜 이메일을 보내면서 쉘 오일 회사가 주유소에서 휴대폰 사용의 위험에 대해 경고했다고 주장했습니다. ② 그때 이후 꽤 많은 사람들이 갑작스런 가솔린 화재를 휴대폰 때문이라고 비난하고 있습니다. ③ 하지만 쉘 오일 측은 그런 경고를 한 적이 없으며, '그런 사고에 대해서도 들은 바 없다'고 밝혔습니다. ④ 화재 조사 결과 주유소에서의 갑작스런 화재 원인은 사실 정전기로 밝혀졌습니다. ⑤ 전문가들에 의하면 휴대폰은 불을 붙일 정도의 강력한 정전기를 발산하지 않는다는데, 이는 '휴대폰이 주유소에서 화재를 일으켰다'는 게 낭설이라는 뜻입니다. ⑥ 하지만 휴대폰을 사용하거나 켤 때 정전기가 나올 가능성이 있긴 있습니다. ⑦ 그 양이 불을 붙일 정도로 강하지는 않지만, 주유소 주인과 휴대폰 제조업자들은 안전한 길로 가기 선호합니다. ⑧ 그래서 이들은 고객들이 주유 중 휴대폰을 사용하지 않기를 당부하며 '불편해도 안전한 게 낫다'고 말합니다. ⑨ 참고로 '주유소에서 흡연은 불을 낼 수 있다'는 말은 절대 낭설이 아닙니다. ⑩ 주유소에서는 절대 금연입니다.

문제 정답 및 해설

1. (d) 지문의 제목으로 적당한 것을 고르세요.
   a. 경고! 주유소에서 휴대전화를 사용할 생각도 마라.
   b. 진짜 용의자는 흡연자들
   c. 또 다른 낭설 적발 : 주유소에서 담배 피워도 된다!
   d. 갑작스런 주유소 화재 : 누구의 잘못인가?

2. (c) 지문 내용과 맞는 것을 고르세요.
   a. 쉘 오일에서는 주유소에서 휴대전화 사용의 위험에 대해 경고했다. ▶ 경고한 적 없다.
   b. 주유소에서의 갑작스런 화재 원인은 휴대전화에서 발생한 정전기였다. ▶ 휴대전화에서 정전기가 발생하긴 하지만 불을 붙일 정도로 강하지 않다.
   c. 불을 붙이려면 강력한 정전기가 필요하다.
   d. '주유 시 흡연은 위험하다'는 건 완전 낭설이다. ▶ 낭설이 아니라 사실이다.

3. 각 문장에 알맞은 표현을 고르세요.
   a. (lots of) 서두를 필요 없다. 시간은 많으니까.
   【해설】 a large number of + 가산 명사 / lots of [plenty of] + 가산, 불가산 명사 / as many as ...만큼 많은 + 가산 명사 ▶ time은 불가산 명사이기 때문에 a large number of, as many as는 올 수 없다. (have lots of [plenty of] time 시간이 많다)

   b. (for) 이것에 대해 나를 비난하지 말라. 당신은 당신의 실수에 대해 비난할 상대를 찾는 것뿐이다.
   【해설】 blame (사람) for ...에 대해 (누구를) 비난하다 ▶ blame은 전치사 for와 함께 쓰인다.

   c. (possibly) 내가 사장님께 한 말을 어떻게 당신이 알 수 있는가? 나는 그와 불과 일 분 전에 말했다.
   【해설】 possible a. 가능한 / possibly ad. 아마 / possibility n. 가능성 ▶ 품사에 따라 의미가 달라지므로 혼동하지 않도록 주의한다. 부사 possibly의 경우 '아마'의 의미로 쓰일 수도 있고, 놀랍거나 짜증나는 상황을 강조할 때 쓰이기도 한다.
   ex) How could this possibly go wrong?
   어떻게 이게 잘못될 수가 있지? (이게 잘못되는 게 가능한 일인가?)

57 코피가 날 때 머리를 뒤로 젖히면 안 된다는 거 아세요?

① 알아두면 좋은 몇 가지 의학적 낭설이 있습니다. ② 코피가 날 때 머리를 뒤로 젖히는 건 좋은 생각이 아닙니다. ③ 많은 사람들이 그러면 출혈이 멎는 데 도움이 된다고 믿지만 그건 낭설인데, 그럼 피가 목구멍으로 들어가 구역질과 구토가 생길 수 있기 때문입니다. ④ 코피를 멈추게 하는 올바른 방법은 머리를 앞으로 숙이고 손가락으로 콧구멍을 단단히 집는 것입니다. ⑤ 사람들은 아플 때 누워야 한다고 생각합니다. ⑥ 일반적으로 맞는 말입니다. ⑦ 하지만 가끔은, 특히 심장 마비의 경우에는 낭설이 될 수도 있습니다. ⑧ 심장마비가 온 사람은 당장 누워야 한다는 게 맞는 소리 같지만, 누우면 숨쉬기가 더 힘들어질 수 있습니다. ⑨ 심장마비가 오면 병원에 가기 전에 눕기보다는 무릎을 굽히고 앉아 있는 게 더 낫습니다. ⑩ 한 가지 더. 꽤 많은 부모들이 아이들에게 츄잉껌을 삼키지 말라고 주의를 줍니다. ⑪ 그들은 껌이 장에 눌어붙으리라 생각하는데 그건 낭설입니다. ⑫ 껌 베이스가 소화되지 않고 남는 건 사실이지만, 소화 기관을 거쳐 배출됩니다.

문제 정답 및 해설

1. (c) 이 글의 요지를 고르세요.
   a. 심장 마비 환자들은 가능할 때마다 머리를 뒤로 기울여야 한다.
   b. 피를 목구멍 안으로 넘기고 싶다면, 껌 한 개를 사라.
   c. 잘못된 의학 정보는 위험하거나 심지어 치명적일 수 있다.
   d. 병을 앓고 있다면 누우면 안 된다.

2. (c) _____, 메스꺼움과 구토를 느낄 것이다.
   a. 코를 세게 쥐면
   b. 심장 마비일 때 눕는다면
   c. 코피 날 때 고개를 뒤로 젖힌다면
   d. 껌을 삼킨다면

3. 각 문장에 알맞은 표현을 고르세요.

a. (vomited) '하루 종일 내 마음을 헤집고 다녔으니 당신의 다리가 피곤하겠군요.' 같은 폴의 싸구려 작전 문구를 듣고 난 후 거의 토할 뻔했다. ▌cheesy 싸구려의, 저급한 pick-up line 여자를 유혹하려는 말
【해설】'vomit, throw up, puke' 모두 '토하다, 게우다'라는 뜻이지만, 동사가 와야 할 자리이기 때문에 throwing up이 올 수 없고, 주어가 3인칭 단수, 현재 주어가 아닌 'I'이기 때문에 pukes가 올 수 없다. 참고로 vomit의 과거형을 vomitted와 같이 -tt-로 쓰지 않도록 주의한다.

b. (Bleeding) 혈액 유출이라고도 하는 출혈은 혈액 손실을 의미한다.
【해설】'bleed'는 동사로 '피를 흘리다', 'bleeding'은 명사로 '출혈' 그리고 'blood'는 명사로 '피, 혈액'이다. 비슷한 의미의 단어인 hemorrhage는 명사로는 '출혈' 동사로는 '출혈하다, 피를 흘리다'로 쓰인다. 문제에서는 동사가 올 수 없고, hemorrhaging과 같은 의미의 명사가 와야 하기 때문에 bleeding이 와야 한다.

c. (lie) 먼저 당신의 책을 탁자 위에 올려놓고 소파에 누우세요.
【해설】lay A on B: A를 B에(on) 올려놓다. / lie down on …에 눕다 ▶ '눕다'라는 뜻의 동사 lie의 과거형이 lay라서 lay와 lie 동사를 혼동하기 쉽다. (lie–lay–lain lying) 이 경우 문장 내의 시제와 문맥, 목적어의 유무를 잘 살펴야 한다. (lie는 자동사, lay는 타동사)
ex) My little boy lay (down) on his bed and sang loudly. (lie의 과거형)
   내 어린 아들은 자기 침대에 누워 큰 소리로 노래를 불렀다.
   Carter laid his credit card on the counter.
   카터는 그의 신용 카드를 카운터에 올려놓았다. (lay의 과거형)

58 어린이들에게 가장 흔한 음식 알레르기가 무엇인지 아세요?

① 많은 사람들이 어린이들에게 가장 흔한 음식 알레르기는 땅콩이라고 생각합니다. ② 그건 사실이 아닙니다. ③ 땅콩 알레르기가 있는 사람들이 많고 땅콩 알레르기 반응이 대단히 위험하긴 하지만, 어린이들 사이에 가장 흔한 음식 알레르기는 우유 알레르기입니다. ④ 알레르기에 관한 또 다른 낭설이 있습니다. ⑤ '나는 고양이 (또는 털을 가진 다른 동물들) 털에 알레르기가 있어.'라고 말하는 사람들이 있습니다. ⑥ 대부분의 경우, 이들은 고양이의 털이 아니라 고양이 침 혹은 고양이 피부 조각 내의 단백질에 알레르기가 있는 겁니다. ⑦ 또 '너무 깨끗한 게 알레르기의 원인이 될 수도 있다'는 건 낭설이 아닐지도 모르는데 위생가설이라는 게 있기 때문입니다. ⑧ 위생가설은 너무 깨끗한 현대 생활방식이 어린이들 사이에 알레르기가 증가하는 데 일조했을 수도 있다고 말합니다. ⑨ 세균이 없는 생활방식 덕분에, 인간의 몸은 과거만큼 세균과 싸울 필요가 없어졌습니다. ⑩ 그 결과, 다양한 박테리아와 곰팡이에 노출되지 않은 면역체계는 꽃가루, 진드기처럼 그다지 해롭지 않은 물질에 과민반응을 보이거나 민감하게 반응하는 경향이 생겼습니다. ⑪ 실제로 박테리아와 바이러스에 자주 노출된 어린이들은 그렇지 않은 어린이들보다 알레르기가 더 적게 나타나는 경향이 있습니다.

문제 정답 및 해설

1. (b) 이 글의 요지를 고르세요.
   a. 고양이털에 알레르기를 가진 사람들은 모든 종류의 털이 있는 동물을 피해야 한다.
   b. 알레르기에 대한 잘못된 낭설이 몇 가지 있다.
   c. 너무 깨끗한 생활 방식이 땅콩 알레르기의 주원인이다.
   d. 인간의 면역 체계는 다양한 박테리아에 노출되어야 한다.

2. (b) 지문 내용과 맞지 않는 것을 고르세요.
   a. 어린이들 중 가장 흔한 음식 알레르기는 우유 알레르기이다.
   b. 어떤 사람들은 그게 있다고 믿긴 하지만 위생가설이라는 건 없다. ▶ 어느 정도 신빙성을 인정받은 '위생가설'이라는 게 실제로 있다.
   c. 땅콩에 대한 알레르기 반응은 대단히 위험하고 심각할 수 있다.
   d. 고양이털에 알레르기가 있다고 주장하는 사람들은 고양이 침 안의 단백질에 알레르기일 가능성이 있다.

3. 각 문장에 알맞은 표현을 고르세요.

   a. (your help) 너의 도움 덕분에 우리에게 콘서트 표가 있다.
   【해설】thanks to + 명사, 동명사 : ...덕분에, 때문에 ▶ to 다음에 동사 원형이 오지 않는다는 점 주의
   ex) You mean, your life was saved thanks to being hit by a car?
   자동차에 치인 덕분에 네 목숨이 구조될 수 있었다는 말인가?
   Thanks to the hurricane, we have no food, no water, no electricity.
   허리케인 때문에 우리는 음식도, 물도, 전기도 없다.

   b. (for) 기억을 책임지는 건 뇌의 어느 부분입니까?
   【해설】be responsible for ...에 책임이 있는, 원인인 ▶ responsible은 전치사 for와 쓰인다.

   c. (hate) 궁금한데, 잭은 그가 그렇다고 말한 것만큼 나를 싫어합니까?
   【해설】의문문에서 이미 does에 3인칭 단수 현재가 표현되었기 때문에 본동사는 원형이 와야 한다. 그래서 dislikes, cursed 모두 올 수 없고 동사 원형인 hate만 올 수 있다.
   * 'do'는 조동사로 쓰일 때 동사 앞에 놓여 의문문/부정문을 만들거나, 지문처럼 동사의 반복을 피하기 위해 반복되는 동사 대신 쓰이기도 한다(대동사).
   .... as much as he says he does ▶ he says 'he hates me'

우리가 섭취하는 설탕 대부분이 단 과자에서 나오는 게 아니라는 거 아세요?

① 부모님들은 자녀들에게 '설탕이 많이 들어 있으니까 단 과자를 줄여라'고 말합니다. ② 맞는 말입니다. ③ 많은 단 과자에는 과도한 설탕이 들어 있고, 그래서 '단 과자'라고 불립니다. ④ 하지만, 동시에 낭설이라고 할 수 있습니다. ⑤ 설탕을 줄이려면 탄산음료와 스포츠음료를 포함한 음료수를 끊어야 합니다. ⑥ 이런 단 음료들이 진짜 범인입니다. ⑦ 미국의 대부분 학교가 교내의 음료수 자판기를 괜히 없앤 게 아닙니다. ⑧ 또 많은 어른들은 설탕이 아이들을 심하게 활동적으로 만든다고 믿습니다. ⑨ 하지만 많은 연구에 의하면, 그건 낭설입니다. ⑩ 생일 파티 때 아이들은 좀 정신없이 행동해서 소파에서 뛰고 큰 소리를 지르는 경향이 있습니다. ⑪ 그건 케이크, 쿠키, 사탕 같은 설탕이 든 과자를 많이 먹어서가 아니라 아이들은 그냥 재미있게 놀고 싶어서 그런 겁니다. ⑫ 설탕이 아이들을 과도하게 활동적으로 만들지 않는다는 건 공식적으로 증명되었습니다. ⑬ 하지만, 설탕에 관한 다른 몇 가지 소문은 사실입니다. ⑭ 예를 들어 설탕은 정말로 심장병을 유발하고 암 위험을 높이며 심지어 늙어 보이게 만듭니다. ⑮ 그러니 건강을 위해 너무 많은 설탕을 먹지 않는 게 좋겠습니다.

문제 정답 및 해설

1. (c) 이 글의 요지를 고르세요.
   a. 설탕은 아이들을 정신없게 만들기 때문에 사악하다.
   b. 설탕을 줄이는 최선의 방법은 쿠키와 사탕을 먹지 않는 것이다.
   c. 먹는 설탕과 마시는 음료를 조심하는 게 좋다.
   d. 늙어 보이고 싶다면 설탕을 피하라.

2. (d) 미국의 많은 학교에서 학교 내 음료수 자판기를 없앴는데, 이유는 _____ 때문이다.
   a. 학생들은 가난한데 음료수는 비싸기
   b. 음료수가 학생들을 바보와 멍청이로 바꾸기
   c. 달콤한 음료수가 학생들을 과도하게 활동적으로 만들기
   d. 음료수에 과도한 양의 설탕이 들어 있기

3. 각 문장에 알맞은 표현을 고르세요.

   a. (for nothing) 아무도 그 안에 살기를 원치 않으니까 너는 헛되이 집을 짓고 있는 것이다.
   【해설】 for nothing 헛되이, 공짜로 / for something 무언가를 위해 / for free 무료로 ▶ 문맥상 for nothing이 가장 적당하다.

   b. (much) 사진 찍기 전에, 빛이 얼마나 많은지 확인하라.
   【해설】 light는 불가산 명사 ▶ much 혹은 little이 와야 한다.

   c. (raise) 닭을 기르고 싶은 사람은 달걀을 사고 닭장을 지을 돈을 모아야 한다.
   【해설】 rise (rise—rose—risen 자동사) 올라가다, 일어서다 / raise (raise—raised—raised 타동사) 일으키다, 키우다, 높이다, 모으다 ▶ 두 단어는 혼동하기 쉬우므로 주의한다.
   ex) raise money 돈을 모으다, raise children 아이를 키우다, raise one's voice 목소리를 높이다, raise one's hand 손을 들다

꿈에서 죽어도 걱정할 필요 없다는 거 아세요?

① 꿈에서 죽으면 현실에서도 죽는다는 낭설이 있습니다. ② 다행히 그건 낭설일 뿐입니다. ③ 낭떠러지에서 떨어지는데 갑자기 잠에서 깨거나, 꿈꾸다 총알에 맞는 순간 모든 게 느닷없이 멈춰버리기도 합니다. ④ 이런 종류의 꿈 역시 죽는 꿈에 포함됩니다. ⑤ 우리가 기억하지 못하는 꿈이 많다는 사실을 감안할 때 거의 모든 사람들이 죽는 꿈을 꾼다고 할 수 있습니다. ⑥ 하지만 죽는 꿈을 꾼 뒤 죽었다는 사람을 찾기는 쉽지 않습니다. ⑦ 그래서 아직 그런 무서운 꿈을 꾼 적이 없다면, 걱정할 필요는 없습니다. ⑧ 그런데 꿈에 관한 재미있는 낭설이 있습니다. ⑨ 어떤 사람들은 꿈은 통제할 수 없다고 말하지만 그건 잘못된 낭설인데, 어떤 사람들은 할 수 있기 때문입니다. ⑩ 그걸 '자각몽'이라고 합니다. ⑪ 놀랍게도 사람들 중 10% 정도는 꿈을 통제할 수 있거나, 자신이 꿈을 꿀 때 꿈이라는 걸 인지할 수 있습니다. ⑫ 이들은 실제 꾸고 싶은 꿈을 통제할 수 있고 현재 꾸는 꿈에서 다른 꿈으로 바꿀 수도 있습니다.

문제 정답 및 해설

1. (a) 지문의 제목으로 적당한 것을 고르세요.
   a. 죽는 꿈에 대해 걱정할 필요 없다.
   b. 자각몽에 대한 진실, 드디어 밝혀지다
   c. 꿈을 통제한다? 마치 꿈이 이루어지는 것과 같다!
   d. 꿈을 통제하는 방법

2. (a) 지문 내용과 맞는 것을 고르세요.
   a. 거의 모든 사람이 죽는 꿈을 꾼 적이 있다.
   b. 열심히 훈련하면 원하는 대로 꿈을 통제할 수 있다. ▶ 훈련을 통해 꿈을 통제할 수 있다는 내용은 나오지 않았다.
   c. 현재 꿈에서 다른 꿈으로 변하게 하는 건 불가능하다. ▶ 약 10%의 사람들이 꿈을 통제할 수 있다고 한다.
   d. 자각몽 전문가들은 무서운 꿈을 꾸지 않는다. ▶ 꿈을 인식하거나 바꿀 수 있다고 했지 무서운 꿈을 꾸지 않는다고는 나오지 않았다.

3. 각 문장에 알맞은 표현을 고르세요.

   a. (woke) 늦어서 미안합니다. 늦잠을 자서 늦게 일어났습니다.
   【해설】 wake up late 늦게 일어나다 ▶ 문장이 과거 시제이기 때문에 wake나 waken같은 현재형은 쓸 수 없다. waken, awake 모두 '잠에서 깨다'는 뜻이지만 awake는 형용사로 더 자주 쓰이고, waken이나 awake보다는 wake up이 '잠에서 깨다'는 뜻의 표현으로 더 자주 통용된다.

   b. (what) 나는 너무 우울하고 지쳐서 내가 해야 할 일을 할 수 없다.
   【해설】 선행사를 포함한 관계대명사 what ▶ I can't do things that I am supposed to do. (내가 해야 할 일들) 밑줄 친 things that이 what으로 쓰인 것.

   c. (dreamed) 이틀 전, 낸시는 자기 남동생에게 공격당하는 꿈을 꾸었다.
   【해설】 문장의 시제가 과거이므로 dream의 과거형을 써야 한다. 동사 dream의 과거형은 dreamed 또는 dreamt이다.

Chapter 7. The Supernatural

61. 서구 문화에서도 손금을 읽는다는 거 아세요?

① 서구인들도 손금을 믿을까요? ② 많은 이들이 서구 문화는 과학적이고 합리적이며 미신과 거리가 멀다고 생각합니다. ③ 하지만, 수상술이라고도 하는 손금은 오랫동안 여러 서구 나라에서 행해져 왔습니다. ④ 그 근원은 인디언의 점성술과 집시의 점술에서 찾을 수 있습니다. ⑤ 어떤 이들은 손금을 읽으면 사람의 성격과 미래를 알 수 있다고 생각합니다. ⑥ 누가 가장 먼저 손바닥의 선을 연구하고 읽기 시작했는지는 아무도 모르지만, 서구인들을 포함해 전 세계 사람들은 손바닥에 선이 많이 나 있으며 그 선이 사람마다 다르다는 걸 알아챘습니다. ⑦ 그들은 그 선이 무언가를 의미하는 게 분명하고 무언가를 밝힐 수 있다고 생각했습니다. ⑧ 믿거나 말거나지만, 미국, 캐나다, 영국, 독일, 그 외의 다른 국가들에 손금에 관한 책이 수백 권이나 됩니다. ⑨ 인터넷에서 손금에 관한 웹사이트도 쉽게 찾을 수 있습니다. ⑩ 물론 이 서구 국가들에서 손금 읽는 사람들도 만날 수 있습니다. ⑪ 이들 자료에 의하면, 네 가지 주요 선은 심장선, 머리선, 생명선, 그리고 운명선입니다. ⑫ (운명선은 모두가 갖고 있는 건 아닙니다.)

문제 정답 및 해설

1. (d) 지문의 제목으로 적당한 것을 고르세요.
   a. 볼 것인가, 말 것인가 : 손금에 관한 모든 것
   b. 손금 보는 사람들 : 지옥의 사자
   c. 손금 보는 사람들, 구류되다
   d. 서양 문화의 손금 읽기

2. (a) 손금 읽는 사람들은 _____ 사람들의 성격을 알아낸다고 주장한다.
   a. 손바닥의 몇몇 선을 읽어서
   b. 손바닥의 숨겨진 선을 찾아내서
   c. 손바닥의 몇몇 선을 만들어서
   d. 얼굴 표정을 조사해서

3. 각 문장에 알맞은 표현을 고르세요.

   a. (on) 인터넷에 광고를 싣는 데 얼마를 내야 합니까?
   ▮ How much do I have to pay to …하는데 얼마를 내야 합니까? place an ad 광고를 싣다. (ad= advertisement)
   【해설】'인터넷에'의 경우 전치사 on을 쓴다. 그러나 newspaper의 경우 신문 지면에 글이나 사진, 그림이 올라오기 때문에 on the newspaper로 쓰기 쉽지만, in the newspaper가 맞다.

   b. (has) 모두가 다 너처럼 날씬한 몸매를 가진 건 아니다.
   ▮ slim 날씬한, 마른
   【해설】 everybody, everyone, each one 등의 표현은 단수동사와 쓰인다.
   * 부분 부정 : 'not (부정어) + all, every, always, entirely, exactly…' 뒤에 이어지는 단어(주어)에 동사의 수를 맞춘다.

   c. (in) 그들은 깨진 거울에 관한 미신을 믿고 있었지만 이를 상관하지 않는 척했다.
   ▮ superstition 미신 the broken mirror superstition 깨진 거울은 불운을 의미한다는 미신 pretend …인 척 하다 care about 신경 쓰다, 관심을 갖다
   【해설】 believe (단순히) 믿다, …로 생각하다 (that + 주어 + 동사)
   ex) I believe he is a good man. 나는 그가 좋은 사람이라고 믿는다.
   　　　believe in (명사) …에 신앙(믿음)을 갖다
   ex) believe in God = have faith in God
   　　　하느님을 믿다, 하느님에 대한 신앙이 있다

62 카퍼필드가 자유의 여신상을 어떻게 사라지게 했는지 아세요?

① 1983년 자유의 여신상이 정말 사라졌다. ② 이 마술쇼는 CBS에서 생방송으로 방영되었고 데이비드 카퍼필드가 진행했다. ③ 그가 여신상을 관객들 앞에서 사라지게 했을 때, 자동차 공중 부양 같은 그의 굉장한 마술에 이미 익숙해졌음에도 불구하고 시청자들은 놀라지 않을 수 없었다. ④ 그는 이를 어떻게 한 것일까? ⑤ 두 기둥 사이에 관객들이 앉아 있었고, 두 기둥 사이로 멀리 여신상이 보였다. ⑥ 먼저 그는 두 기둥에 달린 커튼을 내려 관객들이 여신상을 볼 수 없도록 했다. ⑦ 그가 커튼을 올렸을 때 사람들은 두 기둥 사이의 여신상을 볼 수 없었다. ⑧ 참으로 놀라웠다. ⑨ 어떤 이들은 관객이 앉아 있던 단상이 턴테이블처럼 몰래 움직이는 단이었다고 주장했다. ⑩ 카퍼필드가 커튼을 내릴 때 단이 아주 천천히 움직였다는 것이다. ⑪ 관객과 TV 시청자들은 거대한 여신상을 볼 수 없었지만, 사실 이들은 똑같이 만든 다른 무대를 보았을 수도 있다는 것이다. ⑫ 아니면 카퍼필드가 대단히 밝은 조명을 이용해서 관객들을 몇 초 동안 일시적인 야맹 상태가 되게 했을 수도 있다. ⑬ 어느 쪽이든 여신상은 결국 사라진 게 아니었다. ⑭ 그냥 안 보인 것뿐이었다.

문제 정답 및 해설

1. (b) 이 글의 요지를 고르세요.
   a. 카퍼필드 때문에 자유의 여신상은 다시 만들어져야 했다.
   b. 카퍼필드는 자유의 여신상을 마술로 사라지게 했다.
   c. 마술사는 전 세계인들을 속인 죄로 체포되었다.
   d. 카퍼필드는 여신상을 사라지게 해야 했지만, 할 수 없었다.

2. (c) 지문 내용과 맞는 것을 고르세요.
   a. 자유의 여신상은 1983년에 사라져서 다시 나타나지 않았다.
   b. 데이비드 카퍼필드는 유명하지만, 외모 때문에 인기는 없다.
   c. 어떤 이들은 카퍼필드가 사람들을 속이려고 몰래 움직이는 단상을 이용했다고 말했다.
   d. 관객들과는 달리, TV 시청자들은 여신상이 사라졌을 때 놀라지 않았다.

3. 각 문장에 알맞은 표현을 고르세요.

   a. (aired on) 지난 주 런던에서 사망한 대통령의 장례식은 텔레비전으로 방송될 것이다. ▮funeral 장례식, air 방송하다(=broadcast), be aired on TV 텔레비전에 방영되다
   【해설】주어는 the funeral, 동사는 will be aired : 장례식이 방영되는 것 ▶ 수동태, TV 앞에는 전치사 on이 온다.
   * '방송되다, 방영하다'라는 의미의 동사 air는 능동, 수동 두 가지 모두 쓰인다.
   ex) How many episodes of the show 'CSI' have aired so far?
   CSI 프로그램의 에피소드가 지금까지 얼마나 많이 방영했는가?
   How many episodes of the show 'CSI' have been aired so far?
   CSI 프로그램의 에피소드가 지금까지 얼마나 많이 방영되었는가?
   본문에서는 'This magic show aired...'처럼 능동으로 쓰였는데, 'The game will be aired at 2 pm on ESPN. 경기가 ESPN에서 오후 2시에 방영될 것이다.'처럼 수동으로 쓰일 수도 있다.

   b. (between) 나는 잭과 질 사이에 앉았을 때, 완전히 꿔다 놓은 보릿자루 같은 느낌이었다. ▮a third wheel 불필요한, 없어야 하는 존재
   【해설】둘 사이 between / 셋 이상 among / 옆에 next to ▶ Jack and Jill 두 명 사이에 앉았기 때문에 between이 맞다.
   'feel like a third wheel 꿔다 놓은 보릿자루 같은 느낌이다.(원래 없어야 하는데 눈치 없이 끼어 있는 사람이 된 느낌이다)' third 대신 fifth가 쓰이기도 한다.

   c. (sat on) 잭은 의자 제조업자를 고소하길 원했는데, 그가 앉았던 의자가 무너지면서 그가 부상을 당했기 때문이었다.
   ▮sue 고소하다 manufacturer 제조업자 collapse 무너지다
   【해설】'...에 앉다'라는 표현에서는 동사 sit과 함께 전치사 on이 함께 쓰여야 한다.
   문제 the chair he sat on collapsed(주어는 the chair, 동사는 collapsed : the chair (which he sat on) collapsed)의 의미는 'he sat on the chair, and that chair collapsed'의 뜻이다.

63 미국인 점술사들은 어떻게 광고를 내는지 아세요?

① 미국, 캐나다, 영국 등에도 점술사 또는 점쟁이가 있습니다. ② 인터넷, 신문, 잡지에 나온 이들의 광고도 어렵지 않게 찾을 수 있습니다. ③ 여기 그들이 점쟁이 사업을 어떻게 홍보하는지 보여주는 그런 광고 중 한 예가 있습니다. ④ 도라 참캐스터 : 진짜 심령술사, 35년 경력 ⑤ 더 나은 미래를 위해 오늘 전화하세요. ⑥ 도라는 항상 여러분 곁에 있습니다. ⑦ 제 점술은 200% 정확해서 심지어 다른 점술사들도 조언을 들으려고 저를 찾아옵니다. ⑧ – 온갖 종류의 다양한 사랑의 주문을 제공하는데 이를테면, 상대가 바람을 피우지 않게 할 주문, 누군가 자신을 좋아하게 만들 주문, 연인의 거짓말을 방지하는 주문 등 많습니다. ⑨ 또 저렴한 가격에 사랑의 묘약도 구매하실 수 있습니다. ⑩ – 여러 가지 삶의 문제, 예를 들어 결혼, 직장, 소송, 건강, 심지어 탈모 문제까지 도와드립니다. ⑪ 또 저는 타로 카드 읽기, 영기 정화, 차크라 균형 맞추기, 찻잎 점도 봅니다. ⑫ 제 전문은 전생 봐주기입니다. ⑬ * 처음 전화하신 분은 질문 1회 무료입니다. ⑭ 언제든 부담 없이 전화하세요. *

문제 정답 및 해설

1. (a) 지문의 제목으로 적당한 것을 고르세요.
   a. 서양의 심령술사들은 어떻게 인터넷에 광고를 하는가
   b. 도라 참캐스터 : 심령술사인가 정신병자인가?
   c. 더 나은 미래를 위해 지금 도라에게 전화하세요
   d. 마법의 사랑의 묘약 판매

2. (a) 다른 점술인들이 도라의 조언을 구하는 이유는 _____.
   a. 그녀가 정확한 점술이이기 때문이다
   b. 그녀의 사랑의 묘약이 저렴하기 때문이다
   c. 처음 전화한 사람은 돈을 내지 않아도 되기 때문이다
   d. 도라가 그들에게 그러라고 강요했기 때문이다

3. 각 문장에 알맞은 표현을 고르세요.

   a. (appeared) 먹구름이 사라진 후 하늘에 별들이 나타났다. **|** storm cloud 먹구름 appear 나타나다
   【해설】appear 1. ...인 것 같다 2. 나타나다, 보이다 3. 발생하다 4. (책) 발간되다, (방송 프로그램) 방송되다 5. (영화, TV) 출연하다 ▶ 여기에서는 '나타나다, 보이다' 즉 be seen의 의미로 수동태 be appeared로 쓰지 않고 단순 과거형 appeared가 온다.

   b. (experiments) 우리는 우리 이론을 증명할 다양한 실험을 할 필요가 있다.
   | various 다양한, experiment 실험, prove 증명하다, theory 이론
   【해설】do [conduct] an experiment 실험하다 ▶ various(다양한, 여러 가지의)라는 표현이 앞에 나왔으므로 복수형 experiments가 적당하다. 마지막 an experiment가 틀린 이유는 do various an experiment처럼 쓰지 않기 때문이다. 관사 an을 쓰려면 various를 빼고 do an experiment로 써야 한다.

   c. (advice) 신혼부부를 위한 네 조언이 '결혼하지 마라'라고?
   | newlywed 신혼부부
   【해설】advice n. 조언, 충고 advise v. 조언하다 ▶ 문제에서는 명사 advice가 와야 한다.

64 타로가 원래 카드 게임으로 사용되었다는 거 아세요?

① 타로는 한 세트의 카드로 현재 점치는데 널리 사용되고 있습니다. ② 하지만, 원래 타로는 트라이엄프스, 이탈리아 타로치니 같은 게임에 사용되었습니다. ③ 15세기에 꽤 많은 유럽인들이 이 게임을 즐겼습니다. ④ 당시 주술사들은 타로 카드가 마법, 신비주의와 아무 관련이 없다고 생각했기 때문에 타로 카드를 받아들이지 않았습니다. ⑤ 하지만, 18세기 후반부터 사람들은 인생 문제에 관한 통찰력을 얻기 위한 도구로, 또는 미래를 알기 위한 도구로 타로 카드를 사용하기 시작했습니다. ⑥ 어느 스위스 사람이 1700년대 후반에 종교적 상징주의를 연구했다고 합니다. ⑦ 그는 타로가 고대 이집트 여신 이시스와 고대 이집트 신 중 하나인 토트와 관련이 있을 수 있다고 생각했습니다. ⑧ 그는 '타로'라는 이름이 이집트어에서 온 것이며 '왕의 길'을 뜻한다고 주장했습니다. ⑨ 그의 주장에 따르면 타로는 비밀과 숨겨진 지혜로 가는 왕도를 담고 있다는 것입니다. ⑩ 후에 다른 학자들이 그의 주장을 증명할 근거가 없다는 걸 밝혀냈습니다. ⑪ 그럼에도 불구하고, 많은 사람들은 타로가 이집트 토트의 서와 밀접한 관련이 있다고 아직도 굳게 믿고 있으며, 타로는 여전히 주술인들 사이에 대중화되어 있습니다.

문제 정답 및 해설

1. (a) 지문의 제목으로 적당한 것을 고르세요.
   a. 타로 : 단순한 게임에서 점술 도구로
   b. 타로, 감추어진 비밀의 지혜로 가는 왕도
   c. 토트의 사자, 타로를 만나다
   d. 타로의 비밀이 밝혀지다!

2. (a) 지문 내용과 맞는 것을 고르세요.
   a. 일반적으로 점쟁이들과 주술인들은 타로 카드를 점술에 사용한다.
   b. 예나 지금이나 타로 카드는 점술과 놀이에 다 사용되고 있다. ▶ 전에는 놀이에만 사용되었다.
   c. 18세기 초반이 돼서야 사람들은 미래를 점치는데 타로 카드를 사용하기 시작했다. ▶ 18세기 후반에 들어서 타로 카드가 점치는데 사용되었다.
   d. 학자들은 마침내 타로 카드와 이집트 토트의 서 사이의 관계를 밝혀냈다. ▶ 둘 사이에 아무 관련이 없다는 것을 밝혀냈다.

3. 각 문장에 알맞은 표현을 고르세요.
   a. (are now widely accepted) 놀랍게도 얼굴 이식이 현재 널리 받아들여지고 있다. l to one's surprise 놀랍게도 face transplant 안면 이식

【해설】수동태에서 부사의 위치 : be 동사 + 부사 + pp
ex) We were absolutely surprised by the accident.
     우리는 그 사고에 대단히 놀랐다.

b. (During the early 1900s) 1900년대 초반에, 여성 의류는 대단히 우아하고 화려했다. l clothing 의복 stylish 스타일이 멋진 glamorous 화려한, 매력 있는
【해설】…년대: 관사 the와 함께 …년 뒤에 -s가 붙는다.
ex) during the late 1700s 1700년대 후반 중에
    in the early 1750s 1750년대 초반에

c. (connected) 나는 그의 소설이 그의 사적 경험과 관련이 있다고 생각했지만, 그의 경험과 아무 상관이 없었다.
l novel 소설 personal experience 개인적 경험 have nothing to do with 관련/상관이 없다(= don't have anything to do with)
【해설】be connected to …와 관계[관련]이 있다.

개 유령이 나타난 영화가 있다는 거 아세요?

① 2011년 10월, 몇몇 조사원들이 니거라는 개의 유령을 찾았다고 주장했는데, 니거는 세계 2차 대전 당시 영국인 파일럿 영웅 가이 깁슨이 기르던 개였습니다. ② 1954년에 촬영된 영화 〈댐 버스터〉는 공군 중령 가이 깁슨이 이끈 공습에 관한 전쟁 영화였습니다. ③ 이 영화가 개봉된 후, 어떤 사람들이 영화 후반부에 배우들 뒤로 검정개가 뛰어다니는 걸 보았다고 주장했습니다. ④ 촬영 때 개는 없었기 때문에 사람들은 그 개가 니거의 유령일지도 모른다고 생각했습니다. ⑤ 영화 이전에도, 누군가 깁슨의 매장지 부근에서 검정개를 본 적이 있다는 소문이 돌았는데, 그 중 일부 지역에 현재 RAF 스캠톤 역사박물관이 위치해있습니다. ⑥ 게다가 약 50년간 아무도 사용하지 않은 깁슨의 예전 사무실에도 깁슨의 유령이 출몰한다고 합니다. ⑦ 2011년에 유령 사냥꾼들이 깁슨의 개 유령을 찾고자 길을 나섰습니다. ⑧ 파라노말 링스라는 이 조사단은 적외선 전등, 비디오카메라 같은 장비를 갖고 깁슨의 개 유령을 잠깐이라도 보겠다는 바람으로 박물관 주변을 조사했습니다. ⑨ 조사원 중 한 사람은 그들이 전기 추적 장치를 작동시킬 때 개 혼령의 유령이 자신들에게 말을 시키려는 것 같은 느낌을 받았다고 말했습니다.

문제 정답 및 해설

1. (b) 이 글의 요지를 고르세요.
   a. 개의 유령 또는 유령의 집 같은 건 없다.
   b. 개의 유령에 대한 소문이 있는데 몇몇 사람들은 유령을 느꼈다고 주장했다.
   c. 깁슨의 매장지 근처에 가도 괜찮은데, 거기에 아무것도 없기 때문이다.
   d. 〈댐 버스터〉는 가이 깁슨과 니거가 출연한 전쟁 영화이다.

2. (d) 〈댐버스터〉가 개봉되었을 때, 몇몇 사람들은 _____ 때문에 놀랐다.
   a. 영화가 유령의 집인 RAF 스캠프톤 역사박물관에서 촬영되었기
   b. 니거가 주인인 가이 깁슨과 함께 영화에 등장했기
   c. 주연 배우가 가이 깁슨과 전혀 닮지 않았기
   d. 촬영 때 개가 없었는데도 영화에서 검정개를 보았기

3. 각 문장에 알맞은 표현을 고르세요.

   a. (catch) 어제 밤 헬리 혜성을 잠깐이라도 보기 위해 밤 늦게까지 깨어 있었다. ┃ stay up late 늦게 까지 자지 않고 깨어 있다 Helly's Commet 헬리 혜성
   【해설】 catch[get] a glimpse of 잠깐(흘끗) 보다 ▶ 이 표현은 catch나 get 이외의 다른 동사와 함께 쓰이지 않는다.

   b. (lots of complicated equipment) 많은 복잡한 장비를 설치하는 데 몇 시간이 걸렸다. ┃ it took me hours to ...하는데 몇 시간이 걸렸다 set up 설치하다 complicated 복잡한 equipment 장비
   【해설】 equipment는 셀 수 없는 명사로 -s가 올 수 없다. lots of 는 가산, 불가산 명사 모두 수식할 수 있다. lots of가 complicated equipment를 수식하기 때문에 어순이 lots of complicated equipment로 와야 맞다.

   c. (at the end of the day) 파티를 망치는 사람이 갑자기 '파티가 끝났다'라고 소리친 후, 사람들은 하나씩 집에 갔고 결국 아무도 남지 않았다. ┃ party pooper 파티를 망치는 사람, 흥·분위기를 깨는 사람 yell 소리치다 one by one 하나씩 there was no one left 아무도 남지 않았다
   【해설】 지문에 나온 표현 at the end of는 '...의 끝부분, 후반부'라는 뜻인데, at the end of the day는 '하루의 끝 무렵'이라는 뜻 외에 '결국, 중요한 것은' 이라는 뜻으로도 자주 쓰인다.

   d. (by) 잭스빌에 마법의 배나무가 있는데, 이는 욕심 많은 늙은 농부의 소유였다. ┃ own 소유하다 greedy 욕심 많은, 탐욕스러운
   【해설】 be owned by (수동태) ...에 의해 소유되다 ▶ 문제에서는 'a magic pear tree (which was) owned by a greedy old farmer.'에서 괄호 부분이 생략된 것이다.

66 당신의 얼굴이 당신의 성격을 드러낸다는 거 아세요?

① "관상학" 또는 "관상"을 믿는 사람들은 책 표지만으로 책을 판단할 수 있고 또 판단해야 한다고 생각합니다. ② 관상을 보는 사람들은 얼굴의 특징으로 사람을 알 수 있고 판단할 수 있다고 믿는데, 얼굴의 특징이 어떤 사람인지 드러내기 때문이라고 합니다. ③ 예를 들어 그들은 상대의 눈썹만 보고도 성격을 알아냅니다. ④ 진한 검은색 눈썹이나 활 모양의 눈썹을 가진 사람은 성격이 좋을 가능성이 있습니다. ⑤ 두툼한 눈썹이 납작하게 났다는 건 "냉정"하다는 뜻이고, 부드럽고 얇은 눈썹은 "몽상가"라는 뜻입니다. ⑥ 눈썹 숱이 적은 사람은 거만하고, 두꺼운 눈썹이 넓게 퍼져 있으면 공격적인 사람이라고 합니다. ⑦ 또 관상 보는 사람들은 건강 상태도 알 수 있다고 주장하는데, 내장 기관이 얼굴 부위와 관련이 있다고 믿기 때문입니다. ⑧ 예를 들면, 그들은 코는 심장, 아랫입술은 장기와 관련이 있다고 생각합니다. ⑨ 그래서 당신의 아랫입술이 부어 있다면, 관상 보는 사람들은 당신이 변비가 있거나 설사를 하는 경향이 있다고 말할 수도 있습니다. ⑩ 하지만, 관상이 항상 맞는 건 아닙니다. ⑪ 두터운 눈썹이 납작하게 난 사람 중에 관대하고 친절한 사람이 있고, 아랫입술이 튀어나왔는데 엄청난 양의 음식을 잘만 소화시키는 사람이 있으니까요.

문제 정답 및 해설

1. (d) 지문의 제목으로 적당한 것을 고르세요.
   a. 얼굴과 눈썹 사이의 관계
   b. 부정직한 관상 보는 사람들을 주의하라
   c. 부은 아랫입술의 위험
   d. 당신의 얼굴이 많은 것을 드러낸다

2. (c) 지문 내용과 맞지 않는 것을 고르세요.
   a. 관상 보는 사람들은 얼굴만 보고 당신의 성격과 미래를 추측한다.
   b. 관상 보는 사람들은 검은색의 화살 모양 눈썹을 가진 사람을 친절하고 착하다고 생각한다.
   c. 냉정한 사람들은 항상 납작하고 두꺼운 눈썹을 갖고 있다. 예외는 없다. ▶ 지문 후반부에 보면 관상 내용이 항상 맞는 건 아니고 예외는 있다고 나온다.
   d. 얇은 눈썹을 가진 사람 모두가 다 거만하고 오만한 건 아니다.

3. 각 문장에 알맞은 표현을 고르세요.

   a. (to) 나는 가난이 노숙과 분명 관련이 있다고 믿었다.
   ┃poverty 가난 (a. poor 가난한) must be ...가 틀림없다 homelessness 노숙, 집이 없음
   【해설】 be related to ...와 관련이 있다 ▶ 일반적으로 전치사 to가 쓰이는데 with가 쓰이기도 한다.

   b. (cold-blooded) 파충류는 '냉혈동물'이라 불리는데 모든 파충류의 혈액 온도가 차갑기 때문이다.
   ┃reptile 파충류 cold-blooded animal 냉혈동물 (warm-blooded animal 온혈/정온 동물) temperature 온도, 체온
   【해설】 '냉혈의'라는 뜻의 형용사는 cold-blooded. cold-blood로는 쓰지 않는다. bloody는 blood의 형용사로 '피 비린내 나는, 피가 낭자한'이란 뜻.

   c. (he is) 그가 가르치는 방식은 그가 어떤 선생인지 말해준다.
   【해설】 문제의 what은 의문사가 아니라 목적어 구실을 하는 명사절을 이끌기 때문에 what 다음에 주어, 동사 위치가 바뀌지 않는다. what kind of teacher he is ▶ 그가 어떤 종류의 선생인지를
   ex) What are you doing? 너는 무엇을 하고 있니? (의문문)
   　 I don't know what you are doing.
   　 네가 무엇을 하는지 나는 모르겠다.

우유를 끓어 넘치게 하면 불운이라는 거 아세요?

① 어떤 사람들은 우유를 끓어 넘치게 하면 불운이라고 믿습니다. ② 그럴 수도 있지만, 확실한 건 아무도 모르는데, 그건 운에 관한 수많은 미신 중 하나이기 때문입니다. ③ 사실 서양 문화에서 운에 관해 미신이 굉장히 많습니다. ④ 불운을 가져오는 미신은 다음과 같습니다. ⑤ - 구급차를 보는 건 불운일 가능성이 높습니다. ⑥ 구급차가 보인다면 코를 꼬집거나 검정, 또는 갈색 개를 볼 때까지 숨을 참아야 합니다. ⑦ - 침대에 모자를 올려놓는 건 불운입니다. ⑧ 사다리 밑을 걸어가거나, 또는 해가 비칠 때 올빼미를 보는 것 역시 불운입니다. ⑨ - 울새나 흰 나방이 열린 창문을 통해 방에 날아 들어오면 당신과 가까운 누군가가 곧 죽게 됩니다. ⑩ - 바다에서 낚시할 때 "돼지"라는 말을 하면 안 되는데 불행을 가져오기 때문입니다. ⑪ - 거울을 깨뜨리는 건 7년간 불운을 뜻합니다. ⑫ - 연인으로부터 받은 칼은 좋은 선물이 아닌데, 이유는 사랑이 조만간 끝날 수 있기 때문입니다. ⑬ - 하품할 때 입 가리는 걸 잊지 마십시오. ⑭ 하품하려고 입을 크게 벌릴 때 영혼이 몸을 떠날 수도 있습니다.

문제 정답 및 해설

1. (b) 이 글의 요지를 고르세요.
   a. 행운에 관한 모든 미신은 확실히 진실하고 정확하다.
   b. 서양 문화에 행운에 관한 미신이 많다.
   c. 행운에 관한 미신을 믿는 건 멍청한 짓이다.
   d. '돼지'나 '깨진 거울' 같은 말을 하지 말아야 하는 건 이런 말이 불운을 가져오기 때문이다.

2. (c) 구급차를 보면 당신은 _____ 싶을 수도 있다.
   a. 가능한 한 세게 자기 뺨을 꼬집고
   b. 누군가 죽어가고 있다는 뜻이기 때문에 울고
   c. 검정개를 볼 때까지 숨을 참고
   d. 거울을 깨고 사다리 밑으로 걷고

3. 각 문장에 알맞은 표현을 고르세요.

   a. (eating) 먹을 때 왜 배가 아픈지 나는 궁금하다.
   l I wonder 궁금하다 have a stomachache 배가 아프다
   【해설】주절의 주어와 while의 주어가 일치하고, 주어의 행동이 능동일 때, while 절에서 주어를 생략하고 동사를 -ing형으로 쓸 수 있다. 주어가 일치하지 않을 경우 주어를 생략할 수 없고, 주어의 행동이 수동이면 pp형으로 쓴다. 문제에서 'I have a stomachache'의 주어 'I'와 while의 주어 'I'가 일치하고, 주어의 능동적인 행위(eat 먹다)이기 때문에 'while eating'으로 쓴다.
   ex) I got injured when hit by a car.
   　　자동차와 부딪쳤을 때 부상당했다.
   ▶ 부상당한 주체 = 자동차에 부딪힌 주체 = I, when 절에서 주어가 '부딪침을 당했기' 때문에(수동) I was가 생략된 hit(과거분사)로 쓴다.
   cf. Bill screamed loudly when I was hit by a car.
   ▶ 소리친 주체는 Bill, 자동차에 부딪힌 주체는 I, 주어가 일치하지 않기 때문에 when 절에서 주어 I를 생략할 수 없다. 만약 생략하면 Bill screamed loudly when hit by a car. ('빌이 자동차에 부딪혔을 때 빌이 크게 소리쳤다'는 뜻)

   b. (Sooner or later) 포기하지 마라. 조만간 상황이 좋아질 것이다.
   l give up 포기하다 get better (상황, 질병 등이) 좋아지다
   【해설】for the time being 한동안, 당분간 / sooner or later 조만간 / from time to time 때때로 ▶ 문맥상 sooner or later가 적당하다.

   c. (until) 우리가 살 곳을 찾을 때까지 그녀의 집에 머물 수밖에 없다.
   l have no choice but to …할 수밖에 없다 stay in …에 머물다
   【해설】문맥상 '…할 때까지'라는 의미의 until이 가장 적당하다.

   d. (to lock) 매일 아침, 남편은 한 번도 빼먹지 않고 '외출하기 전에 현관문 잠그는 거 잊지 마.'라고 말한다.
   l never fail to 꼭 … 하다 lock 잠그다 front door 현관문
   【해설】forget to 미래의 일을 잊다 / forget -ing 과거의 일을 잊다
   ex) I forgot to do my homework.
   　　숙제하는 것을 잊었다. (숙제하지 않았다.)
   　　I forget doing my homework.
   　　(숙제했지만) 내가 숙제했다는 사실을 잊었다.
   문제에서 외출할 때 문을 잠그는 것(나중에 외출할 경우 문을 잠그라)을 잊지 말라는 뜻이기 때문에 to lock이 와야 맞다.

13일의 금요일이 어떻게 최악의 날이 되었는지 아세요?

① 금요일에 관한 미신이 많은데 대부분이 "금요일에 다른 침대에서 자면 악몽을 꾼다."처럼 부정적입니다. ② 금요일을 싫어할 수밖에 없는 이유를 성경에서 찾는 사람들이 있습니다. ③ 어떤 이들은 바벨탑 붕괴, 예수 그리스도의 사망, 그리고 노아의 대홍수 등 수많은 성경의 사건이 금요일에 일어났다고 믿습니다. ④ 또 불운의 숫자 13에 관한 이야기도 많습니다. ⑤ 예수를 배반한 유다는 그리스도 최후의 만찬 때 13번째 손님이었습니다. ⑥ 고대 로마시대에 12명의 마녀들이 모이곤 했는데, 이들은 13번째 온 사람은 악마로 여겼습니다. ⑦ 게다가 서양 문화에서 12는 완전하고 완벽한 숫자입니다. ⑧ 그래서 일 년은 12달이고, 황도대에 12궁도가 있고 올림포스 신도 12명입니다. ⑨ 반면 숫자 13은 불운과 관련있는데, 1이라는 잉여분으로 인해 12의 완전함이 깨지기 때문입니다. ⑩ 그래서 13번지 거리나 13번가가 없는 도시가 많고, 호텔과 병원에서 13호실은 찾을 수 없습니다. ⑪ 최악의 요일과 최악의 숫자가 만났으니 13일의 금요일이 당연히 최악을 대표하게 되었습니다.

문제 정답 및 해설

1. (c) 이 글의 요지를 고르세요.
    a. 최후의 만찬과 노아의 대홍수 둘 다 금요일에 일어났다.
    b. 황도대 12궁도는 오랫동안 불운과 관련되어져 왔다.
    c. 13일의 금요일은 최악의 요일과 최악의 숫자의 결합이다.
    d. 12는 완전하고 완벽한 숫자이고 13은 사악하고 멍청한 숫자이다.

2. (a) 지문 내용과 맞는 것을 고르세요.
    a. 많은 서양인들은 금요일과 숫자 13에 대해 부정적인 감정을 갖고 있다.
    b. 전 세계인들은 노아의 대홍수가 13일의 금요일에 일어났다고 믿는다.
    c. 예수를 13번 부인한 유다는 최후의 만찬에 참석하지 않았다.
    d. 미국의 병원에서 13호 병실을 찾는 건 어렵지 않다.

3. 각 문장에 알맞은 표현을 고르세요.

    a. (to return) 그들은 집에 돌아갈 수밖에 없었는데 감독관이 그들을 쫓아냈기 때문이었다.
    I supervisor 감독관 kick out 내쫓다
    【해설】 have no choice but to + 동사원형 = can not help + –ing ...할 수밖에 없다

    b. (are) 정확한 희생자 수는 아직 밝혀지지 않았지만, 소문에 의하면 수많은 사람들이 실종되었다고 한다.
    I exact 정확한 victim 희생자 reveal 밝히다, 드러나다 rumor 소문 miss 놓치다
    【해설】 the number of ... + 단수 동사 / a number of ... + 복수 동사
    문제에서 the exact number of victims에서 주어는 victims가 아니라 the exact number이다. 그래서 단수동사 is가 오고, but the rumor says that...에서 that 이하 문장의 주어는 a number of people (수많은 사람들)이 주어이기 때문에 복수 동사 are가 와야 맞다.
    a number of는 'many (많은)'의 의미로 the number of와 의미가 완전히 다르므로 주의.
    ex) The number of people who are illiterate has increased.
    문맹인들의 수가 늘어났다. (주어는 the number, 동사는 has)
    A number of people were hurt in the train accident.
    수많은 사람들이 기차 사고에서 다쳤다. (주어는 people, 동사는 were)

    c. (considered) 상황을 고려할 때, 네가 이것에 엄청난 양의 돈을 지출하기 전에 다른 선택권을 고려했어야 했다고 나는 생각한다.
    【해설】 considerate 사려 깊은 / considerable 상당한, 많은 / considering ...를 고려하면 / consider v. 고려하다, ...로 여기다
    ▶ should have pp ...했어야 했다, ...했어야 하지만 하지 않았다.
    문두의 considering은 '...를 고려할 때, 감안할 때'라는 의미의 전치사, considered는 동사 consider의 pp형, a considerable amount of의 considerable은 '상당한, 엄청난'의 의미인 형용사이다.

살렘 마녀 재판 때문에 몇 명이 사망했는지 아세요?

① 이 끔찍한 사건은 무지하고 가난한 사람들이 아니라, 지적이고 이성적이고 공정해야 할 판사와 의사에 의해 시작되었습니다. ② 동네 의사였던 윌리엄 그리그스는 살렘 마녀 재판 당시 중요한 역할을 맡았습니다. ③ 그는 일부 동네 사람들을 마녀로 진단하고 재판에 넘겼습니다. ④ 일단 마녀행위(마술)로 유죄를 선고받으면 죽음을 피할 수 없었습니다. ⑤ 17세기 영국 법에 따라, 악마와 친하거나 마녀로 고소당한 사람들은 범죄자로 여겨졌습니다. ⑥ 그들은 정부에 반한 중대한 범죄를 저지른 죄인으로 취급받았습니다. ⑦ 살렘 마녀 재판에서 가장 유명한 재판 중 하나는 1962년에 열렸습니다. ⑧ 약 180여 명이 당국에 의해 마녀 행위(마술) 혐의로 체포되었습니다. ⑨ 그 중 29명이 법원에 의해 마술이라는 중죄로 유죄선고를 받았습니다. ⑩ 이들 대부분이 교수형으로 목숨을 잃었습니다. ⑪ 가일스 코레이라는 남성은 법정에 협조하기를 거부해 무거운 돌에 깔려 압사당했습니다. ⑫ 최소한 7명의 또 다른 사람들이 감옥에서 사망했다고 합니다.

문제 정답 및 해설

1. (b) 지문의 제목으로 적당한 것을 고르세요.
    a. 윌리엄 그리그스, 무지한 농부들에게 공격당하다
    b. 살렘 마녀 재판 : 재판인가, 학살인가
    c. 마술 : 정부에 반하는 최고의 중범죄
    d. 살렘 마녀 재판의 비밀, 마침내 밝혀지다

2. (a) 17세기 때, 사람들은 _____ 유죄판결을 받을 수 있었다.
    a. 마술과 관련된 행위를 해서
    b. 관리들과 친하게 지내서
    c. 법원에 동조하려고 애써서
    d. 무식하고 가난해서

3. 각 문장에 알맞은 표현을 고르세요.

    a. (committed) 범죄를 저지른 남자는 반드시 감옥에 보내져야 한다. ▎guy 남자, 사람 throw into jail 감옥에 넣다
    【해설】 commit a crime / commit crimes 죄를 저지르다 ▶ 범죄 행위의 경우 commit 동사를 쓰고, 이 외에 suicide도 commit 동사와 함께 쓴다.
    ex) commit theft 도둑질하다 / commit fraud 사기 치다 / commit adultery 간통하다 / commit murder 살인하다 / commit suicide 자살하다

    b. (hanging) 내가 코트를 옷걸이에 걸며 '잠깐만'이라고 했을 때 그는 그의 남동생이 교수형으로 사형을 선고받았다고 말했는데, 이는 그가 교수형에 처해지리라는 뜻이었다.
    ▎be sentenced to death 사형 선고를 받다
    【해설】 hang 1. (옷걸이 등에) 걸다 (hang–hung–hung) 2. 매달다, 교수형에 처하다 (hanged–hanged–hanged)
    hang up something on the hanger 옷걸이(hanger)에 …를 걸다 (hang) / hang on a minute[second] 잠깐만 (기다려라) / death by hanging 교수형으로 인한 죽음 / be hanged 교수형에 처해지다 (수동태)

    c. (of) 인종차별로 비난받는 사람들, 즉 '인종차별주의자들'은 우리 가게 출입이 금지된다.
    ▎racism 인종차별 racist 인종차별주의자 ban 금지하다
    【해설】 be accused of …로 비난받다 (수동) / accuse A of B: A를 B의 이유로 비난하다 (능동)
    ex) They accuse him of being a liar.
    　　그들이 그를 거짓말쟁이로 비난하다.
    　　He is accused of being a liar by them.
    　　그는 그들로부터 거짓말쟁이로 비난당한다.

미스터리 '유령의' 집을 아세요?

① 사라 윈체스터가 미스터리 하우스를 지은 건 그녀가 엄청난 부자 과부인데다 초자연적인 힘의 열성적인 신자였기 때문이었습니다. ② 하나뿐인 아기 딸이 사망한 후 그녀는 정신적으로 불안해졌습니다. ③ 설상가상으로 사랑하는 남편과 시아버지까지 세상을 떠나고 말았습니다. ④ 그래서 그녀는 윈체스터 리피팅 암스 컴퍼니의 상속녀가 되었습니다. ⑤ 덕분에 그녀는 하루에 약 1,000달러를 받았습니다. ⑥ (이 금액은 2013년 기준으로 하루에 약 25,000달러를 받는 것과 비슷한 액수입니다.) ⑦ 그녀는 부자였지만 너무 슬퍼서 아무것도 할 수 없었습니다. ⑧ 영매(점쟁이)는 그녀에게 윈체스터 총에 사망한 혼령들이 복수를 시작했다면서 그녀가 집을 지어야 한다고 했습니다. ⑨ 사라는 만약 집 건축이 끝나면 혼령들이 그녀를 죽이리라 믿었습니다. ⑩ 그때부터 사라는 재산과 시간을 윈체스터 미스터리 하우스로 알려진 이 집에 쏟아 부었습니다. ⑪ 이 집에는 아무 쓸모도 없는 계단과 문이 아주 많습니다. ⑫ 방이 약 160개이고 미로 같은 복도도 많습니다. ⑬ 그녀가 이런 식으로 집을 지은 건 혼령을 혼란스럽게 만들기 위해서라고 합니다. ⑭ 그녀의 죽음과 함께 이 집 건축도 끝이 났습니다. ⑮ 사라 윈체스터는 83세의 나이로 잠을 자던 중 사망했습니다.

문제 정답 및 해설

1. (c) 이 글의 요지를 고르세요.
   a. 윈체스터는 부자가 아니었지만 어쩔 수 없이 큰 집을 지어야 했다.
   b. 유령들이 미스터리 하우스를 좋아했던 건 방이 많았기 때문이었다.
   c. 윈체스터는 귀신들을 헷갈리게 하려고 이상하고 어이없는 집을 지었다.
   d. 미스터리 하우스는 귀신이 출몰하는 것으로 유명하다.

2. (a) 지문 내용과 맞지 않는 것을 고르세요.
   a. 윈체스터 리피팅 암스 컴퍼니의 창립자는 사라 윈체스터였다. ▶ 창립자(founder)가 누구인지는 나오지 않았고, 남편과 시아버지가 죽은 뒤에 사라 윈체스터가 회사 재산을 유산으로 물려받았다고만 나온다.
   b. 사라는 부유했지만, 너무 슬퍼서 아무것도 할 수 없었다.
   c. 사라는 자기 가족의 비극의 원인이 귀신들의 복수라고 믿었다.
   d. 사라는 딸이 사망하고 나서 이상해졌다. (It is not that... until... ...하고 나서야 ...하다)

3. 각 문장에 알맞은 표현을 고르세요.

   a. (pass away) 부드럽고 예의 바르게 말하고 싶다면 '뻗었다' 보다 '세상을 떠나다'와 같은 표현을 사용하세요.

| politely 예의 바르게 expression 표현
【해설】 pass away 세상을 떠나다, 돌아가시다 / pass by 지나치다 / pass out 기절하다
문맥상 'kick the bucket (기본적으로 '죽다'의 뜻이지만 어르신에 대해, 또는 예의를 갖추어 말해야 할 때는 잘 쓰지 않는 표현)'과 의미는 같지만 더 정중한 표현인 'pass away'가 들어가야 맞다. .

   b. (to sit) 데이비드는 너무 흥분해서 자리에 앉아 있을 수 없었다.
【해설】 too... to 동사원형: 너무 ...해서 ...할 수 없다 (부정어 not은 없지만 부정문)
ex) His bag is too big and heavy to carry alone.
그의 가방은 너무 크고 무거워서 혼자 들 수 없다.

   c. (surprised) 그의 죽음에 관한 소식은 나를 놀라게 했다.
【해설】 make + 목적어(사람) + surprised, confused, frightened, scared, tired (pp형) ▶ (사람)을 ...하게 하다(만들다)
ex) My kids make me tired. 아이들은 나를 지치게 한다.

71

Chapter 8. Interesting Stories

 어떤 동물이 3개의 심장, 9개의 뇌, 그리고 파란 피를 가졌는지 아세요?

① 이 동물은 정말 세 개의 심장, 아홉 개의 뇌, 그리고 파란 피를 갖고 있습니다. ② 이 동물은 괴물이 아니라 바다 생물입니다. ③ 아홉 개의 뇌 덕분에 똑똑한지는 모르겠지만, 다른 바다 동물보다 더 똑똑하다고 합니다. ④ 아홉 개의 뇌는 이것의 근육에 비하면 놀랄 일도 아닌데, 이유인즉 이것은 몸의 90%가 근육이기 때문입니다. ⑤ 그러니까 이것은 똑똑한 머리와 근육질 몸을 가진 것입니다! ⑥ 이것의 근육에 놀라운 점이 있습니다. ⑦ 이것은 잘린 후에도 움직일 수 있습니다. ⑧ 여러분이 직접 확인할 수도 있습니다. ⑨ 근육질의 똑똑한 이 녀석을 잘라서 양념과 함께 팬에 넣어보세요. ⑩ 요리되는 몇 분 동안 팔이 계속 움직이는 걸 볼 수 있습니다. ⑪ 그러니까... 이것은 똑똑한 머리에 근육질 몸매, 거기다 움직임(멋진 자세)까지 갖춘 셈입니다. ⑫ 그러나 불행히도 이것은 멋진 얼굴은 갖추지 못했습니다. ⑬ 다리도 없고 얼굴도 없고 팔만 많습니다. ⑭ 하지만 이것의 팔은 특별한 능력을 갖고 있습니다. ⑮ 포식자의 공격을 받아 팔 중 하나를 잃어도 팔이 다시 자라기 때문에 이것은 걱정하지 않습니다. ⑯ 그리고 이 녀석은 무섭고 무자비해서 자기 종족도 먹습니다! ⑰ 게다가 독을 가졌고 먹물을 뿜을 수도 있습니다. ⑱ 이게 무엇인지 알 수 있나요? ⑲ 놀라운 이 바다 동물은 문어입니다.

문제 정답 및 해설

1. (a) 지문의 제목으로 적당한 것을 고르세요.
   a. 문어가 대단한 이유
   b. 경고! 바다 괴물 공격
   c. 문어 대 다른 해양 동물들
   d. 무서운 생물이 온다 : 녀석은 근육질이다

2. (d) 문어가 외모는 갖추지 못했다고 말할 수 있는 건 _____ 때문이다.
   a. 얼굴이 전부 근육질이고 끊임없이 움직이기
   b. 너무 많은 얼굴을 갖고 있기
   c. 얼굴이 견딜 수 없게 못생겼기
   d. 얼굴이 아예 없기

3. 각 문장에 알맞은 표현을 고르세요.

   a. (its) 이 페인트(물감)는 어떻게 이 색깔을 갖게 되었는지 궁금하다. I wonder 궁금하다 paint 페인트, 물감
   【해설】 its: it의 소유격 / it's: it is의 줄임
   ex) It is her bag. = It's her bag. 이것은 그녀의 가방이다.
   The snake is shedding its skin.
   뱀이 허물(its skin = the snake's skin)을 벗고 있다.

   b. (the brains) 너는 머리가 좋고 나는 체격이 좋으니 우리는 함께 무엇이든 할 수 있다.
   【해설】 본문 지문에서 문어의 심장이 9개라서 got the brains와 같이 복수형을 쓴 것이 아니라 got the brains, got the muscles, got the looks 등의 관용적 표현은 항상 'the + 복수형'으로만 쓴다.

   c. (robbed) 강도가 난데없이 나타나 내 돈을 빼앗아 갔다.
   l appear 나타나다 out of nowhere 난데없이 rob 강탈하다
   【해설】 got + pp: 수동의 의미가 된다. 지문의 got attacked 역시 '공격당했다' 라는 수동의 의미이다. got robbed = was robbed: 강탈당하다 cf. get injured, get hurt, get caught
   문제에서는 he가 '강도를 당한' 게 아니라 '강도질을 한 것'이기 때문에 got robber나 was robbed와 같은 수동태가 올 수 없다.

성 스테판의 시계탑이 피사의 사탑처럼 한쪽으로 기울어지고 있다는 거 아세요?

① 전문가들은 성 스테판의 시계탑이 피사의 사탑처럼 한쪽으로 기울어지고 있다는 걸 확인했습니다. ② 그들은 영국에서 가장 유명한 주요 지형물인 성 스테판의 시계탑이 북서쪽으로 0.26도 기울었다고 말했습니다. ③ 그 말은 315피트 높이의 탑이 템스 강 강둑으로 가라앉고 있다는 뜻입니다. ④ 기울었다는 게 육안으로 알 수 있을 정도지만, 전문가들은 당장 무언가를 할 필요는 없다고 생각합니다. ⑤ 그들은 피사의 사탑과 동일한 각도가 되려면 대략 4천 년은 지나야 한다고 말합니다. ⑥ 탑 관리인인 마이크 맥캔 역시 이에 동의했습니다. ⑦ 문제는 그 원인을 아무도 확실히 모른다는 것입니다. ⑧ 일부는 탑이 세워진 런던 진흙이 원인일 수도 있다고 주장합니다. ⑨ 진흙 기초가 마르면서 탑을 움직이게 했다는 것입니다. ⑩ 또는, 증거는 없지만 탑 근처 지하철에서의 작업이 원인일 수도 있습니다.
⑪ 어느 쪽이든 전 세계 사람들은 엘리자베스 타워의 미래가 템스 강에 가라앉는 위험은 없기를 바라고 있습니다.

문제 정답 및 해설

1. (b) 이 글의 요지를 고르세요.
   a. 성 스테판 시계탑이 한강으로 가라앉고 있다.
   b. 성 스테판 시계탑의 운명이 현재는 안전하다.
   c. 빅 벤은 세상에서 가장 큰 시계이다.
   d. 마이클 맥켄이 피사의 사탑 관리인이다.

2. (c) 지문 내용과 맞지 않는 것을 고르세요.
   a. 엘리자베스 타워가 한쪽으로 기울고 있지만, 현재 우리가 할 수 있는 건 없다.
   b. 성 스테판 시계탑의 높이는 315피트이다.
   c. 탑의 기울기가 아주 확실하지만, 전문가들만이 이를 알아볼 수 있다. ▶ its tilt is visible to the naked eye (맨눈으로도 기울었다는 게 보인다.)
   d. 성 스테판 시계탑은 런던 진흙 위에 건축이 되었다.

3. 각 문장에 알맞은 표현을 고르세요.

   a. (is) 당신의 이론에 대한 증거가 없습니다. 이를 증명할 정보를 주십시오.
   ▌evidence 증거 theory 이론 information 정보 prove 증명하다

【해설】 evidence, information, news, equipment, money 등의 명사는 관사(a/an)가 올 수도 없고 복수형(-s/es)으로 쓰지도 않는다. 당연히 동사도 단수 동사가 쓰인다.

b. (lean) 같은 사무실에 있는 키가 크고 호리호리한 남자인 네드가 벽에 기대어 서 있는 걸 보았다.
【해설】 lean이 동사로 쓰이면 '기대다, 기울다', 형용사로 쓰이면 '호리호리한, 군살이 없는, (지방 없는) 살코기의'란 뜻. 첫 번째 lean은 형용사(호리호리한), 두 번째 lean은 동사(기대다)이다.

c. (surveyed) 우리는 지난주 100명의 교사를 조사했는데, 네가 알고 싶어 할 만한 놀라운 결과를 얻었다.
【해설】 일반적으로 -y로 끝나는 동사의 과거형은 y가 i로 바뀌고 -ed가 붙는다. (study - studied) 하지만 survey 동사의 과거형은 surveyed (y가 -id로 바뀌지 않고 그냥 survey + ed)이다. 이처럼 -y로 끝나지만 -ed만 붙는 동사로는, 'play-played, stay-stayed enjoy-enjoyed, sway-swayed, pray-prayed' 등이 있다.

73 타지마할을 건축한 황제가 일꾼들의 손을 자른 이유를 아세요?

① 그의 두 번째 아내 뭄타즈 마할이 1631년 14번째 아기를 출산한 후 세상을 떠났을 때, 무굴의 5번째 황제 샤 자한은 크게 상심했습니다. ② 그녀는 수많은 아내들 중 하나였고 그다지 예쁘지는 않았지만, 그는 그녀를 가장 사랑했습니다. ③ 6개월 후, 그는 그녀를 위해 가장 웅장한 무덤, 타지마할을 건축하기 시작했습니다. ④ 그는 타지마할에 관해서라면 무엇이든 아끼지 않았습니다. ⑤ 그는 건축 자재를 인도뿐 아니라 중앙아시아의 여러 나라에서 들여왔습니다. ⑥ 엄청난 양의 건축자재를 건축 현장으로 운반하기 위해 가능한 모든 수단이 동원되었는데, 그중에는 코끼리도 포함되어 있었습니다. ⑦ 2만 명 이상의 사람들이 황제의 죽은 아내의 무덤을 위해 22년 동안 아침부터 저녁까지 고되게 일했습니다. ⑧ 이들은 일을 멋지게 해냈습니다. ⑨ 타지마할의 아름다움은 완벽해서 1983년 유네스코 세계 유산 유적지로 지정될 정도였습니다. ⑩ 그뿐만 아니라 거대한 대리석 구조물의 균형은 너무나 완벽해서 2007년 신세계 7대 불가사의 중 하나로 선정되기도 했습니다. ⑪ 샤 자한도 최고의 무덤이라는 걸 알았고, 그렇게 아름다운 건축물을 누군가 또다시 만드는 걸 원치 않았습니다. ⑫ 그래서 그의 명령에 따라 장인들의 손이 잘리게 되었습니다.

문제 정답 및 해설

1. (c) 지문의 제목으로 적당한 것을 고르세요.
   a. 무덤에 대한 뭄타즈 마할의 기괴한 애정
   b. 샤 자한 : 잔혹한 황제, 아내를 살해하다
   c. 타지마할, 아름답고 완벽한 최고의 무덤
   d. 야무다 강의 기적

2. (b) 샤 자한이 일꾼들의 팔을 자른 이유는 _____ 때문이다.
   a. 최고 장인들이 게으르고 정직하지 않았기
   b. 아무도 타지마할처럼 아름다운 무덤을 만들게 하고 싶지 않았기
   c. 유네스코에서 타지마할을 세계의 신 7대 불가사의로 선정하지 않았기
   d. 그는 가장 끔찍하고 잔인한 황제였기

3. 각 문장에 알맞은 표현을 고르세요.

   a. (spared) 주변 집들은 완전히 파괴되었는데 어떻게 폭풍이 내 집만 남겨 놓았는지 알 수 없는 노릇이다.
   | hard to understand 이해하기 힘든 storm 폭풍 nearby 근처의 destroy 파괴하다

【해설】ruin 망치다 / rupture 터지게 하다 / spare 피하다, 면하다, 겪지 않게 하다 ▶ 문맥상 spare가 적당하다.

b. (available) 소화기는 항상 이용 가능한 곳에 두어야 한다.
| fire extinguisher 소화기 available 입수 가능한, 사용할 수 있는, 구할 수 있는 at all times 항상
【해설】keep ... available: ...를 사용할 수 있게 유지하다 / to no avail 소용없는

c. (devastating) 화산 폭발은 말 그대로 내 고향을 쑥대밭으로 만들었다. 그건 최악의 끔찍한 재앙이었다.
| volcano 화산 eruption 폭발 literally 말 그대로 hometown 고향 disaster 재앙
【해설】devastating a. 파괴적인, 엄청난, 끔찍한 / devastated a. 큰 타격·충격을 받은 / devastate v. 파괴하다

페이트마가 남편의 두 번째 결혼을 허락한 이유를 아세요?

① 두 명의 인도네시아인들이 2006년 고등법원의 허락을 받아 결혼했습니다. ② 이들의 결혼은 나이 차이 때문에 다들 놀라 자빠질 뻔했습니다. ③ 신랑 수다는 105살, 신부 엘라이는 22살이었습니다. ④ 당시 수다는 69살에 굉장히 몸이 아픈 페이트마와 여전히 결혼한 상태였습니다. ⑤ 페이트마는 자신이 아내의 책임을 감당할 수 없기 때문에 남편의 두 번째 부인을 환영했는데, 자신이 아프지 않았다면 남편의 두 번째 결혼을 절대 허락하지 않았을 거라는 말을 덧붙였다고 합니다. ⑥ 엘라이는 자신도 늙고 연약한데 병든 아내를 돌봐야 하는 수다에게 연민의 정을 느꼈다고 합니다. ⑦ 그녀는 친구나 하녀로 이들을 도울 수도 있었지만 어쨌든 그와 결혼하기로 결정했습니다. ⑧ 이 상황을 이해하기 힘들지만, 진정한 사랑에 관해서라면 아무것도 문제 될 게 없다는 말도 있지 않습니까. ⑨ 22살 아가씨는 105살 남자를 대단히 사랑했던 게 틀림없습니다.

문제 정답 및 해설

1. (d) 지문의 제목으로 적당한 것을 고르세요.
   a. 가장 나이 많은 남자 마침내 결혼하다
   b. 병든 아내 사악한 남편에게 버림받다
   c. 미녀와 노인 : 진실하고 감동적인 러브 스토리
   d. 105살 남성, 22살 여성과 결혼하다 : 사랑 이외에 문제 될 건 없다

2. (c) 지문 내용과 맞는 것을 고르세요.
   a. 수다는 이미 엘라이와 결혼해 살고 있는데도 불구하고 2006년에 페이트마와 결혼했다. ▶ 페이트마와 이미 결혼한 상태에서 엘라이와 2006년에 결혼했다.
   b. 법원이 수다의 엘라이와의 결혼을 허락하지 않았기 때문에 수다의 두 번째 결혼은 불법이다. ▶ 법원의 결혼 승인을 받았다.
   c. 페이트마는 남편의 두 번째 아내를 진심으로 환영하지 않은 것으로 보인다. ▶ 'she added that if she were not ill, she would never allow her husband's second marriage.' 문장이 힌트
   d. 신랑과 신부의 나이 차이는 90이 넘는다. ▶ 둘의 나이 차이는 83

3. 각 문장에 알맞은 표현을 고르세요.

   a. (mattered) 너에게 문제가 되는 어떤 일을 내가 저질렀다는 걸 고백하겠다.
   ▌confess 고백, 자백하다 matter 문제가 되다
   【해설】시제가 현재라면 something that matters to you, 과거라면 something that mattered to you가 되어야 한다. I did something...으로 '내가 한 일'이 과거이기 때문에 과거 시제로 맞춘다.

   b. (were) 그가 아니었다면, 그녀는 시험을 실패했을 것이다.
   [해설] 가정법 과거에서 if절에 쓰이는 be동사는 주어에 상관없이 were만 쓰인다.
   ex) If I were rich, I would buy those cars. 내가 부자라면 저 자동차들을 구매할 텐데.

   c. (tying a knot) 존에게 언제 결혼할 것인지 묻자, 그는 끈의 매듭을 매며 내 질문의 대답을 회피했다. ▌avoid –ing 회피하다
   【해설】tie the knot 결혼하다 / tie a knot (운동화 끈 등의) 매듭을 묶다. 동사 tie의 –ing는 tying (tieing로 쓰지 않는다.)

75. 모기의 총애를 받는 사람이 누구인지 아세요?

① 모기는 나름 입맛이 까다로워서 아무 피나 빨아 먹지 않습니다. ② 모기는 길고 얇은 주둥이를 찔러 넣기 전에 먹잇감을 신중하게 선별합니다. ③ 모기가 좋아하는 표적이 되고 싶은데 머리카락이 암갈색이라면, 모기는 암갈색 머리보다 금발이나 빨강 머리를 더 좋아하니까 금발이나 빨강으로 염색하는 걸 고려해보세요. ④ 그리고 모기는 일반적으로 남자보다 여자를 무는 것을 더 좋아합니다. ⑤ 그러니까 금발 여성이 모기의 총애를 받는다고 말할 수 있습니다. ⑥ 머리카락을 염색하기도 싫고 여성도 아니지만 그래도 모기의 총애를 받고 싶다 해도 걱정할 건 없습니다. ⑦ 선택받은 자가 되는 방법이 단 한 가지인 건 아닙니다. ⑧ 모기는 냄새, 특히 지독한 냄새에 끌립니다. ⑨ 그래서 땀을 많이 흘리고 발을 닦지 않아 악취가 풍기도록 유지하면 그렇지 않은 사람보다 배고픈 모기에게 헌혈할 가능성이 훨씬 높아집니다. ⑩ 모기를 끌어들이는 게 두 가지 더 있는데, 바로 이산화탄소와 젖산입니다. ⑪ 이것들을 많이 배출할수록 모기를 더 많이 유혹할 수 있습니다. ⑫ 하지만 어떻게 할까요? ⑬ 간단한데, 비만해지거나 많이 움직이세요. 비만하거나 가만히 있지 못하는 사람들이 그렇지 않은 사람들보다 더 많은 이산화탄소와 젖산을 만들어내기 때문입니다.

문제 정답 및 해설

1. (c) 지문의 제목으로 적당한 것을 고르세요.
   a. 모기에 관한 감추어진 비밀, 드러나다
   b. 모기를 쫓는 최상의 방법
   c. 모기의 총애를 받고 싶은 사람들을 위한 팁
   d. 안절부절못하는 사람들을 조심하라

2. (d) 모기들은 _____ 사람들을 무는 경향이 있다.
   a. 금발이거나 붉은 모발이고 남성인
   b. 키가 크고 마르고 암갈색 모발인
   c. 검정 모발이고 여성인
   d. 금발이고 여성인

3. 각 문장에 알맞은 표현을 고르세요.

a. (rather than) 아내는 독서보다 스포츠를 좋아하지만 나는 밖에서 운동하는 것보다는 차라리 책을 읽는 게 더 좋다.
【해설】prefer to: ...하는 게 더 좋다 / prefer A to B: A보다 B가 더 좋다. prefer to 동사원형 rather than (to 생략 가능) 동사원형: rather than 이하 하느니 차라리 to... 하는 게 더 좋다

ex) prefer sports to reading 스포츠보다 독서가 더 좋다
prefer to reading 독서가 더 좋다
prefer to read books rather than (to) play sports
운동하느니 책 읽는 게 더 좋다

b. (mosquitoes) 내 팔 위의 모기 두 마리를 보았을 때, 나는 그것들을 찰싹 쳤다.
| slap (손바닥으로) 철썩 때리다, 찰싹 치다
[해설] -o로 끝나는 단어의 복수형은 세 종류가 있다.
1) -es : mosquitoes, potatoes, tomatoes, heroes, echoes, torpedoes, vetoes ...
2) -s : pianos * pianoes로 쓰지 않는다.
3) -es / -s : buffalo(e)s, zero(e)s, halo(e)s

c. (moving) 다른 나라로 이사하는 걸 고려해본 적이 있습니까?
【해설】consider는 동명사를 목적어로 취하기 때문에 consider moving... 으로 써야 맞다. 이와 같이 동명사를 목적어로 취하는 동사: mind, enjoy, give up, postpone, admit, finish

두 명의 러시아인들이 놀라운 외계인을 어떻게 만들었는지 아세요?

① 두 러시아인들이 2011년 4월 유튜브에 외계인 비디오를 올렸을 때, 전 세계 사람들은 놀라 자빠질 뻔했습니다. ② 18살의 티머 히랄과 19살의 키릴 브라소프는 자신들의 외계인 비디오가 재미있어서 인터넷 게시판에 흥미로운 댓글이 올라오리라 예상했습니다. ③ 그들이 얼마나 잘 만들었는지 외계인 전문가들과 경찰을 포함해 세계적인 관심까지 끌었습니다. ④ 외계인 전문가들은 또 다른 외계인 장난으로 의심하면서도 비디오 속의 외계인이 진짜 같아서 한번 살펴볼 만하다고 생각했습니다. ⑤ 하지만, 사실 "외계인"은 집에서 구운 빵이었습니다. ⑥ 경찰이 이들의 집을 찾아갔을 때, 티머와 키릴은 밀가루, 계란, 우유로 만든 외계인을 보여주어야 했습니다. ⑦ 그리고 피부의 비밀도 밝혀졌는데, 바로 닭 껍질이었습니다. ⑧ 이 두 십대들은 진짜 생물체처럼 신비하게 보이도록 오븐에 구운 외계인 몸을 닭 껍질로 감쌌던 것입니다. ⑨ 대단합니다.
⑩ 이미 이런 장난에 익숙해진 UFO 모임에서는 '믿을 수 없을 만큼 이상하고 부러울 정도로 독창적인 이번 사건을 어떻게 받아들여야 할지 모르겠다'는 성명을 발표했습니다.

문제 정답 및 해설

1. (c) 이 글의 요지를 고르세요.
   a. 멍청이 같은 UFO 모임이 러시아인 십대들에게 속았다.
   b. 외계인 전문가들은 밀가루와 우유로 만든 외계인에 대해 두 러시아인을 칭찬했다.
   c. 두 러시아인의 소위 외계인은 가짜로 판명되었다.
   d. 러시아 십대들은 부러울 정도로 창의적이다.

2. (c) 지문 내용과 맞는 것을 고르세요.
   a. 두 명의 러시아 십대들은 가짜 외계인을 만든 뒤 체포되었다. ▶ 체포되었다는 내용은 나오지 않았다.
   b. 티머와 키릴은 배가 고파서 그저 빵을 굽고 싶었을 뿐이었다. ▶ 가짜 외계인을 만들기 위해 빵 굽듯 밀가루와 우유로 외계인을 만들었다.
   c. 세상에는 이 외에도 가짜 외계인 사기가 많은 것 같다. ▶ Although alien experts suspected the whole thing would be just another alien hoax와 UFO communities, which are already used to this kind of hoax 문장에서 이 외에도 외계인 사기가 많다는 걸 알 수 있다.
   d. 러시아 십대들에게 속은 외계인 전문가들은 닭 껍질을 싫어했다.

3. 각 문장에 알맞은 표현을 고르세요.

   a. (handmade) 이것들은 모두 나무로 된 수공예품들이다. 전부 손으로 만든 것이라고 보장한다.
   | wooden 나무로 된 handicrafts 수공예품 guarantee 보증하다
   【해설】ready—made 이미 만들어져 나온, 기성의 / homemade 집에서 만든 / handmade 손으로 만든 ▶ handicrafts라는 표현이 나왔기 때문에 handmade가 가장 적당하다.

   b. (real deal) 캐시의 목걸이를 두고 야단법석을 떨 이유는 없다고 생각한다. 진짜 좋은 것이긴 하지만 대단한 일은 아니다.
   | there is no reason to …할 이유는 없다 make a fuss 야단법석을 떨다 necklace 목걸이
   【해설】real deal 진짜, 진품, 실제 상황 / big deal 대단한 일(것)

   c. (watching) 이 영화는 볼만한 가치가 있지만, 저 영화는 볼 가치가 없다.
   【해설】be worth –ing= be worthwhile to 동사원형: …할 가치가 있다.
   ex) It is not worth trying again. = It is not worthwhile to try again. 다시 시도할 가치가 없다.

미국에서 태어난 자이언트 판다들이 왜 중국으로 돌려보내 졌는지 아세요?

① 2010년, 미국 태생의 판다 두 마리, 애틀랜타 동물원의 메이 란과 워싱턴 동물원의 타이 샨이 중국으로 보내졌습니다. ② 중국에 도착한 직후, 너무 안아주고 싶은 판다들은 큰 환영을 받았습니다. ③ 또 미국에서 그랬던 것처럼 몇몇 TV 프로그램에도 출연했습니다. ④ 두 마리 모두 미국에서 태어난 이후 미국인들에게 많은 사랑을 받았고, 미국에서 중국의 친선대사와 같은 존재였습니다. ⑤ 그런데 왜 이들이 왜 중국에 돌려보내 졌을까요? ⑥ 그것은, 중국이 이들의 소유권을 갖고 있기 때문입니다. ⑦ 10년 전, 중국은 천만 달러를 받고 미국에 자이언트 판다 몇 마리를 빌려주었습니다. ⑧ 무언가를 빌리는 돈으로 상당히 비싼 금액입니다. ⑨ 미국과 중국의 합의 하에, 중국은 빌려준 판다들과 미래의 새끼들에 대한 소유권을 보유하게 되었습니다. ⑩ 그래서 메이 란과 타이 샨은 인공 수정에 의해 미국에서 태어났음에도 불구하고 중국으로 돌아갈 운명이었습니다. ⑪ 다시 한 번, 왜 미국은 자이언트 판다를 (구매하는 게 아닌) 빌리는데 수천만 달러를 썼는지 궁금해집니다. ⑫ 그건 멸종 위기의 이 동물을 보길 원하는 사람들은 아주 많은데, 판다를 얻을 수 있는 유일한 길이 중국뿐이기 때문입니다.

문제 정답 및 해설

1. (d) 지문의 제목으로 적당한 것을 고르세요.
   a. 자이언트 판다 : 가장 귀여운 동물
   b. 중국의 불공정한 무역 관행
   c. 미국, 메이 란에 과도한 돈을 지출하다
   d. 두 마리 자이언트 판다 고국으로 돌아가다

2. (c) 미국 태생의 자이언트 판다 두 마리가 중국으로 보내진 까닭은 _____ 때문이다.
   a. 그들이 고국에 돌아가기 원했기
   b. 미국의 죽순은 맛이 없었기
   c. 중국이 이들의 소유권을 가졌기
   d. 욕심 많은 중국이 모든 자이언트 판다 새끼는 중국 소유라고 주장했기

3. 각 문장에 알맞은 표현을 고르세요.

   a. (lend) 그들은 숭고하고 가치 있는 명분에 그들의 지지를 아끼지 않았다.
   ❙ be willing to 기꺼이 ...하다 support 지지, 후원 noble 숭고한 worthy 가치 있는 cause 명분
   【해설】 lend their support 지지를 빌려주다 = 지지하다

   b. (borrow) 만약 나에게 도서관 카드가 있고 사서에게 내 카드로 책 몇 권을 빌려달라고 부탁한다면, 나는 무료로 책을 빌릴 수 있다.
   ❙ library card 도서관 카드 librarian 사서 for free 무료로, 공짜로
   【해설】 borrow (주어가) 빌리다 / lend (주어가) 빌려주다 / rent 빌리는 돈(임대료, 집세)
   ex) He lent me some money. 그는 나에게 돈을 빌려주었다.
   I borrowed money from him to pay my rent.
   나는 집세를 내기 위해 그에게 돈을 빌렸다.

   c. (Ever since) 아내가 앓아누운 이후, 그는 힘들게 살고 있다.
   ❙ ill 아픈, 병든 be ill in bed 아파 앓아눕다 have a hard time 힘들게 살다
   【해설】 since 단순 과거 + 완료 (또는 완료 + since 단순 과거) ...이래로 ...해왔다.

78 케네디 저주가 무엇인지 아세요?

① 케네디가의 저주는 케네디가에 발생한 비극적인 사건을 묘사할 때 사용되는 표현입니다. ② 이러한 불운한 사건이 저주로 인한 것인지 아니면 순전히 운이 나빠서인지는 아무도 모르지만, 반복적이고 지속적인 불운한 사례들이 케네디 가문에 있어왔다는 건 사실입니다. ③ 이 가문의 비극적인 사건들 중 일부는 이렇습니다. ④ 1963년, 당시 미국 대통령이었던 존 F. 케네디가 리. H 오스왈드에 의해 암살당했습니다. ⑤ 그리고 그의 큰아들 존 F. 케네디 2세는 1999년 비행기 사고로 사망했습니다. ⑥ 그가 조종석에 있을 때 그의 비행기가 대서양 바다로 추락했습니다. ⑦ 당시 그의 나이는 겨우 39세였습니다. ⑧ JFK의 남동생 로버트 F. 케네디 역시 1968년에 암살당했습니다. ⑨ 그는 시르한 시르한이 쏜 총에 맞았습니다. ⑩ 1984년에 데이비드 앤터니 케네디는 코카인 과량 복용으로 사망했고 마이클 케네디는 1997년에 스키 사고로 사망했습니다. ⑪ 카라 케네디 알렌은 2011년 헬스클럽에서 운동하던 중 심장 마비로 사망했습니다. ⑫ 2012년에는 RFK 2세 (전 미국 상원의원 로버트 케네디의 아들)의 아내인 메리 리처드슨 케네디가 자살했습니다.

문제 정답 및 해설

1. (a) 이 글의 요지를 고르세요.
   a. 케네디 가문에 비극적인 사고가 많았다는 건 사실이다.
   b. 케네디 저주는 그저 미신일 뿐이다.
   c. 케네디 가문의 많은 가족들이 정치인이었다.
   d. 존 F. 케네디 2세와 카라 케네디는 저주 때문에 사망했다.

2. (d) 지문 내용과 맞는 것을 고르세요.
   a. 케네디 가문의 모든 가족들은 죽을 수밖에 없다. ▶ 가족 모두가 다 죽을 운명이라고는 나오지 않았고, 비극적인 사고로 사망한 가족 일부만 소개되었다. (be meant to 동사원형: …하게 되어 있다)
   b. 케네디 가문에 아무 일도 일어나지 않았고, 그래서 케네디 저주는 사실이 아니다. ▶ 케네디 저주가 사실인지 여부는 알 수 없으나 가문에 비극적 사고가 계속 반복되고 있다.
   c. 존 F. 케네디와 그의 큰아들은 같은 암살자에 의해 살해 되었다. ▶ 존 F. 케네디는 오스왈드에 의해 암살당했고, 아들 존 F. 케네디 2세는 비행기 사고로 사망했다.
   d. 데이비드 앤터니 케네디는 코카인 중독자인 것 같다. ▶ 'David Anthony Kennedy died of a cocaine overdose'라는 표현에서 그가 코카인 중독자(cocaine user)임을 추측할 수 있다.

3. 각 문장에 알맞은 표현을 고르세요.

   a. (assassin) 암살자는 저명하거나 중요한 인물을 살해하는 사람이다. ▮ murder 살해하다 prominent 저명한
   【해설】 assassin n. 암살자 / assassinator n. 암살자 / assassinate v. 암살하다 ▶ 문장 맨 앞에 An이 있고 동사가 is이므로 단수인 assassin만 답이고 복수 형태인 assassinators는 답이 될 수 없다.

   b. (then) 줄리는 2013년, 당시 그녀의 조수이자 친한 친구였던 마리아로부터 사기로 고발당했다.
   ▮ be accused of 고발당하다 assistance 조수, 비서
   【해설】 than은 more than에서 처럼 비교할 때 쓴다. '당시'라는 뜻의 단어는 then.

   c. (stomping) 걸음마를 배우는 한 아이가 발을 구르다 바닥에 넘어졌다.
   ▮ toddler 걸음마를 배우는 아이 fall to the floor 바닥에 넘어지다 stomp one's feet 발을 구르다
   【해설】 while 이하 종속절의 주어가 주절의 주어 a toddler와 일치한다. 이런 경우 종속절의 주어 a toddler를 생략하고, 능동이면 –ing형으로, 수동이면 pp형으로 쓸 수 있다. while a toddler stomped her feet에서 a toddler를 생략하고 stomped가 stomping으로 바뀌어 while stomping her feet가 된다. her feet라는 표현으로 보아 a toddler는 여자라는 걸 알 수 있으므로 he stomped는 올 수 없다.

   d. (former) 2011년에서부터 2013년까지 세계 무역의 전(前) 대표였던 마이클은 내 아버지의 친구였다.
   【해설】 former 전, 이전의 / late 늦은, 고인이 된 / early 일찍이, 조기의 ▶ 이전 즉 前의 의미인 former가 와야 맞다.

79 러슈모어산이 다이너마이트의 도움으로 조각되었다는 거 아세요?

① 사우스 다코타에 위치한 러슈모어산 국립 기념비는 엄청나게 큰 기념비적인 화강암 조각으로 미국의 전 대통령 네 사람, 조지 워싱턴, 토머스 제퍼슨, 테오도르 루스벨트, 그리고 에이브러햄 링컨의 머리 조각상입니다. ② 머리 꼭대기에서 턱까지의 길이가 무려 18미터로 90km 멀리에서도 볼 수 있습니다. ③ 머리 상을 디자인한 사람은 거존 보글럼입니다. ④ 보글럼과 가장 거대한 조각 프로젝트를 위해 소집된 400명의 사람들은 수년 동안 땀을 흘리며 일을 했습니다. ⑤ 조각은 1927년에 시작되어 1941년에 끝났습니다. ⑥ 당시에는 산까지 가는 길이 없었기 때문에 일꾼들은 산꼭대기까지 가기 위해 말을 타거나 걷거나 심지어 등산까지 해야 했습니다. ⑦ 재미있게도 이들은 돌 조각을 조금씩 깨는 식으로 일하지 않았습니다. ⑧ 러슈모어산 표면에 거대한 두상들을 조각하기 위해 보글럼은 다이너마이트를 이용했습니다. ⑨ 다이너마이트로 상당한 분량의 바위를 폭파시킨 후, 보글럼과 일꾼들은 드릴, 망치, 끌로 얼굴을 조각했습니다. ⑩ 이 기념비는 그 크기로도 유명하지만, 매우 위험한 일이었음에도 불구하고 조각 작업 중 사상자가 한 명도 없었다는 사실로도 유명합니다.

문제 정답 및 해설

1. (b) 이 글의 요지를 고르세요.
    a. 러슈모어산은 고도와 아름다운 경치로 유명하다.
    b. 러슈모어산의 거대한 얼굴들을 조각할 때 일꾼들이 다이너마이트를 사용했다.
    c. 다이너마이트 같은 폭발물은 어떤 일이 있어도 사용되어서는 안 된다.
    d. 보글럼은 일꾼들이 오직 망치와 끌만 사용하도록 강요했다.

2. (b) 러슈모어산의 거대한 네 얼굴들을 조각하기 위해 보글럼과 일꾼들은 _____.
    a. 산꼭대기까지 가기 위해 자동차나 마차를 탔다
    b. 다이너마이트의 도움으로 거대한 바위 덩어리를 폭파해서 쪼개냈다
    c. 안전을 위해 오직 손과 막대기만 사용했다
    d. 10년 동안 돌멩이를 조금씩 깎아냈다

3. 각 문장에 알맞은 표현을 고르세요.

    a. (carving) 이 커다란 고깃덩어리를 반으로 자르기 위해 적당한 식탁용 칼이 필요하다. ▌proper 적당한 carve 깎다, 조각하다 chunk of meat 고깃덩어리 in half 반으로
    【해설】carving knife 요리된 고깃덩어리를 써는 칼

    b. (is located in) 지라(비장)는 복부 왼쪽 상부에 위치해 있다. ▌spleen 지라, 비장 upper 위의 abdomen 배, 복부

【해설】be located in ...에 위치해 있다
locate 동사는 '...에 위치를 찾아내다, ...에 두다' 의미의 '타동사' 이며, 위치를 표현할 때는 수동태를 사용한다. 주어가 단수이기 때문에 be동사(is) + located (pp) in이 되어야 맞다. locates in이나 located in은 수동태가 아니라서 맞지 않다.
ex) Where are the lungs located in the human body?
    폐는 인간의 신체에서 어디에 위치해있습니까?
    Africa is located in the Southern Hemisphere.
    아프리카와 아시아는 남반구에 위치해있다.
    The doctor had to locate the bullet wound as fast as he could. 의사는 총상을 가능한 한 빨리 찾아야 했다.

c. (on) 모든 직원들은 9월 1일에 일을 시작해서 12월 중에 일을 끝내야 한다.
【해설】September 뒤에 첫 번째 날(1)이라고 명시되어 있으므로 on을 써야 맞다.
ex) In September 9월에 On September 4th 9월 4일에

> * 날짜를 표현할 때 : 순서에 주의
> 미국 : 달 month ▶ 날짜 date ▶ 년도 year ex) March 29, 2013
> 영국 : 날짜 date ▶ 달 month ▶ 년도 year ex) 29 March, 2013
> 날짜를 표현할 때 서수(first, second, third, fourth, fifth...)를 쓸 수도 있는데, 서수를 숫자로 표기하는 법은 별도로 학습해야 한다. (달력에 31까지만 나오므로 31까지만 설명) 1 (1st), 2 (2nd), 3 (3rd), 4 부터는 '숫자+th'로 쓴다. (4th, 5th, ... 29th, 30th)
> 단, 21은 21st, 31은 31st로, 22는 22nd, 23은 23rd로 써야 한다. (11은 11st로 쓰지 않고 11th, 12도 12nd로 쓰지 않고 12th, 13 역시 13rd로 쓰지 않고 13th로 쓴다는 점 주의)
> ex) 2013년 1월 22일 ▶ January 22, 2013 / January 22nd, 2013 /
>   Jan. 22, 2013 (Jan. = January) / the 22nd of Jan.

기린처럼 보이는 여성들이 있다는 거 아세요?

① 버마의 소수 종족인 많은 카얀인들은 무서운 군사 정부 때문에 버마에서 도망 나왔습니다. ② 이들은 불법 체류자로 타이 국경 지역에서 살 수밖에 없었습니다. ③ 하지만, 당국은 이들이 그곳에 살게 놔두는데, 기린처럼 보이는 카얀 여성들이 관광객들을 끌어들여 돈을 챙길 수 있게 해주기 때문입니다. ④ 카얀 여성들은 기린 여성으로 유명한데, 이들의 목이 보통보다 훨씬 길기 때문입니다. ⑤ 사실 이들이 일부러 목을 길게 만든 겁니다. ⑥ 전통적으로 카얀 여성의 목에 관해서라면 길수록 좋다고 합니다. ⑦ 그래서 긴 목을 만들기 위해 대부분의 카얀 여성들은 놋 (또는 은) 고리를 어려서부터 목에 걸기 시작합니다. ⑧ 수년에 걸쳐 서서히 목에 고리를 늘립니다. ⑨ 무거운 고리 무게가 어깨를 아래로 밀어 목이 길어 보이는 겁니다. ⑩ 이들 사는 동네는 타이 사업가들이 지은 인공 동네입니다. ⑪ 대부분의 관광객들은 오직 목이 길어서 이색적인 볼거리가 되는 카얀 여성을 보기 위해 그곳을 방문하는데, 종종 그 마을을 인간 동물원이라 부르기도 합니다.

문제 정답 및 해설

1. (c) 지문의 제목으로 적당한 것을 고르세요.
   a. 타이 사업가, 카얀 여성들의 최대 적
   b. 불법 이민자들 타이 국경에서 의식을 잃은 채 발견되다
   c. 카얀 여성들 : 이들은 왜 '기린 여성'이라 불리는가?
   d. 지독한 군사 정부, 카얀족을 억지로 기린이 되게 하다

2. (c) 지문의 내용과 맞지 않는 것을 고르세요.
   a. 카얀족의 인구는 다른 종족에 비해 적은 것 같다.
   b. 타이 국경지역에 사는 카얀인들은 불법 이민자들이다.
   c. 카얀 여성들은 돈을 벌기 위해 목을 길게 만들었다.
   d. 타이 관리들이 카얀인들을 그들의 지역에 거주하도록 허락한 유일한 이유는 돈이다.

3. 각 문장에 알맞은 표현을 고르세요.

   a. (immigrants) 우리 부모님은 이민자이시다. 10년 전 이곳 북미에서 새 삶을 시작하기 위해 남한을 떠나셨다.
   【해설】 'here 이곳'이 힌트. 이민을 이곳으로 온 경우 immigrant / 다른 곳으로 이민을 간 경우 emigrant / migration (철새 등 동물, 또는 사람의) 대이동

   b. (concerned) 많은 사람들이 할리우드 여배우들에 관한 한 날씬할수록 좋다고 생각한다.

   l starlet 젊은 여배우 (the) thinner is (the) better 날씬할수록 좋다
   【해설】 as far as ... be동사 concerned ...에 관한 한: be 동사는 ...에 맞추고 concern은 반드시 pp형인 concerned로 쓴다.
   ex) As far as I am concerned, the answer to this question is wrong. 내가 볼 때 이 문제의 정답은 틀렸다.
   As far as your computer is concerned, you don't have to worry about it. 네 컴퓨터에 관한 한, 걱정할 필요 없다.

   c. (to) 물은 종종 생명의 시작이라 불린다.
   【해설】 refer v. 조회하다, 참조하다, 조사하다, ...라고 부르다, 언급하다 ▶ refer에 여러 가지 뜻이 있는데 to와 함께 자주 쓰인다.
   ex) refer to a dictionary 사전을 참조하다
   refer her to a skin expert
   그녀에게 피부 전문가의 도움을 받으라고 하다
   refer his success to God
   그의 성공을 하느님께 (덕분으로) 돌리다
   문제에서는 'be referred to as ...라고 불리다, 언급되다'

Chapter 9. The Amazing Records

81 세상에서 가장 큰 사람이 누구인지 아세요?

① 술탄 코센이라는 터키인이 세상에서 생존한 가장 큰 사람으로, 그는 지금도 키가 자라고 있습니다. ② 2009년에 가장 큰 사람으로 기네스 세계 기록에 오를 당시 그의 키는 247cm였습니다. ③ 그리고 2011년에 그의 고향에서 기네스가 다시 키를 측정했는데, 251cm로 측정되었습니다. ④ 어쨌든 그의 키가 이상하게 커진 원인은 건 뇌하수체 종양이 성장 호르몬에 영향을 미쳤기 때문입니다. ⑤ 최근 그는 종양 치료를 받았고 성장 호르몬의 과도한 수준(수치)을 조절하기 위한 약도 복용하고 있습니다. ⑥ 현재 그의 호르몬 수준은 거의 정상이라고 합니다. ⑦ 하지만, 그는 이미 너무 많이 커버렸기 때문에 걸을 때 목발을 사용해야만 합니다. ⑧ 통제할 수 없이 계속 자라는 키 때문에 그는 학교도 마칠 수 없었습니다. ⑨ 천장이 그에게 너무 낮아 학교 건물 안에 들어갈 수 없었던 겁니다. ⑩ 또 옷과 신발을 구하거나 자동차 안에 들어가는데 항상 어려움을 겪습니다. ⑪ 그럼에도 불구하고 그는 친구들과 컴퓨터 게임을 하거나 엄마가 전구를 갈아 끼우는 걸 도와드리는 등 평범한 생활을 한다고 말합니다.

문제 정답 및 해설

1. (b) 이 글의 요지를 고르세요.
   a. 키가 가장 큰 사람은 항상 목발을 사용해야 한다.
   b. 술탄 코센은 질병 때문에 키가 가장 큰 사람이 되었다.
   c. 술탄 코센이라는 이름의 한 터키인은 현재 세상에서 가장 큰 발을 갖고 있다.
   d. 코센은 학업을 마쳤어야 했다.

2. (d) 지문에 의하면, 뇌하수체 종양은 _____.
   a. 251cm로 측정되었다
   b. 그의 비정상적인 성장 호르몬에 의해 야기되었다 (성장 호르몬이 비정상적이 된 건 종양 때문이다.)
   c. 일종의 불치 암이다
   d. 코센의 신장에 영향을 미쳤다

3. 각 문장에 알맞은 표현을 고르세요.

   a. (growth) 경제 성장률을 면밀히 관찰하는 게 나의 일이다.
   【해설】the rate of economic growth 경제 성장률 (grow v. 자라다, 성장하다 growth n. 성장)

   b. (have already received) 공사장 인부들은 이미 사무실로부터 임금을 지불받았다.
   | construction worker 공사장 인부 payment 임금
   【해설】완료시제에서 부사의 위치: have ( ) pp
   ex) have frequently been used 빈번하게 사용되다 have never heard of 들어본 적 없다

   c. (is measured) 우리는 그의 신장을 일주일에 한 번 측정하지만, 그의 몸무게는 매일 측정한다. | height 신장 once a week 일주일에 한 번 weight 몸무게 on a daily basis 매일
   【해설】but 앞의 문장에서는 주어는 we, 동사는 measure, 의미는 '우리가 측정하다'이다. 하지만 but 다음 문장은 (우리말로는 능동으로 번역되었지만), measure의 주어가 we가 아닌 his weight (그의 몸무게)이기 때문에 measure가 오지 않고 수동태로 be동사(is) + measured(pp)가 와야 한다. '(수치가)…이다'의 뜻이라면 주어가 his weight(3인칭 단수 현재)이기 때문에 동사에 -(e)s가 와야 한다.

82 늑대 소녀가 나중에 무엇이 되고 싶은지 아세요?

① 11살 이 소녀는 의사가 되어 사람들을 도와주고 싶다고 합니다. ② 아마도 소녀는 자기처럼 희귀병을 앓는 환자를 돕고 싶은지도 모르겠습니다. ③ 늑대 소녀로 알려진 수파트라 사수판은 다모증을 가지고 태어났는데, 덕분에 얼굴과 몸에 엄청난 양의 털이 자랍니다. ④ 이 증후는 종종 '늑대인간 증후군'으로 불리는데, 소녀가 늑대 소녀라는 별명을 갖게 된 것도 이 때문입니다. ⑤ 소녀의 외모가 대단히 눈에 띄는 이유는 두 눈과 입을 제외하고 얼굴과 몸 전체에 자란 두터운 털 때문입니다. ⑥ 얼굴과 몸의 털이 꽤나 두꺼워서 소녀는 세계에서 가장 털이 많은 소녀라는 세계 기록을 보유하게 되었습니다. ⑦ 소녀는 기네스 세계 기록에 올라 행복하다고 말했습니다. ⑧ 하지만, 세계에서 가장 털이 많은 소녀라는 건 쉽지도, 재미있지도 않습니다. ⑨ 소녀는 털을 제거하기 위해 레이저 치료를 받고 있지만, 얼마 못 가 털이 다시 자랍니다. ⑩ 또 놀림도 많이 당했고 '원숭이 얼굴'이라고 불리기도 했습니다. ⑪ 다행히 세계 기록을 보유한 이후 친구들과 이웃들이 점차 소녀를 받아들이고 있습니다. ⑫ 기록 보유자라는 걸 소녀가 즐기고 있긴 하지만, 그래도 부모는 어린 딸이 치료받게 되기를 원합니다. ⑬ 그러나 현재까지 소녀의 병을 치료할 방법은 알려진 바 없습니다.

문제 정답 및 해설

1. (b) 이 글의 요지를 고르세요.
   a. 늑대 소녀의 이름은 사생활 보호를 위해 밝힐 수 없다.
   b. 수파트라의 몸은 두터운 털로 뒤덮여 있다.
   c. 늑대 인간 증후군은 전염되기 때문에 수파트라의 이웃들은 그녀를 피해야만 한다.
   d. 세상에서 털이 가장 많은 소녀라는 건 쉽고 재미있다.

2. (d) 지문 내용과 맞는 것을 고르세요.
   a. 수파트라는 한 가지 이상의 별명을 갖고 있는데 그 중 한 가지가 '늑대 얼굴'이다. ▶ wolf face가 아니라 monkey face, 또는 wolfe girl이다.
   b. 수파트라의 외모가 비정상적이지만 친구들은 전혀 그녀를 놀린 적이 없다. ▶ 수차례 놀림을 당했다.
   c. 수파트라는 수북한 털을 제거할 치료를 받을 돈이 없다. ▶ 치료를 받고 있지만 얼마 후 다시 털이 자란다.
   d. 두터운 털이 수파트라의 온몸을 덮고 있지만 눈과 입은 제외이다. (but = except)

3. 각 문장에 알맞은 표현을 고르세요.

   a. (for now) 지금은 안전하다. 하지만, 다음에 무슨 일이 벌어질지 아무도 모른다.

【해설】 forever 영원히 / for instance 예를 들어 / for now 현재는, 지금 당장은 ▶ 문맥상 for now가 적당하다.

b. (except) 이 로봇은 모두를 공격하게 프로그램되어 있는데, 로봇을 프로그램한 사람만 제외이다.
【해설】 everyone 중 예외를 말하고 있기 때문에 except가 들어가야 문맥상 적당하다. (everyone except ...만 제외한 모든 사람)

c. (a 15-year-old girl) 15살 소녀는 거의 여성이 되기 직전이라고 말할 수 있다. I on the brink of ...직전에
【해설】 하이픈(-)으로 연결한 표현에서는 복수 명사라도 -(e)s를 붙이지 않는다.
ex) She is 15 years old. 그녀는 15살이다.
    She is a 15-year-old girl. 그녀는 15살 소녀이다.
    ('15-year-old' : girl을 꾸며주는 형용사)

d. (with) 요즘, 변비 환자들의 수가 날마다 증가하고 있다.
I these days 요즘 the number of ...의 수 (+ 단수동사) constipation 변비 day by day 매일매일, 날마다
【해설】 patient with + 병명: ...병을 가진 환자
ex) patients with hypertension 고혈압 환자들
    (또는 'hypertension patients'라고 쓰기도 한다.)

83. 세상에서 가장 위험한 나무가 무엇인지 아세요?

① 세계에서 가장 위험한 나무는 포이즌 구아바 또는 맨치닐이라는 나무입니다. ② 이 나무는 플로리다 에버글레이즈와 캐리비안의 모래 해안에서 발견됩니다. ③ 그러니 그곳에 갈 때는 이 나무를 만지지도 말고, 비가 올 때 나무 밑에 앉지 않도록 주의하세요. ④ 심지어 이 나무가 불에 탈 때는 숨을 참고 눈을 가려야 합니다. ⑤ 물론 달콤한 향기가 풍기는 사과와 비슷한 나무의 과일을 먹을 생각은 하지도 말아야 합니다. ⑥ 이 나무를 상대하는 최선의 방법은 나무를 멀리하는 것입니다. ⑦ 나무 기둥에서 새어나오는 독성 수액이 피부에 닿으면 엄청난 물집이 생기게 됩니다. ⑧ 만약 수액이 눈에 들어가면 강한 산성 독액으로 인해 눈이 멀 수도 있습니다. ⑨ 같은 이유로 비가 올 때 나무로 피신하면 안 됩니다. ⑩ 수액이 함유된 빗방울은 수액 자체만큼이나 위험할 수 있습니다. ⑪ 이 나무가 불에 탈 때는 그곳에서 달아나야 하는데, 연기로 눈이 따갑거나 심지어 눈이 멀 수도 있기 때문입니다. ⑫ 이 나무의 열매는 보기도 좋고 향기도 좋지만 치명적입니다. ⑬ 나뭇잎, 나무껍질, 수액, (이 나무에 관한 건 무엇이든) 절대적으로 위험합니다. ⑭ 이렇게 해서 포이즌 구아바는 세계에서 가장 위험한 나무라는 왕좌에 등극하게 되었습니다.

문제 정답 및 해설

1. (a) 지문의 제목으로 적당한 것을 고르세요.
   a. 가장 치명적인 나무 맨치닐 * deadliest: deadly(치명적인)의 최상급
   b. 포이즌 구아바 – 최고의 달콤함을 맛보세요
   c. 사과는 비켜라! 포이즌 구아바를 위해 길을 내주어라.
   d. 맨치닐, 냄새도 좋고 맛도 좋다

2. (d) 비가 올 때 포이즌 구아바에서 멀리 떨어져야 하는 이유는 _____.
   a. 이것의 유독성 수액이 당신을 대머리로 만들 것이기 때문이다
   b. 이것의 과일이 크고 무겁기 때문이다
   c. 나뭇잎이 작고 얇아서 비에 흠뻑 젖게 될 것이기 때문이다
   d. 빗방울에 위험한 수액이 들어 있을 수 있기 때문이다

3. 각 문장에 알맞은 표현을 고르세요.

   a. (blister) 이틀 전, 테니스로 손에 물집이 생겼는데 이를 터트렸다. ǀ a couple of days 이틀 pop 터트리다
   【해설】 blister 수포, 물집 / cut 베인 상처 / contusion 멍 ▶ 'pop (터트리다)'라는 동사에 어울리는 표현은 blister뿐이다.

   b. (themselves) 소년 두 명은 서로의 등을 쉽게 긁어 줄 수 있었지만 혼자서 자기 등을 긁었다. ǀ scratch 긁다 back 등 scratch one's back oneself 혼자 자기 등을 긁다
   【해설】 two boys는 복수이기 때문에 himself가 아닌 themselves가 와야 한다.
   ex) They scratched their backs themselves.
   　　그들은 그들의 등을 혼자(스스로) 긁었다.

   c. (is) 문화유산에 대해 배울 수 있는 최선의 그리고 가장 쉬운 방법은 이에 관한 책을 읽는 것이다. ǀ the best and easiest way to …할 최선의 가장 쉬운 방법 cultural 문화 heritage 유산
   【해설】 주어는 heritages가 아니라 way이므로 단수 동사 is가 와야 한다.

   d. (breath) 입 냄새를 야기하는 요인이 몇 가지 있다.
   ǀ factor 요인 lead to …로 이어지다, 야기하다 bad breath (나쁜) 입 냄새
   【해설】 breathe v. 숨 쉬다, 호흡하다 / breath n. 숨, 입김 / breathing n. 호흡 ▶ '나쁜 입 냄새'는 'bad breath' 또는 'dog breath'라고 한다.

세상에서 가장 긴 혀가 얼마나 긴지 아세요?

① 젊은 여대생인 섀널 태퍼의 혀는 엄청나서 세상에서 가장 긴 혀로 기네스 세계 기록에 오를 정도입니다. ② '엄청난' 보다는 '믿을 수 없는'이 더 적당할 것 같은데, 이유인 즉 혀가 10cm 자 길이만큼 길기 때문입니다. ③ 더 정확히 말하면, 그녀의 혀 길이는 9.75cm입니다. ④ 평균보다 두 배나 긴 겁니다. ⑤ 그녀가 혀를 내밀면, 좀 도마뱀처럼 보입니다. ⑥ 그녀는 자기 혀가 길다는 걸 8살 때 알았습니다. ⑦ 그녀와 친구들은 할로윈 때 혀를 내밀고 사진을 찍었습니다. ⑧ 사진을 현상해보니 그녀의 혀는 크기와 길이 때문에 매우 눈에 띄었던 것입니다. ⑨ 주변 사람들이 기록을 위해 촬영된 그녀의 사진을 보았을 때, 반응은 제각각이었습니다. ⑩ 하지만 이들의 반응에 공통점이 있으니, 모두들 놀랐다는 것입니다. ⑪ 그녀는 원래 그렇게 태어나서 혀를 길게 늘이려는 어떤 행위도 한 적이 없고, 가족의 내력이라 생각하지도 않습니다. ⑫ 그녀는 엄청나게 긴 혀를 항상 의식하고 있으며 친구 관계나 이성 관계에 혀가 영향을 미친다고 말했습니다. ⑬ 하지만, 익숙해진 데다 세상에서 가장 긴 혀를 가졌다고 기네스로부터 돈까지 받았기 때문에 긴 혀가 괜찮다고 생각합니다.

문제 정답 및 해설

1. (b) 지문의 제목으로 적당한 것을 고르세요.
   a. 섀널의 기이한 혀에 대한 놀라운 비밀
   b. 비범한 혀를 가진 평범한 아가씨
   c. 섀널이라는 이름의 도마뱀, 세계 기록 보유했다
   d. 혀를 길게 늘일 수 있는 10가지 방법

2. (b) 지문 내용과 맞는 것을 고르세요.
   a. 믿을 수 없게도, 섀널의 혀는 긴 도마뱀과 대단히 흡사해 보인다. ▶ 혀를 내밀면 도마뱀과 비슷하다고 했지, 혀 자체가 긴 도마뱀 모양과 비슷하다고 하지는 않았다.
   b. 그녀가 8살이 되었을 때에야 그녀는 자신이 유난히 큰 혀를 가졌다는 걸 알았다.
   c. 그녀의 긴 혀를 드러낸 사진을 사람들이 보았을 때, 모두가 다 놀란 건 아니었다. ▶ 반응은 다양했지만 공통적으로 다들 놀랐다.
   d. 섀널의 엄청나게 긴 혀는 수년간 훈련한 결과이다. ▶ 원래 그렇게 태어났기 때문에 혀를 늘이려는 시도를 하지 않았다.

3. 각 문장에 알맞은 표현을 고르세요.

   a. (amazing) 그녀의 혀는 참으로 놀라워서 기네스 세계 기록에 등재되었다.

【해설】문장 구문은 so... that 구문: so 형용사 that 주어 동사 (너무 ...해서 that... 이다)
주어가 사람일 경우 주어 + be + amazed: 주어가 놀라다
주어가 사물일 경우 주어 + be + amazing: 주어는 놀랍다 (여기서 amazing은 형용사)
문제에서 주어는 tongue이다. tongue이 놀란(수동) 게 아니라 tongue이 '놀랍다, 대단하다'는 뜻이므로 amazing이 쓰여야 한다.

b. (taken) 최근에 공원에서 찍은 사진을 너에게 보여주고 싶다.
【해설】'our pictures (which were) taken recently'에서 which were가 생략되었다고 보면 된다.

c. (like) 어떤 이들은 유로 존이 위기라고 하지만 나는 지옥이 더 맞는 말이라고 생각한다. 단순한 위기보다 훨씬 더 상황이 나쁘기 때문이다.
▍be in crisis 위기이다 far worse than ...보다 훨씬 더 나쁜
【해설】be more like... (like 뒤에 ...)가 더 나은, 더 맞은
ex) A flashy coat? It's more like a trash coat.
　　화려한 코트? 쓰레기 코트가 더 맞는 말 같은데.

85. 결혼 분야에서 세계 기록을 보유하려면 어떻게 해야 하는지 아세요?

① 결혼 분야에서 세계 기록을 보유하고 싶다면 당장 동네 체육관에 등록해야 할 겁니다. ② 옥타비오 길리엔과 에이드리안 마티네즈는 가장 오랜 약혼 기간이라는 기록을 보유하고 있습니다. ③ 이들은 15살 때 약혼했습니다. ④ 그리고 82살이 돼서야 결혼했습니다. ⑤ 약혼은 1902년에 했고 결혼은 1969년에 했습니다. ⑥ 그래서 약혼 기간이 67년입니다. ⑦ 다음 커플이 2011년 6월에 결혼했을 때 미국 대통령 오바마가 축하 카드를 보냈습니다. ⑧ 왜냐고요? ⑨ 결혼식이 신랑의 100번째 생일에 이루어졌기 때문입니다. ⑩ 행복한 늙은 새신랑 포레스트 런즈웨이와 90살의 새 신부 로즈 런즈웨이는 30년간의 동거 후 공식적인 남편과 아내 사이가 되었습니다. ⑪ 그런데 놀랍게도 포레스트 런즈웨이는 가장 나이 든 신랑이 아닙니다. ⑫ 1984년 해리 스티븐이 가장 늦은 신랑 기록을 세웠는데 지금까지 기록이 깨지지 않고 있습니다. ⑬ 그는 103살에 결혼했습니다. ⑭ 이미 눈치채셨겠지만, 결혼 분야에서 기록을 세우거나 기록을 깨려면 빨리 죽지 마십시오.

문제 정답 및 해설

1. (d) 지문의 제목으로 적당한 것을 고르세요.
   a. 언제 약혼할 것이며 어떻게 결혼할 것인가
   b. 버락 오바마가 누구에게 카드를 보냈다고?
   c. 런즈웨이 부부, 세계 기록을 깨다
   d. 결혼 분야에서 세계 기록을 세우기 위한 유용한 팁

2. (b) 결혼 분야에서 기록을 세우거나 갱신하고 싶다면, _____.
   a. 초등학교 때 약혼해야 한다
   b. 건강하게 오래 살아야 한다
   c. 대통령에게 축하 카드를 보내야 할 것이다
   d. 배우자와 함께 일찍 죽어야 할 것이다

3. 각 문장에 알맞은 표현을 고르세요.

   a. (It was not until 2012 that) 2012년이 되어서야 내 누이가 집으로 돌아와 학교에 다니기 시작했다.
   【해설】It is/was not until A that B: A하고 나서야 B하다

   b. (yet) 그는 이주일 전에 나에게 편지를 보냈다고 말했지만 나는 아직도 그것을 받지 못했다.

   【해설】yet은 부정문과 함께 문장 끝에 쓰이며 '아직 …아니다'의 의미로 해석된다.
   ex) I didn't do it yet. 그것을 아직 하지 않았다.
   Are you going to fix it? 그것을 고칠 거니? – Not yet. 아직 아니야.
   Am I dead? 제가 죽었나요? – Not just yet. 아직은 안 죽었다.

   c. (took place) 어느 역사적인 사건들이 바로크 시대에 발생했는가? I historical 역사적인 the Baroque period 바로크 시대
   【해설】take over 인수하다, 접수하다 / take part in 참가하다 (participate in) / take place 발생하다, 일어나다 (= occur, happen) ▶ 문맥상 took place가 적당하다.

이런 기네스 기록도 있다는 거 아세요?

① 다렐 베스트는 '더 베스트 맨'으로도 알려진 그의 바퀴 달린 결혼식장의 도움으로 가장 빠르고 쉽게 40회 이상의 결혼식을 주례한 목사로 기네스북에 기록되었습니다. ② 그의 예식은 오랜 시간이 걸리지 않고 신랑, 신부 외에 두 명의 증인만 필요합니다. ③ 젊은 독일인 로프 이벤은 가장 먼 거리의 요리용 열판 걷기 기록을 세웠습니다. ④ 물론 그가 걸을 때 열판은 켜져 있었습니다! ⑤ 그는 2009년 4월 18일 이탈리아의 밀라노에서 아주 뜨거운 열판 위를 22.90미터나 걷는 세계 기록을 세웠습니다. ⑥ 열판 위를 걷는 것은 상당히 위험하고 무서운 일이지만 이 도전만큼 위험하고 무섭지는 않을 겁니다. ⑦ 태국 여성 칸차나 케카유는 33일 밤낮으로 5,320마리의 전갈과 유리로 된 방에서 생활한 사람으로 기네스 세계 기록에 올랐습니다. ⑧ 이 특정 전갈들이 치명적이거나 사람에게 해로운 건 아니었지만 2008년 12월 22일에서 2009년 1월 24일까지 그녀는 13번을 물렸습니다.

문제 정답 및 해설

1. (d) 이 글의 요지를 고르세요.
   a. 가장 긴 핫플레이트 위 걷기가 가장 어려운 것이었다.
   b. 전갈과 함께 유리방에서 살려면 최소한 33일을 금식해야 한다. * fast v. 금식하다
   c. 가장 어리석은 일은 유리방에서 전갈들과 같이 생활하는 것이다.
   d. 많은 사람들이 다양한 방식으로 기록을 세우려고 노력한다.

2. (a) 지문 내용과 맞는 것을 고르세요.
   a. 베스트 목사의 더 베스트 맨은 결혼식 예배당으로 사용될 수 있는 탈 것이다.
   b. 로프 이벤이 2009년 기록을 세우려고 시도할 때, 핫플레이트는 꺼져 있었다. ▶ 핫플레이트는 켜져 있었다.
   c. 타이 출신의 한 여성은 세계에서 전갈에게 가장 많이 물린 사람으로 기록되었다. ▶ 가장 많이 물린 기록이 아니라 5,320마리의 전갈과 33일간 생활했다는 기록이다.
   d. 다렐 베스트는 독일인이고, 로프 이벤과 칸차나 케카유도 그렇다. ▶ 다렐 베스트의 국적은 나오지 않았고 이벤은 독일인, 케카유는 태국인이다.

3. 각 문장에 알맞은 표현을 고르세요.

a. (scary) 이 공포 영화는 끔찍해야 했지만, 내 생각만큼 무섭지 않았다. l horror movie 공포 영화 horrific 끔찍한 as I thought 생각했던 것만큼
【해설】무서워하는 주체가 화자가 아닌 '영화가 무서운 것'이기 때문에 scary가 쓰여야 맞다.
ex) My teacher is scary. He is as scary as hell. 우리 선생님은 무섭다. 아주 끔찍하게 무섭다. ▶ 무서워하는 주체가 my teacher가 아니라 이 문장의 주어인 화자이다.
사람 주어가 무서워하는 것이라면 as scared as로 쓸 수 있다.
ex) I am as scared as you are. 나도 너만큼 무섭다.
무서워하는 주체가 화자인 문장의 주어 I.

b. (on) 불을 켜 주십시오. 책을 읽기에 너무 어둡습니다.
l too (형용사) to 동사원형: 너무 (형용사)해서 (동사)할 수 없다
【해설】turn on 켜다, 작동시키다 turn off 끄다 ▶ '책을 읽기 어둡다'는 내용이 이어지기 때문에 turn on이 와야 적당하다.

c. (preside at) 우리 학교 교장 선생님께서 개업식 사회를 맡으려고 앞으로 나섰다. l principal 교장 step forward 앞으로 나서다 opening ceremony 개업식, 시작하는 의식
【해설】preside at[over] a ceremony (어떤 의식의) 사회, 진행을 맡다

87 마르셀 프티오 의사가 어떤 기록을 보유했는지 아세요?

① 마르셀 프티오는 낮에는 의사, 밤에는 연쇄 살인범이었습니다. ② 2차 세계대전 중 나치가 점령한 파리는 대단히 끔찍한 곳이었습니다. ③ 많은 유태인들은 파리를 떠나길 원했는데 사람들이 그냥 사라지는 경우가 잦았기 때문이었습니다. ④ 프티오 의사는 파리를 떠나길 간절히 원하는 많은 유태인들을 꾀어냈습니다. ⑤ 그는 그가 남아메리카로 떠날 수 있게 도와주리라 기대한 이들에게서 돈을 받았습니다. ⑥ 하지만 그 불쌍한 유태인들은 남아메리카 땅을 밟을 수 없었는데, 대신 프티오에게 잔인하게 살해당했기 때문이었습니다. ⑦ 희생자들 대부분은 사지가 잘려 불에 태워졌습니다. ⑧ 1944년, 프티오의 이웃들이 경찰에 전화를 걸어 그의 집 굴뚝에서 고약한 냄새가 난다며 불평했습니다. ⑨ 경찰이 그의 집을 찾아가 지하실로 들어갔을 때 그들은 눈앞에 펼쳐진 광경을 믿을 수 없었습니다. ⑩ 지하실 사방에 팔, 다리 같은 시신 유해들이 나뒹굴고 있었습니다. ⑪ 그는 27명을 살해한 혐의로 기소당했지만, 당국에서는 그가 많게는 150명까지 살해했으리라 추측했습니다. ⑫ 그는 자신은 죄가 없으며, 이중 첩자나 독일 스파이처럼 프랑스의 적들만 살해했다고 주장했습니다. ⑬ 하지만, 판사나 배심원 어느 누구도 그의 말을 믿지 않았습니다. ⑭ 1946년 5월 25일, 프티오는 기요틴에서 참수당했습니다.

문제 정답 및 해설

1. (c) 이 글의 요지를 고르세요.
   a. 프랑스의 적들은 단두대에서 참수 당했다.
   b. 2차 대전 중 많은 유대인들이 사라졌다.
   c. 마르셀 프티오는 많은 사람들을 처참하게 살해했다.
   d. 프티오의 지하실은 그의 비밀 실험실이었다.

2. (a) 많은 유대인들이 프티오에게 돈을 준 건 그들이 _____ 생각했기 때문이다.
   a. 그가 그들이 파리에서 남아메리카로 도피할 수 있게 도와주리라
   b. 그는 사람들을 무료로 치료해주는 좋은 의사라고
   c. 그는 이중 첩자에 독일 스파이라고
   d. 그에게 쓸 만한 넓은 지하실이 있다고

3. 각 문장에 알맞은 표현을 고르세요.

   a. (by) 케이티는 낮에는 평범한 일반 엄마이고, 밤에는 용맹한 범죄수사대원이다. ▮ normal 평범한 average 일반적인 crimefighter 범죄와 싸우는 사람, 범죄수사대원
   【해설】... by day, ... by night 낮에는 ..., 밤에는 ...
   ex) He is Judge Roger by day, Mr. Casanova by night. 그는 낮에는 로저 판사, 밤에는 미스터 카사노바이다.

   b. (saw) 그녀는 자기 눈으로 보고 있으면서도 자신이 본 바를 믿을 수 없었다.
   【해설】can't believe what one see = can't believe one's eyes 자신이 보는 바를 믿을 수 없다
   can't believe what one hear = can't believe one's ears 자신이 듣는 바를 믿을 수 없다. ▶ 'even though she was watching it with her own eyes'라는 표현에서 what she saw가 정답임을 알 수 있다.

   c. (for) 언제 부모님 집을 떠나 기숙사로 갈 것입니까?
   【해설】leave 떠나다 / leave for ...를 향해 떠나다 / leave A for B A를 떠나 B로 향하다
   ex) Jane left London. 제인은 런던을 떠났다.
   Jane left for London. 제인은 런던을 향해 떠났다.
   Jane left London for Paris. 제인은 런던을 떠나 파리로 향했다.

   d. (burglary) 딘은 절도행위로 고발당했을 때 자신이 잘못 고발당한 것이라 주장했다. ▮ burglary 빈집털이, 절도 thief 도둑 steal (stole, stolen) 훔치다 falsely accused 무고한, 잘못 고발한
   【해설】be accused of (고발당하다) + 명사/동명사
   전치사 of 다음에 '주어+동사 절'이 올 수 없다. 그래서 be accused of burglary, be accused of stealing 혹은 be accused of being a thief로 써야 한다.

가장 짧은 전쟁이 단 38분간 지속되었다는 거 아세요?

① 전쟁에 관해서라면 짧을수록 좋습니다. ② 그렇다면 가장 짧은 전쟁은 얼마나 짧은 시간 지속되었을까요? ③ 1896년 잔지바르와 영국 간의 전쟁이 기록된 역사상 가장 짧은 전쟁이었습니다. ④ 이는 '앵글로–잔지바르 전쟁'이라 불립니다. ⑤ 잔지바르의 술탄(지배자)이 1896년 8월 25일에 사망한 후, 그의 조카 바가쉬가 왕위에 올랐지만 대영제국에서는 다른 사람을 마음에 두고 있었습니다. ⑥ 영국은 이 사람이 다루기 훨씬 쉽다고 생각했던 것입니다. ⑦ 그래서 영국은 바가쉬에게 왕위에서 물러날 것을 명령했습니다. ⑧ 바가쉬는 이를 거부했습니다. ⑨ 영국은 바가쉬가 막 이사 온 궁궐 앞에 해군을 보냈습니다. ⑩ 바가쉬가 마지막까지 평화적인 결론을 위해 협상에 노력을 기울였지만, 영국 해군은 공격을 시작했습니다. ⑪ 궁궐은 무너지기 시작했고 민간인, 군인 할 것 없이 사람들이 그의 눈앞에서 죽어가기 시작했습니다. ⑫ 그는 이번 전투를 이길 수 없음을 알았고 독일 영사관으로 황급히 도피했습니다. ⑬ 이후 영국은 공격을 중단했고 잔지바르는 항복했습니다. ⑭ 이 전투는 오전 9시에 시작해 38분에서 45분 정도 지속되었습니다. ⑮ 영국은 꽤 수월하게 전투에서 승리했고 원하는 걸 얻었지만, 잔지바르에 발사한 포탄 비용을 물어내라고 잔지바르에 요구했다고 합니다.

문제 정답 및 해설

1. (b) 이 글의 요지를 고르세요.
   a. 가장 짧은 전쟁이 최고의 전쟁이다.
   b. 가장 짧은 전쟁인 앵글로–잔지바르 전쟁은 약 38분간 지속되었다.
   c. 영국이 먼저 포탄을 터뜨렸으니 앵글로–잔지바르 전쟁은 영국 군대에게 책임이 있다.
   d. 앵글로–잔지바르 전쟁의 원인은 바가쉬이다.

2. (d) 지문 내용과 맞는 것을 고르세요.
   a. 바가쉬는 너무 무서워서 평화 협상을 위한 노력을 할 수 없었다. ▶ 바가쉬는 마지막까지 평화 협상을 하려고 노력했다.
   b. 앵글로–잔지바르 전쟁은 기록된 역사상 최고의 전쟁이었다. ▶ the best war가 아니라 the shortest war였다.
   c. 대영제국은 바가쉬가 왕위에 오르기 원했다. ▶ 바가쉬가 아닌 다른 사람이 왕위에 오르기 원했던 영국은 바가쉬에게 왕위에서 내려오도록 요구했다.
   d. 왕족 중 하나였던 바가쉬는 나서서 술탄이 되었다. (전 술탄의 조카이므로 왕족이 맞다.) * member of the royal family 왕족 가족

3. 각 문장에 알맞은 표현을 고르세요.

   a. (Even though) 그를 수차례 만났음에도 불구하고 아직도 그의 이름을 기억할 수 없다.
   【해설】앞 문장과 뒷문장의 내용을 볼 때 even though (...이지만, ...인데도 불구하고)가 가장 적당하다.

   b. (where) 네 짐을 싸서 네가 속한 곳으로 가라. l pack up 짐을 싸다 belongings 소유물 belong ...에 속하다, ...소유이다
   【해설】the place라는 선행사를 받는 관계부사는 where. where를 생략하고 the place you belong이라고 쓰기도 한다.

   c. (alike) 한 남자는 잔혹하게 피해자를 살해하고 또 다른 남자는 그냥 옆에 서 있기만 했다. 하지만 두 사람 다 똑같이 유죄였다.
   l savagely 잔인하게 victim 피해자 be guilty 유죄이다
   【해설】alike: to the same degree, equally 똑같이, 마찬가지로

69명의 자녀를 낳은 어머니가 있다는 거 아세요?

① 69명의 아이를 낳았다? ② 불가능한 것처럼 들립니다. ③ 사실 쌍둥이, 세쌍둥이... 또는 네쌍둥이를 낳지 않는다면 거의 불가능합니다. ④ 이 슈퍼맘은 다산(多産)의 도움으로 무려 69명의 아이를 낳았습니다. ⑤ 그녀는 쌍둥이 16번, 세쌍둥이 7번, 네쌍둥이 4번을 낳았습니다. ⑥ 대단한 이 이야기가 1700년대에 일어났긴 했지만, 피오도르 바실레프 여사라는 그녀의 이름이 2004년 판 기네스 세계 기록 책에 세상에서 가장 출산을 많이 한 어머니로 기록될 만합니다. ⑦ 그리고 그녀의 놀라운 기록은 아직까지 깨지지 않고 있습니다. ⑧ 기네스북이 믿기 힘든 그녀의 업적을 인정하긴 했지만 69명의 자녀 출산이라니... 믿기에는 너무 심한 것 같지 않나요? ⑨ 어떤 이들은 이를 의심합니다. ⑩ 이들은 이 이야기가 그저 소문 혹은 지어낸 이야기라고 생각합니다. ⑪ 하지만, 누가 이런 이야기를 만들어 내겠습니까? ⑫ 그리고 도대체 왜 그런 짓을 하겠습니까? ⑬ 글쎄, 다양한 이유로 이런 이야기를 만들어내는 사람들이 실제 있습니다. ⑭ 1983년 한 칠레 여성이 58명의 자녀를 낳았다고 주장했습니다. ⑮ 하지만, 그녀가 사망한 후 한 경찰은 이 출산의 여왕이 정부 보조 음식 지원을 받기 위해 거짓말했다는 사실을 밝혀냈습니다. ⑯ 그녀는 겨우 16명의 자녀만 두었습니다.

문제 정답 및 해설

1. (c) 지문의 제목으로 적당한 것을 고르세요.
   a. 최악의 사기극 : 69명의 자녀를 둔 엄마
   b. 69명의 자녀 출산, 누가 비난받아야 하는가?
   c. 믿거나 말거나 : 믿기 힘든 출산의 여왕
   d. 정부 69명의 아이들을 먹이기 위한 조치에 나서다

2. (c) 바실레프 여사가 1700년대에 69명의 아이를 낳았음에도 불구하고 _____.
   a. 칠레인 엄마가 생존하는 가장 아이를 많이 낳은 엄마로 인정받는다
   b. 기네스 세계 기록에서 그녀의 기록을 인정하기를 거부했다
   c. 그녀의 이야기가 기네스 세계 기록 2004년 판에 소개되었다
   d. 수십 년간 아무도 그녀의 엄청난 업적을 인정해주지 않았다

3. 각 문장에 알맞은 표현을 고르세요.

   a. (Had you tried) 네가 이 다이어트를 시도했더라면 체중을 좀 뺄 수 있었을 것이다.
   【해설】가정법 과거 완료 (과거 사실의 반대) : If 주어 had pp, 주어 would/could have pp * if 절의 경우 if를 생략하고 주어와 동사의 위치를 도치시킬 수 있다.
   ex) If I had been smart, I would have done it. 내가 똑똑했더라면 그것을 했을 텐데.
   = Had I been smart, I would have done it. = I was not smart, so I didn't do it.

   b. (doubt) 내 친구들 모두 존과 케이트 사이에 아무 일 없다고 말했지만, 나는 '그렇지 않을걸'이라 말했다.
   【해설】doubt는 동사로 '의심하다, 의문을 갖다' 명사로 '의문, 의혹'. 형용사는 doubtful(불확실한, 의심스러운)이다. (be doubt : X, be in doubt : O) doubt를 써서 '나는 믿지 않는다, 의심스럽다'를 표현하려면, 'I doubt it.' 혹은 'I have doubts (have a doubt).'로 쓴다.

   c. (on earth) 도대체 내가 무엇 때문에 여기 있는 거지? 그리고 도대체 왜 내가 이 짓을 하고 있는 거야?
   【해설】on earth, in the world '도대체, 세상에'라는 뜻의 강조 표현으로 의문사(what, why, who, when...)와 동사 사이에 위치.
   ex) Who on earth did you marry? 넌 도대체 누구와 결혼했니?
   Where in the world did you find it? 도대체 이걸 어디서 찾았니?

90 Chapter 9 | The Amazing Records

브루스 리의 발차기가 얼마나 빨랐는지 아세요?

① 1940년에 태어나 1973년에 사망한 브루스 리 (이소룡)는 무술인, 배우, 무술 지도자, 감독, 그리고 영화 제작자였는데, 입이 벌어질 정도의 놀라운 속도로 움직일 수 있었습니다. ② 말 그대로 속도가 너무 빨라서 입이 벌어질 정도였습니다. ③ 얼마나 빨랐을까요? ④ 그의 발차기는 사람들이 움직임을 볼 수 없을 만큼 너무 빨라서 필름을 천천히 돌려야만 했습니다. ⑤ 그의 주먹 날리는 속도도 마찬가지입니다. ⑥ 그의 발차기와 주먹 날리기가 어찌나 빨랐던지 그 속도를 측정하려는 사람들이 있었습니다. ⑦ 이소룡이 비디오카메라 앞에서 왼발로 발차기 시범을 보였을 때 그의 발차기는 1/5 초밖에 걸리지 않았습니다. ⑧ 현장에서 그의 시범을 본 사람들은 그가 오른발잡이라는 사실에 할 말을 잃고 말았습니다. ⑨ 대부분의 액션 영화들, 특히 무술 영화는 싸우는 장면이 더 빠르고 박진감 있게 보이게 하고자 속도를 빨리합니다. ⑩ 그러나 이소룡의 경우는 반대였습니다. ⑪ 영화 스크리너들은 관객들이 그의 발차기와 주먹을 볼 수 있도록 필름을 다소 느리게 돌려야 했습니다.

문제 정답 및 해설

1. (c) 이 글의 요지를 고르세요.
   a. 많은 무술인들은 오른손잡이다. (right-handed 오른손잡이의)
   b. 액션 영화는 더 활동적으로 보이도록 속도를 높여야 한다.
   c. 이소룡은 굉장히 빨리 발차기와 펀치를 날릴 수 있었다.
   d. 이소룡은 훌륭한 무술인이었지만 좋은 배우는 아니었다.

2. (c) 지문 내용과 맞지 않는 것을 고르세요.
   a. 이소룡은 배우, 감독, 그리고 영화 제작자였다.
   b. 이소룡은 사람들 앞에서 왼발로 발차기를 증명해 보였다.
   c. 영화 만드는 사람들은 이소룡의 영화를 실수로 약간 느리게 돌렸다. ▶ 실수가 아니라 관객들이 그의 동작을 볼 수 있도록 일부러 약간 느리게 돌린 것이다.
   d. 일반적으로 액션 영화는 장면이 더 활기차 보이게 하려고 속도를 높인다.

3. 각 문장에 알맞은 표현을 고르세요.

   a. (took) 그가 이 퍼즐을 푸는데 일주일이 걸렸다.
   【해설】'시간이 얼마 걸리다' : it takes ...
   ex) It will take at least three hours.
   　　최소한 세 시간이 걸릴 것이다.
   　　It took me a whole year to finish the job.
   　　내가 일을 끝내는데 꼬박 일 년이 걸렸다.

   b. (was left) 그녀의 방을 보았을 때 마치 폭탄에 맞은 것처럼 보여서 나는 할 말을 잊었다.
   【해설】주어 + be동사 + left speechless : 주어가 할 말을 잊다, 말문이 막히다
   * leave speechless 말문이 막히게 하다
   ex) You left me speechless.
   　　너는 내 말문이 막히게 했다. 너 때문에 할 말을 잊었다.

   c. (do) 내가 알고 싶은 건 내 남동생이 내가 원하는 대로 행동하게 만드는 방법이다.
   【해설】사역동사 make, have, let + 목적어 + 동사 원형 : ...를 ...하게 만들다, 시키다
   ex) My dad made me do the dishes.
   　　아빠가 나를 설거지하도록 시켰다.

Chapter 10. Proverbs & Idioms

91 표범이 자신의 점들을 바꿀 수 없다는 거 아세요?

① 표범은 자신의 점을 바꿀 수 없습니다. ② 호랑이 역시 자신의 줄무늬를 바꿀 수 없습니다. ③ 표범은 털에 점이 아주 많습니다. ④ 그걸 없애기 위해 아무리 열심히 노력한다 해도, 그 점들은 없어지거나 흐려지지 않습니다. ⑤ 목욕하고, 솔로 문질러 보고, 또는 온갖 종류의 비누를 사용하든… 그래도 '안 되는' 이유는 겉 피부를 문질러 씻어서 해결할 수 있는 문제가 아니기 때문입니다. ⑥ 원래 이 속담은 성경에서 나왔습니다. ⑦ "에티오피아인이 그의 피부를 바꿀 수 있으며, 표범이 그의 점들을 바꿀 수 있느냐? ⑧ 그렇다면 악을 행하는데 익숙한 너희도 선을 행할 수 있으리라." (예레미야 13장 2절) ⑨ 피부색이 짙은 아프리카인이 밝은 피부의 유럽인처럼 피부색을 바꾸는 건 불가능합니다. ⑩ 사악한 사람이 사악한 행실을 쉽게 바꾸지 못하는 건 사악을 행하는데 익숙해 있기 때문입니다. ⑪ 그래서 이 속담은 자신의 본성을 바꾸지 못하는 누군가를 표현할 때 사용할 수 있습니다. ⑫ 예를 들어 게을러서 항상 직장에 지각하는 사람이 있다고 합시다. ⑬ 평소처럼 사무실에 늦게 도착한 그는 미안하다며 다시는 늦지 않겠다고 말했습니다. ⑭ 하지만 다음 날, 그는 모두의 예상대로 지각했습니다. ⑮ 그를 보며 그의 동료들과 상사는 "표범이 자기 점은 못 바꾸지," 라고 말했습니다.

문제 정답 및 해설

1. (a) 이 글의 요지를 고르세요.
   a. 근본적인 천성을 바꾸기는 쉽지 않다.
   b. 피부가 짙은 아프리카인은 피부색을 바꾸려고 시도해서는 안 된다.
   c. 선을 행하는 사람들은 피부에 점이 있는 경향이 있다.
   d. 게으른 일꾼들은 솔로 피부를 문질러야 한다.

2. (b) 예레미야 13장 23절에 의하면, _____.
   a. 에티오피아인은 목욕할 때 솔을 쓰지 않았다
   b. 에티오피아인은 피부를 바꿀 수 없고, 표범도 마찬가지이다
   c. 호랑이와 표범은 사악한 동물이다
   d. 에티오피아인은 악을 행하는데 익숙하다

3. 각 문장에 알맞은 표현을 고르세요.

   a. (fair-skinned) 피부가 희고 금발인 마크는 공정한 사람이다.
   【해설】 fair-skinned의 fair는 '피부가 흰,' have fair hair의 fair는 '금발인,' a fair person의 fair는 '공정한'이라는 뜻이다. 명사 fairy는 '요정'이라는 뜻이다.

   b. (to) 평소 나는 많이 먹는데 익숙하지 않다. 그래서 이제 먹기를 중단해야 겠다.
   【해설】 be accustomed to + 동사원형, 혹은 –ing : …하는데 익숙하다

   c. (neither did she) 그는 그곳에서 무슨 일이 벌어지는지 관심 없었고, 그녀도 마찬가지였다.
   【해설】 부사 neither가 문두에 왔을 때 주어와 동사가 도치된다.
   neither did she ▶ she didn't care … either.

붓 없이도 '시내를 빨갛게 칠할' 수 있다는 거 아세요?

① 붓이 아니라 다량의 술로 '시내를 빨갛게 칠할' 수 있는 이유는 이 표현이 페인트칠과 아무 상관이 없기 때문입니다. ② 이 표현의 의미는 "소란스럽고 시끄럽게 한바탕 마시고 논다"입니다. ③ 이 표현의 유래에 관해 여러 가지 의견이 분분합니다. ④ 가장 잘 알려진 이론은 헨리라는 이름의 귀족에 의해 시작되었다는 것입니다. ⑤ 이 남자는 너무 장난이 심해서 1800년대에 일단의 친구들과 함께 레스터셔 도시에서 난동을 부리며 도시의 건물과 술집을 빨갛게 칠했다고 합니다. ⑥ 어떤 이들은 '홍등가'가 유래일 수도 있다고 주장합니다. ⑦ 과거에 술집과 살롱이 위치한 도시의 특정 지역을 홍등가라고 불렀습니다. ⑧ 이들은 '빨강'이라는 단어가 홍등가에서 나왔을 수도 있다고 생각합니다. ⑨ 아니면 빨간 피에서 유래했을지도 모릅니다. ⑩ 사실 어떤 이들은 피를 흘리게 하고 피로 벽과 건물을 칠하는 등의 정신 나간 행동에서 이 표현이 유래했다고 생각합니다. ⑪ 하지만, 어느 것이 진짜 유래인지는 아무도 모릅니다. ⑫ 어쨌든 밴쿠버에서 2010년 동계 올림픽이 열렸을 때 캐나다인들은 '시내를 빨갛게 칠하자'라는 구호로 자기네 선수들을 응원했는데, 이 표현이 '신나게 즐기자'라는 뜻으로도 쓰이기 때문입니다.

문제 정답 및 해설

1. (b) 이 글의 요지를 고르세요.
   a. 헨리는 홍등가에서 사는 걸 싫어했다.
   b. '시내를 붉게 칠하자'는 건 페인트칠과 상관없다.
   c. 시내를 붉게 칠하면 지방 경찰에게 체포될 것이다.
   d. '시내를 붉게 칠하자'는 피를 흘린다는 뜻이다.

2. (d) 지문 내용과 맞지 않는 것을 고르세요.
   a. '시내를 붉게 칠하다'라는 표현은 술, 파티와 관련이 있다.
   b. 헨리는 건물과 술집을 빨갛게 칠할 정도로 장난이 심했다.
   c. 홍등가에는 술집과 살롱이 많았다.
   d. '시내를 붉게 칠하다'의 유래를 모두 다 알고 있다. ▶ 이 표현의 유래에 관해 몇 가지 의견은 있지만 확실한 유래는 아무도 모른다.

3. 각 문장에 알맞은 표현을 고르세요.

   a. (Which) 커피와 차 중 어느 것을 더 좋아합니까?
   【해설】which : 의문문에서 '이미 제안된(나열된) 것들 중 어느 것 (사람)'이라는 뜻으로, 불특정한 것을 묻는 의문사 what과 의미에 차이가 있다.
   ex) What color is it? 이것은 무슨 색깔입니까?
       Which color is it? (여러 가지 열거된 색깔 중) 어느 색깔을 말하는 것입니까?
   Tell me what is better for him. 그에게 무엇이 더 좋은지 나에게 말해주시오.
   Tell me which (one) is better for him. (이미 나열된 것들 중) 어느 것이 그에게 더 좋은지 나에게 말해주시오.
   prefer는 '...를 더 좋아하다'라는 비교의 의미를 갖고 있다.
   ex) Which one do you like more? = Which one do you prefer? 어느 것을 더 좋아합니까? (아무거나 고르는 게 아니라 이미 언급된 것들 중 더 좋아하는 것을 묻는 의문문)

   b. (from) 새로 온 사람은 그가 얼음과 눈의 땅에서 왔다고 나에게 말했다.
   【해설】come from ...에서 오다. ...출신이다 / come after 뒤쫓다 / come again 다시 오다 ▶ 문맥상 come from이 가장 적당하다.

   c. (was held) 나는 금요일 아침에 교회에 갔는데 거기에서 데이브의 장례식이 거행되었다.
   【해설】누군가에 의해 장례식이 거행되는 것, 즉 수동의 의미 ▶ where 이하 문장의 주어는 Dave's funeral, 동사는 was held이다.
   * 장례식(funeral)이 주어일 때는 항상 수동태(be held)로 쓴다.

93 목숨이 9개인 고양이를 죽일 수 있는 게 무엇인지 아세요?

① 고양이는 목숨이 9개라고 합니다. ② 그럼 무엇이 고양이를 죽일 수 있을까요? ③ 정답은 '호기심이 고양이를 죽였다'는 속담에서 찾을 수 있습니다. ④ 그 의미는 호기심 혹은 캐묻기 좋아하는 태도 때문에 위험한 상황에 빠질 수 있다는 뜻입니다. ⑤ 누군가 원치 않는 질문을 하는데 이를 멈추게 하고 싶을 때 이 속담을 사용할 수 있습니다. ⑥ 고양이는 호기심이 많은 것과 목숨이 9개인 것으로 유명합니다. ⑦ 일반적으로 목숨이 9개인 누군가를 죽이는 건 거의 불가능하지만, 고양이는 자신의 천성적인 호기심으로 죽을 수 있습니다. ⑧ 그만큼 고양이가 호기심이 많다는 것입니다! ⑨ 아마 이 속담은 이렇게 만들어졌을 겁니다. ⑩ 하지만, 원래 고양이를 죽일 수 있는 건 '호기심'이 아니라 '걱정'이었습니다. ⑪ 이 문맥에서 '걱정'은 '근심거리, 슬픔'을 뜻합니다. ⑫ 사실 '걱정이 고양이를 죽였다'는 1800년대 후반까지 통용되었습니다. ⑬ 이 속담이 언제 시작되었는지, 어떻게 '걱정'이라는 단어가 '호기심'으로 바뀌었는지 정확히 설명하기는 매우 어렵습니다. ⑭ 우리가 아는 건, 속담의 원래 모습인 '걱정이 고양이를 죽였다'가 '호기심이 고양이를 죽였다'로 바뀌었다는 것뿐입니다. ⑮ 어쩌면 이 속담의 유래에 대한 호기심을 그만 접어야 할지도 모르겠습니다. ⑯ '호기심이 고양이를 죽였다'라는 말도 있으니까요.

문제 정답 및 해설

1. (b) 이 글의 요지를 고르세요.
   a. 고양이 고기가 맛있긴 하지만 고양이를 죽일 생각은 하지도 마라.
   b. 고양이는 호기심이 많은 동물로 '호기심이 고양이를 죽이다'라는 속담도 있다.
   c. 고양이는 목숨이 9개라서 고양이를 없애려면 고양이를 10번을 죽여야 할 것이다.
   d. 맞는 표현은 '호기심이 고양이를 죽인다'가 아니라 '걱정이 고양이를 죽이다'이다.

2. (d) 1800년대에는 _____.
   a. 사람들이 오직 호기심 많은 고양이만 목숨이 9개라고 믿었다
   b. 호기심 많은 고양이는 사람들에 의해 죽임을 당했다
   c. 고양이에 관한 많은 속담이 생겨났다
   d. 사람들이 '걱정이 고양이를 죽였다'는 속담을 사용했다

3. 각 문장에 알맞은 표현을 고르세요.

   a. (to say) 너는 그렇게 말하기 쉽겠지, 다이앤, 하지만 불행히도 나에게는 그다지 쉽지 않단다.

   【해설】It is 형용사 to 동사 for 사람 : (사람)이 (to 동사)하는 것은 (형용사)하다
   ex) It is impossible for me to do that. 내가 그것을 하는 건 불가능하다.
   It is hard to pass the exam for them. 그들이 시험을 통과하는 건 힘들다.

   b. (unwanted) 수 백 명의 인도 소녀들이 힌디어로 "원치 않는"이라는 뜻의 이름을 갖고 있는데, 그들의 부모가 딸이 아닌 아들을 원했기 때문이다. l share the same name 같은 이름을 공유하다
   【해설】wanted 수배 중인 / savior 구원자 / unwanted 원치 않는, 달갑지 않은 ▶ 문맥상 unwanted가 가장 적당하다.

   c. (into) 놀랍게도 심지어 나도 세상을 더 좋은 곳으로 만들 수 있다. l much to one's surprise 놀랍게도 a better place 더 좋은 곳
   【해설】change A into B: A를 B로 변화시키다 ▶ '...에서 ...로 변하다, 되다'와 같은 change, turn 등의 표현은 into와 함께 쓰인다.
   change A into B / turn A into B

94 실제 도끼를 받지 않고도 'get the axe' 할 수 있다는 거 아세요?

① 받거나 빼앗기는 실제 도끼(axe)가 없어도 'get the axe' 할 수도 있고 'give the axe' 할 수도 있습니다. ② 그게 가능한 건 'axe'에 여러 가지 의미가 있기 때문입니다. ③ axe는 나무를 자를 때 또는 나무를 베어낼 때 사용되는 수공구입니다. ④ 이는 또한 동사로도 쓰이는 데 의미는 '도끼로 자르거나 베거나 다듬다'는 뜻입니다. ⑤ 두 번째 의미는 특히 직장에서의 '해고'를 뜻합니다. ⑥ 그래서 'discharge, removal, layoff...' 등이 'axe'의 유의어입니다. ⑦ 이렇게 해서 'give the axe'가 '누구를 해고하다'라는 뜻을 갖게 되었습니다. ⑧ 마찬가지로 'get the axe'는 '해고되다'는 뜻입니다. ⑨ '해고'라는 말이 나온 김에 알아두면 좋을 또 다른 단어가 있는데 바로 'the sack'입니다. ⑩ 'sack'은 일종의 가방으로 널리 알려져 있습니다. ⑪ 하지만 'axe'처럼 '해고'라는 뜻도 갖고 있습니다. ⑫ 그래서 'get the sack'은 'get the axe'와 뜻이 똑같습니다. ⑬ 한 가지 더. ⑭ 'sack'이나 'axe'를 '해고'의 의미로 사용하고 싶다면, 'the'를 빼면 안 됩니다. ⑮ 만약 'my boss gave me an axe (or sack)'으로 말한다면, 사람들은 당신이 친절한 사장님으로부터 실제 도끼 (또는 자루)를 받았다고 알아들을 것입니다.

문제 정답 및 해설

1. (b) 이 글의 요지를 고르세요.
   a. 누군가 당신을 해고하면(give the axe), 당신은 그에 대한 돈을 지불해야 할 것이다.
   b. "Get the axe"는 "해고당하다"라는 뜻이다.
   c. "Get the axe"와 "give the sack"은 같은 뜻이다.
   d. 도끼는 자루보다 더 비싸다.

2. (d) 지문 내용과 맞는 것을 고르세요.
   a. 게으른 직원 중 하나가 마음에 안 든다면, 도끼를 주면 된다. ▶ 'give him the axe'라고 써야 '그를 해고하다'의 뜻이 된다. 'give him an axe'는 '그에게 실제 도끼를 주다'는 뜻이다.
   b. 'axe'라는 단어에는 최소한 5개의 다른 뜻이 있다. ▶ 지문에는 세 가지 뜻만 나왔다. (명사로 도끼, 해고, 동사로 도끼로 찍거나 다듬다)
   c. 'employment(직장, 고용)'의 유의어는 'discharge(해고)'와 'layoff(일시해고)'이다. ▶ removal, discharge, layoff, axe 등이 '해고'의 뜻을 가진 유의어들이다.
   d. 'get the axe'는 'get an axe'와 완전히 다르다.

3. 각 문장에 알맞은 표현을 고르세요.

a. (layoff) 예산 삭감 때문에 일부 직원들의 일시해고를 당신은 허락해야 한다. l permit 허가하다 layoff 일시해고 staff member 직원 budget cuts 예산 삭감
【해설】permit the layoff 일시해고를 허락하다 ▶ '해고하다'라는 동사 dismiss의 명사형은 dismissal로 문제에서 동사형 dismiss가 쓰일 수 없다. sack은 get the sack이라는 표현에서만 '해고'의 의미로 쓰인다.

b. (are commonly practiced) 아프리카에서 일반적으로 행해지는 종교는 무엇입니까? l religion 종교 commonly 흔하게, 일반적으로 practice 관습, 관행, 행하다
【해설】수동태에서 부사의 위치 ▶ be동사 + 부사 + pp
ex) The first page of a book is generally called the cover 책의 첫 장은 일반적으로 표지라고 불린다.

c. (getting burned) 타는 듯한 태양 아래에서 화상을 입지 않고 축구를 할 방법은 없다. l no way to 동사 ...할 방법이 없다, 할 수 없다 scorching 타는 듯한 get burned 화상을 입다
【해설】without + 명사, 명사구 ▶ without 다음에 주어+동사 절이 올 수 없다.

95 물고기가 배를 드러내면 어떻게 되는지 아세요?

① 물고기가 배를 드러내면, 죽은 겁니다. ② 죽은 물고기를 생각해보세요. ③ 헤엄치지도 않고 지느러미를 움직이지도 않습니다. ④ 그냥 배를 드러낸 채 물 위를 뒤집혀 떠다닐 뿐입니다. ⑤ 'belly-up'이라는 표현도 같은 의미인데, 죽은 물고기의 떠다니는 자세에서 유래된 표현이기 때문입니다. ⑥ 그래서 '배를 드러내다 go belly-up'의 뜻은 '절망적으로 망하다' '실패하다' 또는 '파산하다'입니다. ⑦ 일반적으로 경제적인 어려움에 빠진 상태일 때 이 표현이 사용됩니다. ⑧ 예를 들어 이렇게 말할 수 있습니다.
⑨ "건축업자들은 시멘트 가격이 점점 높아지고 있어서 파산하기 직전이다."
⑩ "그의 부채 문제가 갈수록 악화되는 데도 그는 파산하지 않으리라 확신한다."
⑪ "많은 양어민들이 망하기 일보 직전인데, 이는 발전소에서 방출된 해로운 오염물질로 인해 점점 더 많은 양어장 물고기들이 말 그대로 배를 드러내고 있기 때문이다."
⑫ 하지만 'go belly-down'이라는 건 없습니다.

문제 정답 및 해설

1. (c) 이 글의 요지를 고르세요.
   a. 죽은 물고기를 먹으면 파산한다 (배를 드러내게 된다).
   b. '배를 드러내다'는 표현은 누군가 위암에 걸리면 사용할 수 있다.
   c. '배를 드러내다'는 표현은 물고기와 관련이 있고 의미는 '실패하다'이다.
   d. 양식어민들과 건축업자들이 파산 직전이다.

2. (c) 'belly-up'이라는 표현은 _____ 에서 유래했다.
   a. 채무 문제가 있는 건축업자
   b. 물에서 수영하는 물고기 자세
   c. 죽은 물고기의 떠 있는 자세
   d. 파괴된 절망적인 상황

3. 각 문장에 알맞은 표현을 고르세요.

   a. (means) 일단의 물고기를 종종 a school이라고 한다. 그래서 a school of fish는 a group of fish와 같은 뜻이다.
   【해설】a group of + 단수 동사, a school of + 단수 동사 ▶ '한 떼/무리'라는 의미라서 복수 의미지만, 주어가 'a group, a school'이기 때문에 동사는 단수 동사가 온다.
   ex) a school of fish 물고기 (한) 떼 + 단수 동사
       schools of fish 물고기 여러 떼 + 복수 동사

   b. (higher and higher) 인플레이션 때문에 장보는 비용이 갈수록 높아지고 있다.
   【해설】be getting + 비교급 and 비교급 ▶ 점점 …하다 (진행형)
   (비용, 가격 등이) 상승하다, 오르다 ▶ be getting higher and higher
   (상황) 점점 좋아지다 ▶ be getting better and better
   (크기) 점점 커지다 ▶ be getting larger and larger

   c. (to die) 강도가 그녀를 죽이겠다고 협박하자 그녀는 911에 전화를 걸어 "제가 죽기 직전이에요!"라고 소리쳤다.
   ▎robber 강도 threaten 협박하다
   【해설】be about to 동사원형: …하기 직전이다 ▶ 'to + 동사 원형'인 to die가 와야 맞다.

   d. (was on the verge of) 내 남동생은 대회 승리에 실패한 후 신경쇠약에 걸리려고 한다.
   ▎nervous breakdown 신경쇠약 fail to win 승리하지 못하다
   【해설】be on the verge of + 명사(구) : …하려고 하다, …하기 직전이다 / be about to + 동사원형 : …하기 직전이다 (be about of로 쓰지 않는다.) / be planning to + 동사원형 : …하려고 계획 중이다-현재진행형 ▶ 의미상 was on the verge of가 가장 적당하며, 빈칸 다음에 명사(nervous breakdown)가 왔기 때문에 be planning to는 올 수 없다.

96 'gung ho'가 한자라는 거 아세요?

① gung ho는 한자입니다. ② gung(工)은 '일하다', ho(和)는 '함께, 조화로운'이라는 뜻입니다. ③ 그러니까 'gung ho'의 말 그대로의 의미는 '함께 일하다'입니다. ④ 하지만 사전을 찾아보면 '매우 열정적인, 열심인'이라고 나와 있습니다. ⑤ 사실 'gung ho'가 영어가 된 건 1942년부터입니다. ⑥ 2차 대전 때 미국 해병대 지휘관이었던 에반스 칼슨은 중국에 머물 때 중국 산업 협동조합의 정신에 감탄했습니다. ⑦ 그래서 2차 대전에 참전하자 그는 긴 중국어 발음을 'gung ho' 두 단어로 짧게 줄이고 이를 자기 부대의 슬로건으로 삼았습니다. ⑧ 그때 이후 'gung ho'는 열성과 '할 수 있다'는 태도의 표현으로 미 해병대의 비공식적인 모토가 되었습니다. ⑨ 이 표현을 들어본 적이 없다고요? ⑩ 'gung ho'는 생각보다 많이 쓰입니다. ⑪ 론 하워드 감독의 1986년 코미디 영화 제목이 'Gung Ho'였습니다. ⑫ 켄 블랜차드와 셸든 보울즈가 쓴 'Gung Ho'라는 책도 서점에 있습니다. ⑬ 그리고 'GungHo Online Entertainment'라는 일본의 비디오 게임 회사도 있습니다. ⑭ 보시다시피 상당히 많은 사람들이 'gung ho'라는 표현에 열성적입니다.

문제 정답 및 해설

1. (d) 이 글의 요지를 고르세요.
   a. 중국 한자는 북미인들에 의해 자주 사용되어 왔다.
   b. 칼슨은 일본에 머물 당시 'gung ho'라는 표현을 만들어낸 사람이다.
   c. 'gung ho'는 1942년 이래 지금까지 중국 해병대의 슬로건이다.
   d. 한자로 된 표현 'gung ho'는 '열정적인'이라는 뜻이다.

2. (d) 지문 내용과 맞는 것을 고르세요.
   a. 'gung ho'의 비유적 의미는 '함께 일하다'이다. ▶ 비유적인 의미가 아니라 문자 그대로의 의미가 '함께 일하다(work together)' 이다
   b. 'gung ho'라는 단어는 영어가 아니기 때문에 사전에서 찾을 수 없다. ▶ 영어 사전에 'enthusiastic'의 뜻으로 나와 있다.
   c. 'gung ho'는 1차 세계 대전 이래 미국 해병대의 모토였다. ▶ 2차 세계대전 이래 미국 해병대의 비공식적 모토였다.
   d. 'Gung ho'는 론 하워드가 감독한 영화 제목이다.

3. 각 문장에 알맞은 표현을 고르세요.

   a. (up) 강도가 '꼼짝 마!'라고 소리쳤을 때 나는 사전에서 '꼼짝 마'라는 단어를 찾아보기 위해 도서관으로 달릴 수밖에 없었는데, 그 단어의 뜻을 모르기 때문이었다.

【해설】look은 이어지는 전치사에 따라 의미가 달라지므로 함께 쓰이는 전치사와 숙어로 암기해야 한다. ▶ look up (사전, 자료 등을) 찾아보다 / look at 쳐다보다 / look out 조심하다 (= watch out)

b. (admire) 창문을 좀 보십시오. 아름다운 경치에 감탄하지 않을 수 없을 것입니다. I have no choice but to 동사원형 = can not help + ing ...하지 않을 수 없다
【해설】admire v. 감탄하다, 존경하다 / admirable a. 감탄스러운 / admiral n. 해군장성 ▶ 세 단어 모두 비슷해 보이지만 뜻도 품사도 다르므로 사용에 주의한다.

c. (have enjoyed) 롭과 남동생은 어려서부터 다양한 스포츠를 즐겨왔다.
【해설】have been enjoying(현재완료진행) 또는 have enjoyed (현재완료) 모두 가능하다 그러나 주어가 복수(Rob and his brother)이기 때문에 has enjoyed는 올 수 없다.
현재완료 + since 과거동사 : ...이래로 ...해왔다
ex) I have been blonde since I was born. 나는 태어난 이래 (나면서부터) 금발이었다.(지금도 금발이다)

97. 'easier said than done'의 의미를 아세요?

① 쥐들은 집주인이 '귀염둥이'라는 이름의 크고 살찐 고양이를 데려오기 전까지 집에서 행복하게 살았습니다. ② 귀염둥이는 전혀 귀엽지 않기 때문에 이름이 잘못 붙여진 겁니다. ③ 귀염둥이는 노상 쥐들을 쫓아다녔습니다. ④ 쥐들은 귀염둥이가 너무 무서워서 음식을 찾으러 집안을 돌아다니기가 힘들었습니다. ⑤ 똘똘이라는 이름의 쥐가 손을 들었습니다. ⑥ 그 쥐 역시 이름이 잘못 지어졌는데 똘똘하지 않고 멍청하기 때문입니다. ⑦ 그래서 친구들은 그를 멍청한 똘똘이라고 부릅니다. ⑧ 똘똘이가 말하기를 "제게 좋은 생각이 있습니다. ⑨ 귀염둥이 목에 방울을 달면 녀석은 방울 소리를 내지 않고 움직일 수 없게 됩니다. ⑩ 못생기고 끔찍한 그 녀석이 우리 근처에 오면 우리는 소리를 듣고 녀석이 우리를 잡기 전에 도망칠 수 있습니다." ⑪ 그러자 할아버지 쥐가 말하기를, "그거 쉽구먼. ⑫ 그럼 자네가 언제 고양이 목에 방울을 달 건가?" ⑬ 똘똘이가 화들짝 놀라며 말하기를, "뭐라고요? 제가요? 그건 안 됩니다. ⑭ 녀석의 목에 방울을 달려다 귀염둥이에게 잡아먹힐 게 확실하니까요." ⑮ "실천하기보다 말이 쉽지. ⑯ 자네 친구들이 자네를 괜히 멍청한 똘똘이라고 부르는 게 아니라네," 할아버지 쥐가 대답했습니다.

문제 정답 및 해설

1. (b) 이 글의 요지를 고르세요.
   a. 쥐는 고양이를 패배시킬 기회가 없다. stand a chance to 동사원형, stand a chance of –ing ...할 가능성이 있다.
   b. 말하기는 쉽지만 그걸 실천하는 건 쉽지 않다.
   c. 큰 고양이를 상대하는 최상의 방법은 목에 종을 다는 것이다.
   d. 멍청한 사람들은 말을 하려고 입을 열면 안 된다.

2. (d) Cutie와 Smartie 둘 다 이름이 잘못 지어진 이유는 _____ 때문이다.
   a. Cutie가 똑똑하고 Smartie가 귀엽기
   b. 그들은 미국이 아닌 중국 출신이기
   c. Cutie는 멍청하고 Smartie는 못생겼기
   d. Cutie는 귀엽지 않고 Smartie는 똑똑하지 않기

3. 각 문장에 알맞은 표현을 고르세요.

   a. (misspelled) 'Soul'이 아니라 'Seoul'이라고 해야 한다. 도시 이름이 지도에 잘못 쓰여 있다.

   【해설】misspell 철자를 잘못 쓰다 / misname 이름을 잘못 짓다 / misplace (장소에) 잘 못 두다 ▶ 문맥상 misspelled가 적당하다. 철자에서 s가 두 개라는 점에 주의 (mis + spell).

   b. (touching) 내 남동생은 바닥에 닿지 않고 줄넘기를 할 수 있다.
   ▮ do rope skipping 줄넘기하다
   【해설】without + 명사(구), –ing ▶ 전치사 without 다음에 주어+동사 절이 올 수 없다.
   ex) without touching the ground 땅에 닿지 않고
       without blinking 눈을 깜빡이지 않고

   c. (startled) 놀란 학생들이 크게 비명을 지르기 시작했고 이 소리는 그들의 선생님을 놀라게 했다.
   【해설】the startled students 놀란 학생들: 여기서 startled는 형용사 '놀란'
   cf. the sound startled their teacher 그 소리는 선생님을 놀라게 했다 : 여기서 startled는 동사 startle의 과거형, '놀라게 했다'

98. 'blow it'의 의미를 아세요?

① 해리의 일곱 번째 생일이었습니다. ② 해리는 신이 났고 행복했습니다. ③ 그러다 일이 잘못되기 시작했는데, 그건 그의 잘못이 아니었습니다. ④ 해리는 시키는 대로 했을 뿐이었습니다. ⑤ 아빠가 촛불을 불라고 해서 해리는 초콜릿 케이크 위의 초를 불어 껐습니다. ⑥ 문제는 부는 힘이 다소 강해서 맞은편에 앉아 있던 할머니가 초콜릿 크림을 뒤집어쓰게 되었습니다. ⑦ "할머니, 죄송해요. 제가 망쳤어요(불었어요)," 해리가 사과했습니다. ⑧ "그렇구나," 할머니는 키친 타올로 얼굴을 닦으며 대답했습니다. ⑨ 해리가 풍선을 분 것도 엄마가 그렇게 하라고 했기 때문이었습니다. ⑩ 하지만, 부는 힘이 약간 강해서 풍선이 죄다 터져버렸고 어린 여동생이 울었습니다. ⑪ "미안하다, 동생아. 내가 망쳤어.(불었어)," 해리가 다시 사과했습니다. ⑫ "그렇구나," 엄마가 우는 동생을 달래며 대답했습니다. ⑬ 가족들은 그에게 작은 장난감 나팔을 불라고 말할 때 조심했어야 했습니다. ⑭ 불행히도 엄마 귀를 다치게 할 생각이 아니었지만, 해리는 나팔을 세게 불었습니다. ⑮ "엄마, 죄송해요. 제가 망쳤어요(불었어요)," 해리는 사과했습니다. ⑯ "정말 그렇구나," 아빠는 이렇게 대답하며 엄마를 병원에 데려갔습니다.

문제 정답 및 해설

1. (c) 지문의 제목으로 적당한 것을 고르세요.
   a. 엄마, 약속을 깨는 자
   b. 아빠, 트럼펫 제조자
   c. 해리, 슈퍼 입김 소년
   d. 할머니, 파티 망치는 자

2. (b) 지문 내용과 맞지 않는 것을 고르세요.
   a. 해리의 할머니께서 그의 생일 파티에 오셨다.
   b. 문제는 해리가 장난치려 들고 시키는 대로 하지 않았다는 것이다. ▶ 해리는 부모님이 시키는 대로 했지만 입김이 지나치게 세서 문제가 생긴 것이다.
   c. 해리의 생일 파티는 예상보다 일찍 끝난 것 같다.
   d. 해리의 할머니는 얼굴에 초콜릿 크림을 뒤집어썼다.

3. 각 문장에 알맞은 표현을 고르세요.

   a. (tell you to do) 어떤 이들은 '내 말대로 하고 내 행동대로는 하지 마라'고 말하지만, 나는 '네가 하고 싶은 대로 하지 말고 내가 하라고 말한 걸 하라'고 말하겠다.
   | Do as I say, not as I do. 〈속담〉 내 말대로 하고 내 행동을 보고 따라 하지는 마라.

【해설】 do as I tell you to do ▶ 명령문으로 '내가 하라고 말한 대로 하라' 라는 뜻.
▶ do as ...: as 이하대로 행동하라

b. (should have let) 너에게 거짓말을 한 건 미안하다. 나는 너에게 진실을 알려야 했다.
【해설】 should have pp ...했어야 했는데 하지 않았다. (let은 과거, 과거분사 형태가 동일)
ex) I should have let you know the truth.
   나는 너에게 진실을 알려야 했다. (하지만 알리지 않았다.)
   I shouldn't have told you.
   너에게 말하지 말았어야 했다. (하지만 말했다.)

c. (apologized) 내가 그에게 나의 실수에 대해 사과하자마자, 그는 '너의 사과를 받아들인다.'고 대답했다.
【해설】 apology n. 사과 / apologize v. 사과하다 ▶ '사과하다'라는 의미의 동사가 와야 하고, 이어지는 문장의 시제가 과거 (he answered)이기 때문에 apologized가 와야 한다.

99 'spill the beans'의 의미를 아세요?

① 크리스는 무언가 잘못되었다는 건 알았지만, 뭐가 잘못되었는지는 몰랐습니다. ② 그는 출근이 늦어서 지하철까지 달려가야 했습니다. ③ 달려가는 동안 몇몇 사람들이 자신을 쳐다본다는 걸 알았습니다. ④ 지하철에 뛰어올랐을 때에도 일부 사람들이 다시 자신을 곁눈질했습니다. ⑤ 사무실 건물의 엘리베이터에 탔더니 그의 뒤에 서 있던 사람들이 작은 소리로 웃었습니다. ⑥ 크리스는 좀 짜증이 났지만 무슨 일인지 알아볼 시간이 없어서 사무실로 급히 뛰어들어 갔습니다. ⑦ 사무실 안에 들어가니 모든 사람들이 일제히 그를 쳐다보았습니다. ⑧ 그는 더 이상 참을 수 없었습니다. ⑨ "뭡니까? 왜 모두들 이상한 표정으로 나를 쳐다보는 겁니까?" ⑩ 하지만, 아무도 나서서 무슨 일인지 말하려 들지 않았습니다. ⑪ "제발 무슨 일인지 털어 놓아보세요." ⑫ 그러자 동료들이 한 명씩 입을 열었습니다. ⑬ "어... 당신 바지 지퍼가 내려갔어요." ⑭ "그리고 바지 뒤가 뜯어졌어요." ⑮ "머리카락에 큰 치즈 덩어리가 묻어 있고요." ⑯ "그리고 짝짝이 양말을 신고 있어요."

문제 정답 및 해설

1. (c) 지문의 제목으로 적당한 것을 고르세요.
   a. 짝짝이 양말을 절대 신지 말라.
   b. 콩을 쏟는 자 크리스, 마침내 체포되다!
   c. 모두가 그를 쳐다볼 만도 했다
   d. 크리스, 무례한 동료들에게 질리다

2. (d) 모두가 이상한 표정으로 그를 보고 웃은 건 _____ 때문이다.
   a. 그가 뽀로로 넥타이를 매고 있었기
   b. 그가 실수로 쏟아낸 콩이 비쌌기
   c. 그가 아주 빨리 사무실에 도착했기
   d. 그의 외모에 심각한 문제가 있었기

3. 각 문장에 알맞은 표현을 고르세요.

   a. (a chunk of) 이 청바지를 입으면 내가 고기 한 덩어리처럼 보인다. ▮ a pair of jeans 청바지 한 벌 (two pairs of jeans 청바지 두 벌) look like ...처럼 보이다
   【해설】셀 수 없는 명사를 셀 때 ▶ 계량 방법, 단위에 따라 함께 쓰이는 표현이 다르므로 별도로 암기한다.
   a chunk of 한 덩어리 + meat, cheese, money, sugar ...
   a pack of 한 팩(떼) + cigarette, lies, cards, hounds, hyenas ...
   a bowl of 한 그릇 + soup, cereal, rice, oatmeal, fruits ...

   b. (one by one) 당신의 소유물 전부를 하나씩 책상에 올려놓으십시오. 내가 면밀히 살펴봐야 합니다. ▮ belongings 소유물, 재산 check carefully 자세히 살펴보다
   【해설】step by step 한 단계(걸음)씩 / from time to tome 가끔씩 / one by one 하나씩, 한 가지씩, 한 사람씩 ▶ 문맥상 one by one이 적당하다.

   c. (fly) 어제 내 바지 지퍼가 내려갔을 때 작은 파리가 그 구멍으로 날아들었다.
   【해설】fly n. 바지 지퍼, 파리 v. 날다 (fly–flew–flown)
   Your fly is down. = Your fly is open. 너의 바지 지퍼가 내려갔다.
   A fly flew into the hole. 파리 한 마리가 구멍으로 날아들었다.
   Several flies fly in the sky. 하늘에 파리 몇 마리가 난다.

'mind one's P's and Q's'의 의미를 아세요?

① 자기도 모르게 바지에 오줌을 자주 싸는 어린 소년이 있었습니다. ② 창피하다는 건 잘 알고 있었지만, 소년도 어쩔 수가 없었습니다. ③ 어느 날 소년의 가족은 가족 모임을 갖게 되었습니다. ④ 집을 출발하기 전, 아버지가 소년에게 말하기를 "아들아, 예의 바르게 행동해라. ⑤ 무슨 일을 하든 예의 있게 행동하는 거 잊지 말아야 해. 알겠지?"
⑥ "아빠, 저는 가기 싫어요. ⑦ 또 바지에 오줌을 싸면 어떻게 해요? ⑧ 분명 다른 사촌들 모두 저를 비웃을 거예요."
⑨ 소년의 말은 금방이라도 울 것처럼 들렸습니다. ⑩ "그럼... 무엇보다 소변을 참으면 안 돼. ⑪ 조금이라도 소변 보고 싶은 마음이 들면 주저하지 말고 바로 화장실로 달려가라," 아빠가 대답했습니다.
⑫ "하지만 저는 낯선 화장실은 혼자 못 간다고요." 소년이 말했습니다.
⑬ "나한테 신호를 보내. ⑭ 네가 신호를 보내자마자 나는 무슨 일이든 하던 일을 멈추고 너랑 화장실을 갈 테니."
⑮ "그럼 제가 할 일은 오줌에 신경 쓰고 신호를 보내는(mind my pee and cue) 거네요."
⑯ "내가 뭐랬니, 예의 바르게 행동하면(mind your Ps and Qs) 된다고 했잖니."

문제 정답 및 해설

1. (b) 지문의 제목으로 적당한 것을 고르세요.
   a. 흥을 깨는 사람, 오줌 싸다 (wet blanket 썰렁한 사람, 흥을 깨는 사람)
   b. Ps 와 Qs 대신 오줌(pee)과 신호(cue)를 주의하라
   c. 이런, 소년이 또 일을 저질렀군!
   d. 무슨 일을 하든 그만두어라

2. (c) 소년이 가족 모임에 가고 싶지 않았던 건 _____ 때문이다.
   a. 그가 예의 바르게 행동할 수 없었기
   b. 그의 사촌들이 분명 그를 비웃을 것이기
   c. 가족들 앞에서 바지에 오줌을 쌀까 봐 걱정되었기
   d. 낯선 화장실에 갈 수 없었기

3. 각 문장에 알맞은 표현을 고르세요.

   a. (unfamiliar) 저 사람들 중 낯선 얼굴이 보인다. 전에 한 번도 만난 적이 없는 사람들 같다.
   【해설】familiar a. 낯익은 / unfamiliar a. 낯선 / similar a. 비슷한 ▶ 두 번째 문장의 내용으로 볼 때 unfamiliar가 가장 적당하다. (unfamiliar faces 낯선 얼굴)

   b. (is about to be) 나는 경찰에게 이렇게 말했다. "그는 아직 죽지 않았지만, 곧 죽을 겁니다. 그는 죽어가고 있어요!"
   【해설】dead a. 죽은 / die v. 죽다 (died–died / dying) / death n. 죽음
   ex) He was dead. = He died. 그는 죽었다.
       He is dying 그는 죽어가고 있다.
   문제에서 'he is about to be'는 'he is about to be dead'에서 dead가 생략된 것이다.

   c. (whatever) 네가 원하는 대로 무엇이든 할 수 있고 원하는 때에 언제든 떠날 수 있다.
   【해설】whatever 무엇이든 / whenever 언제든 / wherever 어디든 / whoever 누구든 ▶ 문맥에 따라 적당한 표현을 사용한다. 문제에서는 whenever가 가장 적당하다.
   ex) leave whenever you wish 원하는 때(시간) 떠나다
       whoever I meet 내가 만나는 누구든

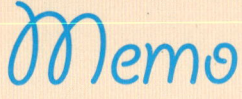

Memo

재미있게 공부하는 영어리딩

Fun! Fun! Reading!

DID YOU KNOW?

펀펀 리딩

『펀펀 리딩』은 이런 분들께 추천합니다.

- 영어책만 보면 지루해서 금방 포기하게 되는 수험생들
- 독해 때문에 항상 영어점수가 늘지 않는 수험생들
- 왜 해석이 이렇게 되는지 친절히 설명해줄 선생님이 필요한 분들
- 문법따로, 독해따로, 문법은 아는 데 독해가 안되는 분들
- 독해뿐 아니라 듣고 쓰는 리딩 훈련까지 입체적 학습이 필요한 분들
- 독해 공부하면서 중요한 어휘도 챙겨보고 싶은 분들

독해서 한 권으로 문법, 어휘, 리스닝까지
모두 학습할 수 있는 All In One Book!